WITHDRAWN

ADVANCE PRAISE FOR

Dear Abigail

"Diane Jacobs weaves a fascinating fabric from the correspondence of Abigail Smith Adams and her two gifted sisters, Mary and Elizabeth, in *Dear Abigail*. The first book to trace the ties that bound, thrilled, and sometimes frustrated America's most beloved Founding Mother to her siblings, *Dear Abigail* provides insights into the tenuous balance between love, empathy, and occasional envy expressed by the three sisters. A must-read for those interested in the lives of Revolutionary-era women."

— NANCY RUBIN STUART, author of *Defiant Brides: The Untold Story of Two Revolutionary-Era Women and the Radical Men They Married*

"Wonder what it was like in British-occupied Boston during the Revolutionary War and what women did while their men fought? The revolutionary lives of Abigail Adams and her two sisters come to life in a drama that shows how women, the generals in charge of their families, did so much to make America what it is today. Jacobs transforms these three different stories into one magnificent epic in an astonishing feat of narrative history and biography."

— CARL ROLLYSON, author of *American Isis: The Life and Art of Sylvia Plath* and *Amy Lowell Anew: A Biography*

"Jacobs elegantly intertwines the personal with the political in *Dear Abigail*. Her intimate accounts of the lives and families of Abigail Adams and her two intellectual, passionately engaged sisters illuminate the history of colonial Massachusetts, eighteenth-century Enlightenment England, revolutionary Paris and, most importantly, the earliest years of the nascent United States."

— SYDNEY LADENSOHN STERN, author of *Gloria Steinem: Her Passions, Politics, and Mystique*

"In highlighting sorority, Diane Jacobs opens a new window on the familiar life of Abigail Adams, wife of American Revolution leader and second President of the United States, John. . . . Deftly weaving military and political events of the Revolutionary period with the personal lives of these fascinating sisters, Jacobs has crafted a riveting curl-up-by-the-fireside story." —*Publishers Weekly*

"[Abigail's] feminist writing, both to husband and sisters, crackles off the page. Readers will cheer when she is finally goaded out of her enforced provincialism by the need to join her husband in his diplomatic mission to Paris in 1784. An intimate, deeply engaging method of following historic events." —*Kirkus Reviews*

"Though Abigail Adams is a perennially popular historical subject, little has been written about her two accomplished sisters, Mary Cranch and Elizabeth Shaw Peabody. This triple biography corrects that oversight. . . . Colonial America, the Revolutionary War era, and the fledgling state of a new nation come to life via the pens of these remarkably prolific, loving, and observant sisters." —*Booklist*

Dear Abigail

Dear Abigail

The Intimate Lives and Revolutionary Ideas of Abigail Adams and Her Two Remarkable Sisters

Diane Jacobs

BALLANTINE BOOKS · NEW YORK

Copyright © 2014 by Diane Jacobs

All rights reserved.

Published in the United States by Ballantine Books,
an imprint of Random House,
a division of Random House LLC,
a Penguin Random House Company, New York.

BALLANTINE and the HOUSE colophon are
registered trademarks of Random House LLC.

ISBN 978-0-345-46506-1

eBook ISBN 978-0-345-54984-6

Printed in the United States of America on acid-free paper

www.ballantinebooks.com

2 4 6 8 9 7 5 3 1

First Edition

Book design by Barbara M. Bachman

For my mother, Patricia B. Jacobs

"ONLY CONNECT!"

—*Howards End*

Contents

. . .

Illustration Credits

. . .

Author's Note

. . .

I N ORDER TO PRESERVE THE CHARACTER OF THE SISTERS' LETTERS, I have maintained their grammar and spelling and, in most cases, placed their words in quotes. The exceptions are occasions when quoting single words or short phrases would clutter the page and undermine the fluidity of the narrative. Sources can always be found in my reference notes.

Family Tree

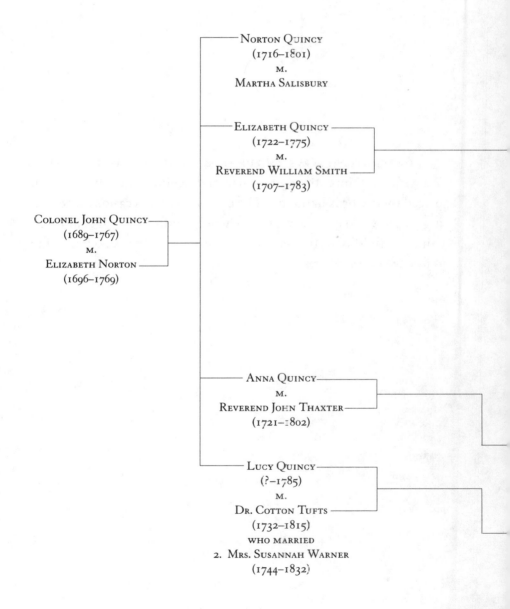

NORTON QUINCY
(1716–1801)
M.
MARTHA SALISBURY

ELIZABETH QUINCY
(1722–1775)
M.
REVEREND WILLIAM SMITH
(1707–1783)

COLONEL JOHN QUINCY
(1689–1767)
M.
ELIZABETH NORTON
(1696–1769)

ANNA QUINCY
M.
REVEREND JOHN THAXTER
(1721–1802)

LUCY QUINCY
(?–1785)
M.
DR. COTTON TUFTS
(1732–1815)
WHO MARRIED
2. MRS. SUSANNAH WARNER
(1744–1832)

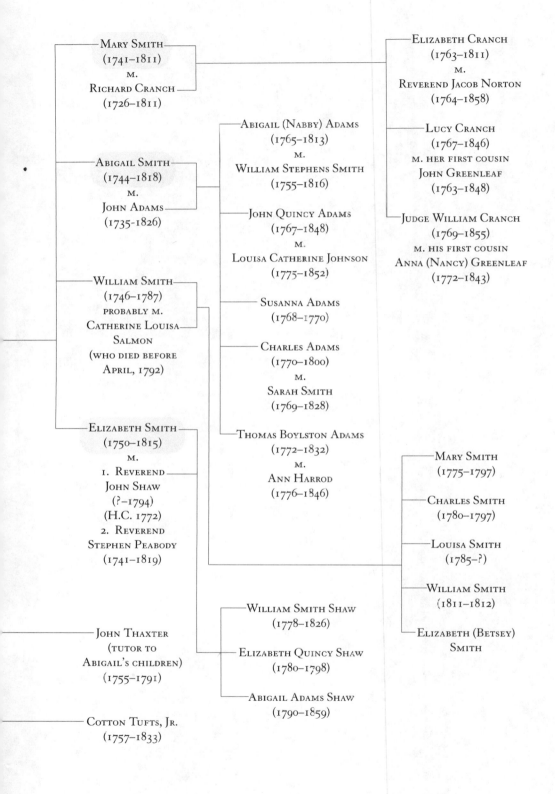

MARY SMITH
(1741–1811)
M.
RICHARD CRANCH
(1726–1811)

ELIZABETH CRANCH
(1763–1811)
M.
REVEREND JACOB NORTON
(1764–1858)

LUCY CRANCH
(1767–1846)
M. HER FIRST COUSIN
JOHN GREENLEAF
(1763–1848)

JUDGE WILLIAM CRANCH
(1769–1855)
M. HIS FIRST COUSIN
ANNA (NANCY) GREENLEAF
(1772–1843)

ABIGAIL SMITH
(1744–1818)
M.
JOHN ADAMS
(1735-1826)

ABIGAIL (NABBY) ADAMS
(1765–1813)
M.
WILLIAM STEPHENS SMITH
(1755–1816)

JOHN QUINCY ADAMS
(1767–1848)
M.
LOUISA CATHERINE JOHNSON
(1775–1852)

SUSANNA ADAMS
(1768–1770)

WILLIAM SMITH
(1746–1787)
PROBABLY M.
CATHERINE LOUISA
SALMON
(WHO DIED BEFORE
APRIL, 1792)

CHARLES ADAMS
(1770–1800)
M.
SARAH SMITH
(1769–1828)

THOMAS BOYLSTON ADAMS
(1772–1832)
M.
ANN HARROD
(1776–1846)

MARY SMITH
(1775–1797)

CHARLES SMITH
(1780–1797)

LOUISA SMITH
(1785–?)

ELIZABETH SMITH
(1750–1815)
M.
1. REVEREND
JOHN SHAW
(?–1794)
(H.C. 1772)
2. REVEREND
STEPHEN PEABODY
(1741–1819)

WILLIAM SMITH
(1811–1812)

ELIZABETH (BETSEY)
SMITH

JOHN THAXTER
(TUTOR TO
ABIGAIL'S CHILDREN)
(1755–1791)

WILLIAM SMITH SHAW
(1778–1826)

ELIZABETH QUINCY SHAW
(1780–1798)

ABIGAIL ADAMS SHAW
(1790–1859)

COTTON TUFTS, JR.
(1757–1833)

Dear Abigail

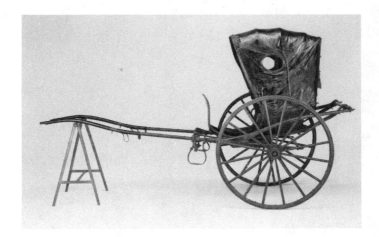

*Abigail pictured herself traveling to
visit Mary in a New England
version of the French chaise,
such as this.*

CHAPTER I

"Never sisters loved each other better than we"

. . .

ONE HOT JULY EVENING IN 1766, 22-YEAR-OLD ABIGAIL, THE wife of rising young lawyer John Adams, stayed up late to write her 25-year-old sister Mary Cranch how much she missed her. Both were living in the outskirts of Boston—Abigail in Braintree and Mary in Salem, but there were twenty-five miles of bad roads and a river between them. Each had teething infants, reams of housework, and husbands setting out to make their marks in the world.

Still, Abigail was determined to get to Salem before the end of the summer. "I have been Scheeming of it this fortnight," she told her sister. But then John was assailed by one law case after another. She couldn't see herself clear until the lower court adjourned, "and then I hope there will not any more Mountains arise to hinder me. Mole hills I always Expect to find, but them I can easily surmount."[1]

Mary had told Abigail she woke up at four to cook and clean, mother her baby daughter, and scurry Richard, her brilliant but impractical spouse, off to work. Abigail joked that she and John dozed until eight at least, enjoying the breeze off the Atlantic and indulging "my inclination to Laziness."

Both Mary and Abigail were deeply in love with their husbands, yet lonely for each other and for their teenage sister, Elizabeth, who was still living with their parents a few miles from Braintree in Weymouth. "Sister Betsy, poor Girl her heart is with you, but when her Body will be, is uncertain, "Abigail lamented to Mary, for their worrying mother always found some excuse—Betsy's cough, the sultry New England weather—to keep her home. So the sisters clung to one another by writing.[2]

They wrote with homemade quill pens and ink produced from their own recipes on Massachusetts bond from the new paper mill in Milton. Composing in moments stolen from spinning or churning butter, or while everyone else was sleeping, with candle wax dripping on their prose, they lamented all the errors they made. Mary had no need to explain that she wrote in great haste: her spotty ink and wild scrawl announced her endless workload. "Burn this letter!" she and Abigail frequently enjoined each other. Betsy made no such request.

Yet, even Betsy, who kept her pen sharp and took pride in her fine cursive, rarely wrote in a tranquil moment. "My brains are all roiled," she characteristically fretted at the end of one letter.

What's more, the colonial postal system, years behind Great Britain's, was so notoriously unreliable that, through no fault of her own, Abigail had just gotten back a letter she wrote Mary a week earlier "like a bad penny." The nearest post office was in Cambridge, so if no neighbor carried it directly, another week might pass before Abigail found a Harvard-bound neighbor willing to send the letter back off.

Still, it was all worthwhile since reading a letter from Mary brought "new spring" to Abigail's nerves and "a brisker circulation to my Blood," creating "a kind of pleasing pain." "I feel so glad that I can scarcely help feeling sorry," she now wrote, and while she conceded this reaction might seem strange, it was perfectly normal when people were connected as deeply as Mary and herself. "Never Sisters Loved each other better than we, I believe I can truly say," she declared.[3]

"I daily count the days between this and the time I may probably see you," Mary agreed; though, being the eldest, it did not behoove her to effuse as much as her middle sister, and while assuring Betsy, the baby, that she longed for a visit, Mary felt impelled to remind her that their parents' needs came first.[4] Honoring those above you and commanding those beneath made life run smoothly: besides, it was God's will.

It would have been obvious to anyone who met them that Abigail,

Mary, and Betsy were sisters. Though Mary was darker and taller and Betsy was the slimmest, all were small and slender with oval faces; narrow, decisive mouths; smooth noses; shining brown hair; and clear skin. Their bright dark eyes conveyed authority and a marked intelligence, and they all shared their mother's energetic, self-confident air and passion for doing good, but were surprisingly delicate—they were the first to catch colds and the last to recover. When she was very young, Abigail had been paralyzed for two weeks with rheumatic fever,[5] and her childbirths had been far more treacherous than Mary's. It was a battle with death for her to produce a child.[6] Betsy, frailest of them all, wilted in the heat and was so weak after one childhood illness that the doctor ordered her not to read, write, work, or even think. It was lucky the "ill humours" attacked her body rather than her mood or she'd be impossible to live with, Abigail observed.[7]

These sisters had been inseparable since their Weymouth childhood. Weymouth—where their father, William Smith, had been minister of the First Congregational Church since 1734—was a crooked, twelve-mile ride away from Boston. It was a typical New England village, smelling of the yellow blossoms of locust trees in the spring and bayberry bushes in the autumn, sweltering in summer and so cold on a winter night that ink could freeze in your pen. Wild ducks flew overhead, and the wind carried fish scents from the ocean. The town had a population of just over a thousand; its dwellings were wood versions of the brick houses the Puritans had left behind in England, and they ran up and down old Indian trails.

The sisters were born in an age of inspiration and conflict, with the Great Awakening stirring evangelical conversions in the Puritan churches and the Enlightenment championing rational thinking in the libraries of Harvard and Yale. It was the era of Voltaire and Rousseau, Locke and Hume, reason and feeling. Such questions as what constitutes a social contract preoccupied the great minds of the time.

In New England, women's fight for social involvement had died a century before with the banning of Anne Hutchinson's weekly meetings in 1637. Where Hutchinson had borne sixteen children and cofounded the colony of Rhode Island, mothers of the mid-eighteenth century generally sought power only in the private sphere. Out of necessity or conviction, they colluded in their own economic and physical dependence. Most mothers set an example of subservience for their daughters and left public discourse to their husbands and sons.

In 1754—the year Mary turned thirteen—the French and Indian War broke out, extending the worldwide Seven Year War to the colonies. Here it became a contest between England and France for American wealth. Most of the Indian tribes allied with the French hoping to thwart the aggressive spread of the British, while colonists from Maine to Georgia identified wholeheartedly with their English kin. American militias rushed to assist the British forces. In the 1750s, young George Washington made a name for himself vanquishing Indians attacking early pioneers.

Around the dinner table at their father's parsonage, the Smith sisters listened silently as the wisest men in Weymouth analyzed battles in Ohio or Pennsylvania or Louisiana. Out the window crashed the waves of the Atlantic Ocean. Across it lay their King and culture. The girls craved British books and British dresses, British concerts and parties and plays. Weymouth, Betsy quipped, was distinguished only "for its inactivity."[8] But its wild, hilly farmland and lofty oak trees also moved her, for she was full of delicate feeling—or, as her epoch phrased it, sensibility.

Females ran in the family. The girls' mother, Elizabeth Quincy Smith, was—like Betsy—the youngest of three close sisters. When Elizabeth Quincy married William Smith on October 16, 1740, she moved across the pond from Braintree to Weymouth, where she gave birth to her first child, Mary, on December 9, 1741. Next came Abigail on November 11, 1744, and last Elizabeth on April 7, 1750. Between Abigail and Elizabeth, in 1746, William Smith was born, assuring them a male heir. In terms of salvation, though, men and women were on the same footing. All four siblings, baptized in their father's parish, set off on the uncertain road to eternal life.[9]

But in the hierarchy of New England, where your family name determined where you sat in church[10] and the order in which you graduated in your class at Harvard, the children of William and Elizabeth Smith were already assured a distinguished place. On their father's side of the family lay a line of successful businessmen going back to Thomas

Smith, who sailed from England and opened a butcher shop ten miles from Weymouth in the village of Charleston in 1663. His son, the sisters' grandfather, became a wealthy merchant farmer, while their maternal forebearers—Quincys and Nortons—were landed gentry, pastors, and statesmen. On an old parchment, their adored grandmother Quincy traced a family tree back to an ancestor who had fought with William the Conqueror at Hastings and another who had signed the Magna Carta beside King John.

In 1633, the first American Quincy, Edward, had arrived in Massachusetts Bay with a band of defiant English Puritans, who called themselves Congregationalists. These men and women rejected England's state religion, Anglicanism, for its ostentation but accepted its emphasis on the inequality of the educated and the ignorant, the wealthy and the poor. Order, they believed, demanded that one man answer to another. There would be no grandiose Bishops or Lords in Puritan America, but also no pretense of egalitarianism; the humble would doff their hats to privilege—just like at home.

Edward Quincy arrived in America as a gentleman with six servants and enhanced his fortune farming the hilly land he named Mount Wollaston in Braintree, which elected him to the first Massachusetts court. Edward's grandson, John Quincy, the girls' grandfather, all but ran Braintree, serving as Colonel in the Army, Speaker in the Massachusetts House of Representatives, and moderator for every town meeting in the precinct for years. A local Indian tribe even chose him as their guardian, praising his fair-mindedness. John Adams complained in his diary that Colonel John Quincy never said anything good about anyone, but admitted he "did not often speak evil" either. He did accumulate the largest library outside of Boston and was as devout as *his* grandfather Edward. The church remained the most powerful agent in New England life, though over the past half century, religion in New England had changed.

Gone, for instance, was the founders' law, which defined anyone who was not a Puritan as a heretic, subject to having an ear lopped off if he practiced his wayward faith. By Colonel John Quincy's time—he lived from 1689 until 1767—Anglicans and Quakers could not only worship as they liked but exert power in town meetings. These local governments were true democracies for their era. Name and fortune for once were irrelevant. Every property-owning male carried the same weight.

Congregationalism, meanwhile, had radically polarized. On the one hand, the so-called "Old Lights" continued to cherish emotional reticence; on the other, the "New Lights" began fanning self-display. Faith, which for the former was inborn or gently encouraged, came for the latter as ecstatic revelation. Writhing was an inevitable consequence as was—in Abigail's words—"foaming."[11]

Reverend Smith managed to appease both camps, though he himself was an Old Light, believing, like John Locke, in the superiority of reason to feeling, and refusing to dwell on man's sins. Abigail spoke for her father when she said, "Gloom is no part of my Religion."[12] Nor was it easy for him to hide his scorn for the Born Again "awakenings" that charismatic evangelicals like the British George Whitefield and the American Jonathan Edwards were fomenting in New England in the middle of the eighteenth century. Reverend Smith voted against the New Lights in clerical meetings, but would not speak against them at the pulpit. As he saw it, remaining impartial made him popular and therefore useful. Usefulness was the most crucial virtue a Congregationalist could possess.

Besides, he loved philosophy and had an aversion to petty gossip—talk about things, not people, he advised his daughters. He prized forgiveness. On the wall of his main parlor hung a Biblical painting of the brothers Esau and Jacob, embracing after a lifetime of envy and hate. Parson Smith subscribed to foreign papers like the literary *Spectator* and *Tatler* and was a shrewd reader of human nature, with a sometimes lurid humor, according to his friends.[13] Loss troubled him. Houses struck by lightning and fire were the sort of events he recorded in his diary. Yet he had faith in human endeavor. In August of 1751, only four months after his church burned to the ground, he had already begun raising another. Here he preached a month later, with his family listening from the best pew.[14]

One evening Reverend Smith amused company by speculating that printing was invented by luck when some careless boy whittled his name onto a tree bark.[15] But nothing of importance was left to chance in his home. Self-control and self-improvement carried the day.

Typically, ministers paid for their great prestige with a low standard of living. Salaries were meager and often—as in William Smith's case—based on the price of crops in a given year. Reverend Smith's diary is filled with jottings about minute rises in the costs of wheat or rye, for he was careful about money and determined to get his fair share. Like most ministers, he also farmed to augment his salary. As little girls, the sisters fell asleep beneath the eaves in their wainscoted second-floor bedroom to the trembling of cow bells. They awoke to the sight of three lofty hills, the sound of woodpeckers drilling nests into the spring trees, and a view of fruit orchards and grazing sheep.[16]

This 1800 watercolor portrays Reverend William Smith's parsonage house in Weymouth where Mary, Abigail, Billy, & Elizabeth were born.

But the Smiths did not rely solely on William Smith's preaching and farming. Thanks to their wealthy relatives, the minister and his wife could afford a silver rather than the standard wood tankard for their dining board and a light, one-horse carriage for two with a calash or hood. They had an upstairs library and paid over a hundred pounds to add a barn-size L-extension to their two-floor wooden home. The house had a slanted roof and sat on the corner of North and East Streets. Windows were taxed, so it was a mark of wealth that they had four, all flooding sunlight into the large formal parlor. Here each of the girls had composed her first letter on a lap desk—and here Betsy now wrote longingly to her married sisters in what John Adams called her "elegant pen."[17]

Unless, of course, she was visiting the Adamses in their smaller house near *their* First Congregational Church, in Braintree. Here Betsy and Abigail would "talk[] and wish[] for" Mary while gazing outdoors at the upward swing of Penn's Hill.[18] Light and perspective mattered deeply to all of the sisters; so even frugal Mary had thrown caution to the wind when she moved to Salem. Mary's house, which Abigail now had her heart set on visiting, had not only brightness but a splendid view of the wharfs and the sea.

The home the girls grew up in had more than a good lookout. "You must remember that very few children have had such advantage as you have and that where much has been done by way of culture good from it is expected," Elizabeth Quincy Smith wrote her son, Billy, when he left home to work in his teens.[19] Billy had been taught Greek and Latin by the finest tutors and plied with new books imported from London. He had the chance to go to Harvard and cared so little for knowledge that he turned it down. Mary loved Billy, more, she believed, than brothers ever loved sisters,[20] but was vexed by his indifference to education when she and her sisters were so avid to learn.

And whereas in England daughters were often educated by their fathers—and the early feminist Mary Astell had gone so far as to advocate college for girls!—in the New World females had half the literacy rate of their brothers[21] and were taught—by their mothers—only reading, religion, and basic math. Dancing and music classes were considered too frivolous in the Smith household, though William Smith's library was open to everyone, and their mother was advanced in promoting reason rather than dogma. "I have always endevour'd to persuade you to act from principle," Elizabeth Smith explained to Billy in a letter that described her method with all four children. "As soon as you were capable of reasoning you [were] treated like a reasonable creature—when any thing was demanded of you the reason was given."[22]

Elizabeth taught charity to her daughters by example, as when she turned down stylish imports and hired indigent neighbors to spin the family clothes, or when she risked her own health to visit sick neighbors. She prayed with her children at night and in the morning and sat with them through two church services on Sunday not only because she was pious, but because she was convinced that fear of God warded off sin.[23] Industry was also a powerful agent for good. She taught her girls the arduous process of mixing grease and ashes to make a barrel of soap on a spring day and how to trap a goose in a stocking so they wouldn't get their fingers bitten off plucking its feathers for their quill pens. From an early age, Mary, Abigail, and Betsy joined their mother in the autumn ritual of making candles by spinning hemp into wicks and dipping them in kettles filled with water and tallow hung on trammels over the kitchen fire. Though her life was hard enough, Elizabeth Quincy Smith felt lucky by comparison to other Weymouth families and told her children they were too.[24]

The girls' mother was a model of thrift, and her warning that it was better to save every apple paring than to waste spoke especially to Mary, who was the most cautious of the three.[25] Mary was also the most easily comforted, always feeling better as soon as she had "open'd my heart" to someone.[26] All three girls were disgusted by females who squandered time or money, for this offended not just God but the sort of man they hoped to wed.

Elizabeth Smith was full of contradictions—so relentless about chaperoning her daughters' fiancés that Abigail suspected she had never been in love herself, but so skillful and kind that Betsy yearned for her nursing for the rest of her life whenever she got sick.[27] The community perceived her as the ideal minister's wife, adept at settling quarrels and avoiding feuds.[28] Yet, while she held a high standard of excellence, her desires were modest. She wanted to shine in the world as it was, and she did.

Mary, with her pleasing ways, seemed the most like her mother, though inwardly she seethed at the neglect of her mind. "Method was wanting in our studies and we had no one to point us to it," she reminded Abigail when they were both out of the parsonage. ". . . Our parents felt the necessity of keeping us from scenes of dissipation and frivolity and left the rest to nature."[29]

Still, on the outside at least, Mary was the dutiful firstborn, while Abigail was openly rebellious and wild. "You will either make a very bad or a very good woman," a family friend told her: obviously suspecting the first.[30] In her teens Abigail committed the sacrilege of opposing her mother's authority, or, as she saw it, made clear she resented how her mother denied her most innocent requests.

As a child, Abigail was often sent away for long visits to her grandmother Quincy, whom she sometimes thought she loved more than her own mother because she did not invidiously compare her to Mary or rebuke her more than once for a crime. Besides, Grandmother Quincy could be wicked herself—whispering to Abigail that it was "a mercy to the world" some people they knew were "kept poor" or they would be even haughtier than they were already,[31] and regaling her with spicy anecdotes from the local newspapers, such as the story of the wife who poured red wine in her husband's pipe.[32]

And then there was Betsy, who was just as high-spirited as Abigail and even less free to express herself. *She* could not run off to her grand-mother's because she was the youngest and—unlike her also unmar-ried and far less industrious brother—always had duties to perform at home. Where Billy wasted his chances to learn, she grasped every free moment to read, and not just enthusiastically, but with a cultivated taste that would have ranged wider, she was sure, if one duty or an-other wasn't always calling her from her father's books. The final insult came during Mary's and Abigail's brief visits when—rather than at last having time to enjoy herself—Betsy was given the further burden of amusing their little girls. "I am almost crazed with the natural Bless-ings of Matrimony," she wrote her cousin Isaac during one such visit. Then she herself got sick, and four months passed before she had the strength to read, which would not be so terrible for this cousin, who was off at Harvard and could "spend whole years in the delightful em-ployment of improving [your] mental powers. Shortness of the time enhances its value and makes the loss greivous to me," she reported with her normal dramatic flair.[33]

"If you happen to have any learning keep it a profound secret," one father implored his daughters in a popular mid-eighteenth-century conduct book, which Elizabeth Quincy highly endorsed.[34] Since girls' literary endeavors were confined to writing letters, and all eighteenth-century letters, but especially girls' letters, were prized for spontaneity and ease, the sisters' mother saw instruction in grammar and penman-ship as beside the point. So Mary's script raced in all directions with no periods in sight, and Abigail's was blockish and tipped back and forth like a metronome. Occasionally (and not always appropriately) colons appeared, but the comma was rare, though both girls wrote compelling prose with a natural rhythm, which was easily comprehensible if you could decipher the words. Artlessness was a virtue of the era: "it is not," Abigail declared, "the studied sentence . . . which pleases, but the genuine sentiments of the heart expressed with simplicity."[35] And she and Mary further approved the literary mode of the day by quoting great chunks of edification from the Bible or Shakespeare.

When Abigail was confused or angered, she sought solace from writing letters. "There are perticular times when I feel such an uneasiness, such a restlessness, as neither company, Books, family Cares or any other thing will remove, my Pen is my only pleasure, and writing to you the composure of my mind," she told John on one such occasion.[36] Letter-writing, she knew, was a passion of her era, stoked by increased literacy and a working post. One of her favorite poets, Alexander Pope, called it "talking on Paper." Candor was its hallmark, as were a stock of literary quotes and learned allusions. But whether it described a trip to Paris or a crisis in the kitchen, the true subject of an eighteenth-century letter was the author's soul.[37] As Pope wrote a traveling correspondent, "You can make no Discoveries that will be half so valueable to me as those of your own mind, temper, and thoughts."[38]

Abigail told Mary, "My letters to you are first thoughts. without correction,"[39] But she also drew on ideas mulled as she lay in bed at night or went about her childcare and housekeeping. And her seeming artlessness was inspired by no less a stylist than the author of the famous epistolary novel *Clarissa,* Samuel Richardson, whom she felt had "done more towards embellishing the present age, and teaching them the talent of letter-writing, than any other modern I can name."[40]

Mary's letters show a gift for gossip and strong opinion. Writing Abigail from Salem, she announces, "I was not born to live among Slaves," meaning her Tory neighbors, who in the mid-1760s were humbly accepting the crippling Stamp Act England had imposed. The sisters deplored this taxation without representation, but the Tories gladly suffered it, Mary complained, and went so far as to attack her opinions at her own table just because she "dare[d] to say one Word against" its perpetrator, King George III. Furthermore, these neighbors were greedy and selfish.

"By what I have heard of them, they have well learnd the lesson of Iago, to Rodorigo, 'put money in thy purse,'" replied Abigail, who prided herself on social observations. "My advice to you is among the

Romans, do as the romans do," she added, unable—even with Mary—
to suppress her need to boss.[41]

Being first, Mary had been forced to grope for titles and authors'
names at parish dinners where "none of the conversation was addressed
to" her. Yet, the conversation there drew her to Plato, Newton, Ben
Franklin, and transcripts of British Parliament debates. Just like the
men sitting over her mother's mutton and pudding, she was formed to
grapple with ideas. Only they didn't know it, they being such otherwise
penetrating men as grandfather Colonel John Quincy; Uncle Isaac
Smith, a successful Boston merchant; and Dr. Cotton Tufts, whom she
called Uncle Tufts. He was a gangly and brilliant young physician and
twice a relative, being the husband of their mother's sister Lucy and a
cousin on their father's side. Visiting ministers and boarding divinity
students also contributed to the chorus of learned men, indifferent to
the young girls' opinions. And then one day when Mary was fourteen,
there was an Englishman at the table who drew her into the conversation at last.

Richard Cranch was tall and lean with a high forehead, delicate
features, and a long open face like the great man who saves the girl in
a romantic novel. Despite the fact that he was a poor man's son, everywhere he went Richard attracted men of rank and learning.[42] He had a
quiet ardor and was "loving and compassionate,"[43] according to a friend
who prided himself on shrewd judgment. Another friend called him a
model "to those who wish to be great and good,"[44] though practical
skills—like knowing how to dress for a winter's day—often eluded
him. He was acutely sensitive, and his health was frail.[45]

The first notice of Richard's arrival in the Smith household is the
reverend's diary record of lending "to Mr. Cranch" a book of John
Locke's letters early in 1755. Richard was then twenty-nine, fifteen
years older than Mary. She was the eldest in her family, he the youngest
in his.

Richard Cranch had five brothers and a sister and came from a
wool-manufacturing family in Kingsbridge, a seaport village like Weymouth, in the county of Devon, England. His grandfather was "a rigid
Puritan,"[46] but Richard, though exceptionally pious, was too curious to
cleave to any single opinion and despised groups like the New Lights
who claimed salvation exclusively for themselves.[47] Primogeniture—

*The scholarly Englishman Richard Cranch
transformed the lives of all three sisters.*

whereby the family estate is bequeathed to the eldest son—doomed
him to inherit nothing, and his only training was at making wiretooth
cards to comb wool. Yet he had taught himself Greek, Latin, and ancient Hebrew and had enormous intellectual powers and a dazzling
array of knowledge on everything from Roman history to mining coal.

Understanding how clocks ticked and water rose through underground pipes came easily to him, though at the moment he had no
plans to capitalize on these talents. He learned for the joy of it and still
had trouble leaving his latest philosophy or math book to go off to
work—which, at the time he met Mary, was co-managing a glass factory in Braintree. His partner was his sister's husband, Joseph Palmer.
The partners clashed frequently, for Palmer had come to America with
the single-minded goal of making a fortune, and Richard sought to
balance study and work.

Nine years before, in 1746, Richard had sailed with the Palmers to
Boston. From there, the Palmers moved to Braintree, while Richard
asserted his independence by staying behind. He rented a shop and set
up a wool-combing business. For years he struggled to make it turn a

profit. To no avail. The business failed, and he reluctantly followed the more successful Palmers to Braintree. Probably it was at his sister's home that Richard first met Mary's father, who invited him to the parish house.

There Richard immediately made friends with the worldlier Uncle Tufts and Uncle Isaac. He quickly recognized Mary's intelligence—not to mention her beauty and goodness. Their passion quickened as he took it upon himself to initiate all three young women into the pleasures of Enlightenment philosophy, epistolary novels, Milton, Pope, Shakespeare, and also some French. Only the subjects most taboo for women—science and ancient languages—were omitted from his curriculum when, with no official assignment or stipend, Richard began tutoring the female Smiths. This entailed organizing a separate regime for each since Betsy was five, Abigail eleven, and Mary fourteen.

Undertaking the education of a woman you love and her two younger sisters would be unusual even for an aristocrat in an eighteenth-century French salon, but it was unheard of for a struggling businessman in the New World.

Abigail could not sufficiently sing Richard's praises in a letter to Betsy, reminding her "To our own and inestimable Brother Cranch do I owe my . . . taste for Letters," attributing "whatever I possess of delicacy and sentiment or refinement" to the books Richard Cranch pulled for her from their father's shelf.[48]

Betsy observed that Richard Cranch expressed more "kindness and affection in one Look" than anyone else she knew.[49] Because she was so young when Richard began tutoring them, Betsy's skills became more polished or "masculine" than her sisters', and in her teens she could stun them by quoting Madame de Sevigne's views on love.[50] She delighted in portraying everything in extreme colors. Her birthday she called "the funeral of the former year." Furthermore, Betsy had the self-confidence not to apologize for her letters or request them burned—indeed, she made it clear that it was well worth remembering her expatiations, not to mention the magnificence of her prose.[51]

It is a shame that none of Mary's courtship correspondence with Richard survives, because language was both the spur and the cement to her passion. Richard was not prosperous, nor trained for a profession, and his social status, not hers, would rise when they mingled their lots. He could not say whether he would learn to make money. All he promised was a life of the mind. This was sufficient for Mary. They announced their engagement or—in the words of the era, published their bans.

RICHARD'S INTELLECT WAS SOON attracting new friends beyond the Weymouth parish. One was a young scholar named John Adams, who saw eye to eye with him intellectually, though the two men differed in many other ways. Born in Braintree in 1735, John was closer to Mary's age than Richard's, and where Richard was tall and slender, John was short and plump. No one would call John's prominent nose and puffy cheeks handsome. He had a bitterly ironic humor and appeared both prim and on guard. His blue eyes were merciless—that is, when he wasn't using them to flirt.

John fell in love easily, but put great emphasis on the importance of marriage and was wary of choosing the wrong partner for life. Though

*On first acquaintance, the critical young
lawyer John Adams dismissed Abigail and her sisters
as "not fond, not frank, not candid."*

he devoted himself to reason, John relied on instinct as much as any woman did when it came to romance. It was instinct, two years earlier, that stopped him from proposing to the town belle whom he was madly in love with and had only the flimsiest *rational* causes to mistrust.

John's own character puzzled many. He was introspective but garrulous, despised gushing, but thrilled as much as Betsy Smith did to the beauty of forests and brooks. Even small changes in his environment fascinated him. His college diary entries all begin with a weather report. A "Charming, pleasant morning," he exudes on a Friday in June and "Had a small flurry of snow" at the end of winter.[52] He was euphoric about the effects of a rainstorm one March: "This morning is beyond description, Beautyfull, the Skie bespangled with Clouds which shed a lustre on us by the refraction of the rays of light, together with the healthy and enlivening air, which was purifyed By the thunder, afford most spirited materials for Contemplation."[53]

Yet John rarely had a good word for human nature. He damned the sisters' grandfather Colonel John Quincy as vain and avaricious.[54] Mary and her sister Abigail, though witty, were "Not fond, not frank, not candid," he decided after spending a single evening with them in the summer of 1759. Their father the minister was ingratiating and "craft[y]," hiding "his own Wealth, from his Parish" with the ulterior motive of getting them to send him gifts.[55] John bewailed that he himself was unstable ("I totter with every Breeze"[56]), indecisive ("I have so many Irons in the Fire, that every one burns"[57]), procrastinating ("I shudder . . . when the thought comes into my mind how many million Hours I have squandered in s[t]upid Inactivity"[58]), and tediously analytical to boot.

John's father was a typical New England yeoman, a farmer in the summer, a shoemaker in the winter, and church deacon all year round. The Adamses were no wealthier than the Cranches; the great difference between John and Richard was that John possessed the entitlements of an eldest son.

Most important was the privilege of going to Harvard. When the two young men met, John had recently graduated and was deciding on a career path. He had entered college intending to pursue the most prestigious work of his times—the ministry. But the rapid spread of the Great Awakening disgusted him. Recently, a council of local ministers had questioned the piety of Braintree's own Reverend Lemuel Briant because he dared to assert that good deeds were more important to God than faith.[59] This was John's view exactly. And tempering was not in John Adams's nature. If he won a pulpit, he confided in Richard, he would use it to denounce the New Light theory of predestination. Life was meaningful, he would insist, not a mere sleepwalking through God's grand design. But what was the point of disputing with zealots? he continued. Their wrath, he suspected, was all you could gain.

Richard's reply spoke more to his own idealism than to John's vocation. The struggle to enlighten the Congregationalist Church was itself a noble calling, Richard argued, and "should Truth under your conduct fail of an entire victory, yet, the brave efforts which I am persuaded you can make would . . . entitle you to the praises of every lover of Truth and liberty."[60] But John had little stomach for lost causes and a hearty longing for worldly success. He began leaning toward a career that would reward his disputative nature.

So it was as a poor but ambitious Braintree lawyer that John Adams came with Richard Cranch to meet the Smith girls two years after they made their first unfavorable impression. He was greeted unenthusiastically by William and Elizabeth Smith, who liked neither his meddlesome job nor his inferior background, and skeptically by the girls, who had found him arrogant the first time they met.

By now Mary was 20 and engaged to marry Richard. Betsy was a precocious eleven and Abigail seventeen, radiant and as quick-witted as John. For once, his heart, instinct, and reason came rapidly to the same conclusion. He must marry Abigail Smith.

But Abigail was not an easy conquest. She had read Samuel Richardson's late novel *Sir Charles Grandison* under Richard's tutelage. Its dashing hero (who rather reminded her of Richard) was the model she had in mind for a mate. John Adams could not fit this picture. His challenge, therefore, was to efface it.

He began by courting Abigail's family. John had no trouble at all reversing his earlier low opinion of *them*. Grandfather Quincy was soon on record in John's correspondence as excellent company; the formerly cagey Reverend Smith was a model of integrity and good sense. My "Wishes are pour'd forth for the felicity of you, your family and Neighbors," he was soon writing with perfect sincerity to Mary, while

THE BIRTH PLACES OF JOHN AND JOHN QUINCY ADAMS
at Quincy Mass.

After her marriage, Abigail set up housekeeping in the smaller
of these two saltbox houses (left); John had been born
in the larger cottage where his mother still lived.

confiding in her middle sister, "Miss Adorable," that "an increasing Affection for a certain Lady (you know who my Dear) quickens my Affections for every Body Else."[61]

John's electricity was contagious. Erotic attraction was in no time bursting off the pages of Abigail's letters as well. When John professed that "The steel and the Magnet or the Glass and feather will not fly together with more Celerity, than somebody And somebody, when brought within the striking distance," Abigail answered, "there is a tye more binding than Humanity, and stronger than Friendship," which was her unabashedly sensual love for him.[62] And where Mary and Richard complemented each other—he being the dreamer, she the pragmatist—John and Abigail were kindred spirits, with common sense to spare and matching wills.

William and Elizabeth Smith were not so easily reconciled to John as he to them or everybody to Richard. Abigail was soon seething because her parents insisted on a long engagement. Why was she a "mere Nun" while Mary and Richard slept in the same bed?[63]

Their all four falling in love within a couple of years had created a kind of *folie a quatre,* or what Abigail called a "sweet communion." When John underwent the dangerous procedure of inoculation against smallpox, Mary and Richard worried almost as much as Abigail; and John told Abigail that he loved Richard and Mary "better than any Mortals"[64] besides his family and her. Which is why in 1766, when Abigail was battling mountains and molehills to get to her sister in Salem, John too lamented the breakup of their happy foursome, telling Mary: "What would I give to have Brother Cranch's long Visage along Side of my short one, with a Pipe in each, talking about this and that and 'tother."

The double courtship in the Weymouth parlor had brought Mary and Abigail closer than ever. Alone in the kitchen or cramped into their small bedroom before they fell asleep, they imagined a future of rectitude, yes, but also enlightened living. They would soon enter the magic circle of marriage and motherhood. And while like their own mother they would stress piety, they intended to be more tolerant than she of secular pleasures like dancing and stylish clothes. More radically, they vowed to educate their girls in history, philosophy, literature, and science too if they showed a knack for it. They would teach their male children fear of the world as well as God. *Their* sons would never come home smelling of rum, like their brother, Billy, had recently, for all his attendance at church in his formative years.

Choosing a partner was the one chance a New England female had to exercise her free will in the larger world. Just as the New Lights were convinced that God predetermined salvation, Mary and Abigail believed their choice of a husband sealed their mortal fate.

Choosing wisely meant happiness, choosing a weak or incapable man meant suffering and shame that neither they nor their family, however powerful, could defray. For Mary, the prospect of marriage was so mysterious and foreboding that she "trembled" the night before her 1762 wedding and cried herself to sleep for days afterward.[65] Twenty years passed before she dared to tell even Abigail of her panic. Still, there was no doubt Mary Smith knew what she wanted. For her wedding verse, she chose the Mary and Martha passage in the Book of Luke where Jesus commends the younger sister Mary for choosing "the one thing needful, the good part," the elevation of her mind, over helping her sister Martha with household chores.[66]

Which is not to say that Mary gladly suffered Richard's unworldliness. A month after their wedding, for instance, Richard refused to argue down the hugely inflated asking price for a worn-out carriage, though Mary's father urged him to bargain. The explanation Richard offered was that the seller was poor and needed the money. John Adams, who was also present at the scene, found Richard's scruples hilarious, and what followed when the same owner offered Richard his flagging horse was funnier still. The owner declared the horse in fine condition.

> Cranch believed every word he said, and was so secret about his Bargain, that he would not make it before me, who was then at his House but he must finish it, abroad, without Questioning the Horses Virtues or Abilities, or asking any Questions about the Price. He is to give 50 pounds for the Horse. I would not give 10 pounds, for he is dull and lean, and weak, looks meanly and goes worse.

"Miserably bumbled by his own Vanity and Credulity,"[67] John Adams gleefully concluded. Mary was less amused.

WHEN AT LAST HER parents agreed to set a wedding date, Abigail had an attack of nerves and got sick. She recovered, however. The ceremony took place on October 24, 1764, and all went smoothly, though Reverend Smith (who was in fact reconciled to John Adams at this point) could not resist a bit of black humor and chose as his wedding text a Biblical passage beginning "For John came neither eating nor drinking, and they say he hath a devil."[68]

And where was Betsy while her sisters were marrying? She was weeping at their weddings and packing them up for their new lives. Betsy helped Mary move first to a house nearby in Weymouth, then to Braintree. Richard's former collaboration with his sister's husband at the Braintree glass factory had convinced him that partnerships were "vexacious."[69] Whatever he did in the future would be on his own.

For now, as well as selling cards for combing wool, he opened a clock and watch repair shop, which immersed him in astronomy and mechanics and gave him opportunity to invent his own pendulums like the well-known Philadelphia astronomer and clock-maker David Rittenhouse, who also had taught himself.[70] It was only, the Cranches insisted, because their neighbors in Braintree proved too poor to patronize watchmakers that they left for Salem. Or was it Richard's desire to prove himself on fresh ground? Richard's sister had her own interpretation and worried in a letter to Mary that her brother was leaving to escape her angry outbursts. She was miserable at the prospect of losing him and promised to practice self-control.[71]

BETSY SMITH NOT ONLY helped Abigail move to Braintree. She lived with the Adamses, when her parents could spare her, and kept her sister company while John traveled from court to court. Abigail's new home stood on twenty-three acres of land seventy-five feet away from John's widowed mother. It was a typical New England saltbox farmhouse, with a lopsided roof, widely spread-out windows, and a tympanum over the front door. What Abigail called her "cottage" was a step down in size and elegance from the Smith parsonage, but the exchange was elating because she was at last in charge.

In February 1763, the end of the French and Indian War chased France out of most of the New World and deepened the colonists' bond with England. Nine months later, on November 20 at midnight, Mary Cranch gave birth to a baby girl whom she named Elizabeth in honor of her mother and the great British Queen. Seven days later, Elizabeth Cranch was baptized in the Weymouth Church by her grandfather. She was the first of a new generation of Smith women, and John and Abigail so closely identified with her parents they called her "my daughter Betcy."[72] A few years later, when Abigail gave birth to a girl, Nabby, and a boy, John Quincy, in quick succession, John could barely suppress his pride to commiserate with Richard:

> Oh fine! I know the Feeling as well as you and in spight of
> your earlier Marriage . . . In a little while Johnny must go to
> Colledge, and Nabby must have fine Cloaths, Aye, and so must
> Betcy too . . . And very cleverly you and I shall feel when we
> recollect that we are hard at Work, over Watches and Lawsuits,

and Johnny and Betcy at the same Time Raking and fluttering
Away our Profits.[73]

For Abigail and Mary, having children made separation all the
more difficult. Were they only together, how many tips about naps and
weaning they would share. What fun they would have with each other's babies! "My dear [niece] Betsy, what would I give to hear her prattle to her cousin Nabby, to see them put their little arms round one an
others necks, and hug each other," Abigail wrote her sister. No one else,
Abigail felt sure, could understand the changes she'd undergone since
becoming a mother, how "every word and action of these little creatures, twines rounds one's heart" and

> All their little pranks which would seem ridiculous to relate,
> are pleasing to a parent. How vex'd have I felt before now upon
> hearing parents relate the chitt chat of little Miss, and master
> said or did such and such a queer thing—and this I have heard
> done by persons whose good Sense in other instances has not
> been doubted. This though really a weakness I can now more
> easily forgive, but hope in company I shall not fall into the same
> error.[74]

As if to stress her point, she quickly turned the subject to public
news and then to her horses and cows and a fine wool cloth called cam-
let she had just finished weaving into a garment for Mary and was debating how to transport.

EARLY ON THE MORNING of November 3, 1766, the Adamses were at
last able to set off on a journey to "my dear Brother Cranches." Their
primitive chaise was more accustomed to outings to Weymouth; its
springs rattled on the rocky, rutted Indian trail known as the Post Road
on the ten-mile ride to Boston. The autumn leaves, brilliant gold and
red just a few weeks before, lay dead on the ground as they drove
through Milton and Roxbury. They proceeded onto the Boston peninsula and ferried across the Bay. In Charleston, the Adamses took a half
hour to stretch, then jolted over the Mystic River by Penny Ferry and

continued north on the inland road. At mid-afternoon, John spotted a tavern with a sign of a soaring eagle and knew they were nearing the town of Malden. Here they heard the daily news, drank hard cider, and ate a good meal at Hill's tavern; then plodded up to the smaller village of Martins, where their horses fed. Now they turned away from the sun and back to the coastline. It was already dark as they drove into Salem.

When finally the Adamses sat drinking tea across from Mary, "all very happy," Mary and Abigail spoke of "riding hoods, Cloth, Silk and Lace." Richard was still at work and, for once, John was content to sit quietly and observe the reunion and wonder, perhaps, at the nature of the sisterly connection that would make Abigail think it worthwhile to "scheme" for months and take a long, exhausting ride in an uncomfortable two-seat carriage just for the pleasure of coming at last to Mary's door.[75]

CHAPTER II

"Oppression is enough to make a wise people Mad"

. . .

Mary would always associate her move to Salem with Parliament's repeal of the Stamp Act later that spring of 1766. The Stamp Act, effective the previous November, had forced colonists to cover all printed material with an expensive badge-shaped stamp brandishing the words "Shame to those who think evil of it" in Latin as a further rebuke. Unlike taxes on British luxury items, which only affected wealthy merchants like her uncle Isaac, the Stamp Act—executed by Parliament's scheming new Chancellor of the Exequer, George Greenville—punished everyone who bought a newspaper or executed a will. Parliament's excuse that Stamp Act money would pay British troops to defend America insulted the colonists' own perfectly capable militias, not to mention their legislatures, which could levy taxes if the need arose—as Massachusetts had proved when its own stamp tax helped fund the British in the French and Indian War. The truth was England was exploiting the colonies to buoy its own crippled economy.

Mary suspected her tiny motherland was also threatened by the wide expanse and seemingly endless potential of America. "America was designed by Providence for the theatre on which man was to make his true figure, on which science, virtue, liberty, happiness and glory were to exist in peace," her brother-in-law John Adams had so eloquently written; and he—and she—were no less loyal to the King for believing that America was the New Jerusalem and that the right to own property was what made a man free. It was a Puritan axiom that free men could not be taxed without their consent. And though Mary was well aware that her indignation against the British tax was stoked by her own British sense of entitlement, for the first time she also understood how very rooted she was in the New World.

This British cartoon shows
"The Horse America, throwing his Master."

AND SHE WAS NOT ALONE. Outraged Bostonians christened a huge old elm near the Commons the Liberty Tree, and hundreds gathered here to protest British injustice. Throughout New England, British ministers were hung in effigy, riots flared, furious colonists attacked stamp collectors and pillaged their homes. Ordinary citizens joined Sons of Liberty clubs, and John Adams's famous radical cousin, Sam— Abigail had met him and told Mary he was charming[1]—instigated a protest against taxation without representation, which the Massachusetts Assembly took further, declaring, "The Stamp Act wholly cancels the very conditions upon which our ancestors, with much toil and blood, and at their sole expense, settled this country and enlarged his majesty's dominions."[2] Parliament's right to make laws did not extend to trifling with the colonies' assets. And whereas, a decade before, those colonies couldn't agree even on a common defense against the French and Indians, now—at a New York Congress attended by delegates from nine regions—the Stamp Act was emphatically denounced by all.[3] Still, many citizens were Tories who supported Parliament's right to tax with or without local approval, and more were undecided what to think and turned to ministers like Braintree's Parson Wibird.

Parson Anthony Wibird was one of the sisters' closest friends and no less than a genius in John Adams's opinion. John praised the minister's subtle mind and poetic imagination as well. Like all Braintree ministers, Wibird favored reason over evangelical "enthusiasm," and his sermons were so sensible that when Benjamin Franklin visited Boston he went out of his way to hear Wibird speak.[4] A devoted friend, Wibird was among the first to visit the Cranches when they moved to Salem. Mary especially loved his wit, but he was hopelessly unkempt and ungainly, with a large, bumpy nose, squinty eyes, and black teeth. One parishioner described his body as "bended, in and out before and behind and to both Right and left . . . When he sits, he sometimes lolls on the arms of his Chair" or "throws him self over the back" and scratches his head so hard his wig "vibrates."

While John Adams was amazed that such a clever man should have "no Industry, no Delicacy, no Politeness," Mary blamed Parson Wibird's eccentricities on his not being married, a terrible fate for a woman, but worse for a man.[5] Wibird was a perfect example of how helpless bachelors and widowers were without wives to cook, clean, and mold them into civilized company. More than most men, Wibird was his own worst enemy. Though John Adams praised his penetrating *remarks* on courtship, Wibird refused to seek out any of the eligible girls in the neighborhood and claimed that he was waiting to be swept off his feet.

In both his squeamishness and languor, Wibird—John observed—approached mating like a fussing turkey, and he was no more aggressive when seeking a job.[6] Braintree's First Congregational Church had to court *him* twice before he nonchalantly accepted their ministership in February of 1755.[7]

Once installed, however, Wibird took to playing with babies and so generally ingratiating himself with everybody that it was all the more meaningful when, a month after the Stamp Act went into effect, he opened his Sunday sermon thundering from the Bible: "Hear O Heavens and give Ear O Earth, I have nourished and brought up Children and they have rebelled against me." No one sitting in the white-spired First Congregational Church could miss the analogy to the British King and his ungrateful colonies. And in the old square meetinghouse in nearby Hingham, Parson Gay more explicitly condemned the Stamp Act protest, reminding his congregants that their very covenant with God depended on subservience: first to God and then to the powerful and elite. The meek would not inherit the earth (though they were free to pick themselves up by their bootstraps), and the Enlightenment ideal of equality ignored the clear superiority of some—in natural gifts, family, education. The King's will was inviolable.[8] Besides, obstructing power could only lead to violence, Parson Gay warned them. If you felt slighted, you should pray and weep.[9]

With Parsons Wibird and Gray all but supporting the Tories, it would have been in character for Parson Smith of Weymouth to keep his dissenting views to himself. Instead, the girls' father, who in the name of diplomacy refused to denounce evangelism, which he hated, spoke out forcefully against the British Parliament, which he revered. He too seized on religion as a model for his political views. But rather than equating sacred and secular order, he preached "Render therefore unto Caesar the things that are Caesar's and unto God the things that are God's" and declared that Puritanism despised unchecked rule even more than it venerated obedience. After all, unlike God, the officials of Massachusetts were elected by democratic town meetings, and while Puritan ministers were selected by committee, they were asked to leave if they failed to please their fold—which happened periodically and with no threat of chaos. Everywhere, Puritan rule called for the consent of the governed.

"The tenor" of Parson Smith's sermon, John Adams wrote proudly in his diary, "was to recommend Honour, Reward, and Obedience to good Rules; and a Spirited Opposition to bad ones." He talked of "Liberty and the Times."[10] Americans were not docile children in William Smith's sermon, but adults capable of influencing their own parents.

In the name of diplomacy the sisters' father, Reverend William Smith, refused to denounce evangelism but spoke out forcefully against the British Parliament, which he revered.

Clearly, the furor of Mary and Abigail and even 16-year-old Elizabeth—who was, of course, more passionately against the Stamp Act than both of them together—had affected him.

Still, Mary and Abigail had old friends who were not especially pleased five months later when Parliament conceded that they had no right to impose internal taxes and repealed the Stamp Act. Boston wildly celebrated the colonies' victory, but in Salem Toryism was so rampant Mary complained of having to make a "labourious inquiery" just to obtain a patriotic newspaper. While she rejoiced at the colonists' victory, she also gave England credit for submitting to reason. She was too full of family feeling to wish for any real break with the motherland, which, after all, produced the watch parts that were crucial to her husband's business and ran the most enlightened government on earth.[11] "Since the Stamp Act is repealed . . . I am at perfect Ease about Politicks," John Adams exaggerated his relief in a letter to Richard. "I care not a shilling who is in and who is out. I have no Point, that I wish carried."[12]

MARY TOO WANTED TO put politics behind her for the time being. For she had her domestic future on her mind, this first year away from home and family. So full of ideas herself, she never forgot how lucky she was to be married to a man with "the happy talent of communicating." Even in Salem he was attracting thoughtful people, like their new friend Nathaniel Ward, who told Richard he wished he could drop in at his house five or six times a day just to listen to the newly-weds talk. [13]

Ward was also awed by Richard's command of Newtonian science. Mechanics, like religion, spoke to Richard's love of perfect systems. Even now, as Richard was setting up his watch business in Salem, he was thrilled to learn that David Rittenhouse, in a farmhouse outside Philadelphia, was beginning work on a machine that would exactly replicate the positions of the planets and stars.[14] And while the world might run on compromise, the watches in Richard Cranch's shop could be made to tick precisely, down to the second—and he saw to it that they did.

In spite of all his other interests, Mary told Abigail, watch work was Richard's favorite activity. His friend Ward thought Richard's pendulum design a great step forward in the field.[15] Ward's only fear was that someone else might reap fame and fortune from Richard's idea because he was too modest or trusting to protect it. Or, Mary might have added, too unworldly to care.

She had begun silently to despair about ever living as comfortably as her parents. Clearly, her "best of men" was hopeless at looking out for his own interests—even after they became hers and the baby's as well. The watch business, with its costly instruments, demanded wealthy clients, and—like Parson Wibird with women—Richard lacked the temperament to woo. Richard certainly was not a born businessman. And while he *was* born to teach or preach, he lacked the credentials. His health ill-equipped him for any more physically demanding work.

As if to prove this point, in the fall of 1766, Richard became so ill that even Abigail, while begging Mary not to despair—"I would not have you cast down my Sister"—could only hope that "perhaps" her beloved Richard would improve.[16]

As he did—slowly, with Mary and her mother taking turns nursing him. But no sooner was Mary free to leave Richard's sickbed than gales of December snow again confined her to the Salem house and blocked the roads so no one could visit.[17] Mary felt the isolation more when she became pregnant. She missed her mother, who was now frequently ill herself, and her father, who, when weather permitted, sent a servant to bring her food and candles on the slimmest excuse.[18] She was their first child, the good one, who was less complicated than the other two girls or their brother. Mary let down her guard and admitted her depression to Abigail in the middle of January. "The winter never seem'd so tedious to me in the World . . . Indeed my Sister I cannot bear the thought of staying here."[19]

"I wonder not at it," Abigail answered, "a person—who has any sensibility, talk what they will of phylosiphy, and fortitude must be greatly affected at leaving so many agreable connections as you have—I feel it myself, but I feel more for you . . . I believe I can truly say. We were happy in our situation. so near each other, and so near our Father['s parsonage]."[20] Two weeks later that father braved the slippery journey from Weymouth to Salem to restore his daughter's good cheer.

In September, Mary gave birth to a second daughter, named Lucy for her mother's sister. Three months before, Abigail had delivered *their* second child, a boy named John Quincy after his dying grandfather.

A favorite topic for the Adamses and Cranches was how they would educate their children. John's diary entry on one such discussion reveals a decided view of his in-laws as well:

> Sister Cranch says, she has had an Opportunity of making many Observations, this Year at [Harvard's] Commencement. And she has quite altered her Mind about dancing and dancing Schools, and r. Cranch seems convinced too, and says it seems, that all such as learn to dance are so taken up with it, that they can't be students . . . What a sudden, and entire conversion this is."

Before this commencement, both couples had agreed that dancing was harmless.

So John remarked of the Cranches' conversion: "That Mrs. C. should change so quick is not so wonderfull, But that his mathmatical, metaphysical, systematical Head should be turned around so soon, by her Report of what she saw at Cambridge is a little remarkable"—not to mention a sure sign of who ruled that home.[21]

But while John and Richard could speak freely about dancing, it was taboo in New England to discuss the recent frenzy in both their houses as midwives ran in and out and the sisters moaned and groped for wine to dull the agony of childbirth. At the time one out of five New England women died from some complication when having a baby; the infant mortality rate was one in ten.[22] "Being brought to bed" is how colonial women described the event that glorified their existence, yet was so anguishing to look at that all men were shooed from the scene. Hospitals were for the very poor, doctors were only summoned in a crisis (though, of course, in the Smith sisters' cases, their uncle Dr. Tufts closely followed the event). Otherwise, expecting mothers "called their women" friends and family "together" for succor while a midwife put them on a low stool or sat them upright with two chairs clasped together to support their legs as she led them through the rituals of birth. Husbands like Richard and John were not only outside the door but often sent away from home altogether. Afterward, they came back to rejoice or despair.[23]

For while some like Mary recovered with the normal prescription of New England air and a nutritious diet, others like Abigail were tormented by a high temperature and painful breast-feeding, symptoms scarily like those of deadly puerperal sepsis. At a time when European medical schools operated on theories promoting purges and bleeding, American doctors like Uncle Tufts saw themselves as naturalists, prodding the body to heal itself with the help of poultices and herbs.[24] Thus Abigail confided in Mary, "Painful experience [teaches] me upon the very first chill, to apply a white Bread poultice because those cold fits are always succeeded by a fever and complaints of the Breast."[25]

WHILE THE SECOND CRANCH and Adams children were being born in the summer of 1767, news arrived that the British Parliament had passed the Townshend Acts (named after Charles Townshend, Lord of the Treasury), a new scheme to make money on the colonies, speciously defended as external rather than internal taxation because it pounced on favorite import items like tea. Since the colonists could legally purchase tea only from England, the tax was as unavoidable as any internal tax—unless, of course, they stopped drinking tea, which Americans loved as much as anyone in London. Parliament was convinced that would never happen.

But in October, Massachusetts became the first colony to boycott tea (as well as British lace and cloth, other victims of the new taxes). The sisters flouted the British tax by making their own "Liberty Tea" from the purple loosestrife plant and "Hyperion Tea" from raspberry leaves. College students took up the rebellion as well. "A *glorious spirit of Liberty prevails among you,*" Elizabeth Smith wrote her cousin Isaac at Harvard, unable to hide her pique that she could not be in Cambridge herself.

Isaac, the son of their prosperous Uncle Smith of Boston, was a favorite with all three sisters. Unlike their brother, who had rejected education, Isaac might well distinguish their family in an elevated sphere. If *they* were boys, they imagined, they would be like this intellectually omnivorous cousin. Possessing the brilliance and fortitude to succeed in any field, he aimed for the highest prize in New England, a good parish where he could preach. Only women had to be handsome; so the fact that Isaac was homely and overweight would not damage his chances—just look at the success of John Adams. Isaac was a year older than Elizabeth, who competed with her sisters for his attention. She sounds a little in love with him in her letters. He was also the first audience for her pronouncements against Parliament and the King.

All three sisters were ardent rebels. In addition to boycotting tea, they renounced the latest English calicos and chintzes. They wore their old dresses, spun their own native linen, cotton, and wool, cheering one another on and contributing whatever they could.[26] Abigail sent Mary yarn for stockings and flax for thread and asked Richard Cranch for a pair of the cards for combing wool, which he was selling along with his watches.[27] "Homespun," which just meant crude garments to the British (whose men did all the serious weaving), became a symbol of virtue in America.

And while Mary, Abigail, and Betsy were scornful of the sewing clubs sponsored by evangelical churches because they lumped patriotism together with predestination, they too were buoyed by faith in a righteous God.[28] In a fervent letter to her cousin Isaac, Elizabeth exclaimed, "At a time when we are threatened with the annihilation of our civil and religious Liberties, which is dearer to us than life, when clouds gather . . . when our King will not hear our petitions, nor redress our grievances: to whom shall we go or whither shall we flee but to the throne of God?"[29]

IN THE FALL OF 1768, when British boats poured into Boston Harbor to enforce the Townshend taxes, Abigail was living within sight of their sails. She was pregnant again, expecting a third child at Christmas. She had left her "humble Cottage in Braintree" and brought Nabby and John Quincy to join John on elegant Brattle Street in the "Noisy Buisy Town."[30] They came to Boston because John was now the most sought-after lawyer there, though Abigail was careful not to boast about his success to the less fortunate Cranches. Instead, she regaled them with stories about her Good Man's expanding waistline and Nabby's lonely Miss Doll. With her younger sister, Elizabeth, she could be less reserved. Elizabeth idolized John and spoke freely about his likely success maybe not just at law, which their parents looked down on, but as a minister in his own right—a spokesman for the American cause.

Of course, John had his weak points—"Temperance, Exercise and

*A 1775 map of Boston
and its environs*

Abigail agonized far less than
John about evil.

Peace of Mind" did not come easily.[31] He was as quick to judge as when he had first met the Smith sisters and so determined to be the center of attention that—before Abigail joined him on Brattle Street—he had stayed out late most nights at political clubs, smoking, drinking, and dominating all debates. Though naturally robust, John could make himself sick with anxiety and anger. Once, he lashed out at an English friend of the Cranches, insisting "there was no more Justice left in Britain than there was in Hell." Afterward, he rued his "Warmth, Heat, Violence, Acrimony, Bitterness, [and] Sharpness of . . . Temper . . . I cannot but reflect upon myself with severity," he agonized in his diary. Though he heaped scorn on Evangelicals, he shared their bleak view of human nature. "The greatest men have been the most envious, malicious, and revengeful," he lamented. Worse—and particularly pertinent, he felt, in his own case—even those "of the most exalted Genius" were "perfect slaves to the Love of Fame."[32]

Abigail agonized far less than John about evil. Her cheerful temperament, she informed a friend, "tis no virtue acquired," because she was born optimistic.

"I sometimes wonder at myself, and fear least a degree of stupidity or insensibility should possess my mind in these calamitous times or I could not feel so tranquil," she explained; ". . . yet I cannot charge myself with an unfeeling Heart. I pitty, commisirate and as far as my ability reaches feel ready and desirous to releave my fellow creatures under their distresses."

Nor were any of the Smith sisters "of that . . . anxious disposition" that saw mischief in every desire.[33] They refused to denigrate ambition. While a Caesar's lust for power might "eradicate every principal of Humanity and Benevolence," the bright side, declared Abigail, was that "Ambition . . . when it centers in an honest mind possess'd of great abilities may [do] imminent Service to the world."[34] A perfect example slept beside her in bed.

Where John fretted about his low lawyer's wages, Abigail knew they'd be happy on a fraction of her grandparents' fortune since wealth was not their priority. Their goals were vaguer and more exalted. For her part, Abigail both relished the protected sphere of domesticity and wished she could explore the world like a man.

When she heard her cousin Isaac was sailing for England, for instance, her first response was pity. The temptations of London were well-known to every colonist. Poor Isaac was doomed to a battle with sin. But when danger failed to materialize, and Isaac wrote home about visits to theatres and bookstores and rides to Canterbury and Paris, Abigail reconsidered their relative positions. "Had nature formed me of the other Sex, I should certainly have been a rover," she meaningfully observed in one letter to her cousin. "Women you know Sir . . . inherit an Eaquel Share of curiosity with the other Sex." And while their physical frailty was certainly a discouragement to crossing the Atlantic, what really kept women in one place for a lifetime were the "dangers we are subject too from your Sex." These included not just rape and murder, but the stigma men attached to women who behaved like them.[35]

Curiosity overcame Abigail's resentment when Isaac wrote her of meeting the famous female scholar Catharine Macaulay, who blamed the Norman Invasion for England's decline since the Magna Carta and demanded more rights for the common man. She had recently published the first few books of a projected eight-volume history of England. Bewilderingly—to Abigail at least—she was acclaimed rather than punished for writing under her own female name.

Abigail yearned to know everything Isaac had learned about this fascinating creature.[36] Who were her friends? Her family? Most important, since poverty was the only excuse for a respectable woman in England to publish even novels, what emboldened Lady Macaulay—who was wealthy—"to engage in a Study never before Exibited to the publick by one of her own Sex and Country, tho now to the honour of both?"[37] And through what mysterious channels did Catharine Macaulay obtain knowledge?

Mrs. Macaulay gave contradictory views of her education. What is known is that her mother died young, and her father either devoted himself to teaching Catharine or—as she at other times reported—was a recluse, and a brother or governess led her to his library. No report exists of Catharine's discussing her upbringing with Isaac, though the historian did, intriguingly, inform another American that she had no tutoring whatsoever and was a thoughtless girl of twenty when she was suddenly drawn to studies of Rome and Greece.[38] At twenty-nine, in 1760 Catharine married a Scottish doctor, George Macaulay. She gave birth to a daughter and published the first volume of *History of England* before she was widowed in 1766. When Isaac Smith met Catharine, five years later, she was writing prodigiously, socializing with luminaries like Dr. Johnson, and managing a house and child.

Because her daughter Nabby turned six during Isaac Smith's 1771 trip to England, the issue of female education was very much on Abigail's mind. Was Catharine Macaulay a realistic model for her colonial daughter, or was she an outgrowth of more enlightened England, as the prodigy Madame de Sevigne was of France? Neither Abigail nor Mary wished to turn their daughters into pariahs. While they were sure their Nabby and Betsy possessed the same learning apparatus as male children, they could not ignore the received wisdom that girls' reproductive systems had a deleterious effect on their minds—and vice versa. Intellectual activity was said to sap fertility. It would be two decades before Macaulay's *Letters on Education* (1790) and Mary Wollstonecraft's *Vindication of the Rights of Woman* (1792) openly ridiculed that widely held eighteenth-century theory.[39] The most radical work Abigail had read lately was a compilation of letters called *On the Management and Education of Children,* which proposed teaching women a smattering of history and literature, primarily for the purpose of improving their conversations with men.[40]

It still rankled that Abigail's own parents had lavished all their learning on Billy. "Why should children of the same family be thus distinguished?" she complained to another cousin, John Thaxter. Besides, pinching women's minds was self-defeating since mothers controlled the early education of boy as well as girl children and so impacted the fate of the whole family, and by extension the community and society at large.

And she did not dissemble about where the blame lay. "Why should your sex wish for such a disparity in those whom they one day intend for companions," she pointedly asked her cousin, unless the "Neglect arises in some measure from an ungenerous jealosy of rivals near the throne."[41]

Abigail knew that her own husband endorsed this rivalry, though she preferred to think he refused to send her Lord Chesterfield's sexually explicit letters *not* to assert his male prerogative but to shield her sensibility, and that he saw no need for laws to protect married women because he was such a good husband himself.[42] John used blandishments to avoid conflict. Rather than lecturing her on obedience, he wheedled: "Nothing has contributed so much to support my Mind as the choice Blessing of a Wife . . . whose pure Virtue obliged her to approve the Views of her Husband."

To society at large, Abigail did cheerfully espouse her husband's opinions. She accepted male hierarchy, for to do otherwise would be to renounce her parents' example and her own Puritan view. But with John himself she was too strong to be strangled by that sort of "virtue," which in any case had conflicting implications for Puritans, who were taught that intellectual growth was necessary to salvation and that frank companionship was crucial to married love. Besides, John Adams was not so jealous of his power that he wanted a docile partner. He boasted that Abigail wrote better letters than he did, relished her "steel[y]" intelligence, and depended on her advice. Each relied on the other's passion for justice. They longed to understand and improve whatever they came in touch with—be it their offspring or their col-

ony. So if marriage reinforced Abigail's resentment at the disparity between the sexes, it appeased her with an admiring partner who shared
her quest for a better world.

Like Richard and Mary, John and Abigail addressed each other as
"Dearest Friend" and meant it.[43] Often, in the privacy of their bedroom, it was Abigail who spoke first on issues that troubled them both.
Slavery was an example. Though her parents' slaves, Tom and Phoebe,
seemed happy enough in the benevolent Smith home, the injustice of
their fate chafed Abigail as she protested her own oppression by the
British troops. "I wish sincerely there was not a Slave in the province,"
she told John, who readily agreed with her. "It allways appeard a most
iniquitious Scheme to me—fight ourselfs for what we are daily robbing and plundering from those who have as good a right to freedom
as we have."[44]

On other subjects, Abigail and John simply came to the same conclusion. It was hard to know who spoke first about facing down the
British, though Abigail drew the analogy between Americans chary of
bloodshed and the ancient warriors who "by an execessive love of
peace . . . neglected the means of making it sure and lasting."[45] What
Patrick Henry said to the Virginia Congress, "If this be treason, make
the most of it!" rang in her ears.

Yet, neither she nor John could feel righteous about an incident that
occurred at the end of the winter of 1770. The colonists of Boston were
then as flammable as tinder. Daily they seethed watching the British set
up barracks in their Commons, fine colonists for the slightest infrac-
tions, and usurp local jobs to moonlight in their spare time. That is,
when they weren't getting drunk, or chasing American women.

On the night of March 5, however, eight British soldiers were just
peacefully guarding the Boston Customs House when they were bombarded with snowballs, garbage, and oyster shells by a rowdy colonial
mob. Soon all the bells in town were ringing. Thirty years before, Boston's indignant poor had rioted against merchants to protest their ex-
port of corn during a time of famine. Now, under the cover of darkness,
they vented their anger at British occupation on the men who happened to be on guard. And they continued assaulting, ignoring British
warnings, until these soldiers, wounded and outraged, retaliated by fir-
ing into the crowd.

The resulting deaths of five colonists, including a former slave, triggered massive indignation. In an instantly famous engraving, Paul Revere portrayed the British as murderers, and Abigail and John Adams saw "no Reason why the Town should not call the Action of that Night a Massacre" since England had no business stationing an army in America at all.[45] The guilt of these particular soldiers, however, was dubious, and in any case, they deserved a fair trial in the Boston courts. It was because of his commitment to British law that John Adams consented to serve as their defense attorney, thereby gaining the limelight but also the rage of friends.

At the trial, Abigail watched him summon all his acuteness about human nature to win over the jury. Speaking of one soldier, clubbed to the ground by a colonist, John Adams asked, "Do you expect he should behave like a stoic philosopher, lost in apathy?" True, the British were troublemakers. "Soldiers quartered in a populous town will always occasion two mobs where they prevent one;" yet the court's mandate was to judge not British policy but the actions of the individual soldiers. "Whatever may be our wishes, our inclinations, or the dictums of our passions, they cannot alter the state of facts and evidence," he argued. And: "It's of more importance . . . that innocence should be protected, than . . . that guilt should be punished."[47]

The jury debated nearly three hours, then acquitted all but two of the soldiers, confirming John's persuasiveness, but enraging the *Boston Gazette* and causing many of Adams's clients to defect. And yet he felt justified enough to boast of his "gallant, generous, manly and disinterested Action . . . Judgment of Death against [the soldiers] would have been as foul a Stain upon this Country as the Executions of the Quakers or Witches . . . As the evidence was, the Verdict of the Jury was exactly right."[48]

Abigail agreed. But the preceding year had taken a toll on her high spirits. The previous February, she had experienced the first real tragedy of her life when the child she had been carrying the day she arrived in Boston—called Susanna after her mother-in-law and nicknamed Suky—died. She was barely a year old. And though Abigail forced herself to believe Suky was happy in Heaven and took to heart the Puritan admonishment that her "usefulness" to the living should not be sapped by grief, her "soul . . . anguish[ed]," as did her husband's.[49] For while losing a child was common enough in New England, there had been no infant deaths in Abigail's immediate family. Somehow it was worse that Suky, like herself, was a second daughter, who would have helped her weave and weed the garden and have kept her company when John Quincy went off to school. And then there was the loss of a companion for five-year-old Nabby. Brothers were fine, but Abigail felt sure no one expanded the heart and social feelings like a sister. It would be years before Abigail could so much as allude to Suky, her pain ran so deep.[50]

FOUR MONTHS AFTER SUKY'S DEATH, in May of 1770, Abigail gave birth to a second boy, Charles, who revived her interest in life, but submitted her once again to the agony of post-partum chills and fevers. Then John became gravely ill with lung pains—which sound like pneumonia—and constant exhaustion. A year passed before Abigail again had the time or inclination to pick up her pen to her sisters.

By then, the Adamses had fled Boston for Braintree—to save his life, John said. And indeed, the sight of Penn's Hill and the stimulation of Parson Wibird's sensible sermons revived both of them, as they threw themselves into the doable tasks of fixing fences and making space for the new baby boy in crowded quarters. They rode and strolled over their farmland; they pondered improvements like cutting ditches and clearing swamps. In 1770, Parliament, pressured by their own merchants, rescinded most of the Townshend Acts,[51] and John once again swore off politics,[52] while Mary and Richard's absence was all Abigail regretted as her spirits rose in a house that held no memories of her dead child.

When a client's case called John to Boston, instead of seeking out his firebrand cousin Sam Adams, who was leading the rebellion against England in the taverns, John now dined quietly with Abigail's brother, Billy, who had become a mild eccentric, surrounding himself with dogs, rabbits, tame ducks, and chickens—as well as too much liquor, to his family's chagrin.[53] Abigail, meanwhile, so devoted herself to teaching that by the time Nabby turned nine she could read any book in the English language, her mother boasted, and six-year-old John Quincy was prepared to chastise himself in a letter to his accomplished 10-year-old cousin, Betsy Cranch:

I have had it in my mind to write to you this long time but afairs of much less Importance has prevented me I have made But veray little proviancy in reading . . . Too much of my time in play [th]ere is a great Deal of room for me to grow better[54]

EVEN MORE IMPRESSIVE THAN Cousin Betsy to John Quincy was his aunt Elizabeth, who frequently visited. Being younger than his parents, breathtakingly pretty, and unmarried made her a romantic figure. Not so to her older sisters, who complained of Betsy's insubordination. "I really think she must take her own way and nobody say her Nay," Abigail complained. But Betsy was a favorite with John Adams, who called her "amiable" and "ingenious," teased her about finding a husband, and took her to visit important friends like Colonel and Mercy Otis Warren when his own wife was obliged to keep house.[55] How Abigail must have resented this privilege.[56] Mercy Otis Warren, a playwright and pamphleteer (under pseudonym) as well as an impeccable wife and mother, was as close as America had come to producing a Catharine Macaulay. It was an honor to be asked to her home.

Of the three sisters, Elizabeth alone wrote out of an ambition to publish her letters—just like Lady Worley Montagu, the British bluestocking who collected her correspondence with such masters as Alexander Pope. Sometimes grandiloquence and a bombardment by adjectives undermine her attempts to sound literary, as in this decidedly precious depiction of the parsonage in a letter to Mary:

At such a window I have viewed with perfect tranquility the softened azure and the variegated cloud—with such a Friend seated upon the verdant Bank we talked down the summer sun . . . beheld the Moon walking in brightness, and almost paid . . . homage to the Queen of heaven.[57]

But her letters also could be forceful, as when she acknowledged that she was more trusting than Mary or Abigail: "How often have I thought it unkind, unjust, and the height of *cruelty* to suspect there was the least Ill, 'where no ill *seemed*.' "[58] She pressed on to argue that presuming the worst of men degraded the human spirit. So too perceiving women as mere coquettes, as did the French philosopher Jean Jacques Rousseau in *Emile,* was an affront to her sex.

Elizabeth hoped to transcend all such prejudice, but pursuing lofty goals was difficult in a humdrum village, no matter how picturesque its natural environment. And it was not easy being the only unmarried daughter of parents who were growing old. Because she "never [could] feel easy to neglect family business," she spent whole days nursing her mother whose "weak state of health devolves [on me] more than is common for young persons in my station of life," she told a friend. She herself frequently got sick and lost the little time she had for "improving [her] Mental Powers" to convalescing so she could care for others once again . . . [59] It was especially during periods when she was confined to bed that writing letters came to her rescue.

For no matter how weak she felt, Betsy could wield words as a weapon. When an acquaintance insisted it was impossible to acquire a knowledge of the world without being deeply infected with its vices, she retorted that knowledge was a precaution rather than a trap, "for as soon as [we] have found out where [we] are mostly likely to be overcome, there let [us] place [our] strongest guard."[60] The Boston Massacre, for example, had taught the colonists to think before acting. "Oh my Brother! Oppression is enough to make a wise people Mad," she lamented in a letter to John Adams, but quickly added that "Reason" and "Prudence" must channel "our turbulent Passions." Random violence had only undermined the colonists' cause.[61]

With her cousin Isaac, who insisted he was perfectly indifferent to politics, she was more combative. "Where," she challenged,

> is the wretch so Stoical as not to be deeply concerned for his Country . . . Liberty fair Goddess . . . now stands tottering on the brink of ruin—Is not this thought enough to rouse every resentful passion in the human breast?

Isaac did not see fit to air his own views on the British. His only commitment, he insisted, was to a moderate, anti-evangelical Puritanism—like Betsy's. He obviously took great pleasure teasing his younger cousin—as when, in a letter from Harvard, he noted unmarried Betsy's supposed "fondness for the single state."

"I abhor *such a single state,*" she lashed back and, to emphasize her point, condemned the contentedly widowed Madame de Sevigne. "Madame it seems . . . recommends Love not as an Occupation, but merely an amusement. I always thought it dangerous trifling with edged tools!" [62]

She objected even more strenuously to Madame de Sevigne's describing romantic love as a dull emotion. "The formal phlegmatic Lover and the cold indifferent Husband" were both anathemas to Betsy.[63] This would seem to eliminate stolid Isaac as a candidate for life partner. But Isaac did possess her passion for literature. Besides, he was young and, she presumed, malleable. Elizabeth had friends who married first cousins. Why shouldn't she?

"There is a natural propensity in the human species to love objects they imagine beautiful," Betsy wrote Isaac at one point. "Beauty strikes the eye and often affects the Heart. But if it is only a set of features, or the tincture of skin that we admire, it is preposterous." True love depended on friendship based on esteem rather than appearance, she assured her short and chubby cousin.[64] And in a subsequent letter to Isaac, Betsy used almost the same words when she described her relationship with him: "Friendship formed in Infancy, which has been cemented by the most rational esteem in maturer years."[65] For his part, Isaac held his tongue.

It was when Isaac was in London and sent Betsy only his "affectionate regard" at the end of a letter to Abigail that she began questioning the depth of his friendship. *She* thought of *him* constantly. So when he boarded a boat for home, "Judge . . . what Grief must overwhelm my Heart," Betsy wrote, imagining him dead in the Atlantic. When he landed safely in Boston during Christmas week 1771: "Welcome thrice welcome to your native soil . . . The glad tidings of your safe arrival . . . too much elated my heart with joy to close my eyelids." Relief, she explained, was as unsettling as fear to a person as sensitive as she.[66]

Yet, though she wrote like a lover, she could not bring herself to say she was *in* love with Isaac—even to Abigail, who interrogated her relentlessly and complained of her reserve. In fact the cousins soon drifted apart, as Betsy threw herself into nursing and housework, while Isaac was ordained and looked for a parish where he could settle and preach. This proved more difficult than any of the sisters could have predicted.

For there was no question that Isaac's family and Harvard record ideally suited him for a major parish in the Boston region. The problem was the radical change in Puritan politics since Parson Wibird and Parson Smith had preached opposite views on the Stamp Act Bill in 1766.

By 1771, there were more than two million colonists in America and approximately 235,000 in Massachusetts alone. Formerly, the individual colonies—so far apart geographically and in competition for foreign buyers—were more like jealous neighbors than siblings. Now British taxes gave them a family cause.

They had slowly recognized the advantage of acting together. For instance, after the Townshend Acts, the Virginia legislature joined Massachusetts to officially condemn external taxes, and Philadelphia merchants overcame self-interest and collaborated in the boycott of British goods. "The colonists are taking large strides toward independency," General Gage, the highest British commander in America, warned the British Secretary of War. Independency: here was a new concept, the colonies as a nation. It was more than most colonists themselves had imagined. They asked only for equal justice under British law.[67]

For a few years after the repeal of the Townsend Acts—while John Adams was clearing swamps in Braintree—colonial opposition waned, only to be woken again in 1773 when a Tea Act imposed yet another burden on Americans. Massachusetts was first to rise to the occasion and refused to accept British tea in her ports.

As the first tea-bearing boat, the *Dartmouth,* appeared in Boston Harbor, secret meetings resumed at Boston's Faneuil Hall and Old South Church. Nine days before Christmas, two hundred Bostonians (poorly) disguised as Mohawk Indians and led by Sam Adams boarded the *Dartmouth* and pitched its entire cargo, 342 containers of tea, into the Bay below. The Boston Tea Party was a solemn attack on that most sacred of British rights—the protection of private property. The leafy water in Boston's harbor spoke to a new level of confrontation. The American protest was no longer purely a battle of words.

But words were more heavily scrutinized than ever. Silence on the rift with England was increasingly interpreted as sympathy for the enemy, or Toryism, threatening a man's social position and even his job. Clergymen in particular were urged to profess defiance against the mother country—an impossibility for Cousin Isaac Smith.[68] No longer able to plead indifference, he acknowledged he "had rather calmly acquiesce in . . . an hundred [unfair] acts, proceeding from a British Legislature . . . than . . . behold the soil, which gave [him] birth, made a scene of mutual carnage."

And further to his detriment, he frankly attacked the Boston Tea Party. Taxes, in Isaac' eyes, were a small price to pay for peace.[69] But he did not proselytize either. He called himself a moderate, never a Tory. Still, one parish after another turned him down.

It was clear there was a crisis that called for the intervention of an older cousin, and Mary Cranch stepped up to the task. Converting dogged Isaac, she saw, was beyond even her powers. So she instead summoned her shrewdness to convince him to play dumb.

"I had rather think [you] understand . . . Divinity better than Politicks," Mary wrote, hinting broadly that his errant views could pass as daftness. "The management of our publick affairs is in very good hands, and all that is requir'd of you is your Prayers and exhortations for a general reformation," she continued in the same vein. He had doubtless failed to note that:

> orthodoxy in Politics is full as necessary a quallification for Settling a minister at the present Day as orthodoxy in divinity was formely, and tho you should preach like an angel[,] if the People suppose you unfriendly to the country . . . and a difender of the unjust, cruil and arbitary measures that have been taken by the [British] ministry against us, you will be like to do very little good.

Mary proposed that Isaac was not vicious, just indiscreet, his principals off-handed and so easy to change. But he refused to bend to her subterfuge. Nor would he propitiate the churches of Boston—even if it cost him his career. He well understood that religion and politics were inseparable. Both involved free will, and he would exercise his own. Nonetheless, his disagreement with Mary was historical, not personal, he made clear. "In what times are we fallen when the least degree of moderation, the least inclination to peace and order . . . the remotest apprehension for the public welfare and security is accounted a crime?"[70] He made a compelling case for the loyalist cause.

Clearly, there was no talking Isaac into a position acceptable to the Puritan congregations of Boston. Now Mary could only pull back and assure him of her family's support. However much they disagreed, he was her cousin. The breach with her metaphorical mother, England, which only eight years earlier had seemed impossible, was conceivable to her now; a breach in the biological family was not. "My high Esteem and great regard for you must be my excuse for the freedom I have taken," she assured him.[71] And he in return wished all the Cranches well.

As ISAAC AND MARY were bending themselves to mend family fences, John Adams relinquished the claims of private happiness and threw himself wholeheartedly into the struggle for American rights. The Boston Tea Party, which saddened Isaac, had elated Abigail's husband. "This destruction of the Tea is so bold, so daring, so firm, intrepid and inflexible, and it must have so important Consequences, and so lasting, that I cant but consider it as an Epocha in History."[72]

Gradually, Boston's cause was embraced by the other twelve colonies. In the spring of 1774, when the British closed Boston's harbor in retaliation for their Boston Tea Party, Virginia responded with a day of fasting, and South Carolina sent carriage-loads of rice up north. Who knew what fresh travesty would follow? If Parliament could tax them, it could banish even the most sacred freedom—freedom of religion, for which their great grandparents escaped England in the first place—John Adams pointed out.

In September of 1774, Adams was one of five patriots elected to represent Massachusetts at a Continental Congress in Philadelphia. All the colonies except Georgia sent delegates. Their goal was *not* independence, but the creation of a Declaration of Rights and Grievances demanding equality under British law.

"All Eyes look up to the American Congress as the Constelation by which the important Affairs of State is to receive its guidance and direction," Betsy wrote John in Philadelphia that October. While her cousin Isaac was now discussing a permanent move to England, Betsy's heart, she assured him, was very much at home. "We all join in wishing you may prosper in your arduous Employment, and may every measure for the good of our Country, be crowned with glorious Success."[73]

At the parsonage, her mother was sick, and Betsy spent all her time ministering to her—or almost all her time, for an attractive new student of ministry had recently appeared to work with her father. Betsy and he had widely different temperaments, but he shared her patriotic spirit, and, best of all, liked to read. His name was John Shaw, and everyone was talking about him.

CHAPTER III

"Sister Delegate"

. . .

ELIZABETH SMITH MET JOHN SHAW IN THE FALL OF 1773, EIGHT months before the Boston Tea Party. The seventh child and namesake of the long-time minister of nearby Bridgewater, Shaw was boarding and studying for the ministry with her father while instructing boys at the neighborhood school. An instructor's salary was meager, but John Shaw loved teaching, which set him apart from most of William Smith's earlier candidates. Nor was his religion as easygoing as theirs. He was a Calvinist, suspicious of the goodness Elizabeth and her sisters saw all around them. He had enemies as well as friends.[1]

And like his Old Light father, who watched his parishioners lured away by the New Lights in the 1740s, John Shaw was wary of opposition. He had little faith in progress. The Enlightenment stress on human potential, which so appealed to the Adamses and Cranches, was misplaced in his opinion since a man's fate was ordained by God before he was born.[2] Enthusiasm on the whole repelled Shaw, although there was something almost evangelical in his pessimism. He had to struggle against his natural reticence to make an impression on the pretty daughter of William Smith.

With her keen sensibility and high spirits, Elizabeth attracted many suitors; a man she alluded to as "Pollio" was courting her at the time she met Shaw. Shaw was more guarded than Pollio, but also more fascinating. He not only knew how to carry a point—he'd been vice-president of the speaking club at Harvard—but listened eagerly to her opinions and appreciated her putting herself out to make him comfortable away from home.

Since Elizabeth, like her sisters, was a liberal Congregationalist, it is curious that she never openly opposed Shaw's Calvinism. Clearly his intensity intrigued her. Perhaps she saw his earnestness as a challenge—maybe she could raise his spirits, brighten his mood. Summer turned to fall, and they were laughing under the red leaves of the giant oak trees and then wandering Betsy's beloved paths through the snow-covered hills. He was twenty-four, unsure where or even whether he wanted to minister; she was twenty-two, and most of her time was consumed by caregiving, since her mother was increasingly sick. Both Betsy and John declared themselves unready for major changes in their personal lives.

Elizabeth felt overwhelmed enough by changes in the outside world, she wrote Abigail, who was visiting Boston, on February 8, 1774. "When I enter on a more particular retrospect of the last seven Years of my Life, I find it replete with Revolutions," she announced, summoning all the solemnity she could muster to persuade her sister to stop treating her like a child. Formerly her ally against their worrying parents, Abigail, now the mother of four (after the birth of a healthy third son, Thomas), had lately taken to laying down laws herself. Her expertise was men: or so she intimated. And she seemed to have completely forgotten her own romance for she declared it a pity Elizabeth could not "reason" herself into love.[3]

"You are either very cruel or very tender," Elizabeth wrote from the isolated parsonage. She envisioned Abigail socializing with all the important people in the big city because of her increasingly famous spouse. And while Elizabeth tried, she said, to interpret Abigail's reproofs as "over anxious concern for my Welfare," she made no bones that she had her doubts, which had only increased when Abigail snubbed John Shaw on a recent visit to the parsonage. Abigail's ostensible reason for disliking Shaw was his severe religious views, but Betsy suspected envy of the attentions he showed her as well.

And Betsy had heard more than enough about the ecstasy of the Adams marriage. So when she finished her discourse on revolutions, she launched into a dirge on disappointed couples "dragging out a miserable load of Life, in domestick Quarrels" and went on to deplore "the weakness, and imperfection of our Natures, the Capriciousness of rational Creatures, and the deceitfulness of the human heart."[4]

Abigail, in return, accused Betsy of wanting to marry Shaw, a fate the family feared for reasons Abigail left Betsy to judge for herself. Noting that May, the "most dangerous month" of the year, was approaching, Abigail advised her younger sister to visit Boston, "an excellent place to quench old Flames and kindle new ones." She proceeded in the same circuitous manner to enjoin Elizabeth "not to seek Temptation, which to avoid were better" and begged her not to flirt.

This letter so enraged Betsy she "feared I should express more Acrimony than would be consistent with that *candid and gentle treatment* due to a Sister." It was the night of March 7, and a candle "snaped and greased" the paper as she wrote. With no siblings home and the winter discouraging even the Tufts and Smiths from visiting, she sat alone in her bedroom. How heartless of Abigail to demand she stand at "Chimney's length" from anyone at all.

While pointedly not building a case for Shaw's attractions as a suitor, Betsy portrayed him as "a Person of Virtue, and Good Sense," a "Gentleman," and "fellow creature." To clinch matters, she drew up a legal-looking document, declaring: "To . . . all those whom it does, or may concern, that We John Shaw, and Elizabeth Smith have no such Purpose in our Hearts, as has been unjustly surmised;" and affixed a signature clipped from one of John Shaw's papers next to her own.[5] In a different hand, she added mock signatures of her parents as witnesses.

She folded this fake document into her very long letter (since the recipient paid, Abigail would be sure to owe a high postage) and awaited her sister's reply.

MARY CRANCH MADE TEA from her mother's hops plant to soothe herself during the spring of 1774.[6] She was finding it a great struggle to set down roots in New England. First, Tory hostility chased the Cranches out of Salem. Now, after four unquiet enough years in Boston, they were being subjected to Parliament's Coercive Acts, which on

June 1 closed the port and loosed 5,000 troops through the streets. As a further humiliation, soldiers were given permission to barrack wherever they wished—even in her own house, if they cared to board with three young children. Boston town meetings were shut down, then secretly reconvened in Concord. Self-deluders might still imagine a reconciliation. Hard-minded Mary could not be so fooled. As the British dug cannons into Beacon Hill and the patriots trained a volunteer militia of Minutemen, she knew only bloodshed would restore peace with honor.

All around her, friends were fleeing to the countryside. Every day some family Mary knew crossed the mucky isthmus called the Neck, which—now that even ferries to Charleston were banished from the river—was the only way onto or off the Boston peninsula. At the end of September John Adams, writing from the First Continental Congress in Philadelphia, urged the Cranches to follow his own family home to Braintree, but Mary had her reasons for refusing to move.

"As to moving . . . I have been so long in an uncertainty what we ought to do: and one Friend advising one way and one another that I feel rack'd," she wrote Abigail. Mary was living on Hanover Street in Boston's North End by the mill pond, surrounded by gray gabled clapboard houses and brick and wooden churches as far as the eye could see.[7] Her artisan friend Paul Revere lived down the road. A leading rebel, Revere was busy riding news to and from the delegates in Philadelphia, where, he told her, there were broad avenues with brick sidewalks and whale oil lamps everywhere so you could travel easily after dark. Boston's pebbled roads were mostly unlit, narrow, and winding. Pedestrians vied with carts and carriages for the center, where the pavement was smoothest, for there were no footpaths on either side.

Despite the cry for homespun, both cities had their share of ladies parading about in manufactured gowns and sleeping on chairs to keep their inflated hair in place. Many men still wore fancy red cloaks like the British. "If we expect to inherit the blessings of our Fathers, we should return a little more to their primitive Simplicity," Abigail wryly commented after one visit to Boston where she observed no difference in adornment since the boycott of British goods.[8]

Still, with just half of Philadelphia's approximately 30,000 citizens, Boston had five newspapers and a larger percentage of rebels than any

Paul Revere lived in this house by the mill pond,
down the road from Mary.

other city on the northeast coast. Being the seat of a thriving Puritan
community on the one hand and a punitive British Army on the other
set Boston apart from the rest of America. The daily threat of war had
a particular impact on women like Mary. For where Martha Livingston, daughter of prominent New York patriots, viewed the battle for
liberty from afar and even declared herself indifferent to its outcome,
since "our sex are *doomed* to be obedient in every state," the men and
women of Boston stood united by a common threat.[9]

Besides, the revolt had begun here. The past decade had made landmarks of places like Faneuil Hall, where Samuel Adams first called
Americans to defend their freedom, and the Old South Church, which
every fifth of March still crowded to the rafters with thousands bewail-
ing the Boston Massacre. There was the 120-year-old elm singled out as
the Liberty Tree to protest the Stamp Act and the tavern distinguished
by a sign of a hammered copper dragon on Union Street where patriots
contrived their plan to dump the caskets of British tea. Indeed, at nearly
every neighborhood tavern, alongside businessmen making deals and
farmers sharing local gossip, politicians now gathered with their anger
and their schemes.

Mary, who had moved to Boston soon after the birth of her now five-year-old son, Billy, had her personal landmarks as well. Two years before, bells from the Old North Church had comforted her through her children's' bouts with measles.[10] The Brattle Street home where the Adamses had lived at the time of the Boston Massacre brought back memories of swapping gossip and being on top of the latest news. And then there was Uncle Isaac's house (near the State House on Queen Street), with its Copley portraits and free-flowing Madeira, which always promised ease when she was tired of being brave and thrifty.

Earlier, Richard Cranch had complained that business was "very dull" because of the rage for British imports.[11] But the recent boycott had been a boon to local producers. And while political uncertainty took its toll on watch sales, the campaign for homemade clothes enhanced the demand for Richard's wool-combing cards. Since there was now a card factory right in Boston, business continued to thrive even with the port closed.

Indeed, for once it was not Richard's failure but his success that tormented Mary. Hating insecurity, she longed to leave Boston, but felt incapable of making the decision now that Richard's efforts were at last bearing fruit. It was hard to explain this to Abigail, whose husband was already a successful lawyer. "I am full of apprehentions of—I dont know what ... Mr. Cranch is so hurried with Work that he does not know how to spare time to see after any thing, and I am so unwell that I am not able too,"[12] she groped for words as well as composure in an error-riddled, barely legible note to her worried sister on August 20. Let the more literary Abigail and Elizabeth take the trouble to prettify their letters. "No copying for me ... I had rather write another," she declared.[13]

HAVING A MESSENGER AS a neighbor kept the Cranches apprised of events in Philadelphia during the fall of 1774. Since mail was easily intercepted, all letters from Congress were guarded and impersonal enough to be read by friends as well as spouses. Paul Revere followed a common practice by bringing Mary and Richard John Adams's letters to Abigail to peruse before sending them on to her.[14]

So while sick with worry about her own future, Mary had the odd experience of reading stories of a far-off First Continental Congress which, wrote John, "most earnestly engaged in Debates upon the most abstruse Misteries of State until three in the Afternoon," after which they dined on "ten thousand Delicacies, and s[at] drinking . . . till six or seven" at night. She learned that normally forbearing John was devouring beer and enamored of a port wine he had discovered in Philadelphia and that he felt surprisingly fit and happy on a regime so completely at odds with their simple Puritan cuisine.[15]

John was rapturous about the fifty-five delegates to the Continental Congress, calling them "a Collection of the greatest Men upon the Continent, in Point of Abilities, Virtues and Fortunes." They were tradesmen and plantation owners, lawyers and wealthy merchants. They shunned the State House because it reminded them of British mandates and met in a modest guild building called Carpenters Hall. John was especially proud of the delegates' willingness to transcend factions, as when members of all faiths agreed to hear morning prayers read by a local Episcopalian. And from the moderate John Dickinson of Philadelphia to Virginia's eloquent radical Henry Lee, the crisis in New England troubled all the representatives who convened on September 5, 1774. Even before the Congress met, George Washington from Virginia offered to personally finance and lead a thousand soldiers to fortify Massachusetts.[16] Now, with sessions in full swing, Massachusetts took the floor to argue its own case in the so-called "Suffolk Resolves."

The man behind the Suffolk Resolves, Joseph Warren, was an outspoken patriot and a gifted physician. Abigail called him the best-dressed man in Boston.[17]

His ideas were bold. Warren's Suffolk Resolves demanded that Great Britain withdraw its blockade from Boston Harbor and rescind all taxes. Obedience to the monarchy was *not* the King's birthright, they insisted, George III was mortal and must earn his right to rule. This was the most radical position yet espoused in Congress. Even Adams worried that Dr. Warren—and hence Massachusetts—had gone too far. So it was with great relief that he could write Abigail, the day after the Suffolk Resolves were read aloud in Congress:

> The Esteem, the Affection, the Admiration, for the People of Boston . . . which were expressed [in Congress] Yesterday, And

the fixed Determination that they should be supported, were enough to melt an Heart of Stone.[18]

Before it adjourned in the end of October, Congress voted to support all the Suffolk Resolves, train a colonial militia, close royal courts, and enforce a moratorium on the import of all English goods.

John's enthusiasm for Congress had apparently worn thin by this time, however. "I am worried to Death with the Life I lead," he wrote in a last letter before heading home to Braintree. The "perpetual Round of feasting" had grown tiresome, and the flourishing of genius had gone too far. Never had he experienced such showing off. "I believe if it was moved and seconded that We should come to a Resolution that Three and two make five[,] We should be entertained with Logick and Rhetorick, Law, History, Politicks and Mathematicks, concerning the Subject for two whole Days, and then We should pass the Resolution unanimously in the Affirmative," he complained.[19]

WHEN JOHN RETURNED HOME, the British were digging trenches to prevent assault from across the neck on the mainland.[20] Then winter came, and British soldiers began crowding themselves into patriot homes all along Mary's street. On February 2, 1775 the Boston *Spy* printed a speech by George III, rejecting everything the Continental Congress had asked for.[21]

To make matters worse, smallpox broke out in early spring, and, fearing an epidemic, the Cranches moved their three children back to Weymouth while they carried on in Boston. This became the occasion for Mary's first known letter to her eldest child, 12-year-old Betsy, who was clearly mature for her years.

"We are in great danger," Mary began her letter, sounding almost like a scared child confiding in a sister. "There is a woman who has [the pox] just below the mill pond. We can see the flag. I dare not stir out."

But "I have found all well at home [in Boston], which makes me very thankful. Every day we have so much to be thankful for," Mary continued, in a more maternal tone. She knew this penetrating child worried less about smallpox or war than about her own moral choices. "If you examine yourself, which you ought to do every day, you will find always something which you wish you had left undone, and something which you might have done better, but let not this discourage you. No innocent amusement is unlawful," Mary comforted her. And if Betsy prayed, God would "direct and instruct you and make your heart right with Him. The preparation of the heart is from God, but be assured, my dear Betsy, that you have the prayers of your Papa and me," Mary concluded her letter, and she signed herself "your friend and mother," stressing the multi-faceted nature of this bond.[22]

AT THE BEGINNING OF APRIL, the smallpox scare diminished, but political tension rose. The British were now bent on confiscating all colonial arsenals. Nearby Concord, with its large stash of guns and cannons, was an obvious target for a raid. Should battle break out here, the sisters had a private reason for worrying. Their brother, Billy, was captain of a Minuteman unit just outside Concord in Lincoln. He had orders not to initiate violence, but to fight if attacked.

At two in the morning on April 19, Mary jolted awake to the warning of church bells. British troops had crossed Back Bay and were marching northwest toward the Lexington Green. Here, at dawn, they surprised and defeated the makeshift Minutemen. By evening, the uncertainty of the past ten years was over. War had begun. It remained a mystery who fired the first shot. But no colonial arsenals were depleted (the townsmen hid their weapons underground or enmeshed them in feathers in their attics), and the Concord Minutemen crippled the remaining British troops as they stumbled back to Boston. Only here did the Redcoats vastly outnumber the rebellious colonists, and they could do what they pleased.

The Cranches arose on the morning of April 20 trapped in a garrisoned city. Gone was their ambivalence about leaving Richard's successful business. But departure at this point required an official exit visa—hard to procure because the British wanted to hold the colonists hostage to discourage attacks from the outlying towns. While her husband began the tiresome struggle to obtain their visa, Mary sought news of her brother. Billy Smith had been spotted guarding Concord's North Bridge just before the British opened fire. No one had heard of him since.[23]

———

"I THINK I AM very brave upon the whole," Abigail Adams, in Braintree, noted matter-of-factly in a letter to her husband. John had rushed back to Philadelphia where a second Continental Congress was addressing the crisis at hand.[24]

She went on to enumerate her own trials since war had broken out. First, there was the scare over her brother, who was hailed a hero in the battle of Concord before dropping out of sight. Days passed before he turned up in Charleston. He was a changed man, he announced when he presented himself to the Cranches in Boston.[25] Gone were his days of drinking and floundering. He had found his calling in the military, he said with certainty. The family was trying to believe this was true.[26]

"Danger, they say makes people valient," Abigail marveled, but reports of Boston under siege sickened her.[27] With the influx of more British troops came disease and a dearth of food supplies. Wounded colonial soldiers were left to die on the road because the jails were full of suspected snipers—which included anyone "loitering" above the street. A watchmaker friend of the Cranches got a warning just for standing on his own roof.[28]

So it was a great relief for Abigail to learn that Uncle Isaac's family managed to escape to Salem and unspeakable joy when the Cranches at last obtained their exit visa, and she could embrace them in her own home. Abigail and Mary lived together for the first time since their marriages. Richard set up business in Braintree and felt confident enough to purchase a large home.

After the Cranches moved to their farmhouse, Abigail invited Continental soldiers and other refugees from Boston into her tiny saltbox house for a night or a week. Doing what she considered her patriotic duty, she was forced to move John's office into their bedroom, rearrange her dairy, and finally relocate farmworkers. To accommodate her close friend Mr. Trott and his large family, for instance, Abigail asked a longtime tenant farmer, Mr. Hayden—who needed less space now that his two sons were away in the Army—to temporarily remove his belongings from a larger to a smaller room. She got a lesson in gender politics when he objected.

Mr. Hayden was an old man with a bad temper. John found him

"sawcy and insolent" but tractable and a reliable hand. Hayden had deferred to John—grudgingly. John's wife he refused to heed. In Mr. Hayden's eye, Abigail was just a woman with no right to boss any man. He said the law was on his side, and this was true. So, reluctantly, Abigail stooped to flattering and pleading. Hayden, in reply, goaded her that he had possession of the space, and "all [your] . . . art . . . shall not stir [me] . . . Tis a time of war get me out if you can."

Now Abigail's only choice was to turn to her husband. Sadly, she could not be sure even of him. "I own I shall be much mortified if you do not support me," she wrote, acknowledging the slim, but humiliating possibility that he could side with Hayden as a fellow male.

And though John immediately replied, "You may depend upon my Justification of all that you have done or said to Hayden," called Hayden "brutal," and demanded that he leave the disputed room at once, the mail was slow, so it took a month for Abigail to carry through on this one simple mission. In the meantime, she had many occasions to ponder the curious position of a wife possessed of the duty but not the power to rule.[29]

And her home was not all she was meant to rule at this point. Abigail had been raised to see her marriage as a partnership and prided herself on excelling in her job as mother and wife. Now her role had hugely expanded to include being a feudal lord in their tiny manor, treasurer of their shrinking finances (John had been at the top of his field in law, but made only a pitiful salary as a delegate), and the single adult available to prepare three boys and a girl for life. Daily, she confronted an array of unfamiliar threats—from the constant possibility of attack by the British to the scourge of caterpillars marauding through her fruit.

As John, in Philadelphia, began championing the cause of a Continental Army, Abigail coaxed Parson Wibird to visit every other day to impress the importance of religion on their children. She hired her cousin John Thaxter to tutor all but baby Tom. John Adams's brother Elihu helped melt Abigail's best pewter pieces so she could turn them into bullets, while another brother, Peter, offered her sanctuary in his house outside Braintree should the British invade the town.

Increasingly, Abigail felt a kinship with warriors in history and literature. She instructed eight-year-old John Quincy to read Charles Rollin's stories of ancient battles aloud to her and recite William Collins's tribute to fallen soldiers,[30] *Ode Written in the Beginning of the Year 1746*, every day before he got out of bed through the long, dry spring of 1775. "I do not now wonder at the regard the Laidies express for a Soldier— every man who wears a cockade appears of double the importance he used to,"[31] she wrote John. And John wrote back that his campaign for a unified colonial Army had succeeded, and she would have been proud to hear him nominate the "modest and virtuous, the amiable, generous and brave George Washington" to command the troops.[32] "Oh that I was a Soldier!" he in turn enthused. "—I will be.—I am reading military Books—Every Body must and will, and shall be a soldier."[33]

Abigail missed John terribly: his dynamism, his ironic humor, even his bouts of prickliness and outrage were dear to her, because she alone could soothe them away. To the world he was all rectitude and resolution, and some mocked him, she knew, for his sprawling belly and pursed public face. To her, he was tender and romantic. And despite her determination to be strong, phrases like "I feel somewhat lonesome" and "my heart felt like a heart of Led" slipped into her correspondence.[34]

She was only thirty-one and clearly missed John sexually when she moaned, "O how I have long'd for your Bosom" or compared his absence to a sacrifice in a letter to a friend.[35] [36] He was Brutus to her Portia (as she had begun signing herself in letters), and how proud she felt when he turned to her above all his brilliant friends for political advice. He also relied on her to subdue his temper and concoct bromides for his maladies. And she felt useless, being so far away, when he wrote of depression or an eye infection they agreed was brought on by overreading, which made him feel blind.[37]

John wrote of a rainy spring promising good crops in Philadelphia while Abigail and Mary were in the middle of a drought, driving home the distance between them. "I rejoice in the prospect of the plenty you inform me of, but cannot say we have the same agreable view here," Abigail observed, not bothering to disguise her resentment.[38] For while she had adjusted to his shorter travels on the court circuit, these absences for indefinite periods in Philadelphia tried even her usually dependable cheer. Nor would she delude herself that they were likely to end soon.

John had anticipated the threat politics would pose to their private happiness on the eve of the first Continental Congress, writing Abigail: "I have a Zeal at my Heart, for my Country . . . This Zeal will prove fatal to the Fortune and Felicity of my Family, if it is not regulated by a cooler Judgment than mine has hitherto been."[39] But public service also reconciled two of John Adams's deepest longings—to achieve worldly recognition and to perform good deeds. Patriotism—allying ambition to a noble calling—spoke to Abigail's deepest passions also. Being a woman, the impact she made on the world would be measured by her husband's glory. So when Congress honored John with prestigious appointments, she rejoiced almost as much as he did. John's faith in ultimate victory was contagious as well. "Great Events are most certainly in the womb of futurity," she echoed him, with a return of her old optimism in early May.[40]

Two weeks later, alarms went off at dawn when four British boats were spotted off the Weymouth coastline. Their object, as it turned out, was merely to steal hay for their horses on nearby Grape Island; but rumor arose that three hundred troops were marching on Weymouth, and Abigail's parents and half their parish fled. (John's two brothers were among the militiamen who raced to burn the hay before the British could lay hands on it.) Writing to John, Abigail found the comic side of the town's overreaction. So terrified was stolid Aunt Lucy Tufts that she had her bed flung into a cart, jumped on top of it, and ordered the driver to race to a neighboring town, "which he did."[41] And Abigail was up to joking about the children's eagerness for mail from Philadelphia. "You would laugh to see them all run upon the sight of a letter—like chickens for a crum, when the Hen clucks. Charles says . . . What is it any good news? And who is for us and who against us, is the continual inquiry."[42]

She also provided news about the larger family. "Poor" Richard Cranch "has a fit of his old disorder," lung disease, she lamented on May 24, and Mary was "very sick with the rash," on June 3. John's brothers were hailed as heroes for facing down the British on Grape Island, and her own brother, Billy, had followed through on his resolution and was now captain of a Cambridge troop. Her sister Elizabeth "possesst a heart as liable to impressions, and as susceptible of the tender passions as any body," Abigail grudgingly acknowledged, but she was maddeningly impervious to advice.[43] "I told Betsy to write you," Abigail reported when John wondered why his "amiable ingenious Hussy" of a sister-in-law failed to contact him.[44] "She said she would if you were her *Husband,*" Abigail huffed.[45]

Word got out in the middle of June that British troops were plotting to cross Boston Bay and conquer Charleston. On the night of June 16, a band of colonial militia crept to the heights of Bunker's Hill to defend that town.[46] The idea was that the British would have to crawl up to catch them. And so it transpired the following dawn, "one of the hottest [days] we have had this season," Abigail began a running report to John in Philadelphia.[47] The Americans, though vastly outnumbered, took full advantage of their height and shot the British like squirrels as they clamored up.

Books had not prepared Abigail for her first real battle. The bellowing of the cannon stunned, but also elated her. She could not eat or sleep. The sky was clear, a high wind carried smells of dust and bullets—maybe the very ones she and Elihu had melted from family pewter—into her newly planted fields. Later in the day, burning scents joined the mixture. But still the battle was almost dreamlike because Penn's Hill blocked her view of the fighting men.

It was not until late afternoon when Abigail overcame her fears and climbed to the top of Penn's Hill that the full experience engulfed her. Below lay Charleston, her father's birthplace—"in ashes," she reported to John.[48] Thick black smoke blinded the rebels as they struggled to beat back the relentless British.[49] Later, when she learned the colonists had finally succumbed only because they ran out of ammunition, "the race is not to the swift, nor the battle to the strong" leapt to her mind; and her heart "burst" when she heard Dr. Joseph Warren had died leading the American troops.

"Not all the havock and devastation [the British] have made, has wounded me like the death of Warren," Abigail wrote John, who she wished could be with her.[50] Her brother too might have perished if he weren't sick (some said drunk, though she wouldn't write it) and unable to fight.[51] And yet, Abigail could find "abundant cause of thankfulness" in the survival of three-quarters of the rebels, while the British had lost half of their men. Quite a pyrrhic victory, didn't he agree?

When Abigail reproved John that his letters were few and short,

John assured her, "my anxiety about you and the Children, as well as our Country, has been extreme." Then he began expatiating on the heavy burden he carried in his most self-righteous tone.[52]

> The Business I have had upon my Mind has been as great
> and important as can be intrusted to One Man, and the Diffi-
> culty and Intricacy of it is prodigious. When 50 or 60 Men have
> a Constitution to form for a great Empire, at the same Time that
> they have a Country of fifteen hundred Miles extent to fortify,
> Millions to arm and train, a Naval Power to begin, and extensive
> Commerce to regulate, numerous Tribes of Indians to negotiate
> with, a standing Army of Twenty seven Thousand Men to raise,
> pay, victual and officer, I really shall pity those 50 or 60 Men.

But he was also, he more conspiratorially confided, witness to a stupendous social comedy. "I will tell you in future," he promised, of "the Fidgets, the Whims, the Caprice, the Vanity, the Superstition, the Irritability" which made his fellow delegates far more hilarious than any characters in books.[53] [54]

At the beginning of July, rain at last fell in Braintree, raising Abigail's hopes for her first harvest. What she could not grow—coffee, sugar, pepper—was impossible to procure. Beverages were running so low she urged John quickly to buy up any available barrel of beer, since soon "there will be neither wine, lemmons or any thing else to be had but what we make ourselves."[55] And she thought it well worth her busy husband's time to send "pins pins!" from Philadelphia for there was not a sewing pin to be bought even for grossly inflated rates in town.

Undeterred, the housewives used what they had and continued spinning. No matter how dire their situation, they were emboldened by the certainty that a powerful God was on their side. When Congress called for a day of fast and prayer, Abigail felt sure the British "trembl[ed] . . . I really believe they are more afraid of the Americans prayers than their Swords."

The day of the fast, Abigail and Mary left "our inanimate old Batchelor"—Parson Wibird—to deliver his tepid, equivocating sermon without them for once and drove the Adams chaise to nearby

Dedham. Here a far more fervent Parson Haven exhorted his large audience to rise to the call of the times.

"We had no occasion to repent Eleven miles ride," Abigail observed in a letter to Philadelphia. Added to her elation at the radical parson's words was the pleasure of finding Sam Adams' wife at the same church. "Sister Delegate" she called the other Mrs. Adams, putting John in his place. The election of husbands forced wives as well to administrate in strange waters. Besides, women were asked to sacrifice from the day they married. "Why should we not assume your titles when we give you up our names."[56]

While Massachusetts united in praying for the demise of the British, Congress was devolving into factions, with one group, led by John Adams, convinced there was no option but a permanent break with England, and another, under Philadelphia's John Dickinson, still grasping for peace.[57] Influenced by Dickinson, in the beginning of July Congress sent off what became known as the Olive Branch petition appealing personally to King George III. Meanwhile, George Washington arrived in Cambridge to prepare an untrained militia to win back Boston, where conditions were increasingly grim. "No man dar[es] . . . to be seen talking to his Friend in the Street," Abigail reported from Braintree. There was a ten o'clock curfew, and—the height of absurdity—displaying a white handkerchief was now against the law.

Abigail also informed John of her newfound popularity. "I never was so much noticed *by some people* as I have been since you went to [Philadelphia]," she noted of suddenly attentive neighbors, who had ignored her entirely when John was less well-known.[58] As John's wife, Abigail was one of the first to meet General Washington, who made a profound impression. "You had prepared me to entertain a favorable opinion of him, but I thought the one half was not told me," she wrote on July 16. "Dignity with ease, and complacency, the Gentleman and the Soldier look agreably blended in him. Modesty marks every line and feture of his face. Those lines of Dryden instantly occurd to me: 'Mark his Majestick fabrick!' "[59]

Abigail was curious about another delegate, the Boston-born Philadelphia printer and inventor of the lightning rod, Benjamin Franklin. "He is a great and Good man," John assured her, praising Franklin's "constancy," "reserve," and steadfastness. Temperamentally they were opposite—Franklin so even-tempered and reticent, John so combustible and impelled to speak his mind. Yet, they were similarly impatient with Congress. Franklin had recently returned from a peace-seeking mission to England as convinced as John that any further attempts at diplomacy were futile. "He does not hesitate at our boldest Measures, but rather seems to think us, too irresolute, and backward . . . I wish his Colleagues from this City were All like him, particularly one," the temporizing John Dickinson, John groaned.[60]

CONGRESS AT LAST TOOK a short break at the end of summer, and on August 11, John announced to Abigail he was nearing home. Abigail greeted the news with mixed feelings. "I have this morning occasion to sing of Mercies and judgments. May I properly notice each," she wrote John, hoping her letter would spare him the pain of learning on arrival that his brother Elihu, the young man who had helped her make bullets, was dead at 34.[61]

Dysentery—the bane of all armies since the Peloponnesian War—and not the British had killed him. It was a vicious disease, swelling the lining of the intestines, causing bloody diarrhea, vomiting, fever, dehydration, and often, as in Elihu's case, death. Dysentery had forced a shrunken Phillip II of France to quit the Crusades and George Washington to tie two pillows to his saddle when fighting Indians in Pennsylvania. It thrived in putrid water and feces and was spread by flies but also exposure to anyone sick. Crowded, unsanitary spots like prisons and Elihu's militia camp were ideal breeding places, and dysentery was famous for wiping out more soldiers than enemy guns or swords.

Elihu was the first family member to die in the rebellion against Great Britain. "The return of thee my dear partner after a four months absence is a pleasure I cannot express, but . . . I feel for the loss of your Brother, cut of in the pride of life and bloom of Manhood!" Abigail exclaimed.[62]

John had scarcely buried his brother before he was summoned back to Congress. Abigail was surprised at how wounded she felt when he prepared to leave. "I find I am obliged to summons all my patriotism to feel willing to part with him again," she confided in a friend. You will

readily believe me when I say that I make no small sacrifice to the publick."[63]

She nearly called him back a week later. Dysentery had struck her
own household with devastating fever, diarrhea, vomiting, and all the
attending smells.[64] Their crowded home was a hospital. Just a few days
after John rode off, Abigail was "seaz'd by the disease" and "sufferd
greatly between my inclination to have you return and my fear" of him
catching it. Her fear for him won out, and she allowed her mother to
nurse her and then help her nurse Tommy when he succumbed. The
shriveling of this youngest son was scarier than the burning of Charleston. Even when, at last, his fever dropped, and he was safe, he remained
skeletally pale and thin.

Soon Susy the housekeeper got sick and went home to her mother,
but Abigail herself took on the nursing of young Patty, another servant,
then watched the girl transform into a "putrid mass."[65] "I had no Idea
of the Distempter producing such a state as hers till now," Abigail marveled to John, and she had to douse the house with hot vinegar night
and day to combat her stench. Moreover, Abigail could get no one to
pitch in with either Patty or the children since her neighbors were terrified of germs. John Quincy and Charles, on the other hand, were so
oblivious to danger they were constantly running in to gape at the
ghastly patient. So Abigail packed them off, leaving only Tommy and
Nabby at home with her.[66]

"The desolation of War is not so distressing as the Havock made by
the pestilence," Abigail wrote.[67] The litany of sufferers was endless.
Some parents had lost five children, there were two to four funerals
daily with no end in sight. Reverend Gay from Hingham lay dying.
Parson Wibird was recovering but still could not "walk a step." Even
healthy ministers had empty parishes because everyone avoided public
places. Uncle Tufts had treated more than sixty patients in Weymouth
alone.

Abigail tried to look to the larger picture, even chastising herself to
John: "The distresses of my own family are so great that I have not
thought about [politics];" and, in a following letter, forcing herself to
discuss protests against the King in Great Britain as well as Patty's
groans. Then, in mid-September, the announcement that her mother
was sick obscured everything else. She returned to the bubble of child-

hood. What made matters worse, Abigail blamed herself for her mother's suffering since: "Her kindness brought her to see me every day when I was ill."

"She is pocess'd with the Idea that she shall not recover," Abigail noted,[68] as she, Mary, Elizabeth, and Billy gathered in Weymouth, and it was hard to dispute their mother's verdict. The perspective of years and her own motherhood had dispelled all Abigail's childhood resentments. She spoke also for her sisters and brother when she praised Elizabeth Smith as "the Best of parents," calling her "tender," "watchful," an ideal nurturer in their infancy, and a wise counselor as they built their own lives.[69] How could any of them feel safe in a world without her?

On October 1, William Smith held Sabbath meeting where he formally inducted Mary Cranch's 12-year-old Betsy into the Congregational Church—he had spent the past six months preparing his granddaughter for this moment—after which he went home to bless his wife before she died at 5 P.M. It was not until three weeks later, after the servant Patty at last was buried and what remained of her household was tolerably well, that Abigail set out to analyze her emotions on the day of her mother's death, telling John:

> That morning I rose and went into my Mother's room . . . with a cup of tea . . . [I] raised her head . . . she swallowed a few drops, gaspd and fell back upon her pillow . . . Her eyes . . . pi[e]rced my Heart . . . [with] the eagerness of a last look . . . It was . . . my dear Father['s] communion day. He had . . . a tender scene to pass through—a young Grandaughter . . . joining herself to the church, and a Beloved Wife dying to pray for— weeping children, weeping and mourning parisioners all round him, for every Eye streamed, his own heart allmost bursting as he spoke. How painful is the recollection, yet how pleasing?[70]

Elizabeth Smith was eulogized in the local paper as the soul of diplomacy, selflessness, and good humor. She was praised for unswerving support of her parson husband and lack of pettiness or pretension despite her high birth.[71]

Nor had she rattled social mores. Unlike Mary, she was content with minimal education. Unlike Elizabeth, she did not aspire to literary fame. And it would never have occurred to her—as it had to Abigail—to impose her will on a *man* like Mr. Hayden, or to immerse herself in public events like the Battle of Bunker's Hill.

"I bewail more than I can express, the Loss of your excellent Mother," John wrote Abigail when the news at last reached him in Philadelphia,[72] but he also gently reminded Abigail of Elizabeth Smith's limitations, namely her confinement of her talents to a parochial sphere. "The Benevolence, Charity, Capacity and Industry which exerted in private Life, would make a family, a Parish or a Town Happy, employed upon a larger Scale, in Support of the great Principles of Virtue and Freedom of political Regulations might secure whole Nations and Generations from Misery, Want and Contempt," John went on to say.[73] In other words, not only the bells of a parish church but the Enlightenment itself was calling his wife to public service. And as the infant America should aspire to surpass Great Britain, Abigail, while honoring her mother's memory, should now cast her own net on a wider world.

CHAPTER IV

"Something great is daily expected"

. . .

Eight months after their mother's death, in July of 1776, Mary, Richard, and their children, Abigail and hers, and Betsy settled themselves in their uncle Isaac's Smith's empty townhouse in Boston. The British were gone, and smallpox was raging. Their plan was to stay there and inoculate their families against this plague for which there was no cure.

Smallpox, which originated in ancient Egypt, had been scourging Europe since the Middle Ages. It came on with violent joint pains, vomiting, fever, and headaches. This was followed by thousands of blisters, which oozed together into pustules that scarred victims' skin for life, if they were lucky enough to survive the experience. George Washington, Abigail had noted, still had pox scars on his face. The disease wiped out whole armies and cities, killing a third of those who caught it through exposure. Even inoculation—where a doctor induced a mild form of the virus under controlled circumstances—could prove deadly, but since having smallpox once insured immunity in the future, it was worth the danger, the sisters agreed.

The sisters thought Cotton Mather a hero for pressing this old Turkish practice[1] on Americans in the 1720s, though then as now it was highly controversial since smallpox in all forms spread wildly. Indeed,

Boston forbade inoculation unless the disease was already out of control—as in the epidemic of 1764 and now, as smallpox deaths mounted, in and out of the Army, in the summer of 1776.

Everyone prepared to be ill with a diet of milk, fruit, and vegetables. All meats, fats, spirits, and salt could intensify suffering, they were told—as could soft beds, so they slept on hard mattresses or on the floor. Reading was believed to intensify eye pain, but they were exhorted to walk, ride, and open their windows wide for air. The sisters had free rein of their uncle's elegant house and John Hancock's sumptuous fruit garden. They fell easily into the collective habits of childhood, sharing housework and expenses, and walking together to meeting, where there was no Parson Wibird to keen on about peace and duty. The Reverend Charles Chauncy (of Boston's First Church) made a point of denouncing the British King.

The traditional way to inoculate smallpox was to carve a gash in the patient's left arm and insert a thread of undiluted toxin. But the sisters chose an experimental alternative (the "Suttonian" method), entailing a smaller puncture and weakened germs, which promised less suffering, scarring, and time away from home. The risk was that the diluted toxin might produce false or no symptoms, leaving a patient vulnerable to catching this highly contagious disease later: as had already happened in several cases. So they would have to be on guard.

In letters to Abigail from Philadelphia over the past year, John Adams had spoken of biological as well as political constitutions. "Without strength and activity and vigor of body, the brightest mental excellencies will be eclipsed and obscured," he observed shortly after the death of his frail mother-in-law, and he was strongly in favor of preventive medicine, which is why he had chosen to be inoculated twelve years before.[2]

On July 11, Richard Cranch and Charlie Adams were first to receive the serum. Mary, Betsy, Lucy, and Billy Cranch followed the next day, along with Abigail, Nabby, John Quincy, and Tommy Adams, their tutor John Thaxter, and Betsy Smith. John Shaw was inoculated at the same time. But he was still unsettled about a career, and Elizabeth was in the middle of a year of mourning: there was no courting; he housed with other friends.

Her husband, Abigail knew, had a vivid imagination for disasters that might befall her or the children while he was in Philadelphia. Only after the deed was done did she acknowledge her mission in Boston. Then she assured John that her own fears "vanished as soon as I was inoculated and I trust a kind providence will carry me safely thro." Mary and Elizabeth were similarly sanguine.

YET THEY HAD ALL BEEN shaken by their mother's death the previous October. Elizabeth, who had lived at home longest, suffered most. She and Mary both got sick after the funeral, but Elizabeth remained "broke and Worne with Grief" even when she was out of bed and back to housekeeping—without her mother. And while Abigail's sending 11-year-old Nabby to stay was a comfort, there was no escaping the distress of watching her father, who couldn't bear eating or even living in his own home. "Child, I see your Mother, go to what part of the house I will," he lamented at the end of October. Meanwhile, rain poured relentlessly on the browning leaves in Weymouth, making everything look worse.[3]

In November, snow fell and Abigail came down with "Jaudice, Rhumatism and a most violent cold."[4] Parson Wibird's pusillanimous sermons urging reconciliation with their "parent state" which was in fact a "tyrant state" infuriated her. "Let us separate, they are unworthy to be our Breathren," she declaimed with perfect certainty on November 12.[5]

Yet a vision of the future eluded her. Sometimes that fall—while missing John and grieving for her mother—even the Enlightenment seemed an illusion, and she found a bitter comfort in the Calvinist view of man as hopelessly flawed. "The great fish swallow up the small" she observed, and what good, really, were revolutions when "power whether vested in many or few is ever grasping, and like the grave cries, give, give."

Abigail dreaded anarchy, she told John, but also feared the arrival of some worse form of government. As safeguards, the people needed laws, but "Who shall frame [them]? Who will give them force and energy?" And was monarchy or democracy the better bet?[6]

For all his fervor, even John had regrets about the independence he was now leading the fight for in Congress. "The Thought that we might be driven to the sad Necessity of breaking our Connection with

G.B. exclusive of the Carnage and Destruction . . . always gave me a great deal of Grief," he wrote Abigail, who knew how confused he still felt about everything British.[7] For even as publicly he was denouncing the King and professing all the colonies equal, privately he boasted that of all the colonists, New Englanders had "purer English Blood" and were therefore best![8]

Abigail was meanwhile struggling not to put on superior airs with her sisters. For while Mary socialized with old friends and Betsy stayed home with their father, with John in Philadelphia she alone was invited to have coffee with General Sullivan and tea with General Lee. Abigail found General John Sullivan, a lawyer and former delegate to the Continental Congress, "a Man of Sense and Spririt," while General Charles Lee (now second in command to Washington) lived up to his reputation for outrageous behavior—ordering his huge dog to mount a chair opposite Abigail and extend his paw for a shake.[9]

Both generals were stationed on the outskirts of Boston, helping George Washington consider his options for recapturing the town. Everyone expected the colonists to cross the harbor and march on Boston. But they could also entrench themselves on a high point on the American side of the harbor, point their guns on Boston, and force the enemy to come out. Though they had ultimately lost because of a shortage of gunpowder, the colonists had nearly defeated the British using this method at Bunker's Hill. Dorchester Heights—with the highest peaks in the region—seemed an ideal spot to stage this sort of maneuver. But the approach to the Heights lay in clear view of the British; so Washington would have to find a way to obscure his troops' movements if he chose this plan.

But strategy was among the least of George Washington's concerns in December. By now, his gun supply was so low Congress had seriously considered fighting with bows and arrows, while 13,000 soldiers would be going into winter coatless but for the homespun contributions of patriotic wives.[10] And the colonists were so short on gunpowder that John urged Abigail to try making saltpeter—the major element in gunpowder—by mixing ashes, urine, and dirt in her own kitchen.[11] She'd be glad to, she said, when she got a moment. At present, "I find [it] as much as I can do to manufacture cloathing for my family which would else be Naked."[12]

Raising money was the underlying problem. Congress could not demand revenue from colonists who still smarted from English taxes,

with a willow stick, and be drawn about in a chair by that stately gentleman, very much to the discomposure of Mrs. John Adams's carpets.

SILVER CREAMER OWNED BY JOHN ADAMS.

The second child of John Adams is the most widely known of the children of the Presidents.

He was born July 11, 1767, and named John Quincy for his great-grandfather who was a distinguished minister and a representative in the colonial legislature, being at one time its speaker. He was born on a Thursday or Friday, and his father carried him on Sunday morning to Weymouth to be baptized by his reverend grandfather Mr. Smith. Nellie Custis I always think of as a romping laughing child, no matter how old I know her to be. John Quincy Adams's name always suggests to me the mature and serene statesman. But as a child we know that he wandered about the woods of Braintree alone, studying

Baby Clothes Made by Mrs. John Adams for her son John Quincy Adams

the habits of animals and the nature of plants, and manifesting a love for books — and withal was a strangely self-examining and self-repressing

boy. He sets himself "stents" of study, and complains by letter to his father that his "thoughts are running after birds-eggs, play and trifles," and asks that gentleman to advise him "in writing" how to "proportion" his play and studies, that he may have the paper for consultation. Some very quaint diaries of his are preserved in the family, begun when he was twelve — little thin paper books stitched together in brown paper covers. This diary-keeping was continued through sixty-five years; and the nineteen thick closely-written quarto volumes form a remarkable record of statesmanship, historical events, and sagacious conclusions concerning public men and international relations—a

SILVER COFFEE-POT OWNED BY JOHN ADAMS.

journal, in fact, of the making of the American nation.

In 1778, when he was eleven years old, he accompanied his father to France. His mother wrote him long letters full of advice. She told him he had been a great reader (he was familiar with Rollins' History at seven) and of course knew there had been and still was a great deal of crime in the world, but she thought he had never realized it. He was now going to have an opportunity to see it, and she warned him against getting familiar with it. She admonished him that he was accountable to his Maker for all his words and actions.

This was not an unusual letter from a mother but he, an unusual son, not only replied in a way which would do credit to a college professor, but we are told by a noted man of the time that during his travels he often behaved with such discretion as to bring the blush of shame to the faces of his older companions.

This learned man, the most cultivated and the greatest reader (perhaps excepting General Garfield) of the Presidents of the United States, was educated fragmentarily, here and there in the great cities of Europe — hardly three years in

Clothes Abigail "manufactured" for her children,
as displayed in a news article.

and there was no hope of foreign aid when they were still officially subjects of the British crown—a good argument, as John often pointed out, for declaring independence. Furthermore, though the Continental Army had twice as many soldiers in New England as the British, they were mostly farmers and artisans, bringing only ardor to a match with European equipment and discipline—and even their ardor was waning. Many had signed up just for a year and now were leaving, disheartened by the lack of action, and filth and sickness in the camps.

The situation improved marginally when weapons from an American raid on Fort Ticonderoga, the British fort overlooking the Hudson Valley, were transported by ox sleds over the Berkshires and arrived safely in Massachusetts as winter set in.[13] A privateer cruising the New England coastline seized a trove of artillery from the British supply ship *Nancy,* and two local mills began churning out saltpeter—though not half as much as General Washington needed.

At Christmas 1775, Congress broke, and John Adams at last came home to his family. He stayed just a month, but it was long enough to restore Abigail. And he cheered her further when—stopping in New York in January on his way back to Congress—he sent her a copy of a new pamphlet he and she, the Cranches, and Betsy were all anxious to read called *Common Sense.*

By the time Abigail received her copy, this screed against kings was already a sensation. The author was unknown, but his argument "carrie[d] conviction wherever it was read," Abigail reported from Braintree. "I have spread it as much as it lay in my power, every one assents to the weighty truths it contains."[14]

Its most intoxicating point was that Americans should not settle for the *mere* rights of Englishmen, that Englishmen themselves were slaves to a barbarous system of hereditary succession, where men without merit were empowered by the accident of birth. Abigail—who just a few months before had been pondering the relative advantages of republics and monarchies—was now reading with pleasure that the author of *Common Sense* believed kings were as likely to be dolts as good rulers, that they reigned without mandate from either God or man. And it was not just kings that *Common Sense* questioned, but the sacredness of all hierarchies.

As Congregationalists, it was second nature for Abigail and her sisters to revere their superiors—be they parents, husbands, ministers, or people of great wealth. But they had also been marked by the Enlightenment's championing of freedom for its own sake. And lately Mary had found it impossible to leave family decisions to impractical Richard, while Abigail fumed when her tenant farmer felt entitled to flaunt her authority simply because he was male. Now here was *Common Sense,* arguing that power was not an estate to be inherited, but a reward for merit. Though the idea was a little frightening, it touched a chord.[15]

Common Sense, it soon came out, was written by a failed English businessman turned journalist named Thomas Paine. Before assailing kings, he had taken a far riskier stance against the oppression of women, who were treated as little more than slaves, he had written in an article for *Pennsylvania Magazine* the previous August: "robbed of freedom and will by the laws; [subjects] of opinion which rules them with absolute sway and construes the slightest appearances into guilt; [and] surrounded on all sides by judges who are at once tyrants and their seducers."[16] Whether you agreed with him or not, Paine wrote with flair and eloquence. *Common Sense* sold wildly and swayed undecided colonists to the revolutionary cause.[17]

Yet John himself felt more skeptical about *Common Sense* than Abigail and her sisters. While he enjoyed what he called its manly style, he disliked the evangelical appeal to the reader's emotions. And while Paine made a fine case for independence, he had little to say about what followed the break with the King. What do you do when anything is possible? For the most part, Paine was vague and romantic, presuming it natural for free men to create virtuous institutions: an egregious misreading of humanity, in John's opinion. And Paine's most concrete suggestion—that America should be ruled by a single legislative body (an idea that smacked of Cromwellism)—was pure naiveté. "A Single Assembly is liable to all the vices of an individual," he declared, which included greed, bigotry, and the temptation to vote themselves into office for life.[18]

"Power whether vested in the many or the few is ever grasping," Abigail had written him during her depression in November, and while by January she had regained her optimism, John clung to this bleaker view. He looked at his own grasping soul and the toll that fighting vanity and ambition took on him personally. Surely basing government on a presumption of man's benevolence was folly. And it was folly too to presume that salvation—whether sacred or secular—lay in a loving heart. Yet John knew that Thomas Paine and the evangelicals were not alone in their emphasis on the passions. An influential school of Scottish Enlightenment philosophers (including the revered David Hume and Francis Hutcheson) argued that action arose from sentiment and, by extension, that government should emerge from the noble feelings of the entire populace not the thoughts of its wisest men. One of John's favorite delegates at Congress, the tall, redheaded Virginian named Thomas Jefferson, held just this opinion. John found the young man brilliant—but wrong on this point.[19]

Since the Stamp Act, John and Abigail had immersed themselves in studies of the good republic, reading Aristotle, Cato, Petrarch, Thucydides, and all the later histories they could get their hands on. But the story of America had no precedent, they agreed. (They were conveniently forgetting England's Glorious Revolution, where England reconceived its government after chasing James II from the throne.) "When! Before the present epoch, had three millions of people full power and a fair opportunity to form and establish the wisest and happiest government that human wisdom can contrive?" John exulted at America's unique advantage.[20] Thomas Paine, he observed to Abigail, "has a better Hand at pulling down than building." Maybe he should conceive the new structure himself.[21]

Meanwhile, *Common Sense* continued spurring colonists to flock to General Washington's secure position on the outskirts of Boston. By February 21, Abigail could report to John, "The army is full. The preparations [for battle] increase and something great is daily expected . . . I impatiently wait for, yet dread the day."[22]

NINE DAYS LATER, at midnight on Saturday March 2, 1775, Abigail had just sat down to write John when suddenly a cannon roared, and the floorboards shook. She raced to the door where a neighbor running by told her the rebels had fired first and the last of the militia had been called to the front lines in Boston.

Returning to her desk, Abigail excitedly quoted *Julius Caesar*: "There is a tide in the affairs of Men/Which taken, at the flood leads on to fortune." At last America was forging ahead.[23] The fact that it was two days before the anniversary of the Boston Massacre made the moment especially poignant. Being alone with the children in a dark house increased her fear. "No sleep for me tonight," she told John and lay in bed listening to her heartbeat keep pace with the cannons ten miles off.

The following day and Monday March 4 were both "tolerable quiet," though her inner agitation mounted. She watched the local militia march off to join General Washington, leaving Braintree and Weymouth to manage on their own. Then, on Monday night, fighting resumed with a vengeance, and Abigail retraced the steps she'd climbed to witness Charleston burn the summer before. It was warm for the end of winter, and the moon was full. Sitting on the crest of Penn's Hill, she lost a larger sense of the battle and became mesmerized by the flying shells and the throbbing cannons. Their sound was "sublime," she thought, "one of the Grandest in Nature," and back home it conspired with rattling windows and shaking walls to assure her little sleep for the third night in a row.

She awoke to learn a great hoax had been perpetrated by the colonists. Hiding themselves behind stacks of hay, the soldiers had wended their way along the Dorchester peninsula. The cannons Abigail had heard were fired to deflect enemy attention to other sides of the harbor while thousands of Washington's soldiers picked and chiseled their way through the frozen sod and up to the loftiest peaks of Dorchester Heights.

British General Howe couldn't believe his eyes when he spotted the entrenchments at sunrise.[24] "My God these fellows have done more work in one night than I could make my Army do in three months," he exclaimed—as Abigail reported to John in her letter. Then Howe boated troops to nearby Castle Island and readied warships for a major fight.[25] "Tonight we shall realize a . . . terrible scene," Abigail predicted—remembering the carnage at Bunker's Hill.

But then there was nothing to report the next day except a drastic change in weather. The temperature dropped; snow, sleet, and crashing winds blinded the British sailors in the harbor and froze the Americans on their hill. The following day remained inclement. Neither side fired. Nobody moved. Boston sat as still as it had all winter. "I feel disappointed," Abigail confessed on Thursday. She had expected something wilder and more definitive—maybe an end to war, though she wouldn't say so to John, who was convinced there were years of fighting ahead. "This day our Militia are all returning, without effecting anything more than taking possession of Dorchester Hill," she announced, disgusted. Had she suffered so much just for this?

Even when General Howe—discouraged by the storm or using the storm as a pretext to avoid a repeat of the bloodbath over Charleston—sent out a truce flag and ordered his troops to evacuate Boston, Abigail continued to feel let down. "Many people are elated with [the British] quitting Boston. I confess I do not feel so, tis only lifting the burden from one shoulder to another which perhaps is less able or less willing to support it."[26]

BESIDES, CANNONS STILL ROARED for hours on end, and Howe insisted he would burn Boston to the ground if the colonists took any step to impede his departure. Over the past days, Redcoats had been spotted looting the town's meetinghouses and mansions and destroying what wooden furniture they could not fit on their ship. (Their stated intent was to deprive the colonists of firewood, but it was clear they were also venting rage. Mahogany chairs, desktops, and tables were among the elegant refuse Mary, Abigail, and Elizabeth saw washed up on the shore.)

On the foggy evening of Saturday, March 9, the colonists crept onto Nook's Hill, just a quarter of a mile from the Neck, a British stronghold. The British fired seven hundred cannonballs upwards, but failed to dislodge them.[27] The rebels commanded the entire region at this point.

On Sunday morning, Abigail stood on Penn's Hill, watching "the largest Fleet ever seen in America" rock in the water below her; the noses of these British ships pointed down harbor, but they did not move. "They look like a Forrest," she told John but added that she still suspected some ulterior motive on General Howe's part.

For enemies were not so tractable, in her experience. Now that most of her farmhands had left Braintree to join the Army, she fought an increasingly lonely war with nature, while each day brought new battles on the domestic front. At the moment, even finding the time to locate a new horse and servant for John seemed a daunting project. And she was short of everything. Her next letter to Philadelphia would be her last unless John replenished her writing paper, she warned him. And by the way, could he send her J. E. Tendon's French grammar book for Nabby, whose tutor—had she forgotten to mention?—was teaching her Latin as well. And what about a copy of Lord Chesterfield's *Letters* for herself? Every small victory over pain and boredom was pleaded and fought for. So how could she believe in the miracle of an amateur army's nearly bloodless triumph over British might?

But a change came over her before she took up her pen to write to John again the following morning. Maybe it was only that the cannons stopped bellowing so she got her first good night's sleep in over a week. She awoke feeling joyous:

> The more I think of our Enemies quitting Boston, the more amaz'd I am, that they should leave such a harbour, such fortifications, such intrenchments, and that we should be in peaceable possession of a Town which we expected would cost us a river of Blood without one Drop shed. Shurely it is the Lords doings and it is Marvelous in our Eyes.[28]

WHEN THE BAD WEATHER dissipated and the wind at last turned fair, on March 17, General Howe commanded his 170 boats to sail away from Boston. Most of the Loyalists who could afford to went with him, leaving a town infested with smallpox, scarred by larceny, and somewhat defaced, but fundamentally just as it was before the battles of Lexington and Concord.[29] Some prisoners had been carted off on the ships, but church bells swayed untouched in their steeples. John's Boston law office was intact and their friend John Hancock's exquisite home missed nothing but a backgammon board. Most important, Uncle Smith's house, which John had imagined burned to the ground, was safe. The valiant Dr. Warren, laid with his vanquished troops on Bunker's Hill, was moved into town for a hero's burial.

By a lucky oversight, the British left behind cannons and gunpowder, which the rebels promptly seized to replenish their stock.

As Howe's troops sped away and the days grew longer, Abigail felt her old "gaeti de Coer" (she meant *gaieté de coeur,* lightheartedness in French) return. She explained to John,

I feel very differently at the approach of spring to what I did a month ago. We knew not then whether we could plant or sow with safety, whether when we had toild we could reap the fruits of our own industry, whether we could rest in our own Cottages, or whether we should not be driven from the sea coasts to seek shelter in the wilderness, but now we feel as if we might sit under our own vine and eat the good of the land.

Her mind expanded, and she began to speculate about upcoming battles. How would other—especially southern—colonies respond to a British attack? Like John, she felt a deep preference for staunch New England Puritans. Despite exceptions like George Washington, Virginians in her imagination were either haughty lords or savage vassals—maybe the very "uncivilized Natives Britain represents us to be," she joked. And, more seriously, how could people who owned slaves have the same sentiments that she did? "I have sometimes been ready to think that the passion for Liberty cannot be Eaquelly Strong in the Breasts of those who have been accustomed to deprive their fellow Creatures of theirs," she wrote John. One thing was certain: southern resentment of British authority was not "founded upon that generous and christian principal of doing to others as we would that others should do unto us."

Still, whatever the shortcomings of individual colonies, the Americans would ultimately triumph. Just as the British had left Boston, someday, Abigail now felt sure, they would leave all American soil and the thirteen colonies would rule themselves. John and Thomas Paine were not the only ones with passionate ideas about a future Constitution. Though pressed for time and paper, Abigail—who'd seven years before lectured her cousin Isaac that women were just as able as men to learn and travel—wrote a half a page explaining even more shocking views to her husband. Cushioning her righteousness with the self-mockery befitting a wife and member of an inferior gender, Abigail, who had read much about power but nothing suggesting that women had rights to it, declared:

In the new Code of Laws which I suppose it will be necessary For [Congress] to make I desire you would Remember the Ladies, and be more generous and favourable to them than your ancestors. Do not put such unlimited power into the hands of the Husbands . . . If perticular care and attention is not paid to the Laidies we are determined to foment a Rebelion, and will not hold ourselves bound by any Laws in which we have no voice, or Representation. That your Sex are Naturally Tyranni-cal is a Truth so thoroughly established as to admit of no dispute, but such of you as wish to be happy willingly give up the harsh title of Master for the more tender and endearing one of Friend. Why then, not put it out of the power of the vicious and the Lawless to use us with cruelty and indignity with impunity. Men of Sense in all Ages abhor those customs which treat us only as the vassals of your Sex. Regard us then as Beings placed by prov-idence under your protection and in immitation of the Supreme Being make use of that power only for our happiness.[30]

John's April 14 response to Abigail's extraordinary request was to deflect her with satire. Assuming a flirtatious voice, he accused the wife whose discernment he relied on of being saucy and compared "Ladies" to children, apprentices, and—in a particularly unfortunate analogy— insolent negro slaves. "Depend upon it. We [men] know better than to repeal our Masculine systems," he asserted, then changing tone assured her:

Altho they are in full force, you know they are little more than theory. We dare not exert our Power in its full Latitude. We are obliged to go fair, and softly, and in Practice you know we are the subjects.[31] We have only the name of Masters, and rather than give up this, which would completely subject Us to the Despotism of the Peticoat, I hope General Washington, and all our brave Heroes would fight.[32]

She should forget about benign despots willingly empowering their adversaries, in other words, and also forgo Chesterfield's *Letters,* which she had recently requested, and he most certainly would not send. "They are like Congreves Plays, stained with libertine Morals and base

Principals," and altogether too bawdy for her, though obviously he had read them.[33]

On April 15, John decided to give Abigail a taste of her own medicine. Venturing into *her* field of expertise—the children—he informed her that their older boys were geniuses (though he'd scarcely seen either in the past two years). Cultivate their minds, inspire their hearts, and rivet their attention on "glorious Objects," he all but ordered her. "Weed out every Meanness, make them great and manly."

Nabby, being a girl, required different instructions. Unlike Abigail's favorite, the British historian Catharine Macaulay, *his* daughter should never possess a masculine mind. Rather, she was to be raised as a model of her own sex, and—distancing himself from mavericks like the fathers of the British bluestockings—he claimed he had nothing to contribute to her knowledge and informed Abigail she was in charge.[34]

Three days later, however, remembering that his wife was having Nabby instructed in Latin, he became apprehensive. Contradicting Abigail directly could provoke a tongue-lashing. So he instead expressed his fears to Nabby, knowing she would pass them on. Studying ancient languages "will do you no hurt, my dear . . . [but] you must not tell many people of it, for it is scarcely reputable for young ladies to understand Latin and Greek. French, my dear, French is the language," he rhapsodized—and encouraged Nabby to get her mother to teach her *this*.[35]

What a barrage of messages, all in a single week, and from a husband so busy he could go a month without writing. Clearly, Abigail's appeal for Congress to "Remember the Ladies" had loosed a demon in America's leading advocate for the rights of men. For here was John the opponent of African bondage suddenly joking about insolent negroes; John the open admirer of his wife's sagacity all but coming out and telling their daughter to play dumb.

John's explosion of words left Abigail in a quandary. Priding herself on being a good wife, she cheerfully accepted that her main role in marriage was to soothe the cares of her adored if sometimes baffling spouse. Being a wife required at least the appearance of submission. On the other hand, it would be cruel to abandon a husband altogether to his follies when it was so easy to correct him with a little tact. Now, for

instance, by simply ignoring John's unfortunate ideas on Latin, Abigail
could look out for Nabby's best interests without ruffling her husband's
pride.[36] This was all in a day's work of domestic administration. But
John's ridiculing Abigail's request to "Remember the Ladies" fell into
a different category, for it threatened the very core of their partnership:
mutual respect. So, in a May 7 letter Abigail came as close as she had
ever dared to questioning the ground rules of marriage, telling John:

> I can not say that I think you very generous to the Ladies, for
> whilst you are proclaiming peace and good will to Men, Eman-
> cipating all Nations, you insist upon retaining an absolute power
> over Wives. But you must remember that Arbitrary power is
> like most other things which are very hard, very liable to be bro-
> ken—

Here *she* broke off, leaving John to come to his own conclusions
about the fragility of male dominance and, in time-honored fashion,
turned to the fanciful subject of love. Women's charms, if not their
rights, were the ultimate check on man's absolute power in marriage,
she lightly noted and went on to talk about how much she wished he
were home.[37]

This ended Abigail's complaint to her husband, but she continued
to brood about male tyranny and wondered if other women shared her
distress. "I think I will get you to join me in a petition to Congress [on
behalf of women]," she sounded out her most accomplished female
friend, the poet and playwright Mercy Otis Warren, recounting her
"List of female Grievances." But a month later when Mercy wrote
back, she completely avoided the subject: clearly, it was not easy to find
allies for this cause in either sex.[38]

WHILE BELITTLING FEMALE REPRESENTATION, John was full of
praise for Abigail's powers of observation—"I really think that your
Letters are much better worth preserving than mine,"[39] he wrote her
that spring, and he called the reports she sent him "clearer and fuller
Intelligence than I can get from a whole Committee of Gentlemen."[40]

John's own astuteness was now much in demand as British rule dissolved and each of the thirteen colonies began creating its own Constitution. When more than one delegate consulted John about forming a state government, he composed a short pamphlet on the subject, which he called *Thoughts on Government*. It was first of all a rebuttal of Thomas Paine.

For just as man was *not* born virtuous, a good government cannot rely on common sense, was John Adams's opinion. Elaborate precautions had to be taken to avoid tyranny by the many or the few. "The very definition of a Republic, is an Empire of Laws, and not Men," he declared with Calvinist disdain for the presumption of human beneficence. And he agreed with Montesquieu that craving control over others was human and with Newton that the natural way to check power was to offset it with a balancing force. Abigail and the Magna Carta had also put some ideas in his head.[41]

So he advocated a tri-part state along the lines of Great Britain's but with telling differences. For instance, the governor—embodying the executive branch of government—should be elected for a year only so as to bind him to the will of his constituents. Like the House of Commons, one chamber of the legislature should present "in miniature, an exact portrait of the people," while the second should be a council comprised of a small group of wise men, *unlike* the hereditary peers in the House of Lords. Both sets of legislators along with the executive should hold short tenures, whereas the judges, who would make up the third, judiciary branch of the government, could only improve with service and should therefore hold office for life.

As important as any other aspect of John's plan was its aleatoric nature: indeed, the fact that it was all an experiment was half the thrill. What didn't work could be fixed. This was the beauty of beginning the world anew. So it was no contradiction when after strongly supporting one-year tenures, John went on to encourage a change to three or even seven-year terms if these proved more conducive to the state's "ease, its safety, its freedom, or in one word, its happiness."

He was particularly clear on the importance of a strong executive branch to preclude dominance by the legislature. But he rejected the idea of a king—calling a republic Arcadia compared to a monarchy—and was even wary of a strong union. If the colonies did choose to centralize, the authority of their Congress should be limited to waging war, legislating trade, and handling inter-colonial disputes, the post of-fice, and unsettled territory.[42] The individual states could for the most part do perfectly well by themselves.

WRITING TO ABIGAIL ABOUT the fierce effort it took him to compose *Thoughts on Government* at the same time that he was working day and night at Congress, John lamented that none of his present endeavors would bring them an easier life. "I shall get nothing [for writing this pamphlet], I believe, because I never get any Thing by any Thing that I do," he complained, while assuring her he was not above commiserat-ing her lack of help on the farm or writing paper for all his preoccupa-tion with posterity and the greater good.[43] Strawberries and an early spring in the dirty city did little to console him. He longed, he said, to walk in their garden and to the cornfields, the orchards, and the Com-mon.[44] "Instead of domestic Felicity, I am destined to public Conten-tions," he brooded. "Instead of rural Felicity, I must reconcile myself to the Smoke and Noise of a city."[45]

So he wished to be home. And yet his overriding desire at the mo-ment was for Congress to make a declaration of independence from Great Britain. It had to be sooner rather than later because without it there was no hope for the foreign assistance—from France in particular—which was crucial to winning the war. On June 7, the Vir-ginia delegate Richard Henry Lee of Virginia raised a motion for inde-pendence in Congress; it was supported by Massachusetts and six other colonies, while another six—Pennsylvania, Delaware, Maryland, South Carolina, New Jersey, and New York—remained unsure.[46]

With everyone hoping for a unanimous verdict, the vote was set three weeks in the future, while a committee to consider the tone and nature of the prospective document immediately convened. It consisted of five members: the most prominent being John, Benjamin Franklin, and the redheaded Virginian who shared Thomas Paine's veneration for the passions: Thomas Jefferson. Considered to be even more elo-quent than the far better-known authors of *Poor Richard* and *Thoughts on Government,* 33-year-old Jefferson was chosen to write the text.

Like Franklin, Jefferson was a scientist and inventor. He had cre-ated a retractable bed and a tilt-top table as well as an indoor weather vane and his own Palladian estate, Monticello. Educated at William and Mary, he was as steeped in history and philosophy as Adams and also adored his wife, a wealthy widow, who was currently pregnant and in poor health. He was a slaveholder who professed to dislike slavery, a statesman ambitious to succeed on the large stage who hated leaving home. As he began drafting the American declaration—in the middle state of Pennsylvania, on a desk of his own design—he longed for southern Monticello as Adams longed for northern Braintree. Though Jefferson was a deist, rejecting Christ and original sin, he shared Adams's obsession with goodness. "Everything is useful which contributes to fix in the mind principles and practices of virtue," he believed.[47]

Jefferson was gangly, fidgety, six-foot-two-and-a-half, and as quiet as Franklin in Congress. But he rode his horse elegantly, spoke up regularly in committees, and, despite his aversion to arguing, proved impregnable to opposing views. For better and for worse, no one and nothing swayed him. He had little use for either the vagaries of individuals or venerated ideals.

"We are hastening rapidly to great Events," John had written Abigail at the end of April, adding that "It requires . . . Serenity of Temper, a deep . . . Understanding and . . . Courage . . . to ride in this Whirlwind" of Congressional discord.[48] By the end of May, he was telling her that affairs were in a critical state.[49] Then, in the middle of June, exultant after Henry Lee raised a motion for separation from England, he wrote, "These Throws will usher in the Birth of a fine Boy."[50]

On July 1, twenty days after that initial motion, Congress resumed its debate on independence with John Dickinson of Pennsylvania arguing against and John Adams for an immediate break from both Parliament and King George III. John spoke fervidly for two hours to a rapt audience. A clear majority of nine colonies sided with him, but in a preliminary vote the delegates from Pennsylvania (out of respect for Dickinson, though most of its citizens favored independence), South Carolina, and Delaware dissented, while New York, with its high percentage of loyalists, abstained. Still hoping for unanimity, Congress agreed to delay the formal vote until the following morning.

That night word arrived that a flotilla of British boats had sailed into New York Harbor, panicking George Washington's unprepared

Army and adding pressure for some buoying news. The next day John
Dickinson, for the sake of unity, announced he would abstain from the
voting, throwing Pennsylvania to the majority. South Carolina and
Delaware joined Pennsylvania, while New York continued to abstain.
The motion was called to the floor and carried.

July 3 was spent amending Jefferson's declaration—much to the
proprietary writer's chagrin. The most significant change, insisted on
by South Carolina and Georgia, was the elimination of a passage implicitly condemning slavery. Jefferson had accused the King of waging
"cruel war against human nature" by capturing and transporting innocent Africans "into slavery in another hemisphere, or to incur miserable death in their transportation thither."[51] This was a daring, if
bewildering, opinion from a southern slaveholder. Jefferson claimed to
be proud of it and to rue its loss. Other of his favorite passages were also
cut or tightened during the nearly twelve-hour debate over wording,
but Jefferson's voice remained, and on the afternoon of July 4, all of
Congress endorsed it.

John Adams could barely contain his exuberance. "Yesterday the
greatest Question was decided, which ever was debated in America,
and a greater, perhaps, never was or will be decided among Men," he
wrote Abigail. What felt hopelessly slow just a month ago now seemed
remarkably expeditious. Looking back to the first arguments with England in the early 1760s, "and recollect[ing] the series of political Events,
the Chain of Causes and Effects, I am surprised at the Suddenness as
well as the Greatness of this Revolution," he exulted. And, of course,
"calamities" and "distresses" might lie in the future; surely the threat of
tyranny by the majority, which he had warned against in *Thoughts on
Government,* would pose a threat in the coming years. And, yes, it
would be far better for the war if independence had been declared
seven months before and foreign alliances were set in place. And yet:
"July [of]1776, will be the most memorable Epocha, in the History of
America.—I am apt to believe that it will be celebrated, by succeeding
Generations, as the great anniversary." It ought, John declared, to be
commemorated and "solemnized with Pomp and Parade, with Shews,
Sports, Guns, Bells, Bonfires and Illuminations from one End of this
Continent to the other from this Time forward forever."[52]

ON JULY 18, A week after they were inoculated for smallpox, and with
no one yet showing symptoms of the disease, Mary and Richard, Abigail, and Betsy joined masses of patriots lining King Street in front of
the Boston State House, the seat of the first elected legislature in the
New World. The ragtag troops who had chased the British out of Boston four months earlier stood before them, respectably armed at least
for the moment. An officer, Colonel Crafts, appeared on the balcony
and began to read:

> When in the course of human events, it becomes necessary
> for one people to dissolve the political bonds which have con-
> nected them with another, and to assume among the powers of
> the earth a separate and equal station to which the Laws of Na-
> ture and of Nature's God entitle them, a decent respect to the
> opinions of mankind requires that they should declare the causes
> which impel them to the separation.[52]

The Smith sisters' lives spoke volumes on the causes for separation,
and the spirit of the declaration was familiar, for they had avidly read the
great thinkers of the Enlightenment who so informed Jefferson's view.
Yet, if his concepts were not original, the occasion was a first in history,
and Richard Cranch as well as Mary, Abigail, and Betsy stood spellbound
at the beautiful expression of what they felt and knew. "We hold these
truths to be self-evident, that all men are created equal, that they are en-
dowed by their Creator with certain unalienable Rights, that among
these are Life, Liberty, and the pursuit of Happiness." And on it went.

"God Save the King" was already a memory. When Colonel Crafts
finished reading the Declaration of Independence, he shouted, "God
Save our American States." The people picked up this chant and ran
with it, as Richard Cranch reported to John in a letter the following
week. There were three cheers that "rended the air," Abigail wrote in
her own description, and they were followed by an elated ringing of
bells; the cannons roared, and rifles shots rang in the air. "After dinner
the kings arms were taken down from the State House and every ve-

stage of him from every place in which it appeard and burnt in King Street. Thus ends royall Authority in this State," she concluded, "and all the people shall say Amen."[54]

By July 22, Abigail was ill with the "excruciating pain in my head and every Limb" that was said to "portend a speedy Eruption," which occurred a few days later, and though she produced only one pox, her symptoms were sufficiently grueling for the doctor to declare her immune. John Quincy's case too was mild but conclusive, while Mary's eldest daughter, Betsy Cranch, the frailest of them all, fainted and lay listless in bed. Her mother and brothers, on the other hand, produced no symptoms. By the end of July, Mary had been inoculated four times and was still healthy as the day she left Braintree, as were Charles and Tommy Adams, who had been inoculated twice. It seemed fitting when Nabby, the calmest of them all, came through with almost no suffering. The doctor, however, insisted that she be inoculated a second time, on the odd chance that her symptoms were "false."

Even after her single pox dissipated, Abigail felt light-headed from the disease. "The smallpox is a great confuser of the mind, I am really put to it to spell the commenest word," she told John.[55] Yet when John gave her an opening, she had no trouble expounding on her favorite topic of women in the new nation. "If you complain of neglect of Education in sons, What shal I say with regard to daughters, who every day experience the want of it," she began. And continued:

> I most sincerely wish that some more liberal plan might be laid and executed for the Benefit of the rising Generation, and that our new constitution may be distinguished for Learning and Virtue. If we mean to have Heroes, Statesmen, and Philosophers, we should have learned women. The world perhaps will laugh at me, and accuse me of vanity, But you know I have a mind too enlarged and liberal [to be vain]. If much depends as is allowed upon the early Education of youth and the first principals which are instilld take deepest root, great benefit must arise from litirary accomplishments in women.[56]

This time John assured Abigail "Your Sentiments of the Importance of Education in Women are exactly agreable to my own," though women who displayed their wits were contemptible, he felt impelled to add.[57]

WITH TIME ON HER hands, Abigail wrote John her fears about the Cranches—who by the first week in August, along with Tommy, her youngest, were in various stages of sickness and recovery, while six-year-old Charles, after three inoculations, had still failed to break out. In Braintree, Abigail told John, Richard Cranch did not have half enough business to support her sister and their family. He was not born for business, as John well knew, and it seemed wrong that a man so "peculiarly formed for the education of youth, and . . . excelling in Philosophy" should not have a professorship somewhere. Knowing John's affection for Richard, Abigail broadly hinted that her husband might recommend their brother-in-law for a tutorship at Harvard.

Abigail saw an ignoble aspect of John's personality when he responded: "I feel as much for my worthy Brother and sister, as I do for my self, and for their family as for mine," but made clear he would not risk his own reputation to further his brother's career. Loving the Cranches and going out on a limb for them were two separate issues in John's mind. So though, of course, he had contacts everywhere in Boston, he peremptorily closed the topic of recommending Richard for a tutorship, claiming: "As to H[arvard] Colledge I know nothing of it." It would be useless to protest, Abigail realized. She determined to help the Cranches behind her husband's back when she could.

Affairs of state were in any case preoccupying both families at the moment. While Abigail waited for Charles to get sick in Boston, John watched for battle to break out in New York, where British strength was mounting as German mercenaries joined their ranks. The attack came at dawn on August 27, when the British surprised and routed 9,000 scared and disorderly Continentals at Brooklyn, pushing them right up to the shoreline at Brooklyn Heights.

To compound John's worries, news arrived from Boston that Charles was finally, maybe fatally, ill with a spiking fever, while Nabby, whose early symptoms indeed proved deceptive, now had "above a thousand pussels as long as a great Green Pea," and couldn't stand on her swollen feet.[58] Her pretty face was unrecognizable.

"I have had a Seige of it, I long for the campaign to be over," sighed Abigail, who[59] was distressed when Nabby remained spotted even after the pox fell off. "A sad Enemy [is smallpox] to soft Features, and fine Faces," lamented a friend who described Nabby's new look as sour.[60]

"My little speckled Beauty," John called her, and noted philosophically that with a few "pitts" she would put more value on ingenuousness and less on appearance. But there was no denying Nabby's beauty would be crucial to finding a good husband, so he cautioned Abigail to hasten her healing by keeping her out of the sun.[61] Though scars never vanished, they could over time recede.[62]

After forty-eight hours, Charles's fever dropped, though he remained languid. Betsy Smith went easily through the disease and on August 13 was disinfected at the border and headed for her father's home.[63] John Quincy left Boston with her, and the Cranches took off for Braintree the week after. In the last week of August, Mary returned to pick up Nabby and Tommy, but Abigail followed doctor's orders and stayed on an extra week at Uncle Isaac's so that Charles could recover his strength.

At first, Abigail was lonely without the Cranches. After nearly two months in Boston, she was also pressed for money. Prices had more than doubled over the past two years, though supplies were now plentiful, and rents had even dropped since the British sailed off in March. The city felt empty. Between the smallpox epidemic and the departure of most of the Continental Army (Abigail had counted fewer than a hundred soldiers left to protect the town), Bostonians were reluctant to return to their homes—especially in the dog days of August, when storms flooded the pebbled streets, but brought little relief from dulling heat and humidity. As Abigail encouraged Charles to exercise in the insufferable city air that all the experts claimed would restore him, she too pined to be gone.

But, being Abigail, she did not pine for long. A week after Mary left, she was already looking at the bright side and enjoying the peace of the empty house. For the first time in months, she had time to sit back and reflect on all that had happened between the death of her mother and the moment Charles's fever dropped. And there was no better place on earth to reflect than in her Aunt Smith's "closet." Here stood bookshelves and a comely little desk with a view of the garden.

Best of all, this was not some part of a bedroom or a kitchen, but a private space built for a woman to use as she pleased. "I do not covet my Neighbors Goods," she wrote John in her hours of freedom, as Charles slept, "but . . . I always had a fancy for a closet with a window which I could more peculiarly call my own."

As she sat musing, her imagination often idled toward John, her dearest friend in the world. One day, while writing at her aunt Elizabeth's desk, her mind wandered, and she daydreamed a story about John coming home. "With the purest affection [she later wrote to him] I . . . held you to my Bosom till my whole Soul . . . dissolved in Tenderness and my pen [fell] from my hand." They were as bound together as ever, their emotions mysteriously in key. When her reverie ended and she opened her eyes in the little empty study, she felt consoled just knowing "that I hold in possession a Heart Equally warm with my own, and full as Susceptable of the Tenderest impressions, and Who even now whilst he is reading here, feels all I discribe." Those who saw John only as a statesman missed half the person. Along with his cool intellect went feelings as keen as an aesthete's.

Abigail had left Braintree intending to come to her uncle's house for three weeks only, but nearly seven weeks passed before September 2 dawned, a sunny morning, and Charles was at last strong enough for them to begin the journey home. The battle of New York remained inconclusive as she set out for Braintree. But after a great struggle she had won her private war, and no one in her family would ever die from smallpox. "I think I never felt a greater pleasure at comeing home . . . in my life," she declared.

CHAPTER V

"A Solemn Scene of Joy"

. . .

AT THE BEGINNING OF 1777, FOUR MONTHS AFTER THE CLOSE of her year of mourning, Elizabeth Smith announced her engagement to John Shaw. She was 27, older than the average New England woman, who married in her early twenties. By Elizabeth's age, Mary and Abigail had each already borne two children, but they had not lived through war or felt the tear of leaving a widowed father. Parson Smith's resilience made Elizabeth's departure easier. At 69, he had recovered from his wife's death and returned to his lifelong habit of exercising to keep up his spirits and health. One afternoon, before dining at Abigail's, he took a forty-mile horse ride and dismissed it as "a triffell for one so young as I am."[1]

John Shaw was now 30, and five years out of Harvard. He had overcome his doubts and like Elizabeth's father decided to preach for a living; though, unlike her mother, Elizabeth brought little fortune to the marriage, and her children would enjoy less prestige than she had growing up, since America increasingly valued wealth and government or military rank over God's work.[2] Two decades after John Adams had to rationalize *not* pursuing the ministry to Richard Cranch, the status of lawyers and businessmen had risen, while ministers were increasingly pitied for their low salaries and constant toil.

Besides, a large percentage of Congregationalist parishes had split in two over evangelism. The rise of Baptism and Methodism had further complicated affairs. And, in the middle of a war, even Puritans who despised cant and crying were demanding some passion from their ministers: lackadaisical Parson Wibird, for instance, was woefully out of step with the times.

Formerly, there was no need to seduce parishioners because all citizens paid taxes to the First Congregationalist Church, no matter what their religious affinity. Now the law had changed, and a minister's salary came from taxes paid exclusively by his own congregants. John Shaw would have to be popular to survive.

But he could survive, even thrive in a large, prosperous parish. As long as salvation remained the crowning glory for Puritans, a minister would command awe. Besides, John Shaw's strengths—piety, a strong intellect, benevolence—suited him ideally for the position. And Elizabeth was born to host parish parties and inspire good works, following in her mother's footsteps. She saw no reason why she could not also steal time to read and contemplate as she had at her father's parsonage all these years. And now there would be added incentive to pursue her dream of writing letters worth publishing as she would be living an inconceivable distance—fifty miles, farther than any female in her family had ever traveled—from her sisters, her father, her nieces and nephews, Aunt and Uncle Tufts, and so many other friends.

Preparations were now being made for marriage, or *housekeeping* as the saying went at the time. Soon Elizabeth, the most easily elated of the three sisters, would experience the married love she had speculated about years ago in letters to her cousin Isaac Smith. She had informed Isaac that love should begin as friendship. If so, she was starting right on course.

Before, it had been Elizabeth who packed her sisters off to grander locations like Salem. This time *they* remained in sleepy Braintree while she took a leap into the greater world. For her fiancé was to be ordained in March at the First Congregational Church in Haverhill, a real town with 2,800 citizens just over the New Hampshire border. When they married next October, she would leave the ocean but gain the splendid Merrimack River and more sophisticated neighbors. Haverhill was known for its wealthy merchants, and merchants were as a rule old-fashioned Calvinists like John Shaw himself. To bind them to him, he would need to overcome a certain archness and impatience with contradiction, but these seemed surmountable problems, and Betsy felt sure she could help. John and Betsy would be only the second tenants in the new white-columned parsonage, which was large enough for many children and, everyone said, quite lovely to behold.

*One compensation for leaving her family
was Betsy's stately new home.*

Unlike Weymouth and Braintree, Haverhill had a post office. And Elizabeth's separation from her father and sisters would be a little less wrenching because of recent improvements in the American post. Begun in 1710 as a moneymaking proposition for the British, it had at first served chiefly as a conduit between Parliament and its colonial governors. It was extremely difficult to find a way to deliver personal letters—especially in New England where roads were too overgrown to accommodate coaches. Indeed, the treacherous paths daunted even single riders; so those who signed on went for days without coming upon a replacement willing to carry on their mail. Drop-off points, usually taverns, were few and far between. To discourage mid-way defections, colonists often bribed their postmen, who tended to bolt anyway. Delivery was in all cases erratic and nearly nonexistent on inland routes. Even if it finally did arrive, a letter took three weeks to reach New York from Philadelphia, until 1753 when Ben Franklin got himself appointed Postmaster General and cut the time in half.

When Franklin left office twenty-one years later, post roads were considerably smoother and ran from Maine to Florida with crossroads and milestones at all the necessary points between. By 1774, Paul Revere, following the postal route from Boston to Cambridge, Cambridge

Just as Betzy was announcing her engagement,
the American postal system gained privacy and speed.

to Watertown, etc., could ride an urgent message to Congress in Philadelphia in just five days, weather permitting. Most postmen, however, were still likely to open your mail and gossip about it. Also, since postmen continued to ride huge distances, they frequently fell asleep or got lost on the job.[3]

Then, at the end of 1776, Congress established a thirty-mile limit for riders, and in February of the new year, just as Elizabeth was announcing her engagement, formed a committee to further enhance privacy and speed. In March, Ebenezer Hazard—a "genius" in John Adams's opinion—became Postmaster General, and by the following month John was assuring Abigail that the post had become "well regulated," and arrived weekly, though he continued railing against frequent British interceptions, which forced him to write "very trifling" letters or risk exposing war plans to the world.[4]

———

AMERICANS HAD BEEN FIGHTING a defensive war since the previous summer. Vastly overpowered by the British and their hired Hessians, Continental troops were humiliated in New York and spent the fall fleeing through New Jersey, British General Howe in swift pursuit. With their numbers drastically reduced and few inclined to sign on again when their contracts ran out in December, they awaited winter on the Pennsylvania side of the Delaware River, expecting any minute to be ambushed by British troops. To compound the problem, anticipating an invasion of Philadelphia, Congress fled to Baltimore. Furthermore, 17,000 enemy troops traveled from Canada to the tip of Lake Champlain, hoping to seize northwestern New York.

Even John Adams had no quarrel with the opening line of Thomas Paine's new pamphlet, *Crisis* (when it came out on December 19): "These are the times that try men's souls." Only through a daring move did Washington manage to avoid the utter collapse of his Army. With just 6,000 sick and disheartened men at his disposal, on Christmas day, an hour before sunrise, he crossed back to the New Jersey side of the Delaware, surprised the British in Trenton, and defeated them in two hours, losing only three men while taking a thousand prisoners. On a roll now, on January 3 the Continental troops pushed on and seized Princeton. These victories, though modest, restored George Washington's reputation and convinced Congress to pass a bill extending enlistments from one to three years or the end of the war, boosting stability, as preparations were made to reinforce troops along Lake Champlain. Then both armies retired for the winter, and Congress left Baltimore to return to its normal seat.

WHEN JOHN LEARNED OF BETSY's engagement in February, he wrote Abigail that she must congratulate Mr. Shaw on his luck. "Tell him he may be a Calvinist if he will, provided always that he preserves his Candour, Charity and Moderation."[5] Abigail replied that she would be unable to convey his message to Betsy "since the mortification I endure at the mention of it is so great that I have never changed a word with her upon the subject," her aversion clearly unmollified by three years' acquaintance with the man her sister loved. "I would not make an exchange with her for the mountains of Mexico and Peru. She has forfeited all her character with me and the world for taste etc. All her acquaintance stand amazd."[6]

She had no compunctions about exaggerating Elizabeth's age to explain her sister's madness: "An Idea of 30 years (Elizabeth was 27) and unmarried is sufficent to make people do very unaccountable things." And she tied up her case with invidious comparisons to her own marital bliss.

As she wrote this diatribe, on March 8, 1777, Abigail—at 33, and five years after Tommy's birth—was pregnant. John had come home for a rare two months the previous November, and they had conceived this child in passion, but not at all by chance. Both of them dreaded another childbirth too much to risk sex just for pleasure. Before she consented to make love Abigail insisted that John promise to be home for her childbirth in case she got pregnant.[7]

Abigail and John made clear they wanted this fifth child to be a daughter. The loss of thirteen-month-old Suky seven years before still rattled them both. John had relived the pain recently when the portraitist Charles Willson Peale gave him a tour of his studio in Philadelphia. A painting of Peale's wife in tears, holding a dead infant on her lap "struck me prodigiously," he confided in Abigail.[8] The birth of two healthy boys had not effaced their longing for another girl child—or twins, as John only half-joked in a letter where he sent love to Nabby, John Quincy, Charlie, and Tommy, then added, "Pray how does the other one, or two?"[9]

This coming child made John a more conscientious correspondent. By March, Abigail could praise him for writing twenty letters to her six.[10] Even if he only had time to scribble a paragraph, he made sure to post at least one letter off every week, and he took a lover's pride at insinuating private allusions to her pregnancy. The thought of being absent with Abigail in her "circumstances" made him miserable, he wrote in one letter, "and yet I rejoice at them in spight of this Melancholy—God almghtys Providence protect and bless you and yours and mine."[11] And in a cheekier mood: "I derive a secret Pleasure from a Circumstance which I suppose at present occasions the most of your Apprehensions."[12]

While her situation made separation even harder than usual, the baby inside her, Abigail told John, was "a constant remembrancer of an absent Friend, and excites sensations of tenderness which are better felt than expressed."[13] And she kept him amused with tales of her external developments. First, she was pale as a "whited wall," then florid and "clumsy" and fatter, their son John Quincy felt impelled to mention, than anyone he had ever seen.[14]

But Abigail was also resentful of John, off at his Congress, with no cumbrous, fragile flesh to drag through snow so high it covered the fences.[15] When the snow held back, following her father's example of regular exercise sometimes improved her mood, and sometimes it did not. She was maddened by her own disgruntlement and fear of illness. This was certainly not the time for her to soften on the subject of John Shaw.

The coming of spring and south winds vexed her more than usual. She compared herself to the Sicilians who, according to a contemporary travel book she was reading, Patrick Brydone's *A Tour through Sicily and Malta,* became too languid to perform the most basic duties when the dread southeast Siroce winds blew in.[16] She was shaken when a neighbor died a week after giving birth. "Every thing of this kind naturally shocks a person in similar circumstances," she wrote John.[17] "How great the mind that can overcome the fear of Death!"

There were days when she wanted to make John suffer, as when she goaded him that her anxieties might disappear "if you could be with me."[18] Even beasts, she reminded him, "had their mate sit by them with anxious care during all their solitary confinement," but not she.[19]

Still, it was the rare day when neither friends nor the larger world could deflect her from private brooding. As always, she empathized most intensely with the Cranches. When nothing turned up in the way of a professorship, Richard Cranch narrowed his possibilities to returning to business in Boston or buying a farm here at home. It was hard to imagine skinny, illness-prone Richard plowing fields and mending fences, but Abigail sat patiently in her kitchen, listening to Mary articulate the pros and cons of each career.

They also swapped outraged tales of the current inflation brought on by Congress's decision to issue paper money to fund the war effort. A dollar was not equal to what a quarter was two years earlier in Massachusetts, Abigail reported to John.[20] Sugar, molasses, rum, cotton, coffee, and chocolate could not be had at any price. Though fresh meat was plentiful, "venal" butchers hiked prices so high that Abigail vowed to shun it "whilst I have a mouthfull of salt meat to Eat." And she would be happier to go without clothes "like Adam and Eve" than to buy them at the present exorbitant cost.[21] Furthermore, she had recently been duped by a five-pound bill counterfeited to look like New Hampshire currency. With counterfeiting added to inflation, people now preferred to barter than to deal with money at all.[22]

The price controls belatedly legislated by Congress to fight inflation were useless, she and John agreed, since shopkeepers ignored them. Printing more paper money would only lower its present worth. And since the best solution to a national money shortage—taxation—was unspeakable in the current climate, Congress should pull back a percentage of the bills already circulating to support the value of the rest. What John saw as even more important to America's credibility with the rest of the lending world was some augury of success on the battlefield.[23] He frequently pointed out that France was a natural ally, but that no one wants to fund a lost cause.

And no one could claim that the Americans were winning. Despite George Washington's advances at Trenton and Princeton, Continental troops were still on the defense. It was no secret that the British plan was to descend through Lake Champlain into the Hudson River Valley, further tightening the vise on New England as summer came in. Fort Ticonderoga, at the base of the lake, was perceived by both camps as a key position. The British felt sure that if they seized this fort they would crush the rebellion. Americans believed that holding Ticonderoga against a British onslaught was their best chance at winning military and financial support from abroad.[24]

General Burgoyne, who led the British campaign, was an aristocrat wedded to traditional European battle strategy. Against him, on the American side, were the British-born General Gates and General Schuyler, a New Yorker, who were jockeying for command. By spring, after nine thousand new enlistments, the Continental troops were still outnumbered, but the gap was shrinking. On May 6, John reported all was "well and quiet" at the bottom of Lake Champlain, where 4,000 Americans now awaited Burgoyne.

As the date for her birthing came closer, Abigail identified all the more intensely with the American troops. She kept John apprised of the building of gunboats in Boston Harbor and the march of freshly recruited New Englanders to join Generals Schuyler and Gates to the west.[25]

After the troops left, she heard rumors that British General Howe might circle back and attack Boston or move on to Philadelphia and catch Congress off guard. She had visions of John being chased she knew not where by the "Barbarous and Hostile" British, or worse still, she herself might be forced to flee.[26] Yes, for once in her life she would put *her* welfare before her husband's. "I confess I had rather [General Howe] should make a visit to you than to me, at this time," she observed.[27] And she went on to lay down the law that if Howe attacked, John must come home to protect her. *No false promises now.*

The woman who had longed for the Battle of Boston trembled at the thought of the British returning. Visions of slaughter and rape afflicted her, and her body was no better than her mind. In April, she came down with a bad eye infection, followed the next month by an alarming rash. The spring was so cold that at the end of May she was still huddling by the fire. Then the first week of June brought an even worse torment: heat.

Missing the wifely concern he was used to, John turned to the metaphor of weight Abigail had employed repeatedly since her pregnancy and wrote that he too had been "loaded constantly" these past ten weeks with a debilitating cold. But soon after he was describing revivifying rides through the splendid Delaware Valley, while by the middle of June Abigail felt so ill she could barely walk in the house.[28]

Richard Cranch bought a thirty-two-acre farm off the Old Coast Road, and Abigail swallowed her reservations and warmly praised his skills. "You would smile to see what a Farmer our Brother C[ranc]h makes," she wrote John at the end of June, "his whole attention is as much engaged in it, as it ever was in . . . Watch Work, or Prophesies."[29]

Mary prepared to join Abigail for her birthing. And now what had long been suspected was finally acknowledged: John would not keep his promise to return to Braintree for his child's birth. Congress could not spare him, and besides, making the weeklong trip on either end to spend two days in Braintree would threaten his health and sap his en-

When he decided to pursue agriculture instead of business,
Richard Cranch bought this commodious farmhouse,
where so much family history would occur.

ergy: "It is nonsense to dance backwards and forwards," he grumbled.[30]
He chose the country over his wife.

But he was miserable about the decision and tried in all the little
ways he knew to placate Abigail. He encouraged her to name the baby
for her mother. He arranged for his brother to support her at the christening and the children's tutor, John Thaxter, to keep him apprised of
household events while she convalesced. For he never really doubted a
happy outcome. "I long to hear a certain Piece of News from Home,
which will give me great Joy," he wrote Abigail as the date drew near.[31]

And with the end of her ordeal in sight, Abigail fretted less about
her husband's absence. The country needed him too.

It was a summer of fierce thunderstorms and unnatural cold spells.
A rogue frost killed much of the fruit, but the hay and corn thrived.
Abigail began creeping up to their room with John's letters and journals "to ruminate over past scenes."[32] She was keenly aware she might
die and thought long and hard about the meaning of her life and marriage. With "my Heart softned and my mind enervated by my suffer-

ings," every loving word John wrote touched her. "I have [no] doubt of the tenderest affection or sincerest regard of my absent Friend," she assured him on the night of July 10.

John indeed felt overcome by tenderness. "My mind is again Anxious, and my Heart in Pain for my dearest Friend," he wrote her that same evening.

> Three Times have I felt the most distressing Sympathy with my Partner, without being able to afford her any Kind of Solace, or Assistance. When the Family was sick of the Dissentery, and so many of Our Friends died of it. When you all had the small-pox. And now I think I feel as anxious as ever.—Oh that I could be near, to say a few kind Words, or shew a few Kind Looks, or do a few kind Actions. Oh that I could take from my dearest a share of her Distress, or relieve her of the whole. Before this shall rea[c]h you I hope you will be happy in the Embraces of a Daughter, as fair, and good, and wise, and virtuous as the Mother, or if it is a son I hope it will still resemble the Mother in Person, Mind, and Heart.[33]

The night before—unbeknownst to John—Abigail had woken with shaking fits. Afterward, when she could no longer feel the baby move, she grew "very apprehensive a life was lost." Dr. Tufts's assuring her otherwise brought little comfort. Every hour the baby failed to kick Abigail became more convinced it was dead. "What may be the consequences to me, Heaven only knows," she warned John, though she knew of no "injury to [herself] . . . which could occasion what I fear."[34]

Abigail's contractions began on Thursday, and she called for her sisters, then composed herself to write John. "Slow, lingering and troublesome is the present situation," she reported, though her mind was clear, her spirits much better than the day before. At one point, she lay down her pen "to bear what I cannot fly from," and when she picked it up spoke cogently of Fort Ticonderoga and the state of their farm. One sentence began teasingly, "I could look pleasant upon you [even] in the midst of [my] suffering," but ended "—allmighty God carry me safely through."[35] She said nothing of the child.

On Saturday, John Thaxter wrote John that Abigail "was deliverred of . . . an exceedingly fine looking . . . daughter, but it grieves me to add, Sir, that it was still born."[36] The mother was well, he said, and this was true.

Abigail recovered far more swiftly than from any of her other pregnancies. Just six days after finding her hopes dashed and no reward for her suffering, she sat up and calmly praised God for the miracle of her own survival, telling John:

> My Heart was much set upon a Daughter. I had had a strong perswasion that my desire would be granted me. It was—but to shew me the uncertainty of all sublinary enjoyments cut of[f] e'er I could call it mine. No one was so much affected with the loss of it as its Sister who mourned in tears for Hours. I have so much cause for thankfullness amidst my sorrow, that I would not entertain a repineing thought. So short sighted and so little a way can we look into futurity that we ought patiently to submit to the dispensations of Heaven."[37]

But it was not so for John, who had received none of the past week's letters and imagined his wife "abed and happy" by this time. He was devastated when four letters including her last arrived in a single post on June 28. "Never in my whole Life, was my Heart affected with such Emotions and Sensations," he replied. ". . . Is it not unaccountable, that one should feel so strong an Affection for an Infant, that one has never seen, nor shall see?"[38]

ABIGAIL COULD STAND BACK enough to observe that bearing a stillborn was not as excruciatingly painful as watching Suky die. Still, her resolve not to repine lapsed periodically over the summer, as when she watched the christening of John's brother Peter's baby, born just twenty-three days after her own and also a girl. This was Abigail's first time out of the house since her confinement, so she was feeling particularly fragile. And when Peter held up the child and announced that he was naming her Susanna, after his mother, Abigail's longing for a girl named after *her* mother (whom she could hold out to John when at last he came home from Congress) burst to the surface, and she felt "our Bereavement . . . with all its poingnacy."[39]

She missed John more than ever. Thinking ahead to their coming thirteenth anniversary, she wrote:

> Tis almost 14 years since we were united, but not more than half that time have we had the happiness of living together . . . The unfealing world may consider it in what light they please, I consider it . . . one of my greatest misfortunes.[40]

With John gone, Abigail reached out to the Cranches. Richard remained truly a brother, and she cheered on his achievements, describing to John how he had already made several tons of hay with his own hands and built a new barn practically by himself. Even he, she said, could not take more pleasure than Richard in farmwork. And it gave Abigail great joy to watch the Adams and Cranch children growing up as close as siblings, especially 12-year-old Nabby Adams and 14-year-old Betsy Cranch.

Another distraction from Abigail's sorrow was her increasing intimacy with places she had never seen. Fort Ticonderoga, formerly just a spot on a map, was now so familiar she called it "Fort Ti" and worried about its fate like a lover's. And France was no longer just the home of fashion and the philosophes, but a beacon of goodwill. Even its monarch, King Louis XVI, adored liberty, it seemed. "The Hearts of the French are universally for us," John had assured her four months earlier, as Congress prepared to send moose, flying squirrels, and rattlesnakes across the ocean to gratify the French ladies' craving for American exotica.[41]

Now, in her mind, Abigail followed these oblations to Paris, where three delegates from Congress—Ben Franklin along with the Connecticut-born Silas Deane and the Virginian Arthur Lee—were currently courting the French Minister of Foreign Affairs, the influential Count de Vergennes. An aristocrat at the height of a long career in diplomacy, Vergennes had little interest in liberty per se. What enticed him was the opportunity to restore a balance of power in Europe by countering the British victory in the French and Indian War.[42] In league with the playwright Pierre-Augustin Caron de Beaumarchais, who had made the American war his passion, Vergennes had supplied the Continental Army on a small scale from the start. But at this crucial juncture Congress needed massive loans and France's formal alliance to sustain the Continental Army through another winter. Up to now, Vergennes had been friendly but noncommittal. "The French . . . tell the English they neither desire War nor fear it," John wrote Abigail.[43] Vergennes was still hedging his bets.

In July, Abigail was devastated to learn that American troops through their own negligence had lost Fort Ticonderoga to the British. A hill overlooking the fort had been left unguarded, and under the cover of darkness the British mounted its narrow pass and forced the Americans to retreat. This was the strategy Washington himself had used at Dorchester Heights. Burgoyne was jubilant and so confident of American ineptitude that he boasted he would reach Albany for Christmas dinner—then demolish town after town and celebrate total victory in New York.

Meanwhile, the British Navy was cruising somewhere in the North Atlantic. Because no one knew its precise location, all the seaboard cities felt vulnerable to attack. When a rumor spread that the boats were heading for Boston, Abigail, still weak from childbirth, summoned all her strength to pack her bags to flee. Then, when the boats failed to appear, she angrily declared, "If allarming half a dozen places at the same time is an act of Generalship How[e] may boast of his late conduct."[44]

She became even more enraged when a neighbor predicted utter defeat for America if Philadelphia fell to Howe. Even if all Washington's forces were destroyed, an army of women would step in and destroy the enemy, she snapped back at this man of little faith.[45] Failure was not an option. She felt zealous to fight the British with her own hands. And yet she sighed at the pettiness of the very people she would deliver from Howe's clutches. When she learned some New England workmen had extorted $100 to carry a small trunk out of Boston during the recent panic, she exclaimed. "O! Humane Nature, or rather O! inhumane nature what art thou."[46]

John despised greed and called Howe "the Scourge of God, and the Plague of Mankind," but he neither feared the British Navy nor despaired over Fort Ticonderoga's loss.[47] "I begin to Wish there was not a Fort upon the Continent," he wrote Abigail. The best policy, in his opinion, was to lure the British off battlefields altogether and into the American wilderness, where their old world theories and cumbrous equipment would seal their doom.

Coincidentally, this was precisely what Washington was currently ordering his generals to do.[48] Let Burgoyne take fort after fort as he rampaged south down Lake George toward the Hudson. For there was land to be crossed between these two bodies of water, and Burgoyne's forty-two pieces of cannon were sure to prolong the trudge.

Americans contributed to Burgoyne's troubles by strewing trees across already narrow passes and propelling boulders into creeks. By refusing to attack, they forced the British to come after them into the countryside, where hundreds of Redcoats fell or were taken prisoner, while Continental militia poured in from both New York and New England, swelling American forces in the north to 16,000, while the British numbers shrank to just 5,800 men as summer drew to a close. On August 16, the Continental troops crossed the border to Vermont and won the Battle of Bennington.

"N.Y. and N.E. [New England] are destroying Burgoyne," John somewhat exaggerated the case a week later. Meanwhile, Howe had finally turned up in Maryland's Chesapeake Bay, seemingly en route to the capital fifty miles north. Defying the British to attack, Washington strutted his troops through the streets of Philadelphia. "Now is the Time . . . for my Countrymen to . . . crush that vapouring, blustering Bully [Burgoyne] to Attoms," John cheered them on.

John described the soldiers marching before Congress as "extreamly well armed" and "pretty well cloathed," but noted some sagging heads and turned-in toes and hats going every which way. These were symptoms of the larger problem of insubordination, he believed. "Discipline in an Army is like the Laws, in civil Society," he told Abigail. No community on earth could dispense with hierarchy, which he did not need to remind her was the backbone of their religious faith. "Obedience is the only Thing wanting for our Salvation—Obedience to the Laws, in the States, and Obedience to Officers in the Army."[49]

But obedience was not all the Army lacked, as John knew better than anyone. If the Philadelphia soldiers were "extreamly well armed," many of the militia who poured in from Maryland and Pennsylvania to fight Howe for the capital had only their own hunting rifles or no weapons at all. Despite his bluster, John did not really expect General Washington to beat Howe in a general engagement. Indeed, he began telling Abigail he *hoped* Howe would take Philadelphia: better that the British should be "cooped up here" for the winter than "run away again to N. York."[50] Already imagining himself quite happy in exile, he belittled the importance of a permanent seat of Congress and placed his hopes on the battle for the north.

Even if all Washington's forces were destroyed, an army of women would step in and destroy the enemy, Abigail declared.

"I long for a decisive battle" there, Abigail agreed. And she got it. On October 17, General Burgoyne surrendered to American General Gates at the Battle of Saratoga. Rather than eating Christmas dinner in Albany, the British general sailed for England in disgrace. As the British lay down their arms, America basked in the repossession of all northern New York. It was a phenomenal coup for Washington, his first major victory since the Battle of Boston. And Congress—now relocated in York, Pennsylvania, the British having chased them from Philadelphia, as John had foreseen—called for the first nationally celebrated Thanksgiving.[51] Letters were rushed off to Paris.

On October 26, the day after her wedding anniversary, Abigail celebrated the American victory by going to church. "Praise to the Supreem Being who hath so remarkably deliverd our Enimies into our Hands," she hailed the righteous God, who had caused good to triumph at Saratoga even as, in his more enigmatic ways, he had chosen to take her child to Heaven four months before. Of course, "God helps those who help themselves," she observed to her husband, praising John's own heroism while broadly hinting it would be nice to put an end to her "more than 3 years . . . of widowhood."[52][53]

As it happened, John was currently in the market for a horse to carry him to Braintree. "I am bound home," he wrote on November 14.[54] He had performed his duty for America and was now prepared to return to his family, his law practice, and the life of a citizen farmer. Or so he told himself.

ON THURSDAY OCTOBER 16, 1777, Reverend Smith officiated at the wedding of his youngest daughter, Elizabeth. All the Cranches and Quincys and Tufts and Smiths and Adamses crowded into the little Weymouth meetinghouse to wish her well. For Nabby, watching her favorite aunt prepare to leave Weymouth was especially moving. But even Abigail rose to the occasion (though she damned it with faint praise in a subsequent letter to John).[55] And William Smith spared John Shaw the mocking he had lavished on John Adams thirteen years earlier. No devil-riddled Johns haunted this service. "There was a man sent from God, whose name was John," the reverend preached.

In the most important part of the service, Betsy Smith vowed to love her husband and vice versa. For a promise of mere faithfulness and obedience was not acceptable. Nor did passive love suffice. More than Catholics or Anglicans, Puritans demanded that a married couple love urgently, that they prefer each other to all else except for God.[56] To prefer your husband not just in your bed or his parish, but through all the long days of life—to side with him even against your parents or sisters—was a large assignment, as Betsy recognized.

"Even blessed with the kindest and most affectionate Partner—and with the most flattering Prospects, it is at best . . . but a solemn scene of Joy," Betsy wrote of her marriage:

To bid adieu to our former Habitation and to give up the kind quarters of our youth and place ourselves under quite a new kind of Protection, cannot but strike a reflecting mind with awe, and the most fearful Apprehensions—as it is *the* important crisis upon which our Fate depends.[57]

There are no descriptions of the wedding, but three months later, Elizabeth—in a markedly lighter tone—wrote to Mary, thanking her for her "very kind enquiries after *Madam* and her *Spouse.*"

I have the pleasure of assuring you they are in fine Health, are exceedingly pleased with their Situation, have every thing they want, more than a Clergyman just entered into a Family could expect, in such perilous Times. She is as happy as she can, or ought to be, at such distance from her dear Friends.

A warming pan, used to soothe a couple's feet in bed, was a popular wedding present at the time.

She made it clear that John Shaw was as marvelous a husband as Richard. "You my Sister," Elizabeth continued, "have experienced how much kindness, affection, and tender assiduity contributed to make you easy even [in Salem]; and Without these Cordials of Life I should be miserable was I situated even in the midst of my numerous Friends."[58] So all was well in the marriage department.

Still, much had changed for Elizabeth since October. For a start, no one ever addressed her as Betsy. According to tradition, she had relinquished this favorite Quincy nickname at the altar and would be Elizabeth Shaw from now on. She lived in a sizable house with flower beds in front and a large, year-round garden off the kitchen. Here—like her sisters and all good New England housewives—she spent hours planting and pruning the fruits and vegetables so highly touted by doctors and difficult to grow in the rocky New England sod.[59]

Elizabeth had begun reading gardening manuals by the likes of the popular English horticulturist Charles Marshall, which gave very specific instructions about nurturing soil and lining fences with protective trees. Peas, squash, corn, cucumbers, and strawberries each had their proper position in the overall scheme, she was learning, and the traditional acre-size plot had to be oblong and slanted away from the north wind. Delicate crops could be shielded with glass or oil paper. So even in freezing January, Elizabeth was out every clear morning planting cucumbers, melon, asparagus seeds, carrots, or lettuce to serve with mutton in springtime. Next month she would add potatoes, shallots, and horseradish, while constantly churning the soil to beat off the frost.[60]

On top of this, she was home spinning John's shirts and coats, and smart clothes for herself to impress the parish. Now that no one could accuse her of dressing to find a husband, she indulged her flair for style to her heart's content. Everyone admired her clothes, made of cambric or lace if she could get her hands on them. She tossed her hair up in the fashionable "high roll," using artificial pads and pomatum to nearly double the size of her coiffure.[61] [62] Meanwhile, she scrubbed and cooked with a newlywed's ardor.

There was no spot on the reputation of the gracious Elizabeth Shaw. From newspaper reports, it seems the town was in love with her. "Among other things I suppose I must tell you what oppinion the People [of Haverhill] have formed of me," Elizabeth could not help boasting to her eldest sister.

> In general, they say my Character [is] very good . . . One says
> that I am a little heavenly body. Others are so favourable as to
> say "that she talks, and is as sociable as one of *Us*," and the Children think that I am a *dear pretty woman.*[63]

Elizabeth herself was mostly pleased with this new society, which included affable Merchant White, the wealthiest man in Haverhill; his wife, Sarah; and their son, Leonard, and daughter, Peggy, the village *belle*. She was ceremoniously entertained at the home of prosperous Mr. Duncan and called upon by intellectuals like Judge Sargeant, who had the distinction of having attended the first reading of the Declaration of Independence. Mrs. Sargeant was born to the elite Pickering family of Salem and led discussions of music and art. And then there was a woman of no social consequence, whom Elizabeth revered for her subtle mind and passion for reading. This person quickly became a friend in the deepest sense, for "How soon must society grow insipid and conversation wearisome unless it is enlivened by a Taste for Literature," Elizabeth Shaw, sounding just like Betsy Smith, averred.

Haverhill was built on a hill looking down on the twining, blue-black Merrimack River. And while she brought food to the poor in their meager garrison houses, Elizabeth lived among the wealthy in their stately shingled mansions with wide, high windows and broad slanted roofs. The view from the parsonage, at the corner of Main and Summer Streets, never failed to raise her spirits. Behind, meadows and woodlands meandered to the riverbank. Out front, and across the pretty Common stood the rising bell tower of the First Presbyterian Church. Here her husband was beginning his professional life in a delicate position.

For the minister John replaced had been, in the language of the time, an Arminian. In other words, he spurned emotion and opposed traditional Calvinism, which said man was saved or damned at birth. In the Arminian view, man chose or rejected God of his own volition. Arminians favored introspection over ardent singing and faith-driven conversions. Many traditional Congregationalists, including Parson

Wibird and Elizabeth's own father, leaned in the same direction (though few dared to acknowledge so in a wartime atmosphere where fire and brimstone were on the ascendant), while John Shaw made a point of rejecting this kind of self-determination and embracing original sin.

John Shaw's anti-Arminian views had certainly promoted his candidacy in Haverhill, where a dynamic evangelical preacher named Hezekiah Smith was luring alarming numbers of First Church parishioners to his new Baptist Church. By hiring John Shaw, the town elders believed, they could stanch the exodus. So high expectations rested on Elizabeth's new husband. He was to appease the anti-rationalists, find a bridge to the evangelists, and—most crucially—outdo his Baptist rival by finding an eloquent voice of his own.[64]

Elizabeth's job was to outdo the Baptists in adhering to severe religious restrictions. While it was all very fine for her to be elegant and charming, what really mattered was that she serve breakfast on the dot at eight, dine at one, pray at nine, and afterward go directly to bed.[65] No urge to write could distract her from dousing the candles on time; sleeping late or wandering into the fields at dawn were not options for the minister of Haverhill's wife. Elizabeth entertained every Sunday evening, never skipping or changing the appointment. Soon there remained few outward traces of Abigail's rebellious sister. For whatever she thought privately, Elizabeth did her best to uphold the status quo. And she found the inner strength to remain cheerful even when she sometimes worried she was stifling her real self.[56]

"We are induced to conform, and suffer many things disagreeable, for the sake of the Blessings and the Comforts that flow from [community]," Elizabeth expressed her guarded faith in majority rule to Mary. "A dismal kind of life I hear you say. I acknowledge it. But while we are in this World Society is essential to Man's happiness . . . Charity, and Benevolence are thus spread from Family to Family, and Friendships are formed that soften the Cares, and mitigate the ills of Life."[67]

How wise and settled she sounds, how free of her old imperiousness and sensitivity to insult; though she does suffer a bit of a setback as her letter draws to a close. John Adams, it seems, in his new role as civilian, had just been arguing a court case in Portsmouth, New Hampshire. Haverhill "would have been but a few miles, if any, out of his way and it would have rejoiced our Hearts to have seen him after so long an absence," Elizabeth fell to musing. And this after he'd just missed her wedding! "I am really troubled with Brother Adams," she huffed.[68]

As it happened, John Adams had good reason for rushing home from Portsmouth. America's three delegates in France were bickering, and one, Silas Deane, had just been recalled. An acquaintance of John's, arriving at the Portsmouth courthouse from Philadelphia, whispered in his ear that Congress had just chosen him to join Franklin and Arthur Lee as the third delegate in Paris.[69] He was to sail immediately and capitalize on America's victory at Saratoga to persuade the French to play the crucial role he had foreseen for them in the ongoing war.

The news arrived at the foot of Penn's Hill before John could warn Abigail. Innocently opening a letter to John from Massachusetts delegate James Lovell, she felt, as she declared in the distraught but also furious letter she rushed off, robbed of all her happiness. The more she thought of the price she was asked to pay, the more aggrieved she grew. For since she loved her husband "above all earthy things," as she was meant to, relinquishing him to the country over the past three years had demanded every spot of public spirit she possessed. She had seen it as no more than her due when the country in turn sent him back at the middle of November. And here it was not even Christmas, and they were calling him up again! Why, she asked, should a man so needed at home endure "the Risk and hazard of a cross-Atlantic voyage?" Why should she "sacrifice" the "tranquility and happiness" of the normal New England wife? And for how many more years would she be asked to run a farm as well as a household? "My life will be one continued scene of anxiety and apprehension, and must I cheerfully comply with the Demand of my Country?" she asked rhetorically, for she knew at once John would see it as his duty to go, and she would agree.[70]

There was certainly no denying that, despite his deficiency in the French language (Abigail was more fluent), he was an ideal candidate. Not only had he been the first Congressman to understand the importance of a French alliance, but his smooth collaboration with Ben Franklin on the Declaration of Independence augured well for their wooing Vergennes in a common voice. And while few of the delegates who chose him had ever met a French *compte* or *philosophe,* they felt sure John's unsullied integrity and intellectual brilliance could not fail to please all civilized men.

The most Abigail could do was beg John to take her with him. Her cousin John Thaxter felt sure she would prevail. "It gives me great pain on your account to indulge an Idea to the Contrary," he wrote Abigail.[71] But, as John Adams saw it, worse than loneliness were the threats of a winter sea voyage and possible capture by the British, who malingered along the coastlines watching for famous patriots to arrest. Plus, there was no denying the greater danger to the children with both parents gone. To carry his argument, John shrewdly expressed a horror of the unkempt female: "No Being in Nature [is] so disagreable as a Lady at Sea."

This last clinched the argument. Worse even than sea wreck was a husband's disgust. "One would not wish . . . to be thought of in that Light: by those to whom we would wish to appear in our best array," Abigail confided to Mary, who, being an eighteenth-century New England female, readily agreed.[72]

To elude British spies, John's preparations to leave were kept secret. A barge picked him up near the Quincy estate at Mount Wollaston and brought him to Marblehead on February 13. There he boarded the ship the *Boston* with John Quincy. At ten-and-a-half, John Quincy was roughly the same age as Benny Bache, who seemed to be faring well overseas with his grandfather Ben Franklin. The advantage in terms of education was worth the risk for a young person, Abigail and John agreed. Furthermore, Abigail recognized with some bitterness, John Quincy was not only their most gifted offspring, he was the oldest male.[73] If his big sister, Nabby, had been the prodigy, no one, of course, would have allowed her to go.

The day John and John Quincy sailed, as well as missing them already, Abigail was quietly seething about the "disparity" between the sexes, just as she had smarted ten years earlier when her cousin Isaac got the privilege of going to London while no one had ever thought of sending her. That "every assistance and advantage which can be procured is afforded to sons" and not daughters still infuriated her, she wrote John Thaxter from her Braintree bedroom as her husband and son headed for Paris. "When a woman possessd of a common share of understanding considers the difference of Education between the male and female Sex ... it is really moritifying," she complained.[74]

Still, "Since they are seperated from me I long to know that they are making the best of their Way to their desired Haven," she continued in a calmer tone. She felt grateful for their "fair weather and ... fine wind." Faith taught her to accept that whatever happened would be for the best in God's eyes. And her instincts said all would end well: "I don't know whether you know it, but I am governd by impulces a little," she confided in John Thaxter, "and cruel as the Seperation is I receive some comfort from a secret impulse that they will have a short and favourable passage."[75]

Yet there was no denying the months, maybe years of solitude and hard work that lay ahead of her. "The most painfull Seperation I have yet been call'd to endure," she described John's departure in a letter to a close woman friend.

And maybe it was not altogether coincidence that her mind turned with more sympathy than usual to her sister in Haverhill at this point. Up until now, unlike Mary, Abigail had felt no motherly obligation to inquire after Elizabeth's new life. Nor had she changed a bit in her opinion of John Shaw But six months after the wedding the energy had gone out of her anger. And then Betsy took the opportunity of John's departure to express *her* sisterly concern for Abigail. "There are

This locket of a woman looking out to sea, John's present to Abigail when he left for France, is made from both of their hair.

many to whom a temporary Separation after so long a connexion, would have been a happy Circumstance; but for you to be separated from him 'whose birth was to your own ally'd' must be a Trial which cannot be described by words," Elizabeth wrote out of her intimate knowledge of John and Abigail's love from its earliest days.[76]

Then Abigail found it only natural to write back and call Elizabeth "my dear sister." "Tho my own felicity is over cast . . . tis with pleasure I hear of your Health and happiness which are dear to me," she began stiffly. But by the end of her note she had swallowed pride to such an extent that she was asking Elizabeth to "Remember me in affectionate terms to Mr. S[ha]w." And, in reply, Elizabeth went so far beyond gloating as to call Abigail "the Object . . . of my veneration."

And how could they help being pleased with themselves and each other? They imagined Mary in the background applauding them as well. For they had proved that sisterhood neither foundered at power struggles nor was dashed by conflicting views. On the contrary, it survived sea change after sea change. It was a palliative to those forbidden foreign travel, a tie to mother and aunts, a gift to pass on in one form or another.

"The heart which is susceptable to all the finer sensations is ever subject to the deepest wounds."

. . .

"I HAD ALMOST TAKEN UP A RESOLUTION NOT TO HAVE WROTE TO aney of my Braintree friends untill I had received letters from them, but you know that second thoughts are often the best and I think I will put [you] in mind that thare is such a person gone out of Braintree as one Nabby Adams."[1]

So wrote Nabby Adams to her best friend and first cousin Betsy Cranch on the fourth of February, 1779, a year after her father left for Europe. In Braintree, the girls were forever in and out of each other's houses. Now, though, Nabby was off visiting their mother's close friend Mrs. Warren in nearby Plymouth. She was fourteen and convinced there was no one luckier in the world than she.

Let her brother sail off to Paris. *She'd* come thirty miles in a carriage—which was quite enough adventure for a girl her age. She knew her mother "must be very lonesome"[2] without her, and being a loyal daughter, vowed, "When ever [Mamma] command me to leive Plymouth I shall obey." Her "secret hope," though, was that she could stay for another month at least, for she was thoroughly enjoying Mrs. Warren's home.

Betsy Cranch, two years older than Nabby, had already visited Plymouth without *her* mama and would concede, Nabby felt sure, that Mrs. Warren was an "instructive" and "improveing" hostess.[3] Being a poet, essayist, and playwright as well as a valiant wife and mother, she set a fine example for aspiring girls. Besides, born an Otis and married to a Warren, Mercy embodied the New England elite. She knew everyone worth knowing, and her "agreeable sons" had marriageable friends.[4]

This was a key attraction, for while they had no intention of wedding before their early twenties, Nabby and Betsy were both of a courting age. Their chief job over the next six or seven years would be falling in love with a suitable husband—to which end they were reading "improving" articles like "The Philosophy of Coquetry," which applauded matches based on "mental attachment" and ranted against sensuality, frivolity, vanity, ornate dresses, and dangling jewels.[5]

Puritan teenagers were bombarded by mixed messages. While one poem or scripture accused men of corrupting innocent females, another, like Genesis, blamed girls for the fall of man. "Beware then, beware how you trust/Coquettes who to Love make pretense," wailed the male narrator in a typical verse of the latter sort, called "Fare well ye green fields," which Betsy jotted painstakingly in her common book.[6] Meanwhile, cautions against arrogance abounded in conduct books like Dr. John Gregory's *A Father's Legacy to his Daughters*.

Since women were expected to excel at manners, daughters of leading families often attended male academies transformed into girls' schools during the summer months. Nabby, for instance, had spent the previous July and August in Boston studying dancing, sewing, music, and the art of polite letter-writing—though it went without saying that initiating or even accepting any correspondence from a male admirer could tarnish a girl's name for life. Thus, a traveling merchant named Henry Drinker wrote ardent letters only to his beloved's sister, and Benjamin Franklin's son courted the girl he wanted to marry by singing her praises to a mutual friend.[7] Of course, sex before marriage was scandalous, even to someone as open-minded as Betsy Cranch. A favorite cautionary tale of the era involved a high-spirited American named

Rachel Warrington, who was seduced by a dashing French officer vowing eternal love. When he absconded, leaving her pregnant, everyone agreed that she had only herself to blame.

For it went without saying that virtue was a woman's mandate. Acquiescence, so becoming to matrons, was decidedly premature for the unwed. Quashing passion required all the fine ideals that, like housekeeping, a woman was believed to grasp with little effort, while men needed prodding. Thus, even an *accomplished* bachelor like Parson Wibird required constant care from the community, while the lowliest spinster "of virtue and prudence [was] a public . . . benefactor," as one popular late eighteenth-century magazine proclaimed. Another noted, "Love and courtship . . . it is universally allowed, invest a lady with more Authority than . . . any other situation that falls to human beings."[8]

And beyond facilitating social intercourse, women could invest this fleeting power in their own happiness. Of course, all women were not equal. Nabby, being John Adams's daughter, would have a wider choice of suitors than Betsy Cranch. Still, in a society that truly valued character and favored love matches, goodness, charm, or beauty might well compensate for financial need. And as John Adams constantly reminded Abigail, a strong woman was crucial to a man's and, by extension, a nation's success.

Unlike her mother, Nabby rarely alluded to politics except when ruing her father's continued absence in Paris. What fascinated *her* was the inner life. She prided herself on her powers of analysis. "You say you have not had the symptoms of love yet: but I sincerely belive you have too fataly experienced them,"[9] Nabby teased her cousin in a typical letter from Plymouth. Nabby described her own nature as "cold" and "indifferent." She was "sometimes . . . at a loss to know whether I have a heart or not." Betsy, on the other hand, was "soft of disposition."[10] Since birth, they'd been a study in contrast, with Betsy following in their mothers' footsteps and reacting intensely to everything and everybody, while Nabby, *sui generis,* took the world in stride.

Nabby clearly enjoyed flouting the female ideal. Even lightning couldn't frighten her, she taunted Betsy, for whom heart palpitations and quivering hands were common occurrences. And whereas Betsy could reach the height of pleasure just by reading Richardson, Nabby was difficult to rouse. Though she was having a pleasant time in Plymouth, "My happiness is not greatly augmented by this visit neither will it be greatly decreased [when I leave]," she reported with an obvious desire to shock her ardent cousin, who both craved new scenes and grieved at the briefest parting.[11] It went without saying that "the heart which is susceptable to all the finer sensations is ever subject to the deepest wounds," in Betsy's view.[12]

Their demeanors were also glaringly different. Betsy, the extrovert, conversed warmly with anyone in earshot, whereas Nabby was too proud to be popular and informed her brother in Paris that she rarely felt inclined to speak.[13] She is rather too quiet, Abigail complained of their daughter in a letter to John around the same time.[14] Nabby also delighted at circumlocution, while Betsy took the family's renowned transparency to a new peak.[15] "Her eye expresses the Exquisite Sensibility of her heart," noted one of many male admirers.[16]

Betsy furthermore had a sympathetic ear for everyone's troubles, and though not beautiful, possessed "a sweetness, and a benign candour . . . which my . . . taste prefers," the same young man went on.[17] She was small, brown-haired, and slim with clear dark skin like Mary's. She had fainted from the smallpox vaccine because she was as fragile as her aunt Elizabeth, while Aunt Abigail declared no man alive was "sufficiently civilized" for her sensitive niece.[18]

But her ideas were bold. She scoffed at all the praise the Boston newspapers were now heaping on society belle Miss Hunter simply because she was beautiful and smart. "Her [looks] were not her acquisition," Betsy preached to her younger sister, Lucy. She hoped that rather than exciting envy, this paragon would inspire emulation so that "an *accomplished woman* may not long be the *most* extraordinary phenomenon" in the world.[19] As ardently as Cotton Mather or Frances Hutcheson, Betsy believed in self-improvement. Happiness, she felt, was "dependant chiefly upon the mind." Yet, while it was a comfort to know that nature and music were accessible even to the lowliest beggar, it was far better to be wealthy and successful than poor and unknown. Indeed, people who made no attempt to help themselves were their own worst enemies, Betsy in the nicest way hinted to a less ambitious friend.[20]

Betsy continually exerted herself to ward off mood swings, which set in especially during the winter months. One Friday night, for instance, while preparing to go to bed, "a sweet pleasing calmness" enveloped her, she wrote in her diary. She experienced "the most perfect composure and serenity . . . each pulse was calm—& beat in perfect unison." She fell asleep sure she had achieved peace at last—then woke up shaking from a nightmare. The demons of her dream refused to dissipate with daylight. Fancy was stronger than reason, she sadly deduced.[21]

But if Betsy was prone to tormenting introspection, she was also agile and energetic, adored fortune-telling games and outdoor activities, like sledding, and was rarely out of love with some boy. She traveled miles to view a parade of the local militia and regularly marched to the top of a nearby hill to watch the sun set over the Cranch farm. She danced until the last minute at assemblies, then stayed up half the night describing in her diary all she had seen and felt.

Sometimes she seemed too good to be true. She refused even to acknowledge her magnetic personality, attributing her popularity with men to a fairy tale sort of luck. At one assembly, she recounted in her diary, she was instantly attracted to a handsome stranger on the opposite side of the room. How sad that he would never notice her, she thought. Then suddenly the young man started walking in her direction. Like her own Prince Charming, he passed by her pretty friends and asked *her* to dance.

The evening ended too quickly. Chaperones shooed them out at midnight, and she had to be home by one. When she went to bed at three, she was still too excited to sleep much.[22] She woke up to a day of housekeeping, sewing lace, and making hair bracelets, reading Bernard's history of England in the morning and a translation of Rousseau's *La Nouvelle Heloise* after tea. Prince Charming faded into memory. She now had her heart set on tracking down a piano so she could play music—for there was no such instrument in her own home.

Betsy could not help noticing that, for all their friends in common, her family was a notch below the Adams on the social ladder. Indeed, much that could be desired was lacking in the Cranch household. For, despite Abigail's initial hopes for her sister, Richard Cranch had not made a success of his farm any more than of fixing watches or selling cards. His genius was protean and undisputed; Braintree honored it by repeatedly electing him to both the County Court and the Massachusetts House of Representatives. Even John Adams—who had refused Abigail's request to recommend Richard to Harvard—on his own initiative submitted one of Richard's inventions for a prestigious science award in Europe and further encouraged his brother-in-law's watchmaking by sending springs and dials from abroad.[23] [24]

But serving science and Braintree were not remunerative enterprises, and the long commutes to court and congress in Boston, coupled with his delicate health, left Richard with little energy to plant and plough. To make ends meet, Mary had begun taking in boarders, a common practice for widows and spinsters, but less acceptable for a married woman and certainly a falling off for the granddaughter of Colonel Quincy and the sister-in-law of America's spokesman in France.

And while Betsy opened her heart to Aunt Adams, Nabby recoiled from Aunt Cranch's belief in "talking everything out." Please don't tell this "even to your Mama" was a familiar refrain in Nabby's letters to Betsy, while Mary, used to her own communicative daughters, could not help taking it personally when Nabby refused to chat.[25]

Not talking was certainly a way to distinguish yourself in such an outspoken family, as was Nabby's professed indifference to impending battles or treaties with France. She made a point that she shared none of her mother's compulsion to understand history or take part in the great events of her time. Nor was she angered by the restrictions placed on females: her goal was to ignore all opportunities for heroic behavior, to marry, mother, housekeep, and without fuss or ostentation enjoy a privileged life.

Physically, she differed markedly from the female members of her family. While they were slight, Nabby was "large in stature" and on the plump side like her father.[26] The remains of smallpox scars still stippled her fine features, but she had a regal bearing, a high opinion of her own importance, a talent for moderation, and was very much the pert young female or, in the words of her older brother, "miss in her teens."[27]

She was full of contempt for girls with bad taste in husbands: "Miss Watson is soon to be married. I suppose . . . she thinks she shall be happyer than at present but some people think her mistaken," she observed of one such deluded female.[28] On the other hand she adored Betsy's nemesis, the celebrated Miss Hunter, whose "beautiful mouth," "sweet . . . countenance," and ability to translate Italian made her, for the moment at least, Nabby's crush. On another day, the bedazzling Elizabeth Mayhew had "a most strange fascinating power over me . . . I cannot account for it." As for men: "I long to be in love," Nabby told Betsy, though she made it clear she was even more anxious to ward off unworthy bachelors in their circle such as "impudent" Mr. Sawyer and Mr. Lincoln with his insufferable conceit. (She was amused when she heard Mr. Lincoln had been complaining about *her* in the same terms.)

With Betsy already famous for feelings, Nabby took pride in her independent spirit and level head. She declared that because love was founded in self-interest she would never be swept off her feet by a cad, and she shocked her friends by leaving a Harvard commencement party early.[29] She shared her father's skepticism about human nature: in her opinion one was more likely to be good because one was happy than happy because one was good. "I believe our happiness is in great measure dependent upon external circumstances," Nabby wrote to Betsy, disagreeing with her cousin's view that we take an active role in our well-being. If success could be attained by effort or merit, why, she reasoned, should she be showered by "ten thousand sources of happiness" while others, who were equally deserving, were starved of the most basic needs? And the possibility of a just God did not bode well for either of them, she reminded her cousin. For "If there is an equal degree of happiness and misery [strewn] in our path," then Nabby and Betsy's good times were limited and might someday soon run out.

NABBY MIGHT WELL HAVE concluded that her mother's luck had run out lately. At the end of 1778, while her daughter was off enjoying herself at Mrs. Warren's, Abigail was stuck at home, mired in snow and "winds blowing like a Hurricane," with only two demanding little boys for company, feeling "solitary indeed."[30] Some days, she said, she felt more unhappy than she would wish even an Enemy to be.[31] A married woman could not go out alone for fear of appearing unfaithful. Abigail could not even look to her faraway husband for comfort because the man who used to open his heart to her had disappeared. In two months, it would be a year since John Adams left for Paris, and in that time she had received only a few exasperatingly short and superficial letters, extolling the felicity of the French climate, but saying not a word about politics or his undying love for her. John's excuse—that he feared the British would intercept his correspondence—struck her as ludicrous. Who cared if the world knew he missed his wife?[32]

Had she foreseen this faintheartedness, she never would have agreed to their parting, she grumbled in a letter she wondered if he would ever see. "You could not have sufferd more upon your [Atlantic] Voyage than I have felt cut of from all communication with you."[33]

She also suffered more than he from the privations of a war that felt endless. The British and Continental armies fought to a stalemate at the gruesome Battle of Monmouth, New Jersey, while the first joint naval venture between America and France—an attempt to retake Rhode Island from the British—was quashed by a sudden storm. When battle ceased for the winter months, the Americans were no closer to independence than after the Battle of Saratoga a year earlier.

To make matters worse, the winter in New England was the coldest in Abigail's memory. Icy roads made even the twelve-mile carriage ride to the Cranches' farm a treacherous chore.[34] The contrast to her husband's situation further infuriated her. The summer before, after she wrote, "I am . . . almost melted" from the heat in Braintree, he effused about the air and manner of living in Paris.[35] Now while she was homebound by snowstorms, his December was so mild he raved about standing outdoors watching candles illuminate Notre Dame.

John seemed equally distant from the drudgery of managing their scant finances. Everything, Abigail was discovering, was a trade-off. She decided to let out the farm, which eliminated her dependence on tenants, but also reduced her already precarious income while the war had inflation bounding out of control.[36] "A hundred Dollars will not purchase what ten formerly did," she felt impelled to inform her distracted husband.[37] Admittedly, his salary was small, but surely he could turn over some of it. He had promised to send European goods for her to sell in New England. Where were those?

Most infuriating of all was John's extolling of French women. "They are handsome, and very well educated. Their Accomplishments are exceedingly brilliant," wrote the man who had urged Nabby not to learn Latin. Then he quipped, "Don't be jealous."[38]

"I regret the trifling narrow contracted Education of the Females of my own Country," she retorted. She went on to praise a recent essay *by a man* sharing her views. The essayist agreed with her that male and female brains were equal *even in America,* and it was "inhumane Tyranny" that men (like John!) deprived girls of school.[39]

"The most Forlorn and Dismal of all states is that of widowhood. How often does my Heart bleed at thinking how nearly my own Situation is allied to that," Abigail wrote Mercy Otis Warren on December 10.[40] And three days later, spurred by a bland letter from Paris, she accused John of only needing her when he was sick: "The climate of France is [so] agreeable I believe to your Health . . . [that in the future] I fear I shall hear from you if possible seldomer than at present."[41]

MEANWHILE, JOHN WAS HAVING troubles of his own across the Atlantic. Though he hid his insecurities in his desultory letters to Abigail, he felt intimidated by the French and out of his depth in the diplomatic world. Not just the language, but the pleasures of Paris were new to him—he had never seen an opera or anything like the stupendously ornate bedchamber at Versailles, where he was received by the King. While his reasoning was as subtle as Voltaire's, he was a stranger to the French taste for insinuation and scorn for plain speaking. And to a man who loved to get down to business, it was a jolt, indeed, to survive winter storms and British spy boats only to learn—upon arriving at last in the Bordeaux harbor—that the treaty between France and America, which he had come to create, had already been written and signed. Worse, his two fellow delegates were very publicly fighting.

The Virginian Arthur Lee, in John's opinion, was honest, but splenetic, confident people were plotting against him, and scornful of anything French. Lee's current nemesis was their fellow delegate, Ben Franklin, who, Lee informed Adams, was duping the Americans and contriving with Louis XVI. Nothing else, in Lee's opinion, could explain Franklin's overblown fame in Paris or his easy access to Vergennes, the French Foreign Minister, who was the embodiment of aloofness to everybody else.[42]

Knowing Lee's temperament and Franklin's talents, Adams dismissed these accusations as envy. But what could explain Franklin's rancor toward Lee?

"It is with much Grief and Concern that I have learned from my first landing in France, the Disputes between the Americans, in this Kingdom," John brooded in his diary. He vowed: "I am at present wholly untainted with these Prejudices, and will endeavor to keep myself so."[43]

But being who he was, it was unlikely John could stand aloof from reports ridiculing the dissension in the American mission. Nor was it in his nature to smile stoically as Lee snooped for spies in Franklin's household and Franklin announced himself too busy to confer with his fellow delegates, though he sat for hours in operas and plays. Had the French flattered the inventor of the lightning rod into turpitude, Adams wondered. Or had Franklin's touting of American industry been a pose from the start? Certainly "early to bed and early to rise" was no longer his motto.

In Adams's view, 78-year-old Franklin had completely abandoned the Puritan ethic. He lived lavishly, hoarded the mission's only two secretaries, refused to save accounts of his transactions concerning the new alliance, and kept all communications with the French to himself. Getting Franklin to sign even the most rudimentary letter required blandishment after blandishment. Franklin's main occupation, besides attending theatre, was visiting famous philosophers, scientists, and writers, or better still, their widows and wives. He went to bed hours after Lee and Adams and slept in while they floundered through reams of perplexing diplomatic papers, getting no help from the man in charge.

"The Life of Dr. Franklin was a Scene of continual discipation," John wrote in the past tense in his diary—as if rehearsing a speech to Congress. "I could never obtain the favour of his Company in a Morning before Breakfast . . . and as soon as Breakfast was over, a crowd of Carriges came to . . . his Lodgings, with all Sorts of People," mostly women and children hungry for "Stories about his Simplicity, his bald head and scattering strait hairs." These visitors lingered, and soon it was time to dress for dinner. Franklin was invited out every night and rarely declined.

John then trotted out another page of invective in support of his reigning theme that no business would ever get done in the American mission to France unless *he* did it.[44] What vexed John even more,

Ben Franklin's flirtation with French "belles" of all ages appalled John.

though he didn't say it, was that Franklin with so little effort had won France's heart. Vergennes continued to ignore any American but him.

Despite John's moratorium on writing politics to Abigail, he managed to convey his view of American diplomacy in France in a letter to his cousin Sam Adams.[45] "Our Affairs in this Kingdom, I find in a State of confusion and darkness," he ominously started. "Prodigious Sums of money have been expended and large Sums are yet due. But there are no Books of Account, or any Documents" explaining what America received from the French in return. This was his oblique way of siding

with Lee and accusing Franklin of helping the French extort American money. He went on to caution Congress that one diplomat was
better than three: "The Inconveniences arising from the Multiplicity of
Ministers . . . are infinite." He left no doubt who the obvious choice
would be.[46]

What John did not say was that he had fallen hopelessly in love with
Paris. More than business or fear of the British intercepting letters, this
explains the sparseness of his correspondence with his New England
wife. He was overwhelmed by French architecture, painting, theatre,
landscape, food, and eloquence. Café Procope—near the Luxembourg
Gardens and the first place coffee was publicly served in Paris—was
ideal for erudite conversation.[47] But France was a treat for the senses as
well as the intellect. "Dined at Monsr. Brillon's . . . Madame Brillon is a
Beauty," he noted in a typical diary entry.[48] He basked in the attention
of the King at "sublime" Versailles.[49] At the Comedie Francais, he sat
in the first box, close to Voltaire, who, though "very old," "has yet much
Fire in his Eyes and Vigour;"[50] and in his library, John discovered Jean
Jacques Rousseau—author of *Emile* and *The Social Contract*—whose
virtue he extolled. (Adams was unaware of Rousseau's policy of shipping his children off to orphanages.)[51] John found the chapel at Les
Invalides "immensely grand,"[52] a trip to Montmartre "one of the pleas-
antest Rides yet"[53] and was spellbound by the waterworks at the King's
palace: "the most curious and beautifull Place I have yet seen."[54]

The whole country was "one great Garden. Nature and Art have
conspired to render every Thing here delightful," John wrote Abigail
soon after he landed.[55] Then, "This is a delicious Country. Every Thing
that can sooth, charm and bewitch is here." (Unconvincingly, he added
that *he* preferred "the Simplicity of Pens Hill").[56] The light show heralding the birth of Louis XVI's first child was the best he had ever
witnessed. After a brief stay in a Paris hotel, he moved outside the city
to Passy, joining Franklin in his "fine airy" and "salubrious" chateau.[57]
Here he took every opportunity to master the French language, but all
he could think to say in English to allay Abigail's increasing sense of
marginalization was, "I write to you so often as my Duty will permit."[58]

So Abigail, at 34, felt abandoned by a husband besotted by the Old
World. But she was not altogether bereft of masculine attention. She
had an admirer of her own.

———

JAMES LOVELL WAS A married man, a father, a teacher, and a spy for the Continental Army. The British threw him in jail for spreading military secrets during their occupation of Boston in 1775. In 1776, when Lovell was released in a prisoners' exchange, Massachusetts hailed him a hero and elected him to join John and Sam Adams at Congress. Here Lovell and John renewed a friendship begun years ago at Harvard. Lovell also secretly began womanizing in Philadelphia at this time.

He was indisputably handsome, though some called him affected. He and Abigail had met briefly, just twice. Their first correspondence dated from 1777, when, as fighting broke out near Philadelphia, Mr. Lovell mailed Mrs. Adams a map of the embattled terrain. "I know You give singular attention to the interesting concerns of America in the present struggle," he explained the unusual gesture of bestowing a gift on a near stranger. He further challenged etiquette by concluding his letter with "affectionate esteem." And his excuse for sending the map to her instead of John was yet another provocation:

> I could, it is true, have deliverred it to your Husband. But I could not with delicacy have told him, *to his face,* that your having given your heart to *such* a man is what, most of all make makes me your—James Lovell

More mystifying than Lovell's transgression was Abigail's failure to reprove him. Usually so sensitive to any threat to her reputation, she chose to put a bright face on this slight. "Your professions of esteem Sir are very flattering to me," she wrote back in uncharacteristically flowery prose.

It was soon after this exchange that Lovell, in his capacity as leading member of the Committee of Foreign Affairs, wrote to inform John of his appointment to Paris. Since John was away at court when Abigail opened the letter, she expressed her first raw feelings on paper to this messenger of doom.

"O Sir you who are possessd of Sensibility, and a tender Heart, how could you contrive to rob me of all my happiness?" she wrote, making no effort to hide her upset. Lovell was a married man with children:

how, she demanded, could he fail to empathize with her sorrow and fears? Had he forgotten how hard it was leave *his* family, even for Philadelphia? She conceded that this appointment did justice to John's talents, but at what a price! She could not sleep or eat, she wrote him, as guilelessly as she would John or Mary, and then, sensing that it was she now who was pushing the limits of polite communication, apologized: "I beg your Excuse Sir for writing thus freely." She would have "poured" her sorrows on John if he weren't away at court.[59]

So Abigail began writing John Lovell as a surrogate for her absent husband. When John left for Paris, Lovell took over John's unfinished law cases and supplanted him as Abigail's purveyor of Congressional news.[60] It was he, for instance, who assured her Ben Franklin had *not* been assassinated. (This was a malicious rumor.) He called her "Madam" at first and signed himself "your most obedient servant." Her initial letters too began and closed in the formal mode. But soon Abigail began signing herself Portia. Before now, she was Portia only to John and close friends like Mercy Otis Warren. Lovell was being admitted to an intimate group.

AND WHILE ABIGAIL WROTE as an equal to her husband and male cousins, her letters to James Lovell were self-consciously female and humble in the extreme. Time and again she alludes to her womanly "fears and apprehensions," her deficiencies as head of a household, her need to be adored and supported by a man.[61] [62]

Each letter was a performance. In the spring of 1778, for instance, four months after John sailed for France and having received no word from him, Abigail read an article in a Newport paper claiming that the British had captured his ship. She expressed her fears in an overwrought and overwritten letter to Lovell, where she declared herself already prostrate with grief. Women were too weak to sustain such blows, she explained, flying in the face both of history and her own professed beliefs. Could Lovell, who had lived through the "Horrours of Captivity and chains," please "communicate to me some share of [your] hidden strength . . . that I may endure this misfortune," she meekly implored.[63]

Lovell pronounced himself only too happy to be of use. Abigail should not, however, presume his motives were lofty. "Call me not a

Savage, when I inform you that your 'Allarms and Distress' have afforded me Delight," he replied in his best mock gallant manner. "If you expect that your Griefs should draw from me only sheer Pity, you must not send them . . . in the most elegant Dresses of Sentiment and Lan-

MRS. JOHN ADAMS.

*Abigail was thirty-three and a desirable woman
when John sailed abroad.*

guage; for, if you persist in your present course, be it known to you before hand, that I shall be far more prompt to admire than to compassionate Them."[64] In other words, he would flirt.

And the woman who admonished her husband to "Remember the ladies . . ." slipped easily into the role of damsel in distress. "I know not whether I ought to reply to your favour," she began her long, temporizing response at the beginning of summer, ". . . for inded Sir I begin to look upon you as a very dangerous Man." On the other hand, she had to admit he was "most ingenious and agreeable," as flatterers went. And she spent another four paragraphs praising his imagination and felicitous writing, while quoting poetry and espousing patriotic thoughts of her own.[65]

Delighted, Lovell proceeded like the rogue in a Restoration comedy. When he opened Abigail's emotional letter during a busy session of Congress, Lovell told her he wanted to scream out "gin ye were mine ain Thing how dearly I would love thee" ("If you were mine, how dearly I would love you," a line from the Scottish writer Allan Ramsay's love poem) before all the delegates. Around the same time, Abigail at last received a passionless note from John telling her only that he had survived the Atlantic trip. What a contrast!

As time passed, and John showed no qualms about neglecting her for business, Lovell, even after a long day at Congress, wrote into the night to allay her slightest fear.[66] She in turn raved about his sensibility, tenderness, and benevolence. She felt no compunctions about telling friends what "a high value" she placed on Lovell's letters or that she was determined to "find some excuse or other to scribble to him soon."[67]

IN THE BEGINNING OF February 1779, while Abigail engaged in an epistolary affair with a married schoolteacher, John Adams received word that Congress had adopted his suggestion and elected a single delegate to replace the bickering three. The surprise was that they chose Ben Franklin.

John's first letter to Abigail flattered her wounded vanity, describing his dismissal as a boon: "I shall therefore soon present before you, your own good Man. Happy—happy indeed shall I be, once more to see our Fireside."[68]

But a week later, on February 20, fearing the first letter might be lost, he wrote Abigail the same information, only now he expressed envy of Franklin and a suspicion that he was being slighted or even punished. "The Congress has not taken the least Notice of me," he complained.[69]

A succeeding letter home (three in the same month!) begins pleasantly enough, recounting a long stroll in the Passy quarter with John Quincy. It is February, but already apples, peaches, and apricots are in bloom. Castles abound, gardens flourish. History comes to life at one's feet. And so he continues, acceding to Abigail's pleas for details about his life on the outskirts of Paris until he can sustain his tone no longer and, about a page into the letter, begins mocking his wife's needs:

> Now Madam don't you think I have spend my Time very wisely in writing all this important History to your Ladyship. Would it not have been as well spent in conjugating two or three french Verbs, which I could have done through all the Moods, Tenses and Persons, of the Active and passive Voice in this Time . . . Suppose I should describe the Persons and Manners of all the Company I see, and the fashions, the Plays, the Games, the sports, the spectacles, the Churches and religious Ceremonies . . . should not you think me turned fool in my old Age—have I Not other Things to do of more importance?"[70]

Two days afterward he commenced a new letter—grumpily: "I suppose I must write every day, in order to keep or rather to restore good Humour, whether I have any thing to say or not." Now he portrays himself as an innocent cut loose from a scaffold of impossible expectations only to wallow "kicking and sprawling in the Mire" of uselessness. "It is hardly a state of Disgrace that I am in," he was capable of appreciating. Still, the "total Neglect and Contempt" of the very Congress that forced him to go abroad *against his will* in the first place was exasperating to say the least.[71]

Then came the conflicting orders. One day he was to go to Spain, the next to Holland or maybe Vienna. Disgusted, on March 8, John declared himself a private citizen and, leaving Passy to Franklin, headed toward the coast, hoping for a speedy passage home.

But it was only after copious mishaps and delays that on August 2, 1779 John and his eldest son finally rowed to shore in Braintree. They returned to a nation immersed in a serious money crisis and a slow-moving war. In the south, General Washington had lost Norfolk but held on to Charleston. In the north, he had surrendered and then won back strategic strongholds on the Hudson, keeping the door to New England open on the New York side. Spain's decision to ally itself with France against England—on June 21—was, of course, heartening, and intimidation by the French Navy checked any concerted British attack on the coast. Indeed, all the talk was of an American victory at some time on some terms. But it remained pretty much a concept at this point.

At last, on the eve of leaving France, John had written Abigail, "No Words, no Actions can express the Ardour of Affection with which I am . . . yours."[72] And at the end of July, Abigail, anticipating John's boat and the end to her need for extramarital attention, had bid Lovell a fond farewell: "Suffer me with the most gratefull sensations to ac-knowledg your kind attention to me during the absence of my dearest Friend."[73]

Elizabeth had called Abigail's separation from John "a Trial which cannot be described by words." Now resentments gave way to the joy of reunion.[74] Neither attempted to write about it—or of the pleasure of having all their children together and the balance of work in the house-hold restored. Almost immediately, John began bringing in money by accepting law cases. He threw himself into farmwork, relieving Abi-gail of the task she most abhorred.

Less than a month after John's return, he was elected to represent Braintree on a committee to conceive a Constitution for the state of Massachusetts. The committee nominated him to a smaller group to compose the document, and they in turn chose John to write the first draft. What he advocated was essentially the same mixed government he had proposed in *Thoughts on Government,* but the spirit of the text also reflected his year abroad.

The previous December, John had written to Abigail, "I shall never repent my Voyage to Europe, because I have gained an Insight into several Things that I never should have understood without it." Being in Enlightenment France, reading and rereading Rousseau, John had begun to probe beyond the excellence of the British constitutional model to an even more hopeful construction of laws.[75]

Indeed, this skeptic, whose ideal government had always relied on

balancing power to redress the inevitable selfishness of the unchanging
human condition, went so far as to speak of progress. In his *Social Contract,* Rousseau had argued that while individuals are physically and
intellectually unequal in nature, civilized men can and should rectify
the imbalance since everyone gains more than he loses by embracing
the general good. John Adams, steeped in Puritan tradition, could not
accept that men of their own free will would sacrifice privilege. And
yet there was something appealing, even persuasive about Rousseau's
picture of government established on the basis of popular consensus. If
virtue could be dispersed throughout society, why not political sagacity,
why not fine ideals?

Clearly, American society was less class-bound than England's. He,
the son of a yeoman, sat side-by-side in Congress with the well-born
Hancocks and Lees. As Abigail argued so relentlessly in support of
education for women, the key to his success was knowledge. History,
politics, law were all learnable, as, indeed, was the pursuit of happiness
itself. And what if every dark human soul was enlightened by wisdom?
Buoyed by exposure to the France of Rousseau and Condorcet, John
dared to believe the human race might improve. And so he made the
radical decision to include in his Constitution a provision for the education of all male citizens. "Wisdom and knowledge ... diffused generally among the body of the people, being necessary for the preservation
of their rights and liberties; ... it shall be the duty of legislatures and
magistrates, in all future periods of this commonwealth, ... to encourage public schools and grammar schools ... private societies and public
institutions ... for the promotion of agriculture, arts, sciences, commerce, trades, manufactures, and a natural history of the country," he
decreed.[76] And though Massachusetts insisted on some minor changes
in other parts of John's first draft of its Constitution, this clause on public education was accepted without amend. It became a milestone—the
first Constitution in history to mandate free education for the common
man.

JOHN HAD NO SOONER finished writing the State Constitution than a
letter arrived from Congress announcing that he had been elected to
return to Paris and represent America at the opening of talks about

trade agreements and the prospect of peace with England and France. He would bear the somewhat misleading title "plenipotentiary minister," for Ben Franklin remained the equivalent of today's ambassador to the French Court. Adams's exclusive power was only in the area of treaties. Still, it was hard to resist the pleading of Henry Laurens, current Chairman of Congress, who, as if speaking John's own thoughts, deplored his sufferings the previous winter. This time would be different, Laurens promised, and he urged John for the sake of his country to accept the offer immediately and speedily prepare to leave for France.[77]

And this he did, while Abigail lamented "O Why was I born with so much Sensibility?" but could not summon up the spirit to protest.[78] She even agreed to send her two oldest boys this time and sacrificed the company of her cousin so John Thaxter could continue to tutor 9-year-old Charles and 12-year-old John Quincy abroad. There was no time limit set, no talk of Abigail accompanying or joining John later. "I cannot resign more than I do unless life itself was called for," she calculated. "Does your Heart forbode that we shall again be happy?" she asked John the day before he set sail.[79] And he replied that he hoped "this will be the last Seperation, We shall suffer," but promised nothing except that he would write faithfully "by the first Opportunity and by all occasions from France."

Out of innocence or guilt, he went so far as to encourage her correspondence with James Lovell, "who complains that Portia don't write him."[80] And so on November 18, Abigail swallowed her pride and reversed her orders of four months earlier. "Your former kindness and attention leads me to rely upon your future Friendship," she wrote Lovell, anticipating years of emotional need.[81]

CHAPTER VII

"The steel and the Magnet"

. . .

MARY WAS BEMUSED BY A LETTER SHE RECEIVED IN APRIL 1781 from her youngest sister. Elizabeth complained that she couldn't keep up her end of their correspondence because her three-year-old and his "saucy" infant sister consumed all the energy she possessed. Her house across from the church on Main and Summer streets fairly howled with her children's longings. Then, when Elizabeth dug into her scant funds to hire a girl to help with the spinning, the cacophony in the house only mounted. "I hate it," she averred. It was the season for sowing flax and shearing wool and making candles. And the flurry of apple blossoms that raised her spirits reminded her she was further obliged to rush into the garden and tie up cabbages, transfer garlic, harvest sweet potatoes, and plant cucumbers, melon, and herbs There was no time to amuse friends or make a name for herself by writing. "For if Ideas present themselves to my Mind, it is too much like the good seed sown among Thorns, they are soon erased and swallowed up by the Cares of the World, the wants, and noise."[1]

Imagination thrived on peace and leisure, Elizabeth wrote, pursuing a familiar theme. But then she made the perplexing observation that Mary had "greatly the advantage of me in the enjoyment of quiet Life." What quiet life? Mary wondered. Where Elizabeth had two children, she had three and a boardinghouse as well as a household to

manage—not to mention a husband prone to ill health, absentminded-
ness, and service to his country at the expense of all else. What spare
time she had was spent commiserating with Abigail on *her* husband's
absence. And this was the life Elizabeth described as "quiet"? How like
a youngest sister to imagine everything was harder for herself!

And yet Mary did have to acknowledge that Elizabeth was the frailest as well as the most exuberant of the three sisters while she, far more
than the others, thrived in the eye of a storm. Everyone's story intrigued
Mary. Every new boarder at the Cranches' was a potential suitor for
her girls. She felt a calling to energize and improve anyone who crossed
her threshold. If Parson Wibird repeated a sermon for the tenth time
at Sunday meeting or Richard failed to fortify himself with flannels in
the cold, it was not for lack of exhortations on her part. She was the
supreme clarifier and temperer of squabbles. No problem was too
slight or too daunting: she advised feuding neighbors and town elders,
took in traveling statesmen and relatives from struggling homes. With
John Thaxter off in France, a bright and ambitious new tutor named
Thomas Perkins had recently come into the family. So the Cranch
farmhouse teemed with outsiders. One guest complained that it was
impossible to think, much less write here. "Every minute something
turns up to prevent me," he observed.[2]

Mary bustled happily through the chaos, her mind ever ticking,
taking everything in: the whiteness of her April orchard, the smooth-
ness of just made butter on bread made precious by the scarcity of grain
this season. With a mother's relief, she watched 18-year-old Betsy's
winter depression lift as the days got longer.[3] She took pride that
14-year-old Lucy excelled in math and science and that Braintree
unanimously voted to return Richard to the County Court.

Whatever the world might think, she was not self-sufficient. After
nineteen years of marriage, she still thrived on Richard's love. Away in
Boston, he called her "as dear to me as my own soul" and longed for the
great happiness he always took in her company."[4]

Now 40, Mary remained a bundle of contradictions. She experienced
everything deeply, as she told Abigail, and was uncomfortable talking
about feelings[5]; she could laugh off Richard's daftness and still be the
world's greatest proponent of common sense. Much as she valued
money, she advised Betsy and Lucy to marry, as she had, for love only.

While Elizabeth Shaw still aspired to leave a legacy of writing, Mary Cranch sought posterity through Billy, her sweet, earnest 12-year-old son. She made it her mission to push him forward—urging him to practice on John Quincy's violin when they couldn't afford their own and to maximize his good memory by taking copious notes on loaned books.[6] No assiduity was too trivial. Matching clothes to one's complexion required taste and judgment, she lectured him. Even Newton paid attention to colors—who was Billy to neglect his looks?

Mary had no doubts that men and women were intellectually equal; so the same tutors taught all her children. But while Betsy and Lucy could enjoy knowledge for its own sake, she implored Billy to muster the practical skills to succeed. Richard joined in, counseling Billy, "You may in future . . . have many opportunities" for prestigious jobs because of John Adams's contacts. Both discouraged selflessness.[7] Affluence was a virtue, they made clear.[8]

A short carriage ride away, at the foot of Penn's Hill, Abigail was also exhorting *her* son to maximize his potential. It was not "in the still of life" but in tumultuous times like the present that great characters were born, she wrote John Quincy in Europe. Nearly two years had passed since 46-year-old John, 14-year-old John Quincy, and 11-year-old Charles sailed from Boston. Negotiations in France had proved futile, convincing John that only an American victory in the war would force Britain to the bargaining table. Certainly, a plenipotentiary minister for peace had nothing to do in Paris at this point. So he had taken on a new mission and moved to Holland to solicit a major loan. Foreign aid was critical in the spring of 1781 since Americans still refused to submit to national taxes. Meanwhile, inflation mounted, and soldiers starved.

For all his privileges, John Quincy also faced danger and hardships, growing up among strangers in a foreign culture where he had to cross the Atlantic to get home. "Great necessities call out great virtues . . . ," Abigail rallied him. "These are times in which a Genious would wish to live."[9]

As the war at home dragged on and Abigail envisioned her husband and son rising to the call of history, she felt herself becoming increasingly invisible. With Boston free of battles for the moment, there was no eccentric general in town offering her his dog's paw. Her role in the revolution was now unassuming, though still considerable, of course. She scrimped on her own needs to help feed war widows and gave up hours when she might otherwise have spun clothes or read philosophy to sit by the wounded and cheer the grieved. Charity blended with patriotism, and she became the good republican housewife.

Imperceptibly, as the years passed, her connection to John, while deep as ever, grew more cerebral, her identification with Mary and Richard Cranch more useful and real. John's crossing from France to Holland worried her less than the Cranches' occasional thoughts of moving to Boston. She saw herself again as the middle Smith girl, relying on wealthy uncles to come up with cash for her in emergencies, turning to Mary's farmhouse or Elizabeth Shaw's parish—or a letter from Lovell—to escape domesticity for the moment and pursue the life of ideas. For where the intellectual wife of a Parisian statesman was free to open her own salon, Abigail could not so much as attend a party without being accused of seducing men. At 37, she was as closely watched as an adolescent. Only at church was she allowed to mingle with those outside her immediate circle. So while John's world expanded, his wife slipped back into the patterns of her unmarried years. Sometimes the gap between their daily experiences seemed as vast as the Atlantic. Still, their hunger for understanding and connection remained intense. So too was their shared commitment to the American cause.

War action was now centered in the southern states. In the past year and a half, England, under General Cornwallis, had stampeded through Georgia and the Carolinas. The Continentals, under General Greene, were currently skirmishing to slow Cornwallis's progress into Virginia, but made a point of avoiding major confrontations, hoping reinforcements would soon arrive from France. In a letter to John, Cotton Tufts marveled at the feats General Greene had performed with vastly inferior forces. Both generals were superb strategists, cool-headed, and beloved by their soldiers; so they at least were well matched.

But as the war moved into its seventh spring, the Americans were disproportionately demoralized. Almost every soldier was owed back wages, and hundreds of Greene's men marched to battle naked with just cartridge boxes shielding their loins.[10] Many southerners had defected when the British overran Charleston and Savannah, and there had been mutinies during a bitterly cold winter in the north.

At Morristown, Pennsylvania, the final straw came when soldiers who had signed on for three years or the duration of the war were forbidden to leave after the shorter period. New recruits, given a $24 bonus to enlist, strode into camp well provisioned, while many regulars had not been paid in a year, Richard Cranch sympathetically relayed news of the rebels' plight in a letter to John Adams. As a result, on January 1, 1781, 1,700 men marched out of the Morristown camp demanding that Congress redress their grievances, which eventually happened, though despair persisted elsewhere. "Glory or Shame, great in Degree of either kind, depends upon the Behavior of the Americans in the coming six months," James Lovell predicted on May 29: he did not feel entitled to anticipate success.[11]

Initially, George Washington, with 3,500 Continentals and 4,000 Frenchmen stationed throughout the country at his disposal, felt victory hinged on retaking New York City, where Clinton sat entrenched with 10,000 men. The major obstacle to advancing on New York was lack of warships. So when, in May, news arrived that a large fleet under Admiral de Grasse at last had sailed from France and was due to arrive by the end of August, Washington prepared for a major battle in the north.

But then, in the beginning of August, Cornwallis settled with *his* 9,500 men in Virginia in the far smaller and more isolated Yorktown. Ringed by low hills and surrounded on three sides by water, it had many advantages as a battle site, particularly as no one expected Washington to strike here. For two weeks, Washington debated the respective merits of the two locations. Then, on August 14, he learned the French fleet was headed toward the Chesapeake rather than the Hudson, and the choice became clear. On August 19, Washington and his northern troops began the long march to Virginia.

He proceeded with such stealth that his troops were well into New Jersey before the British missed them. The Continentals arrived in Philadelphia on September 2, followed by 4,000 French soldiers, and were greeted by light shows and parades and bells. The spirit in Congress had drastically changed over the summer. "We are, at this present Writing, in high Glee with our General in the City and the french Troops encamped on the Commons," Lovell wrote Abigail in Braintree. They had furthermore been informed that De Grasse and 3,000 men on twenty-nine warships had safely arrived at the Chesapeake Bay. "Compleat success" was anticipated, though disaster could still strike if all the allied forces failed to converge before a large fleet of British ships arrived on the Virginia coast.[12]

But the campaign progressed seamlessly. By the last week in September, the French had completely blocked the Yorktown harbor while 16,000 allied troops circled the outskirts and prepared to invade. Cornwallis was trapped, and Washington sensed the momentousness of the occasion, telling his men, "The liberties of America, and the honor of the Allied Arms are in our hands."[13]

On September 29, the British gave up their hillside fortifications without a fight. On October 5, the allies began cutting trenches, and four days later they fired the first shot, and the siege began. For once, America was better prepared and better supplied than the British. They never lost the offensive position, and on October 15, Cornwallis, bereft of alternatives, tried but failed to escape. On October 17, the dreaded British ships at last set sail from New York Harbor, but they left too late to save Cornwallis, who on the same day acknowledged defeat. On October 20, a treaty was signed demanding surrender of the huge battery of enemy weapons and making every British soldier in Yorktown an American prisoner of war.

On October 25, Abigail's seventeenth wedding anniversary, she read "the glorious News of the Surrender of LORD CORNWALLIS" in the *Boston Evening Post*.[14] Washington rushed a courier to Philadelphia where Congress gave thanks and threw banquets. Bonfires were lit in New England and—later, when the news reached Louis XVI in Paris—lanterns hung in the doorways in France.[15]

"American Affairs never wore a more agreeable Aspect than at present," Richard Cranch wrote to John Adams at the end of October.[16] "I heartily congratulate you on [this] great and important Event."[17] Abigail joined in the euphoria, exclaiming, "America may boast that she has accomplished what no power before her ever did." Though final treaties were yet to be forged, she felt confidant George III would

*The surrender of Cornwallis was major news throughout Europe,
as shown in this German newsprint.*

soon resign himself to the sovereignty of the thirteen colonies. The war
that began at Lexington and Concord would end at Yorktown. It was
almost too good to be true.[18]

John Adams could agree only on this last point. "I beg you would
not flatter yourself with hopes of Peace," he wrote Abigail when he
received George Washington's report in Holland. "There will be no
such Thing for several years."[19]

JOHN FELT JUSTIFIED IN mistrusting not just the British but even and
maybe especially the French, on whom he lavished no thanks for the
Yorktown victory. Less than a year before, when the Continentals
seemed to be losing, Versailles had decided to cut its losses and promoted a so-called peace initiative, allowing the British to retain Savannah and New York.[20] Though the initiative failed, it aroused John's
suspicions about French allegiance.

John had left for Paris, aware there was only a slim chance of peace
before America defeated England on the battlefield. So he was not surprised when George III initially refused to talk. What stunned him was

that Vergennes, rather than interceding on America's behalf, first floated this clearly unfavorable initiative, and then refused to negotiate at all.

This was a personal as well as a national insult, leaving John once again at loose ends. With the peace talks quashed and Ben Franklin in charge of all ministerial duties, John had no official business to justify his expensive presence in France. And though he missed home, he dreaded returning empty-handed—especially as he had come in such a flourish, bringing an official and a private secretary, as well as John Quincy and Charles.

At first John threw his energies into establishing the boys in a Paris preparatory school. Here Charles proved as precocious as his brother and was in no time everyone's darling, as at home. ("Charles will be loved everywhere," John Thaxter, who had accompanied them, wrote Abigail of her handsomest son, the one who most resembled her physically, "his delicacy and sensibility always charm.") John next kept his word and purchased European goods for Abigail to sell to augment the farm's income. He began small. "I have sent you, one yard of fine Cambric . . . two of a coarser sort [and] . . . Eight India Handkerchiefs," he wrote in February 1780; but, impressed by her entrepreneurial successes, soon was sending precious fabrics like chintz across the sea.[21] He also immersed himself in study, as he informed Abigail in a particularly eloquent variation on his familiar theme of having no time to write:

> I could fill Volumes with Descriptions [for you] of Temples and Palaces, Paintings, Sculptures, Tapestry, Porcelain, etc. etc. etc. . . . But I could not do this without neglecting my duty— The science of Government it is my Duty to study, more than all other Sciences of Government: the Art of Legislation and Administration and Negotiation, ought to take Place, indeed to exclude in a manner all other Arts.—I must study Politicks and War that my sons may have liberty to study Mathematicks and Philosophy. My sons ought to study Mathematicks and Philosophy, Geography, natural History, Naval Architecture, navigation, Commerce and Agriculture, in order to give their Children

a right to study Painting, Poetry, Musick, Architecture, Statuary, Tapestry and Porcelain.[22]

When John told Abigail it was his duty to study statesmanship, he did not have Ben Franklin in mind as an exemplar. And though he had vowed to present a united front with Franklin, John nonetheless saw it as his duty to stoke the bon vivant's patriotism from time to time. His suspicion was that Franklin was so caught up fawning over the French that he had forgotten that his job was to procure larger loans and more ships for his own country. It was ungainly for an American minister to grovel, which was how John perceived Franklin's habit of smiling and nodding while Vergennes held the floor. And then there were Franklin's sartorial choices. John winced to see the inventor of the lightning rod stroll out of his carriage in a buckskin coat, wigless, with his scant hair flying—confirming the Old World's conviction that Americans were closer to animals than men.

So, with time on his hands—and assuring himself that he was not behaving disloyally toward Franklin—John set out to disabuse France of its image of Americans as humble clowns. His immediate goal was to attract Vergennes's attention. Visiting was out of the question. And since Franklin also had a monopoly on private correspondence, John began contributing articles touting America's importance in the French newspaper *Le Mercure*. Which Vergennes ignored.

And the more Vergennes ignored John, the more impatient John grew to be noticed. How to rouse a man raised on rococo art and pate de foie gras? John determined to adapt heavier tactics and began denigrating France.

And still Versailles was silent. It was not until John received advance reports of a change in American policy that an opportunity to contact Vergennes directly presented itself at last. John's news was that Congress planned to devalue the dollar. The purpose was to stanch American inflation, but it would also discourage the import of foreign goods. So what Adams praised in his letter to Vergennes as American savvy; Vergennes, in a return letter, deplored as an attack on commerce with France. And the two continued trading partisan opinions while John thoroughly enjoyed flaunting America's (and his own) intelligence and presumed that Vergennes, despite plentiful evidence to the contrary, felt as energized as he by debate. Even when Vergennes demanded a moratorium on letters about financial policy, pointedly insisting "I think all discussion in this regard superfluous," John chose to put a literal interpretation on the Frenchman's wishes and simply moved on to a new subject, providing some unwelcome if undeniably wise advice about how France should conduct its side of the war.[23]

This proved the last straw for the embodiment of French circumvention. Vergennes wrote a simple declarative sentence: "The King has no need for your advice to take care of the American situation." (*"Le Roi n'a pas eu besoin de vos Sollications pour s'ocupier des interests des Etats-unis."*) After which even John had to accept that he was not helping the Paris mission and began looking for somewhere else to make his mark. Holland seemed a good idea.

But the battle with Vergennes did not end with John's departure. For while John, a product of the New World, could translate his rage into moving forward, Vergennes, confined to and by the Old World, hankered for revenge. And Franklin, having failed to step in earlier, now bore the brunt of the French minister's need to publicize his torment. Ultimately, this meant agreeing to send Congress Vergennes's copies of Adams's letters along with his own clear-eyed interpretation of what went wrong:

> Mr. Adams . . . seems to have endeavored to supply what he may suppose my Negociations defective in . . . I apprehend that this [French] Court is to be treated with . . . Delicacy . . . Mr. Adams on the other hand, who at the same time means our Welfare and Interest as much as I, or any man, can do, seems to think a little apparent Stoutness, and greater air of Independence and Boldness in Our Demands, will procure us more Ample Assistance.[24]

It was by accident that Abigail first learned that letters from the husband who never had time or privacy to write *her* were being read aloud in Congress. She wrote for confirmation to Lovell, who had hinted at the troubles before but now replied in full. He blamed the crisis on Vergennes. John was not "servile enough to gain the unbounded Affection" of this vain individual.[25] All the Massachusetts delegates sided with Lovell, but Congress voted by a large majority to annul Adams's status as plenipotentiary minister and appointed three others—Franklin, Thomas Jefferson, and John Jay—to join him and limit his power when the time came to sue for peace.

Abigail, who had been chiding John for not writing, instantly forgot his deficiencies as a husband and began championing him as a martyr to the American cause. "In the Name of Indignation can there be any thing more diabolical than [Franklin's letter]?" she exclaimed to Lovell. "False insinuating desembling wretch" she called Franklin, while John was the "Zealous and Strenuous asserter of his countrys rights"; an "Independent Spirit" "sacrificed to a court Sychophant."[26]

America, on the other hand, had reason to celebrate both Franklin's "fawning" and Adams' clamor. By July 14, 1781, the day Abigail addressed her tirade to Lovell, the expanded French Navy John had demanded was en route to the Battle of Yorktown along with a handsome advance of money only Franklin could have enticed from Vergennes.

ABIGAIL RECEIVED JOHN'S FIRST letter in a year on September 25, 1781, days before the siege of Yorktown. For months before, she could only "hope and hope till hope [was] swallowed up in the victory of Dispair," she wrote back. Her heart knew "but little ease—not a line had reachd me from you . . . and whether [you were] living or dead I could not hear."[27]

What intelligence and ease Abigail did manage to grasp during these anxious months came largely from James Lovell. He had forwarded the boxes of fine European goods John had directed to her through Philadelphia; he had kept her apprised of all Congress knew concerning events at home and abroad. While she had to implore John for "an affectionate assurance of regard," Lovell was always wheedling for a more intimate standing.[28] "I love saucyness," he wrote in a daring moment.[29] And Abigail felt increasingly inclined to humor him. She even confessed to feeling hurt at the beginning of 1781 when she hadn't heard from him "for a *very* long time."[30]

Then one of Lovell's letters was captured by the British and exposed in a Tory newspaper. To make matters worse, the specific document, while addressed to his fellow delegate Elbridge Gerry and mostly concerned with Congressional business, included a lewd double entendre in the form of a hieroglyph that was widely recognized as the biological symbol for the male sex. Eyebrows were raised all over New England, and Lovell was quickly condemned for embarrassing his wife.

Abigail's first instinct was to cover her tracks, for appearing upright in the eyes of the world meant a lot to her. The taboo attached to a married man's writing informally to a married woman, no matter that she was the wife of a friend, struck her forcibly—at last. As did the realization that—should a letter between them be opened—both of their spouses might misinterpret certain blandishments Lovell professed. "One must never forget that a woman is the property of her husband," wrote the same wife who had challenged Congress to "remember the ladies" as she began her March 17 reprimand to her friend, the Boston delegate.

Calling her "Lovely" and "charming" was inappropriate, Abigail retroactively reproved Lovell. What would Lovell's wife think if she read these flatteries? What would she herself think if John Adams wrote another woman in a similar vein? (What would her sisters think, Abigail must have wondered to herself.)

"A Husband who tenderly loves his wife should . . . give up the reputation of being a Gallant," she continued her morally superior lecture. And she despaired, she said, of how to answer friends who suspected Lovell cared little for his life's partner since in his five years at Congress he had never found an opportunity to go home.

At the very least, his permanent residence in Philadelphia exposed *Mrs.* Lovell to embarrassment, Abigail prepared to launch into another diatribe, then was stopped by the happy realization that she possessed no concrete proof that the man who'd afforded her so much comfort over the past few years had in fact done anything wrong. Yes, he was verbally glib, but perhaps what he lacked was not feeling but sensitivity to social opprobrium. She decided to give him the benefit of the doubt.

So "No situation [is] more delicate, more critical or more liable to censure than that of a Lady whose Husband is away," she switched approach and sympathized with both his and his wife's dilemma. Lovell's absence punished no one more than himself. "The demands of . . . country must silence the voice of pleading nature," she wrote, and ascribed herself a fellow sufferer at the hands of the unfeeling world.

She prided herself, she told him, on interpreting character. If she concentrated, she could read a man's heart through his eyes. Unfortunately, she had failed to scrutinize Lovell sufficiently when they met in person four years earlier. Yet she remembered a face in which "the traits of Friendship and Benevolence were so conspicuous that they demanded a return in kind."[31]

Since friendship demanded trust, Abigail wanted desperately to exculpate Lovell. On the other hand, she was not ready to renounce him, even if he had erred. Perhaps they should simply drop the subject, she suggested in closing. She hoped to resume their innocent discussions of politics as soon as "you tell me that you have received this in that Spirit of Friendship with which it flowed."[32]

But Lovell would not let her off so easily. Now the offended party, it behooved him to defend himself, and—much as Abigail had lashed out at him when she learned Congress was sending her husband to Paris—he took the occasion to protest the hypocrisy of Boston's elite. The hieroglyph, he freely acknowledged, was an "unbecoming Levity and quite unfit for a [statesman]. But it is not that which will give pain to my affectionate Wife." Abigail could not put herself in Mrs. Lovell's shoes because she was a well-born Quincy. The humbler Mrs. Lovell (married to a mere schoolteacher!) "will be pained with what you would smile at. For she is more apt to fear than to despise" the sneers of New England's upper class.

"I must now be very serious," he went on to correct Abigail on the more vital issue of why he avoided his family. The cause was not, as she flatteringly suggested, lofty patriotism but poverty far worse than her own. He had virtually no money outside of his salary, which was not paid during leaves from Congress. Lovell invited those who criticized his absence to give him a job in Boston. Otherwise, they had no right to accuse him of failing his faultless wife.[33]

Of course, when it came to personal matters, Lovell was no more straightforward than Vergennes on the subject of French assistance to America. Between the lines, what really angered him was not social but moral condescension on Abigail's part. And while praising his wife,

Lovell managed to imply that she was not lovely and not charming, that there was still a place for the lively, quick-witted Abigail to fill in his life. *If* she could address him as a moral equal. And Abigail accepted the wager, writing back: "The Generous acknowlegement of having tran[s]gressed forbids any further recrimination." She was reduced to tears, she said, upon reading of his unjust poverty and would make it her mission to solicit financial help for him from the very gossips they both disdained.

"We will begin a New Score upon the old Stock of Friendship," she went on as faith in her own impulses and longing for male attention combined to make her truly sorry for doubting Lovell's innate goodness. Besides, it now seemed wrong to hold James Lovell to John Adams's standards. Marriage was a deeply private affair, different in every instance. Yet, while she would never know the absolute truth of Lovell's relationship with his wife and family, she felt instinctively that he was in all important ways an honorable man.[34] And while they must abstain from intimacy, they should continue confiding in a compassionate fashion, for their bond was heartfelt—and this itself was rare. "I know you take an Interest in my happiness and . . . I can make you feel," she wrote. "I hate an unfeeling mortal. The passions are common to us all, but the lively sweet affections are the portion only of a chosen few."[35]

As SHE TURNED 16 and then 17, Nabby Adams still showed no propensity for feeling. In one letter to John, Abigail observed that she was "possesst with as much apparent coldness and indifference as ever you saw in one character, and with such a reserve as has many a time awed to the greatest distance the least approach toward her."[36] Where Aunt Elizabeth was sure that Nabby was "full of sensibility,"[37] just waiting for romance to strike her, Abigail proclaimed her daughter hopelessly aloof. Admittedly, she and her sisters, at Nabby's age, had possessed "too much sensibility to be very prudent," but Nabby erred on the other extreme. And while a good, loving daughter, Nabby comported herself like a "princess" and was haughtiness itself to men.[38]

The particular male Nabby was being cold to at the moment was 25-year-old Royall Tyler, who arrived in Braintree and rented a room at the Cranches' house in the spring of 1782. He was a lawyer, intending to start a practice. He was also devastatingly seductive according to reports from Boston friends. Nabby's initial concern was for her 19-year-old cousin, Betsy Cranch. "I was told the other day that [one] could not see him" and resist his charms, she wrote her impressionable cousin. "He . . . is the essence and quintessence of artfulness, and [our friends] fear he will in some way or other ingratiate himself into the good opinion of your se f."[39]

Though Nabby did not yet know it, Betsy was immune to danger. Over the past year, she had fallen in love with Thomas Perkins, tutor for the Cranch and Adams children, who yearned to marry her if he could only earn the money to propose. Royall Tyler, in contrast, was sufficiently prosperous to propose to anyone at any time. His manners and diligence were similarly impeccable, besides which, "I know not a young fellow upon the stage whose language is so pure—or whose natural disposition is so agreable," Abigail reported enthusiastically to her husband abroad.

Tyler's father, a wealthy Boston merchant, had been an early and ardent patriot. Tyler himself, after graduating from Harvard in 1776, had taken a break from his law studies to serve in Rhode Island as General Sullivan's aide-de-camp. And he could turn even a humiliation— like being caught drunk, using lewd language, and smashing windows with a gang of larking students on the Harvard campus—into an opportunity to flaunt his contempt for small-mindedness, demanding of a surprised Harvard disciplinary committee: "What punishment can you inflict upon me? What do I care for a little paltry Degree which may be bought at any time for twenty shillings. If honor in this Country consists in Degrees, you are very welcome Gentlemen to deprive me of yours for I have . . . others already." (He had been awarded an honorary degree by Yale.)

All that could be said against Tyler, in Abigail's view, was that in his early twenties he had dissipated away two or three years of his life and a generous inheritance in high-spirited pranks, like bashing the Harvard campus. It was also rumored (though she didn't mention this to John) that he'd had an affair with his chambermaid at college and had fathered an illegitimate child. Recently, however, she felt sure Tyler had reformed. Besides, he loved literature and wrote poems.

Circumstances brought Abigail and Nabby in everyday contact

with Tyler, for it was at the time when Tyler was moving into the Cranch household that Richard Cranch became mortally sick. After several colds, he developed a serious lung infection. No sooner had he begun to recover than he insisted on going to Boston to take part in a major debate at the House. The day of the debate, May 2, was warm and windy. The room was crowded, and in the afternoon, suddenly cool, damp air replaced the heat. By night, Richard was feverish. He began spitting blood, and the pneumonia resumed. Three weeks passed before he regained sufficient strength to struggle to Braintree. There he collapsed, while, to add to his misery, his legs and bowels swelled— signs of a deadly edema.

Mary never left his side, and Abigail and Nabby went home only to sleep. "In afflictions darkest hour thou hast been my greatest human support," Mary told her younger sister, wondering if she could ever repay the debt.[40] Privately, Abigail doubted any effort could save Richard at this point. Yet, pathetically, even when he could swallow less food than an infant, he imagined he was getting better, and while Mary blinkered herself to the illness's probable outcome and summoned all her strength to pull him through, Uncle Tufts despaired, and Betsy, already depressed by Thomas Perkins's departure, succumbed to gloom.

Randall Tyler was a welcome distraction, indeed, when he came home from his law practice in the evening. How refreshing to confront a compassionate man unencumbered by a personal stake in the survival of Richard Cranch. Not only could he provide emotional support, but he diverted the household with news of war and business. Particularly for Abigail, who had been forced to seclude herself from all but the most intimate friends during the eight years of her husband's absence, the bright young man was a welcome source of knowledgeable and imaginative talk. It did not hurt that Tyler was handsome. And he spoke so eloquently, had such strong opinions, and such an independent outlook, at times he reminded her of a younger John.

Tyler's attachment to Nabby was "too obvious to escape notice," Abigail wrote her husband. Nor was this young man intimidated by their daughter's reserve. He carved her an ice heart to tease away her coldness (which actually thrilled him, Abigail shrewdly observed). Nabby answered his wishes and teased him back.[41]

In the middle of a rainless summer, as the crops drooped and the water at the Braintree Iron Works dried up, Abigail wrote John, "We have little to build our hopes upon of [Richard Cranch's] long continuance with us." John, receiving the news, for once immediately wrote back:

> Your Favour . . . arrived this Day and gave me, all the tender and melancholly Feelings of which My Heart is susceptible . . . How shall I express my solicitude for my amiable, my venerable Friend and Brother? This world contains not a wiser or a more virtuous Man . . . I tremble for his Family. Possibly he may still be spared.[42]

John's slim optimism, it turned out, derived from personal experience. A year before, oppressed by the fetid Amsterdam canal waters, he had caught a mysterious illness and nearly died himself. "I have been within an Hairs Breadth," he continued, "and although recovered to tolerable H[e]alth and Spirits, I am still feeble, and shall never be restored to all my former Force."[43] This was the first time he felt sufficiently out of danger to speak so specifically of his near death to Abigail, who now felt all the delayed anxiety and even more cause to empathize with Mary Cranch.

Nabby, in her understated style, was similarly solicitous of Betsy. "My affection for you is an inducement for my writing you at this time more particularly," she addressed her cousin when she was briefly away during a crisis in Richard's illness.[44] Later she let down her guard completely and assured Betsy, "My heart is warm."[45]

Then the miracle only Richard himself dared to anticipate actually happened. As the parching summer dragged to a conclusion, his swellings decreased, and he stopped spitting blood. "I have the very great pleasure to acquaint you that our dear and worthy Brother is raised in a manner from the dead," Abigail wrote John in September. On October 8, she reported Richard had "recovered far beyond our expectations." He had been well enough this week to go back to Court.[46]

Abigail took sisterly pride in the extraordinary part Mary played in her husband's survival: "The doctors say . . . he owes his life to the incessant, unwearied, indefatigable watchfull care of his wife; who has almost sacrificed her own, to save his Life."

———

THOUGH RICHARD WAS OUT of danger, thoughts of mortality and loss clung to the Cranch and Adams households. Even Nabby had forebodings[47] and mood swings. Though never mentioning lovesickness, she described herself unhappy[48]; Tyler said he was so much in love with her that he could not eat,[49] while Abigail, relieved of the need to comfort Mary, began agonizing over the precariousness of her own husband's health and her loss of married life. She was 38 years old and had begun to feel more like Odysseus's Penelope than Brutus's Portia. On October 25, her wedding anniversary, she looked back to the beginning of their marriage:

> I recollect the untitled Man to whom I gave my Heart, and in the agony of recollection when time and distance present themselves together, wish he had never been any other. Who shall give me back Time? Who shall compensate to me those *years* I cannot recall?

"How dearly have I paid for a titled Husband," she desponded.[50] But she also rejoiced that her "sacrifice" was for the great cause of American independence. And, quoting from John Thomson's 1730 play *Sophonisba, A Tragedy,* she reminded John she too suffered for a larger cause:

> *My Passions too can Sometimes Soar above,*
> *The Houshold task assign'd me, can extend*
> *Beyond the Narrow Sphere of families,*
> *And take great States into th' expanded Heart*
> *As well as yours.*[51]

Besides, where men had obvious incentives to serve their country, a woman's devotion was its own reward. Forbidden to hold office or control property, forced to submit to laws, yet denied the vote, women had every right to be "indifferent to the public Welfare," Abigail continued. "Yet all History and every age exhibit Instances of patriotick virtue in the female Sex; which considering our situation equals the most Heroik of yours."[52]

By Christmas, Royall Tyler was ensconced every night at the Adams fireside. Nabby was no longer indifferent to her suitor, Abigail was happy to report to her husband, though the young man remained in "misirable doubt" of his ability to win her hand. Recently, he had vowed to proceed with or retreat from the courtship, according to Abigail's wishes. "Do with me as seemeth good unto thee," he told Nabby's mother, who was moved by his supplication. "What ought I to say?" she implored John.[53]

John replied unequivocally: "A Youth who has been giddy enough to Spend his Fortune or half his Fortune . . . is not the Youth for me, Let his Person, Family, Connections and Taste for Poetry be what they will. I am not looking out for a Poet," he bristled.

Nor did he "like this method of Courting Mothers. There is something too fantastical and affected in all this Business." As for Nabby's coolness, "In the name of all that is tender don't criticise Your Daughter for those qualities which are her greatest Glory her Reserve, and her Prudence which I am amazed to hear you call Want of Sensibility. The more Silent She is in Company, the better for me in exact Proportion and I would have this observed as a Rule by the Mother as well," he couldn't resist lecturing, despite or perhaps because of the fact that he felt powerless to control his equally strong-willed wife from across the sea.[54]

John's advice was to retreat, a course Abigail had decided upon even before she received his irate instructions. Just after New Year's 1783, she sent Nabby to Boston for the winter, in effect suspending the courtship until spring. Nabby's future should not hang merely on her mother's favorable impressions, she had come to see, and as she had warned James Lovell when he was under attack, gossip had to be discredited, not simply ignored. "The world look back to the days in which I knew [Tyler] not; and remember him as a Beau and a Gay volatile young fellow, and tho I have never heard any vices asscribed to him, yet I think with Some of my Friends a longer period necessary to Establish a contrary character," Abigail decided, sounding more like the circumspect newlywed who had objected to her younger sister's courtship than the rash matron who traded flirtatious missives with a married man.[55]

Now, though, Nabby was in love, which was as natural, she found, as holding her head high and as unsettling as everybody claimed. "The hitherto invulnerable [has] been discovered to be accessible [in so tender] and delicate a place as the Heart," Aunt Elizabeth rejoiced after her fall visit to Braintree, where she found Nabby as affected by love as she'd always foreseen.[56] Yet, while Nabby's passion was so scarily strong it had banished all her famed indifference, her mind remained clear. She never was and was sure she never would be impetuous like Abigail. Nor could she trust the largest decision of her life to a mother so burdened with feelings and cares. More than ever she longed for her father, Nabby confided in Betsy.[57] Indeed, while reading literature so she could talk intelligently with her lover, she was also trying to cultivate an interest in history to intensify her bond with her father when they were at last reunited.

Furthermore, Nabby was visiting Haverhill and revealing all her new sensations to her mother's younger sister. Elizabeth, with her susceptible imagination, soon began reliving her own youth through her niece; "The dear delights of virtuous Intrigues. The solemn partings . . . the contrivances . . . the fond Hopes . . . the surprises." Courtship was a foretaste of Heaven, she enthused in a letter to Abigail, and she rued the disappointment that inevitably followed, even in the happiest married lives.[58]

At the beginning of 1783, John Adams too was longing for past happiness. A year and a half before, John Quincy had left Holland to become secretary to his father's former secretary Francis Dana on a mission to establish diplomatic ties with Russia, while 13-year-old Charles, missing his mother, had sailed home. Now John Thaxter too was planning to return to America, and John told Abigail that he refused to continue "in this horrid Solitude." He could at last leave Holland because he had accomplished his mission. On April 19, 1782, the Dutch government had officially recognized the United States of America. In July,

Holland floated Congress a desperately needed two-million-dollar loan. If bringing about these events "had been the only Action of my Life, it would have been a Life well spent," John declared.

To top it all, in the fall of 1782, John was summoned to Paris for the resumption of peace talks. He arrived just in time to hear the British negotiator officially acknowledge the existence of the United States. "Thus G.B. has shifted suddenly about, and from persecuting Us . . . has unconditionally and unequivocally acknowledged US a Sovereign State," John marveled to Abigail.[59]

Meanwhile, on the French front, Vergennes paid Adams the enormous compliment of seating him on his wife's right side at a state dinner, and John also reconciled with Franklin to the extent that they could work amicably with a third minister, who was far more to Adams's taste, the brilliant New York lawyer John Jay.[60] [61] (Thomas Jefferson was detained in America.)

Though Congress had instructed them to submit to France on any disputed issue, Adams and Jay soon convinced Franklin to ignore these orders, and the preliminary treaty—signed at Versailles at the end of January 1783—made far fewer concessions to England *or* France because all the American ministers spoke in a single voice.[62]

Seven and a half years after Abigail climbed to the top of Penn's Hill to watch the burning of Charleston, the Revolution was over. "Thus drops the Curtain on this mighty Trajedy," John wrote Abigail. "It has unravelled itself happily for Us. And Heaven be praised." And though the treaty still awaited ratification in Philadelphia, John wrote Congress requesting to be released from his present commission and announced he was heading home.

Now all the yearning for Braintree he had suppressed for years poured out in his increasingly profuse correspondence with Abigail. "A Pacquet [of letters] from you is always more than I can bear. It gives me a great Pleasure, the highest Pleasure, and therefore makes me and Leaves me Melancholly, like the highest Strains in Music," John exclaimed. "I . . . ardently long to be at the blue Hills of Massachusetts," he wrote.[63] "I would give the World to be with you Tomorrow," he sighed on another day.[64] He spent extravagantly on the finest material he could find for a "saucy" red dress for his wife to shine in and defied all his rules about epistolary effusing, exclaiming, "No words can express the Feelings of my Heart, when I subscribe myself Yours forever" before signing his name.[65]

But Congress was silent on the subject of John's resignation. He and they both knew that work remained to be done abroad. A commercial treaty with England—crucial to America's survival—needed to be ironed out quickly. Some one or group would have to address this. Secretly, John hoped Congress would appoint him a second time, thus acknowledging how wrong they had been to favor Ben Franklin. If this should occur, John began hinting to Abigail, it might benefit his reputation to accept the job even if it meant spending six months or so more in Europe. On the other hand, he would forgo all satisfactions to his honor rather than spend an extra day abroad without her. "I must go to you or you must come to me," he continued to insist, but now he placed the emphasis on the latter choice.

At this point it was Abigail who equivocated about leaving Braintree. "I had much rather see you in America than Europe," she wrote John on April 7, 1783.[66] After all, he had warned her that a long residence in Europe would ruin their children, three of whom were currently thriving in the United States.[67] And then there was her 76-year-old father, who, unlike most widowers, had not remarried. Her only brother, Billy, had turned alcoholic while a prisoner of war in Halifax during his brief and inglorious stint in the Revolution. As he had subsequently run up debts and deserted his wife and children, the aging minister relied on his daughters for company and care. Once, when Abigail mentioned joining John in Paris, her father rebuffed her: "I cannot consent to you[r] going child, whilst I live."[68]

Furthermore, she was preoccupied arranging her sons' education. Yet another tutor had left for brighter prospects, and—finding no spaces available either in the local Hingham academy or prestigious Andover—Abigail was negotiating with her sister Elizabeth to send Charles and Tommy to Haverhill to be prepared for Harvard by their Uncle Shaw. Needless to say, Shaw was not Abigail's first choice, but "I have done the best I could with them," she told John. Mary's boy Billy Cranch would go as well.

Elizabeth had to summon all her self-restraint to resist exulting at this flattering overture from her older sisters. "I am authorized to say, that [Mr. Shaw] complies . . . with the Request," she primly replied to their initial inquiries. The compliance was conditional, she hastened to add, on their paying $2 per child per week and trusting the Shaws to choose the children's friends. In return came superior teaching, "a good Chamber, good bed, and bedding," and, at meals, "Beef, pork, Corn, and Rye, Butter, milk," and more. Thank you but no, Elizabeth said, she would most certainly *not* need the advance of money they had proposed to contribute for the upkeep of "my dear Newphews." And at no cost at all (she could not help effusing) they would have every attention a mother could give.[69]

After the boys left for Haverhill, Abigail, encouraged—she made a point of emphasizing—by the Cranches, allowed Tyler to return to her parlor. "Be assured that [Nabby] will never make a choice without your approbation which I know she considers as Essential to her happiness," Abigail hastened to add in a letter to her husband that June.

She was still expecting to see John by September. It would be "a dull day to me," she said, if she had to sail to him. Adding to her earlier list of reasons not to go was a new provincialism: "I have not a wish to join in a scene of Life so different from that in which I have been educated; and in which my early and I must suppose, happier days, have been Spent."[70] Recently, even the journey home from Haverhill "enfeebled" her.[71] Gone was the era when she berated the world for commanding girls not to travel. At 39, set in her simple ways, she was sure she could only embarrass John at the European Courts. Her most ardent wish was to remain in Braintree with the Cranches and enjoy the greater world through the reports of friends.

Only now did it occur to John how much Abigail had changed during the six years since she begged him to take her to Paris. She no longer had that fierce desire to see foreign cultures or confidence that she could conquer all. Also, she showed no qualms about managing affairs at home without him. It was her older sister she seemed unable to do without. Like Vergennes, this new Abigail was maddeningly unresponsive. John began a campaign to get her to Europe by accusing her of neglect.

"I am not in Health and don't expect to be," he complained bitterly after three weeks of a Paris heat wave, implying that her absence could kill him. Now that he was the model correspondent, he huffed, she scarcely wrote at all. "You must not cease to write me, until I arrive at your Door," he ordered. And flagrantly reversing a favorite conviction: "I don't care if [interceptors] open your Letters." By refusing to see Europe, she narrowed the range of their conversation. And while he was "Tormented" by Abigail's silence, he also suspected she was usurping his rights as a father. "Pray let me know the History of the [Tyler] Affair you mentioned formerly. I hope there is an end of it," he said, reminding her who was boss.[72]

In early September, on his way to visit his youngest daughter in Haverhill, William Smith stopped to spend the night with Abigail at the foot of Penn's Hill. Though he had been ill for a few days before, his spirits remained high throughout the evening. Then, soon after retiring, he screamed out in pain. The cause was an irreversible urinary track blockage. Soon he could "neither lie nor set," but nevertheless insisted on being driven home to Weymouth. Here, eight years after his wife's death, he lived on for fifteen days with only his strong character to support him through agony no medicine or nursing could assuage.

All his daughters watched over the old minister as he summoned the fire within to preach religious faith to his grandchildren. His old friend Reverend Gray of Hingham "with faultering steps and trembling accents approached the bed," and grieved, "my Brother I did not expect you would get to heaven before me."[73] Abigail affirmed that she would carry on the torch of the Puritan ethic, writing John, "How trifling, and of how little importance does such a scene, make all the wealth, power and greatness of the world appear."[74] She was particularly gratified that even in great pain her father managed to remain cheerful and that he lived to assure her she had been as "good kind [and] considerate a child as a parent ever had."

So too, of course, were Mary and Elizabeth, and after their father's death Uncle Tufts sent them all black gauze for mourning clothes, while Abigail cooked dinner for the grieving Uncle Smith and his family from Boston. Elizabeth for the last time prepared her "desolate" old home in Weymouth to receive family and friends.

In his will, William Smith disinherited Billy—now totally dissolute—leaving him only his wardrobe, but bowed to primogeniture and bequeathed the largest share of his estate to Billy's wife. He freed his only remaining slave, Phoebe, and left his three daughters property on a sliding scale according to their husbands' incomes: Elizabeth received the most and Abigail least. These bequests, slightly enhanced by the remains of the Quincy fortune, were modest: no rise in material comfort would mitigate the pain of their last parent's death.

What did help was the enduring bond between them. "My dear Sister—I believe there were never three sisters more generally alike in their opinion of Things than we," the devastated Elizabeth reached out to Abigail. "I too am one of those Beings that feel vastly more than I express—whether it be Joy, or Grief."[75]

Four months after William Smith's funeral, ten days before Christmas, the family reconvened for anniversary celebrations of the Boston Tea Party at their Uncle Smith's house in Boston. As usual, services at the First Church that day took a patriotic turn.

"For ye shall go out with joy, and be led forth with Peace," the minister quoted from Isaiah 55. And he proceeded to enumerate the events leading up to the American victory. There was the repeal of the Stamp Act in 1766, the meeting of the First Continental Congress in September of 1774, and the battles at Lexington and Concord the next spring. The Declaration of Independence and the victory at Saratoga had followed, along with many defeats and much suffering. Everyone now rejoicing in safety had undergone danger, the reverend reminded them. Abigail, reliving these events with great emotion, thought how doubly true this was of her absent spouse.

But even her father's death could not reconcile her to joining John in Europe. His calls to duty fell on deaf ears. "There was a time when I had brought my mind to be willing to cross the Seas to be with you, but tho one strong tie which held me here, is dissolved, the train of my Ideas for six months past has run wholy upon your return," she held her ground.[76]

On September 7, 1783, John at last received Congress's answer to his resignation, which was an emphatic no, accompanied by what he chose to see as a flattering offer to be one of three American ministers negotiating for special trade rights with Parliament and the British King. Ignoring the fact that he was not made the exclusive arbiter and not even complaining when he learned that Franklin would be one of the teammates, he was convinced that accepting this post would seal his place in history. Still, desperate to see Abigail, he forgot about reason and duty and begged her to join him for love.

"You may embark for London, Amsterdam, or any Port of France," he entreated her. "The moment I hear of it, I will fly with Post Horses to receive you." Or if she preferred an air balloon, that might be arranged as well. No effort would be spared to make life in Europe a honeymoon for his "Miss Adorable." Crossing the Atlantic would be dangerous and expensive, and they would probably not stay longer than half a year, but "I am so unhappy without you that . . . Six months of your Company is worth [all] to me." Besides, the man who had warned her for years against sea voyages now declared the trip would improve her recent headaches and raise her spirits. Even reversing his opinion on Royall Tyler was not unthinkable at this point. Best would be if Nabby could leave Tyler and sail with Abigail. On the other hand, if it was Nabby's clinging to Tyler that was keeping Abigail from coming to Europe, Abigail should throw caution to the wind and "marry her," leave them the house, and hurry off.

Now the impulse that had driven Abigail to brook her parents' disapproval and marry John two decades earlier stirred again. "The steel and the Magnet or the Glass and the feather will not fly together with more Celerity, than somebody and Somebody, when brought within striking Distance," John had teased her about their attraction when they were courting.[77] And where his harangues about duty fell on deaf ears, this reference to their magical connection and his need for her struck home. Memories of their early happiness came rushing back, clashing with pride at the self-reliance she had fought so hard to achieve. Slowly, meticulously, at age 40, for the second time in her life she prepared to risk everything for John. If this demanded far more courage than marrying in the first place, well, so be it.

On May 24, 1784, Abigail booked passage for herself and Nabby on a sturdy, copper-bottomed boat called the *Active*. For servants, she hired a young man named John Briesler, who had worked for her uncle, and a neighbor's daughter of Nabby's age named Esther Field. She said good-bye to James Lovell, who, thanks largely to her, now had a local government job and lived with his family in Boston.[78] She packed heavy winter clothes for the ship.

Abigail turned over financial matters during her absence to her Uncle Tufts, placed Richard Cranch in charge of John's library, and invited the newly freed Phoebe, who had just married a free black named Abdee, to live in the house. They were the most trustworthy people she knew, she assured the new couple, though, being Abigail, in a letter to Uncle Tufts she nonetheless left copious notes of instructions about everything from use of the two gardens to care of the chairs and beds. (The latter required "opening, airing, rubbing, and cleaning.") Phoebe and Abdee could keep a pig in the yard and feast on her fruit.

Charitable donations should be made to poor Braintree widows and spinsters before Christmas, Abigail instructed her uncle. She gave her blessings to Tyler, who now wrote John formally asking to marry his child when she returned from abroad. Richard Cranch agreed to endorse the match.

Fourteen-year-old Charles and twelve-year-old Tommy would remain in Haverhill, studying for Harvard entrance exams. Mary and Elizabeth promised to mother them as Abigail would mother her sisters' children if the tables were reversed. Mary would also take John's aging mother under her wing, send American chocolates to the wilderness of Paris, and perform a million little acts of kindness only such a sister could divine.

Ah, Mary, Mary, Abigail's second best friend in the world and greatest solace during the decade since John first rode away to the Continental Congress: she would be hard to live without. "I have to combat my own feelings in leaving my Friends," Abigail wrote understatedly about their impending separation. Mary was similarly restrained.

So as the departure date grew near, it was the youngest who gave words to her older sisters' anguish:

> Alas! My Sister this will be a *sad* week to my Braintree Friends [wrote Elizabeth to Mary]. My Spirit feels the pressure. Whatever you may think, after you have collected all your phylosophy, and placed it as a mighty rampart about your Heart, one affectionate look from our dear Sisters speaking Eyes, will fix the Fear of separation, and in spite of all your efforts leave you overwhelmed and lost in Grief.
>
> It is too tender, even for me to reflect on.[79]

Later, Elizabeth imagined Abigail's departure.[80] "Ah! My Sister my spirit was witness to the parting Scene," Elizabeth wrote Mary at the end of June. "I saw all the various passions rioting in my Nabby's Face." She could go no further. The prospect of Abigail's reaching Europe seemed far more remote than that of her dying miserably in the middle of the Atlantic. And even if they all survived to some future meeting, their bond would undergo a radical shift. Abigail would be as distant from her sisters as the King of England. On June 20, when she sailed from Boston with her daughter, a cow, a man, and a maidservant, their parents' generation had passed, a revolution had shaken their concept of hierarchy, and two large props of the siblings' loving relationship— shared everyday experience and natural proximity—were violently cut off. Mary, Abigail, and Elizabeth would have to struggle to sustain intimacy across an ocean. That sisterhood could endure such a violent transformation remained to be proved.

CHAPTER VIII

"How many how various how complicated my Sensations!"

. . .

On Sunday June 20, as fair winds sped her off toward mighty England, Abigail could only focus on the humble scenes she'd left. The frank, boxy face of her clapboard house, its lopsided triangle of a roof, and the friendly tympanum over the doorway stood as reproof to the vast, gray-blue ocean before her. So too did green Penn's Hill, her upward view. Abigail's nieces, who were almost daughters, and her mother-in-law and the hardworking neighbors who like a funeral procession had gathered in her yard the day she left Braintree were still weeping and praying in her mind's eye as the boat neared the Boston lighthouse. Only uncertainty stretched before her. "Where is my next abode?" she mourned.[1]

Captain Lyde called for the ten passengers on the *Active* to prepare for seasickness. No sooner had the boat plunged into open water than a crippling nausea struck. The stench of oil and fermenting potash sluicing back and forth in storage compounded the misery. Abigail and Nabby fell onto their listing mattresses, unable even to move a finger without triggering a new bout of throwing up. With a single small grated window in a "stateroom" just eight foot square for three people, Abigail had no choice but to open her door directly on the adjacent men's cabin or perish from the poisonous smells. The servants were as sick as she so there was no one to wash or bring drinking water. Captain Lyde had a rough-looking face and ignored everything but his sails. Meanwhile, the temperature dropped drastically.

Three days later, on Wednesday, Abigail at last felt up to changing into winter clothing and, wedging herself between two gentlemen, crawled onto the upper deck. Here she had to be bound to a chair so she didn't fly away. But her spirits revived, and she determined "to make a Bustle," she announced in an ongoing letter to Mary, who would surely have done the same. Summoning mops, scrapers, and infusions of vinegar, Abigail first supervised a major cleanup, winning everyone's gratitude. Next, she banished the "laizy dirty"[2] cook from the kitchen and began making her own food. Abigail's experience bore out Ben Franklin's warning that ship chefs knew nothing about cooking and were merely the most expendable sailors on board.[3] She memorized the names of the masts and sails, studied how Captain Lyde steered, and almost imagined she'd conquered seasickness when, on their second Monday out of Boston, off the coast of Newfoundland, a nor'easter pounded the ship.

The sea rose high as a mountain, Abigail told Mary later. The waves struck so hard she was sure the boat's flanks would split.[4] Bottles, mugs, and plates crashed to pieces. Her poor milk cow grew lame from standing still and so had to be thrown overboard. In order to sit on deck, ropes no longer sufficed: Abigail needed to link arms with a strong man braced against a lashed-down table. Delicacy was out of the question. She couldn't so much as open a door or walk across her cabin alone. And with Nabby ill and her maid, Esther, feebler than anyone, Abigail became nurse as well as patient, which meant, among other things, pouring the fetid sick pail overboard. The cabin reeked, but after two sleepless nights, she lost even the will to flee the stench. Exhaustion, she wrote Mary, "reduce[s] one to such lassitude, that you care little for your fate."[5]

The storm lasted two days. As the winds died down, Abigail placed a board on her lap, wedged an arm against either side of the cabin, and with a shaking pen poured out her feelings of littleness and awe of God in a letter to Elizabeth in Haverhill. "There is not an object in Nature, better calculated to raise in our minds to sublime Ideas of the Deity than the boundless ocean," she wrote her most religious sister.[6] During the storm, human nature had also risen in her estimation. Captain Lyde, belying his rude appearance, proved consideration itself to the fearful passengers and a natural leader to the mates as well as a brilliant navigator. The physician they were lucky enough to have on board, Dr. Clarke, exhausted himself ministering to passengers and servants with equal care.

Dr. Clarke's solicitousness particularly touched Nabby, who was gloomy without Tyler and frequently collapsed in tears. Nabby's passions were strong, Abigail acknowledged, moved by the transformation in the daughter she had once thought unfeeling. What's more, Nabby treasured her new emotions. Calling melancholy a weakness she would not exchange for joy, Nabby poured out her sorrow in a letter to the most susceptible person she knew, Betsy Cranch.[7]

Still, depression was exhausting. During her first days on ship, it was difficult for Nabby to wake before noon or compose herself to leave the stateroom. Then, as the storm lifted, she joined Abigail outside. Here the general flurry (two men played backgammon, Dr. Clarke ate ham, even Esther was out of bed and knitting) distracted her, and as her spirits rose, her lethargy abated. This improvement confirmed a theory Abigail was just now encountering in a book on domestic medicine. "The passions have a great influence both in the cause and cure of diseases," argued the author, Dr. Buchan. "How mind acts upon matter, will, in all probability ever remain a secret. It is sufficient for us to know, that there is established a reciprocal influence betwixt the mental and corporeal parts, and whatever disorders the one, likewise affects the other."[8]

Variety, Dr. Buchan continued, was essential to human happiness. Scholars, always at their books, were vulnerable to "delirium, melancholy, and even madness;"[9] a change of scene and silly company was as good for the philosopher as exercise for the sick. "How pleasing to the mind is change," Abigail endorsed Buchan's argument in a letter to Mary. "I cannot find such a fund of entertainment within myself as not to require outward objects for my amusement."[10]

And even on a ship she referred to as a prison, she found the diversion she needed. One night it was watching light appear out of nowhere and splay like fireflies over the black ocean.[11] (This was the phenomenon of phosphorescence, not understood in her day.) Another time, it was scrutinizing the amazingly humanlike organs of a porpoise a mate harpooned. She read her health book or John Campbell's *A Political Survey of Britain*, sewed, and played cards. Writing was her favorite activity. She also followed the boat's speed and latitude: by the fourth of July, the captain calculated, they were halfway through their trip.

Now Abigail's seasickness vanished, and she relished all forward movement. Let it rain and blow. Only a calm, with no progress and the ship rocking like a cradle on the swells, was hard to bear. "I begin to think that a Calm is not desireable in any situation in life," she chafed to Mary after three such days. Mary, she supposed, was "scorching under the mid summer heat," while even when the sun shone, Abigail wore a baize robe over double calico gowns and a cloth coat on top of it all to keep warm on ship.[12][13]

As she sat on deck in her double calicos, inevitably Abigail fell into comparing England and America with her fellow passengers. The most learned but least enlightened of them was a Scotsman, who scorned the very notion of earned success. Class and birth were all-important in his view. One day, Abigail could tolerate his snobbisms no longer and decided to put him straight, observing in her most ladylike fashion that:

> Merit; not tittles [gives] a man preeminence in our Country . . . I [do] not doubt it [is] a mortifying circumstance to the British nobility, to find themselves so often conquerd by mecanicks and mere husband men, but . . . we [esteem] it our Glory to draw such characters not only into the field, but into the Senate; and I [believe] no one would deny but what they [have] shone in both.[14]

While honing her skills for touting America in Europe, she also jettisoned her morbid longings for the past. Indeed, every day on board the ship grew easier. Just as variety was a boon to happiness, ritual was a great duller of pain, she found, and went so far as to claim: "I believe I could continue on Board this Ship 8 or ten days more, and find it less irksome than the first 8 or ten hours, so strong is habit and so easily do we become reconciled to the most disagreeable Situation."[15]

Still, she was eager to move on and overjoyed, on Saturday July 17, to spot twenty ships ahead and know she was nearing the English Channel and on her way to the port of Deal. Two days afterward the cliffs of Dover bobbed gently into view. The almost impossible had occurred. She had crossed the Atlantic. And now Abigail's anticipatory fears and the sufferings of the past month seemed trivial in light of the wonder welling up within her. She trusted her thoughts only to her private diary where she managed to scribble, "Can it be that I have past this great ocean . . . [and am] so near the land of my fore fathers? And am I Gracious Heaven; there to meet, the Dear long absent partner of my Heart? How many how various how complicated my Sensations! Be it unto me according to my wishes," she prayed.[16]

In the second week of August, when John Adams's letter about Nabby's engagement arrived for Royall Tyler, Mary Cranch was already out of sorts. It had been a scorching July, threatening drought and another poor harvest. Currency in post-war America was scarce; so the state and national governments had no choice but to impose taxes. Remembering the British, many Americans refused to pay, but Mary believed in the capitalist system and contributed her fair share. The economy as a whole was suffering because America's favored nation trading status with England had ended. Plus, there was a vast disparity between what American wanted from Britain and what Britain was willing to import from them.

At home in Braintree, Betsy was dreaming of music lessons, while the Cranch farm was failing. More than ever, Mary had to scrimp. Furthermore, it had been seven weeks since Abigail and Nabby sailed, and there was as yet no word of a safe arrival. "Time will hang heavy upon me till I hear from you," she wrote.

And then there was the problem of her latest boarder. If no force in the world could stop Nabby from marrying Tyler, then Mary's hints that she disliked him had certainly alienated a future nephew. Worse, if the marriage *could* be averted, she had done little to promote that much-desired end.

She'd been in a difficult position, certainly. The fact that the neighbors were whispering that Mary wanted Tyler for her own girls made speaking ill of him look self-serving, while Nabby's reserve had made it difficult for Mary to raise the subject at all with her niece before her departure. Indeed, she was convinced that the hints she'd dropped had backfired and turned Nabby against her. "She did not love me when she went away," Mary felt sure.[17]

Nor did it help that Abigail, usually so savvy, failed to appreciate Tyler's cunning. Sometimes Mary comforted herself that Tyler was young and could change under Nabby's influence. But it was her role as eldest sister—indeed as head of the family (since their father's death)—to avert disaster, not to hope for the best! And how she rued letting credulous Richard endorse the match to John in that long letter accompanying Tyler's proposal. Richard had called Tyler's addresses to Nabby honorable, described his character as virtuous and polite: all half-truths if not downright misrepresentations.[18] And now Abigail had sailed and John's verdict on the engagement was sealed in the envelope before her.

The moment Tyler got home from his law practice, he snatched it up.

And it was not long before all of Braintree knew John Adams had given Tyler his blessing to marry Nabby. Mary could only cringe inside as her neighbors enthused. More disappointing was the naiveté of her youngest sister, Elizabeth, who imagined—she wrote from Haverhill— that after eighteen months in fear and doubts Tyler must now be ecstatic, when the truth was that Tyler took everything in stride.[19]

Indeed, he let three weeks pass before deigning to reply to John's letter. As for Nabby, not only did Tyler fail to write her—he boasted of his neglect. Furious on her niece's behalf, Mary was now emboldened to write Abigail: "I suppose Mr. Tyler will write he is well,"[20] implying the contrary, and she lamented that she could not yet send payment for the carpet she'd asked Abigail to buy for her in London because you know who was late with his rent.

Mary let more annoyance slip into a subsequent letter, where she reported that after four months' silence, Tyler was now going overboard in the opposite direction. He had ensconsed himself in his room for three days, writing Nabby more than she needed to know.[21] And then there was the matter of his recklessness. Tyler adored sledding, Mary reminded her sister. He festooned his winter sleigh with glass and bought "a Gay horse"—whom he pushed so hard its first three times out that the horse had to rest for weeks. The animal had barely revived when Tyler marched him off toward Germantown in treacherously deep snow. The horse was afraid, and to get him onto a snowy bridge, Tyler employed his favorite tactic of whipping without mercy—at which point the animal got his revenge by breaking away and smashing the sleigh to bits. "Thus ended the Sleighing for the winter," concluded Mary, leaving Abigail to deduce what she would of such a future son.

ELIZABETH SHAW HAD A GIFT for vicarious experience. When she watched the wind whirl her parish weathercock, she rejoiced that the same gales propelled her sister toward England. As she stared at "the Moon walking in brightness" over Haverhill, she imagined Abigail also contemplating its glory in the middle of the sea. With Abigail gone, Elizabeth felt family bonds more deeply. Charlie and Tommy Adams were like sons to her.

And as a mother would, she made them blue velvet jackets and splurged on black satin lasting for their britches. She took pride in Charles's popularity and graceful movements and was first to notice Tommy's homesickness and give him extra kisses and hugs. She applauded the brothers' vying to outdo each other at math and Latin because competition was a Puritan virtue, and was vigilant about their dawning sexuality because lubriciousness was a sin. Charles, for instance, was great friends with a 16-year-old girl named Nancy. But he "is yet a School Boy, and Miss Nancy considers him as such . . . When they play together with battledores, or the like, it is conducted with all the sweet simplicity of little Children," she assured Abigail.[22]

"I take the same prudent care for [your sons], that I think you would," she declared in her first letter to her sister in Europe.[23] And the fact that loving someone else's child came easily to her was lucky because kin-keeping was a mainstay of New England life.

Elizabeth herself had grown up in an extended family, spending weeks with Aunt and Uncle Smith in Boston for as far back as she could remember and later staying for months with her married sisters in Braintree and Salem, when their mother was well enough to spare her at home. Her siblings too had moved freely in and out of the Weymouth parish. Abigail, when she was young, had lived so long with their Quincy grandparents that she talked about being raised by them, while their brother, Billy, had been packed off to Uncle Isaac's when he was an adolescent as much to learn independence as to apprentice for a business career.

Like the British, who made a point of sending their young away at early ages, Puritans valued education outside the parental household. Because kin-keeping was usually the province of eldest daughters, Elizabeth's taking in an older sister's children attracted attention and enhanced her status in the world.[24] Caring for young nieces and nephews also cemented the bonds of sisterhood. "I take a particular pleasure in serving [your children]," Elizabeth told Abigail, "as I consider it, as a medium, through which I am happy to convey my Love, and Gratitude [to you]."[25] And kin-keeping furthermore expanded a child's horizon.[26] Nabby Adams and Betsy Cranch had always felt invigorated by trips to the Shaw parsonage. "Your letters to your friends since you have been at Haverhill . . . bespeak a tranquility of mind which I think the result of an agreeable situation. I dare say you feel intirely happy," Nabby had surmised during one of Betsy's trips.[27]

Discipline and love, the Puritans believed, were the two faces of child-rearing. When the one undermined the other, it was time for a relative to step in. Nabby, who found her own mother formidable, could let down her guard with Aunt Elizabeth, while Billy Smith's daughter, Louisa, wept when she had to end an extended visit to her cheerful Aunt Abigail, and everyone trusted Aunt Mary's judgment most.

Mary was also famous for upholding rigorous standards, where Elizabeth knew she had the tendency to overindulge. Her husband called her Pelican, after the character in the fable who tears open her heart to feed her starving offspring. She was also more likely to spoil because she had just two children of her own. And how opposite they were! The elder, six-year-old William, was a thoughtful, inward-looking child, with lackluster eyes that would "in no ways retard his progress in Literature," Elizabeth assured Mary. "My Book and heart shall never part" was his favorite adage, and there was no need for

Elizabeth to send him off to relatives for discipline since he was almost too docile as it was.[28]

His younger sister, Betsy Quincy, was another matter. A born charmer, she clamored for attention and prattled and mimicked from morning to night. Even at four, she had a droll sense of humor and a cheeky confidence. While William amused himself reading, Betsy Q was either demanding that her mother hold her like an infant or running through the fields of Haverhill like a sprite. Elizabeth could too easily put herself in Betsy Q's shoes to curb her daughter's spirits. The situation called for an aunt's firmer hand.

"I believe I shall bring my . . . wild girl, for you to tame," Elizabeth resigned herself to writing Mary, reminding herself that Abigail had parted for years first with John Quincy and now with Thomas and Charles. But here for once she could not identify with her middle sister, for while nurturing Abigail's brood was as natural to Elizabeth as breathing, parting with Betsy Q for just a summer's trip felt like losing an arm or a leg. Even the packing was torture. How had Abigail done it? "I hope Betsy will be a good Girl and give you as little trouble as possible," Elizabeth wrote Mary after she dropped her little soulmate off in Braintree, but what Elizabeth really hoped was that *she* could survive the rift.

"YOUR LETTER . . . HAS MADE me the happiest man on Earth. I am twenty years younger than . . . yesterday," John Adams wrote Abigail from Holland the moment he learned of her safe arrival in England. That some last-minute business detained him there was a "cruel Mortification," but John Quincy was already en route to London.[29]

Meanwhile, Abigail and Nabby hired a carriage and drove through green and gold countryside "cultivated like a garden." They stopped at Canterbury with its Gothic cathedrals and in Camden dined on an eight-course feast. At dusk they glimpsed the houses of Parliament.

"That I am in the City of London, I can scarce believe," marveled equable Nabby. And it was like stepping out of a page of *Sir Charles Grandison* or the *Spectator* as they descended at a posh apartment in Covent Gardens and then settled, the following morning, at Adelphi's

family hotel off the Strand. Out their window lay the grandest shopping street in the fastest-growing city in Europe. The finest galleries
and bookshops in the world were in walking distance. London was
"large magnificent, and Beautifull," Abigail could scarcely tamp her
glee to write informatively to her sisters. The streets were straight,
forty feet wide, and had sidewalks like Philadelphia. The buildings
were noble, the squares great.

Nabby wrote her cousin Betsy, home in Braintree:
"That I am in the city of London I can scarce believe.

Abigail's hotel suite was elegant as any townhouse in Boston, with
Moroccan chairs in the drawing room and pale green, gold-ridged
walls. The mechanical sciences were so advanced here that pipes from
under the street carried water up to her chamber. Their church had
seats "like a concert hall"; apparently no one was poor. And while British ladies were less feminine than Americans—they wore mere painted
muslin rather than silk and straw hats instead of bonnets—nevertheless,
dressing to go out in London was a queenly affair.[30] "Here is the stay
maker, the Mantua maker, the hoop maker, the shoe maker, the milli-
ner and hair dresser all of whom are necessary to transform me into the
fashionable Lady," Abigail portrayed herself as a female variation on
Moliere's *Bourgeois Gentilhomme* in a letter to her sister Elizabeth.
When they were finished, she was off to see the British Museum and
Westminster Abbey: "You would think yourself in a land of enchantment," she declared.[31]

The British dined early and breakfasted late, so she had to learn to
control her hunger. They were a nation of fast walkers; so she raced to

keep up (and collapsed on her bed afterward). There was a perpetual social whirl, and she filled her days with engagements: "As you know I am fond of sociabil[it y," she reminded her Braintree friends.[32] Everything here was so different—and yet so similar that "I cannot find myself in a strange land ' she concluded. For most of her engagements were with former Americans (including Mr. Joy, an old flame of Elizabeth's, whom, she assured her younger sister, "is still a Character that you need not blush at having an Esteem for").[33] The fact that most of them had been Tories scarcely mattered now that the war was won. And even real Londoners looked like Parson Wibird or Mrs. Fields, Abigail noticed. "I can scarcely persuade myself, but what I have seen this person, that and the other before, there countanances appear so familiar to me, and so strongly mark our own Decent."

Nabby, on the other hand, missed Tyler and her cousins and was more inclined to keep all the new people she met at arm's length. "I do not love that kind of intercourse where no one affection of the heart has any share," she observed in her trip diary. "I would treat everyone with civility . . . but the unmeaning intercourse of a great portion of mankind, I must acknowledge, I have but little taste for." She added, however, that her ideas on this subject might change.[34]

A week after they landed in London, Nabby got her first glimpse of her beloved father. She and Abigail were standing in an art gallery. There, in a large portrait painted by the famous John Singleton Copley, stood John Adams in velvet britches, with a map of America at the end of his fingers and a globe of the world at his feet. Holding a treaty in his fist and with a sword on his hip, he embodied what he'd struggled to create: a powerful nation. Abigail appraised the picture "a very good likeness."

But she was even more delighted with the young facsimile that arrived five days later. "Oh my Mamma! and my dear Sister," cried John Quincy, striding into their drawing room—a 17-year-old figure of fashion, dressed like a count or baronet. At first it was only his eyes and the uncanny resemblance to his father that Abigail recognized. Everything else was foreign. "I look upon him Scarcely realizing that he belongs to me," his mother marveled, though she soon discovered "the same good humourd Lad" beneath the French manners and powdered hair. As for Nabby: "I have the pleasure to inform you Eliza that I have seen my Brother, actually seen him, and do not find him a monster as I expected," she rushed off a letter to Cousin Betsy. On the contrary, John Quincy seemed just the man to take her mind off Royall Tyler, whom she had yet to hear from: "You cannot judge of the disappointment after having flattered yourself with the hopes, of receiving letters, not to find any," she confessed to her friend.[35]

A week later, on August 7, Nabby wrote in her diary:

> At 12, returned to our . . . apartments; when I entered, I saw upon the table a hat with two books in it; every thing around appeared altered, without my knowing in what particular. I went into my own room, the things were moved; I looked around—"Has mamma received letters, that have determined her departure?—When does she go?—Why are these things moved?" All in a breath to [the woman servant] Esther. "No, ma'am, she has received no letter, but goes to-morrow morning." Why is all this appearance of strangeness? Whose hat is that in the other room?—Whose trunk is this?—Whose sword and cane?—"It is my father's," said I. "Where is he?" "In the room above." I flew up, and to his chamber, where he was lying down, he raised himself upon my knocking softly at the door, and received me with all the tenderness of an affectionate parent after so long an absence. Sure I am, I never felt more agitation of spirits in my life.[36]

On the same day, Mary Cranch wrote Abigail from Braintree, presuming the awesome reunion with her husband had already taken place. Had it brought "the most exquisite pleasure or the most Poignant distress?" Mary was longing to hear.

But now for once it was Abigail who declined to speak of feelings, only telling her sister, "You will chide me I suppose for not relateing to you an event which took place in London, that of . . . meeting there my long absent Friend . . . But you know my dear sister, that poets and painters wisely draw a veil over those Scenes which surpass the pen of the one and the pencil of the other. We are indeed a very very happy family once more."[37]

John's initial plan had been to show Abigail and Nabby Holland.

But then Thomas Jefferson—who was replacing John Jay as the third minister on the commission charged to effect a commercial treaty with Great Britain—arrived earlier than anticipated in France. So, on the morning of August 5, the Adams family left Adelphi's Hotel and headed directly for the trade talks in Paris. "I sincerely wish the treaty might have been concerted [in London]. I have a partiality for this Country," Abigail lamented.[38] To pass time on the road, John Quincy read Samuel Johnson's *Lives of the Poets* aloud in the carriage, and John sought to appease Nabby's homesickness for Tyler by exhorting her to look at the world around her and expand her mind.[39 40] The end of all journeys was the getting of wisdom, he reminded her, which was all very fine in theory. But in fact no words could console John Adams's daughter for the shock of arriving in Paris, "a very disagreeable" city filled with "the dirtiest Creatures in the Human race."

How FRENCH IT WAS to love liberty best in the abstract. For all its enthusiasm about the new American democracy, France, in the early 1780s, was a monarchy of the most rigid type. Its legislature had not met in over a century. And while Louis XVI was personally shy and affable, his policies lacked any pretension to seeking a common good. Aristocrats lived well, exempt from taxes, while workers paid punishing tailles and suffered, unassisted, from frequent famines and droughts. Meanwhile, enormous debts incurred from supporting the American Revolution were crippling the entire French economy, as the King lost his worries in hunting and Versailles went on consuming stupendous wealth.

And this same France was the home of the philosophes—Diderot, Rousseau, Voltaire, Helvetius—whom Abigail had revered since Richard Cranch introduced them to her in childhood and whose cry for progress through enlightened education had informed every aspect of her adult life. Voltaire, an Anglophile, remained an enthusiast for monarchy, but Rousseau's *The Social Contract* had made a huge impact on America's Declaration of Independence, demanding liberty, equality, and rule by the general will. Particularly rousing for Abigail were *The Social Contract*'s Puritan-like bursts of humility. "To succeed, one must not attempt the impossible or flatter oneself with giving to the work of men a solidity that things human do not allow," Rousseau insists.[41] Now Rousseau was dead, but his spirit lived on in Paris's answer to Boston's taverns—the powerful salons, run by just the sort of women Abigail had envied, reading John's raves about female intellectuals during his first French trip.

For where propriety obliged good American wives to echo their husbands' positions, women no brighter than Mary, Abigail, and Elizabeth had for the past two hundred years been expressing themselves freely throughout France. Lack of formal education did not stop French women from attracting the great and the good to their salons, for courtship in France was spiced by intellectual discourse, and men went out of their way to teach young women ideas. Indeed, talk often compensated for other deficiencies. So every Tuesday night Madame de Staël—despite being ugly—enchanted liberal aristocrats at her elegant Rue du Bac dinners, and Madame de Roland—despite being low-born—inspired political idealists at her *soirees* in Lyon. On the other hand, Claude-Adrian Helvetius's 65-year-old widow, the beautiful Anne-Catherine de Ligniville, masked a weaker intelligence with charming prattle. The country's most elite scientists and philosophers flocked to her salons near Benjamin Franklin's Passy mansion. Franklin, it was gossiped, rarely missed one of her evenings. Reputedly, he had gone so far as to propose marriage. And though she told everyone she would never replace her late husband, the two nonetheless continued to chat and flirt.

Abigail's first impression, like Nabby's, was that France was vastly inferior to England. The fields merely sprawled, lacking the nice touch of British hedges. The villages along the route from Calais were impoverished, the houses grim thatched huts—devoid even of glass windows. While England appeared opulent, France was squalid. Where the British industrialized, the French enjoyed themselves—romping out to the country and celebrating every Sunday like a major holiday, not to mention spending half their lives guffawing at rowdy *boulevard* plays. All the world was truly a stage for the French people. "In London, the Streets are also full of People, but their Dress, their Gait, every appearance indicates Business," Abigail wrote Mercy Otis Warren, approvingly; whereas, in Paris, "from the gayety of the Dress, and the Places they frequent I judge Pleasure is the Business of Life."[42]

And yet, for all its jollity, Paris had no pavements and fewer public gardens and benches than London. Some of the buildings, though outrageously tall, were tolerable, she acknowledged, but as a rule shops and houses were inelegant, the roads were narrow and clogged with building materials, since the city was expanding.[43] While the French adored science—they'd sent a sixty-foot-high blue balloon careening over the Versailles palace—they sadly lacked the English knack for practical mechanics. Sanitation was so primitive that housewives dumped their dirty wash water out the windows, further endangering any pedestrian foolish enough to joust with the reckless carriages for space in the street. Traveling the short distance from one country to the other, Abigail explained to Mary, was like going from a splendid dinner at Mrs. Warren's to Bracketts Tavern, a charmless old Braintree inn.

Still, there was a beau monde, and to keep up with it—as, being a minister's wife, she must—was catastrophically expensive (especially as Congress had just reduced all ministers' salaries). From gauze to decanters, anything charming was English and came burdened with duties, while housekeeping was exorbitant because a ludicrous custom demanded a separate servant for every task. One man rubbed your floors, another cleaned them. Yet another followed you when you went out to dinner and stood behind your chair while you ate. The *coiffeuse de chambre* sculpted your hair, but refused to dust your bureau. "It is the policy of this country to oblige you to a certain number of servants, and one will not touch what belongs to the business of another, tho he or she has time enough to perform the whole." Even her protean Briesler and Esther were forbidden to perform anything beyond their respective roles as *valet* and *femme de chambre.* And for this they were compelled to dress up and have their hair coiffed, because, even for a servant, "To be out of fashion is more criminal than to be seen" nude.[44]

Frenchwomen were outrageously familiar, she confided to Mary's younger daughter, Lucy. The war hero Lafayette's wife spontaneously embraced her like a long-lost friend on their first meeting. And then there was the famous *salIniste* Madame Helvetius, who showed up at Dr. Franklin's house in Passy oblivious to the inappropriateness of her ancient blue dress, common hat, and ill-placed shawl. Spotting Abigail, 'Ah Mon dieu! Where is Frankling?' she "bawled out." At dinner, Madame Helvetius defied everything Abigail had been taught about female conduct and "carried on the chief of the conversation," meanwhile "frequently locking her hand into the Drs . . . . then throwing her Arm carelessly upon [his] Neck."

"After dinner, she threw herself upon a settee . . . She had a little Lap Dog who was next to the Dr her favorite. This She kisst and when he wet the floor she wiped it up with her chemise . . . Thus my dear you see that Manners differ exceedingly in different Countries. I hope however to find among the French Ladies manners more consistant with my Ideas of decency, or I shall be a mere recluse." Indeed, with so many

Madame Helvetius had been a beauty
in her youth.

fewer American residents here than in London, she imagined a dull winter ahead.

And even after her initial shock passed and she could perceive Madame de Lafayette's spontaneity as art—the French studied to seem natural, she told her sisters—and Madame Helvetius's dishabille as a sign that she was distinguished enough to disdain common rules, Abigail still could not shake the pangs of an exile. Visiting Paris's heavy, dark Catholic cathedrals made her long for a visit from sensible Parson Wibird. She spent a full page in a December 12 note to Mary describing John Quincy's Herculean efforts to retrieve a packet of the Cranches' letters from the French authorities and her unspeakable joy when she saw Mary's handwriting at last. Of course, she studied French (by reading a play every day), and once a week she entertained visiting Americans and foreign ministers, since such was her duty, but she still spent hours of every day writing home. And this was not because she felt impelled to keep up with a large swath of important acquaintances. Time and again, the recipients of her long and imaginative correspondence were the same four women: Elizabeth Shaw and Mary, Betsy, and Lucy Cranch.

Yes, even as her marriage thrived and she basked in the pleasure of getting to know her adult son John Quincy, Abigail felt a constant need to connect with her distant sisters and nieces. Walking in the Tuilleries or visiting St. Sulpice, she wondered what *they* would think or how *they* would survive so many wet days without sun or intimate company. She knew they would share her repugnance at France's loveless marriages, often arranged before puberty. The disparity between the decadence of Versailles where the three-year-old dauphin was worshipped like a deity, and the grim indigence of the common Frenchman would depress them as well. She longed for both the ideal of American democracy and the reality of living without hairdressers and floor-rubbers in virtuous America. "I have really commiserated the unhappy Refugees more than ever, and think no severer punishment need to be inflicted upon any mortals than that of banishment from their Country and Friends," she wrote Mary.[45]

And she chose to tell Elizabeth about her visit to a French orphanage, which raised her spirits because (for once in France!) it was clean and orderly and in the course of a year rescued six thousand babies abandoned like old clothes in boxes on the Paris streets. But what sort of people could renounce their babies to boxes? And the orphanage spoke volumes on the rampant licentiousness in Paris, where an astounding 52,000[46] prostitutes were *licensed* to corrupt married men.[47]

Still, she could not declare herself altogether miserable in exile. "Where is my next abode?" she had wondered, full of trepidation, as she crossed the Atlantic. Well, the answer was: in a house rented from a French count four miles outside Paris, on the edge of the Bois de Bo-

Abigail's first residence after leaving her cottage in Braintree was this mansion on the edge of the Bois de Bologne in Auteuil.

logne in a fairy-tale village named Auteuil, a cynosure for artists and intellectuals. In place of her little wood house was a three-story white stone mansion with a jaunty mansard roof and a reception hall larger than Mercy Otis Warren's. Fanciful sculpture embossed the outside, and rococo figures cavorted on ceilings within. The walls were plated with gold, the bedrooms papered with swirling scenes of rural enchantment. There were forty beds to sleep in and too many chambers to count. Everywhere you looked were sets of floor-high glass windows opening like doors in the middle. There was a large room set aside just for indoor walking. She at last had a closet of her own like her aunt Elizabeth's to write hundreds of letters home in, and best of all was the enormous garden out back.

Abigail only wished she could whisk Betsy Cranch up in one of the new air balloons and transport her to this little verdant paradise. "Why you would be in raptures," she began a meticulous description of arbors, orange trees, exotic plants, potted flowers, and grape vines for her fellow aesthete. The garden took up five acres of land and was laid out geometrically. The trees were so neatly trimmed you could imagine walking through air or their limbs.

Two doors down, Nabby had a similar view of the garden, but no thoughts of walking on treetops. Neither falling in love nor arriving in Europe had caused her to see the world as her mother and Betsy did, as she lightly made clear in a letter to the similarly prosaic Lucy Cranch:

> This crow quil that I now write [with] and the beautiful flower garden of which I have a fine prospect from the Window I am now sitting at, and the voice of a pretty lass in a garden adjoining, would inspire your Sister Betsy's imagination with . . . images sufficient to compose ten pages of poetry—while I can only view them as they realy are, and admire the variety of the flowers and their various colours . . . and can only observe upon the crow quil, that it is much smaller than a goose quil, and that I can write much better with it. Don't you think so too?

By now, Abigail and Nabby were more bemused than vexed by their contrasting temperaments; fortunately—for they spent almost every moment of the day together, from breakfast, where it was Nabby's job to serve her mother and brother tea and her father chocolate, to dinner at two, tea between five and six, and a last game of cards before Abigail went to bed and Nabby and John Quincy stayed up to relish each other's company and rehash the day's events. (In between family activities, Abigail and Nabby each read, wrote, and studied French in adjacent rooms.)

Besides, travel opened so many new pleasures to both of them. First and most magical was the elaborate process of going out at night to what Parisians loved most: "entertainments." Preparation got under way with an hour of reading Moliere or Voltaire while Madame Paulina curled and poofed your hair in the Auteuil manor and continued as you dressed, took a ride in the fine coach John had purchased in London, and approached the Place de l'Opéra or Jardins de Luxembourg with an expectant crowd. The new Comédie-Française, with its porticos and Doric columns, was especially splendid. Life-size sculptures of the muses stared down on two thousand seats. "The scenery, the musick, the dresses, the action," not to mention the acting and words, were all captivating, reported Abigail, who had never before seen a play out of book covers,[48] while Nabby raved about the dancing, calling it "superior to any thing you have an idea of," in a letter to a Braintree friend.[49]

Gradually, France and the French grew on both of them. "I have found my taste reconciling itself to habits and fashions, which at first disgusted me," Abigail admitted to Mary in February.[50] For instance, the first time she saw the host at a dinner party yank a partridge leg and smell it "to see if it is in a condition to offer to the Ladies," she was revolted. Now, though, she admired the thought behind the deed. And so too the French opera dancers ("Girls cloathd in the thinest Silk: and Gauze . . . poising themselves in the air, with their feet flying . . . shewing their Garters and draws") who initially scandalized her with their near nakedness over time came to dazzle her with their grace and skill.

She also began to like the "wasp's" shape of French dresses, with their lack of trim and their emphasis on thick shoulders, and the novel structure of dinner parties, where general conversation was discouraged, and you spoke exclusively with the man assigned to sit by your side. The ease of the French manners grew on her. The volubility of Parisian women in public fed her own propensity to speak out. Still, so far her only new friend in France was an American.

IN JULY OF 1784, as he settled into a pretty house in a cul-de-sac near the opera on the Right Bank in Paris, Thomas Jefferson was eight years older than when he wrote the Declaration of Independence. At forty-one, his buoyant hair was less red than sandy. His tall, slim figure was a little fuller, and he was considerably more at ease. But he was still a slaveholder, still a Deist, he still valued passion over reason, Thomas Hutcheson over John Locke. Jefferson had spent the war years in Virginia, as a progressive legislator and then governor. That his most radical initiatives—to extend franchise and widen public education—were voted down frustrated, but did not discourage him; he remained committed to the ideal. He also remained by nature a homebody. But his adored wife had died in childbirth three years earlier. Monticello had become a painful reminder of her absence. So when Congress offered him this ministry in Paris, he leapt at the chance to escape.

Here he was, joined once again with his colleagues from the Declaration committee, at another critical moment in American history. The current crisis was in fact a direct outgrowth of independence. America was free, but poor. Riddled with debts, Congress had less than $400,000 at its disposal. A bill to impose duties on foreign products had been defeated; so at the moment, taxes were the major source of badly needed funds. But these taxes were collected by the states, who—strapped for money themselves—were loath to release them to the federal government. Some states like New Jersey outright refused. The Articles of Confederation, entitling Congress to act, were weak and, what's more, there were no national courts to enforce them. To empower Congress to compel tax payment at this point required a new law supported by all thirteen former colonies, a near impossibility in the post-war climate where the states, jealous of their autonomy, were competing among themselves.

So Congress was looking for salvation outside the country. Franklin, Adams, and Jefferson were on a mission to generate federal capital through foreign trade—specifically with England, but they were open to all deals. And it seemed a reasonable presumption that the world would cooperate. After all, America had much to offer.

But it soon became clear that America's abundance was as repellent to would-be investors as was its lack of a dependable federal government. Certainly the French, who'd allowed America's war to exhaust their treasury, were not eager to facilitate the new nation's trade at the expense of their own. England added resentment to protectionism and was going out of its way to thwart America wherever it could: providing arms for Indian tribes to attack settlers in the new western territories as well as stymieing the New England fish industry by placing trade restrictions on American imports in the Caribbean. Abigail described the British ministers as "very sour and bitter haughty and imperious," and also so petulant that, to punish their former colonists, they acted against the good of their own businessmen, who would profit from a rapprochement. Perhaps worst of all, the English Navy no longer shielded American vessels. So Boston merchants were now vulnerable to attack by Barbary pirates prowling the coast of southern Europe, which was traditionally a good market for American flour and wheat.

The British were in no rush to accommodate the urgency of the American ministers, who spent the fall in Passy waiting for England to set a date to talk. Jefferson therefore had plenty of time to observe his older colleagues. He had reason to be awed by their accomplishments. Franklin, now 78, had masterminded the French end of the Revolution. John, 49, had won the Dutch loan, which kept the Treasury afloat.

Yet, exile, Jefferson perceived, clearly had taken its toll on both of them. John now felt compelled to avoid city air and walked four miles every day in the Bois de Bologne to stave off the fevers he picked up in Holland, while Franklin had developed gout from all his decadent living in Paris and currently had a kidney stone so severe that he could no longer contemplate a carriage ride farther than the short distance from Passy to the Adamses' mansion in Auteuil. Their connection to the mood in America had also abraded. They could not comprehend why the ungrateful states were already bickering, or, knowing what they did about the French monarchy, share his own simple faith in the inevitable triumph of enlightened rule. Indeed, John's bleak view of human nature inclined him more toward Franklin's improvisations than Jefferson's calculated action.

Still, they all rose to the occasion of what, considering Franklin's age, was bound to be their last assignment together, as did Abigail in her indispensable role as John's counselor and spouse. And while Franklin's ill health gave John an excuse to cease inveighing against his unearned fame and moral turpitude, Abigail authentically reveled in the old man's charms. He was "vastly social and civil to me," Abigail reported. And she thought even better of Franklin for his yearning to go home to Philadelphia, though "I think whatever his inclination may be, his infirmities will prevent him."[51]

As for Jefferson, none of the Adamses could say enough of his character, wit, noble aspirations, or rhetorical brilliance. Nabby found him charming and "a Man of great Judgement." John called him "my worthy Friend" and the only man in France he could confide in "with perfect freedom and unreserve."[52] John, with Abigail at his side, was himself the happiest man in Europe, as he told *everyone*. And happiness made him so generous he was soon alluding to John Quincy, who became a Jefferson devotee on first meeting, as "our son," and standing by contentedly as the handsome young widower from Virginia flirted with his wife.[53]

Abigail met Jefferson five days after she moved to Auteuil when he drove up in his handcrafted phaeton to dine with them. Her first mention of him is in a September 5 letter to her sister, where she wryly commiserates with his sufferings at the whims of the Versailles Court. A Prussian prince had died, and Louis XVI was demanding eleven days of official grieving. Since "Fashion is the Deity every one worships in this country . . . Poor Mr. Jefferson had to hie away for a Tailor to get a whole black silk suit made up in two days, and at the end of Eleven days should an other death happen, he will be obliged to have a new Suit of mourning Cloth, because that is the Season when Silk must be cast off."[54]

The French obsession with fashion became a standing joke between Jefferson and Abigail, but Jefferson—with his townhouse and his phaeton—had vanities of his own. From the moment he crossed the Pont de Neuilly, he felt bound—as John and Abigail, with their Puritan roots, never could be—by a deep temperamental affinity to Paris. The bridges, the architecture, the salons, the theatres all gratified the particular nature of his intelligence and precisely fulfilled his aesthetic needs. An aristocrat himself, he was nowhere near as offended as Abigail by Paris's luxury nor was he blinded to its beauty by the filth piling up on the streets. *Nor* did he need to warm to the ease and irony of French manners: they were just his cup of tea. His love of equality drew him to the Palais Royale, formerly Cardinal Richelieu's private gardens, which the Duc d'Orleans had transformed into an extravaganza of cafes, shops, circus and art shows, brothels and gambling houses, and an arena for political debate, open to all classes. And while Jefferson could laugh with Abigail about the execrable state of French carriages, "I do love this *people,*" he told her, by which he meant everyone, rich and poor, except the deluded monarch and priests. "With a better religion and a better form of government," French life would be enviable, even for an American, he suggested.[55] And it was only half in jest that he began referring to the French as "we."

Exchanging impressions after the opera or wandering side-by-side past the Duke de Chartres's fine collection of Rafaels in the Palais Royale, Abigail could not help but catch Jefferson's enthusiasm.[56] She also nursed him when, as the weather turned colder, he became seriously ill, and she helped cheer his 12-year-old daughter, Polly, who had been plucked from her accustomed Protestant life in Monticello and placed in a French convent school. When Jefferson mourned the death of Polly's younger sister that January, Abigail was just the person to comfort him, while Jefferson was the first man since Lovell she felt inclined to establish an intimacy with on her own. Unlike Lovell, Jefferson had a spotless reputation. She took increasing pleasure in his company, she told him, and to Mary confided that he was "one of the choice ones of the earth."[57] [58]

AT THE END OF SEPTEMBER, 1784, when Mary came to bring four-year-old Betsy Q home to her mother in Haverhill, she found Elizabeth in bed "violently" sneezing and coughing and John Shaw in a panic because he had never seen his wife so sick. Maternal anguish had been the theme of the previous weeks. First, Betsy Q had collapsed with a high fever in Braintree. Then, no sooner had the Cranches nursed *her* back to health than Billy Shaw came home to the Shaw parsonage one afternoon, lay down, and three days later was still trying to raise his head.

"My dear Billy, my *only Son* . . . you cannot think how much I was dejected with his sickness," Elizabeth wrote Abigail. "My anxiety for my son prevented my sleep, and my spirits were so low, that I was on that account more exposed to the malignity of his Disorder." Even as Billy recovered, a cold storm blew in, and Elizabeth ignored the dampness seeping through the hinges and went on with her housekeeping: "It would have been better for me if I had kept my Room," she had to admit.[59]

So Elizabeth embraced the current wisdom that wet air bred illness, but adhered even more strongly to theories like Dr. William Buchan's that insisted on the impact of mood on disease. Mary's comforting presence, her goodness in taking two weeks from her own life to nurse Elizabeth until she was out of danger, were better than doctor's orders, this youngest sister believed. Indeed Mary's care felt like their mother's when they were children: a cure for all woes. "It seemed a good Providence sent her," Elizabeth wrote Abigail, expecting her sympathy.[60]

But Abigail, far from the scene, could only take alarm that the illness had happened in the first place. The years fell away, and she saw Elizabeth not as a 35-year-old wife and mother, but as a child with questionable values, careless of the perils of the world. As when she first suspected her younger sister of flirting, Abigail felt impelled to reprove her and, seeming to implore but in fact admonishing, tossed off a letter telling Elizabeth:

> "Let me beg of you, and if you will not hear, Let me desire Mr. Shaw to assert the authority of a *Husband* and forbid your ever touching *wet* cloaths, or Ironing, which is but a slow poison for you in your state of Health. You know my sister that . . . your constitution is hereditarily feeble.

And she went on to give orders about riding often and eating fruit and milk products, then rushed the letter off.[61]

Only afterward did it occur to Abigail to wonder at her tone and the current balance of power and indebtedness between herself and her younger sister. She gazed at the sketches of Charles and Tommy she'd hung in her bedroom and thought how much reliance on Elizabeth's stewardship of her absent children had contributed to her peace of mind these past months. "I thank you for your kind maternal care toward my sons," she wrote with true gratitude in a letter a few weeks later. And she came as close as she could to apologizing for all her former high-handedness, explaining:

In a Letter which I wrote you the latter part of December, I have given you a long lesson respecting Your Health: which altho it might savor something of the Quack, and a little of the Authority of Eldership, Spoke not my Heart, if it manifested not the tender solicitude of a Sister anxious for the Health of one deservedly Dear to her.[62]

And Elizabeth, bowing to no one when it came to large spiritedness, answered:

I thank you my Sister for your kind solicitude for my Health. Be assured I received it just as you intended, as an effusion of your Love, and Benevolence, and I never entertained even in Younger Life, an idea that *You* wished to assert the superiority of eldership. If at any time your counsel and Advice, ever opposed my Inclination, I always believed it to arise from the heighth of goodness, and from too great an Opinion of, and Love for me.[63]

Whatever her resolutions toward Elizabeth, Abigail had by no means lost the urge to rouse and enlighten. She informed Ben Franklin that he should save himself the pain of getting in and out of a carriage by purchasing a sedan chair and wrote Uncle Tufts reams of suggestions on the theme of furthering the Adamses' prospects at home. But the primary focus of her urge to exhort was her future son-in-law.

While traveling across the Atlantic, Abigail had picked up her campaign to inspire Tyler to be more like Nabby's father. "True greatness . . . must be Elevated by aspiring to great things and by dairing to think yourself capable of them," she rushed to inform him, as soon as she recovered from seasickness. "Reflection is a pole star which will point to truth," she added; and "Nothing makes a Man truly valuable but his Heart."[64]

Then, six months passed, and no word arrived in Auteuil from Mary's boarder in Braintree. Even with John Quincy's doting, and famous strangers like the Swedish ambassador extolling her charm and beauty, Nabby was sick at heart. When packets from the Cranches arrived carrying no letter from Tyler, Nabby "looked sad but said noth-ing," and even Abigail's confidence in his potential for improvement faltered at times.[65]

In December she broke down and wrote explicitly to Mary:

> The young gentleman who lives in your family I hope you will Guard and Guide advise and counsel . . . what a source of anxiety has it been to me!! . . . Remind him often of the expecta-tions of his Friends, remind him of what he hopes one day to be, tell him the Eyes of the World are more than ever fixed upon him.

Briefly, she toyed with the idea that Tyler might defy even Mary's and her own best efforts to reform him. "He stands not immoveable; if this should be necessary," she told her sister, then quickly dismissed the thought with "I hope it will not."

Mary, on the other hand, continued to see Tyler as beyond meliora-tion, and she was overjoyed to find him—on the rare day when he was not out ruining his sled or otherwise enjoying himself—sulking in her parlor after reading a letter from Nabby in France.

> He looked very cross [she wrote Abigail]. It was nothing but a scolding letter, he said. I told him I was very glad of it. Such an one was all he deserv'd and that had my cousin pos-sessed my spirit he would not have had [a letter at all] . . . Ask'd him whether after setting such an example of neglect and exer-ciseing the Power he knew he had to give Pain, He thought he ought to expect any more. He was nettled and I design'd he should be.[66]

To add to his delinquencies, Tyler began neglecting to deliver let-ters Nabby sent him to pass on to friends in the Boston area. He with-held one of three envelopes he was instructed to deliver to Mrs. Guild in April, while a letter for Miss Broomfield that arrived in his bag in the autumn did not reach her hands until spring. Nabby "must never wonder why She does not receive answers to her Letters," Mary ob-

Elizabeth assured Abigail that she suspected nothing
but sisterly concern in what others might interpret as bossing.

served as temperately as she could to Abigail. "She will receive Petitions from many of her Friends to have their Letters not incloss'd in Mr. T's Pacquit . . . [since] It is one of his whims not to deliver Letters for a long time after he has receiv'd them . . . You may read this to [Nabby] or not, as you think best."⁶⁷

Even Elizabeth was beginning to question her unbounded enthusiasm for Tyler; but, like Mary, she knew the danger of offending a future nephew. And more than anyone, she appreciated the discretion

> Love for me——— Let me assure you I have acted agreeable to your Injunctions, though I cannot say it was without Mr Shaws interposition, & have not Ironed or touched the wet Cloaths this Winter. I have been obliged to content myself by employing my Time in a way that would expose my Health less, & I hope as useful to my Family: As we have had twelve in it all Winter, I find there is sufficient sewing, & no occasion for my being idle. My Health this Spring is much as usual, I have no cough, but my Lungs are still weak.——— When I see how many hardships Others can endure I am almost tempted to repine at my own feeble Constitution, but that would be opposite to that Humility of heart, which makes happy— Gratitude for present Mercies, & cheipd Resignation to the dispensations of Providence in all time to come is a Temper of Mind I would wish devoutly to cultivate.———
>
> Your Children are still in fine Health they have been two Quarters to dancing School, & they both dance excellently, but Mr Charles exquisitely— you know what an Ear he has for Musick, & that has been of great advantage to him in his movements— He is graceful in all his motions, & attitudes, he, as if his Profile had been faithful to the maternal charge, has held up his head much better than formerly.— At the close of each Quarter the have had a Ball, in our new assembly

needed to alert Abigail of her protégé's faults without ruffling her pride. The Tyler she knew had been so solicitous, so tender, so susceptible to feelings (the very definition of a lover in Elizabeth's opinion). Even now he continued to write *her*; explained that only the rain prevented his visiting Haverhill; and took obvious care selecting gifts—a pocket case for Charles, "elegant" geographical cards for Thomas—to propitiate the Adams boys. Surely, there was some excuse for his odd behavior toward Nabby.

"It is not sufficient to hear only upon one side," she counseled, and reminded Mary that, as the eldest, she was the prime minister of the family: "You have my Sister a critical, delicate, part to act. You are at all times apprized of the necessity of Candour, and impartiality in our in-quires . . . Your own prudence, and goodness of heart, will direct you in the Path of Duty.—And I sincerely hope it will ultimately tend to the Peace, Satisfaction, and happiness of all."[68]

CHAPTER IX

"A joy in which our reason plays no part is but a sorrow."

· · ·

In March 1785, news reached France that North African pirates had captured an American trading ship in the Mediterranean, absconded with its cargo, and imprisoned its crew. No longer under the protection of Great Britain, America was forced to deal directly with Morocco, Algiers, Tunis, and Tripoli, who were in the habit of extorting fabulously expensive "presents" to guarantee foreign merchants safe passage through the Mediterranean Sea. They thought it reasonable to presume similar emoluments could be expected from Congress. Indeed, the Emperor of Morocco was soon offering "to enter into an alliance with America upon the same footing with other nations, which you know is with Cash in hand," Abigail reported to her cousin John Thaxter.[1] On March 19, the three American ministers met at Passy to consider how to respond.

John excepted, they made a sorry spectacle. Franklin, waiting impatiently for a Congressional release so he could go home to Philadelphia, was now almost totally incapacitated by his kidney stone. Jefferson, sick for the past six months with a cold that daily worsened, had suffered over every mile of the road from his Paris townhouse to Franklin's door. Once gathered, the ministers studied European precedents but could come to no consensus about an American initiative. Franklin, increasingly docile, was not the problem. Surprisingly—particularly for John, who had come to anticipate like-mindedness from his younger colleague—it was John and Jefferson who adamantly disagreed.

For while Adams perceived the piracy in practical terms as a challenge to American commerce, Jefferson read it as a moral evil and an affront to his lofty ideals. Submitting to blackmail was insupportable, in Jefferson's opinion. Instead, a navy should be raised to defend Americans' right to sail where they pleased. "1. Justice is in favor of this opinion," Jefferson argued his case to Adams. "2. Honor favors it. 3. It will procure us respect in Europe, and respect is a safeguard to interest."[2]

John, on the other hand, while equally attuned to the niceties of honor, found idealism a luxury America could ill afford in its current financial crisis. His closest adviser came to the same conclusion. Justice was a fine goal, in the Adamses opinion, but navies were prohibitively expensive, and, as Abigail pointed out with her usual frankness, since "England France and Holland treat and pay, would it not be folly and madnes in America"—still reeling from years of suffering for independence—"to Wage War?"[3]

For the moment, the issue remained at a standstill, as did most of the American ministers' work in Paris, to their growing chagrin. The only business they'd managed to effect in the past year was a treaty of commerce with Prussia. The French, the Dutch, and the Spanish all refused to make any concessions in favor of American trade. The previous November, the British, finally replying to America's numerous overtures, did at least agree to negotiate—but only in England. They proposed that a single American envoy be appointed and sent to London. Franklin, Adams, and Jefferson forwarded the offer to Philadelphia in December. In April, they continued to wait for Congress's reply.

Still, considering Franklin's health and Jefferson's lack of diplomatic experience, it was safe to presume that Adams would be selected for the new position, and Abigail began grappling with the inevitability that she would soon be leaving Auteuil. Now London, which she had vastly preferred just eight months earlier, seemed a poor replacement for Paris. She already missed walking with John in the Bois de Bologne and browsing with Jefferson in the Palais Royale—not to mention nightly excursions to plays and operas. While she continued to mock the French frenzy to theatricalize real life, she could not pass up the spectacle of the King appearing in church to wash a dozen poor boys' feet during Lent season. Nor could she resist joining the crush of showy carriages inching toward Longchamps in the traditional three-day parade during Easter week.

Meanwhile, the Parisian *lack* of show in dress was now her preferred style. She bought simple French satin petticoats for her nieces and lamented that, in gaudy England, she and Nabby would have to pack away their new trimless gowns. Also, "The exchange of climate must be for the worse," she wrote her Uncle Tufts (who was still shivering in Weymouth in April).[4] For as the nightingales sang and the sun shone and the days grew longer, she was under the enchantment of the spot where God's mysterious will had placed her. Who could improve on Paris in spring?

And who in England would fill the place of Madame de Lafayette, who had embraced her like a friend on their first meeting and now—unlike so many "Great Folks" Abigail would be happy to leave behind her—was truly a friend in the deepest sense? She could almost be an American, Abigail explained to Mary. For, contrary to the European norm, she was "exceedingly fond of her Children and attentive to their education," and moreover "passionately attached to her Husband!!! A French Lady and fond of her Husband!!!"[5] Abigail needed six exclamation points to express the rarity of such a soul.

For John, with his delicate health and love of nature, it was the geography itself he would most regret leaving. He sounds almost as if he is speaking of Braintree when he writes Richard Cranch: "I shall find no where so fine a little Hill, so pleasant a Garden, so noble a Forest and such pure Air and tranquil walks as at Auteuil."[6]

On April 27, Jefferson rushed from Paris to inform the Adamses that Congress had appointed a former denizen of George III's most-wanted enemies list—John Adams—the first official American envoy to England. Franklin was released to go home if he was physically able, and Jefferson was unanimously elected the new minister to France. (Asked by Vergennes, "Is it you, Sir, who replaces Dr. Franklin," Jefferson famously replied, "No one can replace him, Sir; I am only his successor.")

At this point good-byes had to be said in earnest. In Nabby's diary entry describing a wistful parting scene with Madame Helvetius, even the scrappy dog who peed at Franklin's and the widow's eccentric glass-encased memorial to her husband are portrayed as hard to leave. Nabby is no longer shocked to be received by a 60-year-old woman spread out under bedclothes and surrounded by canines on a settee. Rather, she notes, with only praise intended, "Madame Helvetius was . . . quite at her ease."[7]

Jefferson, of course, was even harder to part with. "I shall regret the loss of Mr. Jefferson's society," Abigail understatedly observes in a letter to her uncle.[8] And, writing Mary, she rejoices at squeezing four evenings with this "choice one" into a final week in France.

But the saddest change of all had nothing to do with the move to London. Months before, it had been decided that 18-year-old John Quincy must end his long European education and prepare to attend Harvard with his brothers and cousin at home. It was his preference, and his parents completely approved it. Still, "I dare not trust myself with thinking upon the subject," Abigail told her older sister, and she begged Mary to take care of John Quincy as she would of Mary's Billy (who was reportedly flourishing at college) if tables were reversed.[9] [10]

John was to lose a secretary, Abigail a translator, Nabby one of the few people in the world she cared for intensely and with whom she was neither silent nor, as Madame de Lafayette described her, "grave."[11] Thrown together with no other friends of their age during the past ten months in Paris, they had grown almost as inseparable as lovers. Both felt marked by coming of age in Europe. And while shopping at a magnificent milliners or watching the King celebrate the birth of his son with no holds barred, they experienced the same mixture of fascination and outrage at life in a monarchy, always contrasting the reign of Louis XVI to their hopes for democracy at home. John Quincy told his cousin Billy that Nabby was everything a boy could want in a sister, and contemplating life in London without this brother, Nabby lamented, "I would walk, [but] my Brother is gone. I would ride, [but] my Brother is gone. I would retire to my chamber. Alas, I meet him not there. I would meet him in his appartment—but—where is it? I would set to my work, and he would read to me—but, alas, this is Passed." They vowed to sustain their closeness by writing minutely of their separate experiences, and Abigail too looked forward to sustaining her flourishing relationship with John Quincy through letters, though it would not make up for their intimate discussions in Auteuil.

Abigail would particularly miss consulting with her son about Nabby. Still wary of prejudicing John against Tyler, she had made John Quincy her only confidant on his sister's romantic affairs. That Nabby's ardor continued as strong as ever, both agreed, spoke for the advantage of a speedy marriage, but, on the other hand, Tyler's negligence about writing—compounded by the poor part he played in the incidents regularly reported by Mary—made an equally good case for breaking off the engagement.[12] Neither Abigail nor John Quincy could come to a decisive conclusion, but they agreed to act with caution. Recently, Uncle Tufts too seemed to argue against haste when he warned Abigail not to send Nabby home prematurely. And Abigail in turn confessed to her uncle that while any sensible person worried about the choice of a life's partner, "I have had more fears and more anxieties for [Nabby] than ever I felt for myself."[13]

On May 12, John Quincy left Auteuil for Lorient and a French packet ship to America. "I [have] lost all the companion I had,"[14] Nabby wailed to her cousin Lucy, and John Quincy was soon writing his sister, "You would think I carry sentiment too far, and that I am weak . . . [but] a tear involuntarily started from my Eye," when her first letter reached him the day before he sailed.[15]

That same day, May 20, the rest of the Adamses prepared to set off for the English Channel. As they entered their carriage, Abigail's pet bird began madly fluttering, and seeing that the French bird might die if she persisted in her plan to transport it to London, she handed it back to a servant and, grieving its loss, drove off.[16] Two days before, Abigail had made her last trip to Paris, that avatar of all her French experiences. "I took my leave of it," she remembered that evening, "but without tears. Yet the thought that I might never visit it again gave me some pain, for it is as we say a dieing leave when we quit a place with that Idea."[17]

WHILE NABBY ADAMS WAS OFF in Paris longing for letters from Royall Tyler, Betsy Cranch sat in her old room in Braintree, waiting for

*"Could I once acquire that perfect equality of temper which no possible
event could disturb I might be truly happy,"* Betsy Cranch believed.

the man *she* loved to come home. Like her mother two decades earlier,
Betsy had fallen in love with her tutor: Thomas Perkins. Born in

Bridgewater, Perkins graduated from Harvard three years after the Declaration of Independence was issued and then came to board and teach at the Cranches, where he soon was inseparable from their eldest girl. Everyone admired him. Perkins had all Betsy's father's virtues: intelligence, compassion, a deep capacity for feeling. He was also as penniless as Richard Cranch had been two decades earlier when he arrived at the Weymouth parsonage and began wooing prosperous Mary Smith. Betsy had watched her parents' happy marriage strained by financial hardship, and she made clear to the man who loved her that she would not suffer need.

So as the Revolution drew to a close, in 1783 Perkins completed a course of law under Royall Tyler. The following year, as the economy began collapsing in New England, he accepted a loan from Betsy's father and set out for the west.

The west, for Perkins's post-war generation, symbolized everything from the end of the rainbow to a last resort. Its vastness was double-edged, for chaos as well as freedom thrives on opportunity. The west gave America the advantage over Europe, as Cousin John Thaxter shrewdly observed in a letter to Abigail, "When a Nation has reduced to Cultivation the last Inch of its Soil, it has passed the Zenith of its Virtue. I contemplate with pleasure the vast Extent of our back Territory, and view it not only as a Mine of Wealth but a future Nursery of hardy and virtuous Citizens."[18]

But it also exposed the hypocrisy of America's claim to respect private property and mocked its championing the equality of man. For what was wilderness to the white man was, of course, Indian territory. And Indians were wreaking vengeance by assaulting the settlers—who were so far mostly squatters and speculators, "nearly related to an Indian in [their] manners," warned one wary Congressional delegate[19] and often with British help.[20] So Betsy, who thrilled at Abigail's descriptions of gardens and clothes in Paris, got no such pleasure imagining the long, treacherous journey to Kentucky. Still, it was here that Congress was selling land for as little as $1 an acre and miles of contested property were opening doors for lawyers willing or eager to take risks. Without encouraging him, or promising to marry Perkins even if he came back wealthy, Betsy managed to convey that she approved of his move.

Elizabeth Shaw speculated about Perkins's departure: "Mr. Perkins you say is gone to Kentucky determined if possible to procure a Fortune," she wrote Mary. "If he should succeed I suppose he will depend upon that to supply him" with the courage to propose. She imagined the lovelorn boy, pining for Betsy in the wilderness as she conjured it in her romantic mind and prose:

> The Woods—the Rocks, the hollow mountains will all resound with the plaintive Notes of this heart—less Swain— There he will sit lost in the heart-thrilling meditation, while his spirit is borne away up Love's swift wings, and embraces the amiable object of his tender Regard—[21]

Mary, on the other hand, assured Abigail that Betsy's relationship with Perkins was merely a close friendship. She was the most popular girl in Braintree and free to fall in and out of love as she pleased.

Then, a fall and a winter passed, and there was no word from Perkins. With her keen sensibility and imagination for disaster, Betsy saw her lover eviscerated by Cherokees or stampeded by buffalos or seized by some baneful disease. Her attachment grew, and she blamed herself for Perkins leaving in the first place. Throwing caution to the wind, she now made a private vow to marry him—that is, in the unlikely case that he lived.

And he did, though it was a year before a letter announcing his safe arrival in Danville, Kentucky, reached Braintree.[22] What an adventure it had been! "A man must be insensible not to be charmed with the beauties of the Blue Ridge Mountains," Perkins began a rollicking account of the early stages of his trip. "The murmuring . . . streams, the variety of fowls and birds, the prodigious herds of cattle and horses which graze on this mountain, the different kinds of wild [trout] with which it abounds . . . almost made me imagine myself on enchanted ground." The wagonloads of people he passed "seemed absolutely infatuated by something like the old crusading spirit," as if they were headed toward Jerusalem. Some days he rode long distances quickly; others, his horse was buried up to the knees in mud from rain storms, "the rugged ascents and descents . . . seemed absolutely impassibe," and it was "hard work to go a mile in an hour."

When he crossed to the west side of the Allegheny Mountains, syca-
more, cherry, and oak trees rose to greet him. Meanwhile, he still had
195 desolate miles to slog through. The paths, he was told, were ragged,
and Indians had devastated several parties of adventurers who failed to
take proper precautions the summer before. Proper precautions meant
traveling with a large group of companions. Still, Perkins, impatient to
be moving, rode into the wilderness alone one Sunday at dawn and
continued without seeing a soul until sunset. Then "some little apprehension of danger from the Indians, the loneliness of my situation, the
howling of wolves and croaking of ravens on every side, made me feel
some what gloomy," Perkins wrote Betsy. A quarter of a mile off the
road, he tied his horse to a tree, dragged his heavy saddle and measly
bag of corn to the side of a steep rock, where he covered himself in a
blanket and, with a pistol in each hand pointing out at the labile darkness, prepared to sit guard all night.

Life became easier the following day, when he caught up with a
party of five hundred. But progress remained slow (approximately ten
miles a day) and the weather treacherous. "I believe no company ever
had so disagreeable a time of it through the wilderness. Out of 22 days
we had only 4 in which it did not rain and thunder most excessively."
Moreover, a measles epidemic struck the group, and scalped heads
blotted Perkins's path right up to his triumphant arrival at the first
Kentucky settlement, where, he was happy to report, the soil was pre-
ternaturally fertile, the climate far better than Boston's, and his prospects good. He was currently riding 250 miles each month to capitalize
on all available business.

The relief Betsy felt at Perkins's safety confirmed her love and determination to marry him and, for a while at least, satisfied her need to
look forward to better times. But she was 22 years old, and her mind
flew to more dramatic scenes than a distant reunion with a provident
Kentucky lawyer. She had a passion for philosophical books, which
urged readers to solve the riddle of life, like Rousseau's *Candide* or John
Bunyon's *Pilgrim's Progress.* Her Puritan faith also cried out to be tested,
while sensibility, the dominant literary mode of the late eighteenth century, spurred her quick feelings and lofty ideas. How Betsy wished she
could live inside a novel by Samuel Richardson—whether *Pamela* with
its portrait of righteousness rewarded or *Clarissa* with its tale of virtue

doomed. She had more to say to Richardson's rogues than to any of her neighbors in Braintree. Indeed, the villainy of *Clarissa*'s Lovelace felt more real to her than the Battle of Boston, and, where Perkins's lonely trails and croaking ravens merely frightened her, the splendid backgrounds of Richardson's ravishments demanded to be seen. Loving Perkins did not stop Betsy from wanting to travel. In one of her many pipedreams she imagined herself trailing the ideal Charles Grandison through the British countryside. "My desire to see England is as ardent as ever. I think encreasing," she reported to Abigail. "I am a good mind to run aboard a ship, and say nothing about it to any body. Would you receive such a vagrant?"[23]

While Europe was out of the question, there were other alternatives to wasting away in Braintree. Betsy's father scrimped together the money to buy her a secondhand harpsichord and—when her restlessness persisted—proposed a trip to Boston where she could study her beloved music with an exclusive master during the summer months. Arrangements were swiftly made for Betsy to board with Richard and—while he was busy at the state Court and Legislature—practice Bach and Haydn and socialize with family and friends. She also determined to keep a diary. Here she could exhort herself to struggle to improve while accepting the lot God determined for her, and, like a novelist, describe all her physical sensations and analyze her joys and fears.

With her hopes revived on April 25, as the Adamses were preparing to leave Paris for London, Betsy wrote in the mode of a Richardson heroine about her own travel plans to her aunt. "I shall be quite a rustick Lass among the polished Belles of Boston, I intend however to be happy," she professed, and went on to anticipate early-morning walks past Faneuil Hall and through the Boston Common as well as reading Racine and Moliere to improve her French. She had strong feelings about the importance of transforming her surroundings. "I believe it will be good for me to change this scene, which has been so continually before me; not that the present is unpleasing, for I do not expect to find an equal proportion of pleasure any where else; but because the mind is apt to contract; to be biggoted to certain forms and opinions by being always confined to a certain spot, to a particular set of acquaintance."[24]

From her mother's view, broadening Betsy's social circle was the best reason of all for this visit. Her eldest daughter at 22 was still in search of a husband, as far as Mary and Richard knew.

But then, Betsy was "rather feeble this warm weather," Mary reported to Abigail when she dropped her eldest daughter in Boston, and went on to worry: "How this town will suit her I know not. Musick may Possibly amuse, it does not often Serve as a brace." And while in early July Mary declared the visit a triumph—"Betsy is very attentive to her Harpsicord and . . . in better health than I have known her for many years,"—when the "dog days" arrived, Betsy collapsed and had to go home to convalesce in Braintree. Here she was all too soon cleaning out Aunt Abigail's cedar chest and making Lucy a bonnet.[25] Then, just as she was resigning herself to another long selfless fall of helping her overburdened mother, a new opportunity arose.

This time the chance to escape came in the form of an invitation to spend October and November with Peggy White, the child of Aunt Elizabeth's good friends in Haverhill. Peggy was Betsy's age and, as her father was a prominent Haverhill businessman, a desirable connection. The previous year Peggy had been seized by a crippling depression. "The sight of this dear Girl affected me greatly," Mary Cranch had written Abigail during that period, and described beautiful Peggy "seting upon a couch, dress'd in a Queens nightcap with a white ribbon bound round her head and a white long loose Gown on, her Hands cross'd before her, and her Eyes fix'd upon the Flour."[26] This terrible illness ran in the family. Peggy's uncle had killed himself in a similar state. Peggy, however, was now fully recovered: chubby, high-spirited, and eager for Betsy to stay two months and study music with her on the family's new pianoforte. They would share the price of lessons, which anyway were only a shilling a piece.

So on October 10, Betsy took off for the Whites' enormous three-story house on elegant Water Street, just east of the Shaw parsonage. She arrived to a scene of gracious living, complete with spacious rooms, a river view, a staircase all the neighbors envied, exquisite furniture, and gardens everywhere you looked. She had her own room and, with servants to spare, no more duties than Nabby in Paris. Rather than cleaning her own house or checking on Abigail's, Betsy now spent mornings reading history and afternoons making lace. The Whites treated Betsy as part of the family, and a lively social life quickly ensued. Walks by the river, teas, and fortune-telling parties became common occurrences. Music lessons proceeded as scheduled, Peggy was in no time "my darling Peggy," and the Whites' household was always full.

Among the most frequent guests was Betsy's cousin John Quincy, who had arrived home looking the epitome of a foreign gentleman and now was following in his younger brothers' footsteps and preparing for Harvard exams at their aunt's. Meeting for the first time since childhood, the cousins took to each other immediately. Betsy, John Quincy teased Nabby, almost "supplies your place as a sister."[27] He praised her sweetness, vivacity, and exalted taste in reading, while Betsy was struck by his antic sense of humor and the resemblance to both his parents, especially her beloved aunt.[28]

Besides Peggy and John Quincy, Betsy's intimate circle consisted of Peggy's easygoing brother, Lenny; Peggy's wealthy admirer, Bailey Bartlett; the Shaw's female boarder, Nancy Hazen; and Betsy's first cousin once removed John Thaxter, who had tutored all the Cranches and Adamses when they were children and now was a rising lawyer in Haverhill.

John Thaxter was in many respects the opposite of Thomas Perkins. Where Perkins's manner was sincere, Thaxter's was ironic. Where Perkins was blunt and unassuming, Thaxter was polished and self-assured. As the grandson of a Quincy, he had many connections to smooth his way in the world. Short, small-boned, and physically delicate, John Thaxter could never have crossed the Alleghenies. But he loved to speculate about the place of the west in America's future. He had been John Adams's law clerk in Braintree at the start of the Revolution and his secretary in France and Holland at the end. It was he who in 1783 carried the peace treaty across the Atlantic to Congress. He was eight years older than Betsy, a great favorite with both her parents, and one of the few men to whom her aunt Abigail wrote about both political and intimate news.

He was also a charmer. In their early teens, Nabby and Betsy were both a little in love with him, and even Abigail teasingly forbade him to prefer any woman but his future wife to herself: to which remark he replied with feigned horror, "Wife. The idea makes me shudder."[29] During Thaxter's years in Paris, Betsy remembered, he and Abigail had a standing joke about his supposed passion for an American girl he refused to identify. "An abundance of Love to all the young Ladies of my Acquaintance, and particularly to my fair American, if it is yet discovered who she is," he ended one letter; and Abigail got it into her head that "fair American" was one of the myriad Betsyes and Elizas they knew in the Boston area and wheedled and threatened, but couldn't get him to acknowledge even this.[30] In 1785, Thaxter was still assuring Abigail he was a confirmed bachelor and "at a great remove from Matrimony" while everyone in Haverhill took it for granted that he would soon propose to Peggy White's cousin Betsy Duncan, the prettiest girl in town.[31]

And, with her strong intellect, education, and good spirits, beauty was the least of Betsy Duncan's assets, according to John Quincy, who did not praise easily. He was "monstrously severe" on female follies, Betsy Cranch reported in her diary, and considered falling in love the "greatest misfortune that can befall a young man," as he acknowledged in his. John Quincy frequently found himself in this unlucky position, he confessed to his cousin, and though he'd vowed not to marry for another decade, she watched him fighting off a violent passion for the Shaw's female boarder, Nancy Hazen, who clearly enjoyed perturbing his cool veneer.

It seemed romance was in the Haverhill air this autumn. Many nights Betsy and Peggy sat by a window, watching the moon rise over the terraced lawns sloping to the Merrimack River and imagined joyful futures where Thomas Perkins made a great success and rode safely home from Kentucky and Bailey Bartlett proposed. Other times they listened to the adults lament the threat of poverty hanging over Haverhill now that the British had cut off their trade with the West Indies. And then there were the talks of inner conflicts, which interested Betsy most. Once she and Lenny White went off by themselves and had "quite a sentimental con[versation]" which she later reported in her diary: "We talkd of happiness—in what it consisted—from what sources most generally derived . . . all we should aim at—or suffer ourselves to expect in this world."[32]

———

As the discussion continued, Betsy went a step further and argued that the mind was self-sufficient and could create its own contentment, while Lenny, like Nabby Adams, suspected happiness largely depended on luck.

All was not peaceful abstract talk at the White's house, however. Among the adult denizens at Water Street were the merchant James Duncan and Mrs. White's sister, his second wife. A few months before, this Mrs. Duncan had succumbed to the family curse of depression, and Peggy's mother, worried that she was suicidal, made a pact with Mr. Duncan that some member of the family would always keep her in sight. Lately, Betsy could see, delirium had compounded Mrs. Duncan's miseries.

So this poor distracted woman was a constant source of worry, whereas social tension surrounded another favorite guest at the Whites' house, the town's charismatic Baptist preacher, Hezekiah Smith. The Baptist faith was as a rule a working-class religion, but it was now a generally accepted fact that Betsy's uncle John Shaw was a rigid and uninspiring preacher; and Smith was capitalizing on Shaw's oratory weakness to lure more and more wealthy First Congregationalists to his far more dynamic church. The Whites were among these defectors, which, Betsy could not help noticing, complicated their long friendship with her silently suffering aunt.

And, as on the Kentucky trail, disaster could strike at a moment's notice. At the end of October the worst rainstorm in forty years hit Haverhill. Hundreds of uprooted trees crashed down the river, which swelled to the highest point in memory and drowned two men, besides deluging cellars and sluicing the lower streets. More terrifying still was the internal devastation Betsy witnessed two weeks later when, returning from an afternoon tea party, she found Mrs. Duncan ranting in the Whites' great room.

It was hours before Mrs. Duncan was calm enough to walk up the hill to her own house with her husband. Then when he left her alone in her room for a moment, she fled. By now it was completely dark, and drizzle was falling. Mr. Duncan hurried back to the Whites' house, hoping to find his wife with her sister: to no avail. All night long the citizens of

Haverhill marched through blinding rain, scouring wells and barns, chasing down soggy streets, clamoring back and forth over the narrow wooden bridge that straddled the Merrimack. Betsy Cranch swallowed her fears, and, to appease Mrs. White, who still hoped her sister might be hiding on the premises climbed up to the garret and flashed her candle in the creaking closets and down the ghostly halls. At dawn, Mrs. Duncan was found, dead, off a wharf in the river. John Quincy marveled that she had drowned in just two feet of water. Mrs. White and Peggy, emotionally frail under the best of circumstances, were frantic with grief.

On the surface, Betsy Cranch remained composed, reserving her bleak conclusions for her diary, where she wrote in her careful script:

> The ways of providence are dark and intricate—impenetrable
> to the most refined human understanding—how weak! how
> transcient! How futle! are the schemes of Mortals![33]

Mrs. Duncan was eulogized by Hezekiah Smith and buried on Friday, November 11. John Thaxter's beloved Betsy Duncan was Mrs. Duncan's stepdaughter. Thaxter confirmed his intention to marry her by sitting with the family in the Baptist Church.

The overwrought Whites opened their hearts to Betsy Cranch and insisted she extend her visit. ("Peggy would not let [Betsy] stir from her side," Mary Cranch reported to Abigail; so, though "I know not how to spare her [myself] . . . I cannot take her away," and she consented to a longer stay.[34]) Then, when Peggy recovered more quickly than anyone expected, the two girls slowly resumed their old routines. Meanwhile, Betsy Duncan had to seclude herself in mourning, and John Thaxter was forced to cease his courtship for the time being.

Now, like the Whites, Thaxter turned to Betsy Cranch for comfort. And how she enjoyed commiserating with him over their absent loves! Once they spent an entire evening contemplating "past . . . pleasures . . . which time cannot wholly deprive us of."[35] Another time Betsy was surprised to find herself in "remarkable good spirits" after the two had a lively chat.[36] And watching Thaxter read a letter about a childhood friend's death, Betsy rejoiced to observe a "tear . . . filld his eye and for a moment overc[a]me manly Fortitude—this is not the weakness of human nature—it is its glory," she declared.[37]

On December 1, the river froze, and the young people rushed to go sledding. As Christmas approached, one lively event followed another, and Betsy convinced her mother to allow her to stay until spring. Though her mood fell briefly after she read about Indian raids in the western counties, Betsy was increasingly content to presume Thomas Perkins was well and happy and to love him from afar. Even at this remove, she reminded herself, he was crucial to her present happiness, for "*Hope* keeps the mind active—some favourite object in pursuit is always to be wished for—perhaps every one does not think so but let them examine their own Hearts critically and I believe they will find it true."[38]

THE NEW ENGLAND SOCIAL SEASON began after New Year's, and the first young people's assembly in Haverhill was set for January 17. Betsy Cranch was one of just sixteen young men and women formally invited to the party. Couples for most of the evening were decided through lots, so you were free only for the few voluntary dances. The Friday before the assembly, Betsy Cranch matter-of-factly noted in her diary that John Thaxter had asked her for all of these.

The day of the affair too, Betsy was determined to stanch her excitement, writing only that her mood was "low" in the morning and that she was "far from pleasd" at the prospect of attending the ball without Peggy: who was staying home out of respect for her aunt. She mocked "the important business of dressing for the Assembly," which entailed pulling a linen shift over her head and affixing bone stays to mold her torso into a cone shape; and disdained even to mention the color of her pleated gown or the design for the triangle called a "stomacher" inserted in the opening around her waist. Nor did she note that—thanks to Abigail—she was the only girl in town with a hand-quilted pink petticoat fresh from the Palais Royale in Paris. Betsy's reports of the dance itself were also uncharacteristically laconic: there was no enthusing over minuets or moonlight, only a brief mention that Bailey Bartlett escorted her into the "excesively cold" ballroom, that she was "pleasd" to draw one of the three Osgood boys as her partner, and had "the honor of Mr. Thaxters hand" at the free dances *because,* she felt impelled to remind herself, Betsy Duncan was not there.

And then, directly after alluding to Thaxter, she suddenly let down her guard and enthused: "The evening . . . was the most agreable of any one I ever spent in publick company." She came home at one and didn't even try to sleep until 3 A.M. Clearly, Thomas Perkins was not the only man on her mind.

More hints that Betsy and Thaxter were falling in love soon followed. "I had a few words in private with [Thaxter]," Betsy wrote meaningfully in her diary the following Friday. After that, rarely a day passed without her noting that they'd met up at the Shaws' or the Whites' or one of the two Protestant meetings. Thaxter cut a romantic figure, for he had lived abroad and worked in government, and Betsy Cranch, his former star pupil, was at the height of her beauty and the most contemplative girl in town. Reading between the lines of Betsy's veiled diary entries, the attraction between them is palpable. At the second assembly, on January 31, Thaxter again chose Betsy for the voluntary dances. The next morning, he hurried to call on her at the Whites' house before heading off to work.

On the fifth of February, Betsy left the Whites' to spend her final weeks in Haverhill with John Quincy at Aunt Elizabeth's. Here her life was more rigorously scrutinized, and she was frequently chastised for staying out late. The issue reached a climax when Elizabeth, pleading her responsibilities as a minister's wife, threatened to send Betsy home for missing curfew. And while John Quincy chafed at the household's austerity ("The family I am in presents as perfect a scene of happiness, as I ever saw: but it is entirely owing to the disposition of the persons," he wrote in his diary. "A life of Tranquility is to them a life of bliss . . . [whereas] Variety is my theme, and Life to me is like a journey, in which an unbounded plain, looks dull and insipid."),[39] Betsy accepted the reproof uncomplainingly, for an unmarried girl was not in a position to question rules.

Living at her aunt's, Betsy was in any case grateful to be able to see Thaxter almost daily, sometimes with no one else present, as on Saturday night, February 11, when "Mr. T . . . sat in the study with me half an hour and had some conversation about some subject interesting to ourselves." But she was also rereading Thomas Perkins's letters from Kentucky. Behind all his enthusing about soil and climate lay the undeniable fact that he was a book lover making due with a miniscule library and a social creature enjoying few civilities in a wilderness full of savages—all for the love of her. And, unlike Thaxter, who three months before was on the verge of proposing to Betsy Duncan, he loved *only* her.

Still, Perkins was far away and could not, like John Thaxter, call her name up the parsonage stairs first thing on a Saturday morning, or sit beside her on a sleigh skidding down the Merrimac, or share her anguish over loving two people at once. If only she could have talked to the fictional Charles Grandison, who shared her dilemma! "P[egg]y and myself had some very interesting conversation and she inform'd me of one circumstance which confirmed me in certain resolutions that I had before made which were necessary to my peace of mind," Betsy stammered evasively to her diary. She was building up a case for ending the infatuation. Yet, "Ah who shall pretend to fathom the deep recesses of the human heart?" she sighed, and added what in anyone else would seem bitterness: "'Know then thyself'—uncommon knowledge indeed."[40]

The month before Betsy Cranch was scheduled to leave Haverhill, her mood fluctuated radically, and her journal took on the overwrought tone of Rousseau's *La Nouvelle Héloïse,* which she had recently read. Like Rousseau's heroine, Julie, she felt torn between two very different men in her life. Thinking about Thaxter made her feel guilty toward Perkins, which led to dark musings; so on Tuesday, February 24, she is certainly discussing more than the landscape when she laments: "there is such a sameness in the fact of the Country at this season that it admits no description." Two days afterward, Aunt Elizabeth, hoping to give her niece some perspective on her troubles, took out her own old journals. Elizabeth's "youthful . . . effusions" immediately struck a chord with Betsy, who vowed also to study her aunt's self-control. "May I be aided to transplant all her virtues into my own heart and life," she implored God. On March 13, however, Betsy reported:

> Mr. Txr came and spent half an hour with me—quite sociably—we talked of *one* subject that affected me much and in consequence of it I slept very little that night. O! how frail is human nature.[41]

Then she woke up resolved to follow her conscience. That evening when all her friends drove off to the Haverhill assembly, she overcame the temptation to dance even one more time with Thaxter and stayed home. "If I lose some enjoyment—I may also escape some regret that my enjoyment might occasion," she lectured herself; moreover, "'A joy in which our *reason* bears no part is but a sorrow.'"[42] Nonetheless, on a rainy afternoon two days later she was still endeavoring "to recover my usual . . . sprightliness." The following afternoon, watching the sun set from the Shaw's west window, she "felt a kind of wild sadness" and burst into tears.

But she would not accept defeat and willed herself to recover. Soon she was reporting in her diary: "My slumbers were those of a heart at ease." It was foolish, after all, to die like Rousseau's Julie for the unattainable. Better accept *Candide*'s message and make the best of the world as it is. Besides, Betsy would always have memories of Thaxter and Haverhill. "The recollection of the past winter shall serve as my pleasure and amusement when secluded among the Shades of sweet retirement," she consoled herself on the eve of returning to her parents.[43] In her mind's eye she saw Perkins, his pilgrimage fulfilled, riding home from Kentucky. She steeled herself to follow the path of all the good women before her and entrust her happiness to him.

THE ADAMSES' JOURNEY AWAY from Paris was grimmer even than their entrance ten months earlier. Now a cold drought as well as poverty disfigured rural France. "The country is an heap of Ashes. Grass is scarcely to be seen and all sorts of Grain is short thin, pale and feeble while the Flax is quite dead . . . Sheep and herds of cattle . . . stalk about the Fields like Droves of walking Skeletons," John wrote Thomas Jefferson from a carriage stop on the road to the English Channel. And while he assured Jefferson that he pitied the French their famine, he also leapt on it as fresh proof that the Old World needed the fruits of America's more diverse climate and resilient soil. After a year of frustrated attempts, John was gearing up once more to promote American trade to England: perhaps "these rainless, heatless Heavens" would serve his cause.[44]

Also on the road to Calais, the Adamses were reading a parting present from Thomas Jefferson: his new, privately published *Notes on the State of Virginia*. It was a long book, packed with revealing opinions as well as vivid depictions of climate and fauna, acute remarks on the state's scientific wonders, and reams of historical facts. Jefferson's enthusing about the fertile and mineral-rich land west of the Alleghenies mirrored Thomas Perkins's observations in letters home from Kentucky, but where Perkins reinforced the stereotype of American Indians as mere savage predators, Jefferson—in keeping with his enlightened political philosophy—eloquently defended the red man as exactly the same as if not superior to the white, writing:

> [The Indian is] brave, when an enterprise depends on bravery . . . endures tortures with a firmness unknown almost to religious enthusiasm with us . . . is affectionate to his children . . . his friendships are strong and faithful to the uttermost extremity . . . his sensibility is keen . . . his vivacity and activity of mind is equal to ours.[45]

What a contrast then were his remarks later in the same book on the black man, whom he vehemently disparaged as vastly inferior to Caucasians in reason ("one could scarcely be found capable of tracing and comprehending the investigations of Euclid"), imagination ("Among the blacks is misery enough, but no poetry"), and even smell (the odors from slaves' apartments "are enough to breed the Plague if they do not suffocate you on the spot") and looks ("Are not the fine mixtures of red, the expressions of every passion by greater or less suffusions of colour in the one, preferable to that eternal monotony . . . that immoveable veil of black which covers the emotions of the other race?"). Indeed, on the basis of appearance alone, Jefferson questioned the black man's right to reproduce at the same rate as Europeans, arguing "The circumstance of superior beauty, is thought worthy attention in the propagation of our horses, dogs, and other domestic animals; why not in that of man?" His solution to slavery was (sometime in the vague future) to send all black men back to Africa. The idea of two free races co-existing in a democratic America was unthinkable in Jefferson's view.[46]

From the early days of the Revolution, Abigail had condemned slavery, declaring: "It allways appeard a most iniquitious Scheme to me—fight ourselfs for what we are daily robbing and plundering from those who have as good a right to freedom as we have." Now it was on the subject of slavery that she experienced a first irreconcilable difference with the Virginian she on so many other counts revered. And while John warmly praised his colleague's production—even enthusing, "The Passages upon slavery, are wort Diamonds"—Abigail, in her lengthy correspondence with Jefferson from London, implied her disapproval by never acknowledging the book.[47]

There was in any case much else to report from London, which was far more various than Abigail had noticed on her first visit. For while it was the wealthiest city in the world, full of thrilling mansions, imposing squares, and magnificent dress shops, it was also home to the middling farmers of Epping, the flashy actors and whores of Drury Lane and Covent Garden, the busy publishers of St. Paul's Courtyard, the staunch nonconformists of Newington Green, the hacks of Grub Street, and the hapless immigrants weaving frippery for the beau monde in squalid Spitalfields. The poor, though better-hidden, were even more prevalent than in France.

In terms of production, England was decades ahead of France, having created the original central waterwheel and rotary steam engine. Its first factory was a 1719 silk mill. Cotton and metal works swiftly followed. Copper was wrung from the Cornish countryside, coal from Yorkshire and Wales. By mid-century, agriculture was taking a backseat to industry and commerce. British entrepreneurs grew rich as lords and began exerting their influence on culture as well as the class system. Currently, for instance, a major concert of Handel's *Messiah* was being mounted with private funds alone. Yet, while the new rich basked in their heightened powers, they took the example of their domestic King and spurned decadence. "Moderation" was their watchword, and they embraced George III's code of home and hearth.

As in America, women bore the burden of upholding morality and, the rare Catherine Macaulay excepted, eschewed intellectual pursuits. An "angel in the house" was what a man sought in marriage; so even bluestockings deferred to their husbands' opinions and denounced outspoken Frenchwomen as both masculine and oversexed. A favorite butt for moralists like Hannah More was female self-expression. Madame Helvetius's and even Madame Lafayette's dress, so "natural" in Paris, would be a scandal in London, where originality was out of favor and "politeness" reigned, with its mandate to restrain yourself to please others. Nabby wrote her cousin Lucy that she missed the feminine sentiment of the Comédie Française in the action-packed Drury Lane dramas she saw on her first days in London. "The spirit of the age affects all the arts," David Hume had written, and mainstream British theatre was as eager as its industry to flaunt active male virtues and (even in satire) affirm the mightiness of the status quo.[48]

While still mourning the little warbler so leery of travel she had been forced to part with him in Paris, Abigail arrived in London serenaded by two heartier songbirds presented to her by a gentleman she'd been kind to on the Dover ship. The Adamses crossed the Thames on May 26, 1785 in the midst of lavish celebration of King George III's forty-seventh birthday and a concert at Westminster Abbey. Their old lodgings, the Adelphi, had no vacancies; so America's first plenipotentiary minister was forced to move on to the noisier, dirtier Bath Hotel where, Abigail noted, a mere four rooms cost one-third more than her entire estate in Auteuil.

In letters to Jefferson, Abigail and John both insisted that they were homesick for Paris. "The Noise and bustle" of arrogant London "almost turnd my Brain," Abigail reported, while John waxed nostalgic for his daily walk in the Bois de Bologne. By comparison, London was damp and smoky. Its famed sidewalks reeked of kitchens and stables just feet from the road. "Such whiffs and puffs assault you every few steps as are enough to breed the Plague if they do not suffocate you on the spot," he lamented, appropriating Jefferson's conceit.[49] To which Jefferson replied, "The man must be of rock who can stand all this," and, rightly judging the difference in his own and John's characters, told Abigail, "To Mr. Adams it will be but one victory the more. It would ill have suited me. I do not love difficulties." And, of course, they rued the unnatural halt to a growing friendship. "I own I was loth to leave my Garden because I did not expect to find its place supplied," Abigail told Jefferson. "I was still more Loth on account of the increasing pleasure, and intimacy which a longer acquaintance with a respected Friend promised, to leave behind me the only person with whom my Companion could associate with perfect freedom, and unreserve: and whose place he had no reason to expect supplied in the Land to which he is destined."[50] [51]

All these protests were true enough, but they also concealed the Adamses' enormous emotional response to their mission. England—its land, its government, its literature—had been their imaginary home since birth. Even its architecture was similar: Boston's Old South Meeting House was clearly modeled on Christopher Wren's churches. With its brick base and soaring white weather vane, the formidable St. James Palace bore a distinct kinship to the rebels' Faneuil Hall. Separating from England had been the major task of their adult years. King George III, though in fact three years younger than John and a perfect stranger, was symbolically the father they overthrew but still sought to please. Months before signing the Declaration of Independence, John was still bragging that New Englanders were superior to other Americans because they had "purer English blood."[52]

In fact, John and George III had many traits in common. Both were domestic creatures, celebrating the ideal of a close-knit family, loving their gardens, and reviling profligacy of any sort. Both revered reason and fought to stanch their own unruly passions; accepted the concept of a Great Chain of Being and, to varying degrees, embraced hierarchy as a bastion against the chaos of an unstratified world. Each loved art and literature. George III had hosted Dr. Johnson in his library in Buckingham House (now Buckingham Palace), which was among the grandest in Europe. But emotional differences between the King of England and the American ambassador were also significant. George was reserved, whereas John was volatile. While John had married Abigail of his own choice and in passion, George had renounced the British love of his life Sarah Lennox for the German Princess Charlotte to further national interests and please his mentor, Lord Bute. Both were fatherless oldest sons, but John treated his brothers as autonomous individuals, where George viewed his siblings as children and went so far as to break all contact with his favorite brother, when William ignored his order to marry a foreigner and announced he had taken an English bride. It was logical to suppose George III's proprietary view of family extended to the American colonies.[53]

So it was with trepidations as well as pride that John, less than a week after he arrived in London, set out at 1 P.M. on June 1 for his for-

mal introduction to this king at St. James Palace. It was raining as he
left Abigail and Nabby behind at the Bath Hotel. Arriving at Court, he
briefly mingled with bishops and lords going about their normal business in the antechamber leading up to the King's reception. "While I
stood in this place, where it seems all ministers stand upon such ocas-
sions . . . you may well suppose I was the focus of all eyes," he later
wrote. Then the door opened, and he approached the King, bowing
like any other visitor to a North European Court.

John began reciting his short speech, according to custom, by acknowledging that he came at the will of his country, "to cultivate the
most friendly and liberal intercourse." He went on to say what was
obvious, that the very presence of an American minister in London
marked a new era in the history of the English-speaking world. Then,
his voice faltering, he turned in a more original direction:

> I think myself more fortunate than all my fellow-citizens, in
> having the distinguished honor to be the first, to stand in your
> Majesty's royal presence in a diplomatic character, and shall es-
> teem myself the happiest of men, if I can be instrumental in rec-
> ommending my country more and more to your Majesty's royal
> benevolence, and in restoring an entire esteem, confidence, and
> affection, or, in better words, the old good humor, between peo-
> ple, who, though separated by an ocean, and under different
> governments, have the same language, a similar religion, and
> kindred blood . . . I beg your Majesty's permission to add that
> although I have some time before been intrusted by my country,
> it was never, in my whole life, in a manner so agreeable to my-
> self.

John told Jefferson only that the King had received him with more
"Respect" and "Kindness" than he had anticipated. Abigail similarly
underplayed the occasion in her own long letter to the confirmed Fran-
cophile, merely noting in passing that John received the attention he
deserved. Far more eloquent on the quick feelings of these two former
arch-enemies is John's June 2 letter to John Jay in Congress. The King,
he writes to Jay:

listened to every word I said, with dignity, but with an apparent emotion. Whether it was the nature of the interview, or whether it was my visible agitation (for I felt more than I did or could express,) that touched him, I cannot say; but he was much affected, and answered me with more tremors than I had spoken.

For his part then, the King felicitated John on his presentation, expressed personal pleasure that Adams had been chosen to represent America at his Court, and insisted that while he had been "last to consent to the separation" of their two countries, he "would now be the first to meet the friendship of the United States, as an independent power," providing the sentiments expressed in John's speech prevailed. George III even hinted at the possibility of a favorable trade arrangement, saying, "The moment I see [America's] disposition to give to [Great Britain] the preference, that moment I shall say, let the circumstances of language, and blood have their natural and full effect."

Then, reaching for a lighter note, George III teased Adams about his reputed dislike of French manners, and John smartly deflected the issue, replying, "I must avow your Majesty I have no attachment but to my own country." To which the King replied: "An honest man will never have any other" and, bowing, signaled the audience to a close. At this point John, the lawyer son of a farmer yeoman, mocker of pomp, author of *Thoughts on Government* and the Massachusetts Constitution, for the second time that day performed the requisite three bows, and stepped backward out the door.[54]

ABIGAIL'S TURN CAME THREE weeks later. "Tomorrow at the Queens circle my Ladyship and your Niece make our compliments. There is no other presentation in Europe in which I should feel so much as this," Abigail wrote Mary on Wednesday, June 24, knowing her sister would vicariously share her bittersweet joy. Mary would also appreciate the giddy unreality of a Weymouth girl's meeting a queen under any circumstances, and she would settle for nothing less than a meticulous depiction of how everybody present spoke and looked.

Starting with the Adams women . . . "I directed my Mantua Maker
to let my dress be elegant, but plain as I could possibly appear with
Decency," Abigail informed Mary, "accordingly it is white Lute string
coverd and full trimd with white Crape festoond with lilick ribbon and
mock poit lace, over a hoop of enormus extent." The color scheme was
reinforced in her cap's two white feathers; she wore a "blond lace handkerchief" and pearls at her ears and neck. Her hair, piled high, looked
"very tastey." As for Nabby:

> Well, methinks I hear Betsy and Lucy say, what is cousins
> dress, white my Dear Girls like your Aunts, only differently
> trimd, and ornamented, her train being wholy of white crape
> and trimd with white ribbon, the petticoat which is the most
> showy part of the dress coverd and drawn up in what is calld
> festoons, with light wreaths of Beautiful flowers. The Sleaves
> white crape drawn over the silk with a row of lace round the
> Sleave near the shoulder another half way down the arm and a
> 3d upon the top of the ruffel [with] little flower[s] stuck between.

Queen Charlotte, on the other hand, wore purple and silver and
"was not well shaped or handsome," while most of the Court ladies
were "very plain ill shaped and ugly, but don't you tell any body that I
say so."

Abigail's presentation to the Court was far from private. Arriving at
2 P.M. at the Queen's Chamber, she, Nabby, and John joined a large
standing circle of overdressed aristocrats, randomly positioned
throughout the large room. The King and Queen then entered, the
King (trailed by his Lord of Waiting) proceeding to the right side, the
Queen (with her Lady) heading left, and both whispering, as they had
two hundred people to greet. "Only think of the task the Royal family
have, to go round to every person, and find small talk enough to speak
to all of them," Abigail marveled. The King came to her first and
seemed "a personable Man," but had a ghastly red face and white eyebrows. Programmed banalities smoothed the encounter: she removed
her right glove, he kissed her left cheek and asked if she'd walked that
day. "I could have told his Majesty that I had been all the morning pre-
pareing to wait upon him, but I replied no Sire," Abigail quipped to

Mary. "Why don't you love walking says he? I answered that I was rather indolent in the respect. He then Bow'd and past on."

She stood two hours more before meeting the Queen, who commiserated briefly about the Adamses' trouble finding housing, then intro-

Engraved for the Lady's Magazine.

A View of the BALL at St. James's on the
King's Birth Day June 4, 1782.

"There is no presentation in Europe in which I should feel so much as this," Abigail wrote Mary of her upcoming visit to St. James.

duced Abigail and Nabby to her sister and daughters, who were "pretty rather than Beautiful" and dressed similarly "in lilack and silver with a silver netting upon the coat, and their heads full of diamond pins." No protocol could dissipate the emotional nature of this meeting. "The Queen was evidently embarrased when I was presented to her. I had disagreeable feelings too." But the princesses were "afable" and "compassionate," behaving with "the ease and freedom of old acquaintaince"—rather like the French.

It was 6 P.M. by the time all guests had been greeted and dispersed to their carriages. "Congratulate me my dear sister it is over," Abigail at last found the energy to write Mary the following morning. All in all, the experience confirmed her democratic convictions. Certainly, the old adage that "fine feathers make fine Birds" did not hold true for the Queen and her set. "I saw many who were vastly richer dresst than your Friends, but I will venture to say that I saw none neater or more elegant," she prided herself.[55]

A recent acquaintance who did impress Abigail was the young American colonel sent to replace John Quincy as John's secretary. This William Stephens Smith had graduated from Princeton and fought with "great fidelity, bravery, and good conduct" during the Revolution, in the words of George Washington himself. Smith was furthermore witty and handsome.[56] Indeed, Abigail gave Mary the cue that he was becoming an important person in the Adams household by observing that he reminded her a bit of the youthful Richard Cranch.

CHAPTER X

"The Die is cast"

. . .

"I THANK YOU MY DEAR SISTER FOR THE IMPORTANCE, YOU HAVE given me," Mary wrote Abigail, after regaling all of Braintree with Abigail's account of meeting the British King and Queen. "There is not another court in Europe where you could have had such a triumph . . . I find the knowledg of My having a Letter descriptive of your dress and reception . . . will introduce me anywhere."[1]

Though she knew Mary was teasing, Abigail was quick to anticipate the envy even this best of elder sisters must feel at the sudden disparity in their world positions and pointed out, in her following letter, that no brush with aristocracy assuaged her loneliness for home. Indeed, she insisted, Mary's letters were far more valuable to her than hers were to Mary. For "I believe our social affections strengthen by age as . . . the social converse and society of Friends becomes more necessary," Abigail speculated. Except for John and Nabby, Abigail was friendless, where Mary saw Parson Wibird daily and was within a day's ride of Elizabeth Shaw. For all her opportunities to dress up, Abigail, like Betsy Cranch, was forced to derive much of her emotional comfort vicariously. It was Mary's vivid (and barely decipherable!) sentences that transported ailing Aunt Tufts and thriving Charles and Tommy Adams to her drawing room—otherwise filled with strangers. "I go along with you, and take an interest in every transaction which concerns those I love," Abigail spelled out her reliance on her older sister, who, like a novelist, gave voice to the human spirit. Abigail's reports were mere gossip by comparison. "I enjoy more pleasure from those imaginary scenes [you create for me], than I do from [visiting] . . . St. James. In one I feel myself your Friend and equal, in the other I know I am looked down upon."[2]

Abigail went on to say that even considering the odd silk she had the luck to be able to send the Cranch girls from Europe, she was still deeply in her older sister's debt. Only consider all the mothering Mary did for the three "orphan" Adams boys in their parents' absence! To which Mary, in the same spirit, replied that lending what talents she possessed to the improvement of her nephews was a privilege: "You know not my dear Sister how attach'd I feel myself to these children . . . They feel like my own . . . and if I can but gain as much of their Love as you have of my children I shall feel very happy."[3]

And Mary *was* more than usually happy in the summer of 1785. To make an impact on the future was her passion. So helping Richard steer a course for Massachusetts at the House of Representatives invigorated her, while nurturing gifted young men like Billy Cranch and John Quincy and Charles and Tommy Adams to run the nation in the next half century seemed the most exciting job in the world. And it was a job requiring a large variety of skills and accomplishments. One moment she was rummaging through John Adams's old clothes to find material for a waistcoat to clothe 13-year-old Tommy, and in the next she was negotiating terms for John Quincy to study Greek and room with the Shaws. And then there was the matter of striking just the right balance between pleading and name-dropping to persuade Harvard to reverse their ban on freshmen living on campus in Charles Adams's case. "I hope to make him happy yet," she promised Abigail.

And when Aunt Mary had won Charles not just any spot on campus but a corner room in nice Hollis Hall near his cousin Billy, the job of furnishing it both well and economically began. She commandeered a square tea table ideal for Charles's study from Abigail's cottage and stopped in Boston on her way home from Harvard and bought him a looking glass and a pine table painted to look like marble, which he could eat at or use to play cards. She arranged for Charles to accompany Billy on his weekly visits to Richard Cranch at his Boston lodgings when the House was in session and siphoned off some of the cinnamon Abigail had sent her from Paris to make both boys cakes for snacks. On August 17, Mary could write confidently to Abigail: "Now I think [Charles] is equip'd and will go [to Harvard] tomorrow with the best advice I can give him. You may assure yourself my dear sister that I shall watch over him with the Parental Eye of tenderness. In sickness and in health He shall be my peculiar care."[4]

Mary could also report that Harvard had advanced Billy a half year for his exceptional schoolwork, and even the Cranches' perennial financial woes seemed of little consequence in light of her overall good mood: "Money is very scarce," Mary wrote Abigail, ". . . but I do not design to stress myself. Something unforeseen may turn up."[5]

What did put a damper on her happiness, however, was the behavior of Nabby's fiancé, Royall Tyler, which was increasingly scurrilous, if the worst could be believed. Mary'd had few opportunities to lecture Tyler lately because he now spent most of the year defending clients at court in Boston. Here he had begun lodging with the family of his friend Joseph Pearse Palmer (who was the Cranches' nephew on Richard's side). During the war, the Palmers had lost their large fortune. Now, having exhausted his options in Massachusetts, Joseph Palmer— soon after Tyler arrived in the household—took off to seek work in Maine. This left Tyler alone with Joseph's 30-year-old wife, Betsey. Betsey was beset by creditors, and Royall Tyler began paying her bills.

What prompted this gallantry was now a matter of heated speculation among the Cranch and Adams circles. For while one side acclaimed Tyler a hero, the other reviled him as a cad. Was he or was he not sleeping with Betsey Palmer? was the operative question. And while all Mary's inclination was to join his defamers, honesty demanded proof—which she did not have. So Mary agonized about whether or not to spell out the situation to Abigail and composed and burned two candid letters before, retreating to insinuations she stammered, "There are many things which would do to be said, that it would not be prudent to commit to writing." And: "You conclude your last Letter by saying that "You hope—[Tyler] is very busy and to good purpose. I hope so too, but I know very little about him for he is very seldom in Braintree and when he is very little at home.' What she could relate was that Tyler had gotten so fat he had to enlarge his waistcoat, and she

struggled to find a way to imply that he had a more than casual relationship with the Palmers, finally writing in the margin, "As to Mr.
Palmer's Family Mr. Tyler must give you an account of them. He
knows more about them than any one else."[6]

In *her* correspondence to London, Elizabeth confined herself to
mild complaints about Tyler's failure to visit after she scolded him for
not writing Nabby. And Uncle Tufts, struggling as ever to be fair-
minded, waited months before replying to his worried niece's queries
and then ventured only that: "If the Marks in favour [of Tyler] . . . are
not such as to establish a full Confidence those against it are not such as
to exclude all Hope."[7] Then, regretting even so nebulous an admission,
he implored Abigail to burn his mail.

The beginning of fall passed peacefully in Braintree and Cambridge
and Haverhill. Charles settled easily into Harvard. Mary visited Elizabeth and found her "in better health than I have seen her for several
years," though Elizabeth's comic little Betsy Q, now five years old, had
a boil and was thin. As the leaves turned brilliant red and orange, Aunt
Tufts continued her slow march toward eternity, while twice every
Sunday Parson Wibird wriggled and twisted his wayward limbs at the
First Church pulpit, rarely surprising his flock with a new idea.

Then, on the night of October 22, Mary received a letter dated August 15 from London. The news was almost too extraordinary to believe: Nabby Adams of her own free will had definitively broken her
engagement with Royall Tyler!

As Abigail described the wonderful event to Mary, "My dear sister . . . I have for some time observed a more than common anxiety in
the appearance of your Neice . . . A few days since, something arose
which led her in conversation to ask me, if I did not think a Gentleman
of her acqauintance a Man of Honour? I replied yes a man of strict
honour, and I wisht I could say that of all her acquaintance." Rather
than protesting her mother's implied criticism of Tyler, Nabby questioned her own role in the fraught affair, asserting "a breach of honour
in one party would not justify a want of it in the other."

"I thought this the very time to speak," continued Abigail. "I said if
she was conscious of any want of honour on [Tyler's part] . ., I and
every Friend she had in the world, would rejoice if she could liberate
herself."

Was her father one of those Friends? Nabby inquired. If so, "I have too long ... known ... fear, suspicion, doubt, dread and apprehension ... and I am determined to know them no longer," she announced. At this point, John quickly supplied his approbation. "He told her ... that he was a perfect stranger to [Royall Tyler], that his Character had been such as to induce him to give his consent not so freely as he could wish: but because he conceived her affections engaged. But if she had reason to question the strictest honour of the Gentleman ... he had rather follow her to her Grave, than see her united with him."

Nabby had no new suitor, Abigail assured her sister, nor had Abigail ever revealed, even to John, Mary's letters announcing Tyler's misdeeds. Tyler had only himself to blame for his dismissal. "I have always told him that he was his own greatest enemy. Such he has proved ... It is not worth his while to make a Bustle. I don't think it will kill him. He would have been more solicitous to have kept his prize, if he had known the value of it." Abigail hoped friends at home would refrain even from mentioning Tyler's name to her daughter in the future. Out of affection for Tyler, Joseph and Betsey Palmer, she foresaw, might want to solicit Nabby to reconsider her decision. This would be useless, Abigail counseled, for "the die is cast."

"My dear Niece has acted with a Spirit worthy of her Parents," Mary rejoiced in a letter to London the following morning. "She may assure herself of the approbation of every Friend she has." And while Mary still forbore relating the sordid rumors about Tyler and Betsey Palmer, she gleefully guaranteed her sister that the Palmers would not protest. As for the possibility of Tyler's having a rival in London, the thought never crossed Mary Cranch's mind.

FOUR MONTHS EARLIER THE Adamses had concluded an exhausting house search and ensconced themselves in a mansion at the corner of Duke Street and Grosvenor Square. Grosvenor Square! What associations those two words brought to mind. And now, Abigail knew, her sisters would respond to them! For here it was that their favorite literary hero, Richardson's Charles Grandison, settled into domestic bliss with Harriet Byron—always their model of womanhood because of her virtue and cultivated mind.

Like her hero Charles Grandison, Abigail settled in Grosvenor Square.

Thirty years after the publication of *Sir Charles Grandison,* Grosvenor Square remained one of the most prestigious addresses in London. The Adams home, number 9, was a 1725 Georgian redbrick building with a facade as English in its regularity as the teasing friezes on their white stone house in Auteuil had been French. For all their deriding of British snobbery, the Adamses were as pleased as any upstarts to be so well located. No foreign minister would blush to reside here, Nabby assured John Quincy in America. Though "a little out of repairs," the house had three spacious floors, an attic, and the conventional British basement kitchen—whose dimensions were all wrong for Abigail's French furniture; so (she moaned to Mary) she was forced to replace what she owned at enormous expense. Exorbitant also was the price of hiring the too many servants the British—like the French—required of anyone who was anyone. Among Abigail's original staff was a proverbial drunken coachman, who fell off his box while waiting for John to emerge from a meeting and crashed to the ground, smashing the carriage windows and splitting the front in two.

Fashionable London's custom of separating the sexes was also jarring. Rather than drawing a male dinner partner, as in Paris, Abigail and Nabby were seated with the other ladies during a meal and then herded off to the dreaded card room afterward. Still, the scene of the Adamses' daily life was agreeable. The grand entry hall was enhanced by a majestic stone staircase. A dining room, where Abigail served an 114-pound tortoise to fifteen foreign ministers, and John's office were on the first floor; a library and drawing room on the second; and the bedrooms were on the third. Out her window Nabby could gaze at a lord's chimney. From a drawing room adjacent to theirs, a Lady Lincoln Parlores "peeps at us," Nabby reported to her brother, and the Adamses with equal abandon returned her stares.[8]

Soon Abigail felt well compensated even for the loss of her Auteuil garden. In the middle of August, she enthused to Mary:

> We are . . . situated . . . in a fine open square, in the middle of which is a circle inclosed with a neat grated fence; around which are lighted every night about sixty Lamps. The border next the fence is grass, the circle is divided into five grass plots. One in the middle is a square upon which is a statue of George 2nd on horse back. Between each of the plots are gravel walks and the plots are filld with clumps of low trees thick together which is calld Shrubbery, and these are surrounded with a low Hedge, all together a pretty effect.[9]

With due respect to the brilliant actress Sarah Siddons, Abigail continued to prefer France's theatre as well as its shoemakers (she commissioned Thomas Jefferson to order her two pairs of satin pumps from Paris), but a performance of Handel's *Messiah* at Westminster Abbey surpassed all. Seated beneath massive medieval arches, surrounded by gargoyles and statues of dead monarchs, with Geoffrey Chaucer's tomb in one corner and Isaac Newton's in another, and blocks of colored light stippling ancient wood and marble, Abigail was greatly moved even before an infantry of musicians from all over the world marched to the head of the nave. Now the excitement built. And, "When it came to that part, the Hallelulya, the whole assembly rose and all the Musicians . . . Only conceive six hundred voices and instruments perfectly

chording in one word and one sound! I could scarcly believe myself an
inhabitant of earth," she exclaimed to Betsy Cranch.[10]

Abigail was less enamored of the typical British party, one of which
she describes in a letter to Mary, whom she imagines surrounded by
worthy neighbors who've never gambled at cards in their lives:

> There were about 2 hundred persons present last evening,
> three large rooms full of card tables. The moment the ceremony
> of curtsying is past, the Lady of the House asks you pray what is
> your Game? Whist Cribbage or commerce, and then the next
> thing is to hunt round the room for a set to make a party. And as
> the company are coming and going from 8 till 2 in the morning
> you may imagine she has enough to employ her . . . The Lady
> and her Daughter, last night, were most fatigued to death for
> they [were] . . . toiling at pleasure for seven hours in which time
> they scarcely Set down. I went with a determination not to
> play . . . but here you cannot live with any character or conse-
> quence unless you give in.

So she submitted to playing at a table "with three perfect strangers,"
the greediest of which, "an old experienced hand" at cards, opened
with a high bid, which Abigail met reluctantly and then—she couldn't
help boasting to Mary—proceeded to trounce the woman at four games
before striding off with her win. "I never play when I can possibly
avoid it," she resumed her obloquy, "for I have not conquered the disagreeable feeling of receiving money for play but such a set of gam-
blers . . . the Ladies here are. And such a Life they lead. Good Heavens
were reasonable Beings made for this? I will come and shelter myself
in America from this scene of dissipation and upbraid me whenever I
introduce the like among you . . ."[11]

Abigail admitted to Mary that England outshone its former colony
in the arts and industry. But in what really mattered America held the
upper hand. "We have native Genious capacity and ingenuity equal to
all their improvements," she confided, and furthermore a far abler and
more dignified working class.

WHEN THEY WEREN'T RUSHING off to concerts or card games, all the Adamses were having themselves painted by Mather Brown, an up-and-coming American portraitist. Nabby's finished picture shows an attractive young woman swaddled in white gauze, her powdered hair classically molded and topped by a wide-brimmed straw hat, with huge feathers, pitched upwards as if to fly off her head. Gone is the baby fat that had everyone in Braintree calling her a "big" girl. Nabby is as thin as a greyhound, Abigail tells Mary. And while the unbreachable inner life and reserve remain, Nabby's eyes look playfully out at the viewer, her lips are almost smiling; like a woman of the world, she owns her costume, but her frank face talks back to all its wispy formality. "Pappa is much pleased with [the portrait]," Nabby wrote her brother; "and says he has got my character, a mixture of Drolery and Modesty . . . It is a tasty picture I can assure you, whether a likeness or not."[12]

Nabby had changed more than anyone else in the family during the

John said this Mather Brown portrait of Nabby conveyed her "mixture of Drolery and Modesty."

little over a year since she arrived in Europe. In Braintree she'd been large and handsome. Now she was the "American beauty" to everyone from Thomas Jefferson to the ladies at Court. The size of her waist was the least of her metamorphoses. Loving but mistrusting Tyler had banished the last remnants of her famed indifference. She began carrying sad poems[13] in her pocketbook and expressed disappointment as frankly as Betsy Cranch. (She sounds exactly like her emotional cousin when, upon failing to receive a long-awaited letter from John Quincy, she chides him: "Thus at one moment all my pleasing prospect vanishes . . . Mortifying reflection that we are not permitted to look forward with any degree of certainty even to the next hour.") Gone too were her self-sufficiency and aversion to visiting and dinner parties. With her brother gone and Tyler silent, she threw herself into socializing with her mother's new American friends, like Boston-born Mrs. Rogers, kept up a lively correspondence with Thomas Jefferson, and could boast to her brother that the great British Dissenting minister Dr. Price engaged her in discussion of affairs of state. Her sorrow notwithstanding, her acceptance of the inevitable had blossomed into curiosity, and the dreaded absence from Braintree had become an opportunity to expand her mind. In a letter to her brother written in the summer of 1785, around the time she was breaking her engagement to Royall Tyler, Nabby sounds almost like the young Abigail pining to go to England, when she announces to John Quincy:

> For my part I should like above all things to make one of a
> *Party to go* round the world . . . I can't see why people who have
> the *inclination* (and *ability*) which to be sure is the most essential
> of the two, should not gratify themselves, by . . . seeing as many
> and curious parts of the world as it should Lead them to visit. If
> they are possessed of proper Principles, it will not injure them,
> but make them wiser and better and happier. Pray don't you feel
> a great deel wiser, than if you had never been outside the State of
> Massachusetts Bay, . . . though [it is] a very respectable place.[14]

The pleasures and follies of society remained Nabby's chief interest. But now politics, toward which she'd professed abject indifference in Massachusetts, absorbed her as well. The historical hatred between

England and France was a topic of scrutiny in one long, reflective letter to John Quincy; in another she devotes nearly a page to marveling that an Irishman she met at a dinner party should surprise everyone with his thoughtful comments on Britain's mistakes during the American Revolution while thoroughly misunderstanding the nature of the American republic itself. Nabby could also speak knowledgeably about the Massachusetts Navigation Act and her father's so far frustrating attempts to interest the British in a trade agreement. She was pleased that she could translate Jefferson's cipher and thus keep apprised of political developments in France.

Nabby shared the whole family's ire at the vicious scribes of Fleet Street, who thought it the greatest joke in the world that Americans had presumed to appoint a foreign minister and alluded to John Adams as a "commercial agent" on a good day and "proscribed Rebel" on a bad.[15] One journalist compared Abigail in her new carriage to a milk-maid riding "an old chaise to market with a little fresh butter." Meanwhile, every discord between the American states was exaggerated into the imminent demise of what was never a government to begin with, in England's opinion. And while aristocratic ladies made their obligatory calls at 9 Grosvenor Street every Tuesday, disparagements of the American Congress did not stop with the press. "There are those who have the ear of the ministry and persuade them that there is not union sufficient in the States to accomplish [our diplomatic mission]," Abigail reported to her Uncle Tufts, knowing how close these subversives came to the truth.[16]

And yet America had its British defenders. The famous radical minister Dr. Price was among the earliest and most vocal. Price was a Dissenter from the state religion as well as an acolyte of Locke and a brilliant financier. He was a rationalist who denied miracles, though he believed in Christ. Like New England Congregationalists during the Revolution, Price was convinced that love of God meant attacking injustice. And no less than Madame Helvetius, he enjoyed conversing with the opposite sex. Indeed, he made a point of joining the rare London club that admitted females. Abigail particularly admired how he doted on his sick wife, while Nabby was dazzled by his highly original belief in reincarnation. Now in his mid-sixties, the preacher was self-effacing to the point of mumbling his (brilliant) sermons and many evenings he absentmindedly wandered up to his neighbors' doorstep wearing only a dressing gown: "He would talk and read the Bible to us, till he sent us to bed in a frame of mind as heavenly as his own," that neighbor recalls.[17]

Yet Price was very much of this world in his determination to ennoble government. He was one of the earliest and most vocal British supporters of the Declaration of Independence and, in the spring of 1785, shortly before the Adamses arrived in London, further enraged the average Englishman by publishing a pamphlet rejoicing that America's victory in the Revolution marked "a new era in the history of mankind." Like John Adams who—despite his bleak view of human nature—perceived the world on a trajectory of improvement, Price fervently believed in progress. Long before they met, the enlightened minister felt a strong kinship with the author of the Massachusetts Constitution, particularly on the subject of religious rights. Having himself been denied a university education and all government work because of his dissent from the Anglican religion, Price praised Adams's guarantee of full citizenship to every Christian in Massachusetts as "liberal beyond all example."

But why stop with Christians? Price challenged Adams to embrace an even more radical agenda. "Montesquieu probably was not a Christian. Newton and Locke were not Trinitarians and therefore not Christians according to commonly received ideas. Would the United States, for this reason, deny such men . . . all places of trust and power among them?"[18]

Price preached at Gravel Pitt Meeting House in the Dissident village of Hackney, and the newspapers thought it hilarious that the Adamses drove six miles northeast to this sparsely adorned parish every Sunday to sit with the least elegant families in England and hear such a homely man speak.[19] Mayfair's Grosvenor Chapel, with its Greek Revival style and soaring bell tower, was just feet from the Adamses' doorstep and far more suitable for a foreign minister—and moreover closer in design to a New England Church. Even Abigail, who was soon naming Dr. Price among her closest friends in England, was dismayed by the meekness of non-Anglicans. "Dr. Price has the most liberal sentiments of any Gentleman I have heard converse since my residence here," she wrote a friend in Boston that August, continuing:

He is indeed one of the best of Men, but the dissenting clergy in this country appear a very different set of Men from those who inhabit ours. They are cramped contemned and degraded, they have not that independent appearance, and that consciousness of their own worth which gives an Air of dignity to the whole deportment. Dr. Price notwithstanding his literary fame, and his great abilities, appears like a man who has been brow beaten. In America he would be revered and caressed, as his merit deserves.[20]

Abigail's religion, the foundation of her life, every bit as much now as when she was a girl in Weymouth, had undergone a sea change since she left America. The obscurism of Catholicism in Paris had disgusted her, as did the smugness of British Anglicanism, but she was no easier on the Puritan Church. Her brother-in-law John Shaw's view that the accident of birth determined your final judgment had always appalled her. Nor could she accept the Calvinist premise that faith was more important than effort in the eyes of a compassionate Lord. Yet, while Abigail had questioned the Puritan hierarchy of wealth, she had never doubted that knowledge and virtue distinguished one soul from another. Now, buoyed by John's success and her own rapid advancement in taste and culture, she went further to predict the triumph of *inequality* even in the next world. "We are told in scripture, that there are different kinds of glory, and that one star differeth from another. Why should not those who have distinguished themselves by superior excellence over their fellow-mortals continue to preserve their rank when admitted to the kingdom of the just?"[21] she wrote her scholarly niece Lucy Cranch.

Between June 5 and July 31, during the hot, rainless summer of 1785, Dr. Price stammered out his philosophy of religion in a series of charged sermons denouncing ignorance and superstition while heralding man's potential for goodness and also his entitlement to pleasure on earth. Price was John's closest friend in England. For John, Price's visionary politics was a relief after all his dealings with shortsighted courtiers. But Abigail was most moved when the doctor expounded on God as a superior friend.

What a boon it was to hear a minister declare that everyone can and must cultivate a relationship with the Almighty on a personal level; that as much as God is just in his dealings with nations, he is wise about domestic affairs. In her forty-second year, sitting in a pew in the Gravel Pitt Meeting House, Abigail at last found a parson attuned to the household God she had consulted on every aspect of her life since childhood. At 19, she had sought God's advice about choosing a husband her parents disapproved of. As a young mother, she had beseeched his council when she was deciding whether inoculation against smallpox was worth the risk to her children's lives. Recently, it was God—more than Mary, more than John—Abigail had turned to when deciding whether to leave her two adolescent sons behind and join her husband in Europe. She had felt God's presence in all her discussions with John Quincy at Auteuil on the subject of Royall Tyler. Now again she was consulting her deity on Nabby's behalf.

For she had not been telling Mary the full truth when she wrote that Nabby broke her engagement to Tyler solely on the basis of *his* unworthiness. There was also the matter of John's new secretary, the man who—Abigail had earlier confided in Mary—reminded her of a young Richard Cranch.

COLONEL SMITH WAS HANDSOME, brave and learned with a muscular physique, naturally dark skin, weathered from constant exposure to sun on the battlefield, an aquiline nose, and deep-set penetrating eyes that radiated sensibility. Only the fact that he did not dance cast a shadow on his romantic perfection. He was the first of ten children born into a New York merchant's family. Ten years older than 19-year-old Nabby, he had been a hero in the Revolutionary War.

Colonel Smith and Royall Tyler were both financially comfortable, but where Tyler had to live down a reputation for womanizing and squandering his fortune, Smith was the embodiment of virtuous youth. Immediately after graduating from Princeton, he signed on to fight for his country and so excelled as an officer in the Battle of New York and the siege of Newport that in 1779 he was appointed adjutant-general under Lafayette and in 1781 made aide-de-camp to George Washington himself.

Writing of Smith's performance in the war, Washington praised his "gallantry, intelligence, and professional knowledge."[22] In 1785, Congress appointed him secretary to the American mission in London, and Smith arrived to take up his new position on May 25, a day before his boss.

Ease and a hint of lassitude hang over William Smith in this Mather Brown portrait, painted in London.

The colonel and the Adams family were well matched in their personal philosophies. They all revered Dr. Price's liberal Christianity, valued duty above success and patriotism over financial gain. "Rectitude" was their watchword, and each of them disliked pretension and chafed at the requisite visits to Court. Colonel Smith reported himself "much pleased" by his first meeting with the three Adamses,[23] while John all but raved in a letter to Congress that his new secretary had "as much honour and spirit as any Man I ever knew. His principals are those of his Country, and his abilities are worthy of them . . . In short you could not have given me a man more to my taste."[24]

Colonel Smith easily fell into John Quincy's role as obliging young man in the household. During the day he took care of national business, at night he escorted the ladies to the theatre or conversed with them in the drawing room about everything from the children's boxing matches they witnessed with horror daily in Grosvenor Square to the latest news on the Barbary pirates to the Queen's clothes. Smith praised Abigail to a friend as "discerning."[25]

Soon they were so intimate that it was to Smith Abigail turned when she was dismayed to find herself cringing at the love scenes at a Drury Lane production of *Othello*.[26] Theoretically, she explained, she believed there was no difference between the races, yet:

> Whether it arises from the prejudices of Education or from a real natural antipathy I cannot determine, but my whole soul shuderd whenever I saw the sooty . . . More touch the fair Desdemona . . . Through the whole play . . . the character of Othello is manly open generous and noble . . . but . . . so powerfull was prejudice that I could not separate the coulour from the man.[27]

And while there is no record of Smith's response to Abigail's remarkable admission, it is certain that he shared her analytical bent. He also was outspoken, incapable of hiding his feelings, and as impetuous as any young man they knew. There was the day, for instance, when he drove up to introduce a visiting friend to the Adams household and found Abigail and Nabby already in their carriage preparing to ride out. Abigail called to the colonel that she regretted he was not free to join them. At which point, he leapt out of his carriage and into theirs, leaving his friend to greet John unannounced. Nabby related this incident in a July 4 letter to John Quincy, concluding, "Perhaps you will say the Coln. Sacrifised politeness to Gallantry."[28] It was clear *she* approved of the move.

As for William Smith's opinion of Nabby: in mid-June, when he escorted her and Abigail to the Queen's reception, she was already "fine" and "amiable" and pretty. But by the time he leapt into her carriage, Nabby's perfection was beyond dispute. She was "more than painters can express, or youthful poets fancy when they love," he marveled to a friend in America. And while he'd been infatuated before, his love for Nabby—like Charles Grandison's for Harriet—had begun in friendship and was founded on esteem.[29] The fact that she was engaged to Royall Tyler did not in the least dispel William Smith's determination to marry her—though he saw no reason to acquaint his boss with the news. Abigail, on the other hand, was Smith's confidante from the beginning. She did not discourage his attentions to her daughter, though she teased that he was under the dangerous influence of Cupid and did "not always conduct himself with the prudence I could wish."[30]

In this original image by Isaac Taylor, Charles Grandison shows the same gallantry as William Smith by leaping out of his carriage to help a lady.

More seriously, she warned that haste might be his downfall. "There are entanglements . . . from which Time the great solacer of Humane woe only can relieve us," Abigail wrote, knowing Smith would understand the allusion to Nabby's by now clearly unsuitable engagement. "And Time I dare say will extricate those I love from any unapproved Step, into which inexperience and youth may have involved them. But untill that period may arrive Honour, Honour is a Stake—a word to the wise is sufficient."[31]

Appealing to Colonel Smith on grounds of honor was precisely the right tactic, for while he proclaimed indifference to professional advancement, he was avid to merit respect and his highest goal in life was to deserve a spotless character. His other desires were few but strong. He wanted Nabby as he had never wanted any woman. To win her, he came to realize, he would have to remove himself from the contest and allow events to unfold.

And so, on August 4, while Nabby confided her scruples about Tyler to her parents, Colonel Smith wrote John requesting a leave of absence to observe a review of the Prussian Army in Berlin. And John replied in the affectionate tone he would have used with John Quincy:

> You will give me leave to say, that your assistance and advice has been at all times so useful and agreeable to me, that I should lose the advantage of it with reluctance if it were only for a few weeks or even days. Nevertheless . . . the general review of the Prussian Army is an object worthy of [your visit].

Besides, everyone was out of town, there was only the rare letter to be copied or appointment to be arranged. John was loath to detain his young protégé in a place "so dull, and so disgusting and unwholesome" as London in August, and, urging him to return as soon as possible, wished him an edifying trip.

Two days after William Smith left Grosvenor Square for the Continent, on August 11, Nabby wrote Tyler a very cool farewell:

> Sir
>
> Herewith you receive your letters and miniature with my desire that you would return mine to my Uncle Cranch, and my hopes that you are well satisfied with the affair as is.
>
> A.A.

Sometime during the fall Tyler responded to Nabby's brief note with the love letter she had long yearned for, replete with eloquent protests that the correspondence she supposed he'd neglected had in fact been lost at sea. For three days, Nabby pored over Tyler's words, reliving each stage of the courtship, not sure whether she even wanted to believe him, yet determined to behave as she should. Finally, once again, she left the ultimate decision to her father. If he believed Tyler's justifications, she would forget Colonel Smith. And Adams was clearly moved by Tyler's entreaties—so moved, in fact, that Abigail saw no recourse but to put her sister's word on the line and at last show John Mary's letters. Adams was appropriately astounded and Tyler swiftly dismissed.[32]

It was around this time that Abigail began planting seeds for the announcement of a new romantic interest, telling Uncle Tufts, who had taken her father's place as family elder: "Col. Smith . . . appears a Gentleman solid sedate tho warm and active when occasion requires. He is sensible and judicious, dignified sentiments of his own Country and a high sense of honour appear to govern his actions." To John Quincy she enthused about the colonel's happy temper and prospects: he was a young George Washington and would surely lead the American Army in the event of another war.

Meanwhile, this paragon of virtue crossed the Channel, made a leisurely journey through Holland and wended his way to Berlin, arriving on August 31. There he joined figureheads from all the great capitals of Europe and absorbed the latest military knowledge while favorably impressing such notables as Frederick the Great (whom he described as "the great king and the grand merchant strangely blended"). After a month, and without asking John's permission, Smith moved on to Prague and Vienna. He later described this extended journey to John Jay as a mission to promote American trade with Europe.[33] But he flattered Abigail with a more poetic explanation, writing *her*:

My dear Madame

Your benevolence I know will excuse the particularity of this address, when you confide in the assurance of its proceeding from a sincere heart . . . I feel myself complimented by your confidence and believe I am not capable of abusing it. I hope for an advocate in you, should Mr. Adams think my absence long. Tell him that—what will you tell him? Can you say with Stern that it is a quiet Jorney of the heart in pursuit of those affections, which make us love each other, and the world better than we do?, or will you say he is flying from—? . . . but I will not dictate, say what you please. Whatever you say and whatever you do . . . I will subscribe to it.[34]

Meanwhile, fall swept the noxious air away from London, the nobles scurried home from their country visits, and business was in full swing. As John resumed pressing for a favorable trade agreement with Britain, Barbary pirates were again threatening American vessels, and Adams and Jefferson rushed to prepare treaties to stave off war with Morocco and Algiers. Long letters flew back and forth between London and Paris, with no secretary to copy on John's end. When John's eyes inflamed from overwriting, he hired an American friend, Charles Storer, to help out for a few weeks before Storer sailed for Boston. At that point John, who'd despaired so much at Nabby's learning Latin, summoned his daughter to work. "Your Pappa is overwhelmed with writing," she wrote her brother at the end of November. "I know not what he would do if it was not for Your Sister who copies for him. So much writing and to so little purpose, is very mortifying. Colonel Smith has not yet returned." Nor, for the past ten weeks, had he communicated with anyone in the family, so by late November Abigail was convinced he was sick or dead.

And how did John Adams, with his preternatural sensitivity to insult, interpret Colonel Smith's extended absence? Surely, Abigail did her best to defend his motives, and in the short run she was successful, for in the middle of September she could still assure the sentimental traveler that "Mr. Adams has not been impatient tho he has sometimes wished for you."[35] But how John's mood fared as October and November came and went without a word of explanation from the peripatetic colonel is not recorded. John being John, it is safe to assume that pique at times triumphed over anxiety for the young man's health.

And this was a time when John felt particularly exasperated, as his primary mission in London—to talk England out of imposing trade duties on American imports—seemed more utopian by the day. Humiliated by their own military defeat, yet heartened by the chaos of the American government, the British glibly rebuffed John's most generous offers, hoping to hasten the downfall of the United States. Adams in turn became increasingly oppositional. "We must not, my Friend, be the Bubbles of our own Liberal Sentiments," he wrote Jefferson in Paris. "If we cannot obtain reciprocal Liberality, We must adopt reciprocal Prohibitions, Exclusions, Monopolies, and Imposts."

Paris is where Colonel Smith ultimately wound up in the end of November. The city was in black, mourning the recent death of the King's cousin, but Smith arrived looking only to the future and eager to conquer all obstacles ahead. He spent most of his short time in France with Thomas Jefferson. And Abigail, who had been eager for Jefferson's impression, was gratified to receive a letter from him, effusing:

> I congratulate you on the return of Colo. Smith, I congratulate you still more however on the extreme worth of his character . . . Your knowledge of him will enable you to judge of the advantageous impressions which his head, his heart, and his manners will have made on me.[36]

Three weeks before Christmas Nabby, John, and Abigail returned from a five-hour tribute to Shakespeare at the Drury Lane Theatre and had just sat down for a chat when who should walk into their sitting room but the colonel himself. His first words were a sheepish "Dare I see you Sir?" to John; after which, he produced "a peace offering" for his long absence in the form of their mutual American friend Colonel Humphreys, whom he'd torn away from his budding career as a writer and whisked across the Channel from France. Having acquitted himself, in his own view at least, the colonel sat down in his old chair and proceeded to regale his audience with developments in the Barbary crisis and to gossip about Jefferson's mounting debts.

In her letter describing the scene to John Quincy, Nabby acknowledges that John has a right to be angry at the colonel, but implies that he is not, or not so much as to disturb her joy. With her engagement to Tyler safely ended, she was free to bask in this young man's attractions—his lean body, his perfect almond-shaped eyes, like the hero in a Roman sculpture, his sensual lips, and most of all, the electricity between their two natures—he so fluent, she so reserved. Nabby had gone out into the world, but she still thrived in intimate circles, as she frequently reminded her cousins in Braintree, and her conversation would never do justice to the richness of her inner life. William Smith respected Nabby's frequent silences, particularly with Abigail around to talk.[37]

And Abigail, like Nabby, welcomed the colonel without reservation. No sooner did she set eyes on him than she ceased to wonder about his absence and resumed singing his praises to one and all. The colonel continued to confide in her. As far as he knew, his boss was unaware of his passion for Nabby, and so eager was he to move forward that in a significant breach of etiquette, he skipped the long, formal process of requesting John's permission to begin courtship and instead asked Abigail to intercede on his behalf. "I seek *your* friendship, and aspire to your Daughters Love," Smith wrote Abigail, flattering her centrality in the family, and went on in a characteristically modest vein to plead his cause. First, it went without saying that he adored Nabby. Furthermore, he was loyal, well educated, and a gentleman from head to toe. Like all the Adamses, he despised ostentation. Unlike John, he lacked the zeal to shine in the world. His goals were domestic. He sought "the peaceful walk of Life," contentment and seclusion, as Nabby did. His family was comfortably situated. So while he was perfectly competent to learn law or business, career was not his first priority. He would, however, rush to serve his country whenever the need arose.[38]

Confronted with Nabby's pleading looks and Abigail's emphatic approval, John put aside any reservations he may have nurtured during his secretary's absence and immediately acceded to the young man's request. The courtship began.

Abigail was nearly as euphoric as Nabby. A year and a half earlier, speaking of her emotional reunion with John in London, she had written Mary: "Poets and painters wisely draw a veil over those Scenes which surpass the pen of the one and the pencil of the other."[39] At the beginning of 1786, she began insinuating that another such event had occurred in her family—this time, though, she was bursting to elaborate, only protocol forbade her to speak. So her letters home danced around the delicious topic. She balanced praise of Colonel Smith with raves about his friend Colonel Humphreys. She wrote repeatedly that Nabby was the injured party in the affair with Tyler and that it would be perfectly respectable for her to love another suitor, while never admitting that she did. In one letter to Mary, Abigail suddenly launches into an assault on the legion of gossips who for some unstated reason

will soon be slandering her daughter ("The World . . . I expect will as-
scribe to her fickleness and perhaps infidelity"); then sheepishly acknowledges, "I know I leave you in a puzzel."[40]

Which was not true in the least. Mary felt perfectly sure Nabby was
in love with Colonel Humphreys. She was only baffled that Abigail
should underestimate her own sister's powers to deduce. That there
was a suitor at Grosvenor Square any fool could discern from Abigail's
letters. Clearly, he was American, or her patriotic sister would never
approve. And while a less discerning reader might suspect the man was
William Smith, who was also frequently mentioned, *he* was only a colonel, while David Humphreys was both a colonel and a poet of some
renown. A poet. What scion of the book-loving Smiths could resist
such a romantic figure? And Humphreys was "The best poetical Genious our Country can boast," according to Abigail's latest effusion.
Mary declared herself ready to embrace Tyler's replacement with open
arms.

Tyler, meanwhile, was stirring up trouble from Boston to Braintree,
Mary reported. The villain in his version of the tale of the wobbly engagement was herself, whom he accused of poisoning Nabby's mind
against him, though he was still not man enough to acknowledge that
he'd been definitively dismissed. He attributed the silence from London to "a little misunderstanding," and insisted he'd set matters right
in person once he'd unveiled his latest coup. This masterwork, Mary
informed Abigail, was a windmill now being erected in an area near
the schoolhouse. A bolting and a chocolate mill were scheduled to follow. "I wonder if the Law business is to go by the wind also," Mary
quipped.

Around the same time Mary was congratulating Abigail on Nabby's good fortune, Betsy Cranch received a long earnest letter from
Nabby revealing a surprising change in her cousin's attitude toward
luck. Gone, it seemed, was the young fatalist who three years before
had insisted that happiness depended exclusively on external events.
Now Nabby, like Betsy, was focusing on inner joy.[41] "Happiness must
result from contentment and contentment arises from our satisfaction
with ourselves," Nabby wrote her cousin; and success is "dependant
upon the arrangements of our own Minds," not—as she had formerly
believed—a roll of the dice. Nabby did not enjoy being thrust into the

limelight. Indeed, her greatest wish was to be liberated from London high society with its hostile strangers and to live humbly at home with those she loved. "The ties of my earliest years, cannot be replaced," she told Betsy, who ought to be grateful to have her sister, Lucy. "For near two years I have had no [female] intimate or Companion . . . How much I often wish for you," she sighed.

When she could return from Europe was uncertain. Yet it cheered Nabby to know her happiness would transcend even a long exile: so powerful was her reliance on self.

Besides, not everyone in Europe was a stranger. She switched to the bantering tone she had used when doling out gossip from a visit at Mrs. Warren's. "Do not suppose my Dear Eliza, that there may not be some *one* individual that may interest my Mind, and whom my judgment and reason may approve . . . But I shall Confess too much if I don't take care," she peevishly added then quickly signed off.[42]

The current gossip in Braintree was all about young Lucy Apthorp, who had just stunned her neighbors by marrying a British officer she'd known less than half a year. Betsy and John Quincy both wrote the news to Nabby, Betsy discreetly asking what her cousin thought of "sudden matches," while John Quincy made no bones about his scorn for both the officer and their old friend. "Can an acquaintance of less than three months, give any two persons sufficient insight, into each others characters, to assure them, that they must trust to each other their happiness for life?" he with his normal moral certitude demanded.[43] Nabby, usually just as fast to denounce anything unusual, now with uncharacteristic humility demurred. She could not, she said, presume to divine Lucy Apthorp's motives, though she did suspect that couples who "Consider, and reconsider and delay, till they are doubtfull what they would do" were at least as foolish as those who marry in haste. Besides, the faux pas, if it existed, lay less in Lucy's timing than in her choice of a mate: "If the Gentleman had been an American whose Character was known and approved it would have been a very different case."

And this was precisely what Abigail hoped to convince their friends in America at the end of February when she at last identified Nabby's suitor and announced they were engaged. To John Quincy she wrote most defensively. "You will say, is not this sudden?" she anticipated his initial disapproval, and went on to cite analogous happy events in literature and to praise William Smith's strict forbearance during the agonizing months before Tyler was dismissed.[44] To ward off clucking in the Haverhill parish, Abigail appealed to her sister Elizabeth's romantic nature and flattered her that Nabby would doubtless open up to *her* first. ("Your Neice has always been more communicative to you, than to any other of her friends.")[45] And it was not until she'd expatiated further on the resemblance between Nabby's husband-to-be and Mary's ideal Richard that Abigail at last let down her guard and confided her apprehensions about this and all marriages to her closest female friend in the world:

> The book of futurity is wisely closed from our Eyes. If our prospects are built upon a virtuous foundation it is all we can do towards ensuring their success. My own lot in Life has been attended with so many circumstances, that at my first sitting out, I could have formed no Idea of, that I did not think it worth my while to object to the present connection of your Neice, because it was probable that she would be separated from me, and that I could not see what her future destination in life might be. It will feel very hard however to me to part with her.

Abigail did not, she on a happier note concluded, worry about Nabby's choice in a spouse.[45]

The reaction from home was univocal. John Quincy was so relieved his sister had escaped the horrible fate of marrying Royall Tyler (of whom he'd heard worse than his mother could imagine from people whose honor was beyond dispute) that almost anyone seemed preferable. "I rejoice, I greatly rejoice," Mary agreed, and Elizabeth too spontaneously expressed her approval, then wrapped herself in her literary mantle and in one of her loveliest passages informed Abigail why Nabby had fallen in love again so soon:

> I consider the human Mind something like a musical Instrument, where if any of the Notes are silent, or out of tune, it produces a vacuum, a discord, which interrupts the harmony of the whole Machine. The Mind when once touched by the tender

Passion of Love, and set to certain number of Ideas, will never
after be in Unison, unless it find some Object capable of vibrat-
ing those delicate Keys. And experience informs us, that it does
not require so great an Artist to put an Instrument in Tune, as it
did at first to form one.[47]

While always paling beside the significance of Nabby's coming
marriage, other events did compete for the sisters' attention during the
first half of 1786. Out of frugality and resentment, American businesses
continued to not pay their debts to English merchants. Great Britain
continued to ridicule the ambassador of a penurious and irresponsible
so-called nation that still had no power to control its states.[48] Abigail
grew fatter while Elizabeth grew thinner. The peach trees drooped in
the Adamses' orchard in Braintree, and months after the fact news at
last reached London that Aunt Tufts had slipped away.[49] The attachment of her grieving nieces endured and deepened. "Never was there a
stronger affection than that which binds in a threefold chord your
Mamma and her dear sisters," Abigail, feeling emotional one day in
February, wrote John Quincy. "Heaven preserve us to each other for
Many Years to come."[50]

As much as they needed to report news, the sisters sought to convey
the texture of their daily lives, as when Mary broke off a letter to Abigail, exclaiming "Adieu I must run" because Elizabeth had arrived
from Haverhill, or when Abigail described herself writing to Mary
while Colonel Smith sat cozily "prating" to Nabby on the settee. Memories of the Revolution united them. As she watched the inauguration
of a new bridge to Charleston, Mary's thoughts flew back to the Battle
of Bunker's Hill, as did Abigail's when she caught sight of a portrait of
the martyred Dr. Warren in a London gallery.[51]

Whereas the sexes had equal rights to view pictures at London
galleries, Abigail and Nabby were left home sulking when John and
Colonel Smith drove off to Sheridan's new hit, *The School for Scandal.*
Abigail in particular resented the reason for their exclusion, which was
that women were forced to pay a huge surcharge to see popular plays.
On principal, she refused.

By contrast, only women had the dubious privilege of being invited
to the Queen's birthday party, where Nabby appeared in pink and sil-

ver and Abigail was at the height of fashion in a "spanish fly" bright green satin with crepe and a gold fringe. The rooms at St. James were so clogged, the women's dresses so festooned that the floors fairly gleamed with rattled trimmings. The British noblewomen groveling to the Queen looked like giant apes in Nabby's opinion, and it was a pity the King could come up with no more imaginative greeting than, "Do you get out much this weather?"—the same question he'd asked her for months.[52]

During Harvard's winter break, Charles Adams and Billy Cranch visited Aunt Elizabeth in Haverhill. Jefferson shortly afterward came to England and made a tour of the British gardens with John. Late winter snow deluged London as well as Braintree. A "worthy, sensible" parson—in Mary's opinion—was selected to succeed their father in the Weymouth meetinghouse,[53] and Dr. Price stirred the Adamses with a sermon discouraging nationalism and urging philanthropy toward men of all religions.[54] Letters crossed the Atlantic via Captain Lyde or Callahan or Cushing. "It adds greatly to our happiness if we can communicate it," Mary wrote Abigail[55]; while Elizabeth, hurt by her niece's failure to confide the progress of her courtship, lectured Nabby that *"Reserve will wound"* and asked, "Is *Love really a narrower* of the *Heart?*"[56]

In March, John Quincy passed his exams and was admitted to Harvard while Colonel Smith stepped up his pleading with John and Abigail to let him marry posthaste. Dissident marriages were illegal in Great Britain. So the lovers would need an Anglican minister, and luck was in their favor when John's choice, the Bishop of Asaph (a friend of Dr. Price's), announced he would only remain in London through the middle of June. To secure Asaph, the Adamses agreed to push the wedding forward and quickly applied for and received a special license from the Bishop of Canterbury (which as a rule was granted exclusively to nobles and Members of Parliament, Abigail could not help boasting to Mary), to suspend the church service and allow Nabby to marry at home. Lodging was soon found for the couple on Wimpole Street. Abigail began pricing china and linen and wishing more than ever for a balloon to transport one of her nieces across the ocean to keep her company now that Nabby was poised to leave.

On June 11, the eve of Nabby's wedding, Abigail lay awake in bed remembering her own journey to the altar. How long her engagement had been drawn out because of her parents' disapproval of John Adams. How uncertain her future had seemed as a lowly lawyer's wife. By contrast, Nabby was about to marry a man her parents blessed and the world honored. And yet she too faced the unknown of sexual love and the age-old struggle to separate from her family.

"Any agitation of mind, either painfull or pleasurable always drives sleep from my eyes," Abigail confided to Mary, explaining that the prospect of Nabby's wedding stirred joy and sorrow in almost equal degree. For "Satisfied as I am with the person [she has chosen], the event is too Solemn and important [for me] not to feel an agitation equal to what I experienced for myself when my own lot was cast."[57] And Mary perfectly understood Abigail's maternal identification: she would tremble too in her place, she felt sure.[58]

When finally Abigail fell asleep, who should appear in her dream but Royall Tyler, come to plague her once again with the unsettled matter of why he fell out of love with Nabby. Or worse, maybe Abigail had misread him, and he loved her daughter still? In any case, Abigail continued to "feel" for Tyler, she admitted to her older sister. Once she'd loved him enough to want him for her daughter, and she saw his virtues still. Though he lacked prudence and judgment, there was "good Sense . . . benevolence and kindness" in his nature. A different history and education might have made him a fine match. Even now she could not denounce the man who'd amused her on those lonely nights by her fireside in Braintree. She wished him well.

But she also wished him off her conscience; so it was a relief when the momentous day of June 12 dawned, and the apparition of Royall Tyler vanished. Abigail set her gaze on the future as the "fine portly" Bishop of Asaph consecrated Nabby's marriage to William in front of a small party of acquaintances, including the John Singleton Copleys, and two of the groom's close friends. Sadly, there was no Betsy or Lucy Cranch to stand by Nabby, who with her usual composure endured the embarrassment of pronouncing the Anglican "I Abigail take thee William" (Puritan women were only required to curtsey). Afterward, the bishop told Abigail he foresaw great happiness for the newlyweds. For now, though, Nabby was sadder even than her mother imagined, since beyond the pain of leaving her parents was the worry that her parents would be lonely without *her*. And she was certainly right on the second score, Abigail acknowledged to Mary. John was no less affected than she herself.

It was the first of July, nearly three weeks after the wedding, when Nabby left for housekeeping a half mile away at Wimpole Street. The following morning, Abigail concluded her report to Mary: "Mr. Adams went into his Library after Breakfast, and I into my chamber where I usually spend my forenoons. Mr. A commonly takes his daily walk about one oclock, but by eleven he came into my room with his Hat and cane, "and, Well I have been to See them: what, said I, could not you stay till your usual Hour? No, I could not, he replied, I wanted to go before Breakfast."[59] Now a whole afternoon loomed before dinner, when they had next agreed to meet.

CHAPTER XI

"The Disunited State of America"

. . .

IT WAS THE LAST WEEK OF AN UNUSUALLY WARM SEPTEMBER, WHEN 1,500 Massachusetts farmers, lugging pitchforks and sprouting hemlocks from their caps, like Continental soldiers, strode up to the Supreme Court at Springfield, Massachusetts. The year was 1786. The foreclosure of yet another farm was on the docket, and the unruly crowd determined the trial should not take place.

The leader of this embittered group was 39-year-old Daniel Shays, the son of Irish indentured servants. A day laborer, Shays rose to the rank of captain during the Revolution and afterward went home to Massachusetts, where he purchased 251 acres of farm land, thus becoming a citizen, almost a gentleman by American standards. Indeed, his life seemed to validate the promise of equality in America.

Then came the post-war depression, accompanied by deflation and exacerbated by a new burden of taxes levied to repay merchants who had helped fund the war. Many of these merchants held mortgages on the farmers' property. When the hard-hit farmers were unable to pay their mortgages, court after court sided with the lenders and ordered foreclosures on their land. Shays himself barely escaped debtors' prison. His urgent petitions for clemency to the governor and legislature proved futile. As Shays saw it, this was a clear case of taxation without representation. So taking a leaf from the recent Revolution, on September 25 he and his determined band stormed and occupied the court at Springfield, preventing the latest foreclosure and emboldening thousands of fellow sufferers to oppose injustice.

A righteous minority had triumphed but a government by law had failed. Four men died in the taking of the courthouse and the citizens of Massachusetts, never inclined to pay tax collectors in the first place, had fresh encouragement to flaunt government orders. So there was no money in state coffers to compensate legislators like Richard Cranch, who had already worked two years without salary. "The people will not pay their Tax, nor their debts of any kind, and who shall make them?" Mary wondered. "The Publick owes us three Hundred pound and we cannot get a shilling of it," she complained in a letter to Abigail. Luckily, they had scrimped and "liv'd with great caution" or they too would be in debt, "a thing I dread more than the most extreme Poverty."[1]

Mary spoke sarcastically of "the disunited State of america." "We are all in a confusion," she sighed, "and what will be the consequence I know not. Anarchy I fear . . . There is not the least energy in governement." And indeed, delegates to the federal Congress, disheartened by their powerlessness under the weak Constitution, had been staying home in droves. Recent sessions had been canceled for want of a mere quorum.[2] Two months later, when the weather turned bitter cold and Shays's revolts spread unchecked throughout western Massachusetts, Mary despaired that America was following the trajectory of all other failed republics and "hastening fast to monarchy"[3] as the only alternative to chaos.

Abigail, reading reports of Shays's rebellion on a warm, foggy November day in London, came to the same conclusion:

"I could not refrain shedding tears . . . to behold my countrymen who had so nobly fought and bled for freedom, tarnishing their glory, loosing the bands of society, introducing anarchy confusion and despotism, forging domestick chains for Posterity. For the experience of ages, and the Historic page teach us, that a popular Tyranny never fails to be followed by the arbitrary government of a single person."[4]

John and Abigail were in perfect accord that "order is heavens first Law" and its disruption a disaster for any republic. The false peace of their lives abroad frustrated them—like the balmy days England enjoyed all that winter while record snowstorms closed Harvard weeks before the scheduled break and blasted their Braintree home. Abigail envied her sisters their proximity to the crisis for, as she explained to Elizabeth, "The more quarrelsome and turbulent you grow, the more anxious I am to be with you, not that I think it pleasant fishing in troubled waters, but because immagination paints higher then reality, and the danger apprehended is always worse than that which is experienced, in short I have seen my Countrymen armed one against the other, and the divided house falling to the ground."⁵

Elizabeth took a different stance than both her sisters, replying that the current crisis was moral not political. Wherever she went among her husband's parishioners, she heard opinions "dictated by Fear, Ignorance, Malice, Envy, and self-interest the most powerful of all . . . No One is willing to believe *themselves* the *Cause* of any Evil they feel" so they turned the blame outward and accused the government. She, on the other hand, believed change was a religious experience and must arise from within.

AT THE END OF DECEMBER, Nabby, now five months pregnant, and William Smith planned a trip to Bath to inspect the Palladian Crescent and (Puritan scruples notwithstanding) luxuriate in the fashionable resort at high season. Abigail joined them, while John stayed at his desk in London.

It was not the—ever unsatisfying—business of seeking trade concessions from England that kept John from joining the family party. Rather, frustrated by his idleness in London and reading about Shays's Rebellion and its affront to the very existence of constitutional government at home, John was impelled to reexamine the huge, thorny issue of what political system best suited the new American republic. The book he began writing was partly a defense of his own Massachusetts Constitution, partly a revised view of America after nearly a decade abroad. It took the form of a riposte to a letter written by the French philosophe Baron Anne-Robert Turgot. Turgot's point was that America had failed to live up to its mandate. Rather than imagining a new social contract, it was slavishly emulating the very system it (and France!) had fought so hard to overthrow. According to Turgot, America's worst mistake, manifest in eleven of its thirteen state Constitutions,[6] was perpetuating England's two-chamber congress. Liberty and equality, Turgot argued, depended on rule by a single legislature: anything less pure and simple would blight the general good.

John retorted that the general good was perfectly served by the British Constitution, which was in fact "the most stupendous fabrick of human invention" ever effected on earth. Its greatness lay in shunning precisely what Turgot sought. For men were not born equal. Without safeguards, rule would always fall to the privileged few. Look at ancient Greece! Single legislatures inevitably devolved into martial law or anarchy. In order to guarantee the greatest good to the greatest number, a mixed government composed of an executive, judiciary, and two-part legislature was crucial. And as John had chided Thomas Paine when *Common Sense* cried out for unicameral rule eleven years earlier, equality must be constructed, not presumed.

So far John's *Defence of the American Constitutions* sounded very much in accord with Abigail's correspondence with Mary and with Adams's own 1776 *Thoughts on Government*. For all his chagrin at the impotence of the Continental Congress in his new book, Adams continues to emphasize the importance of government on a state level and only in passing notes the need for more federal control. "A government where the laws should prevail would be the kingdom of God," John reiterates, quoting Aristotle. Only now he goes further and stresses the importance of the executive role.

"I tell [John] they will think in America that he is s[e]tting up a King," Abigail, fearful for the book's reception, wrote John Quincy. "He says not, but he is for giving to the Governours of every state the same Authority which the British King has, under the true British Constitution, balancing his power by the two other branches."[7] Unlike *Thoughts, Defence* praises the refinements made over the years by European monarchies, but it also declares up front that the worst republic is preferable to a king: "It would be better for America . . . to ring all the changes with the whole set of bells, and go through all the revolutions of the [ancient] Grecian states, rather than establish a monarchy among them, notwithstanding all the great and real improvements made in that kind of government."[8]

The difference in tone between the two works is marked. The gov-

ernment envisioned in *Thoughts* (written just before the Declaration of
Independence) wholeheartedly embraces Enlightenment faith that the
world is getting better. America is the future, England the past. Fear,
"the foundation of most governments," is the younger Adams's nemesis, for (he wrote) "it is so sordid and brutal a passion, and renders men
in whose breasts it predominates so stupid and miserable, that Americans will not be likely to approve of any political institution which is
founded on it."[9] Rather, "noble principal" and man's "most generous
affections" were to impel the framers of the new state Constitutions.
There would be frequent elections not only to limit the influence of any
single individual but to draw on the best in all.

Defence (1787), on the other hand, has little to say about the nobility
of humanity. It is not that man is fundamentally wicked, as Hobbes
and Calvin had claimed; he is simply weak. Passions—notably greed
for money, praise, and power—do and always will consume him. As in
the self-loathing of his early diaries, John peered into himself to discover:

> The cunning with which [these passions] hide themselves
> from others, and from the man himself too; the patience with
> which they wait for opportunities; the torments they voluntarily
> suffer for a time, to secure a full enjoyment at length; the inven-
> tions, the discoveries, the contrivances they suggest to the under-
> standing sometimes in the dullest dunces in the world, if they
> could be described in writing would pass for great genius.

Laws no longer spring from "generous affections," but are twisted
into being by mistrust. Adams approvingly quotes Montesquieu, who
says craving control over others is innate to the human condition, and
also Machiavelli, who insists that, whatever the truth may be, government should be created on the *premise* that man is bad. And it is not just
Turgot that Adams disputes in this later work. The old differences between himself and Jefferson were widening as well. For where Jefferson, whose spirits had been restored after his wife's death by a trip to
Paris, saw change as beneficial, Adams, with his Congregationalist
background, prized stability above all else. Negotiating with Europe
had made both men wary of foreigners, but they arrived at opposite

conclusions. Where Jefferson continued to favor frequent elections, Adams now repudiated them, writing his friend in Paris:

> As often as elections happen, the danger of foreign Influence recurs. The less frequently they happen the less danger.—And if the Same Man may be chosen again, it is probable he will be, and the danger of foreign Influence will be less . . . Elections, my dear sir, Elections to offices which are great objects of Ambition, I look at with terror. Experiments of this kind have been so often tried, and so universally found productive of Horrors, that there is great Reason to dread them.[10]

Quite a statement from the man who a decade earlier wanted governors replaced every year!

IT WAS ON NEW YEAR'S EVE, 1786, while Abigail was enjoying "the clear sunshine and fine air of Bath,"[11] that the most vicious snowstorm in seventy years struck Massachusetts. Mary watched neighbors forced to climb out their bedroom windows onto snow drifting nearly to their roofs. Harvard now had been closed for weeks, and Charles and Tommy Adams were ensconced with their cousins Billy, Betsy, and Lucy at the Cranches' in Braintree. But John Quincy had determined to take his chances gathering firewood in Cambridge and, like his father at Grosvenor Square, he stayed behind to work. He too was contemplating the state of the American government. But his vision of the future was more salubrious than John's. "I am . . . in hopes that in two or three months . . . tranquility, will be perfectly restored," he wrote his mother. And he went on to inform her that the precise argument John was now struggling to articulate—that "a pure democracy, appears to much greater advantage, in speculation, than when reduced to practice"—was already gaining wide acceptance in America and was in essence old news. What is more, though he had spent his whole youth abroad, he never felt tempted to advocate Europe as a template. On the contrary, when debating politics with his classmates, "I find . . . that I am the best republican here."[12]

In January, Boston merchants took matters into their own hands and raised a militia that, on order of the governor, routed the rebellious farmers and in effect put the revolt to an end. But the common man's cause had been heard, the justice of Massachusetts law questioned. Besides, Shays, though convicted, was quickly pardoned, exasperating those like Abigail, who still insisted the farmers acted out of purely imaginary grievances and were overjoyed to see them trounced.[13] But many at home read the militia's supposed victory as a stalemate. After all, how could the government boast of transforming the social contract when, just like the English, they addressed popular resentment at the barrel of a gun?

In September of 1786, a small group of nationalists encouraged by the activists Alexander Hamilton and James Madison had called for a meeting of all the states to address the threats arising from the weakness of the current federal Constitution. Initially, little interest was generated. But Shays's Rebellion raised the specter of class warfare, and now state after state began signing up to attend. In the end, even Congress endorsed the means of its own undoing and called for the gathering of a Constitutional Convention in Philadelphia on the second Monday in May.

"I WENT TO MEETING in the morning—our Parson [Wibird] is as dull as Death which was his subject," Betsy Cranch jested in her diary in April 1786, shortly after her return from Haverhill. The sea out her window was blue; pink and white blossoms were bursting in the Cranch orchard. When not suffering old Parson Wibird's foolishness in church, she was reading the inspiring sermons of Dr. Price and François Fénelon, and—John Thaxter having obligingly receded into memory—dreaming of the love of her life. For while Thomas Perkins was still slogging through the wilderness, he was with her in spirit and influenced everything she did—or so she wrote in her diary.

And she felt increasingly confident that what she did was important to both God and the nation. Far more than Europeans, post-war Americans were giving equal value to private and public spheres. Being a good wife required conversing with your husband in addition to mending his cloak or framing a quilt or getting up before dawn Monday mornings to scorch your arms in the family wash or to make cheese.

Six years before, when Betsy was seventeen and had just begun thinking about courtship, only about half as many women as men in the United States could sign their names.[14] But the world was changing. The frivolous girls school where Nabby Adams polished her dancing during the Revolution now vied with female institutes like Philadelphia's Young Ladies' Academy, which taught "male" subjects and exhorted "wisdom is the principal thing."[15] A bold new proselytizer named Judith Sargeant Murray was writing screeds in the *Gentlemen and Ladies Town and Country Magazine* imploring young women to prepare for independence and longing for the time when "The term helpless widow, might be rendered as unfrequent and inapplicable as that of helpless widower."[16]

Aunt Abigail insisted that possessing knowledge actually made a woman prettier,[17] while Betsy's own mother mocked the old bromide that men shun learned women, insisting that *her* girls would never settle for husbands whose minds were inferior to theirs.[18]

Betsy was not only learned, but rife with sensibility, and no day was complete before she took out her diary and examined her mood. During the summer of 1786, happiness predominated. Harvard was out, and each afternoon brought some new activity, like scrambling with friends over rocks to the ocean, or rambling through heaths of grazing sheep. Or sailing play boats with Aunt Elizabeth's comic little six-year-old Betsy Q. After a day in picturesque nearby Squantom, Betsy Cranch concluded that Arcadia was at her doorstep. And even when the August heat and an implosion of visitors added to the stress of making and mending clothes for the boys to return to college, and she felt "almost a stranger to myself" because she had scarcely a moment to write or read, there was the delight of receiving a letter from Thomas Perkins reporting that he was healthy and prospering.

Though still formally unacknowledged, their courtship was moving forward. Betsy and Perkins no longer communicated through third parties but openly wrote each other as if they were engaged. In her letters to London, Mary discussed Perkins like a member of the family.

On October 5, Betsy drove to Bridgewater to call on *his* "good Folks." Their humble house and grounds spoke to the poverty that had driven Perkins to Kentucky to improve his lot. Yet she "felt a pleasure at viewing every spot" and was determined to anticipate his return rather than fret about possible calamities. For "Hope cheers the Heart through the gloom of Suspense; and Fancy irradiates the future scene." Perkins was a frequent subject of conversation wherever Betsy traveled. He had "taken full possession of [her] Heart,"[19] Aunt Elizabeth observed.

A balmy October passed, with Shays's Rebellion dominating the conversation. The arrival of a book on English gardening from Aunt Abigail got Betsy thinking about restructuring the Cranches' grounds. Then there was an outing to Harvard to hear Billy and John Quincy address chapel, and always ironing and mantua-making and asserting her literary prowess by copying passages from great authors in her commonplace book. One she quoted at length was Milton's warning against too much passion in marriage: "Love is attended by a constant inquietude, which is by no means compatible with that tranquility which ought to subsist in the married state."[20]

On October 30, a snowstorm suddenly blasted New England into winter. Richard Cranch returned from Boston with a three-month-old letter scripted in a strange hand. It carried the worst possible news. The savages Betsy feared had not killed Thomas Perkins, but pneumonia had—in just a few days last August, when she had likely been darning a sock for Tommy Adams or sewing a pair of pants. And he died delirious in a strange land without her. "It is right, support me heaven!" she cried upon hearing the news.[21] But two weeks passed before she could acknowledge in her diary, "Yes, the dreaded event has taken place and Heaven deprives me of the friend on whom my Heart lean'd."[22]

"THE [CRANCHES] ARE IN AFFLICTION on account of the death of Mr. Perkins," John Quincy wrote in *his* diary, noting that Betsy's "particular attachment" and "great sensibility" deepened the wound. "Her grief is silent, but is painted expressively on her countenance."[23] Aunt Elizabeth anguished for her niece, while Mary watched Betsy at one moment struggle to triumph over misfortune, only, inevitably, to succumb to grief in the next. Then Betsy would turn to God and beg for resignation. It was only in a letter to Aunt Abigail that she openly bemoaned her fate. The British gardening book her aunt had sent now seemed an apt metaphor for all the pleasure that neither knowledge nor imagination could secure for her. Before reading it:

> I had not by any means, an adequate idea of the perfection to which They had brought the art of ornamenting their farms and grounds in England; I think they must be enchantingly beautiful; I felt when I finished it, as if I almost regretted having read it: for having never before had Ideas of such perfection, in my mind, wherewith to compare what I saw, I could think these beautiful and they satisfied me ... but now my standard is altered, and all appear uncouth and imperfect, I am wishing to alter this, pull down that ... turn the course of a rivulet, widen a brook, and a thousand other whims and impossibilities are coming into mind ... but alas all in vain![24]

And, yes, she still believed that luck did not *assure* happiness. She might be just as miserable if her gardens were perfect and Perkins alive and headed home. But where did knowing this get her?

For a change of scene, in the middle of the winter, Mary sent Betsy to Uncle Tufts's in Weymouth. There a Mr. Jacob Norton, straight out of Harvard, was boarding while he preached on a trial basis at First Church. Four years after Reverend Smith's death, his post was again vacant. Three candidates had rejected Weymouth's meager salary, so the town was willing to overlook Norton's youth and extreme Calvinism and admire his fire and intellectual bent. What is more, he was handsome. "Mr. Norton appears to be quite agreable—loves philosophical conversation," Betsy Cranch noted on January 25.[25]

But her spirits remained low, even as she reported that he had begun calling on her family. "How small, few, and uninteresting are the events ... which my secluded life afford," she commented at the end of the winter. In May she had a relentless pain in the back of her head and could barely rouse herself to help boil hams and bacons and tongues and make cider and biscuits for the commencement party her mother had spent a year arranging for Billy and John Quincy, which would take place on July 18. Then she missed both the solemn occasion and afterward the comedy of their old servant gorging alamode beef[26] and plumb cake off the guests' dishes as he cleared them at Mary's feast.[27]

Betsy was not "well enough to be in such a Bustle . . . her nerves are so weak that she cannot bear to be in the company of Strangers," Mary explained to Abigail, though she bathed in cold water and rode horseback, as the doctor proposed.[28]

She was still thin, pale, and febrile on the anniversary of Perkins's death. "He sought for fame, honour and fortune! . . . o elusive hope!" she lamented in her diary on August 22 and went on to berate herself for obsessively contemplating Perkins's unfulfilled promise and, by extension, her own "languid dullness" and never-ending grief.

But just four evenings later, after a perfectly average day of morning work and afternoon visiting, Betsy felt completely different—like her old self: "Every pulse beat[s] harmoniously," she marveled in her diary.[29] And while she attributed the change to improved circulation after a bracing walk with John Quincy, Mary thought otherwise. She hinted her more romantic suspicions to Abigail: "Was you hear I would whisper something."

ON JANUARY 24, 1787, John Adams wrote Congress that he was determined to leave Europe the moment his London commission expired the following January. It would be foolish to remain longer. The turmoil in Massachusetts, the discord between the states, the impotence of the Continental Congress all made negotiating favorable trade agreements with the British downright impossible. Besides, his public life was in shambles. While Congress dawdled for months and then wrote only the most desultory response to his urgent petitions, the constant ridicule of him in the British press was driving him mad.

And yet, after nearly a decade abroad, he also felt alienated from his native country. As he saw it, through no fault of his own, his prodigious efforts on America's behalf had come to naught—or, to be specific, had come to Shays's Rebellion. His life was a "series of Remorses," he in a particularly pettish moment informed his brother-in-law. Besides, over time, and despite all his complaints about London's fog and pomposity, talks by the Cranch fireside had become a vague memory while he sought outings to British theatres and country houses to calm his nerves. Eccentric old Dr. Wibird felt as remote as China when John sat on a hard bench in Hackney, drinking in Dr. Price's sermons. The Braintree

cottage was like a doll's house beside Grosvenor Square. More importantly, he feared for what Enlightenment authors approvingly called
his fame, or honor in the world, as he reveals in a long complaint to
Thomas Jefferson:

> For a Man who has been thirty Years rolling like a stone
> never three years in the same Place, it is no very pleasant Specu-
> lation, to cross the seas . . . in a State of Uncertainty what is to be
> his fate; what reception he shall meet at home; whether he shall
> set down in private Life to his Plough; or push into turbulent
> Scenes of Sedition and Tumult; whether be sent to Congress, or
> a Convention or God knows what.[30]

As for England itself, John's feelings remained as ambivalent as
when, long ago, he boasted to Abigail about the superiority of their
British ancestry while exhorting the Continental Congress to break
with the King. Leaving London now, he grumbled to Richard Cranch,
was "an irksome undertaking—to break up a settled habitation . . . at
any time of life is no small matter, but when people grow into years and
are weary of changes, it is more disagreeable."[31]

Abigail felt otherwise. A month after John alerted Congress of their
departure, she exulted to Mary, "So . . . my dear sister I most joyfully
accept your invitation and will come home God Willing e'er another
year expires." In case Mary had any doubt, Abigail quipped, "I shall
quit Europe with more pleasure than I came to it."[32]

In a sense, she had never left her sisters. Throughout the previous
four years, the children had always entangled them. There were Mary
and Elizabeth's constant ministrations to Tommy, Charles, and John
Quincy Adams and Abigail's heroic struggle to assuage her indebtedness for their caregiving by finding the perfect silk or book on gardening for her sisters' girls. And there was the eternal need of sisters to
outshine one another, tempered, of course, by the Puritan insistence on
a hierarchy of birth. Abigail was surely the sibling to best at the moment. So in one letter to London, even Mary felt impelled to boast of
substitute parenting the Adams boys during the Harvard break, and
she describes them "all sitting in a row before our chimney board in the
little Parlour" and then taking up their flutes to accompany Betsy

Cranch at the harpsichord and Billy on violin."[33] And Abigail, eager for any excuse to show deference to her older sister, answers: "You drew such a lovely picture of our children dwelling together in unity around your Hospitable Board that I am sure no amusement here ever gave me such heartfelt satisfaction as I received from your description only."[34]

Elizabeth, ever the youngest, was more openly competitive. It was not enough for her to boast of homely pleasures in America. She had to outdo Abigail in language as well as life. "Return, to America for one moment, my Sister," she all but orders Abigail in one letter, and then launches into a narrative about a July boat excursion to a little island off the coast of Haverhill, with the obvious intent of displaying her literary gifts. For while Mary's letters are breathless as conversation and Abigail prides herself on using the first expression that comes to her head, Elizabeth, as pressed for time as either of them, continues to strive for poetic effect. Madame de Sevigne's lyrical depictions of landscapes are clearly her model as she preciously sets the scene for her pastoral trip:

"A little before Sunset we all embarked in our new Boat with a sail spread over the Top, the School Benches answered for seats ... the Doors, Windows, and Banks of the River all Thronged with People." Forty-five minutes later, when the passengers arrived on the island, they erected a shady booth "covered with ... large Clusters of Grapes interwove with Wreaths of Flowers.

"Fancy yourself most conveniently seated in this Bower," Elizabeth invites Abigail, "your Sons, Neices, and particular Friends noticed, by the most polite attention—sweet Merrimac [River] gently gliding beneath your feet—Health-Peace, and Plenty smiling around you— Good-humour-without ribaldry—Ease—Complacency—every Necessary, and Convenience, all conspiring to make you happy.

"Here a lofty Oak—and there a branching Elm—and little Thickets of Wood," she further embellishes her description; then, eager as ever to signal a favorable comparison, concludes, "Whether in all your Travels, you will find a happier Circle, than I have described, I something doubt."[35]

Even an ocean couldn't stop the three sisters from intuiting one another's whereabouts, as on the day in May when Abigail wrote Mary,

"Is not Sister Shaw just making her annual visit to you? O how I envy you."[36] And Mary wrote back, "By my last letters you will see that you were right in your conjecture that Sister Shaw was with me and we were also right in ours, for we thought that you would suppose it and we took a peculiar pleasure in supposing that we were at one time all thinking the same thing."[37]

Mary and Abigail also agreed on the debased state of American women. In anticipation of the Constitutional Convention, Mary broke with friends of both sexes when she exhorted Abigail *not* to apologize for writing about politics. Rather than losing themselves in luxury, women should study public policy and take part in it as well by influencing their husbands and sons. "Let no one say that the Ladies are of no importance in the affairs of the nation . . . We do not want spirit. We only want to have it properly directed."[38]

Always eager to improve her intellect, Abigail, who had just signed up for twelve philosophical lectures, took Mary's argument a step further:

> My dear Sister I have ever observed that it is a most Dangerous thing for a Female to be distinguished for any qualification Beyond the rest of her sex. Whatever may be her Deportment, she is sure to draw upon herself the jealousy of the men and the envy of the women. Nor do I see any way to remedy this evil but by increasing the number of accomplished woman, a monopoly of any kind is always envidious. [39]

Their minds were even more attuned in the days leading up to Harvard's 1787 graduation. The previous July, Mary, with her usual foresight, had written Abigail that though "a year seems in this changeable world a long time to look forward . . . if our children should live till the next commencement, we must think of some little intertainment for them." Since Billy Cranch and John Quincy Adams were best friends, the two families could split the cost and plan a single party after the ceremony in Cambridge. This Mary was born to orchestrate; the Adamses need only approve her views.

First, there was the menu to settle. Pig legs had to be treated before,

> 6
>
> dangerous thing for a ~~female~~ to be distinguished for any qualification beyond the rest of her sex. whatever may be her Department she is sure to draw upon her the jealousy of the men and the envy of the women, nor do I see any way to remedy this evil but by increasing the number of accomplished women, a monopoly of any kind is always envidious I have never received a line since m Stay since she left england. which I have wondered at considering the intimacy which subsisted between us when here. I thought her reasons good for chusing to go to America. it was natural for her to wish to be with her relations during the long voyages of captain Hay. rather than to reside at Board abroad. I knew she endeavoured to influence him to go with her. but he was in good business here. & saild with more safety in a british Ship. than he could in an American vessel subject to the capture of Algerines as he thought at that time. he was about taking a voyage when she left him. in which he expected to be absent 15 months I think I should have done as she did, if I had been in her place I knew Captain Hay met with a disapaintment. by his owners loosing his Vessel. by which means captain Hay was detained here a long time — nor do I know how long he has saild when circumstances are unknown, it greatly alters appearances
>
> Mrs Elworthy I saw at her House not long ago. she was well then. they live in the city & have but very small appartments not calculated to see company. they are people of business honest industerous & obliging. but their whole House is very little larger than your office — mr John Cranch

winter, swathed in bacon slabs if they were to serve beef rump stew–which was the customary main dish, "excepting [for] those who chuse to lay out a thousand dollars for an intertainment which nobody is the better for," Mary informed Abigail, who, bowing to this insuperable manager, answered that she and John "submit wholy to your opinion and judgement."[40] "We neither wish on the one hand to be lavish nor on the other Parsimonious," she sounded the family creed.[41]

In a sign of the changing times, John Quincy and Billy were chosen to give speeches in English rather than Latin. Because of the depressed economy, Harvard asked that no clothes be bought or sewn for this year's affair. Recently, Abigail had sent Mary, now 46, and Elizabeth, 37, colorful silks, ideal for graduation. ("I was deliberating for some

Mary and Abigail were both chagrined by the
debased state of American women.

time whether [the silk] should be virgin white; or sky [blue]," she had
teased Elizabeth, "upon the whole I concluded that you had more pre-
tentions to the Skys . . . so I bought the blew, which is vastly the present
taste."[42]) The eldest sister promptly set her green silk aside to follow
Harvard's orders, while the youngest dismissed the rules as spiteful in
her own attention-starved position and seized the pleasure of designing
a "sky-born" gown posthaste.

When Billy and John Quincy returned to Braintree to hone their

speeches a month before graduation, added to the normal tumult of the
Cranch household were screeching saws and thudding hammers: Mary
had ordered tables and chairs built from scratch for over a hundred
guests. On July 16, two days before commencement, while Mary and
Billy were consumed with preparations and John Quincy paced the
house, praying for the ceremonies to be canceled, and Elizabeth swelled
with pride at her own crucial role in her nephews' education, Abigail,
John, and Nabby were longing to be spirited across the Atlantic.[43]

All three sisters felt deeply involved in the 1787
Harvard Commencement.

   Then July 18 dawned cool and fair on both sides of the ocean. Miraculously for New England, the mid-summer air felt like fall. Graduates strolling the Harvard common were seen clapping their hands on
their sides to keep warm.[44] "I give you joy of the day," Abigail wrote
John Quincy, who was competing with a classmate named Freeman for
best orator of his year. Each boy spoke on the deterioration of public
faith in America. John Quincy moved those who were close enough to
see him with what Mary called his "faculty of [throwing] expression
into his countinance." But, overall, Freeman was gauged the more eloquent speaker, and Elizabeth, who prided herself on impartiality, con-

firmed this verdict in her letter to Abigail, while Mary (who couldn't even attend the ceremony because she was preparing the party) reported a general consensus that John Quincy surpassed not merely Freeman but everyone who had ever spoken at the school.[45]

And while nerves had undermined Billy Cranch's delivery, his cry for balance of power in government (sounding his uncle's cause) was also a triumph. "Never did you see two Happier Faces than theirs when they return'd from meeting," Mary told Abigail, "I do not believe they will ever feel so happy again."[46]

"The Day—the mighty Day is over," Mary exulted when she was alone with memories and surplus flour. They had fed a hundred guests dinner, treated three hundred more to wine and sweets, and still had a plumb cake in reserve for John Adams's mother. Parson Wibird had once again lost the battle with inertia and stayed home in Braintree. (His excuse was a broken chaise and not wanting to wear boots in the summer.) Nevertheless, the governor, several senators, professors, and tutors paid their respects at the Cranch reception and pontificated on this and that like their royal equivalents in the castles of England and France. "I had as much small Talk to do as their Majestys upon a presentation day," Mary clucked in her letter to Abigail, but no Queen, she felt sure, was ever so proud.

ON APRIL 2, 1787, four months before her brother's graduation party at Harvard, Nabby Adams Smith gave birth to a healthy baby boy in her mother's house in London. He was named William after his father, and christened at his grandparents' home on Grosvenor Square by Dr. Price. Nabby had endured the pregnancy with her normal fortitude, while Abigail, remembering the agony of her own childbirths and the heartbreak of producing a dead girl almost exactly ten years earlier, was house-bound with a high fever during her daughter's final month. "What we suffer for our children is much more distressing than what we feel for ourselves," Mary commiserated from Braintree.[47]

Nabby passed through her ordeal no better or worse than most women, Abigail afterward informed her sisters. Abigail's own fever persisted, but her spirits rose. "My Grandson be sure is a fine Boy," she boasted to Lucy Cranch at the end of April.[48] She taunted Elizabeth

Shaw that she was a *"great Aunt . . . you may put up with the term,
since your sister is obliged to . . . with that of Grandmamma,"*[49] which
sounded "quite unfashionable and vulgar" and not at all how she saw
herself at 43.

William Smith's safe birth was a tonic in a year filled with illness
and worse on both sides of the Atlantic. Not only was Abigail bedridden with rheumatic fever, but the Shaw family caught a virulent "throat
distemper"[50] that swept through Haverhill. The sisters prove true to
character in their letters of comfort: Elizabeth, the poet, imagines her
"sisterly spirit" crossing the ocean to succor Abigail, while Abigail, considering herself the family medical expert, instructs Elizabeth to consume her favorite remedy, the Bark, a medical plant whose chief
component is quinine, and smoke her clothes and burn pitch and tar to
purify the air.[51]

But there was no cure for mortality. After years of invalidism, Cotton Tufts's wife, Lucy, slipped away in October of 1785 at her home in
Weymouth. Aunt Smith of the marvelous closet died after a convulsive
fit the following May, and heartbroken Uncle Isaac followed just over
a year later. Their Boston townhouse, that haven of charm and enlightened living, where the sisters as children had escaped for weekends and
later gathered with their own children for inoculations against smallpox, was reduced to part of a small estate.

Even closer to home, there was "our unhappy connection," the sisters' code phrase for their dissipated brother. Alcoholic Billy Smith had
failed in myriad business schemes, become permanently estranged
from his family, borrowed recklessly, and concealed himself so successfully that one desperate lender, unable to find the guilty party in America, began harassing Nabby's husband, William Smith, in London for
her uncle's debts. When Billy died of jaundice away from home on
September 10, 1787, at less than 40, Mary and even Elizabeth were at a
loss for words. "Your own mind will furnish you with the best Idea of
what I feel," Mary wrote Abigail; and Elizabeth echoed her—"Our
feelings I suppose are similar upon this occasion": sorrow and shame.[52]
Abigail, in a reply to Mary, could not resist searching further for the
cause of their brother's dissipation, intimating that he was overin-
dulged:

When I reflect upon [his] Death . . . I can only say, the judge of all will do right. I cannot however upon a Retrospect of His Education refrain from thinking that some very capital mistakes were very undesignedly made. The experience which you and I have since had with regard to the different dispositions & tempers of children would lead us to very different conduct. I say this to you who will not consider it, as any reflection upon the memory of our dear parents, but only as a proof how much the best & worthyest may err, & as some mitigation for the conduct of our deceast Relative.[53]

AT THE END OF MAY 1787 the Constitutional Convention began meeting in Philadelphia. Its mission was to determine the fate of nearly three million Americans, comprising the largest republic on the face of the earth. The fifty-five delegates were a wealthy, well-educated elite, mostly lawyers, mostly men who had served their states on other vital occasions. Conspicuously absent were John Adams and Thomas Jefferson. But their colleague, Madame Helvetius's darling "Frankling," had miraculously survived his Atlantic voyage, and Ben Franklin was hoisted to the statehouse, as to the Adams's Auteuil mansion, on a Paris sedan.

The Philadelphia summer was torrid as usual, the statehouse especially airless because windows had to be closed against an infestation of large black bugs. Still, business got rapidly under way. Within the first week the delegates voted to replace the current single-chamber Congress with a tri-part government modeled on John Adams's Massachusetts Constitution. George Washington was unanimously elected president of the committee, while Virginia's James Madison and New York's Alexander Hamilton led what became known as the Federalist mission: the struggle for a strong central government.

Madison and Hamilton were a study in contrasts: Madison, a small, wizened, 36-year-old bachelor, careful in demeanor and perpetually in black; and Hamilton, a dapper, impulsive, redheaded bastard from the West Indies, a Revolutionary War hero who had married Elizabeth, the daughter of General Philip Schuyler, now one of the most powerful men in New York. Madison, a close friend of Thomas Jefferson's, was a Virginian planter, steeped in southern agrarian values, Hamilton a New Yorker, urban through and through. While Madison envisioned power vested primarily in the legislature, Hamilton, like Adams, believed in a strong executive to the point where he too was accused of monarchial leanings. Madison was renowned as a fervent champion of religious freedom, Hamilton (who had founded the first bank in New York in 1784) as an economist. What bound them was intellectual brilliance coupled with a profound knowledge of political theory and the conviction that the old Constitution must be overthrown, not simply fixed. Their cause was the end of state dominance and the birth of a true nation.

Those who opposed them, the so-called anti-Federalists, demanded that the power of the states endure. Fluctuating between these two camps were delegates who feared monarchs and delegates who feared mobs; advocates for and against a state religion; followers of Hutchinson and of Hobbes; those who wanted elections on a one-citizen-one-vote basis; and those committed to special dispensations for the small states or the large. But all were bound by fear of bankruptcy, civil war, and foreign invasion. When, on September 19, they at last left Philadelphia to petition their constituencies, the majority of delegates had endorsed a Federalist Constitution, though a minority, including Massachusetts's Elbridge Gerry, voted against it, fearing the disempowerment of their states.

Before the Convention, Cotton Tufts, still smarting from Shays's Rebellion, had predicted an imminent Revolution.[54] Now he worried that, while solving the problem of insurgency, the new Constitution opened the door to monarchy, which was worse. The Constitution "has warm advocates for and warm Enemies against it," he equivocated about his personal view in a letter to Abigail.[55] Mary and Elizabeth waited for John Adams to speak before committing themselves, while John Quincy scoffed at the "new continental form of government" and presumed his father, whom he saw as a tired old warrior yearning to quit the battlefield, thought the same.[56] But in fact John was delighted by the Constitution. "It . . . [will] preserve the Union . . . increase Affection, and . . . bring us all to the same mode of thinking," he enthused. A

Bill of Rights was missing, but that would come later, Adams assured the more skeptical Jefferson in Paris.[57] John wrote Cotton Tufts that he pitied opponents of the Constitution like his cousin Sam Adams who "may do no harm in the End: but I should be Sorry to see him, worried [by his shortsightedness] in his old Age."[58]

What is more, the world-weariness John professed in recent letters home was misleading. Nabby with authority informed her brother.

> Respecting your desire that your father should . . . spend the remainder of his days in retirement—I cannot agree with you . . . He has it in his Power to do as much perhaps the most towards establishing [his nation's] Character as a respectable Nation—as any man in America . . . Besides my Brother independent of other important considerations—he would not I am well convinced be Happy in Private Life.

She went on to hint that, should the new Constitution pass, 52-year-old Adams had his heart set on a position in national politics. "The Americans in Europe—say he will be elected Vice President," she observed.[59]

The Constitution needed to win nine out of the thirteen states to achieve ratification. By the end of December 1787, Delaware, New Jersey, and Pennsylvania had voted their assent. Braintree chose Richard Cranch and Parson Wibird to represent them at the upcoming Massachusetts convention. Wibird, Mary exasperatedly informed Abigail, was sure to decline the position for the same reason he had missed commencement: "He cannot bear to put out of . . . course . . . He will not change his Lodgings because he has not done it before nor marry for the same reason and I know no other why we do not have a new sermon. I am not sure that I have heard one from him since you went away."[60] Her prediction notwithstanding, Wibird accompanied Richard to the Convention and voted for the Constitution, which Massachusetts passed by nineteen votes on February 6, 1788, to the delight of the now confirmedly pro-Federalist Cranches, John Quincy, and Uncle Tufts. Georgia and Connecticut also ratified, so the Constitution in principal needed only three more states to pass. But the fight was far

from over. For no one believed a United States government could stand
without the support of New York and Virginia, and anti-Federalists
had formidable strongholds in both.

New York State was especially problematic. No sooner was the document released than New York's Governor Clinton began rounding
up his vast patronage to defeat it. By the winter of 1788, the governor
had accrued a two-thirds majority, while Alexander Hamilton and his
Federalists could only be sure of the city of New York. Clearly a bold
strategy was needed to defeat Clinton. So Hamilton, together with
James Madison and John Jay, under the rubric of "Publius," composed
The Federalist, a series of eighty-four essays written at lightning speed
and exalting the Constitution in language accessible to all educated
men.[61] Successive chapters of *The Federalist* ran three times a week in
four out of the five New York City newspapers and were reprinted
throughout the country, causing heated debate wherever they appeared.

Like John Adams's *Defence,* Hamilton and Madison's endorsement
of the Constitution demanded a strong central government to resolve
America's social unrest, inter-state rancor, indebtedness to foreign
powers, and military disarray. It endorsed separate executive, judicial,
and legislative sectors with senators elected by the state legislatures for
six-year terms and representatives by direct vote for two. It denounced
factions as inimical to the common good.

But here the similarities ended: the differences between these two
documents—though few and conspicuously ignored by Adams at this
moment—were crucial. Adams saw the United States as merely another in a chain of nation states, tumbling down from the Greeks and
Romans. "There is no special providence for Americans, and their nature is the same with that of others," he dismissed the vision of American singularity, and he scoffed that while equal *rights* could be legislated,
to profess that "all men are born . . . to equal influence in society . . . is
[a] gross fraud."[62] For *The Federalist,* on the other hand, the United
States *was* a radical departure from Europe. Here for the first time in
history, industry and talent could transcend birth. Furthermore, America's uniqueness was not merely the accident of time or geography. God
had chosen Americans for their noble mission. And while Publius acknowledged that humanity is fallible, he presumed that Americans

possessed an *esprit général* unique even from the British and defined it as "republican," explaining:

> As there is a degree of depravity in mankind which requires a certain degree of circumspection and distrust: So there are other qualities in human nature, which justify a certain portion of esteem and confidence. Republican government presupposes the existence of these qualities in a higher degree than any other form.[63]

So for Publius as for Hume and Montesquieu—and in sharp contrast to Adams with his baleful view of human nature—faith in public virtue is the cornerstone of representative government: no republic on earth can "constrain" an evil world.

DURING THE SUMMER OF 1787 the Adamses took a long, restorative tour to see the countryside and meet Richard Cranch's immediate family in Devonshire. In the fall, the embattled Continental Congress at last formally accepted John's resignation, which also put Colonel Smith out of a job, and the two families prepared to leave England in April—Abigail and John for Boston, Nabby, her husband and baby for the colonel's family estate in New York. Nabby, putting her husband's professional interests first, had steeled herself for the separation. Abigail was less easily consoled.

Writing to Colonel Smith's mother, Abigail grieved: "I have frequently been call'd in the course of my Life to very painfull seperations from some of my nearest and dear connections, but this is the first time I have suffrd a seperation from [Nabby], and it is the more painfull, as she had always been my companion and associate and I have no other Daughter to supply her place." She also worried about Nabby's reception by the New York family. During their four years together in Europe, Abigail had come to cherish Nabby's serenity, but she had also watched strangers misinterpret her daughter's failure to converse as pride. Even the colonel called Nabby's disinclination to talk her only imperfection. "[Nabby] has my dear Madame a natural reserve in her manners which I hope will not make an unfavorable impression upon her Friends," Abigail launched a private appeal to the Colonel's mother, blaming Nabby's silence on the long-ago death of Susanna and her own failure to produce more girls. "The Relationship of a sister is a character she has no remembrance of, and must in some measure plead for her native reserve."[64]

Abigail began packing in February. Captain Callahan's ship the *Lucretia,* which had so often brought letters from Braintree and Haverhill to England, would now carry *her* back to her sisters and sons. Almost everything she had acquired abroad would go with her: the high-backed red damask chairs, pinched at the seat like cinched waists; the Louis XV furniture; the bed from Holland; the hand-painted silk screens European women wore to prevent makeup from dripping off the nose or forehead; the gold-encrusted mirrors, which would surely raise eyebrows at home.

Abigail also booked passage for her loyal servants John Briestler and Esther Field, though Esther was suffering from every imaginable malady, and Abigail doubted this frail creature would survive the trip. Even at her best, Esther needed "as much care as a Young Turkey."[65] Indeed, Abigail was already writing Esther's elegy, calling her a "Good Girl" and lamenting "I shall feel her loss most severely," in a letter to Uncle Tufts in January.[66] Then, the first week in February, Esther came to her in tears, begging forgiveness. On top of everything else, she had just discovered that she was six months pregnant, as great a shock to herself, she insisted, as to the doctors treating her all year. The father was Briesler. They had planned to marry in America. Abigail called Esther ignorant and foolish, but immediately arranged a wedding and booked passage for an old nurse to assist with what Abigail imagined as a foregone disaster: birth at sea. "Tis vain to complain," Abigail sighed in a letter to Mary. Besides, she could not bring herself to blame Briesler, that prince of servants, who "looks so humble and is so attentive, so faithfull and so trust worthy, that I am willing to do all I can for them."[67]

The Adamses' last weeks were filled with leave-takings at Court and elsewhere. John made a last-minute business trip to Holland, while Abigail reversed her course of two years earlier—moving out of the Grosvenor Square mansion and back into the overpriced Bath Hotel. First Abigail, then Nabby came down with sore throats. Baby William turned a year old on April 2 in Falmouth and three days later set sail in his parents' arms for New York.

The Adamses, on the other hand, left London later and waited weeks in Portsmouth and then Cowes for favorable winds. After four years of almost constant adventure, Abigail soon exhausted the books and needlework she had brought for the journey and had nothing to do but think. "If I live to return to America, how much shall I regreet the loss of good Dr. Prices sermons," she began musing about her favorable experiences in Europe. She also carried happy memories of the roomy houses she had kept in Auteuil and London, the afternoons strolling through the Palais Royale, the theatre, ballets, and concerts in both countries, the friendship of Madame de Lafayette and Thomas Jefferson, the wedding at Grosvenor Square, the birth of Nabby's first child. Still, "I do not think the four years I have past abroad the pleasentest part of my Life," she wrote in her diary. "Indeed I have seen enough of the world . . . and shall be content to learn what is further to be known from the page of History."[68]

CHAPTER XII

"With much joy and pleasure"

. . .

WHEN ABIGAIL WAS HOMESICK IN HER LARGE, ORNATE MANSIONS in Auteuil and London, her cozy Braintree farmhouse seemed like Heaven by comparison. It was toward Penn's Hill she saw herself sailing when John resigned his commission to England. She asked Mary to take measurements of her floors and windows so she could shop on Bond and Jermyn Streets and spruce up the rooms.

"We have taken the dimensions of your little room and the other, but I cannot think you will cut a cloth to them," Mary quickly dismissed Abigail's illusions about returning to the bliss of the early years of her marriage.[1] The house where she had cradled babies at her bedside would shudder under the weight of three grown-up sons—not to mention the inevitable eminent visitors. And surely Abigail had forgotten the wisp of a white and yellow office where John wrote the Massachusetts Constitution. Mary was already conceiving a magnificent new library in a grand house she had designed in her head.[2]

The logical spot for the Adamses, Mary counseled, was one of the finest properties in Braintree. The Borland manor—constructed in 1731 as a summer place by a West Indian sugar planter and owned most recently by none other than Royall Tyler,[3] who had defaulted on his payments—was now up for sale. The location was perfect: just a mile and a half from their current home. There were seventy-five acres of prime farmland and dozens of orchards for John to prune.

Abigail took her sister's point and lost no more time in nostalgia. The Adamses commissioned Cotton Tufts to buy the Borland estate in John's name—which he did on September 26, 1787, for two hundred pounds less than the asking price. It had a view of the sea and seven rooms plus a garret, but was sorely in need of repairs.

The west room was dim and needed new windows, Uncle Tufts reported; the brick chimneys were fragile, the walls cried out for fresh paint or cloth. (He was adamant that Abigail buy domestic rather than foreign wallpaper.) Abigail soon came up with her own list of requisites: a writing "closet" as at Aunt Smith' s, one room painted "French grey," iron backs for the chimneys, brass locks for her doors. "I should think it would not be best to make many alterations in [the house] till you return,"[4] Mary cautioned, but painting inside and out had to start by spring at latest because the smell was pernicious to Abigail's health.

Increasingly, Mary pined for her sister's arrival. "The time till you return will seem longer to me than all that has past since you went away," Mary exclaimed in September 1787.[5] Betsy Cranch concurred, "You can never know my dear Aunt how severely we have felt your absence; not all our other friends could possibly supply your place."[6]

Elizabeth Shaw was no less dramatic: "You cannot think how anxious I have been to hear from my Sister Adams," she wrote Mary on May 8, frantic with fears that Abigail might drown at sea. "The idea of her being separated from us I cannot think of without a gushing tear," she prematurely lamented. On the other hand, Elizabeth dreaded being eclipsed by Abigail's safe arrival. Already, she imagined, the luster she and her husband had accrued from educating the family had dimmed. She had been looking for Betsy Cranch to visit, "til my eyes ake," Elizabeth announced in a rare complaint to Mary; then marshalling grudges she had nurtured since childhood, "You must all come and see me now . . . before sister Adams arrives, for I shall not then get one of you to look this way" for a year.[7]

Six weeks after leaving Falmouth, on May 13, Nabby, Colonel Smith, and one-year-old William landed in New York Harbor. Everyone presumed the Adamses, Esther, and Briesler (and maybe their newborn!) could not be far behind. Massachusetts Governor John

Hancock planned a reception for John to rival Philadelphia's for Ben Franklin. But over a month passed with no sign of his ship. "We are almost tired with expectation of Aunt Adams—every hour we are looking for their arrival," Betsy Cranch wrote in her diary on June 14.[8] Three days later Callahan's boat appeared in Boston Harbor. Parson Wibird rushed the news to the Cranches, where Richard promptly got sick, Betsy suffered "a flutter of spirits," and Mary ignored her family's various nervous disorders and joyfully set out for town.

At the end of a miserable eight week and two day passage, Abigail arrived on June 17 in Boston Harbor to the explosion of cannons from castle and fortress and the roar of huzzahs from citizens swarming like seagulls to the end of the pier. She had not, after all, died at sea or been condemned to the life of a statesman's wife in Europe. Expatriation was behind her. As through the lens of a telescope, she now watched the weathervane on top of the Old State House come into focus and the blur of well-wishers individuate into several thousand grateful Americans. For all the royal jubilees Abigail had yawned through in Europe, she had never witnessed the likes of this welcome for a statesman on American soil—and, moreover, there was no bowing or scraping, all was in perfect taste.

The frustrations with Vergennes and Ben Franklin, the recalcitrance of the British, the months of waiting for Congress to answer John's letters faded like the Old World behind her. What she remembered was the triumph of the loan John wrested from Holland, his successful partnership with Thomas Jefferson, the Treaty of Paris that ended the war. A grand carriage swept the party off to a private reception at the governor's lordly mansion, where the Adamses read the Court's official statement praising John's "many successful labours in the service of your country" and effusions from the Boston journalists, who referred to him as "Excellency," a refreshing contrast to his dubbing as "proscribed rebel" or "commercial agent" by the British press.

At the governor's house, John and Abigail "received the most pointed civility and attention, as well as from the ladies and gentlemen of Boston," Abigail reported with characteristic understatement to Nabby. It was here too that Abigail and John first set eyes on the

Cranches (Richard had recovered and joined Mary): another one of those events they discreetly refused to describe.

Betsy Cranch exulted in her diary, "With much joy and pleasure did we once more see this good, great and excellent man," on June 19 when John Adams arrived with her parents in Braintree. (Abigail had stayed behind to wait for John Quincy.) The next morning, John and Richard walked out to greet the neighbors, who were similarly "overjoyed," as were the town elders—Mr. Black, Mr. A. Alleyne—who called to pay their respects. John's mother was in raptures at mid-day dinner. "Her eyes had seen their desire," Betsy marveled at the power of maternal ardor in a panegyric worthy of her favorite authors, before she succumbed to "an exceedingly bad head ache" which kept her upstairs all afternoon.

But by evening she had recovered. And at 9 P.M., with a mild west wind rustling the June orchards and a full moon in a clear sky, "My dear Aunt Adams arrived," Betsy concluded the story of the Adams's homecoming:

> My joy was too great for words to express—my heart was too full for uttererance and my tears only could express it—never did I feel so strong, so sudden an emotion of joy—after some minutes I could speak and we past the evening in the height of pleasure . . . We sat up till 12 o'clock.[3]

WHEN THE NEWS OF the Adamses' arrival reached Haverhill on Friday, June 20, Elizabeth Shaw's rancor vanished, and her only wish was to rush to her sister's side. "Thanks be to an ever watchful and kind Providence that has conducted my dear Brother and Sister safely to their native Shore," she wrote with unalloyed joy to John and Abigail. "With all the tender affections that ever warmed a Sisters Heart, I bid you welcome—welcome once more to America—welcome my dear Brother to a Land for which you have for many years toil'd." And, expanding from her own experience, Elizabeth predicted:

> The dangers Mr. Adams has encounterd, & the eminent Services he has rendered his country, cannot be fully known [but] to

his nearest Connections—and though a grateful people may yield him a tribute of praise yet all the applause, and glory he justly merits may not be given him till some future age— when . . . Envy and malice cannot operate—& All the Causes of them are removed—[10]

Like Betsy Cranch, Elizabeth suffered as keenly from joy as from sorrow. No sooner did her heart leap than her body collapsed. This time she was struck by an eye infection. "My ill humours are always operating some where or other—I think you once told me it was a favour to my friends it was in my blood and not in my temper," she wrote Abigail on Sunday. On Tuesday she felt well enough to set off with Parson Shaw for Braintree, where she arrived Wednesday in time to dine with her two sisters, as if it were twenty-odd years earlier, before her own exodus to Haverhill and the war.

Once again all three sisters gathered around Mary's table. Outside, the sun shone and the apples and pears ripened in the orchards and the hill they had so often climbed before teatime rose to the same splendid view of the shore. Nothing substantial had changed, except that Nabby was missing. John Adams was visibly moved by this family reunion. He remembered his first meeting with the Smith sisters at their father's parsonage and how he had categorically dismissed them as "not fond, not frank, not candid." How wrong he had been, yet how enduring were the similarities between them. No one, he proclaimed, could "conceive of the happiness [he] felt at seeing their faces together again."[11]

Wednesday June 25 was also a momentous day for Betsy Cranch, who had been 11 years old when her uncle John left for the first Continental Congress and now cooked the reunion dinner for her parents and uncles and aunts. Shortly afterward, at tea, came the occasion she had longed for and dreaded since her engagement the previous December: the presentation of her fiancé, Jacob Norton, to Aunt Abigail, the family's sternest judge.

Jacob Norton's father was Betsy's grandmother's first cousin. Norton had graduated from Harvard in 1786 and was ordained minister of the Weymouth parish the following year. He was 23 and seemed older. Like Betsy's uncle John Shaw, he was an intellectual and ardent Calvinist, passionately opposed to rationalists like Dr. Price, whom Betsy

and her parents had read and revered. Unlike Shaw, he had a charismatic presence that drew congregants as difficult to please as Uncle
Tufts. Aunt Elizabeth told Mary that all the young girls fell in love
with the young man when he preached in Haverhill. He ignored them
and set his heart on Betsy Cranch.

Norton was poor like Thomas Perkins but hardly adventurous or
lighthearted. A sense of humor was not his strong point. Yet, he was
ardent. His love letters assured Betsy of "inviolable and constant attachment," while stressing a bleak view of human nature (his own in
particular) and an easily flustered mien. In reply to one gentle reproof
from Betsy, for instance, he stammered: "Think not that I am insensible of being a proper subject for the pruning knife as well as the hewers
axe . . . I . . . am so benighted that I can very scarcely see whether my
pen emits its ink or not." It was clear he had much to learn from the
family he was marrying into when he announced, as part of their engagement agreement, that Betsy should write two letters to his one.
While she signed the document, Betsy soon was lecturing: "I never
consented to [your demand] of . . . two letters for one—nor shall I ever
agree to it." Puritan men could rule the world but not their wives.

Falling in love again made Betsy "tolerably happy," but did not assuage her fears. What if the worst occurred and Norton stopped loving
her or, almost as bad, was killed? Remembering her first fiancé's fate,
she had nightmares where Norton was struck by snakes or smallpox.
"Nothing gives me greater anxiety [than] the . . . health of my best, my
dearest friend," she wrote in her diary. "If Heaven spares his life and
health, I may be happy but . . . Many, many possible events . . . may
destroy my fun[d]est. hopes. I can think of my own dissolution with
calmness but [not] his."[12]

Nor was Betsy calm about this June 25 meeting between her judgmental aunt and the Calvinist with no financial prospects. Fearing
Abigail's disapproval, she raced from the tearoom, heart "fluttering,"
when Norton appeared. But she returned to find everyone smiling.
The only hint that Abigail was not altogether satisfied appears in a letter to Nabby a few weeks later, where, after seeing Norton almost daily,
she dissimulates: "I am not enough acquainted with [Betsy's fiancé] to
judge him, he bears a good character and I hope will make [Betsy]
happy." Clearly, he was no Colonel Smith.[13]

The Adamses stayed a week with the Cranches before journeying the short distance to their new property. The Brieslers came with them. Esther had lost a baby girl at sea, but was pregnant again and happy to be reunited with her mother, and her husband was grateful to have survived the worst seasickness of anyone on Callahan's ship and to have family life in view.

John Adams quickly recovered from the euphoria of his hero's welcome and reverted to his familiar brooding about the ingratitude of America. "I will tell you, my dear child, in strict confidence," he wrote Nabby less than a month after landing in Boston, "that it appears to me that your father does not stand very high in the esteem, admiration, or respect of his country, or any part of it. In the course of a long absence his character has been lost, and he has got quite out of circulation."

This complaint was false, and John knew it. The author of the Massachusetts Constitution remained highly approved of despite his wrangling with Ben Franklin and Vergennes. Equally disingenuous was John's insistence that all the best government positions had been seized, leaving him only two choices: "private life at home or to go again abroad."[14] He said nothing about the vice-presidency, which the whole family knew was what he sought.

Abigail's hands were so twisted with arthritis that she was unable to write until three weeks after her landing. Once she took up her pen, she sadly reported to Nabby: "I see no person who seems so much alterd in the course of four years as your worthy Uncle Cranch," who was thinner than ever and had aged ten years. Betsy and "tranquil" Lucy Cranch were if possible more "deserving" than when she left them, whereas Parson Wibird "like most old Bachelors is become nearly useless, and fears his own Shadow."

After her mansions in Auteuil and Grosvenor Square, the Borland manor, which had once seemed so grand, "in height and breadth . . . feels like a wren's house," Abigail confided to Nabby. The garden was a "wilderness," the interior a mere "Barrack," and the "swarm of masons, carpenters, and farmers" working at odds with each other to repair inside and out wracked her nerves. What's more, it was imperative that she build a new kitchen, dairy, and library after the winter, so she could look forward to a similar inundation in the spring. "But I must leave off, or you will think me as [dazed] as Esther; indeed," she joked, "I feel almost bewildered."[15]

Nabby and William and baby William Smith were now living twelve miles from New York City in a fine house with a "good garden" on fifty acres of flat, sandy land near William's family in Jamaica, Long Island. Once a fur-trading post for Native Americans (who gave the town its name, Jameco, meaning beaver), it had been the site of one of the bloodiest Continental losses during the Revolution. Afterward, Jamaica became quarters for the victorious British troops.

With the soldiers gone, Jamaica was quieter even than Braintree, but fortunately, Nabby had immediately ingratiated herself to the Smith family and in turn was making a valiant attempt to love them like her own. "It is a family where affection and harmony prevail; you would be charmed to see us all together," Nabby assured her mother.[16]

But her many letters home speak to a longing for her parents and brothers and cousins. "This seperation of families is to me the most painful circumstance in Life," she wrote John Quincy, and time was no healer in her case; only frequent correspondence assuaged the pain. She informed Abigail that she had no friends but the Smiths outside of Massachusetts: "There is no family [in the area] where I can make a home, and go when inclination would induce or business necessitate me, with freedom and reserve." Anticipating her mother's remonstrances, Nabby reminded Abigail that she never had been or would be "disposed to acquire or contract new acquaintances. Unless there are some very apparently attractive traits of character to induce me to cherish the friendship of persons with whom I become acquainted, I do not find much satisfaction from them."[17] What she did not say was that her sociable husband was deemed so inconsequential that he was rarely invited anywhere, nor was he looking for work. Six months earlier during a diplomatic mission to Portugal, William had celebrated "the active life," in a letter to Nabby, insisting, "Sloth and inactivity will sicken me; but [work] will ensure me health and spirit."[18]

Now, however, hoping for a political appointment, he sat idly by while New York prepared to vote on the Constitution. In early summer, Governor Clinton and his anti-Federalists still carried almost two-thirds of the vote, but Alexander Hamilton was gaining momentum. He managed to delay the meeting of the delegation until after Virginia voted, hoping the Federalists would win in Madison's state and set a precedent. He threatened that New York City would take its wealth and prestige and secede from the state if the Federalists lost. Businessmen and artisans representing sixty trades supported Hamilton's threat with a massive rally throughout the island.[19] The poor equated federalism with wealth and stayed home.

"The Happiness of our family seems ever to have been so interwoven with the Politicks of our Country as to be in a great degree dependent upon them," Nabby wrote John Quincy.[20] Writing to Nabby, John Adams deplored this bondage and made clear he hoped her husband would not fall victim to its thrall. The Smiths could not live long or well on William's modest inheritance. And though "Mr. Smith's merit and services entitle him to expect employment under the public," John urged him to secure his independence by preparing himself for the New York bar. Nothing good would come from waiting for a political appointment.[21]

On June 21, 1788, New Hampshire supplied the ninth favorable vote needed to officially ratify the Constitution. But in Virginia, two great patriots—James Madison and Patrick Henry—remained at loggerheads, with Henry stooping to scaremongering, insisting a unified nation would free the wealthy planters' slaves. "It is strange that the men of large property in the south, should be more afraid that the Constitution will produce an Aristocracy or a Monarchy, than the genuine democratical people of the East," George Washington wrote Lafayette, who was eagerly following the contest in Paris.[22] Fortunately, the poor Virginians were also divided. And, after a monthlong battle, the back countrymen of West Virginia helped tip the balance in favor of nationalism, and the Constitution was ratified by a margin of ten points on June 25.

At this point, the New York delegates were wrangling above a jail in a Poughkeepsie courthouse. The chief defender of ratification was Hamilton, who vowed "the convention shall never rise until the Constitution is adopted"; his most vocal opponent was Governor Clinton's spokesman Melancton Smith, who prided himself on his "plebian" mien.[23] Where Hamilton was eloquent and prolix, Smith was wry and appealingly understated. But he was also reasonable, and three weeks after the Virginia victory, Smith changed sides and endorsed the Constitution, which won approval by a mere three votes.

America was no longer the aggregate of thirteen states but a bona fide republic, the embodiment of a century of Enlightenment thought. And yet, as the slim majority in New York made clear, this Federalist victory was fragile. A government by laws could yet be overthrown like the tea in Boston Harbor. America's tolerance for peaceful disagreement would be tested time and again as each state chose its senators, representatives, and "electors," the latter of whom were to vote for the executive branch. (A state was allotted the same number of electors as the sum of its senators and representatives.) The results of the electors' vote then would be tabulated and read aloud at the first meeting of Congress in New York, the provisional capital. The winning candidate would become President, the runner-up Vice-President. George Washington was by far the popular favorite. John Adams was frequently mentioned as a likely second-in-command.

For the time being, however, John sought to steel himself against disappointment, telling Abigail: "My mind has balanced all circumstances and all are reducible to two Articles Vanity and comfort . . . if they mortify my Vanity they give me Comfort.—They canot deprive me of Comfort without gratifying my Vanity."[24]

Writing to Thomas Jefferson in Paris shortly after New Year's, 1789, John affected the indifference expected of an eighteenth-century statesman: "The new Government has my best Wishes and most fervent Prayers for its Success and Prosperity: but whether I shall have any Thing more to do with it, besides praying for it, depends on the future suffrages of Freemen." He signed the letter "with an affection that can never die" and meant it, though it was growing increasingly apparent how much their political views diverged. Jefferson welcomed revolt—"like a storm in the atmosphere"—while John prized stability to the point of advocating long terms for all members of the government and a president with powers very like a king's. Jefferson continued to fear the few and Adams the many.

And then there was the matter of France. To boost its seriously impoverished Treasury, in 1788, Louis XVI had petitioned the French courts to raise taxes, and to everyone's great surprise, the courts rebuffed the King and refused. When Louis in retaliation closed the courts and banished the magistrates, the French took a cue from the Americans, whose war had depleted their coffers, and rioted. At Pau, crowds beat down the locked doors of the courthouse; at Grenoble, they pelted the King's troops from their rooftops. The Palais Royale, where Abigail and Jefferson had gazed at art two years earlier, was overrun by protestors from all classes. Pressure was placed on the King to convene the nobles, the clergy, and the "people," who, respectively, comprised the three houses of the Estates-General, the French legislature, which had last assembled in 1614. On August 8, 1788, Louis reluctantly obliged his subjects and agreed to a meeting the following May.

Jefferson, who was on the scene, cast a cynical eye at all these proceedings. Much as he advocated revolution in America, he saw scant hope for republicanism in France, with its entrenched monarchy and history of servile citizens. Since the calling of the Estates-General, the two upper chambers had "shamelessly combined against" the people, he reported to Adams, adding that nothing good would come from the upcoming meeting. The King would seize even more absolute power and definitively stifle the poor.[25]

Adams took the French discontent more seriously. Despite his talk of Americans being no different than the rest of humanity, he was quick to stereotype the few nations he had seen. For him and for Abigail, France was the land of boulevard theatre, on and off the boulevards, and he could well imagine the families they had watched playacting in the Bois de Bologne every Sunday being ripe for some new dramatic thrill. Revolution, if it came, "must terminate in Improvements of various kinds. Superstition, Bigotry, Ignorance, Imposture, Tyranny and Misery must be lessened," even in France, he acknowledged. But he could not imagine the French with their penchant for extremities sustaining a republic for long. "The world will be entertained with noble sentiments and enchanting Eloquence," but also the specter of "confusion and carnage, which must again end in despotism," he predicted in a letter to Jefferson.[26] Fortunately, the American character was as yet unformed and its government had the chance to start from scratch.

LIKE HER MOTHER AND aunts a quarter of a century earlier, Betsy Cranch understood all too well the momentousness of marriage. According to Puritan law, she would stand in relation to her husband as man did to God, which felt to her like a step down from her current position as cherished daughter. She in turn would have to become a household god on wash day and at the spinning wheel and with the children she would bear. Seeing England was now definitely out of the question, and whether the gaiety she had felt that winter in Haverhill would ever return was up in the air. Certainly, as a clergyman's wife, she would always have to worry about money, and having the leisure to study or even rest depended on holding down the size of her family, which meant convincing her husband to regulate sex. But Betsy's greatest anxiety about marriage arose from the Bible's demand that she love her husband *more than anyone.*

In late August, she had written asking Nabby, the current seer on such topics, whether being a good wife would conflict with loving her family and friends. And though Nabby blithely assured her that "So far from lessening our general friendships or contracting our dispositions to give pleasure to our friends—[marriage] enlarges our sphere expands the heart . . . and is the means of promoting in our minds all the social affection," Betsy remained perturbed.[27] Next she appealed to Parson Wibird, who just as glibly cited her passages from the Bible to the effect that she should "leave [her] parents" and "cleave" to her husband, which contradicted all her instincts. Less inclined to cleave to Jacob Norton than wary of casting her fate apart from Mary, Richard, Lucy, and Billy, she found many reasons to postpone the whole affair.

First, she made clear that Jacob Norton had a long ladder to climb before meriting her hand in marriage. Weeks after their engagement, she was still holding him at arm's length while referring to her brother, Billy, as "*my best* and *dearest* friend,"[28] and she further demoted Norton in the hierarchy of devoted connections by chiding his failure to visit when he knew she was depressed. "I will not tell you what influence your presence may have upon my mind. You ought not to be too sensible of your power—those who can govern may tyrannize," she averred.[29] A true child of the 1770s, she grasped the revolutionary discourse and applied it to her home.

As always after such an attack, Norton was hurt, confused, and wondered if Betsy really loved him. Then he turned penitent and called himself "vex'd . . . to the heart" or "a more stupid companion and correspondent to you than to almost any other person." He declared himself eager to change and grateful for her admonishments. His rigid calculations were exasperating, he acknowledged, and he begged her not to cringe at his methodicalness, which was a natural outgrowth of training for the Church.

Sometimes Norton's solemnity and Betsy's anxiety proved contagious. One night when he came to visit, Norton caught the nervous twitch in Betsy's eyelid. Another time, finding themselves alone after leaving off friends on a sleigh ride, both lovers felt listless and subdued, but soon lost their gloom in animated conversation: a deep bond between them was love for ideas. And Norton could raise Betsy's moods as well as depress them. On March 11, she was spending a dull evening alone with her parents when, unexpectedly, her dashing young fiancé materialized at the door. What a spring his presence brought to her spirits! "Never did I experience more forcibly a sudden transition from low spirit to a calm and cheerful state of mind," she observed.[30]

While Mary Cranch worried that Norton's Calvinism might alienate the rationalist half of his Weymouth congregation, Uncle Tufts thoroughly approved of the young minister and was eager to see the couple wed.[31] In early March, expatiating in front of the Cranch fireplace, Cotton Tufts urged Betsy and Norton to forget the practical details, "Trust in Providence," and marry soon. Norton found this a delightful recommendation and wrote to Betsy afterward, hoping she did too.

"I wish to give you the . . . answer you desire," Betsy cautiously began her exegesis against precipitate marriage. But she found her uncle in too much of a rush, lacking the wisdom he could usually be counted on to dispense. "Your happiness is my first wish," Betsy assured Norton, and she was as eager as he to begin housekeeping. But where? "You have caught the *Bird* and now must find the *cage*," she warmed to her subject. Why, Norton didn't even own a house at the moment. Furthermore, should he buy, say, her grandfather's parsonage, which was now in her parents' possession, their troubles would be far from over because it would take ages to repair.

"You ask me if I should not be afraid to quit my dependence on my Parents *at present,*" she alluded to Norton's most penetrating question, and then changed the topic by accusing him of failing to define *"at present"* and throwing in that haste "might cause repentence" and was always wise to eschew.[32]

Like his Biblical namesake, Jacob Norton continued to plough down the difficult road to wedding the right woman. He began visiting Braintree more often and made no more pleas that they marry soon. He disciplined himself not to take Betsy's nervous outbursts personally. Rather than questioning *her* love, he called her "My Love" and urged her "to feel happy."[33] In the spring he bought the parsonage where Betsy's mother and aunts had grown up watching hummingbirds glide around the giant peach tree that still exploded with blossoms at the sashed windows. A Biblical oil painting showing the twin brothers Jacob and Esau resolving their differences hung as ever in the small square entry hall. Norton threw himself into home improvements, which included hanging Betsy's lush cream-and-mauve-colored curtains embellished with country scenes on the windows. He chased a cavalry of wasps from upstairs.[34]

Reading to each other at night, they marveled at James Cooks's nautical voyages or felt morally uplifted by the allegories Dr. Johnson collected in *The Rambler.* They walked vigorously around the harbor at Betsy's favorite little village, Squawtown; afterward "we were happy," she had to admit. A week later, following a trip with Norton to Lincoln, she was "supremely happy" and spoke glowingly of "my dearest friends kindness."[35] In May, elated by the scent of apple blossoms on the orchards, she cut out her bridal gown and bought wallpaper for her grandfather's parsonage, where she would someday live.

Still, she felt no compulsion to do so immediately and leapt at a new reason to postpone marrying when in the beginning of November Nabby's second child was born, early. Abigail rushed to be with her daughter, instructing Betsy not to marry before she returned from New York.

———

MARY CRANCH WAS DEVASTATED, not so much by the wedding delay
as by intimations that this was far from her sister's last journey. "I cannot bear this separation—and must I hope it will be continue'd?—Can
I be so publick spirited? If I am I shall sacrifice a very great part of my
private happiness."[36] And Abigail wrote Mary, similarly chagrined.

Feeling that he would seem to be pushing himself forward by so
much as appearing at the seat of the new government, John did not accompany Abigail on her journey to New York. In the eighteenth century,
there was no precedent for political campaigning in America. During
colonial times, all the major positions like governor had been appointments by the British, while elections since the Revolution had been based
on character and social position rather than political views. The press did
its share to advocate or discourage particular candidates. But for an individual to solicit votes for himself was considered crass and probably a
sign of not deserving them.[37] So John stayed close to home in Braintree.
Mary found him in his meadow beaming at fifteen young heifers. She
went away convinced he wanted nothing more than to spend the rest of
his life farming, exactly the reaction John wanted. If only it were true![38]

Abigail missed her husband more than usual. As soon as she arrived
in Long Island and found the baby—named John Adams after his
grandfather—very well and Nabby recovering, she was clamoring to
return home. "I think every Seperation more painfull as I increase in
years," she wrote John after three weeks of overcast skies and rain during which she never went further than Nabby's Jamaica garden. Still,
the Vice-Presidency was as much on her mind as on Adams's. Colonel
Smith, she wrote John, had seen Alexander Hamilton, who showed
him a letter from his friend James Madison, saying that John had Virginia's support for the job.

Colonel Smith became acquainted with Hamilton on one of his
"seldom" visits to an exclusive club in the city. When he was at home,
Abigail noncommittally observed to John, her daughter's husband collected turkeys and ducks. She was more biting on the subject of her
son-in-law's lassitude at the end of a letter to Mary. Here, after sympa-
thizing with John Quincy's loneliness as he studied for the Bar exams,
she added, "but how much better is this, than having no given object no

pursuit. I had rather a son of mine should follow any mechanical trade whatever than be a Gentleman at large without any occupation"—in other words, William Smith.[39]

Finally, the rain stopped, and cold, dry weather settled over Long Island. Nabby's strength returned, and she became as eager as Abigail to see Betsy wed. The problem was the two hundred mile journey. Frigid winter roads made traveling in William Smith's carriage hazardous, while hiring a coach cost more than Abigail was willing to spend. A sleigh ride was the obvious answer, if only there were sufficient snow on the ground. But dry weather persisted. "Tell Betsy she must not steal a march upon me, if she waits an other month mrs. Smith will come and be Bride maid," she promised Mary in mid-December.[40]

New Year's passed with only a flurry. Abigail took off for New York, where she was feted as the wife of the future Vice-President, while Betsy made use of this new extension to further fret and dread her fate. Mary too was beside herself. Betsy, she wrote Abigail, "wishes you to be here when she is married—but I believe you must come soon if you are—It has become such a serious matter with her I really wish it was over—she will have no health till it is."[41]

Then the skies opened up, the rivers froze, and snow sailed over New York and New England. Colonel Smith gathered the family and drove his horse-drawn sleigh north. The weather was fine, the roads smooth, the inns as good as could be expected. "Our Musk and Lemon Brandy were of great service to us, and we never [failed] to Toast the donor," Abigail informed her New York friend Sarah Livingston Jay.[42] Ten days after they took off, the Adams party arrived for tea at the Cranches on January 30. It was the first time Betsy had set eyes on Nabby's husband, or Nabby on Betsy's betrothed. Nor had they seen each other since 1784 when Nabby left for England. Thomas Perkins was now dead and Royall Tyler long out of the picture. It seemed ages since Nabby and Betsy had whispered together in their mothers' kitchens, or marched off to assemblies, or paid visits to Boston and Mrs. Warren's in search of eligible men. The burning question of their adolescence—who would they marry?—had been answered, for better or for worse.

On February 3, Betsy resigned herself to packing for the move to Weymouth. On February 7, she was able to pray, "May I become useful in the new situation in which I am to be placed—may I trust in God." But on the eve of her wedding, calm eluded her, and, wondering if she would ever write again, she despaired in her diary: "Would to Heaven I could commend my mind into a more composed frame!"

On February 11, Betsy Cranch became Mrs. Jacob Norton in a ceremony at Braintree's First Church presided over by Parson Wibird and attended by two generations of Adamses and Cranches.[43] A few days later she moved into the parsonage and was six months pregnant at the end of the year. By all reports, Betsy came to cleave to Jacob Norton as tenaciously as any wife in the Bible.

But the transfer of loyalty did not occur immediately, as is clear from a letter she wrote shortly after her marriage, informing Lucy: "I cannot for all Parson Wibird's injunctions divest myself of the Idea that my parents demand—and have a claim to my duty before any other connection whatever."[44] Her mother, she explained, was lonely, and with all due respect to her husband, Betsy was racing to her.

ELIZABETH SHAW HAD NOT been so outraged since Abigail accused her of flirting twenty years earlier. It was the week after Betsy Cranch's wedding, and the Adamses—who had been home from Europe for eight months without setting foot in Haverhill—had once again failed to pay their respects to the Shaws. Nabby, Elizabeth reminded Abigail, had said her parents "intended" to arrive on February 13. Elizabeth had accordingly made up beds, laid a fine table, and invited four prominent couples from the parish to tea. Imagine her humiliation as "The Clock struck three, four, five, six"—and there was no sign of the Adams carriage. She was "most *unmercifully* disappointed," she fumed the next day in a letter to Abigail, adding with biting irony that she ought to sue the Adamses for the damage to her reputation: "The People say, they believe, you do not care much for your Haverhill Friends," despite the fact that the Shaws practically raised the Adamses' youngest sons.

In a lowest blow, Elizabeth challenged Abigail's provenance. "I could not help contrasting the disappointment we had met with, with the punctuality which our dear Father always observed towards his friends, & say, that if you had one drop of his Blood stiring in your veins," you would know how to behave toward your kin.[45]

Abigail did not immediately answer this implied accusation that she was flaunting her superior age *and* rank.[46] If she had, she might have defended herself on the grounds that Nabby's saying her parents "intended" to visit Haverhill was somewhat less than a promise, or that she had only just returned to Braintree and might any day be summoned back to New York. Elizabeth could call it a slight if she liked, but Abigail had no time to make apologies, much less a day's trip to Haverhill. She was dealing with a daughter recovering from childbirth, an unemployed son-in-law, and a high-strung husband she needed all her powers to calm.

For while John had talked himself into resignation to the will of the people, not knowing whether America had made him a farmer or a Vice-President was torture to his pride. The electors had cast their votes, on the fourth of February, but the results could only be announced by Congress, and with their members detained by icy roads and snow gales, the Senate and House of Representatives had yet to convene. February passed, then March. Further problems arose when the brilliant new Federal Hall in New York where Congress was to meet fell behind on its construction schedule. It was not until April 6 that both houses of Congress finally sat to read the votes.

At dawn on April 7, a messenger from the Senate named Sylvanus Bourne set sail from New York and arrived two days later in Boston. The electors' votes had at last been revealed by Congress. Bourne had in his hands a certificate officially declaring John Adams Vice-President of the United States.

George Washington was President of the nation and had been elected unanimously, whereas Adams won second place by a mere majority of 34 out of 69 votes. Adams's joy was considerably tempered by the low number of votes in his favor. Had he known that a man he had presumed a strong ally, Alexander Hamilton, had advised electors from other states to vote against him, he would have suffered more. (Hamilton, who did not know Adams personally, claimed that there was no animus involved in his petitioning for Adams's opponents. What impelled him was fear that Adams was too attractive a candidate and might defeat even Washington if Hamilton did not step in and divert some votes.)

A hero's send-off the following Monday revived John's spirits as he once again left Abigail at home to run the farm and began his voyage to the temporary capital at New York City. The sun shone, crowds thronged, and cannons saluted him as he passed through Boston, while a cavalcade of forty, like the French carriages parading toward Long-champs on Easter week, followed behind. Everywhere he stopped he was celebrated. Hartford presented him with a large swathe of its famous broadcloth. New Haven gave him the key to the city, while on April 20 at 4 P.M. troops on horseback followed by Congressmen in carriages escorted Adams into New York and dropped him at the mansion of his old friend from the Paris negotiations, John Jay. Commenting on John's effusive reception, Abigail wryly noted, "I enjoyed the Triumph . . . and perhaps my mind might have been a little Elated . . . if I had not lived Long enough in the world to have seen the fickleness of it."[47]

Her sisters were even less enthusiastic about the victory. "By the News Papers, I find you have met with a temporary Loss—the United suffrages of my countrymen have once more taken Brother Adams from *you,*" Elizabeth summoned her flowery prose to compassionate Abigail from Haverhill.[48] Mary went further and spoke of "mourning." All too soon, Abigail would arrange her affairs and run off to join John. What a cruel irony that less than a year after Mary gave thanks for her sister's return from Europe, she was losing her to New York.[49]

As Vice-President, Adams's chief job was to preside over the Senate. The day after he arrived at John Jay's, he made his first visit to its chambers in the new federal government building, a mass of friezes and pillars superimposed over the tidy bricks and stepped Dutch roof of the old City Hall. Stars lined the foot of the pediment where an eagle spread its wings and thrust its striped chest out at the city. Olive branches enfolded thirteen arrows, denoting the states, on the tablets over the grand windows on the second floor. Created by Major L'Enfant, a French engineer who had fought in the Revolution, the exterior of Federal Hall was an amalgam of ancient and new, solemn and jaunty, the first Federalist building in America; and L'Enfant's interior was no less grand.

The ground-floor hall was paved with marble. The House of Representatives had octangular-shaped windows and was large and majestic. The Senate, studded with pilasters, was "light and graceful," according to contemporary reports. A distinguishing touch was the chair where Adams would sit as president of the Senate. It was raised three feet from the floor and crowned by a canapé of crimson damask.[50]

When John Adams had visited New York in August of 1774 on the way to the first Continental Congress in Philadelphia, he complained that its denizens were crude and garish. "I have not seen one real Gentleman," he observed in his diary. There was "no Modesty—No Attention to one another. They talk very loud, very fast, and alltogether. If they ask you a Question, before you can utter 3 Words of your Answer, they will break out upon you, again—and talk away."[51]

In 1789, New York remained far less civilized than Boston or Philadelphia. Like Paris, its streets were narrow and winding. A recent ordinance requiring sidewalks was honored in the exception, as were laws demanding streetlamps that worked. Filth was widely deplored but seemingly impossible to eradicate. From a distance the island looked lopsided, with the majority of its populace huddled between Broadway and Greenwich Street and no further north than Broome Street (then called Bayard's Lane).

Two decades after the great fires of 1776 and 1778 had consumed most of the old Dutch houses, the prevailing architectural style was framed buildings with brick fronts, as in London or Boston. Fashionable society consisted of about three hundred people, whom the French visitor Brissot de Warville described as stylish and extravagant; the women not only sported British fineries but displayed a "scandalizing" amount of flesh.[52] Their chief amusements were balls, tea parties, and jaunts to out-of-town gardens. The literary world was practically nonexistent, but the one playhouse in town, the John Street Theatre, thrived. It was there, three years earlier, that Royall Tyler's *The Contrast,* had premiered. *The School for Scandal* was playing to packed houses when John arrived from Boston. The seaports were also prospering, commerce was more than ever New York's raison d'etre, and the population had swelled to 29,000, with an ever-widening disparity between rich and poor.

New York had suffered British occupation longer than any other American city, and, while flattered to be chosen the provisional seat of the new government, it mistrusted invaders of any sort. Its journalists were quick as the London press to satirize. John Adams, with his self-important air—accrued as a defense against sneering European diplomats—and his New England stolidity—which bordered on stodginess—was an ideal target. Moreover, despite its flattering title, his position as president of the Senate demanded only the virtue he most conspicuously lacked: forbearance. His orders were *not* to contribute to the general debate or vote, except in the rare case of a tie.

John was anxious the morning of April 21 as he set out to address the Senate, and Abigail was not on hand to caution him against unrepublican displays of pride. Still, he got off to a good start, acknowledging how difficult it would be for him to stifle his opinions and pleading "if from inexperience or inadvertency, anything should ever escape me inconsistent with propriety, I must entreat you, by putting it to its true cause and not to any want of respect, to pardon and excuse me." But John could not resist just as candidly ruminating (in what sounds like a parody of Cassius's "I was born free as Caesar" monologue in Shakespeare's play) about his own importance versus that of the Commander in Chief. "I am Vice President. In this I am nothing, but I may be everything," he alluded to George Washington's mortality. John got into further trouble musing on their relative power when Washington came to his ground: "Gentleman, I feel a great difficulty how to act . . . I am . . . President of the Senate. When the President comes into the Senate, what shall I be?" His colleagues were soon referring to him as "His Rotundity" under their breaths, which tried John's never formidable tolerance of jokes at his own expense.[53]

The inauguration on April 30 was a mixture of triumph and exasperation. Every inn in town had been booked by the rich and famous, so ordinary travelers pitched tents and slept on the ground.

The day before the ceremony, Washington boated in from across the river. According to one of thousands of awed observers:

> Carpets were spread to the carriage prepared for him; but he preferred walking through the crowded streets . . . He frequently bowed to the multitude, and took off his hat to the ladies at the windows who waived their handkerchiefs and threw flowers before him . . . His name in every form of decoration appeared on the fronts of the houses.[54]

Even the French emissary had to acknowledge that Washington had "the soul, look, and figure of a hero" (though he couldn't resist adding that Americans on the whole should make no such claim).[55] On the night of April 29, bands blasted and fireworks splayed and enormous backlit patriotic portraits swung above the crowds: one, at Broadway, showed Justice and Wisdom beaming down on the new government; in another, at the John Street Theatre, Fame descended from Heaven to grant the first President immortality—suspiciously close to divine power.

The specter of monarchy also hung over the inauguration proceedings at Federal Hall, where George Washington appeared in a splendid yellow coach with six white horses. Outside, crowds clamored on the rooftops and rendered the new President's initials on everything from tobacco boxes to front doors.[56] John stood by Washington on the second-floor balcony as he swore the designated oath to uphold the Constitution, then in a spontaneous gesture added divinity into the bargain by kissing the Bible and declaring "So help me God."[57]

From Federal Hall, the President and Vice-President proceeded to services at Saint Paul's followed by an exclusive reception in Washington's elegant mansion on Cherry Street near Fraunces Tavern. John was criticized by the press for looking too regal in his foreign suit, when in fact his suit was made from the broadcloth presented to him in Hartford and exactly the same as Washington's, which drew only praise. Yet what Adams took from the day was essentially positive. "The President has received me with great Cordiality, of affection and Confidence, and eve[ry] Thing has gone very agreabley," John, exhausted but content, wrote Abigail the next morning.[58]

But matters soon deteriorated. Determined to elevate America's dignity in the eyes of Europe, Adams backed a suggestion that Washington be addressed, hilariously, as "His Highness the President of the United States of America and Protector of the Rights of the Same." Then, for nearly a month, John allowed debate on this subject of titles to drag out in the Senate, flagrantly ignoring his mandate to remain silent, enraging his enemies and trying the patience of his friends. Even Washington eventually became disgusted. By the time it was determined that the President should be addressed merely as President, Adams's preoccupation with titles had earned him understandable, if false, accusations of wanting a king.

To make matters worse, doubtless remembering how his carriage was compared to a milk cart by journalists in London, he drove a coach fit for nobility (as did Washington), wore his hair powdered (as did Washington), and dressed like a member of the House of Lords. As in his dealings with Vergennes, he seemed to have lost all sense of discretion, not to mention humor, and opened himself to sobriquets like "Duke of Braintree" wherever he went.

From Braintree, where Abigail was managing the farm, contemplating a second move in a year, and overseeing the birth of Esther's second daughter, she sensed trouble and subtly counciled John to tone down his remarks. After reading his first address to the Senate in the newspapers, she quoted Dr. Johnson to the effect that "The Generals Triumph and Sage's disputation, end like the Humble Labours of the smith or plowman in a dinner or a sleep." To prove her point, she devoted as much space to her own mundane, but enormous troubles managing the farm and the cold weather in Braintree as to the president of the Senate's speech.[59]

She also wrote that she was lonesome: "I do not like to sleep alone." By the middle of the month, John too was so desperate for intimacy and council that, summoning all the urgency he had needed to bring her to Europe, he appealed to Abigail to collect their belongings and come to New York at once. He had rented a large house a mile outside the city, on the east corner of Varick and Charlton Streets. It was called Richmond and had everything the Boreland estate lacked—sturdy walls, pruned orchards, a view of the Hudson River. All it needed was furniture, which Abigail could easily supply by dismantling their ramshackle Braintree house. "As to Money to bear your Expences you must if you can borrow of some Friend enough to bring you here. If you cannot borrow enough, you must Sell Horses Oxen Sheep Cowes, any Thing at any Rate . . . —if, no one will take the Place leave it to the Birds of the Air and Beasts of the Field: but at all Events, come."

Less than a year after she arrived in Boston Harbor, Abigail began packing the red damask chairs and the Dutch bed, already damaged from their cross-Atlantic voyage. "It is a very unpleasant Idea to me . . . to pull down and pack furniture . . . just as I have got it well arranged," she bristled. She insisted on spending a week unruffling the offended Elizabeth at her parsonage in Haverhill. This was no mere obligation, but a true meeting of souls. Unlike Mary, Elizabeth retained her lifetime zest for literature. Speaking with her was invigorating, and Abigail's joy was only diminished, she wrote John, by his insistence that she race to him. When Abigail got home from Haverhill, though the weather was still cool, she had the pleasure of savoring her own winter apples; the "wilderness" she had tamed into a garden was ready to sprout asparagus; and the orchards were in bloom. "In short I regreet leaving," she bluntly informed John, but went on to assure him, "I know you want your own Bed & pillows, your Hot coffe & your full portion of kian [a bowel stimulant]. How many of these little matters, make up a large portion of our happiness & content, and the more of publick cares & perplexities that you are surrounded with, the more necessary these alleviations." Whatever occurred in the outside world, it was her highest ambition, she wrote, to assure his domestic happiness, and it "shall be my constant endeaour to / prove in all situations & circumstances/ affectionately yours."[60] She promised to come to him quickly.

But when the first week in June arrived with Abigail still settling affairs in Braintree, "Never did I want your assistance more than at present, as my Physician and my Nurse," John stooped to begging, for he had been struck, he said, by the alarming illness that had almost killed him in Holland eight years before. His health was so poor, he might be forced to resign his office, he shamelessly wheedled. Abigail was appropriately electrified. Five days after hearing her husband

These white Louis XV chairs are the formerly red damask chairs that Abigail transported from Paris to London to Braintree to New York.

would die if she waited to set her household in order, she dropped everything and left for New York.

As always, for Abigail the hardest part about going to John was leaving Mary, who had no adventures ahead to offset the loss of her best female friend. For the first time, Mary was visibly depressed at their parting.

"It grieved me to see you so dull, you used to keep your Spirits better," Abigail, already cheered by calls from eminent citizens, exhorted Mary from her Rhode Island inn. "A merry Heart does good like a medicine we shall hear often from one another, and the seperation be rendered less painfull by that means."[61]

"I do not know why I have found it so much harder parting now than before, but it really is so," Mary answered. She had "more difficulties to incounter now" than when Abigail left for Europe; she was older, "and my prospects are gloomy." Both her dreams and her fears had come true. Richard, with his brilliance and devotion, had proved an ideal lover and companion. After nearly three decades of marriage, he was still writing her tender letters vowing that he esteemed her "company and conversation . . . above all the world besides."[62] But he was useless as a breadwinner; so Mary's possibilities in life were severely limited. She could aspire only to pay her debts, see her friends, and pinch no more than she already did. "Honor without profit we have had enough of," she bitterly dismissed Richard's service to the courts and legislature of Massachusetts. With Elizabeth in Haverhill and Abigail in New York, she felt cheated of "the kind soothing of my Sisters." And while religion exhorted her to be cheerful, "I cannot always succeed—Patience and resignation are the great dutys I have to exercise [but] Hope and Trust must be their attendants or the Heart would faint."[63] She was not a martyr.

Two weeks later, Mary explicitly acknowledged the wide gap between her lot in life and her sister's. "You are in the midst of the busy world I almost out of it," she wrote Abigail, who had safely arrived in New York and, finding John far healthier than he had led her to anticipate, been swept up in a social whirl.

The contrast in their lives had not escaped Abigail, who after a few weeks away from home included in a letter to Mary a general statement to the people she loved: "I have a favour to request of all my near and intimate Friends it is to desire them to watch over my conduct and if at any time they perceive any alteration in me with respect to them, arising as they may suppose from my situation in Life, I beg they would with the utmost freedom acquaint me with it. I do not feel within myself the least disposition of the kind, but I know Mankind are prone to deceive themselves," she added.[64]

But her private words for Mary reflect an even deeper view of connections. No stroke of luck, she felt sure, could separate sisters. Their souls were intertwined from birth. So Abigail found it perfectly natural to circumvent John's approval and, using Nabby as a go-between, send Mary all the pocket money she could spare from her own relatively small budget. Anticipating her sister's anguish, she reminded her, "Do not talk of obligations, reverse the matter and then ask yourself, if you would not do as much for me?" Or for Elizabeth? she might have added. Fate, in Abigail's view, was not a democratic process. Nor did she think much of equality on earth. Hierarchy guaranteed order, which was crucial to the survival of mankind. But family ran on a loftier system of government. She and her sisters differed only in birth order, where Mary reigned supreme. Otherwise, they always had been and always would be equal, harbingers of the more perfect world to be.

CHAPTER XIII

"The most insignificant office that ever the Invention of Man contrived"

. . .

WHATEVER ABIGAIL SAID OR FELT, HER MOVE TO NEW YORK marked a new stage in the sisters' relationship. More and more, they were assuming distinct identities. Mary was everyone's surrogate mother, taking special interest in Elizabeth's precocious 10-year-old Betsy Quincy, watching over easygoing Thomas Adams at college, and making sure John Quincy looked up from his books to wash and exercise and did not propose marriage to any of the women with whom he frequently fell in love. More than ever the ideal manager, Mary took pride at whipping the Adamses' manor into shape and clearing out half of Richard's office so her darling Billy could begin practicing law.

Elizabeth, on the other hand, increasingly resented wasting her energy on housework and for the first time blamed her husband in part for her chores. "If Mr. Shaw could take Scholars, the profit of which would furnish us with cloathing, I would never turn the [spinning] Wheel again for I perfectly hate the work," she wrote Abigail.[1] Drudgery notwithstanding, Elizabeth managed to pick up an interest in theatre by devouring newspaper descriptions of the New York productions and begged Abigail to get her a copy of Mary Wollstonecraft's *Vindication of the Rights of Woman,* which claimed an intellectual life for the female sex. Whatever moved her to joy or pain or anger propelled her to express herself in letters. "Out of the abundance of the heart, I find the hand will write," she said.[2]

Meanwhile, Abigail was on yet another voyage: to discover what it meant to be the wife of a statesman in America. Indeed, this being the inaugural administration, she would help define the role. She fell in love at first sight with her New York estate called Richmond Hill, situated in today's West Village, then on the northern outskirts of town. You approached by a winding road bounded by exotic brush and clumps of oak trees, Abigail wrote Mary. In the garden oleander, lavender, olive and lime trees ran rampant, while the house, with its classical pillars and tympanum, was orderly and "sublime." It stood at the pinnacle of a steep hill.

Below on the Hudson, boats streamed in with spices from the West Indies or out to New England bearing correspondence for the Cranches and Shaws. New York, New Jersey, and Long Island were all easily within its purview. No wonder General Washington had chosen this spot for his headquarters during the early days of the Revolution. For Abigail, her new home was as gracious as her "wren's house" in Braintree was cramped. On the second floor, a glass door opened from a large hall onto spacious galleries, just the sort of elegant touch she could never have found on stodgy Grosvenor Square. And while Richmond Hill was almost the same distance from New York City as Auteuil was from Paris, the fanciful landscaping gave it the advantage of feeling infinitely more remote.

Abigail felt too happy for her days in Richmond Hill to last, she confided with uncharacteristic superstition to Mary a few months later. Her happiness was greatly enhanced by the presence of Nabby, who had come with her husband and baby to live with the Adamses, and Charles, who joined them after finishing Harvard and began studying law with Alexander Hamilton at his father's request.[3] Charles was the fair child, the one who had always had a special place in her heart because he had been born shortly after the Boston Massacre to comfort her for the loss of her infant girl. He was also the son who charmed

Abigail fell in love at first sight with this property,
Richmond Hill, which George Washington had chosen for
his headquarters during the Revolution.

everyone. Somehow, the drive for perfection that shaped his father and older brother had escaped him, nor was his character so intensely upright as theirs. Letters between Abigail and Mary make veiled allusions to Charles's drinking. Furthermore, he had been accused of participating in a campus riot, and "such is the company in which he is seen that he cannot fail to bear a part of the reproach even if he is innocent," Abigail wrote John Quincy.[4] So she was determined to reform him under his father's roof.

Besides her children, Abigail imported her doting 16-year-old niece, Louisa (the late Billy Smith's daughter) to help with needlework and ironing. Her loyal servants, Esther and John Briesler, who had been children themselves when they accompanied her for the adventure to Europe, now carried their infant away from their own families in Braintree so they could lead the household staff. Altogether, there were eighteen people residing at Richmond Hill.

Her life was by no means easy, Abigail assured her sisters. Adams's $5,000-a-year salary allotted by Congress was insufficient to support two homes and always had her scrimping. Just helping John Quincy get started practicing law in Boston was a burden she could scarcely bear. And no more than Mary and Elizabeth had she a moment to cultivate her intellectual interests. "I have never before been in a situation in which morning noon and afternoon I have been half as much exposed to company," she complained to Mary, adding that she was constantly expected to fill all twenty-four seats at her table. No sooner did she finish dining all the Senators with wives than she had to move on to the Senators without wives and after that begin all over again with representatives from the House. Worse, she had to be "at home" to every passing carriage. Speaking of carriages, "I can no more do without Mr. Briesler, than a coach could do without wheels," Abigail informed Mary, reprising her complaints from overseas about the dissolute and incompetent local servants. Hands she could find anywhere, "but what are hands without a Head?"[5]

By mid-summer, Betsy Norton was pregnant, and Mary had recovered from her depression. "I am naturally very cheerful," she reminded Abigail, and she was eager as a page-turning reader to hear all the delicious gossip from New York.

Abigail in turn was delighted to supply depictions of the characters she encountered—from the drunken cooks she chased out one after the other, to the "foaming loud speaking" Congregationalist clergymen who "work[ed] themselves into such an enthusiasm as to cry" and made her long for Dr. Price or even the reasonable if soporific Parson Wibird at home. She accompanied John Jay's beautiful and accomplished wife, the former Sarah Livingston, to hear debates in the House of Representatives. Here she found one of the leading legislators, James Madison, "a very amiable character a man of virtue and probity," while she was appalled to discover Adams's old colleague Elbridge Gerry (who was elected representative from Massachusetts, despite his opposition to the Constitution) looking "ghastly," "worried," and "mortified"; he was "always in a minority" and "very frequently wrong."[6]

Then there was Martha Washington, whom Abigail called upon her first morning in New York and found slighter than she had supposed, with teeth as white as her hair, dressed simply but in the finest cloth and bearing an easy and artless manner. Martha had been a wealthy widow with a young son and daughter when Washington

married her forty years earlier. Both her children died early, but her
son lived long enough to leave four offspring, two of whom, a boy and
a girl, accompanied the Washingtons to New York. Martha was en-
dearingly fond of them and quite the grandmamma,[7] Abigail approvingly reported. Mrs. Washington's letters to Abigail are filled with
motherly concern about Nabby and her children and Abigail's tall, shy
young niece, Louisa, whom she invited to take dancing lessons with her
brood. The President too had a paternal streak and once picked all the
sugar plums off his dessert cake to send home with the Adamses for
Nabby's younger son, John.

The Washingtons and Adamses frequently dined together. They
watched plays like *The School for Scandal* at the John Street Theatre,
in adjacent boxes festooned with patriotic symbols, and one weekend
met for lunch in Harlem after the men took an excursion to Long Island on their own. Martha was a second Madame Lafayette in her
warm welcome to all the Adamses, and once she began receiving the
elite of New York society every Friday night at eight o'clock, in her
variation on a British levee, she made a point of always seating Abigail
to her right. When that seat was occupied, Abigail told Mary "the President never fails of Seeing that it is relinquished for me, and having
removed Ladies Several times, they have now learnt to give it to me,
but this between ourselves, as *all distinction* you know is unpopular."[8]

Abigail's own increasing attachment to titles and privilege was surprising. Acknowledging concern over where she sat was quite a change
from her mockery of the minutia-obsessed nobility in England and
France. It is tempting to attribute her new attitude to sheer pride, for
Abigail was human, after all, and watching the upper classes leap to
their feet in her presence had to be gratifying after enduring the scowls
of aristocrats at Versailles and St. James. Besides, Abigail's Puritan her-
itage predisposed her to hierarchies, and after Shays's Rebellion she,
like John, came to see marks of rank—which she had earlier derided as
"putting on airs"—as necessary to maintaining order, even in a brave
new world. Humility from above would only stoke disrespect in the
masses, was their logic. Yet it was clear that Abigail had not dismissed
republican virtues. Her ambivalence about class distinctions shows in
the inconsistency of her letters home.

On one day she is praising American simplicity, reporting to Mary

Abigail was pleased to report that Martha Washington's receptions, held every Friday at eight, were far less ceremonious than the British Queen's.

that Mrs. Washington's levees are far less ceremonious than the British Queen's. Instead of marching for hours around exhausted suppliants, Martha sat comfortably. And rather than standing in a circle endlessly waiting, each guest was met at the door and immediately escorted inside. The lady then curtseyed to Mrs. Washington and sat for a chat with the President, whose grace, dignity, and ease left "Royal George far behind." After the reception, the lady was free to mingle and help herself to lemonade and ice cream. She could leave at her leisure. Clearly the message of Abigail's story is that modesty surpasses pomp.[9]

But on another day, Abigail admits "I know very well by experience the strong attractions which England possesses."[10] She boasts to Mary that Martha Washington's New Year's party was as lustrous as the King's birthday, as if this were the ultimate compliment, and praises the women present as every bit as brilliantly dressed as princesses at St. James. The fact that George and Martha were preparing to move into the grandest mansion in New York also pleased Abigail because it elevated them far above the "common people": a group she no longer extolled as the backbone of America, but rather feared as a greater menace than the rich to the security of the United States.

The Adamses were not alone in their confusion about pomp and protocol. Almost every Federalist was perplexed about whether to follow or repudiate the British ideal. The President was no exception, though he set an example for those less transparent than Adams by saying as little as possible on the subject and avoiding both extremes. Abigail praised Washington to Mary as "polite with dignity, affable without familiarity, distant without Haughtiness, Grave without Austerity, Modest wise and Good." So universally beloved he held the nation together, he also "has so happy a faculty of appearing to accommodate and yet carrying his point that if he was not really one of the best intentiond Men in the world he might be a very dangerous one."[11]

He was undoubtedly dangerous for John Adams, who failed to read him as subtly as Abigail and was too straightforward himself to comprehend how a man who plucked sugar plums for his Vice-President's grandson could exclude this same man from every important political decision the federal branch of the government took. And by the fall Washington had made crucial decisions. He had appointed Thomas Jefferson Secretary of State, John Jay Chief Justice, and Alexander Hamilton Secretary of the Treasury.

While another of Washington's former aides-de-camp, Edmund Randolph, was appointed Attorney General, William Smith was overlooked for every important position and had to settle for being "Marshall for the district of New York City," which he described as mortifying, and John and Abigail agreed. From a practical point of view, Colonel Smith's new salary could not support a family, so this was a direct blow to Abigail's daughter as well as the Revolutionary hero. Perhaps Washington had reconsidered his earlier praise for Smith's "gallantry" and "intelligence," or simply preferred other candidates, or feared being accused of nepotism on John's behalf. Or perhaps Washington neglected Smith in order to distance himself from Adams, with his European bearing and emotional outbursts.[12] John Quincy took the view that George Washington, though a friend, feared his father's wide influence. He consoled Nabby about her husband's disappointment, blaming it on John Adams's finest qualities: "You and I, my dear Sister, shall always find, that our near affinity, to a man, who has sacrificed himself and his family to his country, will be a real impediment to our success in the world." Mary Cranch, who had previously hinted to her sister that her husband would appreciate a government appointment, now gave up hope that Adams could procure *anyone* a job.

And every day John himself grew increasingly convinced that his Vice-Presidency was, "the most insignificant office that ever the Invention of Man contrived or his Imagination conceived."[13] Satirists rushed in to confirm Adams's nullity or howl at even his most democratic views. In a lampoon called "The Dangerous Vice," for instance, an anonymous Boston poet,[14] attributes Adams's demand that statesmen be decently paid (so the poor as well as the rich can afford to govern) to the greed of a dandy wallowing in the "soft lap of pamper'd luxury . . . wasting thousands" and pining for *"thousands more."* So much for Abigail's frugal housekeeping. And in a similar vein, Boston newspapers, which dared not attack the universally beloved George Washington, gleefully smirked at Adams's every faux pas and so constantly alluded to a secret acrimony between the two leaders that Billy Cranch felt compelled to ask his cousin John Quincy whether there was such a chill in relations between the President and Vice-President that they did not speak.[15] While Abigail assured Mary that these reports were perfectly baseless, she and John canceled their subscriptions to the offending newspapers, while loathing more than ever the power of the press.

When it was not distracted by the Vice-President's idiosyncrasies, the press had much to report as the first administration got under way. Ideas for a federal bank and a small standing Army were batted about Congress—both were ultimately accepted. The House of Representatives officially declared a month of mourning when the country's oldest patriarch, Ben Franklin, died peacefully in his sleep at 84 in his daughter's house in Philadelphia, an ocean away from Madame Helvetius. Noah Webster transformed the American language with his new spelling book, while Thomas Jefferson arrived home from France and declared America so changed that he felt like the only republican he knew. The country, on the other hand, found Jefferson gratifyingly uncorrupted by Europe: a still handsome, distinguished, self-effacing widower, he was as beloved as the author of the Declaration of Independence as Adams was mocked as a would-be English squire. Politically as well as personally, Jefferson immediately ingratiated himself with Washington, who relied on his Secretary of State's advice in cabinet meetings, which Adams, whom Jefferson habitually had deferred to in Paris, was rarely invited to attend.

It was Jefferson who convinced Madison to fight for a Bill of Rights guaranteeing personal liberties (freedom of the press, religion) not mentioned in the Constitution. Jefferson was also instrumental in breaking the deadlock between southern and northern legislators regarding Alexander Hamilton's plan for the federal government to found a national bank and assume the states' debts. What Hamilton aimed for was the establishment of a national debt, like Great Britain's, which would stabilize the monetary system and inspire trust in the country by regularly paying interest to its creditors. Predictably, the mercantile northern states, with many foreign debts outstanding, were enthusiastic about Hamilton's strategy, while the agrarian southerners, who had paid back most of what were smaller loans in the first place, violently opposed the bill. Behind their reluctance to pay for the north's expenses was fear that "consolidation," the loss of state autonomy, was a first step toward embracing monarchy in the British mold.

Hamilton's old ally Madison was particularly vociferous in his opposition. Increasingly, Madison, from Virginia, identified with states' rights and the south. To no avail did Hamilton coax his co-author on *The Federalist* with promises of reduced taxes for all the states or threaten that America could not speak in thirteen separate voices and do business with the world. It was only Jefferson's intercession with Madison that convinced the latter to temper his rhetoric, ultimately enabling what became known as the "assumption bill," (allowing current debts to be handled on a national level) to narrowly pass through Congress and setting the foundation for a national treasury far more powerful than the states'.

In return, Jefferson and Madison wrested their own concession from Hamilton and his allies. The Constitution had mandated that a permanent seat of government be established on no more than ten square miles at a spot of Congress's choosing. But a year after convening, the legislature was still bickering about the location, with New Englanders arguing for nearby New York, the middle states committed to Philadelphia, and southerners envisioning a new city rising out of Virginia swampland along the Potomac River. To compensate Madison for allowing Hamilton's assumption bill to pass through Congress, the north now agreed to the Potomac city. The President immediately got to work on what looked like a decade-long project, hiring L'Enfant, who had built New York's Federal Hall, to design the new capital. All that remained for Congress to consider was whether they would spend the next ten years in Philadelphia or New York.[16]

Many read this compromise as a fulfillment of the Enlightenment belief that affection combined with self-interest could hold a republic together. Abigail's reaction was more skeptical. Twenty years before, she had questioned how southerners who kept slaves could fight for freedom with the same zeal as northerners, and her doubts had grown on the ride from Paris to London when she read Jefferson's diatribe against the black race. "I firmly believe that if I live Ten years longer, I shall see a devision of the Southern & Northern states," she now predicted in a letter to Mary.[17] President Washington, however, was doing everything in his power to secure a permanent union, his first step being a trip to New England in the fall of 1789 to prove he was equally committed to south and north.

The press followed in loving detail Washington's monthlong journey through sixty northeastern towns and villages at a time when their leaves were at their most brilliant. Everywhere, cheering mobs fought to catch a glimpse of the hero of the Battle of Boston. That city completely lost its head and, besides staging a mammoth parade, erected an arch inscribed "To the Man who unites all hearts." Only the weather refused to bow to the great leader and was "dreadful raw and uncomfortable," Mary informed Abigail. Nonetheless, half of Braintree, including even Parson Wibird, rushed to town and came home sniffling from their hours waiting to glimpse the President with what the newspapers dubbed the "Washington cold." Meanwhile, the President got such a worshipful reaction from the very Bostonians who were accusing John Adams of demagoguery that Lucy Cranch complained to her aunt Abigail: "Was there ever such a people who acted so inconsistently as some of ours do, to clamour and rave if there is a shaddow of power given their rulers and at the same time pay them homage in a manner that would disgrace the subjects of the Grand Turk—."[18]

ONE TOWN PRESIDENT WASHINGTON was not scheduled to visit was Haverhill, New Hampshire. Then, at the last minute he decided to make a surprise stop and on November 4 drove up in his four-horsed British carriage, followed on horseback by six black slaves, and checked in at the local inn.[19] At the time, Elizabeth and John Shaw were out of town making their fall visit to Weymouth and Braintree, and their 12-year-old son, Billy, was less interested in *anyone's* arrival in town than in his books. But his younger sister, Betsy Quincy, was in raptures at the President's God-like appearance at her doorstep. The next morning she got up two hours before daybreak and loped across town to Washington's lodgings. There she and a friend were respectfully greeted by the President's secretary, who went upstairs, and a short time afterward down the President came. He took both girls on his lap and kissed them. This kiss earned Betsy Quincy write-ups in the local newspapers, where it became symbolic of the President's paternal goodness, while in Elizabeth Shaw's mind it assumed a talismanic power for Betsy herself. "I often mention it to Betsy Quincy as an incentive to every thing that is praiseworthy . . . I presume [she] will never forget [it] through the whole period of [her] Existence," Elizabeth proclaimed.

At the time of Washington's kiss, Elizabeth Shaw was 39 and pregnant with her third child. Since American women bore approximately nine children and continued procreating well into their forties, Elizabeth's condition was far from rare. Admittedly, not everyone was like the 17th-century poet Anne Bradstreet, who found an almost mystical calling in reproduction, but neither did society give a thought to the fact that long-married partners were still mating when they had rotting teeth and gray hair.

But Abigail Adams was not the world in general. Elizabeth knew what she was doing when she hid her condition from her most opinionated sister, who, like Mary and their mother before them, had produced her last surviving child at 28. It was Mary who gingerly broached the topic to Abigail in a letter at New Year's, 1790. Clearly, more than anxiety for her younger sister's health was involved in Abigail's instant disapproval, though she stressed Elizabeth's frailty in her response to the shocking news.

"I was really surprised to learn that Sister Shaw was likely to increase her Family," Abigail wrote Mary. "I wish her comfortably through, but shall feel anxious for her feeble constitution." Abigail no more deigned to write Elizabeth of her March due date than she had congratulated her on her engagement thirteen years before. On the subject of Betsy Norton, who was also due in March: "I doubt she will find her Health mended by becoming a mother," Abigail cautioned the already frantically worried Mary.[20] And when Nabby gave birth to yet another son before weaning her second, Abigail groaned to John Quincy: "Heaven grant that she may add no more to the stock" unless Colonel Smith could support them in better style.[21]

In her opinion, it was the mother, through lack of power or prudence, who was to blame for the birth of inconvenient babies. Abigail was not simply concerned about Elizabeth's health and family finances in this "foolish business," as she described the Shaw's decision to start a "Second crop ... after all these years." Abigail, the sister who had spoken most openly about sexual yearning during her courtship and fought her mother most ardently to marry sooner than the family wished, now implied there was something unseemly, maybe even sordid about lovemaking in what John Quincy termed "old age." Certainly, John Quincy was echoing his mother's sentiments when he wrote his cousin Billy Cranch after a visit to their aunt and uncle in Haverhill, "I wonder people at [the Shaw's] time of life are not ashamed of getting children. I was so much scandalized, that I could hardly refrain from expostulating to them upon the subject."[22]

Still, with or without the Adamses' approval, bellies continued to swell throughout the winter of 1790 in the parsonage houses of Weymouth and Haverhill. Elizabeth defied all expectations, and when her neighbors were still insisting she barely looked pregnant, shooed her husband out of her bedroom and "called her women" in. Knowing what to expect made everything easier. The warm room, the hushed voices of friends murmuring encouragement as she squatted on the midwife's stool and endured the trauma that ended with a snip of the umbilical cord: these experiences she had lived through two times before, and fortunately her labor was short and relatively easy. On the second day of March 1790, out of Elizabeth's small and slender body clamored a nine-pound girl. "Rejoice with me," Elizabeth exhorted Abigail. "She has little bones ... is as plump as a partridge, quiet as a Lamb, and [a neighbor] says she has a mouth *like you,* but you know every one will flatter upon those occasions." Anticipating Abigail's envy that the baby was a girl on top of her disapproval of late-life childbearing, Elizabeth further sought to propitiate her sister by naming the

child Abigail Adams "in respect and gratitude to a much loved Sister—
and we hope she will not be offended that we have given her this name,
endeared to me by a *thousand kindnesses.*"[23] In subsequent letters, Elizabeth marveled at the infant's resemblance to Abigail, Charles, and
Nabby, but to no avail. As with Elizabeth's engagement—when Abigail had informed John, "The mortification I endure at the mention of
it is so great that I have never changed a word with her upon the
subject"—she simply ignored this late-life baby. The next surviving
letter from Abigail to Elizabeth is dated a year later, and even then she
focused on her own travails, never so much as mentioning Abigail
Adams Shaw.

Abigail found it far easier to empathize with the Cranches. "You
will soon be as fond of your Grandchildren as ever you was of your
own," she assured Mary, and waited impatiently for news that her niece
who felt like a daughter had gotten safely to bed. And when news arrived that a perfect little Richard Cranch Norton was born a week after
Abigail Adams Shaw, Abigail did "sincerely rejoice" and lament that
she was not home to "personally tell [Betsy] how much her safety and
happiness is dear to me." Betsy's labor was surprisingly easy, but when
later her breasts "broke" (ached) and her fever rose, Mary turned to
Abigail, the sister who had suffered most to love her husband and bear
a family. And Abigail hurried off letters prescribing herbal baths and
poultices with such specificity that it was clear she had not forgotten
her own agony in all the intervening years.

WHAT SHOULD HAVE CHEERED Abigail at the moment was the presence of Thomas Jefferson in the capital. Yet her letters during this period contain only two lines pertaining to the first Secretary of State. To
Mary she writes, in the spring of 1790: "mr. Jefferson is here, and adds
much to the social circle."[24] And she tells a friend in London: "mr. Jefferson . . . took leave of me last week to visit his family in Virginia."[25]
Both observations imply warm feelings for John's old colleague, but
there is none of the close analysis of Jefferson's splendid character or
detailing of dinners and outings together that filled her letters during
the Paris years.

John had spoken for Abigail as well as himself when he professed "an affection that can never die" for Jefferson a year earlier, and on the Adamses' part, nothing had changed since then.[26] Jefferson's loyalty, on the other hand, was more complicated. While he continued to admire Adams's intellect, he was determined not to be identified as the friend of a so-called monarchist, and increasingly confided in fellow Virginian James Madison rather than speaking directly to Adams about their ideological differences. This last was so much true that when Jefferson wrote Adams, "you and I differ in our ideas of the best form of government,"[27] Adams could sincerely respond, "But my dear Sir, you will give me leave to say, that I do not know this. I know not what your Idea is of the best form of Government. You and I have never had a serious conversation together that I can recollect concerning the nature of Government. The very transient hints that have ever passed between Us have been jocular and superficial."[28]

The most conspicuous difference between Adams and Jefferson during the first two years of the American government arose over France. Much had happened there since late 1788 when the two men last traded opinions on the country's instability. At that point, Louis XVI reluctantly had acquiesced to a meeting of the three houses of parliament (made up of nobles, clergy, and the "people" or middle classes). Jefferson had been convinced this meeting would only further entrench the corrupt monarchy, while Adams had suspected the people would follow America's example and revolt.

Adams was proven correct. Rather than binding France together, the King's lavish reception of the three houses of Parliament in May 1789 alienated the middle classes, who broke off from the nobles and clergymen and formed a unilateral national assembly of their own. Sympathizers from all classes, including Lafayette, quickly joined them. Across the Channel, idealists like the Adams's Dissident friend Dr. Price hailed a new era for mankind, and even the traditionalist Edmund Burke, who would soon become one of the harshest critics of the Revolution, found it impossible not to admire the "spirit" of the French. On July 14, the citizens of Paris seized the Bastille prison. On August 26, the National Assembly declared a constitutional monarchy, with a single-chamber legislature co-governing with the King.

While Jefferson quietly cheered on the insurrection, Adams immediately perceived his great nemesis—the tyranny of the many—raising
its ugly head in France, especially after angry mobs went on to prove
the King's power a sham by forcing the royal couple from their palace
in Versailles and back to the hub of the turmoil in Paris. As Adams had
made clear to Jefferson a year earlier, he saw no reason to equate the
French, who lacked any history of liberty, with the American colonists
raised as free men under British rule. Dr. Price might perceive the taking of the Bastille as a natural outgrowth of the American Revolution,
but Adams read hypocrisy in the rebels' utopian rhetoric. He anticipated chaos and blood.

As did Abigail, though she was more sympathetic than John to the
French fervor for liberty and initially equated their sufferings with her
own, writing in a letter to a friend in London: "Alass poor France how
many direful scenes has she yet to pass through before order will be
Reestablished. however great the Blessings to be derived from a Revolution in government, the Scenes of Anarchy cruelty and Blood which
usually proceed it and the difficulty of uniting a Majority in favour of
any System, are sufficient to make any person who has been an Eye
witness to the demolition of one government Recoil at the prospect of
over turning Empires and kingdoms."[29]

Though they could not at the moment imagine they would play any
part in the unfolding drama, most Americans were fascinated by the
developments in France. The irony of cheering on the rebels did not
escape them, for the checks that saved America's Army from bankruptcy were signed by Louis XVI. American journalists took both sides
on the conflict against the French monarchy, with the *New-York Daily
Advertiser* warning "the [French] people incline to the most cruel executions," while the *New-York Gazette* tempered its criticism, "Paris has
lately been troubled by some insurrections; happily a few only, who
deserved it, became victims to them."[30]

John's response to enthusiasm for the French righteous anger was a
series of articles published anonymously called *Discourses on Davila.*[31]
His message, as in *Thoughts on Government* and *Defence of the Constitutions,* was that a nation run by a single legislature, whether in Philadelphia or Paris, is doomed. Once again, he drummed home the advantages

of a three-pronged mixed government with a bicameral legislature, and because he pointed to England as a successful example, many, including Jefferson, misread *Davila* as pro-monarchy, though Adams spoke only of the importance of an "executive," never a king.

Davila is not an elegant work. The writing sounds rushed, and the long-winded quotes from the Italian historian Davila about the French civil wars are merely an excuse for Adams to draw unflattering conclusions about the French character. What *is* extraordinary about these articles—particularly coming at the end of a year where Adams was forced to sit silently while others took the limelight in the Senate—is their psychological implications. Whereas John's earlier works follow Locke and locate man's primary impulse as self-interest, *Discourses on Davila* further narrows self-interest to mean yearning for recognition by the world: "a desire to be observed, considered, esteemed, praised, beloved, and admired." Exactly what Adams as Vice-President was denied!

This determining passion need not be the heinous lust for power Adams located in his own psyche as a young diarist. It could be simply "a desire to excel another, by fair industry in the search of truth." But exposed to competition, inevitably it would deteriorate into envy or blind ambition. Benevolence was no match for it. The only way to foil this avidity for attention was to acknowledge it existed. Hence, Adams exhorts the French to forget their rhetoric of natural goodness and "Act and think like yourselves!" as flawed human beings. Their job was to "Consider that government is intended to set bounds to passions which nature has not limited," and dispense with the idea that a single assembly can express the general will. "Rivalries must be controlled, or they will throw all things into confusion; and there is nothing but despotism or a balance of power which can control them," he averred.

John's admonishments to the French were, of course, also alerts to Americans that their freedoms were rare and precarious. "It has been said that it is extremely difficult to preserve a balance of [power]," he pointedly reminded them. "This is no more than to say that it is extremely difficult to preserve liberty. To this truth all ages and nations attest. It is so difficult, that the very appearance of it is lost over the whole earth, excepting [England] and North America."[32]

———

IF *DISCOURSES ON DAVILA* aimed (as it surely did) to warn Americans against a sudden upheaval of even the worst government, it only succeeded in reinforcing Adams's image as a slave to stability and lover of kings. His frustration mounted in the month of April 1790, as more snow deluged New York than during the whole winter beforehand, and John struggled through the slush only to sit silently under his red damask canopy in the Senate and watch his passion to excel thwarted at every turn. It was then that events suddenly threatened to end the Vice-President's "nothing[ness]" with a blow nearly as perilous for America as the taking of the Bastille was to Louis XVI.

The cause was a virulent strain of influenza, which struck in late April all along the eastern coast. Elizabeth Shaw's house was "a mere Hospital," John Quincy reported after a visit to Haverhill, where his diligent uncle could not get out of bed to preach Sunday services. In Braintree, Mary Cranch "hardly [knew] of a person who has not been or is [not] now sick," including her wailing grandchild. Friends were perishing all around her. John's mother could "hardly crawl," Mary reported. Betsy Norton was "thin as a [lantern] you can see thro her nose."[33]

At Richmond Hill, Abigail, who at first mistook this flu for her perennial rheumatism, languished in her room with a spiking fever, as did Charles and Colonel Smith in theirs. Soon Nabby and the servants were also incapacitated. The only healthy person in the whole house was John.

In the middle of May, Martha Washington wrote a friendly note asking Abigail whether the Vice-President continued in fit condition. The question was in fact far more urgent than it sounded, for her own husband was gravely ill. George Washington was 58 years old, scion of a family that degenerated early and died young. With his determined jaw, height, and unassailable demeanor, Washington was easy to envision as an epic hero, but age had begun to wear at his health. Two months after he assumed office, he had developed a tumor that needed to be removed from his left thigh. For nearly a week Washington lay in critical condition, with his street roped off to preclude the scraping wheels of carriages from irritating his nerves.[34] Eventually, he recovered, and it never occurred to the adoring New Englanders who made themselves sick paying homage to Washington during his tour that autumn that their leader was assailable too.

But the following spring Washington's lingering weakness from the amputation was further complicated by liver problems—a "Billious disorder," as Abigail informed her Uncle Tufts. Rather than consult a doctor, Washington decided to "exercise it away" with a brief tour of Long Island. Here influenza was raging, but the President felt restored. Still, his constitution had not thoroughly recovered when he returned home and was struck by the flu.

From the start, his case was dramatic. He collapsed with fever and chest pains. Then his lungs filled with pus, he gasped for air, and his temperature soared. Fluid suffusing his ears made it impossible for him to follow conversations, so he seemed uncomprehending. One day he was "seizd with Hicups and rattling in the Throat . . . mrs. Washington left his Room thinking him dying," Abigail reported to Uncle Tufts in Massachusetts, where, to avoid panic, news of the crisis had been carefully kept from the public.[35] The doctors "apprehended him in a most dangerous state" and administered their strongest remedy for inflammation, "James powder" (a concentrate of antimony and phosphate of lime). Now all they could do was wait. A year earlier, John had stunned the Senate, implying that he was one step away from the throne, since if Washington died he would become "everything" to the nation. For three days in the middle of May 1790, what then had seemed the height of pomposity rang like prophesy for the few who knew of Washington's rapid decline.

Had craving attention, as John defined it in *Discourses,* been their driving passion, the Adamses ought to have rejoiced at the prospect of Washington dying and John becoming President—a position he had made clear he felt he deserved. But Abigail was no Lady Macbeth, she assured her sister. Her deeper desire, like John's, was for the triumph of the American experiment—the grand purpose of the Cranches' and Shaws' as well as the Adamses' lives. This, Abigail knew, required a living George Washington. Two years after the signing of the Constitution, no one else on earth—much less her own unpopular husband—could bind the ragtag thirteen states as he had his soldiers during the war. Abigail said she dreaded his death because "it appears to me that the union of the states, and concequently the permanency of the Government depend under Providence on his Life, at this early day when neither our Finances are arranged nor our Government Sufficiently cemented to promise duration."

As Washington continued in danger, the likelihood grew that Abigail would replace Martha in the Presidential mansion, host dignitaries at federal levees, and watch her husband hold sway over the same Cabinet that had snubbed him for months. Adams's salary would rise from the Vice-Presidential $5,000 to the Presidential $25,000. But she took no pleasure in such thoughts, for they came with an image of John plagued by jealous enemies and weighed down by a mourning nation. When she let her mind go further, Abigail envisioned herself a widow, John having been carried "to an early Grave with misiry & disgrace." Indeed, even without this added strain, John was only three years younger than Washington and could perish as easily.[36]

"I feard a thousand things which . . . I never before realizd [might befall me], and the apprehension of it only for a few days greatly distresst me," a still agitated Abigail wrote Mary after, "thanks to Providence," Washington's fever finally broke, and his breathing eased.[37] But the recovery was long and painful. For weeks Washington's eyes perpetually teared while, because his ears were still stopped, he could only faintly hear reports from his Cabinet and Congress, which led to rumors that he was senile.[38] And though his intellect was in fact as sharp as ever, listlessness did drape over him like a carapace. Suddenly his oft-professed eagerness to leave statesmanship and retire to Mount Vernon seemed sincere.

WHILE WASHINGTON SLOWLY RECOVERED his stamina, the Residence Bill, determining the site of the U.S. capital, and Hamilton's petition for national assumption of states' debts were both reaching a crucial phase in Congress. The Adamses were strong supporters of Hamilton's economic agenda. In May, Abigail fretted over the havoc that would ensue if his assumption bill failed to pass during the current Congressional session. Correctly, she blamed the deadlock on Madison, whom until recently she had considered an ally, telling Uncle Tufts that he led the Virginians like a flock of sheep.[39]

At the same time assumption was being fought over, the new government easily came to a consensus to expand America's borders. So far, tales of shrunken heads and midnight massacres had discouraged western settlement by all but the desperate, like poor Thomas Perkins. Everyone agreed that peace had to be established for the country to grow. And most legislators concurred with Washington that it cost less to pay for peace than to pay for battle—besides, it was fairer. So in the summer of 1790 the American government took a step toward conciliating the disgruntled first settlers by inviting representatives of the Creek Indians of Georgia to come to New York.

Their leader was the half-Scottish Alexander McGillivray, who was 30 years old, classically educated, and spoke perfect English. Abigail described him to Mary as "not very dark . . . grave and solid, intelligent and much of a Gentleman, but in very bad Health." He wore an American-cut suit of striking scarlet, while his kinsmen were "very fine looking Men [with] placid countenances and fine shape" who thrilled New Yorkers with their feathers and crowns. The city greeted them like royalty, staging a lavish parade to Federal Hall and visits to the homes of the President and governor. Afterward, they were lodged in style at an inn near the Adamses and, between attending lavish ceremonies and negotiating terms of a treaty, managed to fit in daily visits at Richmond Hill.

"These are the first savages I ever saw" and "they behave with much civility," Abigail continued her report to Mary. "Mico maco, one of their kings dinned here yesterday and . . . confered a Name upon me the meaning of which I do not know . . . he took me by the Hand, bowd his Head and bent his knee, calling me Mammea, Mammea."[40] Since they could not converse, the Adamses and tribesmen spoke through signs, which were sufficient to convince Abigail the Creeks were "Friendly, manly, generous gratefull and Honest:" just as Jefferson had described them in *Notes on the State of Virginia*.[41]

The negotiations lasted a month, the upshot being that the Creeks relinquished two-thirds of the state of Georgia to the American government in exchange for Washington's assurance that he would protect in perpetuity their remaining third. Egregious as it now sounds, by eighteenth-century standards, the agreement was generous on America's part. The Senate approved it on August 7, and the treaty was signed

at a ceremony six days later where Washington presented McGillivray
with a string of beads signifying friendship and every member of the
Creek delegation rose and shook Washington's hand. "A truly curious
scene" was Abigail's tantalizing assessment of this occasion. Afterward,
she watched on as the Creeks built a "great Bond fire dancing round it
like so many spirits hooping, singing, yelling, and expressing their
pleasure and Satisfaction in the true Savage Stile."

On July 26, the assumption bill passed Congress. The Residence Act
had preceded it two weeks earlier, denoting the Potomac as the ultimate site of the capital. As to where the federal government should
convene until 1800, the vote in the Senate was evenly divided between
New York and Philadelphia; Adams had the deciding vote and was
free either to make his wife happy or to force her to pack her red damask chairs once again and move even farther from home. John did not
hesitate to vote for Philadelphia, Abigail explained to John Quincy, because he was firmly committed "never to suffer private interest to Bias
his judgment but to sacrifice ease convenience and interest for the general welfare of the country."[42] Philadelphia, redolent of culture and science, home to Benjamin Franklin and the first Congressional Congress,
was more likely to unite the nation than mercenary, restless, anti-
intellectual New York. The fact that New York was identified with the
increasingly controversial Hamilton also did not help its case.

Still, philosophize as she might, Abigail was heartbroken. "Do you
not pity me my dear sister?" she wailed to Mary. "The idea of going
farther from you is painfull to me." Besides, just a year after leaving her
unfinished house in Braintree and with her hopes of a brief summer
visit to New England dashed by the upcoming move, she again embarked with "as much Boxing and casing, as if we were removing to
Europe." Indeed, "Our furniture might well be stiled moveables," she
grumbled. "I am going amongst another new set of company, to form
new acquaintances to make and receive a hundred ceremonious visits,
not one of ten from which I shall derive any pleasure."

Abigail had "many other things upon my mind, and spirit which I
cannot communicate by letters," she continued, doubtless alluding to
the unpredictable Charles, who would stay behind and board with his
sister. To make matters worse, his younger brother Thomas had graduated from Harvard and let his father talk him into studying law when

Abigail was sure he was better suited to business. Worst of all, Abigail would be leaving Nabby and her grandsons, just at the point that Colonel Smith was so discontent with his low-paying marshallship he had begun talking about going abroad. For the first time, Abigail openly acknowledged remorse at Nabby's marriage to the man she once considered the ideal husband. She used Colonel Smith as catalyst for an admonishment to John Quincy: "I will give you one piece of advice, never form connextions untill you see a prospect of supporting a Family, never take a woman from an Eligible situation and place her below it."[43]

With Charles and Nabby staying behind in New York and John Quincy on his way to Boston to start a law practice, Abigail fretted to Mary: "At present you have your Family with and near you, but it is my destiny to have mine Scatered." And she confessed, "I feel low spirited and Heartless."[44]

In this, Abigail was not alone. For a tendency to depression seeped through the family and was as liable to appear in varying degrees of intensity as her brother's fatal alcoholism and her younger sister's literary bent. Though for some, like Betsy Norton, depression could arise from no more than a change in the weather, usually a traumatic event triggered the prolonged languor and sadness that often afflicted the descendents of Elizabeth Quincy and William Smith. The summer of 1790 was a hard time for the Cranches, Shaws, and Adamses with this tendency. As Abigail languished under the pressure of moving for the third time in two years, Elizabeth Shaw in Haverhill had also succumbed to bad news.

"My mind [does] not feel strong enough for anything," she wrote Abigail with an uncharacteristic lack of metaphor and simile.[45] The source of her "tumult" was the sickness of a little neighbor boy, who had been named John Adams after the Vice-President and was just slightly older than her own infant girl. He was the child of Betsy Norton's former love, cousin John Thaxter, who had married Betsy Duncan and remained in Haverhill. Thaxter's son was cutting his eyeteeth when the mysterious illness struck his bowels. For two weeks the parents hung over his listless cradle. Then he expired. The fact that Elizabeth was still nursing her own infant, Abigail Adams, made the death doubly difficult. "Bearing the same name, & People talking so much about them, makes me look upon my little Aba Adams, & consider her,

as widdowed even in her Cradle." Elizabeth was further deflated because she had counted on Thaxter's son to play with Aba, since her
own brother and sister were practically adults. Far more than her older
sisters, Elizabeth relied on faith for transcendence and declared with
conviction, "heaven allwise—has determined . . . and Submission—
however hard must be our part."[46]

In the summer of 1790, Mary too was feeling miserable, because of
her husband's lingering cold, loneliness for Abigail, and worry over her
eldest daughter's continued breast pain and weakness, she confided in
a long letter to Richmond Hill. Like Abigail vis-à-vis Colonel Smith,
Mary at last let go and complained about Jacob Norton's failure as a
breadwinner: "[Betsy] poor girl is wasted to nothing almost. She wants
better living than a country Clergyman can afford."[47] Only wine could
alleviate Betsy's lassitude, and Mary insisted Norton supply a glass or
two daily. Mary's own financial circumstances were as pressed as ever,
thanks to Richard's poorly paid public service. Still, Mary felt better
after confiding in her sister, in large part because, no matter how different their stations, she imagined them both struggling for the same goal:
the happiness of their families. It was not so much God as human contact that brought her solace. "I hope we shall not always feel so many
calls as we have done for these several years," she included Abigail in
her lament over recent privations. "You & I have been better wives than
the world will ever know or give us cridit for."[48]

DEPRESSION AND TALK OF depression were not confined to the family's females. John Quincy was as vulnerable to low spirits as anyone he
knew. With no cause whatsoever, he could lose "all my mirth" like
Hamlet, he reminded his cousin Billy Cranch. How much worse then
was his mood in June 1790 when he was forced either to defy his parents or cease to court the woman he loved. The woman was Mary Frazier, whom he had met while clerking forty miles from Boston in
Newbury-Port.[49] Mary was perfection itself in John Quincy's opinion,
and he told a friend that "all my hopes of happiness in this life, centre
in possession of that girl."[50] The problem was that John Quincy had
spent his early adulthood studying and was now living extremely frugally on the small allowance his parents could afford.

Nobody doubted John Quincy's potential. In his mother's words, only "some dire misfortune or calamity" could impede his ultimate success.[51] And at first Mary Frazier was willing to wait for the man she loved to fulfill his destiny. But in the spring of 1790, urged on by a calculating cousin, Mary suddenly insisted that John Quincy sign a formal engagement or never see her again. John Adams had forbidden his sons to propose before they could support a family; John Quincy, who agreed with his father in principal if not sentiment, submitted to the older man's will and dropped his suit. But oh, how he suffered. "My ambition and vanity are at present . . . swallow'd up by a stupid indolence, and an unmeaning listlessness," he went on confiding in his cousin Billy, and his demoralization was further stoked when he opened a law business in his father's old office in Boston—but not a single client walked through the door.[52]

"I have often found myself in the same Situation," warmhearted Billy Cranch quickly wrote back to his ailing cousin, determined to empathize with John Quincy's depression, though it was clear from his letter that he had never experienced more than a fleeting bad mood.

> I have sometimes puzzled myself about [depression] . . . I think it a disorder or Disease to which a man may as necessarily be subjected as to the Stone or the Gout. The best remedy I believe is determined opposition. My depressions seldom last more than a few hours. I can generally reason them away. If neither Reason nor opposition will prevail, I take the first opportunity to run away from them. Some trivial Circumstance generally occurs . . . which I convert into a source of Pleasure and I soon make out to dissipate the Gloom.[53]

Unlike Billy Cranch, Nabby Smith, who had once worried that she was immune to feelings altogether, now found herself afflicted by a surfeit of love and gloom. The cause was Colonel Smith's decision to act on his business impulse. He set sail for London, while Nabby remained at home in New York with the children. This was Nabby's first real separation from the man she continued to love passionately, and it could not help but trigger memories of her father's trips to Philadelphia when she was not much older than her eldest boy. She wrote candidly to Betsy Norton of "a blank in my mind . . . which nothing can fill up" and told her mother she felt "alone in the world."[54] Abigail's long and heartfelt reply, recalling the stretches of time when John was absent during their marriage, opens a window on her own mature view of what constitutes connectedness as well as her profound commitment to her only female child:

> Why do you say that you feel alone in the world? I used to think that I felt so too; but when I lost my mother, and afterwards my father, *that* "alone" appeared to me in a much more formidable light. It was like cutting away the main pillars of a building; and though no friend can support the absence of a good husband, yet, whilst our parents live, we cannot feel unprotected. To them, we can apply for advice and direction, sure that it will be given with affection and tenderness. We know not what we can do or bear; till called to the trial. I have passed through many painful ones, yet have enjoyed as much happiness through life as usually falls to the lot of mortals; and, when my enjoyments have been damped, curtailed, or molested, it has not been owing to vice, that great disturber of human happiness, but sometimes to folly, in myself or others, or the hand of Providence, which has seen fit to afflict me.

"But my pen runs on," she gracefully concluded. She was called from her thoughts by duty, the very tonic that had so often proved this middle sister's salvation when she had no power to change the course of events.[55] [56]

DURING THEIR LAST SUMMER in New York, Abigail and Martha Washington became increasingly friendly. In the beginning of June, they took an excursion together to tour the Passaic Falls in New Jersey. At the end of August, when Martha left for Mount Vernon, she embraced Abigail, "tenderly saying god Bless you my dear Madam we will meet again at Philadelphia."[57]

This reunion was about all Abigail could anticipate with pleasure as she began packing up her house on the Hudson. As the leaves changed, she more than ever longed to be in New England and on the night of October 10, she sat down in her dressing gown to describe to Mary how she dreamed of eating her own apples and pears. Abigail told her sister, "We are all well," but no sooner did she snuff out her writing candle than she began uncontrollably shaking and for two hours writhed with pain in her head and back. Then, for five days she was as delirious as George Washington had been in his crisis. The cause was difficult to diagnose, though in retrospect it seems to have been malaria. St. John's powder proved useless. On the tenth day, Abigail began her own favorite remedy, "the Bark," which was powdered bark from the cinnamon-colored Peruvian cinchona tree.[58] Her fever diminished. But at this point, she could barely ride out for air in a carriage, and she remained weak a month later when—with Congress due to reconvene on December 6—Adams could delay no longer, and he; Abigail; Thomas; Nabby's middle son, John; Louisa; and the loyal Brieslers slowly drove south.[59] Twenty miles a day was the maximum Abigail could tolerate.

No sooner did she arrive at her new house on the vastly inferior Schuylkill River—"the Schuylkill is not more like the Hudson, than I to Hercules," Abigail moaned to Nabby—than her youngest son, Thomas, came down with the rheumatic fever he had inherited from her and lay near death for five weeks. Abigail, still weak herself, never left his side except to greet the endless chain of visitors who fought their way in around trunks and boxes, or to tackle the overwhelming job of housekeeping with yet another cast of debauched servants and the inevitable appalling rise in the cost of goods. Her house was brick and named Bush Hill, though there wasn't a twig around it, the occupying British having cut down all the trees. The Adamses liked its situation, two-and-a-half miles from the health hazards of urban living, but the clay roads made travel to Philadelphia difficult. Bush Hill had been empty the past four years, and workmen were only now lathering paint on when Abigail, with her aversion to the smell, stepped out of her carriage. Soon after, it snowed, and the already cold chambers became icier still. Half the staff caught one germ or another. The unfortunate John Quincy chose this moment to plan a cheering visit to his parents. Charles came from New York and proved "a great assistance," but still "I want my dear sisters," Abigail exclaimed.[60]

And Mary wrote back, equally sorry not to be with her, "What a succession of troubles have you had to incounter & not one of us to help you through.[61]

Sometimes Abigail was so exhausted she had to lie on her back to greet visitors. Always, she longed for Nabby, whom she assured, "You cannot regret your separations more than I do, for morn, noon, and night, you rest upon [my] mind and heart."[62] But once Thomas began to improve, she was also quick to thank God for her blessings. High on this list was her two-year-old grandson, John, the middle and difficult child she had taken off Nabby's hands and brought to Philadelphia just as her own grandmother once had taken *her* in. John was "much more evil than good," Abigail frankly reported to Nabby, but she was determined to reform him and meanwhile derived considerable pleasure from his wicked tricks. He was also a boon for his surprisingly indulgent grandfather. "[John] has spent an hour this afternoon . . . driving his grandpa round the room with a willow stick," Abigail bemusedly reported on one day.[63] A month later they had developed a ritual. Every night after his supper, John Smith commanded John Adams to pull him in a chair around the dining room, "which is generally done for half an hour, to the derangement of my carpet" and the Vice-President's glee.[64]

The week before Christmas, with Thomas at last on the mend, Abigail left home for the first time to visit the Washingtons' lavish double brick Philadelphia house behind a wall high enough to screen off Market Street in the government district. The weather was cold and wet as usual. The journey was arduous, with the horses up to their knees in spattering clay before they reached the pavemented town. Once inside the city, there were pigs, rabid dogs, and rats everywhere, and the air reeked as much as in the French capital from the loamy mixture of garbage and manure thrust down the streets. Abigail was eager to join the Washingtons and especially Martha, but no keener to see new faces than she had been in Paris, London, or New York, and so once again was pleasantly shocked to discover fashion, intellect, and even kindness existed outside of her own state. The Washingtons received guests in their opulent first-floor dining room. "The room became full before I left it, and the circle very brilliant. How could it be otherwise, when the dazzling Mrs. Bingham and her beautiful sisters were there; the Misses Allen and Misses Chew; in short a constellation of beauties?" Abigail described this scene with far more enthusiasm than her reception at George III's palace. Soon she was praising the Philadelphia production of *The School for Scandal* and even looking forward to the very card parties she had despised in London as an opportunity to meet the intriguing residents of this surprisingly civilized town.

A year and a half from the momentous day when Congress first sat in Federal Hall, it reconvened in a new two-story brick building near the State House in Philadelphia—fittingly, it seemed, to many of the delegates. For having a population of 45,000, Philadelphia was larger than any other city in America, with 6,600 houses, 415 stores, and 26 places of worship. All sorts of wondrous things were happening there. Around the time the Adamses were moving in, the pleasure spot Gray's Gardens was installing a seventy-foot waterfall and greenhouse to grow tropical fruit, John Bill Ricketts was planning to open a circus on Market Street, and in an era when even a china washbasin was a luxury for Americans, a wealthy merchant named Joseph Carson paid four pounds and fifteen shillings to have a bathtub installed in his own home. The prudish ban on theatrical performances had been lifted a year before, and Old Southwork Theatre was thriving. So too was trade. In 1790, a record 1,354 ships arrived in the Philadelphia harbor, as opposed to 750 before the Revolutionary War.[65]

Though Abigail complained of the "dead and flat appearance of the brick walls of the houses," she admired Philadelphia's wide straight avenues and broad pavements. "You never see a person in the middle of the street!" she marveled at the contrast to Boston's chaotic traffic in a letter to her sister Elizabeth. Willow trees ("a favorite tree with me from the peacefulness of its branches which float and wave to every breaze") interspersed with 'tall strait and elegant popular[s]" marched in a phalanx down the sidewalks, "contribut[ing] greatly to the beauty."[66]

Philadelphia was also associated with more historical events than any other city in America. Here the first Continental Congress had sat and both the Declaration of Independence and the Constitution had been written. Here too Washington had been appointed general of the Confederate Army, and he was clearly aware of the significance of the spot where he stood when he addressed the House and the Senate on Wednesday December 8, two days after Congress convened. "The abundant fruits of another year have blessed our Country with plenty," he informed them and went on to enumerate the many successes of 1790, notably the commercial triumphs enabled by Alexander Hamilton and the growth of the nation, thanks to the addition of Vermont and Kentucky's pending statehood.[67] The laws and amendments vital to a working government had been set in place. Though he did not say it, Washington, like the country, had overcome great peril and emerged triumphant. There was every reason to hope that the worst had passed.

The President's speech helped buoy the spirits of most of his fellow countrymen. A few days after the address was printed in the Boston newspapers, the value of public securities rose over ten percent. "Content will follow . . . and a general Confidence in the national Government," Uncle Tufts predicted from Weymouth.

Elizabeth Shaw waxed euphoric on the subject, writing Abigail, "I believe there was never a Country more blessed than ours—The People are now enjoying there hard earnings—[There] is no murmering— no complaining in our streets—no n[ews] of Tax[e]s . . . Health through—the Land—Peace and Plenty crown the Year."[68]

The turn in John's mood was even more remarkable. It was high praise indeed when this denizen of so many momentous American Congresses pronounced the current session "the most assiduous, the most harmonious, and the most efficacious I ever knew."[69] (Pennsylvania Senator Maclay, on the other hand, represented the growing number of anti-Federalists when he responded dyspeptically to Washington's address in his diary: "Republicans are borne down by fashion and fear of being charged with want of respect to General Washington. If there is treason in the wish, I retract it, but would to God this same General Washington were in Heaven! We would have him brought forward as the constant cover to every unconstitutional and unrepublican act.")[70]

Abigail was particularly gratified at Vermont's joining the union because it would add another northern state to offset Madison, Jefferson, Washington, and their Virginia contingent. But then again, maybe she had been wrong about the inevitable battle between the two sections of the country, and the initial animus would dissipate rather than grow over the years. Thinking back on the achievements of 1790, Abigail saw the government coming together like the building of a Roman temple: "One pillar rises after an other, and adds strength to the union ... and tho the old squabling spirit is not entirely extinct, it appears to be near its dissolution."[71]

To further her happiness, at the beginning of the new year, President Washington appointed Colonel Smith supervisor of New York State as well as New York City, which promised, Abigail approvingly noted, "a handsome sum," certainly enough to support Nabby and his three boys.[72] Whatever they thought of William Smith personally, the Adamses had no doubt that he was crucial to their daughter's happiness and clearly considered his current absence a crisis because each wrote a separate letter to London imploring their son-in-law to accept the job. Abigail sent Nabby official papers confirming the appointment to rush to him by private vessel. She wanted the colonel to see the requirement that he appear in New York before July 1. Return "with all possible despatch," Abigail implored her son-in-law.[73] She no longer could count on this young man's judgment, nor penetrate his ambition. She knew him to be impulsive and impatient for success. Still, just a few years before he had listened to her advice and gotten what he wanted. She could only hope he would do so again.

Colonel Smith's return to New York was not the only plan in which Abigail's heart was deeply invested. Ever since the summer before, she and Mary had been scheming to meet the next time Congress rose. It was as if they were again newlyweds plotting for 22-year-old Abigail and her rising lawyer husband to visit the young Cranches in Salem where Richard just had opened a watchmaking shop. How distant had Salem then seemed from Braintree, how obdurate the obstacles they would have to overcome to be together for a precious day or two. And how the sisters had prided themselves on their cleverness when they at last brought the visit off. Then Mary had felt sure she could bend life to her bidding, and some of that confidence returned now, at the end of the coldest January she could remember, as she wrote her 47-year-old sister, who was currently the wife of the Vice-President and living in Philadelphia: "I past by your House this afternoon and the thought of seeing it again inhabited by my dear Brother and Sister gave a chearfulness to its appearance which it has not had since you left—and believe me my Sister Joy and Sorrow are so nearly alli'd in their effects that some of the few tears which remain'd unshed at your departure forc'd themselves from my Eyes."[74]

CHAPTER XIV

"Too painful to think upon"

. . .

"I BELIEVE SISTER CRANCH HAS FORGOT THAT I AM LIVING, FOR I have not had a Line from her these three months, or she is wholly absorbed in your charming company—must I forgive her?" Elizabeth feigned a jesting tone in a letter to Abigail on June 24, 1791. Not only had Mary failed to write, but Abigail had been home from Philadelphia in Braintree for a month and still had not contacted her younger sister. What had become of their lasting bond?

The parsonage in Haverhill felt sad, with the nephews dispersed and no scholars boarding. As she sat down to write, Elizabeth was overwhelmed by housework and her brood. Baby Abigail screamed while 13-year-old Billy Shaw sequestered himself reading. Eleven-year-old Betsy Quincy would be a delight, especially with her new penchant for hilariously mimicking everyone's foibles, if only she could control her soaring moods. Elizabeth was sick from the heat wave that had withered her bright green garden. The fields around the parsonage were browning, the pea and asparagus plants drooped, adding to the "gloom" that already hung over the town.

Her neighbor and cousin John Thaxter, Elizabeth's sole relative in Haverhill, was dying. Less than a year after losing his son, Thaxter himself had contracted pleurisy, then consumption. All three sisters adored this debonair cousin. But Elizabeth, like the heroine in a Gothic novel, had a "dark secret": a reason she could not disclose for dreading his loss.

When Thaxter did pass away—on July 6—Elizabeth feared for herself as much as she grieved for his family, but the source of her excessive anxiety she could not reveal—even or especially to her older sisters, for it involved her husband.

It was still painful for Elizabeth to remember Abigail's disapproval of John Shaw at the time of their engagement, but it remained a source of satisfaction that both Abigail and Mary later entrusted her husband to educate their sons. To have her marriage respected by her older sisters was more urgent now than ever.

There were certain subjects "too tender to write or converse upon," she had once told Abigail and Mary. Now she acknowledged there were subjects even "too painful to think upon."[1] The truth was that at some point during their fourteen-year marriage, John Shaw had begun drinking heavily and had become a verbally and maybe physically abusive spouse.

Elizabeth was not alone in her reticence. The importance of projecting the image of a perfect family has almost always discouraged public disclosure of marital conflict in America. In a brave exception, the first Puritans declared wife-beating a criminal action, but by the mid-eighteenth century, maintaining the stability of the family was considered more crucial than punishing the wicked by both state and church. In Elizabeth's time, society was as likely to condemn the victim as the perpetrator for any rift in the household. Well-known in Haverhill was the saga of a woman named Elizabeth Ela, who was shamed by her neighbors into recanting accusations against her violent spouse.[2] Even in the rare case where separation or divorce was granted, humiliation was a woman's reward for seeking help from the outside. Elizabeth Shaw, with her pride of character and position, had many reasons to dread airing her grim predicament. Help had to come, if not from her judgmental sisters, then from some younger member of their clan.[3]

So it was a great relief when—eleven days after Thaxter's death— Billy Cranch, now called William, arrived to take over not only Thaxter's law firm but his place as Elizabeth's protector in Haverhill. William moved into his old room at the Shaws' parsonage and in no time was cheering his aunt. "Your son is indeed very dear to me," Elizabeth wrote Mary. "He is just such a Friend as everyone wants near them—I think he is exceedingly like his Father—He [makes] every body love, and respect him."[4] William was born with the inner peace that escaped his more volatile siblings and cousins. When he expressed doubts that he could equal John Thaxter's business success in Haverhill, John Quincy assured him, "You have a fund of happiness within yourself that is worth more, than all the law business" in the world.[5] Although Elizabeth told Abigail she saw William as her defender, she did not explain what or whom he was defending her from.[6]

William Cranch was now in love with his cousin Nancy Greenleaf from Boston, but too poor to marry her. Elizabeth could easily empathize with his frustration because she had endured a protracted courtship herself. Romantic love had given full play to all her most delicate feelings. Even recalling that excruciating pleasure now lifted Elizabeth's spirits, which rose further still when the Adamses and Cranches arrived in August for a long visit. The sisters' time together fully restored her faith in the threefold chord.

Then, just after Abigail returned to Philadelphia, in the beginning of October, Elizabeth's own Billy—doubtless lost in a daydream—tripped into a hole and broke his leg. Elizabeth's only son was accident-prone as well as absentminded. Mary spoke euphemistically of his "peculiarities," and Elizabeth herself complained that Billy could never find two socks that matched. Five years earlier he had lain unconscious for twelve hours after skipping into a clothesline. This time he was wide awake but in agonizing pain.

Medical experts of the time (like Abigail's favorite, Dr. Buchan) treated broken legs with bed rest. The patient was laid on his side with the wounded leg slightly bent and immobilized by moistened leather or pasteboard splints.[7] "A merry heart doth good like a medicine" was Elizabeth's creed as well as Abigail's; so she joked and cajoled—but nothing worked. "I am anxious for Billy Shaw least he should be a criple all his day's," Abigail wrote Mary at the end of October.[8]

In April, Mary was still reporting to Abigail that the boy had not improved. Now she also worried about her sister: "Elizabeth possesses a great share of fortitude but tho her spirits sustain the load of woe and cares . . . which Providence has seen fit to exercise her yet her Body bows under it."[9]

As the months passed, even Elizabeth's famous fortitude teetered. "I [fear] that if my sons life [is] spared, I [will] have the misfortune to see him a miserable criple . . . Perhaps no one ever had a greater dread of seeing Persons useless than Myself."[10]

Depressed by her son's health as well as the woe that could not be spoken about, Elizabeth strove more than ever to be useful herself. She remained the smartly dressed hostess at parish functions and a middle-aged seeker in her private soul. Still she determined to write letters worthy of publishing. Still she sought connections to the wider world.

"I never wished to read History more in my Life," Elizabeth wrote Mary.[11] And even when hobbled by an attack of inflamed eyes that made her dizzy if she read for more than a few minutes, she made sure she kept up with the news.

The French Revolution seized her imagination. She rejoiced at the sansculottes ardor for liberty and determination to "remember the ladies"—the very directive promoted by Abigail that America had ignored. She envied French wives who, under a 1792 law, gained the right to divorce their husbands, and marveled that a delegate to the National Assembly (the Marquis de Condorcet) declared what would be unthinkable in Britain or America—that women deserved to vote.

She perceived the influence of French radicalism in the electrifying 1792 *Vindication of the Rights of Woman* by London journalist Mary Wollstonecraft. Its argument for female education gave voice to her own dreams. And while the book so infuriated John Adams that he read with pen in hand and argued back at it in the margins, *Vindication* thrilled Elizabeth by flouting the myth of gendered minds. "Nonsense!" Wollstonecraft scoffed in response to Rousseau's smug remark that "a perfect man and a perfect woman should be no more alike in mind" than in complexion. Men were superior in physical strength only. The intellects of all humans were formed for the same work.[12]

While elated by French ideals, Elizabeth grieved at the savagery of the guillotine and the tragedy of a nation divided: "Is anything more to be deprecated than a civil War?"[13] She was horrified when the National Assembly under Danton and Robespierre denounced religion, sickened when it ordered priests and noblemen "purged."

She watched with growing alarm during the winter of 1792–3 as

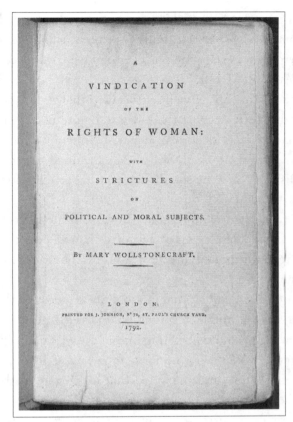

A

VINDICATION

OF THE

RIGHTS OF WOMAN:

WITH

STRICTURES

ON

POLITICAL AND MORAL SUBJECTS.

BY MARY WOLLSTONECRAFT.

LONDON:
PRINTED FOR J. JOHNSON, Nº 72, ST. PAUL'S CHURCH YARD.
1792.

This is the title page of the original 1792 printing of Mary Wollstonecraft's groundbreaking book, A Vindication of the Rights of Woman.

Louis XVI was tried and then condemned for treason. She winced at newspaper reports of his doleful two-hour trip through Paris to the scaffold, of his rapid decapitation while—worst of all—the mobs gaped and leered. To her further disgust, hoards of Americans, including Thomas Jefferson, cheered on the murderers. John Adams perceptively observed that, as he had been the only American minister to incur Louis XVI's dislike during his tenure in Paris, he was now aberrant among his own colleagues for mourning the King's death. And he enhanced his singularity by reminding America of its indebtedness to Louis, without whose loans and Navy they would still be subjects of the *British* King.[14]

Elizabeth too grieved for "the unfortunate Lewis" whose only crime, she pointed out in a letter to Mary, was "that he was born, and a King at this particular period of time." The French Assembly had squandered its riches. "They felt the advantages arising from a greater degree of *Knowledge and Liberty* than their Fathers had possessed, but had not virtue enough to sustain, and make a wise use of it—They thought they could not obtain *too* much of so great a *Good*—They precipitately made vast strides, and the pendulum of power has vibrated with such violence, as has thrown them into such Scenes of horror, and confusion as we now see—"[15]

She went on in a gloomy tone to equate her own dimmed hopes with the fate of French idealism. Lofty goals were "tender leaves" unlikely to survive the winds of fortune. "Every day we are taught by some Occurrence, or other on what an uncertain tenor, we hold every earthly Enjoyment."[16]

EVENTUALLY, THE SORENESS IN Billy Shaw's leg subsided. One spring day, he sat up and tugged his mangled bones over the bed. The splints came off, and by June he could study in a chair and limp to dinner. Summer came, and he stumbled into a carriage and took off to visit his aunts.

Mary and Abigail leapt at the chance to unburden their younger sister, whose physical distance from them seemed harder to bear each year. Emotionally, the three sisters drew closer, their efforts to connect stronger. Abigail in particular made a point of taking Billy under her wing. Suppressing her lifelong temptation to suggest improvements, she wrote Haverhill singing only his praises. "It was very pleasing to me that he was approved by you," Elizabeth wrote back and roused herself to look for a bright side to Billy's disaster: "Joseph [in the Old Testament] could not have given Bread to his Brethren and supported his aged Father if he had not . . . been cast into the Pit, & sold to the Ishmalites."[17]

And even if it was to do no future good, the fall left Billy's genius undiminished. He was his father's single remaining scholar, and in the fall of 1793, when Billy resumed studying for the Harvard exams he would undergo the following summer, John Shaw showered all his knowledge and ambition on his only son. Billy easily won admission to Harvard. What was hard for both parents was letting their first child go.

"Your Father calls upon his William and really mourns for his scholar . . . he seems quite lost, he has had the care of you so long that he does not know what to do without you," Elizabeth wrote Billy his first month in Cambridge. Writing and conversation were vital for success in the world, Elizabeth sounded the family creed and, like Mary and Abigail when their sons left for Harvard, exhorted: "Committing our thoughts to paper makes us more attentive—more close observers—of everything which obliges us to think." Writing a mother was particularly salubrious.

"You used to love to come sit with me after study . . . Write as you would converse."[18]

In the same letter, Elizabeth reported the sad news that William Cranch was leaving the Haverhill parsonage. Over the past three years, he had made great strides as a lawyer and amassed almost enough savings to propose to the woman he loved. He was twenty-five and attached to his aunt Elizabeth: "My affection for her is like that I feel for my sisters," he wrote Mary. It would have been comfortable for him to stay put.

Instead, he plucked up courage to accept riskier work for the land development firm Morris, Nicholson, and Greenleaf in the nation's future capital city, Washington D.C. The "Greenleaf" in the firm's title was his fiancée Nancy Greenleaf's brother, a gifted self-promoter determined to capitalize on the speculating fervor of the times. At present, the city of Washington was little more than unpopulated swampland. The plan was to scoop up properties currently selling for practically nothing[19] and in six years' time turn them around at huge profits when Congressmen and Cabinet members competed for homes in the town.

"It is an unstable world we live in." Elizabeth grieved over the departure of both her son and William Cranch in a letter to Abigail. "We sisters seem to be called to be separated from some of our dearest Connections all at once—For I must think, I shall *feel* the separation from Mr. Cranch, even more than his own Father and Mother. For I had considered him as fixed *among us*—as a dear Relative and worthy Friend, as a Protector to me, and my Children[20], one I hoped to have lived and died with . . . ought I to murmur or repine?"[21]

Certainly, Elizabeth repined on Tuesday, September 23, when William Cranch departed for Washington.[22] John Shaw was now the only man at the parsonage. Elizabeth was again at the mercy of we do not know what form of domestic abuse. That Sunday Parson Shaw preached his usual two services. Afterward, congregants poured into the parsonage for the party Elizabeth had prepared weekly for the past seventeen years.

There is a form of liver disease called steatosis where the patient loses weight and experiences dramatic mood swings, but can appear healthy to the casual viewer. No guest at Elizabeth's party suspected that her husband was an alcoholic and that his liver had eroded. Even Elizabeth, who did know, detected no dramatic change in his eating habits or general health. So she was not alarmed when "At half after nine [John] said he was weary and wanted to go to Bed," she later told Mary. He called "for his [night]cap. I gave it to him little thinking it would be the last kind office he would ever know."

Her husband breathed heavily in his sleep, "but as he so frequently did I was not apprehensive of Danger," Elizabeth continued. Then when she tried to rouse him the following morning, "Alas he was deaf to the voice of his Friend, and to the tender calls of his children crying Pappa." No amount of shaking could wake him. Three hours later, his panting ceased.

John Shaw was only 47 years old when he died of a corroded liver the last Monday in September. With Billy Shaw in Cambridge, William Cranch en route to Washington, and her sisters a day's ride away in Braintree, Elizabeth—beset by her needy daughters—felt "like a Tree of the forest whose surrounding wood was cut down . . . perfectly alone."[23]

Although liberated from her husband's torment, she was also instantly poor and homeless. There were no *Rights of Woman* in the American Constitution, nor did Puritan churches provide housing or food for the family of a parson no longer alive to preach. And how could she possibly afford tuition and living expenses for Billy at Harvard?

AT THE END OF SEPTEMBER 1794, John Adams was at home enjoying the last days of his summer break from Congress. When he learned of Elizabeth's predicament, he straightaway drove the day's ride to Haverhill and—to put her mind at ease—promised to pay all William Shaw's college fees. Elizabeth felt so beholden she told Abigail she "could go Barefoot to Mecca"[24] to thank him, but John knew that what he did was only fair.

"Your Uncle who was also to you for some time a Preceptor and [surrogate] Father went off suddenly and left a widow and children in Distress," John wrote John Quincy. "I must assist them as much as I can. They have deserved it by their kindness to me and mine upon all occasions."[25]

John's generosity toward Elizabeth was particularly touching, as the Adamses were now struggling to save money for themselves. After paying his greater expenses, a Vice-President retained only little more pay than a village minister. When he returned to Philadelphia in 1794, John scrimped by lodging, rather than renting a house, and avoided hiring a manager by leaving Abigail behind to run the farm.[26] Memories of European pomp were fading fast. Wealth was never out of fashion, but showing it off in Philadelphia at the end of the eighteenth century would have been as gauche as driving a shabby carriage on a London street. "I am so well satisfied with my present simplicity, that I am determined never to depart from it again," John confirmed his return to Puritan austerity.[27]

He was also determined to ingratiate himself with the Senate, where he sat silent as a monk, day after day. "I am happy to learn that the only fault in your political character, and one which has always given me uneasiness, is wearing away," Abigail applauded his diplomacy. "I mean a certain irritability which has some times thrown you off your Guard."[28]

It was not only prudence and the political value of thrift that kept Abigail from Philadelphia. She also relished life in Quincy, as her district of Braintree had recently been renamed in celebration of the Quincy family.[29] The familiarity of a small town and proximity to her sisters meant more than ever to her. And John was gone only when Congress sat. The postal system had improved, and they felt free to write intimately. When 59-year-old John asked 50-year-old Abigail if she still worried about him as much as she used to, she answered with one of her most stirring declarations of love:

> My days of anxiety have indeed been many and painful in
> years past; when I had many terrors that encompassed me

around I have happily surmounted them, but I do not find that I am less solicitous to hear constantly from you than in times of more danger, and I look for every Saturday [when your letter arrives] as a day in which I am to receive a Boon. I have received a Letter every week since you left me . . . for which receive my Thanks, particularly [for] the part in which you say you are not less anxious to see me than when seperated twenty years ago—Years subdue the ardour of passion but in lieu thereof a Friendship and affection deep Rooted subsists. which defies the Ravages of Time, and will survive whilst the vital Flame exists.

John did not explicitly comment on this emotional passage, though he slyly contradicted its verdict on passion, signing a following letter. "I am, with all the Ardour of Youth yours."[30]

TWO YEARS BEFORE, AMERICA had peacefully chosen a second government. Washington was unanimously re-elected President, and Adams remained the nothing who would be everything if Washington died.[31] Alexander Hamilton as Secretary of the Treasury and Thomas Jefferson as Secretary of State again dominated the Cabinet.

While on the surface there were no radical changes, Abigail declared the future grim. A fissure was deepening between Federalists—like Washington, Hamilton, and Adams—and anti-Federalists—like Jefferson and Hamilton's former ally James Madison. The latter group now dubbed themselves "Jeffersonian" or "Democratic" Republicans and accused the Federalists of undermining Enlightenment ideals.[32] "The Halcion days of America are past," Abigail lamented. They had lasted a mere four years.

In the eighteenth century, a "halcyon" government was by definition unified. Differences of opinion were symptoms of disease.[33] The one conviction Jefferson and Hamilton shared was that factions were noxious. Their own conflicts had to be explained as failures on one side or the other. For Hamilton, Jefferson had abandoned nationalism to embrace southern agrarian interests; for Jefferson, Hamilton had betrayed equality to promote commerce in the north.

Each side had journalists to defend their stands and vilify their enemies. To combat John Fenno's Federalist *Gazette of the United States*—which had printed Adams's *Davila* essays—Jefferson convinced the poet Philip Freneaux to publish a Republican-slanted *National Gazette*. Benjamin Franklin's grandson, Benjamin Franklin Bache—John Quincy's former playmate in Paris—espoused similar views in his *Aurora*. These two papers attacked not just Hamilton but George Washington himself.

"Our Antifederal scribblers are so fond of Rotations that they seem disposed to remove their Abuses from me to the President," John joked to Abigail shortly after the elections, when the Republican attacks began. "Baches paper which is nearly as bad as Freneaux's begins to join in concert with it," and to accuse Washington rather than himself of monarchial excess. "I may be expected to be an advocate . . . for Equality in this particular," John observed: no one could doubt he had suffered his share of journalistic barbs.

While John sat placidly in the Senate, during the second administration, the animus between Hamilton and Jefferson intensified. As Jefferson himself later acknowledged, the Secretary of the Treasury and he were "daily pitted in the Cabinet like two cocks."[34] Everything from the definition of an ideal republic[35] to the importance of English trade provoked a quarrel.

Their most heated disputes entailed foreign alliances. On February 1, 1793, Revolutionary France declared war on England. As Jeffersonians leapt to defend the French and Hamiltonians sided with England, President Washington made a point of distancing himself from both. Like Elizabeth Shaw, he despised the savagery of Danton and Robespierre. Yet he would not dream of assisting his former archenemy, George III. The broken American military was in any case unfit to fight even in self-defense.[36] Washington saw neutrality as the only choice.

Publicly, Adams too espoused neutrality, but in a letter to Abigail he obliquely supported Great Britain by challenging a signal tenet of the American as well as the French Revolution: the equality of men. He made the controversial declaration that rule by law did not demand equality. Men were equal only in the broadest sense:

By The Law cf Nature all Men are Men and not Angells—
Men and not Lyons—Men and not Whales . . . That is they are
all of the same species. And this is as much as the Equality of
Nature amounts to. But Man differs by Nature from Man, almost as much as Man from Beast. The Equality of Nature is
Moral and Political only and means that all Men are independent. But a Physical Inequality, and Intellectual Inequality of the
most serious kind is established unchangeably by the Author of
Nature—and Society has a Right to establish any other Inequal-
ities it may judge necessary for its good.[37]

In other words, government was not compelled to uplift the weak
or shower influence on the powerless. If God had wanted an undiffer-
entiated populace, he would have created it himself. Adams had retained his Puritan belief in hierarchy, while Jefferson, for all his
aristocratic airs, was committed to leveling power. John still feared the
many (as he had observed long ago in Paris), Jefferson the few. Adams
was not a monarchist, but he did believe in an intellectual elite. This
remained the great ideological distinction between Adams and Jefferson, and indeed, between most Federalists and Republicans.

Equality was a momentous issue for all Americans, a crucible for
thinkers like Mary, Abigail, and Elizabeth still struggling to understand their own break from the British King.[33] Had they seceded from
Britain to form a separate but similar union? Or had they severed the
bonds of kinship so that all Americans could be equally free?

THE DISPUTE BETWEEN FEDERALISTS and Republicans exploded when
in April 1793 France sent 29-year-old Citizen Edmond Charles Genet
as French Minister to Philadelphia. (By accepting Genet, the United
States became the first government in the world to recognize Revolutionary France.) His general mission—as Ben Franklin's had been in
Paris—was to stoke enthusiasm for his country's revolution, and he
was met by a sympathetic audience, since American Federalists as well
as Republicans could identify with France's love of freedom and contempt for hereditary rule. Genet lacked Franklin's patience, however.

Emboldened by a rapturous reception when he arrived in Charleston, South Carolina, he began blurting specific demands, such as that Americans seize British vessels trolling in their waters and help France "liberate" Spanish and English territories throughout the New World.

Genet was hailed by a mass of ecstatic Philadelphians when he reached the capital. George Washington chose not to appear. Nor was Washington moved when Genet rose to serenade guests with La Marseillaise at a formal dinner. Only reluctantly did the President officially agree to receive the French minister, and then it was just to announce that he would countenance no aggression against a European nation on American soil.

Genet was flummoxed. How alienated Washington appeared from the rest of the country where French flags whirled and cries of *"liberte, egalite, fraternite"* greeted him everywhere he went. In New England, even moderate clergymen like Parson Wibird enthused about the French in their Sunday sermons. Clubs endorsing France proliferated, and it was soon a hazard to be British even in the theatre, where American actors playing Englishmen often were booed off the stage. Jefferson, unofficially, and his newspaper, officially, made an issue of encouraging Genet to pursue his militant agenda, and it came to the point where the French minister was sincerely deluded into believing America would overthrow its unanimously elected President rather than disappoint the crusading Republic of France.

Citizen Genet was the son of Edme Jacques Genet, a modest publicist/translator John Adams befriended when touting the American Revolution in the Paris of Louis XVI fourteen years earlier. John had not forgotten young Edmond as John Quincy's childhood companion[39] and on their single meeting in Philadelphia he found his old friend's son well spoken and polite. But John confided to Abigail that Genet was politically ignorant, harboring a romantic view of popular government.[40]

Coming from King-murdering France, Genet interpreted America's free criticism of the President as a prelude to violent insurgency.[41] Hence, he felt at liberty to displease Washington, ordering supporters of France to harass British trade boats and scheming to unseat the Spanish so the French could expand through the American south. It was a mark of Washington's faith in the stability of his five-year-old government—and in the American character—that he felt unthreatened by Genet's chicanery and initially left the Frenchman to undo himself. Meanwhile, Genet lost Jefferson's support as the Federalists began exploiting the French minister's faux pas to embarrass the Republicans in Congress The coup de grâce occurred when Genet's forces seized a British ship in an American harbor, flagrantly defying the President's command. Four months after the minister's arrival, Washington and Jefferson jointly demanded that he return to France.[42]

On December 31, 1793, Jefferson abruptly announced his resignation from the Cabinet. The reason, he told his daughter, was emotional fatigue, brought on by thankless battles with Hamilton—which was certainly a plausible cause. But he also felt mortified by the Genet affair and politically stymied. The Adams family struggled to understand the true reasons behind their old friend's decision.

This contemporary cartoon, entitled "Mad Tom In A Rage," mocks Jefferson's anti-Federalism.

"Good riddance of bad ware," John initially quipped to Abigail.[43] But he tempered this salvo in a letter to his middle son, Charles, acknowledging that Jefferson's "abilities are good—his Pen is very good—and for what I know the other Ministers might be the better for being watched by him."[44] So evidently Adams had his own suspicions about Hamilton and his acolytes in the Cabinet and, in spite of their many differences, he continued to admire "the choice one," as Abigail had described Jefferson long ago.

In a letter to John Quincy, Adams speculated that Jefferson's prodigious personal debts or his inability to sway Washington to the French cause may have triggered his return to Monticello. Or perhaps, for all his lofty sentiments, Jefferson was driven by the same base yearnings that had troubled Adams all his life. "Ambition," John wrote his eldest son, "is the subtlest Beast of the Intellectual and Moral Field. It is wonderfully adroit in concealing itself from its owner, I had almost said from itself. Jefferson thinks he shall by this step get a Reputation as a humble, modest, meek Man without ambition or vanity. He may even have deceived himself into this Belief. But if a Prospect opens, the world will see that he is as ambitious as Oliver Cromwell." [45]

Abigail, on the other hand, clung to the impression she had formed of Jefferson in Paris. "I have always reluctantly believed ill of him," she wrote John.[46] Besides, she was no foe of ambition, which produced Washingtons and Adamses as well as Cromwells and Robespierres.

AFTER JOHN SHAW'S DEATH, Elizabeth retreated to her bedroom. Care of bewildered 14-year-old Betsy Q and four-year-old Abby fell to the housekeeper. For five weeks, their mother could not rouse herself even to shed a tear.

"The death of my Uncle Shaw was a most affecting stroke to me," William Cranch wrote Mary from Washington. "The sickness of my dear Aunt Shaw goes to my heart—I feel her distresses—I see all the frightful fancies that must crowd upon her imagination. I participate in her anxieties for her dear children. The time of my entrance into [Haverhill] was marked by the death of our friend Mr. Thaxter; my exit by that of my uncle—I regretted that I was not there at that awful moment—I might have made the stroke less severe to my Aunt, and perhaps might have discharged some small part of the many kind offices I owe her." He sent his aunt $40 and hinted that his parents should do the same.

John Quincy also sent her money as well as the only known eulogy for his difficult uncle. Uncle Shaw, he wrote Elizabeth, had been "a

friend whose affections were always warm and expansive [and] . . .
from whose conversation I had always been sure to derive both instruction and delight . . . At whatever distance of time and place your nephews are separated from you, they can never cease to feel deeply interested
in your welfare," he assured his aunt. [47]

And where were Elizabeth's sisters when she most needed them?
Chafing that they couldn't race to comfort her because they were bound
to stay home and work: Mary to nurse her constantly ill husband and
eldest daughter, Abigail to prepare her fields for the coming chill. But
once the first potatoes were dug and the orchards hung with seaweed
to protect the fruit from freezing, Abigail stole a week off from farming and hurried to Haverhill to exhort her sister to bear her fate as best
she could.

The mission was not altogether successful.

"I . . . FOUND MY SISTER as well as I expected, tho' at times low in
spirits," Abigail reported to John after her visit.[48]

Low-spirited was an understatement, in Elizabeth's own opinion.
Five weeks in bed had wiped away any illusion that her plight was a
bad dream. She had reams of debts to pay but no income, distracted
children clinging to her apron, but no encouragements to calm their
fears. Formerly touted the first lady of Haverhill, she was now an object of charity. Self-reliance, her prized possession, seemed gone for
good. And what a contrast she saw in the life of the honored wife of the
Vice-President. Besides, for all her good intentions, Abigail could not
resist reminding Elizabeth to be grateful for the town's good deeds.

It was a great boon that Haverhill had paid for her husband's funeral! How generous that the church refused to evict her—at least
until a new minister arrived to preach. When the townspeople signed a
deed promising Elizabeth free firewood, "No person could wish to be
more loved and regarded by a people," Abigail marveled.[49] [50]

"I have always been exceedingly fond of Haverhill. I have lived Seventeen Years in this Place loving, and I believe beloved," Elizabeth
agreed.

But she also was forced to remind Abigail of the vagaries of human
nature when—suspecting that Elizabeth was discouraging a potential

new minister—the town took back its offer to send firewood. By the time this minister convinced the church elders that Elizabeth was in fact urging him to accept the position, it was winter, and she had been forced to buy her own. "I need to be possessed of more wisdom than the serpent, joined to the innocence of the Dove, more meekness than Moses, more patience than Job." Elizabeth made no attempt to hide her resentment in a letter to Mary.[51]

Her ideas on how to cope fluctuated. One day she panicked and determined to sell all her furniture. The next she saw an alternative and, besides taking in boarders like Mary, resolved to collect her husband's debts. "I see my feelings must be hurt," she resigned herself, when old friends resented her businesslike demands for money. Shaw, they remembered, had always retreated when his debtors balked. Elizabeth stood firm. "I pity them but myself and children are the real sufferers."[52]

Slowly, though, her spirit revived. During meals with their new boarders, Elizabeth and Betsy Q sat silent—Elizabeth wrote Mary at the end of December—appearing, they hoped, preoccupied by sad thoughts. But frequently the mother had to "swallow hard" and Betsy Q dove into her handkerchief to repress giggles at the self-importance of the other diners. "I am fearful it is wrong and yet it is the . . . natural Byas of my Temper."[53]

By April, Elizabeth had regained her interest in spinning similes and metaphors. In a draft of a note to Abigail, she compares letters with carriage rides,[54] which "for a while remove the Hills and Vallies that seperate us." She was well enough in June to take a real carriage ride to escort Betsy Q to summer in Quincy, where her aunts doted on the comic 14-year-old. Abigail declared she had never met a better-tempered girl.[55]

No less eccentric in her own way than her brother, Betsy Q had recently developed a tendency to slump. Straight-backed Abigail would surely teach her to stand upright like a lady, Elizabeth flattered her sister. And since Betsy Q remained as rambunctious as the day she had sprinted off at dawn to greet George Washington on his New England tour, Elizabeth begged her sterner sisters to "check" Betsy Q's "temerity" and "pluck . . . weeds" from her unruly mind: "You canot think what a comfort it has been to me to think that you love her."[56]

All advice was not welcome, however. During this June visit, Abigail urged Elizabeth to marry any man who could support her. And Elizabeth, while acknowledging her sisters' beneficent motives, refused to enter such a state of intimacy for money alone. She could no more be talked into marriage now, at 45, than talked out of it in her twenties. Hardships had not soured her idealistic view of marriage (to love your spouse was also, of course, a Puritan precept). Nor had gray hairs diminished her desirability to men.

Indeed, it soon became clear that, just nine months after Shaw's death, Elizabeth was already fighting off an avid suitor. To explain how painful this process had become she drew an analogy to Sophocles who "being asked what harm he would wish his *enemy,* answered that he might *love* where he was not liked." She, on other hand, believed no greater ill could befall a sensitive individual than to be loved and unable—or unable *yet*—to reciprocate.[57]

The suitor Elizabeth alluded to was Minister Stephen Peabody, a Harvard graduate, nine years her senior, who a quarter of a century earlier had lived and studied divinity at the Smith parsonage. To help pay for his board, Peabody had transported Mary, Abigail, and Elizabeth on outings. Nineteen-year-old Elizabeth is one of the few people he alludes to in his cryptic diary entries from that period, noting: "I rode to Nataskel, over the Beech, with Miss Betsy . . . A very pleasant ride for 4 or 5 miles over the Beech."[58] In another, "Miss Betsy came home with her Father. Been gone more than six weeks."[59]

Peabody had a formidable presence: over six feet tall, he had dark brown eyes, swarthy skin, large bones, a formidable girth, and a mass of curly hair. He was gregarious and polite unless insulted, at which point, according to a student, "an awful shadow would gather on his visage, his eye would roll fiery glances in every direction, and the dauntless volly of rebukes would pour from his lips."[60] Because his family was poor, Peabody reached 22 before he could afford to go to Harvard. Maturity did not, however, stop him from loving a lark or becoming a ringleader in student protests—such as a mass undertaking to improve the quality of the butter served at meals![61] (He won his point.). He could play almost any instrument, had a booming voice, and loved to sing. His physical strength was epic, he was a gifted wrestler and a born wood chopper and planter. Yet, hugeness notwithstanding, he had a well-proportioned face and gentleman's mien.

Peabody became the first minister of the First Church of Atkinson, New Hampshire, on the border of Haverhill. In 1773, he married a deacon's daughter, Polly Haseltine, and with her dowry money built a commodious house where he was known to keep the door unlatched and a fire burning all night in the sitting room so anyone passing through town could warm themselves there. Peabody loved his wife, who lacked his robust health and was frequently sick with coughing fits. He doted on his only daughter; in 1791, she demanded to attend the boarding school for boys that he had founded four years earlier, and to please her he began admitting girls.

It became a habit over the years for Peabody and the other neighboring ministers to gather on Thursday nights at Parson Shaw's in Haverhill. Later, they would stroll to the parish, where the men took turns preaching to their peers. Friendships grew up over these regular meetings, and the Shaws and Peabodies began socializing. The two men were a study in contrast—the first timid about collecting debts,

Stephen Peabody was over six feet tall, and polite unless insulted.

cerebral, and widely disliked by his parishioners, the latter a formidable accountant, so emotional he was given to weeping in public, and beloved by all. In his diary, Peabody praised Shaw's more intellectual sermons and described his wife as "amiable." Secretly, he considered Elizabeth Shaw the female ideal.

When Polly Peabody died on September 19, 1794, after a long ill-

ness, Peabody mourned—even bemoaning in his otherwise strictly fac-
tual diary, "The sensations I had were inexpressibly keen and severe!
Here I was called to part with a most dear and valuable Partner never
more to meet her in life!"—but he lost no time seeking Elizabeth's
help. According to local legend, within a week after his wife's death
Peabody was consulting Parson Shaw's wife about whom he should
marry.

"What sort of woman do you want?" Elizabeth purportedly inquired.

"One just like yourself," he replied.

Only ten days after Polly's death, Shaw was dead also, and Stephen
Peabody began his courtship.

It soon became clear that he was not Elizabeth's only suitor. Her
older cousin Isaac Smith, with whom she had argued so passionately
about love and literature as an unmarried woman, began paying calls
on her as well. Everything about Isaac had fascinated the young Elizabeth, and his strong intellect remained a welcome challenge to her
own. He now lived fifteen miles away, where he was preceptor of the
prestigious Byfield Academy. The son of a merchant, he came from a
better and wealthier family than Peabody. Elizabeth's trusted housekeeper, Lydia Springer, made it clear she preferred him to the boisterous Atkinson minister and gave him tips on winning his cousin's hand.
Isaac, however, had not changed much since the days when he refused
either to accept or condemn the American Revolution. He was in no
hurry to propose anything so rash as marriage without weighing all
sides.

The fatal decision came on a stormy night, Lydia Springer reported
to local journalists. At around the same time, both suitors set out for the
parsonage to propose to Elizabeth, but Peabody, living nine miles
closer, arrived first. When Isaac at last lumbered up to the door, Lydia
chastised him, "You are altogether too late, sir; Parson Peabody has
long ago dried his coat by the kitchen fire, and has been sitting with
Mrs. Shaw a whole hour in the parlor."[62] Lydia's opinion notwithstanding, it was surely more than luck that determined the recipient of Elizabeth's hand in marriage. Time had taught her the limits of erudite
company, and, more even than financial comfort, she longed for a de-
monstrative and considerate spouse.

She had not, however, neglected her children's financial interests in agreeing to marry and move to Atkinson. Stephen Peabody had agreed to support her *and* preserve separate estates, a rare agreement in the eighteenth century, so that the small property she had inherited from her father would pay interest exclusively to herself and then to William, Betsy Q, and Abby after her death.[63] Yet, "I would be paying [my future husband] but an ill compliment" by stressing the "pecuniary" aspects of the engagement, she assured Abigail and Mary. She had grown to love the man himself.

It was now the end of September 1795, almost exactly a year since her first husband's funeral. Rumors about John Shaw's alcoholism and anger had reached her sisters in Quincy, and she now had no choice but to address their fears.

"Many, very many were the virtues of my Friend," Elizabeth began her long incantatory explanation of the unraveling of her marriage. "How often have I said that if my head were waters and my eyes a fountain of Tears, I would weep day and night, if it could wash out [my husband's] sin and free him from the *worst of slavery* and make him stand fast, in that *Liberty* in which Christ had made us free." John Shaw's "slavery," like their brother's, was to liquor, though she never says so explicitly. Nor does she speak of his striking her in a drunken outburst or bludgeoning her with words. She makes clear, though, that his addiction poisoned her existence and tarnished the ministry. Elizabeth at last confessed to Mary and Abigail that her husband's death—"what I should consider under happy circumstances as my greatest affliction"—was in fact "the greatest Blessing that could befall me." She had grieved, yes, but only for her own impoverishment. "How often have I said that if I had any hopes of a happy hereafter for my friend, I should infinitely prefer . . . to see him stretched a pale corpse before me than to endure the anguish—the torture that I daily experienced—yet many, very many were the virtues of my Friend."

Words, she said, were inadequate to her feelings, though she employs words here with the fervor of an Old Testament prophet. She perceived "the footsteps of divine love and pity," in Shaw's removal from her life. For the children too, his death was a blessing since "alas," they were "too old not to perceive there was some thing very wrong."[64]

She goes on to wonder how her sisters heard about Shaw's offenses.

Maybe from Billy Cranch, who must have noticed "the tremor of my
Nerves, the anguish of my heart," though he was "too generous to
claim any merit, and too delicate ever to give the most distant hint" of
interceding with Shaw on her behalf.

Indeed, for all her suffering, Elizabeth still felt lucky, she insisted.
"Such good sisters—such Nephews, Neices as I am blessed with sel-
dom fall to the lot of any one." And she finished in a rapture worthy of
Charles Grandison:

> To be esteemed, and loved is and has been the solace of my
> Life, the soft soother of my woe, the chief ingredient that has
> sweetened my Cup of Life—In the mutual interchange of kind
> offices, in the exercise of benevolent affections I wish to spend
> my time here, till I am admitted to purer regions, and then with
> more extensive views, and enlarged powers I hope to spend an
> Eternity with those blessed Spirits who fly to do the will of their
> great Original.

Elizabeth did not invite her sisters to her December wedding, which
proved all for the good, she assured them afterward, since: "Everything
took a contrary turn, all my plans were deranged and . . . had I lived in
ancient days I should have stood agast and believed all the Gods and
Goddesses had conspired against me, and had engaged the elements
upon their side—raging with more violence than that which dispersed
the Grecian Fleet."

It was a season of illness throughout the parish. Some were "dead,
others dying." The morning dawned with a howling snowstorm. Any
reasonable man, Elizabeth presumed, would postpone the wedding
and stay home, so she could scarcely believe her eyes when Peabody
drove in from Atkinson, punctual as usual. Surely he was "too wise," or
at least too superstitious, to be *married* in a tempest, Elizabeth confronted her betrothed when he arrived covered from head to foot in
snow.

"What if it does storm, is it not often a prelude to a calm sunshine?"
Peabody calmly answered.

"I was silent," Elizabeth continued, "though at that moment I
thought I would have given the world not to have been the chief actor

in this gloomy solemn scene." Only duty propelled her through gusts of wind to the parish, where the townspeople shivered. No sooner did she open her mouth to say "I do" than someone shouted, "Fire." Wouldn't you know, the house in flames was hers!

And even when the fire was quickly doused, with nobody injured, and the ceremony duly gone through, she was still miserable to be leaving her neighbors and the parsonage where she had become as famous as Abigail in her more constricted sphere. And what a strain to leave home in her late forties. Elizabeth felt herself "one of the most pitiful objects in nature, and very unfit for the duties" that loomed.

Peabody felt otherwise. As Elizabeth reported to her sisters, he was as happy as any man just married to the love of his life. This "kindest of Friends" "supported and encouraged" his new wife with every slushy step of the horses' hooves toward Atkinson. There Elizabeth dreaded a confrontation with Peabody's adolescent daughter, Polly, who had lost her mother barely a year before. But the girl "met me at the door with so much sweetness, benevolence, and affectionate respect, as has left an indellable impression upon my heart that has bound me to her forever."

When a month had passed, Elizabeth declared herself cheerfully settled. Chief among her pleasures was this epic new husband, who was transforming her vision of married love. She began a concluding sentence to her sisters, "My Friend looks supremely blest, in the power of making"—then blotted out the next word and replaced it with "others happy."[65] If we speculate that the blotted word was "love," then this tale of woes has a comic romantic end. "To make love" only became a euphemism for sex in the twentieth century. In the sisters' time, it meant to pay amorous attention, court, or flirt. How satisfying to imagine large, clamorous Peabody flirting with petite, genteel Elizabeth, perhaps among a few freezing travelers gathering for comfort at their hearth. Even without the word "love," this final sentence sounds the triumph of the human spirit. A beautiful middle-aged widow has survived a drunken first husband, the torments of poverty, assaults by winter weather, and a house on fire to start life anew with an adoring spouse.[66]

CHAPTER XV

"Second to no man but Washington"

. . .

GEORGE WASHINGTON'S SECOND TERM IN OFFICE WAS PLAGUED by a series of small crises. No sooner had the furor over Citizen Genet subsided than some 6,000 men staged a riot in Pittsburgh. The object of their rebellion was the first internal tax leveled by the federal government—an excise tax on whiskey, imposed to help fund Hamilton's bill assuming state debts. The chief sufferers were western grain farmers, and while their precedent was Shays's Rebellion, they also honored the French example by shouting anti-monarchial slogans and carting guillotines. Washington himself led 13,000 troops to quash what became known as the Whiskey Rebellion, and while the President's easy victory restored peace and enforced the tax, it also widened the chasm between those who favored order and those who endorsed unfettered revolt.

Discord between Federalists and Republicans was further inflamed when Great Britain took advantage of America's military weakness and began attacking her trading ships. Washington dispatched Adams's friend John Jay to England, where he signed a treaty successfully averting war. But Jay's Treaty was economically disadvantageous to America, particularly to the southern plantation owners. Washington defended Jay's concessions as inevitable, considering America's vastly inferior military power. Madison, though, opposed any capitulation to Great Britain. And while Jay's Treaty was ultimately ratified by both houses of Congress, Republican anger at the Federalists and Republican identification with France also grew—particularly when Robespierre followed the King to the guillotine and the Terror came to a close.

During these traumas, Adams sat quietly at the head of the Senate. He remained as opinionated as ever, but saved his views for his politically avid children and spouse.[1] He was neither so pro-British nor so anti-French as the public suspected, he told Abigail. Like Washington, he supported Jay's Treaty because of America's military weakness, but he remembered his own thankless mission to England and begrudged this "stepmother" any victory on personal as well as patriotic grounds. And while the extremism of the French Revolution appalled him, Adams could not forget Yorktown or categorically dismiss the dream of an ideal government Rousseau had inspired. John regarded France as he regarded Jefferson. He was more of a friend to both than others supposed, he told his wife.[2]

Abigail unequivocally denounced the anti-Federalists (she could not bring herself to call them Republicans), but once Robespierre was replaced by the more benign five-man Directory, she reconsidered her position on the French themselves. "I ruminate upon them as I lye awake many hours before light," she wrote John. "My present thought is, that their victorious Army will give them a Government in Time, in spite of all their conventions, but of what nature it will be, it is hard to say."[3]

IN THE MID-1790s, Abigail and Mary both watched their children dispersing.

In the spring of 1794, John Quincy was slowly expanding his Boston law practice. Though he enjoyed arguing his Federalist views in anonymous news columns, he expressed no appetite for politics as a career. But his parents had their own expectations, as John, in an April 1794 letter to John Quincy, bluntly reminded him: "You come into Life with Advantages which will disgrace you, if your success is mediocre—And if you do not rise to the head not only of your Profession but of your Country it will be owing to your own Laziness, Slovenliness, and Obstinacy."⁴ Abigail had long ago prophesized that "only some dire misfortune or calamity" could bar John Quincy from greatness. So, later in the spring, when George Washington appointed their 27-year-old prodigy minister to Holland, both parents were thrilled but not surprised. John Quincy, on the other hand, felt ambivalent about statesmanship. He knew its toll. But he also knew displeasing John and Abigail required more courage than he possessed at the moment. In early fall, he left Boston and the law practice he had established through his own merits and sailed back to Europe to the thrill and thrall of diplomacy—drawing his brother Tom along as secretary.

Recently, Nabby had returned from England, where Colonel Smith's land speculations thrived beyond anyone's expectations. The Smiths now possessed what a public servant could never hope to acquire: wealth. No Puritan scruples kept the colonel from displaying his affluence, and while the Adamses admired his triumph, they chided his taste. "He boasts too much," Adams complained to Abigail; and he predicted that Nabby would not have the colonel's permission to travel by mere stagecoach with him to Quincy: "Her Adventurer of a Husband is so proud of his wealth that he would not let her go I suppose without a coach and four."⁵

Abigail's concern was all for her modest, introspective daughter, who at 30 was no more eager to join crowded drawing rooms than she had been inclined to linger at Harvard commencement parties thirteen years before. Though Colonel Smith too had professed commitment to "retirement" and "the peaceful walks of life" during their courtship, he was now using his new money to ingratiate the beau monde.

Loyalty to one's husband had limits, Abigail, surprisingly, announced in a 1794 letter to Nabby. She had been reading European authors like Mary Wollstonecraft and Madame Roland, controversial women who defied social conventions, yet were powerful enough to get their books published in Philadelphia and New York.⁶ Like her sister Elizabeth, Abigail was especially drawn to Wollstonecraft's *Vindication,* with its validation of the female intellect and scorn for simpering wives. Emboldened, Abigail now began preaching what she long had practiced: that women should think for themselves. After all, she had remained in Quincy for her own physical and emotional wellbeing rather than following John to Philadelphia for *his.* "You may sometimes join in . . . society," Abigail counseled Nabby; but the main point was to honor her "grave and thoughtful" nature and the enlightened education that had pointed her toward intellectual pleasures, the only reliable joys on earth.[7]

Soon after she returned from Europe, Nabby became pregnant and on January 28, 1795, overjoyed the whole family by producing a long-yearned-for girl, the first in her generation. Nabby's procreative mission was fulfilled, at least in Abigail's opinion. The infant had fair skin, blue eyes, and fiery red hair, unlike anyone else in the family, and the Smiths named her Caroline Amelia.

Nabby's brother Charles was spending as much time as he dared with the Smith family. Though his parents gave lip service to his reformation, in letters to each other they continued to refer to him as "Silly Charles," and John confided in Abigail that he wrote to Charles more often than to either John Quincy or Thomas "to see if I can fix his Attention and excite his Ambition."

Two years before, Charles had fallen in love with Colonel Smith's sister, Sally. As with John Quincy, John and Abigail insisted that Charles establish himself in business before marrying. Charles agreed to end the courtship, and officially did.

But that March, when John Adams wrote Charles asking whether he had severed his "attachment" to the Smith family, Charles replied that he had resisted visiting the Smiths in Jamaica, "but were I to declare that I did not entertain the same opinion of Sally Smith that I ever did, I should declare a falsehood." Six months later, at twenty-five, and with his career still in infancy, Charles ignored his parents' warnings and married 26-year-old Sally Smith. Nabby applauded this defiance, rejoicing in a letter to John Quincy in Holland: "After all the Hair Breadth scrapes and imminent danger [Charles] has run, he is at last safe Landed and I believe is very happy." Abigail and John, charmed by Sally's good sense and beauty, soon agreed.[8]

Though she was not invited to Charles's wedding, Abigail attended two others in the same year. William Cranch—after four years of repining—at last had the money to wed Nancy Greenleaf, and his sister Lucy married Nancy's brother (and William's close friend) John. The synchrony was fitting because Lucy and William were now as inseparable as Abigail and Mary. "We shall be doubley united in the bonds of fraternity," William had rejoiced when Lucy confided she was in love with John. "There is scarcely another Event among the uncertainties of futurity which can bring such real Satisfaction to my heart."[9]

Mary and Abigail, however, were skeptical about both spouses, doubting Nancy Greenleaf's strength of character and dreading Lucy's dependence on her husband's family, since John Greenleaf was blind and could not work. Lucy's own concern was for Mary and Richard. Homely and 28, the scientifically gifted Lucy knew her parents had never expected her to marry and, because Richard Cranch was ill with increasing frequency, she worried that her mother could not nurse her father without her help. "Ought I to think of forming a connection . . . that shall take me away from my parents?" she had asked her brother.[10] William had answered with a resounding yes, and then built a long, lawyerly case to persuade his dubious mother that John's only flaw was his blindness and in any case marrying a blind man was better than never marrying at all![11]

ON JANUARY 7, 1796, John wrote Abigail that he was convinced George Washington would retire at the next election. Thanks to Hamilton's economic strategies, the country was financially sound. The federal government's assumption of state debts had vastly lowered state taxes, and the ensuing enrichment of the populace (western grain farmers excluded) had diminished the urge to revolt. Championing of France died down as quickly as it had risen.[12] But the urge to factionalize did not. Both the 64-year-old President and his wife were exhausted, worn down by political quarrels and demoralized by the persistent attacks of the Republican press. Unlike Jefferson, Washington truly longed for rural tranquillity. "The President looks to me worried and growing older," John reported in February. The 1796 elections were fast approaching. If the highest position in the land was up for election, John began wondering out loud if he should run. "I am weary of the game, yet I dont know how I could live out of it," he frankly told Abigail.

Abigail was less candid in her reaction, speaking eloquently of the joys of rural living, while implying that John should aim for the prize. "There is not a beam of light nor a shadow of comfort or pleasure in the contemplation of [your becoming President], if personal considerations alone were to weigh," she contradicted her recent acknowledgment that she was increasingly attached to "Fame" and "Reputation." And while she did not overtly stoke his ambition, no more did Abigail counsel her husband to quit public life. "I dare not influence you," she demurred with unconvincing reticence.

What she did believe was that John should never agree to serve as Vice-President under Jefferson, his rumored opponent. "Resign. Retire. I would be second to no man but Washington," she proclaimed.

In the last week of March, John was invited to dine with the President and his ministers. After dessert, Washington "detained" him while the others went off. Never in their relationship had Washington been so "frank and open about Politicks," John reported to Abigail. "I find his opinions and sentiments are more . . . like mine than I ever knew before, respecting England and France and our American Parties. He gave me Intimations enough that his Reign would be very short. He repeated it three times at least."[13] John dared not speculate on what this unusual confidence from Washington portended. "The Heart is deceitful and I do believe as well as suspect that I know not mine."[14]

On September 19, 1796, George Washington published his Farewell Address to a nation that had come into the world under his leadership. The prospect of continuing under *anyone* else, he knew, would unsettle the electorate, and he did his best to smooth the transition by stressing that America depended not on men but on laws. He also took the occasion to warn against parties and to remind the mercantile north and the agrarian south of their complementarity. Geographical divisions were again becoming a threat to the union, he lectured both sides—just what Abigail had predicted to Mary, years before. Nor could the danger of foreign alliances be overestimated. "The nation which indulges toward another a habitual hatred or a habitual fondness is in some degree a slave," Washington declared and urged his fellow countrymen to deal with the rest of the world only through peaceful commerce. He did not suggest a successor, though he made clear that he hoped his legacy of evenhandedness and dispassion would endure.

By now, the campaign to be second President of the United States was in full motion—which is to say that both Adams in Quincy and

Jefferson at Monticello—the two favored candidates—were studiously avoiding any appearance of wanting the job. There was a third candidate as well, Thomas Pickney, former Governor of South Carolina, who was now in the middle of the Atlantic, having successfully negotiated a treaty with Spain. Though less known than the other two, Pinkney had the advantage of being, like Washington, a southern Federalist. He was also openly pro-British. Alexander Hamilton favored him and once again used his influence behind the scenes to thwart Adams, who this time at least was well aware of his intrigues.[15] The only other candidate mentioned was the Republican Aaron Burr.

The race was close up to the last minute. As in the past, each state determined its own election date. More than before, sympathies were split along geographical lines. And the results leaked out much sooner than in 1788 or 1792. So when the polls were tallied in a southern state, Adams (with his normal tendency to overreact) was sure Jefferson had won the entire election, prompting Abigail to wail, "O! Save my Country Heaven if we are to receive a President from the French Nation."[16] Another day a northern state decisively voted in his favor, and the Adamses' hopes rose.

By the beginning of December, Adams was freely acknowledging his dread of losing to his old colleague, writing Abigail on December 7, for instance:

> I laugh at myself twenty times a Day for my feelings, and meditations and Speculations in which I find myself engaged. Vanity suffers. Cold feelings of Unpoplarity. Humble reflections. Mortifications. Humiliation. Plans of Future Life. Economy. Retrenching of Expenses. Farming. Return to the Bar. Drawing Writs, arguing causes, taking Clerks. Humiliations of my Country under foreign Bribes, Measures to counteract them. All this miserable Nonsense will come and go like evil into the Thoughts of Gods or Men, approved or unapproved.[17]

Though the official report would not come until February, when the electors' votes were read out loud (by Adams himself, as the current president of the Senate!) in Congress, the voting was finished by mid-December. Adams—by a small margin—had won.[18] Jefferson, with the second highest tally, automatically would be his Vice-President. John had spent the last eight years by turns scared and ambitious to assume the executive position. He now felt ready for both the honor and the obligations of being on the same footing as the French Directory and George III. "I have been Daddy Vice long enough," he wrote Abigail on December 20.[19] He was strong and healthy and felt "no Consternation at the Prospect" of moving up.

Abigail clearly protested too much when she wrote their old friend Elbridge Gerry on New Year's Day: "At my Time of Life, the desire or wish to shine in publick Life is wholly extinguished."[20] What rings more true is the mixture of anxiety and defiant optimism suggested by a dream she described to John. In it, she was driving along in her coach when suddenly a flock of huge black cannonballs materialized in the air above. All were poised to crush her. Yet they "burst and fell before they reach'd me," she marveled, "crumbled all to Attoms" and left her unharmed. Two guns discharged at her left ear but they too could not arrest her progress. She "proceeded undaunted upon my course"—as, she made clear, she fully intended to do as the President's wife.[21]

CHAPTER XVI

"Yours are mine and mine are yours"

. . .

"WE HAD A FORTNIGHT SINCE SUCH A STORM OF HAIL AS YOU NEVER beheld," Mary wrote Abigail from her farmhouse in Quincy in the summer of 1797.

The storm in Quincy "lasted about an hour," Mary continued in her usual elder sister's tone to the new First Lady; it "was attended with Thunder, lightening and a torrent of Rain with a violent wind. The hailstones were gigantic, three and four inches round." They lashed feathers off the chickens "Thresh'd the Barley, broke the corn, pick'd the vines and laye the cabbages . . . all to pieces." They also broke every window on the west side of the Cranch farmhouse and were so slow to melt that a week later myriad solid balls of ice still lurked in a hollow on the grounds. Mary did not sit idly by and mourn the natural fiasco. She scooped up hailstones by the "pailsful" and carted them home to make punch.[1]

Turning hail to punch was Mary's latest riposte to the grim Calvinist view of predestination. At 56, she was as loath as ever to perceive anything short of death as immune to her resourcefulness and quick wit. Which did not mean she escaped suffering. Like her sister forced to endure floods of visitors in "vile and debauched" Philadelphia, Mary was highly attuned to vexations in her town and home.[2]

No longer was there any fear of hierarchy between them, the sisters attested. Their "troubles were known and felt in common . . . yours are mine and mine are yours," they agreed.[3] And, with age, they endured the same inevitable change in perspective: "As we descend the Hill of Life, our gay and vissonary prospect vanish," Abigail spoke for both of them; "as the Shadows lengthen, we see through a different medium."[4] What is more, their joys and sorrows both increasingly were complicated by an expanding web of kinship.

On Mary's side: the previous January, rampant speculation had driven her son William's land firm in the soon-to-be Washington D.C. out of business, sending its partners, including William's brother-in-law James Greenleaf, to debtor's prison and reducing William's income from \$1,800 a year to not a cent. Worse, three years before it was set to become the nation's capital, the city on which he'd staked his livelihood remained little more than a swamp. His best bet was to resume practicing law, but jobs were scarce in this woebegone community, and his law books had gone up in flames on the ship transporting them from home.

Following the family tradition, William's solace came from the happiness of his marriage to Nancy Greenleaf. "Whatever disagreeable occurrences I meet with abroad, I am sure to find peace, tranquility, and happiness at home," he had told his mother. Only now Nancy was sick and his own famed equanimity shattered.[5] For the first time in his life, William, whose "fund of happiness" had been the envy of his cousin John Quincy just a few years earlier, succumbed to the depression that had hobbled his sister Betsy Norton all her life.

Betsy Norton, meanwhile, continued frail and fertile, producing a torrent of male children year after year. Illness often forced her to leave her beloved boys for long stays with Mary, who was inevitably nursing her husband, Richard, from some new lung complaint at the same time. And while Mary and Richard's youngest daughter, Lucy Greenleaf, was spry and healthy, she and her blind husband lost their only source of income when James Greenleaf's land business collapsed. What's more, Lucy was pregnant! A blind husband was sufficient liability. "I did hope [she] would not have . . . children," Mary moaned.

And then there was the grand matter of finding a new minister for the Congregationalist First Church of Quincy, a quest of infinite importance to Mary and Abigail both. Guidance of the soul was more crucial even than government of a nation, since one's most vital mission in life was preparation for the next world. Religion, the great subject of their youth—the one arena deemed as crucial for girls as for boys to excel in—grew more pressing as death increasingly preoccupied all three sisters. They comforted one another for their trials on earth by pointing to the future. "If it was not for the sure and certain hope of a superior state of existance beyond this transitory scene of Noise, Bustle, pain and anxiety—we should be of all Beings the most misirable," Abigail comforted Mary in one crisis.[6]

For Congregationalists, religion was not just faith, but an ongoing subject of inquiry. Church attendance was mandatory for salvation, so ministers had an outsize effect on the community's attitude toward everything from child-raising to the nature of God. Talk of Dr. Price and Parson Wibird had filled large portions of the sisters' letters when Abigail was in Europe. Now Dr. Price was dead, and Wibird was aged, filthy, and most of the time incapable of stumbling next door to church, much less delivering even his most thread-bare sermon.

According to Quincy custom, an aged minister, whether or not he worked, would continue to room free of charge and draw about a tenth of his former pay from his successor's salary.[7] The issue for the town was finding that successor. Over the past year, the First Church had been trying out ministers. Now the congregants were tired of substitutes and wanted to hire a permanent preacher as fast as they could.

Being an old and honorable community, Quincy presumed it would easily attract one of the best young Harvard-trained ministers. In 1797, it boasted 120 households and was the home of the President of the United States. Everyone farmed, but there was also a cod fishery and a respectable industry in shoe- and boot-making during the winter months. Profits came from exports to the American south and the West Indies. There were a handful of prosperous landowners, notably the Adamses' two neighbors, Mr. Black and Mr. Beal, whose approval was obligatory to any decision. The main road to Cape Cod passed through Quincy; Boston was just ten miles away by land or sea.

Quincy chose Richard Cranch to lead the search for its new minister. Despite ill health and failure in business, he was the most revered man in town. Entirely self-taught, he knew Greek, Latin, and Hebrew,

had steeped himself in literature and philosophy, held an honorary degree from Harvard, and (according to John Adams) knew more about
Judaism as well as Christianity than any other clergyman in the northeast. He practiced a rationalist monotheism and denied the divinity of
Christ before the word "Unitarian" existed in America. He was or had
been a judge, state assemblyman, and first postmaster of Quincy. More
important than all these accomplishments, his wife was the world's
master expeditor Mary Cranch.

Though as a woman, Mary, of course, could hold no public position,
from the start it was understood that she and Richard would work as a
team: he handling communication between the town and potential
ministers, she interpreting the community's sentiment behind the
scenes. Like Harvard commencement a decade earlier, the First Church
election furnished Mary and Abigail with a feast for conversation. As
when she was buying pigs' legs and serving punch to their sons' tutors,
Mary assumed responsibility for reporting each new development to
her impatient sister.

One Sunday, for instance, a promising candidate named Dr. Lark
took the pulpit in Quincy. In the middle of his sermon, his eyes closed,
and he seemed asleep. In fact, Mary recounted to Abigail, the man had
been struck by epilepsy and dropped dead without regaining speech!

Historically, the Braintree/Quincy Church was liberal. A century
before, Anne Hutchinson had conducted radical Bible reading sessions
from her Braintree farm, and even during the Great Awakening, the
town elected lighthearted Reverend Lemuel Briant and defended his
bold attacks on evangelism to the fire and brimstone preachers from
neighboring towns.[8] Parson Wibird was less bold but equally opposed
to mysticism and predestination. He concurred with Abigail that, in
her words, "True religion is from the Heart between man and his creator, and not the imposition of man or creeds and tests."[9]

The town's current two candidates were similarly anti-dogma. Both
were highly qualified Harvard graduates. Peter Whitney had more
eloquence and a subtler intellect, Jacob Flint a stronger popular appeal.[10] Like America itself, Quincy was now larger and more factional-
ized than when Wibird won his post by unanimous vote a generation
earlier. So while the Adamses and Cranches preferred Whitney, what
they wanted most was to unify the divided town.

Hoping to avoid a long battle, Richard set elections for fast-approaching May 1. Mary scurried to visit neighbors and cajoled friends to hold a round of tea parties to turn out the vote.

"You will be surprised I believe when I tell you Mr. Whitney had a large majority," Mary rejoiced in a letter to Abigail three days after elections. Predictably, the first ballot split down the middle. But on the second, Peter Whitney handily beat Jacob Flint, 60 to 8. Crucially, both Mr. Black and Mr. Beal supported the decision. Avoiding for now the delicate question of money, Richard sent Whitney a formal request to "settle," which meant sign an agreement to serve as minister to Quincy for life. "The harmony is so unexpected I hope we shall have him," Mary confided to Abigail. She felt sure at least of a quick response.[11]

Instead, Whitney announced he was leaving to visit his father in Northborough.[12] From there, he wrote "a very unpolite and ungentlemanly" rejection, which was then read aloud to the town. "It was a fixed principal with [Whitney] never to settle where there was much division. In short he must be" everyone's choice![13] Mary scoffed to the First Lady in Philadelphia. Adding insult to injury, Whitney went on to claim Quincy could not afford wages commensurate with his gifts. How would he know (since money had not been mentioned in the offer)? Mary warned Abigail that she would not like Whitney's explanation: which was that Mrs. Adams had told him so the summer before.

"The man must have lost his senses," Abigail exclaimed to Mary from the writing closet that was normally her refuge from cares in Philadelphia. She could not deny making the statement:

> because it has always been my opinion that the people would not be willing to support two ministers, but little did I think of having my Name quoted on any occasion in Town meeting. If he had respected my publick Character only, he would have had some scruples upon that Head . . . I am mortified to find [a] Gentleman of whom I had formed so favourable an opinion guilty of such a want of decorum. It will however serve as a lesson to me to be very close mouthed.[14]

The frown of the British Queen paled beside this humiliation in Quincy. And Abigail was not the lone victim of the town's outrage.

Richard was also attacked—for telling Whitney more than he needed to know about his struggles to get the vote out—while the candidate himself was denounced even by friends as a "clerical coquette."¹⁵ As a cold June set in, one group of congregants continued to pine for Whitney; the other swore they would never set foot in a church where he preached. Quincy was split down the middle, Mary balefully reported to her sister, and Richard had acquired the sinister habit of groaning in his sleep.

UNITY WAS PROVING EQUALLY elusive for the new President in Philadelphia. On May 16, 1797, President John Adams called for a special session of Congress, the first ever convened in the United States. His subject was the impending war between France and England. The French government was now ruled by a five-man Directory, which had discarded much of the Revolution's initial idealism but spurred its determination to "liberate" all *anciens regimes.* In other words, to conquer Europe. When Washington and then Adams refused to side with the Directory against England, France began threatening the New World too.

Still, in their hearts, the Directory (like Genet) could not believe the American *people* were neutral. The real villain, they felt sure, was America's Federalist regime. James Monroe, appointed minister to Paris three years before, had encouraged this delusion; so Washington recalled Monroe and, just before leaving office, sent Federalist Charles Pinckney to fill his place.

Now the Directory had humiliated Washington and Adams both by refusing to receive the new minister. It furthermore threatened to seize all American vessels that transported British freight. Though outraged, John was determined not to act out of passion and reinforced his commitment to peace in this special joint session in the middle of May. Avenging Pinckney was useless, he reasoned. America should instead renew attempts to negotiate with the Directory, while bolstering troops and creating a navy, so aggressive measures could be taken if these peaceful gestures failed.

John Adams—piercer of grand illusions—was at the height of his own idealism. He had begun his term in March, confident he could fulfill a lifetime's dreams. Washington had brought independence. Now, under his own aegis, America would solidify its identity. To do so, the country needed to avoid war not only with foreigners but within

This 1789 engraving by Amos Doolittle shows President John Adams
surrounded by the arms of the sixteen states. Below the eagle, a banner
reading "Millions For Our Defence Not A Cent For Tribute"
honors American defiance in the XYZ Affair.

itself. For all his skepticism about man, Adams continued to believe that law could move mountains. His family was thoroughly behind him. "It is union which gives power, strength and energy to every kind of Government," Elizabeth Peabody articulated John's strong opposition to factions.[16] By agreeing to serve as Vice-President under Adams, Thomas Jefferson seemed committed to working—as in France—as a team.

So John was shocked at the wild partisanship that greeted his temperate appeal to Congress. The "High" Federalists (mostly northerners tied financially to England) demanded war with France to retrieve American honor; the Republicans (mostly agrarian southerners still smarting from the urban bias of Jay's Treaty) underplayed the Directory's refusal to meet Pinckney as a misunderstanding and denounced monarchial England as the enemy of all free men.

This rigid split was a hard blow to John just two months into his administration. And while a torrent of hate from Benjamin Bache's *Aurora* newspaper was to be expected, ambivalence in New England was not. What did Massachusetts and New Hampshire think of the President's address? Abigail asked her sisters. "Every body but fools and knaves are charmed," Mary replied, evasively. When further pressed, she acknowledged that their Quincy neighbors were curiously silent—they could or would not take either side.[17] Elizabeth more explicitly criticized John when reporting the reaction in Haverhill and Atkinson:

> If I could tell you without giving offence, I would mention a remark I have heard made upon [John's] composition . . . that *his* mind could contain a concatonation of Ideas much better than those inferior Persons who perused them, and that his sentiments were so excellent that [he should make them] obvious to every one.[18]

Abigail arrived in Philadelphia just in time to witness the dramatic reaction to John's special session. She had missed the inauguration and the first months of his term. True, one good cause after another delayed her, but John did not pretend to be sympathetic. He made clear she should let half of Quincy die if necessary and rush to him. "I think of you and dream of you and long to be with you," he had begun his campaign gently in January.[19]

In February, he took a darker tone and pled. If only she could address his financial woes!—which included costly, drunk servants; harassing pleas from charities; an outrageously expensive carriage; and a house with no wife or furniture that gobbled up nearly a fifth of the meager $25,000 salary Congress deigned to pay. "[Our] Prospects . . . appear . . . worse and worse," he groaned.[20]

"It would have given me great Pleasure to have some Family present," he grumbled after his March inauguration. "I was very unwell, had no sleep the night before, and really did not know but I should have fainted."[21] Besides, he was losing his eyesight, and private debt would force him to resign and leave the country stranded in six months' time at most.

"I sometimes suspect that I deserve a Character for Peevishness and fretfulness, rather than firmness," he acknowledged in one letter and in another assumed a pious tone: "I pray you to come."[22]

"I can do nothing without you,"[23] he protested a week later, and a week after that (only half self-mockingly) insisted that even his mother's illness should not detain his wife:

> My dear and venerable Mother—Alass—I feel for her . . . [But] it seems to me that the Mother and the Daughter [Abigail] ought to think of the President . . . His Cares! His Anxieties, His Health!—don't laugh—his comfort—that his head may be clear and his heart firm, ought to be thought on more.[24]

Just as fifteen years before, when the dilemma was whether to join John in Europe, Abigail temporized about leaving the healthful country for the fetid city, the farm for politics, Mary and Richard for her spouse.

Now a new factor contributed to her reluctance to leave New England. Over the past five years, she had grown increasingly close to her sister Elizabeth. They visited frequently and confided in each other more urgently than ever before. Increasingly secure of her importance in the family hierarchy, Elizabeth readily turned to Abigail with personal problems—such as an onslaught of mysterious sweating and sleeplessness in her forty-ninth year. "Your complaint my sister arises from your period of life," Abigail enlightened her and consoled, "I suffer from the same cause." She used "Elixer Vitorl the bark and whatever can invigorate your constitution"—and bemoaned that medical science had as yet to devise a cure.[25]

With neither as competitive as in their youth, Abigail praised and even strove to imitate the high literary tone of Elizabeth's letters. On February 10, for instance, Abigail raved in a reply to Elizabeth:

> What a charming Letter have I received from my ever Dear and valued Sister. Surely she openth her mouth with wisdom and upon her Tongue is the law of kindness. Not an avenue of the Heart, which her pen cannot trace, not a chord which her skill cannot strike. How soothing, how comforting, how encourageing are her words.[26] [27]

The letter Abigail refers to "rejoic[ed] with trembling" at John's election, the "trembling" arising from Elizabeth's fears that Abigail would catch the yellow fever that had recently swept through Philadelphia if she decided to join John.[28] Abigail's reply expressed her loving concern for all Elizabeth's children, but especially for the young comic who had enlivened the Adams and Cranch households on her frequent visits during the summer months. "How does that Laughter Loving Girl BQS [Betsy Quincy Shaw] do? I have mist her spirits this winter," Abigail wrote.

Abigail felt especially in need of cheer at this time because John's mother was seriously ill, as was her niece, Mary Smith, who lay weak, coughing up blood, and flushed with fever, in Mary Cranch's spare room. The cause of Mary Smith's lassitude and emaciation was consumption, or tuberculosis, which in the late eighteenth century accounted for one out of four deaths in Canada and the United States. Only a quarter of those who caught it ever recovered. Half would be dead within two years. No cure existed, which is why even when it meant forgoing remedies—bleeding, Peruvian bark, mercury—which, if applied early, were said to prolong life, many consumptive patients simply denied they were sick.[29] Certainly, it had been hard for Mary, Abigail, and Elizabeth to acknowledge that their dead brother's child was afflicted.

DAFFODILS AND FORSYTHIA BURST out during a brief heat wave in the middle of April. The next week, it snowed, quashing all the nascent blossoms and giving Abigail a fresh reason to delay her departure for Philadelphia. Every day John's mother's condition worsened. "The good old Lady is sure she shall dye now her Physician and Nurse [Abigail] is about to leave her," Abigail staved off one of John's pleas for her to hurry to him.

Then, on April 21, 89-year-old Susanna Boyston Adams Hall passed peacefully and without regrets. She had outlived most of her generation—through colonial rule and the Great Awakening, into the Revolutionary era and beyond. She had borne a family and survived to see her eldest son become the first American ambassador to England and now President of the nation he had helped conceive.

Mary Smith, in contrast, was on the brink of death before her twenty-second birthday. Abigail saw the two-fold character of humanity fester in her fragile form. "The distressing pangs of dissolution of an agonizing nature are separating the soul from the body of my dear niece," Abigail wrote John, two days after his mother's death.[30] The girl asked Abigail to remain in Quincy for as long as she lived. Abigail saw the will of God in her petition.

"I want no courting to come [to Philadelphia]. I am willing to follow my husband wherever he chooses; but the hand of Heaven has arrested me . . . It is not for me to say when I will leave here."[31]

Mary Smith died the last week in April. After Abigail buried her and John's mother, she in a state of grief and turmoil took off on wet, "rut[ted]" roads to join John. The first caterpillars were spinning their webs when she stopped on her way at Nabby's farm twenty miles outside New York in rural East Chester.[32]

No good news awaited here. The land speculations that made Colonel Smith rich had backfired, and the Smiths now lived as frugally as Betsy Norton and William Cranch. The theatres, operas, and political whirl that had brought out the best in both of them were ancient history. And while stoic about the loss of mansions and carriages ("she never enjoyed a life of dissipation," Abigail reminded Mary), Nabby was heartbroken by the change in her spouse. Gone was Colonel

Smith's domestic temperament. He now disappeared for months, chasing harebrained schemes, writing to her rarely, and leaving his wife without support or society to raise her sons and baby girl.

True, Nabby's father also had been a poor correspondent to her mother and had left Abigail to scrape together a livelihood not just for months but for years; the difference was that Abigail was never friendless. When Nabby was living in splendor in New York City, Mary Cranch had refused to sympathize with her complaints of "feeling alone in the world" and intimated that Nabby's pride alienated new acquaintances as it had rebuffed Mary's attempts at intimacy when she was growing up.

Now, though, Mary saw past her old hurt and pitied Nabby's painful shyness. When Abigail wrote Mary that Colonel Smith had "gone a journey, I [know] not where" and Nabby's "Heart [was] too full" to talk, Mary offered no veiled judgments, remarking simply, "My heart aches for my dear Mrs. Smith."[33]

As adolescents, Nabby Adams and Betsy Cranch had never tired of discussing the origin of happiness. Betsy was sure it came from within, from exertion and a blameless conscience, Nabby that it was determined by external events. Now Nabby refused to blame God or herself for her sorrows. Her fall in the world confirmed her childhood belief in fate. Abigail, though, could not help lamenting: "My reflections upon prospects [in East Chester] took from me all appetite to food, and despresst my spirits, before too low."[34]

What did raise Abigail's mood was reaching John, who drove to meet her twenty-five miles outside Philadelphia on May 10. "I quitted my own carriage and took my seat by his side," she wrote Mary, and went on to describe their day on the banks of the Delaware with the restraint of a happy lover struggling not to boast.

Her spirits continued to rise, as the hopelessness of lingering over deathbeds gave way to the pleasure of action. While the President (having won his point) frantically searched for the right two men to join Charles Pinckney in a second attempt to negotiate with the French Directory, Abigail threw herself into the First Lady's role.

Because her own study was dark, she rose an hour earlier than John and composed long letters to Mary and Elizabeth from his cheerful library. There three large windows faced south toward the fishing boats in the seaport, and she could catch the first sparks of dawn from a fourth exposure pointed east.[35] Her schedule was, as always, rigorous:

> From [5] until 8 I have a few leisure hours. At 8 I breakfast, after which until Eleven I attend to my Family arrangements. At that hour I dress for the day. From 12 until two I receive company, sometimes untill 3. We dine at that hour unless on company days which are tuesdays & Thursdays. After dinner I usually ride out untill seven.[36]

After all these years, entertaining Congressmen and housekeeping with a flutter of servants in a strange house she had to furnish on a budget no longer daunted Abigail. Besides, there were continuities. John Briesler, whom she had brought as a boy to Europe fifteen years earlier, was at her side to hire and fire all the male servants, while his wife, Esther, Abigail's head housekeeper in Paris and London, when not consumed by parenting still helped with chores.

Yet there was all the difference in the world between being wife of the Vice-President, whose role was ceremonial, and wife of the President, who was responsible for every executive choice. "The task of the President is very arduous, very perplexing and very hazardous," she confided in Mary, her initial rush of spirits abating. "I do not wonder Washington wishd to retire from it." Invectives against the Republican newspapers cropped up as usual in all her correspondence. When Adams picked two moderate Federalists—John Marshall from Virginia and Massachusetts' Elbridge Gerry (who was rabidly anti-British)—to join Charles Pinckney as delegates to the French Directory, Republican newspapers attacked with exaggerations and outright lies. Worse still, as Abigail was sure Mary could imagine, was their response when John broke his vow never to promote relatives and appointed their highly eligible son, John Quincy, minister to Berlin.[37] Abigail declared the *Chronicle* was worse even than the *Aurora,* because while they shared the "true spirit of Sat[an]," the Chronicle compounded this with "Lies, falshood, calimny and bitterness of [its] own."[38]

A realist in so many other respects, Abigail was never able to accept that eighteenth-century newspapers, supported and often financed by one party or the other, inevitably distorted truth for political advantage. No public figure escaped their ire, though John, with his easy anger and tendency to overreact, came in for more barbs than most. Certainly he had none of the impunity granted to Washington in his first year. And rather than growing inured to the journalistic blasphemies that had followed the Adamses since John's ambassadorship in London, Abigail experienced each careless allusion to her husband as "His Rotundity" as a fresh wound.

Congress drifted on into summer, still arguing about the wording of the dispatch the delegates would bring to the Directory and whether or not to approve John's proposal to arm ships against the marauding French. "I verily think our General Assembly [in Boston] get thro their Business with more dispatch than your Venerable Body," Mary quipped from Quincy when Abigail complained to her. Petitions for and against "The Dog Act" had preoccupied the Massachusetts session. The upshot? A $1 tax would be levied on all dog owners in the state. "The design is to extirpate the race. How happy for the country if Congress could as profitable get rid of [its] Mad Dogs," Mary joked.[39]

In the middle of June, Abigail had a new concern—that Philadelphia's notorious heat would spoil her Fourth of July celebration. What she considered a tedious ordeal in the best of circumstances entailed inviting 150 members of Congress, plus the governor and foreign ministers to imbibe huge quantities of cake, punch, and wine. This ritual was initiated by the Washingtons, Abigail sighed, and—in order to appear equally patriotic—she and John must carry it on. Independence Day was Mary's 1787 graduation party writ large and confined to hoards of strangers, Abigail explained. Long tables had to be laid both outdoors and in to accommodate the enormous list of guests. She could be no more burdened if she were Queen Charlotte at St. James. "You will not wonder that I dread it, or think President Washington to blame for introducing the custom," Abigail fretted on June 23.

"I got through the 4 July with much more ease than I expected," she wrote when it was over.[40] But her relief did not last long. The day of the party had been cool, but "The weather is Hot as we can bear," Abigail wrote Mary three weeks later as August approached. "The whole city is like a Bake House."[41] And she felt under siege not just by the climate. Anyday, the peace America had enjoyed for the past fifteen years could end. "We are critically situated . . . the next vessel arrives may bring us a Formal declaration of war," she wrote her Uncle Tufts, adding that the economy was already suffering from French aggression.[42] And to Mary: "From every side we are in Danger. We are in perils by Land, and we are in perils by sea, and in perils from false Breathern."[43] What contributed to Abigail's mounting fear was John's health—"Such close application for so long a period without any relaxation but a ride of a few miles, is too much for him & I see daily by a langour of his countanance that he wants rest."[44] More than ever, she needed her sister. "I want to hear from you again. You must write me once a week," she demanded. Would Congress ever finish or even forgo its business so she could drag the ailing President from the filthy city and for at least two months go home to rest?[45]

DRAMATIC WEATHER ALSO STRUCK Quincy during the summer of 1797. "Last Sunday evening we had a terrible Tempest," Mary wrote Abigail a few months after the torrential hailstorm. The wind was "violent," and "I never saw so much Lightening. Colomns of Fire" shot down a neighbor's chimney and crashed straight through to the cellar, electrifying everyone in the house as it plunged.[46] Some had to be rubbed with vinegar for hours before the shock wore off.

The search for an "assistant to Mr. Wibird" moved forward. By the end of June, Mary and Richard had reconciled themselves to losing Peter Whitney and were now hoping to appease their divided community with the lackluster but politic Mr. Flint. An acquaintance described Flint as "a large man with a forbidding countenance" and a tyrant to his family. There was also "something disagreeable to me in Mr. Flint's voice," Mary confessed to Abigail, but he mixed easily with the parishioners, and, while she still preferred Whitney, "we may not get a better man on the whole."[47] What was vital was filling the spiritual vacuum. Flint's was now the only name on the ballot, and the Cranches did everything in their power to boost his morale.

Mary made sure he was wined and dined by all the important members of the community, while Richard determined to avoid election-day surprises and conducted a preliminary vote by questionnaire. On June 26, Richard announced ninety-two responses in Flint's favor.[48]

Still, Mary sensed trouble—"I hope we may not get into strong parties," she worried in a letter to Abigail—with good reason, for even among families, discord ran rife. Whitney's strongest defenders protested his loss by refusing to support another minister. So though Mr. Flint easily won the plebiscite, in what the town minutes describe as a "sermon-length letter," he followed in Whitney's footsteps and rejected the job. Insufficient love and money once again were the cited cause.

IT WAS MID-SUMMER WHEN Mr. Flint rejected Quincy's offer. Around the same time, worse news came from Washington, where William Cranch's wife, the former Nancy Greenleaf, had no sooner given birth to a large baby boy than she collapsed from fear and humiliation over the ramifications of her brother James Greenleaf's enormous debts. The doubts Mary and Abigail harbored about Nancy's character before the wedding long ago had vanished. Indeed, Nancy was so crucial to William's happiness that Mary anguished almost as fervently for her daughter-in-law as for her son himself.

Nancy "has lost her appetite, flesh and her spirits and is very weak and has a great fat baby to nurse and tend," Mary worried to Abigail, who wrote back, sending sympathy and money. "Slip the inclosed into [Nancy's] Hand when you see her, and say nothing about it," Abigail insisted.[49][50] At the same time, she and the President were helping William find work.

"We are doomed to always be the oblig'd," Mary fretted in her reply to Abigail; though in the next breath she was rattling off the many feats she had accomplished at the Adams home. Mice had been chased from Abigail's oven and clover and vegetables brought to perfection in her field. "The Rose Bush under your window is . . . full of bloom and fragrance," Mary proudly reported, and she predicted that the strawberries would be sweet to her sister's tastebuds in August, if she and John could drag themselves from the crisis over France in Philadelphia to spend precious time at home.[51]

And so they were and so they could. Abigail was home long enough to consume pears as well as strawberries, to steal hours in her mice-free kitchen unburdening herself with her best female friend in the world, and to become a strong partisan in favor of the new young minister the ever-persisting Cranches had unearthed to audition for the opening at the First Church. This man was Kilburn Whitman, a scholar of law as well as divinity, with charm to spare and frankly anti-Calvinist views. Unlike Mr. Whitney and Mr. Flint, Mr. Whitman was married, and his wife was, in Mary's words, "a spritely sensible affable industrious little woman . . . Everyone will love her," she cooed.[52]

It was in the context of electing Mr. Whitman to serve Quincy that Abigail made her most remarkable statement about female rights since her "Remember the Ladies" letter twenty years before. After returning to Philadelphia, in November 1797 she instructed Mary, "Present my compliment[s] to Mr. Whitman, and tell him if our State constitution had been . . . liberal . . . and admitted the females to vote, I should certainly have exercised it in his behalf."[53]

Abigail's temerity reflects her familiarity with French and British radicals (notably Condorcet and Mary Wollstonecraft), but more important, it shows her enhanced confidence in the judgment of the women she knows. Was Mary, who read all the debates in Congress, less qualified to choose a candidate than Richard, or sister Elizabeth, an educator, than her new husband Stephen, or she than John? Certainly not. How much distance Abigail had traveled since, as a circumspect young woman two decades earlier, she described females as "Beings place[d] by providence under [men's] protection," and pleaded for husbands to consider their wives when creating laws.[54] Gone is the flirty, urging tone, replaced by forthrightness. Life had cured Abigail of self-effacement. And though the possibility of a woman *running* for minister or governor or President remained inconceivable, she now felt entitled to hold different views from her husband, to enjoy equal suffrage, and—most thrillingly—to frankly desire power—outside the home.[55]

AT FIRST, MARY FELT confident Mr. Whitman could sail into the First Church with or without female enfranchisement. Dynamic at the pulpit and ingratiating in town, he combined the best traits of his two predecessors. Almost everyone who liked Mr. Whitney wanted Mr. Whitman. Opponents of Mr. Flint were easily seduced by Mr. Whitman's vivacious sermons. And while "Those who were warm for Mr. Flint have not got over their disappointment and feel cross," among them the only crucial votes were Mr. Black's and Mr. Beal's. Mr. Beal's vote was secured immediately, and, as he was getting to know him, Mr. Black entertained the candidate "handsomely," Mary was pleased to observe.[56]

But Mr. Black, being less liberal than the Beals, Adamses, and Cranches, had to be persuaded that Mr. Whitman was as theologically correct as he was amusing over tea. Specifically, Mr. Black wanted the minister to declare that he accepted the strict Calvinist view that Christ was immortal and that faith rather than good works was the key to eternal life. This was not only untrue in Mr. Whitman's case, but a certain means of antagonizing the large liberal portion of the congregation; so, using all his lawyer's skills, Whitman deflected the issue as deftly as he could. That "a man does not wear Calvinism on his face" was no reason to reject his candidacy, Abigail scoffed to Mary. The town agreed and voted him in.

The sisters had their own ideas about Mr. Black's obstinacy. In tirades that came to consume more space than national politics in their letters, Mary blamed religious differences, while Abigail attributed her neighbors' recalcitrance to self-importance; the Blacks wanted "to make themselves of concequence," she jeered, adding: "The President will be very angry with some of his Neighbors, if through their means we lose so good a Man."[57]

Soon Mary was deprecating the Blacks as the head of the "opposition" while reminding Mr. Whitman of the brilliance of their political system where anyone could think as he wanted, but the opinion of the greatest number of citizens prevailed. To Abigail, on the other hand, Mary lamented, "I hope we shall get fixed soon or we shall split all to pieces." She was beginning to have doubts that the majority ruled.

The majority of Quincy residents certainly seemed eager to accept Mr. Whitman, who arrived in town to report his decision the last week in November and "dined with Captain Beal on Thanksgiving," which gave Mary hope. "I . . . think if Mr. W. accept we shall be very peaceful with him," she reassured herself in a letter to her sister. On the downside, though, Mr. Black was ignoring Mr. Whitman, who clearly felt snubbed.[58]

"How much chagrined shall I feel if you write me that Mr. Whitman has given his answer in the Negative," Abigail answered. "I hate

Negatives when I have sit my Heart upon any thing. Half the year [in Philadelphia] I must sit under as strong Calvinism as I can possibly swallow and the other half, I do not know what is to come."[59]

What came, on November 30, was a third negative in five months from a candidate favored by the majority of Quincy's citizens. Like his two predecessors, Mr. Whitman demanded unanimous approbation, Mary dutifully related to Abigail; who wrote back that she was "mortified" at the loss of so clever a preacher. "We must be doomed to a—a droomadery," she sulked.[60]

Mary, though, recovered with astonishing speed and was soon comforting her sister that "The study of law will be more for [Mr. Whitman's] advantage ... than the gravity of the pulpit." Besides, she had someone else in mind.

During her vacation in Quincy, in the late summer of 1797, Abigail brought her grandsons ten-year-old William and eight-year-old John Smith to be educated at Stephen Peabody's Atkinson Academy. Mary, now 56, sat beside 53-year-old Abigail in the carriage rolling toward 47-year-old Elizabeth. *Plus ça change,* they must have mused, remembering how two decades before, when they were Nabby's age, they had committed their own sons to the Shaws.

Unlike John Shaw, however, Stephen Peabody was no scholar. His library was tiny, according to one boarder, his reading confined to newspapers, and he had forgotten whatever Greek he once knew. Nabby's boys would study not with Peabody himself but with a preceptor, Mr. Vose, whom Peabody had hired for his rising academy. What drew Abigail to Elizabeth's new home was not the man but the woman in charge.

The Smith boys "could not have better care ... if they were with their mother," Mary declared, while Abigail marveled at Elizabeth's writing prowess, telling her, "What ever you write is always precious to me. No one better knows how to touch every feeling of the human Heart."[61 62]

Though the finest in the village, the Peabody's home was not as elegant as the parsonage in Haverhill; the gabled meetinghouse had no bell tower or steeple; and many of the five-hundred-odd residents lived in squat redbrick cottages and were poor. Some twenty boarders as well as Elizabeth's own seven-year-old Abby appeared daily with hair to be combed and socks and shirts to be mended, either by Elizabeth or her eldest daughter, Betsy Quincy, who was now 17 and indispensable to the run of the house. "Betsy Q is reaping the benefit of your good counsels and maternal tenderness," Elizabeth had flattered Abigail over the summer. "I have comfort in her good temper. I think it improves every day."[63]

An abundance of work did not deter Betsy Q from regaling whomever was in earshot with ironic comments any more than it stopped Elizabeth from dressing more fashionably than anyone in the state. And Elizabeth still had her flower garden and a small orchard as well as a courtyard where she planted lilacs and roses to shield the armful of household laundry she hung to dry on the fence.

An Academy student named Samuel Gilman, who boarded with the Peabodies around the time the Smith children arrived in Atkinson, recalls "Ma'am Peabody" as better-educated and more polished than her Harvard-trained spouse. She elevated dinner conversations with quotes from Shakespeare and Dryden and raised sartorial standards, wearing a mesmerizing headdress of white interleaved muslin stitched with fine lace thread. She had a "delicate, transparent complexion," a "beautiful speaking eye," and a youthful aspiring spirit, seeking accomplishment as well as universal good. "Her conversation powers were of a superior order," Gilman noted. At the end of the day, while her husband sang, played his violin, or regaled their borders with anecdotes (frequently leaping from his seat to gesticulate), Elizabeth sat straight-backed in her rocking chair and read.[64]

THE REUNION OF THE THREE SISTERS in middle age was a high point of the summer of 1797. Soon after, Abigail left for Philadelphia, stopping to visit Nabby in East Chester, where there was still no news of Colonel Smith. Life seemed even gloomier and more uncertain to Nabby with her children in Atkinson. "For these two years past I have had so many trials and struggles in my mind to contend with that I only wonder that I have maintained my senses," she wrote her brother, John

Quincy.[65] To add to her troubles, the Peabodies were slow to communicate. On the November 15, Nabby still had not heard a word about William and John.

"Sister Peabody has so many cares that she has not much time to write, but I wish she would to Mrs. Smith," Abigail confided in Mary, and she went on to recount how she had written Betsy Q as well as Elizabeth, hoping to elicit a solacing report from one of the two. Pressing further would rattle her cherished detente with her younger sister, so "Pray do you represent the matter to her," Abigail, as so many times in the past, begged Mary, who enthusiastically agreed. Only rather than conciliating, Mary—uncharacteristically—inflamed the situation by ordering Elizabeth to write at once.[66]

A month later, in December, it was Elizabeth's complaint Mary reported to Abigail. "Had [Nabby] been left to follow her own plan of education her children would have done her more honour," Mary lost no time blaming the children's misbehavior on the Colonel Abigail once had touted as the ideal mate. "Sister says she finds it difficult to make Mr. Peabody believe that their mother is a woman of breeding and politeness. Parents must be united in their mode of education or their children will suffer," she could not refrain from lecturing, and she added salt to the wound by downright boasting that her own Betsy had never looked better and Lucy was thriving (despite a blind and impoverished spouse).

But while Mary felt secure enough to flaunt her seniority, Elizabeth was eager to renounce all competition in honor of preserving her new sense of equality with the President's wife. Besides, how could she not empathize with a suffering mother? When she at last wrote Abigail, at the end of December, Elizabeth blamed overwork for her earlier silence and presented a far less devastating portrait than Mary of life with Nabby's sons. "Your Grand Children are well, and are in a very good way," she began her letter, and in her version of the tale, there was no problem with William, who "loves to be quiet," only John was obstreperous and:

> beats all for noise. I ask him what you did with him and how his mamma could bear it. We have talked, coaxed, flattered, and assumed a sterner manner, and all does not avail . . . But it is not

from ill will, but a shocking habit of speaking as sharp as a boat-swain, or a coachman driving over pavements.

"He is a dear boy notwithstanding and we all love him," she quickly added, assuring Abigail (disingenuously) that at John's age her own children had been just as defiant. Meanwhile, she vowed to write more frequently and keep the family apprised of the progress that was sure to transpire.[67]

Then a month passed, with no further word from Elizabeth. When she did pick up her pen, it was to implore Abigail not to make "frequent writing a criterion of my love." For while "I have the pleasure to tell you, your grandsons behave exceedingly well and are become quite the favorite of the Family," her days were "fraught with cares," because her beloved Betsy Q, now 18, around the same age as Nabby when she fell in love with Royall Tyler, was incapacitated by an undiagnosed disease. There was no doubt what Elizabeth suspected when she enumerated Betsy Q's symptoms: a chest pain, aching limbs, temperature, and difficult breathing. Nor did she make much of an effort to mask her premonitions, writing: "I always feel anxiety when my Friends have pulmonick complaints. They often undermine the constitution, and like a worm in the bud destroy unseen."[68]

Abigail wrote back at once and wholeheartedly rejected Elizabeth's unstated theory. Betsy Q's malaise perfectly fit the description of rheumatic fever, which they all had suffered and survived. It came on (just like the unmentionable tuberculosis) with chest pain, swollen limbs, and flushing. "I am scarcely ever free from it, yet do not think it worthwhile to complain." And while there was no cure, Abigail sent her own prescription for powders and advised bleeding for relief.

Mary—eager to atone for her recent troublemaking—urged that Betsy Q make a trip to Quincy. Elizabeth accepted, and, forgoing bleeding and powders for the moment, relied on the mysterious talents of an eldest sister to restore her daughter's health. But Mary, watching her daily, could make no impact on Betsy Q's cough, which she described as troublesome, in a letter to the capital. It was the beginning of March, and while Betsy Q was strong enough to help her "fork" asparagus and "sew" lettuce, "I do not know what to do with her," Mary fretted. "She says she had [a cough] all last winter. It does not confine her nor make her sick but it racks her." And while Betsy Q was now begging to return home to her mother, a winter chill still hung over New England, so Mary was loath to let her go.

By the end of March, Betsy Q was, in any case, back in Atkinson to greet her brother, William, when he arrived on a break from Harvard. The weather cleared for a few days, and, as suddenly as it had come on, Betsy Q's fever fell, and the cough disappeared. With spring in the air, Elizabeth dared to hope that her fears had been groundless. But three weeks of intense cold followed the fleeting fine weather, and by early April Betsy Q's cough and fever had returned in full force.

"I confess I am afraid to hear from Betsy Shaw," on May 10 Mary confided in Abigail. "She has never been well since her fever in the winter. Her mother says she is in good spirits but that does not please me. She has fever enough to keep them up." A friend visiting Atkinson was "shocked" at the child's deterioration. "I think her very critically situated," Mary meaningfully wrote.

The impact of Mary's words did not escape Abigail, who saw Nabby's worries and new troubles from the French pale by comparison to her sister's plight. "I can allow for your long silence," Abigail wrote Elizabeth,

> tho I wish it were not imposed upon you by your numerous cares and unavoidable avocations. The anxiety which you feel for the Health of a Beloved child, whom I pray God to restore to Health and preserve to you, is I well know more exhausting to the spirits, and wearisome to the Body than labour. What ever scenes you may be call'd to pass through, may you be sustain'd and supported by that Being in whom we trust satisfied that however greivous his dispensations, they are wise and just and we will strive to adore the Hand that "strikes our comforts dead."[69]

When at last Elizabeth wrote Abigail, her letter was long and rambling, full of apologies—"I have a heart that would communicate, or that would afford you pleasure if I had time, but the business of the Family presses so hard upon me that when I feel determined to write coats, jackets and stockings call so loud for my attention that my purposes are quite altered," etc. What most distracted the youngest Smith sister had nothing to do with mending garments. In the most candid letter she ever composed, Elizabeth for once refused to underplay her pain or prettify her language and expressed the cause of her near distraction in straightforward prose:

> The cares and anxieties, the hopes and the fears, that I should do too much or not enough for my poor Betsy, I did not wish to trouble you with, or to tell you that my mind has been so agitated least the fatal messenger was on the wing . . . that I have scarcely been fit for the duties of life, and though I wish to be resigned to the will of heaven, and to think like a saint, yet such is the frailty of our nature, that we *all feel* the imperfections of humanity in a most powerful and humiliating degree.

She was well aware that she blasphemed. Though she was the most religious of the three sisters, she could not keep herself from preferring her human child to God. Nor could she help praising Betsy Q's "cheerful happy temper" and "unreserved manner," bringing justice into the equation. Between the lines, she railed against the unfairness of blighting the good. Yet "you need not tell me I do wrong. I am very sensible of my error," she assured the sister who had listened as intently as she when their father preached resignation in the Weymouth meetinghouse. "If I should be deprived of her I must say it is the heaviest stroke I have ever yet experienced." And still, she strove for acceptance. Elizabeth ended her gloomy passage, praying "Should I be called to so severe a trial, may I have that temper which can say, 'thy will be done'—as I ought."[70]

There was always a chance that, like the Biblical Isaac, her child would be spared.

This both of her sisters ardently wished, and Stephen Peabody, reporting on the pleasing progress of Nabby's children to the Adamses at the beginning of summer, raised Abigail's spirits by attesting that Betsy Q was "a little better and in a way to recover." Mary, receiving the same news, was not so cheered. "Betsy Shaw is something better," she wrote Abigail in Philadelphia, "but her cough has not left her nor her fever. The loss of her would be almost too much for her mother," she feel-ingly added and concluded with unwonted eloquence: "Tis strange what little thread our Lives hang upon that we should plan for an hour but as the chance for executing it was against us."[71]

In June, it was Mary who at last used the awful word "consumption" and pronounced Betsy Q "firmly settled" in a tubercular state. The child had night sweats, she wrote Abigail, and was so frail she could "ride but a few miles in a day." Shortly afterward, William Shaw sent news that Betsy Q was bedridden. No amount of pleading could coax a word from Elizabeth herself.

And who would blame her? Just when the sisters most needed to be together, Abigail was pinioned in Philadelphia as John struggled with one political crisis after another, and Richard Cranch was too sick and Betsy Norton too fragile for Mary to contemplate leaving town. "Tis hard for [Elizabeth] to suffer without a sister by to soothe and comfort her," Mary grieved, knowing she spoke for Abigail also. "She has every thing in Mr. Peabody that a kind good Husband can be, but she wants the assistance of a sister. Such a lovely child as Betsy Shaw and such comfort as she looked to receive from her is hard to be parted with.

"I feel so myself at the thought that I want the support I would give."

Whatever else in the world changed, the sisters' love still knew no boundaries. But the geographical distance between them grew increasingly hard to endure.

CHAPTER XVII

"One of Sister Cranch's Letters is worth half a dozen others"

. . .

WHILE ELIZABETH WATCHED BETSY Q SICKEN IN HAVERHILL, John Adams, in Philadelphia, had spent the fall and winter of 1797 anxiously waiting to hear from the three delegates—John Marshall, Charles Pinkney, Elbridge Gerry—he had sent to negotiate peace with Foreign Minister Talleyrand and the ruling Directory in France. All he knew was that the Americans had reached Paris safely in October. Since then, any number of foreign boats had landed in the Philadelphia seaport, but not a word from the emissaries had appeared.

Lack of news did not stop the Republican press from continually impugning evil designs toward the French on the part of the Federalists. "Scarcely a day passes but some . . . scurility appears in [Benjamin] Baches paper," Abigail continued her harangue against journalists.[1] Then when January passed and there was still no report from the delegates, Abigail had her own reasons for fearing the worst. "Vague and contradictory accounts are in circulation respecting our Envoys," she wrote Mary the first week of February. The absence of official communication, she conjectured, meant the Americans had bad news and thought it dangerous to express.[2]

A month later, private dispatches at last arrived from abroad and confirmed her suspicions. Indeed, the reports were so explicit about

French treachery that all John felt safe to reveal to Congress was that the mission had failed. "It is a very painfull thing that he cannot communicate to the publick dispatches in which they are so much interested," Abigail lamented to Mary, "but we have not any assurance that the Envoys have left Paris." As well as the lives of these three men, the future of American foreign policy was at stake. For who would agree to negotiate in a foreign country unless assured his activities would remain secret until he returned?[3]

The Republicans reasoned differently. In a shocking misreading, Vice-President Thomas Jefferson concluded that John was repressing material favorable to the French government out of Francophobia, while Bache's pro-French *Aurora* ranted about abuse of executive power, and private citizens sent death threats to the President's house.[4] Pedestrians hummed French songs as they ambled down Market Street, while between curtain calls in the theatre, audiences shouted for the performers to sing the French revolutionary anthem, "Ça ira."

"Material for a mob might be brought together in ten minutes," Abigail wrote Mary, even more distressed than she had been at the Battle of Boston, and her sister wrote back, "Tis hard, very hard indeed, that the People should shew such a jealousy and want of confidence in the President after such proofs as he has repeatedly given of his wisdom and faithfulness and his unshaken attachment to the true interest and safety of his country. What mules they are!"[5]

To a confidante in Boston, Abigail addressed her first acknowledgment that a friend had become a political enemy. Jefferson was conspiring against his own administration and, she felt sure, intriguing with the French.[6][7]

On April 2, the House of Representatives voted to compel the President to reveal the dispatches. The following day, Adams complied. "The Jacobins (the Federalist derogatory term for Republicans) in Senate and House were struck dumb," Abigail savored a political triumph despite her professed anti-partisanship. For the dispatches from the American delegates revealed egregious disrespect for America, conveyed by three underling French statesmen the emissaries described in code as "X,Y and Z."[8] This triumvirate was chosen by the French Directory, who refused even to meet the American delegates in Paris before they submitted to humiliating demands.

X, Y, and Z named four conditions for opening diplomatic negotiations. The first, on the surface at least, involved a matter of principal. Pinckney, Marshall, and Gerry must apologize for their President's refusal to stand with France, as France had stood with America, in war against England. But the last three were blatantly mercenary: America must dismiss all debts incurred by Frenchmen, advance a "considerable loan" to the French government, and, the coup de grâce, donate fifty-thousand pounds for Talleyrand and the Directory's "private use." To this insult to their national pride the American delegation fearlessly retorted, "It is no, no, not a sixpence," at the risk of their own imprisonment or worse.[9]

Not just Republicans, but all of Congress was "struck dumb" by these revelations, which were leaked to newspapers and soon available to the outraged country at large. Those whose sympathies had been wavering were now ardently anti-French, especially when the Directory signaled its rejection of American neutrality, and the very Navy that fifteen years earlier had come to George Washington's rescue at Yorkville began seizing American trade vessels on the high seas. John's push for a "half war" or, as Abigail phrased it, a war "to defend ourselves"[10] against France was swiftly accepted by Congress, who endorsed his call for a moratorium on commercial relations with the Directory and the creation of an American Navy to protect the shoreline and England-bound ships. Congress itself initiated a bill to enlarge the Army by 12,000 men and create a provisional Army of 10,000 for the President to summon if war ensued.[11]

The great surprise for Abigail was the alacritous change in public sentiment. Gone were the sansculotte cockades and the humming of French revolutionary tunes in the capital. The theatre became a battleground where, during intervals, the sorry few still calling for "Ça ira" were trounced by a majority demanding the newly composed "Hail Columbia"—a patriotic anthem honoring Adams and set to the tune of the President's March. One night Abigail slipped incognito into the theatre with her friends the Otises. Between plays, actor Gilbert Fox leapt on stage and performed "Hail Columbia," she wrote Mary, enthusing as she had from abroad about the ballet and opera. "At every Choruss, the most unbounded applause ensued." After the final curtain, the audience "call'd again for the song, and made [Fox] repeat it to the fourth time. And the last time, the whole Audience broke forth in the Chorus whilst the thunder from their Hand was incessant . . . In short it was enough to stund one."[12]

Even more stunningly, Abigail's much-maligned husband was suddenly a hero. Not only did theatre crowds applaud him, but military officers and ministers who had shied away from politics since the close of the American Revolution broke precedent to applaud his handling of what became known as the XYZ Affair. Fan letters deluged his desktop; and in the first week of May, 1,100 young Philadelphia merchants—wearing black cockades on their hats in defiance of the tri-colored French hats—paraded two-by-two to pay homage at the President's home. Ten thousand citizens of all ages spread to the limits of Market Street to watch them—the crowd was so thick "One might have walkd upon their Heads," Abigail observed.[13]

John so thoroughly enjoyed his fame that he felt free to write as he liked in the responses he penned personally to every piece of fan mail. In one reply, he turned a thank-you note for a Boston group's warm letter of praise into a rant against adulation except in a case as extreme as the XYZ Affair. Mary read the letter when it was printed in a Boston newspaper and, after a few propitiations, suggested to Abigail that John's language was too "delicate" for the common man to grasp. "Instead of [discerning] the high complement contain'd in those words 'It must be an unnatural state of things to make it necessary or even proper, etc.'" "Many supposed the President was not pleas'd and censur'd rather [than] approbated their addressing him with their professions of support."[14] "He must not attempt to flatter again," she added. "He never did know how to do it."[15] Abigail wholeheartedly agreed and revealed that she had freely expressed her misgivings to John when he showed her an early draft of the letter. "I did get an alteration in [his revised draft]," she for the first time in print acknowledged a substantive disagreement with the President—though only to Mary.[16]

Abigail and John were in perfect accord that religion was as crucial in statesmanship as in private life. "A man can not be an honest and Zealous promoter of the Principals of a True Government without Love of God," Abigail declared, implicitly blaming Jefferson's wrongheaded support of the French on his deism.[17]

To stress the importance of religion and defuse partisanship John

called for a national day of prayer and fasting on Wednesday, May 9, a
month after the reading of the delegates' report in Congress. But while
most citizens spent the day safely in church, a brawl between gangs of
young Republicans sporting tri-color cockades in their hats and Federalists wearing black broke out in the yard of the Philadelphia State
House. This incident, coupled with an intercepted letter threatening
that French émigrés were plotting to set fire to Philadelphia, riled Federalists, some of whom authentically feared foreign invasion, while
others seized the occasion to push for war on France.

As with their fury at "enemy" newspapers, the Federalists' terror of
immigrants was not entirely chimerical. Just as it was true that Bache's
Aurora misled those unable to deconstruct its hyperboles, many of the
foreigners who had entered America over the past decade did bring
strong prejudices from home. The predominant groups were Britains,
who hated the French, and French and Irish exiles, who hated the English. What Federalists overlooked was that most of these immigrants
harbored mixed feelings about their own countries also—or why would
they have moved? Some of the French, for instance, were nobles fleeing the guillotine.

But even for President Adams, who was deeply ambivalent about
both France and England, eager to maintain neutrality, and had spent
his life struggling to subdue passion in his theory and in his soul, reasoning palled. The gravity of the Directory's insult and the intensity of
the threats at home—burn a city?—ensured a high level of anxiety
throughout the nation. Abigail and Mary were by no means exempt
from leaping to extreme views.

"I wish the Laws of our Country were competant to punish the
stirer up of sedition, the writer and Printer of base and unfounded cal-
umny. This would contribute as much to the Peace and harmony of our
Country as any meausre, and in times like the present, a more carefull
and attentive watch ought to be kept over foreigners. This will be done
in future if the Alien Bill passes," Abigail at the end of May wrote
Mary, approving the Alien Friends and Sedition Acts that Federalists
were currently championing in Congress. If passed, the Alien Friends
Act would allow the President to bypass the Constitution and banish
foreigners at his private discretion. The Sedition Act would jail and
fine newspaper editors maligning the U.S. government in print.[18]

"I am glad Congress are bringing forth such spirited Bills," wrote Mary from Quincy. Conveniently forgetting that her own husband was born in England, she went even further than Abigail in her support of shipping off foreigners and censuring the press. "What a shame," she observed, that Congress needed to be consulted in the first place. They wasted "so much time in debating upon what" the President could easily decide himself![19] And Elizabeth Peabody completed the circle of revolutionary sisters who seemed to believe, as this youngest sister phrased it, that "Limited monarchy is the best government," at least while John Adams ruled.

Even before the Sedition Bill passed Congress, Benjamin Bache was thrown into jail for seditious libel. Jefferson took the high road, which was also politically advantageous, and removed himself to Monticello to escape the daily attacks on freedom of speech.[20] Adams had not written the bills, nor—ever after the Alien Friends Act passed—did he banish a single foreigner. But he conspicuously failed to oppose the radical Federalists eager to confiscate Republican newspapers and exile Frenchmen, hundreds of whom leapt onto boats of their own accord and fled the U.S. President as they had run from Robespierre.

By the end of June, another furious heat enveloped Philadelphia, and the dread yellow fever—not yet known to be transmitted by mosquitoes, but already equated with summer and coastal cities and believed to originate in the West Indies—had arrived, heightening the already palpable fear in the capital. Though less prevalent than smallpox, yellow fever was equally mortal and more terrifying because there was no inoculation, and doctors held radically different theories about its cause. The Adamses' friend Dr. Benjamin Rush, for instance, attributed the first major epidemic five years earlier to puddles of coffee festering at the Philadelphia dock.

Though it was more prevalent among the poor, Dr. Rush himself and Alexander Hamilton had caught this mysterious disease in the 1793 crisis. Its trajectory was deceptive, for a few days after an initial fever, headache, bloody nose, and nausea seized the body, all complaints greatly alleviated, and the patient had the illusion of getting well—only to be struck more forcibly soon afterward. This was a turning point where two outcomes were equally likely. In the better case, the patient slowly recovered; in the worse, the virus devoured the intestinal tract and caused excruciating pain as the liver and kidney collapsed.

Abigail and half her household suffered "bowel complaints" as sultry June turned to savage July, mosquitoes multiplied, and Congress continued to debate the two most controversial bills in America's short history. Social activities among the powerful also continued. "What a medley are my letters," Abigail mused, for they veered from politics to disease, and, even in the midst of a crisis, might end with a verbal picture of the beau monde. "The young Ladies generally have their Hair all in Curls over their heads and then put a Ribbon, Beads, Bugles or a Band of some kind through the fore part of the Hair to which they attach feathers," she wrote Mary, who was helping to plan a niece's wedding. The latest gowns "have only one side come forward and that is confind with a belt round the waist. Some sleaves are drawn in diamonds, some [trimming] drawn up and down with bobbin[21] in 5 or 6 rows. In short a drawing room frequently exhibits a specimin of Grecian, Turkish, French and English fashion at the same time, with ease, Beauty, and Elegance equal to any court."[22]

In the middle of July, with insects "torment[ing]" Abigail "so that it is next to impossible to write without both hands flying at the same time,"[23] Congress passed the Alien Friends and Sedition Acts, and the Adamses were at last free to leave Philadelphia for Peacefield, as they had christened their Quincy home.[24]

John was pale and had lost so much weight, "His Rotundity" looked starved. "Bowel complaints" had also weakened Abigail, who hoped to escape public fanfare and minimize the inevitable exhaustion of the trip. Still, cheering crowds slowed them on every step of the journey.

ONE MORNING THE PREVIOUS winter, Abigail, entering John's study, had found him "gravely" squinting over the fire at a letter of Mary's he had scooped from her share of the post. John's excuse—that "One of Sister Cranchs Letters is worth half a dozen others," and that if he did not get her mail "clandestinely," he rarely saw it at all—did not move Abigail. "I scolded . . . hard" Abigail assured her sister until "the President" promised "he will not open any more Letters to me, and will be satisfied with such parts as I am willing to communicate"—in other words, not much.[25]

In the spring, Mary was still begging Abigail, "Do not be impatient my Sister if I do not write twice a week always. I believe I often do. Others have a demand upon me also and grumble if I do not write frequently." Primary among those others was her son William, who was still in the capital city, still seriously depressed out of shame over his involvement in his brother-in-law Greenleaf's speculations and his so far unsuccessful attempts to build a law practice of his own. Abigail, who told Mary, "Next to my own children I love those of my sister," was also eager to promote William, hosting him on his many trips to Philadelphia, writing him long letters of advice and encouragement, sending money, and relying on him as on her own sons.[26]

Now, as the Adamses traveled toward Peacefield, William was shepherding their new in-laws around Washington. Yes, in-laws, for John Quincy, though still a low-paid ambassador to Berlin, had found a woman worth overriding his parents' discouragements about starting a family before establishing a private career. The previous summer, on July 26, 1797, he had married Louisa Catherine Johnson, daughter of an Englishwoman, Catherine Nuth, and Joshua Johnson, formerly a prosperous Maryland merchant and now America's foreign consul in London. Louisa had grown up in a privileged circle, and Johnson had promised a generous dowry to help start her married life. Instead, no sooner was the wedding announced than the consul confessed he was as financially ruined as Colonel Smith and the Greenleafs. Soon after, he fled his London debtors for Washington, where he owned property and hoped to redeem his name. With John and Abigail (caught up in the XYZ Affair) mired in Philadelphia, William Cranch assumed the role of official family representative and took John Quincy's in-laws under his wing. William refused to accept thanks for helping the Johnsons since, he told Abigail, "The fraternal and affectionate friendship which has so long existed between your son and myself, has indeed been one of the greatest consolations of my life."[27]

Increasingly, the sisters reached out to one another through their offspring. While Elizabeth's husband, Stephen Peabody, schooled Abigail's grandchildren, Mary and Abigail, powerless to revive Elizabeth's suffering Betsy Quincy, compensated by lavishing attention on her intelligent but highly eccentric son. On June 21, 1798, William Shaw graduated from Harvard and settled himself at Mary's. "Willm has the best heart in the world but will never be broke of his pecularities," Mary predicted to Abigail after a week with the clumsiest and most tongue-tied of the sisters' children. "They will injure him in the Beau-mond at least and I am sure they would as a publick speaker." William Cranch chimed in that his cousin's large, inky handwriting was execrable and his spelling poor. William Shaw's letters were also strained and humorless, though erudite. "There is need of very shining talents to counterbalance [such defects] or they will subject him to ridicule," Mary concluded. Obviously, no such gifts were apparent to her.

Abigail thought otherwise, or in any case was so determined to alleviate her younger sister's fears about the boy's future that before leaving Philadelphia for Peacefield, she convinced John to hire the possessor of these "oddities" as his private secretary. And Elizabeth so appreciated her sister's kindness that she left Betsy Q's bedside and for the first time in months picked up her pen to express her thanks. "William is very good, attentive, and obliging," John was soon telling Abigail, "and sister may make herself easy on his Account."[28]

At the same time, John rose above private resentments and nominated Colonel Smith as adjutant general of the American Army, now enlarging to meet the French threat. His motives were not just nepotistic. For while John and Abigail held no illusions about Colonel Smith's character as businessman or husband, much less father,[29] they well remembered the triumphant young Revolutionary hero who infatuated them all at Gloucester Street after the war. Abigail in particular believed in her former protégé's military genius. When the Senate trounced the colonel's nomination, she continued to contend, "He has fought and bled in the service of his country, and I believe would have cordially done so again, if called to the task."[30] The disappointment to Nabby saddened Abigail as she prepared to leave Philadelphia. And suspicion that her son Charles, like Colonel Smith, had run up debts endangering his brother John Quincy, as well as his own family further depressed her mood. Charming, handsome Charles, who so resembled Abigail physically was "the only Child who ever gave me pain," she said.[31]

———

BUT WHAT MOST TROUBLED Mary as well as Abigail in the days before Congress rose in the summer of 1798 was fear for the life of the third fold of their chord: Elizabeth. How easily they could imagine themselves in her position. "Sister is so distressed that I should not wonder if she should go before her Daughter," Mary spoke to the grief of surviving a child, especially a girl, upon whom a mother depended for companionship in the future.[32] And Abigail echoed her older sister's anxiety in a letter to John Quincy in Europe, who remembered Betsy Q as the young mischief-maker in the household when he was studying for Harvard with his Uncle Shaw. Betsy Q had grown up less beautiful than Aunt Elizabeth, but in "otherways everyway Lovely and desireable," Abigail assured him, "and to lose her would be a stroke, which her mother would not know how to support."[33]

At the end of August, Betsy Q was strong enough to kiss the reformed William and John Smith, now 11 and 10, good-bye when they left to join their mother and grandparents in Quincy. The languishing girl "followed them in her mind, and said she could see the dear good Boys hug their Mama. She was very fond of the children and I saw it was very hard for her to part with them," Elizabeth said.[34]

A month later, when Nabby brought her children back to the Peabodies, Betsy Q was not at home to greet them. No announcement of her death survives. The first mention occurs in a letter Nabby wrote John Quincy in September after returning to her parents' from Atkinson. "Our Dear Aunt Peabody has lost her Daughter . . . in a consumption . . . it has almost broke her heart."[35]

Though Elizabeth does not specifically mention Betsy Q's death, it is clearly the catalyst for the raw letter she had composed to her son William a few days earlier:

> I am sometimes ready to believe (what is almost a paradox) that the less sensible are the most happy—that we must be too wise, or too stupid to be moved at the vicissitudes and accidents which encounter us upon every side, before we can enjoy this life—for it is a dangerous, thorny, devious, ragged road through which we have to pass.

Briefly, she mentions the comforting prospect of an afterlife, but only as an anodyne, aberrant in the general misery of existence.[36]

ABIGAIL LAY NEAR DEATH herself at Peacefield all summer. She arrived home on August 8, went to her bedroom, and did not walk out for eleven weeks. The doctors could not arrive at a diagnosis. No one mentioned yellow fever, though the disease was by now rampant in Philadelphia and this must have been a fear. If it *was* yellow fever, the symptoms were irregular: no nose bleed and only an intermittent fever, though she had the obligatory diarrhea and incapacitating weakness, as well as what John termed "almost a Diabetes," which at that time meant vomiting, thirst, and dry skin.

Nabby, in Quincy for the first time in five years, found Peacefield dreary. "The Illness of our Dear Mother has cast a gloom over the face of every Thing here, and it scarce seems like home without her enlivening chearfulness," she wrote John Quincy.[37] Abigail was too far gone to summon that merry spirit that "makes good like a medicine." Even as Nabby and Mary labored to save her, for the better part of three months she was convinced she was dying, to the point where she formally took leave of her children and discharged them to their father's care.

Their father could think of nothing but his beloved wife. Even the Presidency lost its urgency, and he dragged out his absence from the capital, telling Abigail, "If I had less Anxiety about your health, I should have more about public affairs, I suppose."[38] And: "Your sickness . . . has been to me the severest Tryal I ever endured."[39]

It was not until the second week in November, with Abigail still weak, feverish, depressed, and unable to sleep, but showing signs of improvement, that John at last tore himself from his wife's bedside and reluctantly headed south to confront affairs of state. By cruel coincidence, Richard Cranch became "dangerously sick" just as John was leaving; confining Mary to her farm. The first time Abigail ventured out, in the third week of November, it was to visit Richard, who was still gravely ill but now expected to live.

At the end of November, a snowstorm struck Quincy. Abigail went for a sleigh ride, slept through the night, and at last reported, "My Spirits and Health mend."[40]

"I want your society, Advice and Assistance," John lamented en route to Philadelphia. But now it was Abigail who pressed to join John and resume her job as First Lady, while John was adamant that she stay home and rest. "I cannot encourage the Idea of your coming on to Philadelphia. The horrid Roads and cold damp Weather would put an end to you," he wrote.[41] Though she continued to fret that she was shirking her duty, Abigail had to acknowledge she was not up to the journey and content herself with asking John to "Tell me who and who inquires after me as if they cared."[42]

There was no easy trajectory back to health after so long an illness. One Sunday, Abigail for the first time in four months drove to her pew for meeting; the next she was too ill to go anywhere. Only her writing steadily progressed.

The subject of her first letter to John was the rumored rout of Bonaparte's forces by the English naval commander Horatio Nelson in Egypt. The story was quickly confirmed and greatly reduced anxiety among Federalists that France would attack England, much less America, any time soon. Or rather, it reduced anxiety on the part of "moderate" Federalists, led by Adams, while it seemed merely a temporary reprieve to the "ultras," led by Alexander Hamilton, who viewed France as bent on aggression no matter what. Though he now held no public office, Hamilton wielded great influence over the growing band of "ultras" and even the moderate George Washington, whom he convinced to come out of retirement to lead an army against imminent attack. Reluctantly, John endorsed the buildup. But—trusting private reports from John Quincy in Berlin and, for once, *not* consulting Abigail—John planned for a very different approach to France.

It was a sad Thanksgiving for the family, in Philadelphia, Quincy, and Atkinson. With the "ultras" pressing for war and the Republicans clamoring to restore freedom of the press to the newspapers, John spent his day off alone with William Shaw and the Brieslers. "No company—no society—idle, unmeaning Ceremony," he groaned to Abigail and went on to cite Colonel Smith's and Charles's debts as further cause for pain. "You and I seem to have arrived prematurely at the Age when there is no pleasure," he continued in the same vein. The depressed President had made the remarkable decision to reread deist philosophers like Benjamin Franklin, then had gone further and taken a radical leap to imagine himself in their heads. Such "Soidisant Phylosophers insist that Nature contrives [misery] . . . to reconcile men to the thought of quitting the World," he wrote Abigail. "If my Phylosphy was theirs I should believe that Nature cared nothing for Men, nor their follies nor their miseries nor for herself,"[43] he continued, with so much relish it was clear he had entertained this blasphemy. And while he concluded that, *even if he was wrong,* he was a happier man for ascribing to a benevolent deity, Adams insisted he regretted his political career. "My [only] Enjoyments have been upon my farm."[44]

At *his* farm in Quincy, Richard Cranch was too ill to travel even to Abigail, who in turn was too weak to join the Cranches and spent the day trying to summon the gratitude she knew she should feel. "No Husband dignifies my Board," she wrote John, "no children add gladness to it, no smiling Grandchildren Eyes to sparkle for the plum pudding, or feast upon the minced Pye. Solitary and alone I behold the day after a sleepless night, without a joyous feeling. Am I ungrateful? I hope not."[45]

Saddest of all was Elizabeth in the conspicuous absence of her elder daughter. Besides being sick at heart, she had a bad cold, and struggled through the motions of serving puddings and pies to her boarders like a clock, she told Abigail—summoning up a flicker of her famed imagination—which "could not speak a word, but kept in silent motion."[46] To her dismay, the rest of the household was anything but reposeful—led on by her boisterous husband, the students' voices thundered and instruments squeaked.

"Everything seems a burden since your dear Sister's death," Elizabeth appealed to her son, William, who was swept up in his new job and had not offered the consolation she wanted. "While [Betsy Q] was well and smiling by my side, my work was easy—she made every burden light and pleasant . . . and some might say [I am] very foolish to shed so many unavailing tears—But I cannot help it . . . such is the disappointed state of my mind—I try—soar for a while, and then down and sink."[47] That God's purpose was beyond human comprehension, His justice perfect, had been a touchtone of Elizabeth's faith since childhood. More even than her sisters, she lived by the precept "God's will be done." And yet, she now confessed, she had cherished the— blasphemous?—hope that God would spare Betsy Q on *human* grounds, *because she was blameless*—which made turning to religion after her death cold comfort. Like John Adams, she was dangerously close to doubting a beneficent deity when she listed instilling "christian virtues" as only fourth on her list of reasons to exert herself, well behind "the *belief* that I am promoting the cause of Literature"[48]—in which God had no hand.

IN THE WINTER OF 1799, as John Quincy continued to insist the French were ready to negotiate with American diplomats, Adams's "quaisi" war with France was going nowhere. There were neither enough "ultras" in Congress to muster votes for a real war nor enough Republicans to force an alliance with the revolution to free the world. The fact that the Republicans came within four votes of passing a bill to repeal the widely hated Alien and Sedition Acts was a sign of the country's dwindling faith in the President. The President did not, however, doubt either his eldest son or himself.

So as the government prepared to rise for summer break, Adams sent a shock through Congress, proposing that America drop its grudge over the XYZ Affair and send a Maryland Federalist, William Vans Murray, to resume the pursuit of peaceful relations with France. The French leaders in turn would have to agree to receive America's minister *before* Murray set sail—as John Quincy assured the President they would.

A 39-year-old moderate, currently minister to Holland, Murray had been an Adams disciple ever since the two met in London fifteen years before when John was ambassador and Murray a law student.[49] At the time, Murray made known that he admired John's *Defense of the Constitution,* and the two were of like minds on practical matters as well.[50] John had no intention of flattering the Directory: the fact that Murray was not a major figure on the American political scene was an advantage, he reasoned.

Federalists in Congress, however, interpreted the selection of an unknown in such a vainglorious endeavor as either mad or evil, while Jefferson could only understand it as calculated to force Congress to rebel and declare war. Members of both parties backhandedly complimented Abigail by declaring that if she had been in Philadelphia

Adams never would have made such an outlandish decision, or as she phrased it, everyone "wisht the old woman had been there." Abigail, meanwhile, confounded them by loyally supporting her husband, declaring his policy a "master stroke."

Bitter confrontations with moderate as well as "ultra" Federalists followed Adams's dramatic announcement. But, with Congress eager to adjourn before yellow fever again descended on the capital, a compromise was soon effected, whereby the President agreed to send three delegates instead of Murray alone. Both houses grudgingly approved the revised plan and fled the onslaught of germs.

Assurances of French goodwill arrived at Peacefield over the summer break. In mid-November, the three delegates (Chief Justice Oliver Ellsworth and North Carolina Governor William Davie as well as Murray) set sail. With them, Adams believed, rode his place in history. If they succeeded, he could avert war; set a precedent for neutrality in all future European conflicts; confirm his diplomatic shrewdness; and, with luck, win the upcoming 1800 election and a second term. The alternative was unthinkable.

In the fall of 1799, Mary Cranch was 58, Abigail Adams was 55, and Elizabeth Shaw Peabody was 49 years old. Though they moved in separate spheres and each was so overwhelmed she felt as if, in Mary's words, she "belonged to everyone," their inter-connectedness was inviolable. For the good of their children, their husbands, their communities, but mostly for their private comfort, they were more dependent on and available to one another than ever before. As women, they were increasingly convinced of their importance in the larger world. Mary had no doubts that her role in reconciling a minister to Quincy and Quincy to a new minister was at least as vital as Richard's. Abigail determined to risk her health and follow John to Philadelphia this year—not, as with her journey to Europe, just to nurture her important husband, but to fulfill the First Lady's consequential role.

"I will never consent to have our sex considered in an inferiour point of light," Abigail wrote Elizabeth. "If man is Lord, woman is *Lordess* . . . As each planet shine in their own orbit, God and nature designed it so."[51] And Elizabeth downright boasted about her epic capacities as educator, informing her son, William: "To take a number of other Peoples Children and rear them up to man, and maintain rights, preserve property peace and order, I have sometimes thought required the patience of Job, the Wisdom of Solomon, the Eyes of Argus the lungs of Stertor, and the strength of Hercules."[52]

Mary began the final Thanksgiving of the eighteenth century visiting Parson Wibird, who was now a ragged, listless, "Dirty Beast" she was nurturing to the grave. Then, to dinner, many of whose delights came from Abigail's kitchen. "The Turkey was very good," Mary reported to her sister. "The raisins made a fine Pudding, and the Flour is excellent. The Sugar corrected the acid of the Cranberry and we drank our wine with thankful hearts." It was no small matter that Lucy Cranch Greenleaf; her blind husband, John; and their baby had traveled from Boston to join in the festivities, and that, for once, Betsy Norton was neither too pregnant nor too ill to sit up with her family at the table she had so frequently fled with depression or a headache in her youth.

Being together was reason enough for John and Abigail to rejoice on Thursday, November 28, at the President's mansion.[53] They had the added pleasure of sitting down to their own turkey and puddings with a transformed William Shaw. "We have rubd of so many of his peculiarities that he has scarce one left for us to laugh at," Abigail proudly reported to Mary, who could scarcely believe the eccentric who had tripped and stammered his way through holiday visits had survived over a year as secretary to the President of the United States.[54]

It was the Adamses' last Thanksgiving in Philadelphia; the government was scheduled to move south to Washington D.C. in the spring. A month before, John and Abigail had celebrated their thirty-fifth anniversary. "Few Pairs can recollect so long an Union," John proudly observed at that time.

Elizabeth was still grieving on her second Thanksgiving without Betsy Quincy. Furthermore, her nine-year-old, Abby, was sick and William gone.

"I must confess to you, my sister [Elizabeth wrote Abigail], that when I came to the Table Upon our Thanksgiving Day, and found my family collected, and almost every one [unrelated to me], my full heart sickened at the sight of food, and I had an hard contest with myself . . .

But it looks so cheerful, to see a large family, especially when composed chiefly of young persons," that, rather than "check the gratitude" of the others, she joined in their praise.[55]

When Elizabeth lost faith in her gift or confidence that she could find strength to write under the load of work that beset her, Abigail was there to cheer and encourage. While she acknowledged that the mind is "imprisoned in its own little tenement" and, when bombarded by quotidian duties "has no time to rove abroad," she reminded Elizabeth that she had "in early life treasured up a store of . . . knowledge, which time has matured," and urged her: "Dry not up the talents the return of which are tenfold whenever you bring them into action."[56] Rearing students was good and useful, but Elizabeth Smith had been "born to shine in higher spheres."

Abigail herself was suffering silently at the moment. Charles, the college prankster she and John had committed so much energy to reform, had succumbed to the same vice as Abigail's mismanaged brother.

Abigail's third son, Charles, charmed everyone in his youth.

By the autumn of 1799, Charles Adams was alcoholic, bankrupt, and had deserted his wife, Sally. She in turn had fled with her two small daughters to the already overwhelmed Nabby. This latest news struck John and then Abigail when they made their respective stops at Nabby's in East Chester en route to Philadelphia. John had no trouble connecting his failure to reform Charles with his increasing powerlessness to sway the "ultras" in his Cabinet and Congress. He expressed his fury and frustration in both realms when he told Abigail he "renounce[d]" their son.[57]

Abigail made no such repudiation. For better or worse, he was hers. "But shall we receive Good and not Evil?" she stretched to reconcile Charles's fall with her religion, in a letter to Mary. A cloud hung over even Charles's innocent children. "I cannot look upon them my dear Sister with that Joy which you do upon yours. They make my Heart ache, and what is worse, I have not any prospect of their being better off . . . Any calamity inflicted by the hand of Providence, it would become me in silence to submit to, but when I behold misiry and distress, disgrace and poverty, brought upon a Family by intemperence, my heart bleads at every pore."[58]

IN THE MIDDLE OF DECEMBER, Americans for a few months forgot their differences and joined to mourn their embattled President's predecessor. Sixty-seven-year-old George Washington—struck suddenly by a bacterial infection—was dead. "No man ever lived, more deservedly beloved and Respected," Abigail wrote Mary Cranch—a rare encomium to a statesman other than her spouse. ". . . If we look through the whole tennor of his Life, History will not produce to us a Parrallel," she added, though John, of course, came near.[59]

For everyone, it was a time to look backwards—to the young Virginian's leadership at the First Continental Congress, his winning the Revolution that produced the United States, his induction into the office of President, and, crucially, his willing retirement from it, affirming that America's elected executive, unlike George III or Louis XVI, would step down after no more than eight years.

All three sisters had personal memories. Elizabeth recalled Washington's one-night stay in Haverhill and the famous kiss he planted on Betsy Q's cheek when she burst into his inn at dawn. Mary remembered Parson Wibird rising out of his sloth to hear Washington speak in Boston and trudging home with the "Washington Cold." Conscious of their long friendship, Abigail now sent a personal note of sympathy to Martha Washington at Mount Vernon, while Mary promised to put the Adams pew at the First Church "in mourning by fastening a band

of gauze upon the edge . . . and tying it together in a number of places
with a Black ribbon."[60]

The President and First Lady both rose to the occasion of leading a
nation in sorrow, though John begrudged the adulation for a *former*
President when he was so widely disliked. And Abigail did not fail to
comment on the sartorial preoccupations in the capital, writing Mary:

> Last frydays drawing Room was the most [crowded] of any I
> ever had. Upwards of a hundred Ladies, and near as many Gen-
> tlemen attended, all in mourning. The Ladies Grief did not de-
> prive them of taste in ornamenting their white dresses: 2 yds of
> Black mode in length, of the narrow kind pleated upon one
> shoulder, crossd the Back in the form of a Military sash tyed at
> the side, crosd the peticoat & hung to the bottom of it, were worn
> by many. Others wore black Epulets of Black silk trimd with
> fring[e] upon each shoulder, black Ribbon in points upon the
> Gown & some lain Ribbon, some black [chenille], etc. Their caps
> were crape with black plumes or black flowers. Black gloves and
> fans . . . The assembly Room is burnt down, and they have not
> any place to display their gay attire, and as they expect it will be
> [the government's] last winter [in Philadelphia] they will have
> the opportunity, they intended shining.[61]

When mourning ceased in the spring, preparations both for the
move to Washington, D.C. and the elections of 1800 resumed with a
vengeance. Four men had been nominated for the Presidency and
Vice-Presidency—Adams and Charles Cotesworth Pinckney by the
Federalists, Thomas Jefferson and Aaron Burr by the Republicans.
That there was still no news from France did not help Adams's candidacy, nor did he make the most of his incumbency by lingering in Philadelphia over the summer or returning before the last minute in the
fall. Still, he was not indifferent to the election's outcome. He hated to
lose far more than he dreaded remaining in office. And, for all her au-
thentic yearning for Peacefield, domestic life, her sisters, and the familiar smells and habits of Quincy, Abigail shared her husband's ambition.
Jefferson would clearly be Adams's primary adversary in a close contest, and she was ready for the fight.

———

"ELECTIONING IS ALREADY BEGAN," Abigail had written Mary when she first arrived in Philadelphia. There was a similar commotion in Quincy as the town prepared for yet another vote on a pastor for the First Church. The latest candidate was none other than Mary and Richard's initial choice, eloquent Peter Whitney, the very man who had divulged Abigail's private warning about Quincy's never being able to afford a second minister when he brazenly rejected this same position three years before. His demand to be everyone's first choice also had incensed those who valued humility—or at least the pose.

Apparently, Mr. Whitney had soon regretted his rejection. He "mistook the meaning of the committee," he pleaded with Mary, who related the situation to Abigail in Philadelphia, giving her own view that: "Notwithstanding his imprudence in this affair [Mr. Whitney] is a very worthy man and wishes it was possible to reinstate him[self] in the good opinion of the People but thinks you can scarcly forgive him. I told him that you consider'd it as a great want of delicacy yet I was sure you would overlook it . . . but I did not see how it was possible to bring him and the Town together again he has so greatly affronted them."[62]

It had taken twenty-three months, but Mary Cranch had done just that—almost. Again, she was just short of a unanimous endorsement. This time it was not Mr. Black, but Abigail's distinguished neighbor on the other side, Captain Beal, and a small contingent of his supporters who opposed the candidate of choice. In Mary's opinion, Mr. Beal's opposition was "sour" and unconvincing.[63] His real motive was revenge on Mr. Black for defeating *his* favorite, Mr. Whitman, in the earlier vote. The two great friends no longer spoke and even ordered their wives to cease contact. Isolated from her beloved Mrs. Black and avoided by others chagrined at her husband's opposition, Mrs. Beal felt miserable, Mary reported to Abigail, but she was only a woman and had to submit to her spouse.

The town felt no such obligation. Maybe it was a matured view of majority rule or thoughts of the coming Presidential election, which promised to be close, that gave both Quincy and the candidate a more realistic idea of what constituted general approbation. Perhaps too it was rejection of Rousseau's fantasy of a "general will" as manifested in

France's National Assembly or a nod to America's new two-party system or simply the fact that Captain Beal's disapproval held less weight with the populace of this particular village than did Mr. Black's. But on December 8, 1788, Mary reported to Abigail that, without anyone changing sides, negotiations between Mr. Whitney and Richard's committee to elect a minister were progressing "very smoothly."[64]

"It will be a real subject of rejoicing with me, if we obtain Mr. Whitney," Abigail cheered her on.[65]

On December 9, Richard addressed a formal offer to the young preacher. It promised only the normal $500 to buy a house and the $500 salary his predecessors had rejected and did not represent a unanimous call from the town. Nonetheless, Mary felt confident that Peter Whitney would accept it.[66]

And so, on January 5—with acquired humility and characteristic flourish—Whitney informed the "Honored and Beloved" parishioners of the First Church of Quincy, Massachusetts, that he accepted the post. And proving himself a political as well as a religious adept, declaimed: "May God Almighty bless the connection, which is soon to be formed between us! In this near and intimate relation may we ever experience, how good and how pleasant it is for brethren to dwell together in unity!"[67]

"Unity," "the general will," "the general good": these catchwords of the Enlightenment—however impracticable—betrayed a noble longing. And there were moments when men and women did manage to speak in a single voice: the election of George Washington was one of them and so, in its modest way, was Quincy's reception of its new minister. "Captain Beal has taken [Mr. Whitney] by the Hand . . . and invited him to dine," Mary was soon reporting to Abigail. What is more, the town had banded together to support the Cranches as they approached their next and final goal.

Which was Mr. Whitney's ordination, scheduled for the fifth of February, forty-five years to the day after Parson Wibird took his vows. Not since her son's Harvard commencement had Mary faced a challenge so worthy of her managerial and creative talents. No fine point escaped her—from the need to appoint suitable neighbors to host dinners, to the availability of Abigail's utensils ("We shall want you," she wrote her sister, "but as [we] cannot have you I must ask leave to borrow a number of things of you such as knives forks Plates spoons, etc."), to the idea of raising $40 rather than just $20 so the town could present Parson Wibird as well as Mr. Whitney with a plush new gown.

The buildup to the ordination proved as dramatic as the Peabody wedding, and Mary picked up what Elizabeth called her "narrative pen" to relate the story to Abigail in fulsome detail. The day before "a violent storm of rain" turned the roads to rivers. The out-of-town guests arrived in "dripping condition" and raced to Mary, who was sick, "could not speak loud enough to be heard and was very much oppress'd . . . I think I never felt more disagreeable in my life.

"We had to kindle Fires in all the rooms to dry and make [the out-of-towners] comfortable . . . We had provided halters and fill'd our stable cow house and Barn Floor with their horses, provided beds for as many as we could stow away, gave them a good supper Brandy and wine . . . It was Two in the morning before we all got to Bed."

Mary was prepared with "Ham Cake Wine cider Brandy" for the even greater onslaught that swam up to her house on ordination day for breakfast, during which time a stove that had refused to light all winter suddenly "caught on fire and burnt with fury." Thanks to the rain, it did no harm and was quickly doused. As for the ordination: "everything was conducted with peace love and harmony." Afterward, Mary dined fifty guests on a variation of her commencement menu ("Roast Turkeys and geese Roast Beef Chicken Pye and apple pye squash and Rice Puddings in plenty besides a large Round of alamode Beef), and though she told Abigail "I have had a fatiguing time of it," she clearly basked in her hard-won success.[68]

From Philadelphia, Abigail applauded: "I congratulate the town in having made so wise, and as I think, judicious a choice. The President frequently expresses his satisfaction that we are once more a setled people."[69] She went on to compassionate Mary's "fatigues" and then to rue the debilitating nature of all campaigns—sacred or secular, before or behind the scene. "Trials of various kinds seem to be reserved for our gray Hairs," she lamented; then remembered to look ahead. In a few months, Congress would recess, and she would be free to return to Peacefield: "I will not forget the blessing which sweeten Life. One of those is the prospect of meeting my dear sister soon."[70]

CHAPTER XVIII

"As always I hope for the best"

. . .

ABIGAIL'S JOURNEY TO WASHINGTON D.C. WAS AS MUCH A LEAP into the unknown as crossing the Atlantic. She traveled with only servants. John had left Peacefield two weeks earlier, and her niece Louisa had stayed behind at the Cranch farmhouse. A shocking event had occurred. Mary took sick and was barely conscious throughout the end of the summer. She was now teetering between life and death.[1]

It was the beginning of November, 1800, the weather was bright, the leaves browning, when Abigail left Philadelphia, turning southward. The path was clear, but dreary, a mere tedium of forests, "destitute of natural as well as artificial beauty."[2] Baltimore, a thriving town dropped into a cliff sixty miles from the new capital, briefly relieved the monotony, but, it was gone in a flash, and then the woods resumed, unsettling Abigail like the infinity of the ocean. The roads were dilapidated, and bridges vanished so they had to splash through angry streams without a soul to salvage them should the carriage collapse. Worse, eight miles out of Baltimore, after stopping to see the town of Frederic, they lost their way and wandered two hours on dirt roads, pressing down or breaking off tree boughs in order to move at all until at last a black man in a cart appeared out of nowhere and pointed them to the post road. Now thickets resumed, opening every sixteen miles or so to a threadbare village—thatched cottages without glass windows and only a few black faces in sight.

At 1 P.M. on Sunday, November 16, Abigail drove into the capital. "As I expected to find it a new country with Houses scattered over a space of ten miles and trees and stumps in plenty . . . so [it is]," she wrote Mary. Washington was a city in name only, like the "wilderness" she had traversed to arrive. Stonecutters were drilling and bricklayers pulleying their fired clay in a rush to complete the President's mansion, "a castle of a House—so I found it— . . . in a beautiful situation in front of which is the Potomac with a view of Alexandr[i]a. The court around is romantic but . . . wild." Made of porous Virginia sandstone, the "castle" was sealed with a mixture of ground limestone, salt, ground rice, and glue that produced an illusion of sheer whiteness.[3] It was twice as large as the Quincy meetinghouse, though no single room was finished and thirteen fires had to be fed day and night to fend off the autumn cold.

Because there were no stores nearby, you had to travel a mile through pathless mud to George Town, "the very dirtyest Hole I ever saw," just to go marketing. Despite the abundance of trees, firewood was scarce because no woodcutters could be found south of Philadelphia. Bell installers were similarly elusive, so you had to walk great distances to communicate with a husband two floors above or a servant at the opposite end of the house. The whole mansion was damp, and the large reception hall on the first floor was fit only to hang laundry. But an oval space upstairs, designed to replicate George Washington's favorite room in the Philadelphia mansion, was filled with Abigail's mahogany furniture and already "very handsome." One day, under the auspices of some future President's wife with far more money than Abigail had at her disposal, it would be sublime. For now, she was "determined to be satisfied and content, to say nothing of [the] inconvenience." It would have had to "be a worse place than even George Town" for her to balk at a three-month stay.

Whether she stayed three months or four years, this house was not built for her but "for the ages to come," she presciently observed, implicitly expressing a faith in America's future, whatever she would say afterward. But even in its infanthood, it was fit for the first family of a great nation. Instead of gazing into the dark, as she had in Philadelphia, Abigail could look out from her room and see sunlit boats drifting down the Potomac as she wrote Mary in Quincy or Elizabeth in Atkinson.

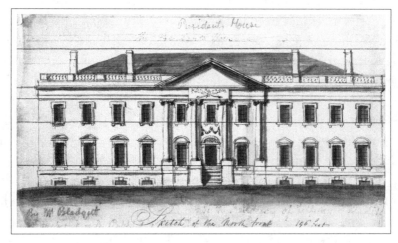

Abigail called the White House, even in its infancy, a castle and predicted it would one day be sublime.

Abigail was grateful she had brought her own thirteen northern servants, who were superior to any twenty slaves or former slaves employed by other statesmen's wives. These blacks were nothing like her industrious Phoebe in Quincy. "You can form no conception of the listlessness, the indolence and apparent want of capacity for business of these [southern] black people," she wrote her sister Elizabeth. But then, "How is it possible," she asked, that a captive, reared with "no sort of stimulous, but their driver . . . should have any ambition?" The fault lay not with the blacks but with the pernicious institution of slavery itself.

There was no library when she arrived at the President's House, but she found both John and William Shaw comfortably settled in partially furnished studies. John was as well as possible, considering that Alexander Hamilton had a month before disseminated a fifty-four-page rant, impugning the President's judgment and even sanity and urging Federalists to shun him and vote for his Federalist running mate, Charles Coteworth Pinckney; though Hamilton's long, twisted argument, quickly picked up by the newspapers, would surely benefit Jefferson more than anyone else. In days to come, Abigail would have time to contemplate the damage wrought by Hamilton's outburst.

Now, though, all political worries were overthrown by the blissful sight of a letter from the Cranches, where her sister Mary gave proof that she was still living by scratching a few agitated, barely coherent lines in her unmistakable scrawl:

> Welcome thou best of women, thou best of sisters, thou Kindest of Friends, the soother of ever[y] woe to the city of Washington ... Take their sweet offspring to your benevolent Bosom and say to them Thus would your grandmama do if she could hold you in her arms. I tremble, I can scarcely hold my pen. Others must tell you how I am afflicted with Boils, forty upon my back ... More would [I write] if I had strength to— [4]

CHOOSING TO LEAVE THE POSSIBLY dying Mary in order to fulfill her role as First Lady on the eve of elections had been one of the hardest decisions of Abigail's life. With Mary's daughters ill themselves, Abigail had been Mary's primary nurse through the end of October. "My Heart was rent," Abigail wrote, when she left Mary to the care of their niece Louisa and female neighbors. "I was never so divided between duty, and affection, the desire I had to remain with you, and the necessity I was under to commence a long and tedious journey ... To the great Physician both of body and soul I committed you and yours, and s[e]t out with an anxious mind and heavy heart." [5]

"I did not expect to see you again when you left me," Mary replied in her much-restored voice the first week of December, when she was at last able to sit up in a chair. "I could not trust myself with a last adieu. The care you took that I should want for nothing overcame me to such a degree, that tears not words spoke my grateful heart."

Mary's son William Cranch also attributed his mother's survival to Abigail's nursing, exclaiming of his aunt's goodness: "Human benevolence never approached nearer to divine." [6]

Then listlessness and excruciating boils confined Mary for five weeks to her chamber. Her greatest feat was leaving bed to walk to the fireplace, and she managed it only by clinging to Richard and another strong body for support. At first, eating was an agony. But as she improved, neighbors began tempting her with favorite dishes. When, for the first time, she ventured downstairs on Thanksgiving, "O! What a Goose I had on our Table . . . and what an appetite I had for it," she exulted in a letter to Abigail. Best of all was savoring the rewards of a lifetime of beneficence. "Tis true we have been a distress'd Family but we have had every alleviation that Friends could bestow."[7]

WITH MARY SO NICELY RECOVERING, Abigail would have been cheerful despite John's dwindling chance of winning the elections had politics been her only chagrin. But arriving at Nabby's in East Chester on her way south from Quincy, she had found her son Charles deathly ill. His face was bloated, his body shriveled. Liquor had scalded his liver, he could neither eat nor sleep. The man who had charmed everyone lay struggling for composure. When not deranged by pain, he was affectionate and remorseful. "His mind was constantly running upon doing justice, and making reperation."[8]

"His Physician says, he is past recovery," Abigail wrote the Cranches. Charles's wife, Sally, had forgiven him, his father had not—either on principal or because he did not realize Charles was on his deathbed. Abigail chose to believe the latter. "I shall carry a melancholy report to the President, who, passing through New York without stopping, knew not his condition."[9]

By the time Abigail drove into Washington, it was rumored that the peace mission had succeeded in Paris, but there was no official corroboration to boost John's chances with the Presidential electors, who would cast their votes in two weeks, on December 3. Election results turned on a penny, she wrote Mary, though privately she felt confident John would lose. In all but five of the now sixteen states, the legislature, rather than popular vote, decided the Presidential electors. Thus, John could anticipate taking New England where Federalists dominated the assemblies, and Jefferson would easily win most of the south where Republicans ruled. The pivotal contests were in the mid-Atlantic states, especially the traditionally Federalist New York, and in South Carolina, where Adams had a chance because his co-runner, Pinckney, was a native son.

So it was a significant blow to Adams when Republicans won an upset triumph in New York's Congressional elections. Worse, on December 2, South Carolina removed all chances of a Federalist victory by selecting electors pledged exclusively to Jefferson and Burr. Though the votes would not be formally tabulated until February, it was soon apparent that Adams and Pinckney had lost at 65 and 64 votes, respectively, and Jefferson and Burr had tied at 73 votes apiece. According to the Constitution, the House of Representatives now would take charge and elect one of these two Republicans to be America's third President. The vote would take place sometime before March 4, when Adams's term officially came to a close.

It was the end of an era for John and Abigail. Since 1774, when Boston elected him delegate to the first Continental Congress, John Adams's business had been leading America—as signer of the Declaration of Independence and the Treaty of Paris, as the United States' first minister to Great Britain, as head of the Senate, and now, for the past four years, as President of the United States. Knowing his own heart, he had mistrusted any nation dependent on human goodness. His Massachusetts Constitution was a template for rule by law. At the same time, his lust for personal greatness and power had been gratified. Now his days of glory were over. After more than a quarter of a century at the center of a great national drama, John was to return—not of his free will, like Washington, but because the American people had refused him a second term in office—to the private sphere. It was a humiliating diminishment.

Always ambivalent about public life, initially Abigail was less devastated than her husband by his defeat at the polls. While she complained of the nation's "ingratitude," she was also happy to be done with levees, lambasting journalists, and inconvenient moves. She could go home to Quincy with its promising new minister, to her sisters, to the life she'd led as a young wife.

Then, nine days after the Presidential vote, a treaty with Napoleon, assuring honorable peace between France and America, arrived from the three delegates in Paris. Had the incident occurred even two weeks earlier, John's success at averting war might have won him a second term.

Confronted by this bitter irony, Abigail could not help lamenting her practical losses. "We will live in independence, because we will live within our income," she wrote her youngest son, Thomas. But she raged at America's indifference to the financial comfort of its aging statesmen. How unjust it was that there was no stipend set aside for the President's old age. "The Country which called into service an active, able and meritorious citizen placed him in various ... elevated situations, without the power or means of saveing for himself or family what his professional business would have enabled him to have done, at advance years can dismiss him to retirement (and poverty in the worlds sense)."

Though always submissive to God's inscrutable wisdom, Abigail was more than ever baffled by his methods. "He who permits not a sparrow to fall, unnoticed, assuredly overrules the more important interests and concerns of Kingdoms and nations." With the Federalists ousted, Abigail predicted "calamity" for America. But she claimed command of her own dominion. "If I did not rise with dignity," she declared with Puritan humility, "I can at least fall with ease, which is the more difficult task."[10]

Charles had died "without a groan," two days before the electors cast their ballots.[11] This death was not unexpected like the loss of her one-year-old Susanna in 1770 when Abigail was a young lawyer's wife in Boston nor a blight on innocence like the death of her sister Elizabeth's Betsy Q. But Charles's complicity in his own demise did not lessen the pain for a parent. Abigail canceled her levees and went into mourning. "I know, my much loved, Sister, that you will mingle in my sorrow, and weep with me over the Grave of a poor unhappy child," Abigail took comfort in the certainty of Mary's solicitude.[12] And she lent her own solicitude in a feeling letter to Charles's widow, writing:

> From my own thought and reflections I trace the sorrow of your soul and feel every pang which peines your Heart ... You have the consolation of having performed your duty, no remembrance of any unkindness has deterred your fulfilling it ... [Charles] was kind and affectionate, beloved by all his acquaintance, an Enemy to no one but a favorite where he went, in early life no child was more tender and amiable; but neither his mind or constitution could survive the habits he but too fatally persued ... May I be enabled in silence to bow myself in submission to my maker whose attributes are Mercy as well as judgments.

"The President sends his love to you and mourns, as he has for a long time, for you," Abigail closed her letter, meaningfully signing herself "Your affectionate Mother,"[13] thus binding herself to Sally for life.

And John dismissed the loss of the election, telling Thomas, "The melancholy decease of your brother is an affliction of a more serious nature . . . Oh! That I had died for him if that would have relieved him from his faults as well as his disease."[14]

IN QUINCY, IT WAS CLEAR that Parson Wibird was heading swiftly toward the next world. *His* final days, however, were untroubled by affection or remorse. His dearest wish was to avoid washing or changing clothes. His greatest struggle was to continue living independently in his current dwelling when, in Mary's words, "his life was in danger from every kind of vermin. He was cover'd with sores from his Shoulders to his Face" and clearly suffering from dementia compounded by lifelong stubbornness and aversion to work. He certainly confirmed Mary's conviction that bachelorhood was a grave mistake.

The community agreed it was "absolutely necessary to remove" the old preacher to the home of Captain Brackett, who generously volunteered to care for the parson in his basement room. The challenge was to convince 75-year-old Wibird to leave the saltbox house at the wind of a hill where for the past forty-five years he had looked down on the churchyard.

Predictably, Mary, now in robust health, took charge of the mission, which—in one of her most sumptuous letters to the First Lady—she makes sound like a military operation or a brawl with a big, grumpy, oppositional child. The day she scheduled for the move dawned unseasonably sultry. It took two men "to tear" Wibird's "Breeches drawers and woolen socks" from his tortured and reeking skin, "he threatning to scream murder all the time." Afterward, Mary laboriously redressed him in Richard's clean clothes lined with rags sluiced in ointment to poultice his livid rashes—receiving, of course, no thanks from him.

"Such an object of filth I am sure you never beheld," she continued. "We [had] sent a cart before to take away his Trunk, etc. . . . [and] spent several hours endeavouring to perswaid him of the necessity" that he follow his worldly goods. But "He was obstinate and cross, altho the Blood was streaming from his Shoulders and stomach."

All day Wibird oscillated between rage and docility. When Richard arrived and "told [the parson] that he should go and call'd the other Gentlemen to take hold of him and put him into the chaise," suddenly Wibird stopped resisting and "jumped of[f] the Bed and . . . came away very peacbly." But no sooner did he arrive at Captain Brackett's than his self-pity swelled. He had been "taken by violence," he bellowed to the Brackett household. Afterward a group of neighbors arrived and congratulated him on his change of life "as if he had just been married," and he beamed like a groom.

Richard Cranch devoted the next two days to placing his old friend's books on shelves and arranging his lifetime's possessions. "Every thing is neat and clean on and about him now and he looks like a human Being," Mary felt pleased to report.[15]

Abigail, responding, could scarcely disguise her contempt for the "forlorn creature," once witty and learned, who had now succumbed to a lifetime of sloth. Unlike Charles, Wibird lacked even the decency to rue what only he had brought upon himself. The "deeds of charity," lavished by her dear sister Mary, were wasted on this laggard. "Mr. Wibird is punished in life not for sins of commission but of omission," the worse of the two evils, in Abigail's opinion, for it flouted the sacred Puritan injunction to be useful on earth.[16]

IN ATKINSON, ELIZABETH GRIEVED the death of her nephew Charles, whom she had shepherded through adolescence, and feared that the change of administration in the capital harbingered the "scourge" of civil war. She knew certainly that it put her son, William, out of a job. And Jefferson was so "undisciplined" that, if elected, he would "set the world on fire," she direfully predicted. Her words specifically refer to Ovid's myth, where the mortal Phaeton nearly destroys the earth because he cannot steer his father the Sun God's chariot. But they also speak to the creative power of passion and, unconsciously perhaps, to Elizabeth's own youthful dreams of distinguishing herself in the world of letters and the fervor that ignited her still when she picked up her pen.[17]

In the winter of 801, the Atkinson Academy was prospering, and Elizabeth's growing daughter, Abby, was, at least for the time being, in good health. "We have a flock of fine Children," Elizabeth wrote Abigail of the promising new class at the Academy.[18] These young people called her mother, and she took great satisfaction in raising them as her own. "Perhaps you [would] smile if I [told] you . . . many parental duties devolved around your Sister—some [students] I had to encourage and direct, others, kindly to reprove, and admonish, though the latter is always disagreeable; for praise and approbation is more pleasing and congenial to my nature than reproofs."[19]

Elizabeth had come to terms with her dreams of distinguishing herself during her lifetime. She was too busy making ends meet to follow Madame de Sevigne into publishing fame. Still, she would not relinquish her ambition to make a difference in the world outside her parish. Educating boys and girls to build America would be her legacy, as would a small trove of delicately crafted letters to her sisters and particularly to Abigail, who preserved each precious note in her desk drawer.

Elizabeth knew she would never recover from her sorrows. It took only a single cough or threat of fever in Abby to rouse all the painful memories of her older sister's death. One day Elizabeth wrote Mary that the "repeated stroke" of calamity had "broken" her. "I feel as if I was only the shadow of what I once was as if only a little solitary piece of my heart remained."

But her native cheer, passion to be useful, and curiosity time and again revived her spirits. As when she had debated literature and politics with her cousin Isaac Smith from her father's parsonage, Elizabeth brought her fierce intelligence to bear on everything from child discipline to the mysteries of the universe. Typical was the irrepressible optimism embedded in a letter she wrote William at the turn of the century. A comet, she reported, had three weeks before suddenly appeared in the sky above Atkinson. Its provenance was obscure; its future path impossible to predict.

"From the slenderness of its body, and its complexion, we find its velocity is great. And from its frequent corruscations, which emited in a black and white colour, resembling *sheets of written paper* . . . it might be attended with some baneful, deleterious influences upon *our System*."

But Elizabeth could not accept such a dire interpretation. "As always I hope for the best," she declared, and chose to believe the meteor "a happy Omen" that "may terminate in auspicious Days."[20]

In January of 1801, Mary Cranch for once was not confined to performing deeds of mercy for Quincy's woebegone. She was preparing for her beloved sister to come home for good. During the Adamses long absences over the past decade, Mary and Cotton Tufts had transformed Peacefield—following Abigail's instructions, of course.

The home Abigail returned to now would be very different than the Boreland estate she had described as a "wren's house" in comparison to her European mansions when she had taken possession of it twelve years earlier. In 1797, Abigail had ordered the creation of a large new wing, so there was now a library that held all John's books on its second floor and a parlor for her own use below. Always preoccupied with light, she had added windows and fireplaces. The interior had been whitewashed many times over in the decade since Abigail left to

RESIDENCE OF EX PRESIDENT ADAMS.

As she retired from public life, Abigail was dreaming up
new improvements for her beloved Peacefield.

join the nation's first Vice President in New York. Still, it remained true to its original structure. Peacefield was classic New England Federalist, wood plank over wood plank, with no stone columns, tympanums, or other allusions to the Old World. It was a larger, more commodious version of the parsonage Abigail, Mary, and Elizabeth grew up in, the house of a minister—albeit a minister of state rather than a minister of the Lord. It was not and might never be finished, for Abigail was always dreaming up improvements. Right now, though, she was preoccupied with pine wood, which, she wrote Uncle Tufts, must be cut and corded for her impending arrival in Quincy. She needed her two-seat 'chariot"[21] mended and a commodious carriage built from scratch, for the Adamses would be leaving their current means of transport in the capital, to be inherited by either Jefferson or Burr.

Though John would have to remain in Washington until the inauguration of the new President on March 4, Abigail was planning to leave even before February 11, when the House was scheduled to vote. No matter that it was the worst season to travel. She felt as impelled to go home now as, thirty-five years before, she had been determined to

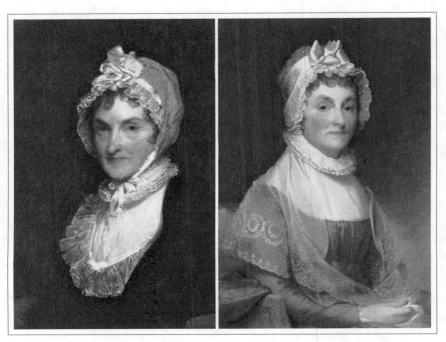

The similarities between Elizabeth Shaw Peabody (left) and Abigail Adams are unmistakable in these late-life portraits, both by Gilbert Stuart.

join the newly-wed Mary in Salem. Then there had only been "mole hills" between them. Now there were mountains and rivers as well.

But her courage did not fail her, nor did her lifelong determination to stare down defeat.

On the eve of her departure from Washington, Abigail took time to describe to her younger sister how it felt to confront obscurity after a quarter of a century in the public view. Her future was as unknowable as that of the comet over Atkinson. America, the mission of her generation, might any day dissolve like Rome. Still, she took heart from the very limits of the human imagination and set out for Quincy determined "not to become querilous with the world, not to molest or disturb the new . . . government but hoping for better prospects than present themselves now to our view."[22]

Epilogue

. . .

On February 11, 1801, the head of the Senate read the electoral ballots for President aloud to Congress.[1] As expected, the Federalists had lost, and Aaron Burr and Thomas Jefferson had each won 73 votes apiece. It now fell upon the House to select a winner. But a small group of Federalists were so determined to thwart the election of any Republican that it took seven days and thirty-five votes to break the deadlock. During that time, anything might have happened—coups, successions, even civil war. The model of bloody France hung over all the proceedings. Certainly, Federalists and Republicans both suspected the worst of their foes. But nothing momentous transpired. And while Jefferson called his first Republican Presidency nothing short of a "revolution," many others, Adams included, proclaimed a victory for the Union and government by law.

Yet, so bitter was Adams at his own loss and what he perceived as Jefferson's betrayal that he boarded a stage coach at 4 A.M. on March 4 to escape the inauguration later that day. During Jefferson's two terms in office, no word passed between them. Then, on a New Year's day well into Madison's Presidency, Adams sat down at his desk at Peacefield[2] to write Jefferson a brief note, concluding, "I am Sir with a long and sincere Esteem your Friend and Servant."[3] Jefferson swiftly replied: "A letter from you calls up recollections very dear to my mind. It carries me back to the times when, beset with difficulties and dangers, we were fellow laborers in the same cause, struggling for what is most valuable to man, his right of self-government." [4] What followed was perhaps the most fascinating correspondence in American history, ranging over everything under the sun and lasting fourteen years until Adams's and Jefferson's almost simultaneous deaths on July 4, 1825, the fiftieth anniversary of America's Declaration of Independence from the British King.

During the last days of his Presidency, John Adams appointed Mary's son William Cranch Judge for the circuit court of the District of Columbia. Five years later, Jefferson raised him to Chief Judge, and Mary's son went on to serve the court with honor for five decades. Though Mary and Richard were never strong enough to travel the 450 miles to the capital city, they sustained a close relationship with William and his family through the ever-improving postal system. Whenever William felt disheartened, he turned to his father in particular. And Richard never failed to assure him of human resilience—insisting that imagination "presents objects to our view through a very false medium. Bad is never so bad as imagined, good is never so good."[5]

When it came time for his own sons to prepare for college, William sent them to his aunt Elizabeth in Atkinson as he had been sent to her in Haverhill years before. He lived to be eighty-six, happy in his work and his family, and enjoyed the modest fame and prosperity that had always eluded his kin.

After his Uncle Adams lost the Presidency, leaving him jobless, Elizabeth's son William Shaw studied law and served for a few years as clerk of the U.S. district court in Boston. But William's first love was books, and in this respect at least he gratified his mother by becoming the first Secretary of the prestigious Boston Athenaeum library, where he served for sixteen years. Elizabeth never convinced William to socialize much less wed and start a family, but he did dig from his small savings to pay for his surviving sister to marry the man she loved. A decade later, William Shaw succumbed to the family curse of alcoholism and died in 1826 at forty-eight.

IN 1805, ABIGAIL'S YOUNGEST SON Tommy married Ann Harrod, daughter of the owner of the Mason Arms (the tavern and boarding house where George Washington kissed the young Betsy Quincy Shaw) in Haverhill. They settled near Abigail and John in Quincy and produced seven children, while Tommy dutifully followed his father's wishes and set up a law practice, served briefly in the Massachusetts legislature, and farmed. Thomas was a gifted letter-writer with a flair for business and a strong loyalty to his family. Unfortunately, as Abigail had noted years before, he was not cut out for law. Tommy failed in this career and became an alcoholic like his brother Charles and cousin William Shaw, dying when he was fifty in 1832.

John Quincy Adams more than made up for his younger brothers' failures. He served as Senator from Massachusetts under Jefferson and was appointed ambassador to Russia by Madison in 1809. After the fall of Napoleon, John Quincy followed in his father's footsteps to represent America at the Court of St. James in London. Abigail lived to see her eldest son appointed Secretary of State by President Monroe in 1817. In 1824, John Quincy was elected the sixth President of the United States, and though—again like his father—he lost his bid for a second term, he never retired from politics. He lived to be 81 and spent his last seventeen years in the U.S. Congress, where he carried his mother's torch, calling repeatedly for an end to the unequal treatment of the black race. He was survived by his youngest son Charles Frances Adams, who published the first volume of Abigail Adams's letters to her husband and friends.

Betsy Cranch Norton and Nabby Adams Smith both suffered bad luck in their marriages. Betsy's husband Jacob Norton remained a poor clergyman, avid to make long trips to clerical meetings and to socialize at home at the expense of his wife's health. Delicate physically and emotionally, Betsy lacked the stamina to single-handedly raise their eight children. Frequently ill and without the money to hire help, she relied heavily on Mary. If Betsy could move back into her parents' home for a substantial period of time, Abigail speculated, she might have a chance to fully recuperate.[6] But Betsy was determined to fulfill her role as homemaker and, following Mary's example, cared for her husband even when she was sick. "She is now a shadow," Abigail reported in 1810.[7] Betsy Norton died of consumption less than a year later at 48 and was eulogized as a paragon of female excellence. Those who knew her longest mourned her youthful aspirations, keen intelligence, and lively spirits. Her diaries record for posterity the feelings of a late eighteenth-century girl.

"Last Sunday morning arrived here through all the Dust and Heat of the week my dear Daughter," Abigail wrote her sister Elizabeth, in July, 1811. It was a doleful story. Nabby had driven six days in a shabby wagon from the small upstate New York farm to which Colonel Smith's speculations had reduced them. She was desperate for a re-union with her parents, whom she had not seen in three-and-a-half years, and they were too weak to travel to her. Another reason for Nab-by's heroic journey was that she had discovered a painful lump in her chest which was diagnosed as cancer and wanted a Boston physician to advise her about how to proceed. Though in great physical pain, she appeared as serene as ever. She was researching her cancer treatment with the same thoroughness that she applied to deciding whether to break her engagement to Royall Tyler over two decades before.

At the end of the summer—in an age when there was no anesthesia—Nabby decided to endure a long, excruciating operation, and the tumor was removed. That she was cured at first seemed certain, but less than a year later, the cancer returned. She survived a final trip from the up-state farm to die in her parents' house on August 15, 1813. She was 48, like her cousin Betsy. "Humble in prosperity; cheerful in affliction," one obituary eulogized Nabby's aversion both to display and self-pity.[8] Colonel Smith arrived a week before his wife's death and lived three years after. The Smiths were survived by two boys and an only daugh-ter. Though her grandmother stated time and again that this daughter Caroline Smith was not pretty, she was in all other ways a second Nabby for Abigail, and a healing bond developed between the two.

Lucy Greenleaf defied her mother's predictions and sustained a fifty-year marriage with a blind husband, using her steady hand to sign his documents, darning his socks, loving him through thick and thin. She was as even-tempered as Betsy Norton was excitable. Elizabeth gave a good description of her— "sensible, modest, gentle—tranquil—not greatly elated or depressed."[9] Lucy called on her superior intellect and knowledge of science to nurse her older sister, parents, cousin Nabby, and Aunt Abigail in their final illnesses. She bore seven chil-dren and lived to be 78.

Elizabeth's youngest daughter, Abigail Adams Shaw—known as Abbe—lead an unusual life for a woman of her era. Unlike her female cousins, she was formally educated at the Atkinson Academy where she met her husband, a classmate, Joseph Barlow Felt. Felt went on to study divinity at Dartmouth, and, after their marriage, in 1816, became a Congregational minister and then a noted antiquarian and writer on the subject of Massachusetts towns. In 1837, he was made librarian of the Massachusetts Historical Society, and appointments increased as his reputation grew. Unlike Elizabeth, who sacrificed her ambition to write to the demands of poverty and a large family, Abbe did not suffer grave financial worries nor—after she nearly died giving birth to a stillborn—could she have children of her own. She thus had the leisure to support causes like the anti-slavery movement and worked with her husband on his publications,[10] carrying on her mother's love of words.

"WHAT A WRECK DOES age and sickness make of the Human Frame!" Abigail exclaimed in an 1811 letter to Elizabeth.[11] "Such a struggle [we make] for existence, which appears scarce worth holding when obtained."

While their options diminished, Mary, Abigail, and Elizabeth clung tightly to each other, writing and visiting more frequently, mourning the deaths of nieces and nephews as if they were daughters and sons. Elizabeth made the difficult choice to leave her frail husband alone so she could nurse her eldest sister when she collapsed with a chest pain in meeting. [12]And while Abigail still swore by the elixir of a cheerful spirit and sent wine and sherry to all her relatives on the slimmest excuse, Mary, as in the days when she had led the search for a new preacher, lamented that she "belong[ed] to everyone," which included eight grandchildren after Betsy Norton's death.

As, early in life, they had dissected the agony of childbirth and traded lurid accounts of menopause in middle age, now they kept track of their own degeneration. "For four days and nights my face was so swelled and inflamed, that I was almost blind. It seemed my blood boiled," Abigail—with evident relish—described the onslaught of a virulent skin infection in a letter to Elizabeth.[13] And Mary grew so emaciated by tuberculosis, Abigail lamented, "her bones are almost bare." [14] They agreed that they were hopeless invalids. "We look old, withered, feeble and most good for nothing."[15]

But their lives were not all suffering. Abigail was cheered every time she received word from her younger sister, and Elizabeth thoroughly enjoyed hearing this once harsh critic repeatedly extol her prose. The popular British Gothic novelist Mrs. Radcliffe wrote not a wit better than the former Betsy Smith, Abigail insisted. And even in the Spring of 1811, when they were all weighed down by Betsy Cranch Norton's death, the mourning Elizabeth could still transport the mourning Abigail with a letter the latter placed "among my richest treasures."[16] And if nothing else helped, there was always Abigail's wine to fend off despair.

Sure as they were of Heaven, they were never ready to leave this world. Mary and Richard died, days apart, in 1811, while struggling to live for their grandchildren.[17] Elizabeth, healthy until the day before, went off in her sleep in the Spring of 1815, leaving an irreplaceable void in the Atkinson Academy that widened four years later when Stephen Peabody followed.[18]

Abigail, the middle child, lived the longest. There were moments when she still found reason to rejoice—"my heart glows with gratitude," she wrote at the end of an especially hard year, and she never lost her passion for the politics of churches or nations.[19] It has been speculated that she grew more conservative after Nabby's death because, in her agony, she seemed to be accepting the Calvinist belief in the divinity of Jesus Christ, when she wrote: "My own loss . . . can only be alleviated by the consoling belief that my Dear Child is partaking of the Life and immortality brought to Light by him who endured the cross."[20] And yet, just a few years later, she was arguing John Quincy into Unitarianism, insisting: "There is not any reasoning that can convince me, contrary to my senses, that three, is one, and one three."[21] In a late letter she appears bent on emphasizing the differences between the sexes, scorning "learned lad[ies]" like Madame de Stael and insisting, "Nature has assigned to each sex its particular duties and sphere of action."[22] But in a letter of the same era, she recommends one of Rousseau's most intellectually challenging volumes, *Letters From The Mountain,* as appropriate reading for young girls.[23] No single ideology could claim her, nor could any one party. She supported the Republican President Madison in the war of 1812 so strongly that she refused to attend church when Reverend Whitney preached the opposite view.

Abigail died of typhus fever, seven years before John and two years after Elizabeth.[4] Now the living cord was broken; Mary, Abigail, and Elizabeth lay buried in New England sod. But their letters were released into a wider sphere, and so they live on. Find these sisters in the history of their country and their sex.

Acknowledgments

. . .

S O MANY WONDERFUL PEOPLE AND INSTITUTIONS ENABLED THE creation of this book.

I would be ungrateful, indeed, if I did not first mention the capacious Massachusetts Historical Society, repository of most of the Adams, Cranch, and Shaw/Peabody letters and papers, which made this book possible in the first place. My particular thanks to Peter Drummey and Celeste Walker, who pointed me in the right direction, to Elaine Grublin and Sara Sikes, who made research from New York City infinitely easier by sending me early drafts of upcoming volumes of Adams family correspondence, and Anna Cook, who cheerfully endured my relentless search for images to accompany the text.

I am deeply grateful to Jaclyn Penny and all the librarians at the American Antiquarian Society, which holds Stephen Peabody's diary as well as most of Abigail's later letters to Mary; to the staff at the Library of Congress' Shaw/Peabody collection, where I found Elizabeth's teenage declarations to Isaac Smith; to the Albany Institute of History and Art, with its rich store of Cranch correspondence; to the learned Jaclyn Payne and her cohorts at the Haverhill Special Collections Library; to Kristi Wermager at Carleton College, who sent me large swathes of Betsy Cranch's diaries; to Ed Fitzgerald and Marianne Peak at the Quincy Historical Society; to Christa Zaros at the Long Island Carriage Museum; to Patricia Klingenstein and Eleanor Gillers at the New-York Historical Society; to Elisa Benavidez Hayes at the Arizona State University Art Museum; to New York's Mount Vernon Hotel

Museum and Garden; to Kimberly Reynolds and Sean Casey in the Rare Books section of the Boston Public Library; and to Catherine Wood, a floor below, at the Norman B. Leventhal Map Center.

Especially crucial to the writing of this book was Caroline Keinath of the Adams National Historical Park, who tirelessly supplied me with family images and arranged for a long and illuminating tour of the saltbox house where Abigail took up housekeeping, and of Peacefield, where the Adamses lived out their final days. My gratitude also to Ginny Karlis, who spent two afternoons shepherding me around a meticulous restoration of Reverend Smith's parsonage, where the sisters were born, and to Mike Ryan, who narrated the sad and sordid life of their brother, William Smith. Hope Patterson spent hours acquainting me with the differences between various branches of Congregationalism, while Parson Sheldon Wells Bennett recounted fascinating stories about Parson Wibird and the search for his successor at Quincy's First Congregational Church.

For encouragement and advice I want to thank Beryl Abrams, Dan Bergman, Edith Gelles, Jim Harvey, Marion Meade, Ruth Kaplan, and Anne Yarowsky. Mary and Justin Klein housed and fed me for long periods of undisturbed writing time in their beautiful Cape Cod house. I want to thank my own sister, Suzanne Davidson, who is the essence of loyalty, and am grateful to my father, Richard Alan Jacobs, whose lifelong interest in American history encouraged my own. Countless close friends have also contributed to my ideas about family.

Beryl Abrams, Ann Powell, Gerry Rabkin, and Anne Yarowsky responded perceptively to my early chapters. Betsy Lerner lent her time and profound insights to both my first and my final drafts. But my most consistent, most fastidious, most penetrating reader from start to finish has been Kathy Chamberlain, my friend and colleague, who purely by chance is the scion of Mary Cranch and the purveyor of many previously unseen treasures from the Cranch and Norton troves.

Thanks to the astute Ryan Buckley, Rebecca DiLiberto, and Betony Toht for their historical research; to Chris Ziegler-McPherson, for her resourceful fact-checking; and to the infinitely knowledgeable and fastidious Winny Lee, without whose assistance there would not be a single illustration here.

No one could wish for a more involved, generous, and gifted editor than Susanna Porter, whose optimism and understanding steadied me during some times I prefer not to recall. She has been ably assisted by the imaginative Dana Isaacson, who came up with most of my titles, and Priyanka Krishnan, who with great expertise (not to mention cheerfulness) led me through every step of production. Many thanks to Joseph Perez for my beautiful cover.

The book is dedicated to my unconquerable 90-year-old mother, and no list of tributes would be complete without mention of Gerry Rabkin, who passed away, and our daughter, Masha, who grew up, during the decade it took me to complete *Dear Abigail*.

Selected Bibliography

. . .

Ackroyd, Peter. *London: The Biography.* New York: Doubleday, 2001.

Adams, Abigail. *Letters of Mrs Adams, The Wife of John Adams,* introductory memoir by Charles Frances Adams. Boston: Wilkins, Carter, And Company, 1848.

Adams, Abigail. *New Letters of Abigail Adams,* edited by Stewart Mitchell. Boston: Houghton Mifflin, 1947.

Adams, Abigail. *The Adams Family in Auteuil, 1784–1785, As Told in the Letters of Abigail Adams,* with an introduction and notes by Howard C. Rice, Jr. Boston: Massachusetts Historical Society, 1956.

Adams Family Papers, 1639–1889, microfilm edition, 608 reels Boston: Massachusetts Historical Society, 1954–1959.

Adams, John and Abigail. *The Book of Abigail and John: Selected Letters of the Adams Family 1762–1784,* edited and with an introduction by L. H. Butterfield, Marc Friedlaender, and Mary-Jo Kline. Cambridge, MA: Harvard University Press, 1975.

Adams, John and Jefferson, Thomas. *The Adams-Jefferson Letters,* edited by Lester J. Cappon. Chapel Hill: The University of North Carolina Press, 1959.

Adams, John. *A Defence of the Constitutions of Government of the United States of America,* excerpts, with an introduction by Neal Pollack. New York: Akashic Books, 2004.

Adams, John. *The Adams Papers Diary and Autobiography of John Adams,* vol 1–4, ed. L. H. Butterfield. New York: Atheneum, 1964.

Adams, John. *The Earliest Diary of John Adams.* Cambridge, MA: Belknap, 1966.

Adams, John Quincy. *The Diary of John Quincy Adams, vols. 1 and 2.* Belknap Press, Harvard University, Cambridge 1982.

Alden, John R. *A History of the American Revolution.* New York: Knopf, 1969.

Applewhite, Harriet B. and Levy, Darline G., ed. *Women & Politics in the Age of Democratic Revolution.* Ann Arbor: University of Michigan Press, 1993.

Bailyn, Bernard. *The Ideological Origins of the American Revolution.* Cambridge, MA: Belknap Press, 1992.

Bailyn, Bernard. *To Begin the World Anew: The Genius and Ambiguities of the American Founders.* New York: Knopf, 2003.

Berkin, Carol. *A Brilliant Solution: Inventing the American Constitution.* New York: Harcourt, 2002.

Berkin, Carol. *Revolutionary Mothers: Women in the Struggle for American Independence.* New York: Knopf, 2005.

Bober, Natalie. *Abigail Adams: Witness To A Revolution.* Alladin Paperbacks, 1995.

Bobrick, Benson. *Angel in the Whirlwind,* New York: Penguin, 1998.

Boorstin, Daniel J. *The Americans: The Colonial Experience.* New York: Vintage, 1958.

Brewer, John. *The Pleasures of the Imagination: English Culture in the Eighteenth Century.* New York: Farrar Straus Giroux, 1997.

Brookhiser, Richard. *America's First Dynasty: The Adamses 1735–1918.* New York: Free Press, 2002.

Buckland, Gail. *The White House In Miniature.* New York: Norton, 1994.

Burrow, Edwin G. and Wallace, Mike. *Gotham: A History of New York City to 1898.* New York: Oxford, 1999.

Butterfield, L.H., ed., *Adams Family Correspondence, vol. 1.* Cambridge, MA: Belknap Press, 1963.

Butterfield, L.H., ed. *Adams Family Correspondence, vol 2.* Cambridge, MA: Belknap Press, 1963.

Butterfield, L.H. and Friedlaender, Marc. ed. *Adams Family Correspondence, vol 3.* Cambridge, MA: Belknap, 1973.

Butterfield, L.H. and Friedlaender, Marc, ed. *Adams Family Correspondence, vol 4.* Cambridge, MA: Belknap, 1973.

Caroli, Betty Boyd. *First Ladies: From Martha Washington to Michelle Obama.* New York: Oxford University Press, 2010.

Chernow, Ron. *Alexander Hamilton.* New York: Penguin, 2004.

de Tocqueville, Alexis. *Democracy In America,* vol 1. New York: Vintage, 1990

Douglas, Ann. *The Feminization of American Culture.* New York: Farrar, Straus and Giroux, 1998.

Earle, Alice Morse. *Home Life in Colonial Days.* Stockbridge MA: Berkshire House, 1993.

Ellis, Joseph J. *American Sphinx: The Character of Thomas Jefferson.* New York: Vintage Books, 1998.

Ellis, Joseph J. *Founding Brothers: The Revolutionary Generation.* New York: Vintage, 2000.

Ellis, Joseph J. *Passionate Sage: The Character and Legacy of John Adams.* New York: Norton, 2001.

Ellis, Joseph J. *His Excellency George Washington.* New York: Vintage, 2005.

Ferguson, Moira, ed. *First Feminists: British Women Writers 1578–1799.* Bloomington: Indiana University Press, 1985.

Ferling, John. *Adams vs. Jefferson: The Tumultuous Election of 1800.* New York: Oxford, 2004.

Fischer, David Hackett. *Paul Revere's Ride.* New York: Oxford, 1994.

Forbes, Esther. *Paul Revere and the World He Lived In.* Boston: Houghton Mifflin, 1999.

Franklin, Benjamin. *The Autobiography And Other Writings,* ed. L. Jesse Lemisch. New York: New American Library, 1961.

Gay, Peter. *The Enlightenment: The Science of Freedom.* New York: Norton, 1969.

Gelles, Edith B. *Abigail Adams: A Writing Life.* New York: Twayne, 1998.

Gelles, Edith B. *Abigail and John: Portrait of a Marriage.* New York: William Morrow, 2009.

Gelles, Edith B. *Portia: The World of Abigail Adams.* Bloomington and Indianapolis: Indiana University Press, 1992.

Greven, Philip. *The Protestant Temperament: Patterns of Child-Rearing, Religious Experience, and the Self in Early America.* New York: Knopf, 1977.

Hareven, Tamara K., ed. *Themes in the History of the Family.* Worcester: American Antiquarian Society, 1978.

Harris, Sharon M., ed. *Women's Early American Historical Narratives.* New York: Penguin, 2003.

Hawke, David Freeman. *Everyday Life In America.* New York: Harper & Row, 1988.

Hazlitt, Margaret. *The Journal of Margaret Hazlitt,* edited and annotated by Ernest J. Moyne. University of Kansas Press, 1967.

Holton, Woody. *Abigail Adams*. New York: Free Press, 2010.

Homberger, Eric. *The Historical Atlas of New York City*. New York: Henry Holt, 1994.

Jacobs, Diane. *Her Own Woman: The Life of Mary Wollstonecraft*. New York, Simon & Schuster, 2001.

Johnson, Paul. *A History of the American People*. New York: HarperCollins, 1998.

Jouve, Daniel. *Paris: Birthplace of the U.S.A.: A Walking Guide for the American Patriot*. Paris: Grund, 1994.

Kerber, Linda K. *Women of the Republic*. Chapel Hill: University of South Carolina Press, 1980.

Langdon, William Chauncy. *Everyday Things In American Life 1607–1776*. New York: Scribner's, 1937.

LaPlante, Eve. *American Jezebel: The Uncommon Life of Anne Hutchinson: The Woman Who Defied The Puritans*. New York: HarperCollins, 2004.

Larkin, Jack. *The Reshaping of Everyday Life 1790–1840*. New York: HarperCollins, 1989.

Larson, Edward J. and Winship, Michael P. *The Constitutional Convention: A Narrative History from the Notes of James Madison*. New York: Random House, 2005.

Levin, Phyllis Lee. *Abigail Adams: A Biography*. New York: St. Martin's Press, 2001.

Marsden, George M. *Jonathan Edwards: A Life*. New Haven: Yale University Press, 2003.

Marshall, Megan. *The Peabody Sisters: Three Women Who Ignited American Romanticism*. New York: Houghton Mifflin, 2005.

McCullough, David. *1776*. New York: Simon & Schuster, 2005.

McCullough, David. *John Adams*. New York: Simon & Schuster, 2001.

Morgan, Edmund S. *Benjamin Franklin*. New Haven: Yale University Press, 2002.

Morgan, Edmund S. *Inventing the People: The Rise of Popular Sovereignty in England and America*. New York: Norton, 1989.

Morgan, Edmund S. *The Birth of the Republic 1763–89*. Chicago: University of Chicago Press, 1992.

Morgan, Edmund S. *The Puritan Family: Religion and Domestic Relations in Seventeenth-Century New England*. New York: Harper & Row, 1966.

Mossiker, Frances. *Madame de Sevigne: A Life and Letters*. New York: Columbia University Press, 1985.

Nagle, Paul. *The Adams Women: Abigail and Louisa Adams, Their Sisters and Daughters*. New York: Oxford, 1987.

Norton, Mary Beth and Alexander, Ruth M., ed. *Major Problems in American Women's History*. New York, Houghton Mifflin, 2003.

Oliver, Andrew. *Portraits of John and Abigail Adams*. Cambridge, Massachusetts: Belknap Press, 1967.

Paine, Thomas. *Common Sense*. New York: Penguin, 1986.

Paine, Thomas. *Rights of Man*. New York: Penguin, 1984.

Pleck, Elizabeth. *Domestic Tyranny: The Making of American Social Policy against Family Violence from Colonial Times to the Present*. Urbana: University of Illinois Press, 2004.

Porter, Roy. *English Society in the Eighteenth Century*. London: Penguin, 1990.

Richardson, Samuel. *Sir Charles Grandison*. New York: Oxford, 1986.

Roof, Katharine Metcalf. *Colonel William Smith And Lady: The Romance of Washington's Aide and Young Abigail Adams*. Boston: Houghton Mifflin, 1929.

Ryerson, Richard Alan, ed. *Adams Family Correspondence vol 5*. Cambridge, MA: Belknap, 1993.

Ryerson, Richard Alan, ed. *Adams Family Correspondence vol 6*. Cambridge, MA: Belknap, 1993.

Ryerson, Richard Alan. "The Limits of a Vicarious Life: Abigail Adams and Her Daughter." In *Proceedings of the Massachusetts Historical Society*, Volume C, 1988. Boston: Northeastern University Press 1989.

Schama, Simon. *Citizens*. New York: Knopf, 1989.

Schiff, Stacy. *A Great Improvisation: Franklin, France, and the Birth of America*. New York: Henry Holt, 2005.

Silverman, Kenneth. *A Cultural History of the American Revolution*. New York: Thomas Y. Crowell, 1976.

Silverman, Kenneth. *The Life and Times of Cotton Mather*. New York: Harper & Row, 1984.

Sprigg, June. *Domestic Beings*. New York: Knopf, 1984.

Stuart, Nancy Rubin. *The Muse of the Revolution: The Secret Pen of Mercy Otis Warren and the Founding of a Nation*. Beacon, MA: Beacon Books, 2008.

Tanselle, Thomas G. *Royall Tyler*. Cambridge MA: Harvard University Press, 1967.

Taylor, C. James, ed. *Adams Family Correspondence vol 7*. Cambridge, MA: Belknap, 2005.

Taylor, C. James, ed. *Adams Family Correspondence vol 8*. Cambridge, MA: Belknap, 2007.

Taylor, C. James, ed. *Adams Family Correspondence vol 9*. Cambridge, MA: Belknap, 2009.

Taylor, C. James, ed. *Adams Family Correspondence vol 10*. Cambridge, MA: Belknap, 2011.

Taylor, C. James, ed. *Adams Family Correspondence vol 11*. Cambridge, MA: Belknap, 2013.

Tillyard, Stella. *A Royal Affair: George III And His Scandalous Siblings*. New York: Random House, 2006.

Todd, Janet. *The Sign of Angelica: Women, Writing, and Fiction 1660–1800*. New York: Columbia University Press, 1989.

Ulrich, Laurel Thatcher. *The Age of Homespun: Objects and Stories in the Creation of an American Myth*. New York: Knopf, 2001.

Ulrich, Laurel Thatcher. *A Midwife's Tale: The Life of Martha Ballard, Based on Her Diaries 1785–1812*. New York: Knopf, 1990.

Whatman, Susanna. *The Housekeeping Book of Susanna Whatman*. London: Century Hutchinson, Ltd., 1987.

Wills, Gary. *Explaining America: The Federalist*. New York: Penguin, 1982.

Wills, Gary. *Inventing America*. Boston: Houghton Mifflin, 2002.

Wineapple, Brenda. *Hawthorne: A Life*. New York: Knopf, 2003.

Withey, Lynne. *Dearest Friend: A Life of Abigail Adams*. New York: Touchtone, 2002.

Wollstonecraft, Mary. *A Vindication of the Rights of Woman*. New York: Penguin, 1985.

Wood, Gordon S. *The Americanization of Benjamin Franklin*. New York: Penguin, 2004.

Wood, Gordon S. *The Creation of the American Republic 1776–1789*. Chapel Hill: University of North Carolina Press, 1998.

Wood, Gordon S. *Empire of Liberty: A History of the Early Republic, 1789–1815*. New York: Oxford, 2009.

Wood, Gordon S. *The Radicalism of the American Revolution*. New York: Knopf, 1992.

Zagarri, Rosemarie. *Revolutionary Backlash: Women and Politics in the Early American Republic*. Philadelphia: University of Pennsylvania Press, 2007.

Notes

. . .

A LIST OF THE ABBREVIATIONS USED IN THE NOTES SECTION:

AA	—	Abigail Adams
AFC	—	Adams Family Correspondence
A/J Letters	—	*The Adams-Jefferson Letters*
Angel	—	*Angel in the Whirlwind*
ESP	—	Elizabeth Shaw Peabody
JA	—	John Adams
JQA	—	John Quincy Adams
Letters	—	*Letters of Mrs. Adams, the Wife of John Adams,* collected by Charles Francis Adams
LOC	—	Library of Congress
MC	—	Mary Cranch
MHS	—	Massachusetts Historical Society
MHS microfilm	—	*Adams Family Papers,* 1639–1889, microfilm edition 608 reels (Boston: Massachusetts Historical Society, 1954–1959)
MOW	—	Mercy Otis Warren
New Letters	—	*New Letters of Abigail Adams*
RC	—	Richard Cranch
TA	—	Thomas Adams
TJ	—	Thomas Jefferson
WC	—	William Cranch
WS	—	William Smith

CHAPTER 1

1. Letter from AA to MC 7/15/1766, AFC vol. 1, pp. 5
2. Ibid.

3. Letter from AA to MC 6/27/1776. Mount Vernon Hotel Museum and Garden.

4. Letter from MC to AA 1/15/1767, AFC vol. 1, pp. 59–60.

5. Letter from AA to JA 11/11/1783, AFC vol. 5, pp. 266–269. In the eighteenth century, "rheumatic fever" was a variation of inflammatory fever, which attacked the joints and caused swelling and high fever. It often, as in Abigail's case, began in childhood and continued chronically throughout later life. The tendency to rheumatic fever was hereditary, and Abigail's son Thomas would suffer as severely as she did. Often, the disease struck with the change of seasons—fall into winter and winter into spring. The treatment was bleeding, a light diet, mustard, wine, an ounce of the "Peruvian bark" (which contained quinine) and bed rest even after the fever abated. Dr. Buchan, an expert of the era, recommended that the patient wear flannel next to the skin.

6. *New Letters,* 4/21/1790, pp. 45–46.

7. Letter from ESP to AA and JA 6/22/1788, AFC vol. 8, pp. 275–276.

8. Letter from Elizabeth Smith to JA 10/14/1774, AFC vol. 1, pp. 168–169.

9. According to the first Puritans, there was nothing you could do to gain salvation. Performing virtuous deeds and living an upright life were signs that you'd been blessed, not ways to get to Heaven. Whether you were saved or not was predetermined by God. However, by the time the Smith children were born, this view had been tempered so that many Congregationalists believed, like Reverend Smith, that eternal life was a reward for doing good on earth.

10. Their father was given first choice of a pew, and the family sat in number 10.

11. Letter from AA to MC 7/4/1790, *New Letters,* pp. 53–54.

12. Letter from AA to MC 11/26/1799, ibid., pp. 215–217.

13. The friend was Parson Wibird. Summer 1759, *Diary and Autobiography of JA,* vol. 1, pp. 108–109.

14. Diaries of William Smith in Proceedings of the Mass. Historical Society 10/1908–6/1909, volume 42, recordings on 4/23/51, 8/7/51, 9/1/51.

15. *Diary and Autobiography of JA,* vol. 1 entry 11/19/1760, p. 170.

16. Hazlitt, Margaret, *The Journal of Margaret Hazlitt,* University of Kansas Press, 1967, p. 64.

17. Letter from JA to AA 7/7/1775 AFC vol. 1, pp. 241–243.

18. Letter from AA to MC 1/31/1767, AFC vol. 1, pp. 60–62.

19. Letter from Elizabeth Smith to WS 4/28/1763, LOC, Papers of William Cranch.

20. I surmised as much because Mary later wrote her own son Billy in 8/1783, "I have always been afraid that you would not have so great an affection for your sisters as they have for you. I do not think that Brothers in general have." LOC, Papers of William Cranch.

21. Kerber, K. Linda, *Women of the Republic,* University of North Carolina Press, 1980, p. 193.

22. Letter from Elizabeth Smith to WS 4/28/1763, LOC, Papers of William Cranch.

23. Ibid.

24. Letter from Elizabeth Smith to WS 4/28/1763, LOC, Papers of William Cranch.

25. Letter from MC to AA 6/10/1798, MHS microfilm.

26. Letter from MC to AA 7/30/1789, AFC vol. 8, pp. 393–395.

27. Letter from ESP to MC 3/20/1785, LOC, Shaw Family Papers.

28. Obituary of Elizabeth Quincy Smith, *New England Chronicle or Essex Gazette,* 10/19/1775.

29. Letter from MC to AA 4/11/1800, MHS microfilm.

30. Letter from AA to ESP 6/10/1801, MHS microfilm.
31. Letter from AA to MC 10/?/1787, AFC vol. 8, pp. 192–194.
32. *Diary and Autobiography of JA,* vol. 1, pp. 273–275.
33. ESP to Isaac Smith, date illegible, LOC, Shaw/Peabody Collection.
34. Gregory, Dr. John, *A Father's Legacy to His Daughters.*
35. Letter from AA to Lucy Cranch 8/27/1785, AFC vol. 6, pp. 312–314.
36. Letter from AA to JA 9/23/1776, AFC vol. 2, pp. 133–134.
37. Anderson, Howard, Daghlian, Philip B., Elrenpreis, Irvin, ed.; *The Familiar Letter in the 18th Century,* University of Kansas Press, 1966, p. 273.
38. Ibid., p. 45.
39. Letter from AA to MC 5/26/1798, *New Letters,* pp. 179–182.
40. Letter from AA to Lucy Cranch 8/27/1785, AFC vol. 6, pp. 312–314.
41. Letter from AA to MC 10/6/1766, AFC vol. 1, pp. 55–56.
42. Letter from Mary Cranch Palmer to MC 10/9/1765, Historic New England collection, Boston, Mass.
43. The friend is John Adams, who also writes in *Diary and Autobiography of JA,* summer of 1759, vol. 1, p. 108: "Cranch was fond of his Friend . . . and would have been fond of his Wife and Children" if he had them.
44. Letter from John Thaxter to AA 8/16/1782, AFC vol. 4, pp. 362–364.
45. Letter from Mary Cranch Palmer to MC 10/9/1765, Historic New England collection, Boston, Mass.
46. RC's "an account of myself for the Information of My Posterity," Cranch Family Papers, MHS.
47. Sibley's Harvard Graduates, vol. 2, pp. 370–376.
48. Letter from AA to ESP 5/21/1798, MHS microfilm.
49. Letter from ESP to MC 6/6/1785, MHS microfilm.
50. Letter from ESP to Isaac Smith, Jr. 6/10/1769, LOC, Shaw Family Papers.
51. Letter from ESP to Isaac Smith, Jr. 4/13/1768 AFC vol. 1, pp. 63–66.
52. *Earliest Diary of John Adams,* vol. 1, p. 46 and p. 51.
53. Ibid., p. 52.
54. *Diary and Autobiography of JA,* vol. 1, pp. 93–94.
55. Ibid., pp. 108–109.
56. Ibid., p. 73.
57. Ibid., p.76.
58. Ibid., Letter to Samuel Quincy, p. 67.
59. Briant won the case, which accused him of being an Arminian, but he died shortly afterward.
60. See letter from RC to JA 10/1756, The Adams Papers, vol. 1, pp. 23–24.
61. Letter from JA to Abigail Smith 4/20/1763, AFC, vol.1, pp. 4–6.
62. Letter from JA to AA 2/12/1793 and AA to JA 8/11/1763, pp. 18–19, *The Book of Abigail and John.*
63. Letter from AA to JA 4/12/1764, pp. 28–30, ibid.
64. Letter from JA to Abigail Smith 2/14/1763, AFC vol. 1, p. 3.
65. Letter from MC to AA 9/24/1786, AFC vol. 7, pp. 341–344.
66. Harriet Norton Young recalls being told this story in "Some Letters of Jacob Norton, assembled by Kathy Chamberlain." She notes that this passage comes from 10 Luke 38–43 in the 1611 King James Bible.
67. *Diary and Autobiography of JA,* vol. 1, 12/28/1762.

68. The passage is from Matthew 11:18.
69. Letter from RC to WC 6/18/1811, MHS, Cranch Family Papers.
70. Wills, Garry, *Inventing America,* pp. 100–114.
71. Letter from Mary Palmer to MC 10/9/1765, Historic New England.
72. Letter from JA to AA 4/1764. AFC vol. 1, pp. 16–19. In fn 11 on p. 19 AFC identifies the "Betcy" JA refers to as Abigail's sister. I think its position makes it clear that the reference is to baby Betsy Cranch.
73. Letter from JA to RC 9/23/1767, AFC vol. 1, p. 63.
74. Letter from AA to MC 10/13/1766, AFC vol. 1, pp. 57–59.
75. *Diary and Autobiography of JA,* vol. 1, entry 11/3, pp. 319–320.

CHAPTER 11

1. In a letter from AA to MC 7/15/1766, AFC vol. 1, pp. 53–55, Abigail writes: "I have had upon a visit here, from Saturday till Tuesday Mr. Samll. Adams and wife, and indeed Sister they are a charming pair. In them is to be seen the tenderest affection towards each other, without any fulsome fondness, and the greatest Complasance, delicacy and good breeding that you can immagine, yet separate from any affectation . . . Had you been at [your old house in the Germantown section of Braintree] you should have been an Eye Witness of what I have told you."
2. Bobrick, Benson, *Angel,* Penguin Books, 1998, p. 75.
3. A very modest plan for united defense (basically the work of Benjamin Franklin) was proposed by delegates to the 1754 Albany Congress, but their constituencies at home turned it down. Ben Franklin mocked the disunity of the colonies in his famous cartoon showing a snake sliced in pieces under the banner "Unite or Die."
4. *Diary and Autobiography of JA,* vol. 1, pp. 12–16.
5. Ibid., vol. 1, pp. 92–93.
6. Ibid., vol. 1, pp. 74–75.
7. CFA, *Three Episodes of Mass. History,* pp. 642–643.
8. There is an excellent discussion of the Puritan vision of order and of the seventeenth-century theologian John Norton's writing on the subject in the first chapter of Edmund S. Morgan's *The Puritan Family.*
9. *Diary and Autobiography of JA,* pp. 279–280.
10. Ibid.
11. MC to AA 1/15/1767, AFC vol. 1, pp. 59–60.
12. Letter from JA to RC 6/29/1766, AFC vol. 1, pp. 52–53.
13. Letter from MC to Billy Cranch 5/22/1785, LOC, Cranch Family Manuscripts.
14. Wills, Gary, *Inventing America,* pp. 101–102. See Wills' brilliant discussion of David Rittenhouse and the 18th c. clock in chapters 7 and 8, pp. 100–114.
15. Letter from MC to AA 12/22/87, Cranch Collection at Albany Institute.
16. Letter from AA to MC 10/13/1766, AFC vol. 1, pp. 56–57.
17. Ibid.
18. Letter from WS to RC 6/10/67, Cranch Collection at Albany Institute.
19. MC to AA 1/15/67, AFC vol. 1, pp. 59–60.
20. AA to MC 6/27/1766 (my dating, it has been officially dated 1776, but the content strongly suggests it was written a decade earlier), Mount Vernon Hotel Museum and Garden, 421 East 61st Street, New York, NY 10021.
21. Diary entry in *Diary and Autobiography of JA* 7/22/71, pp. 45–47.

22. Hawke, David Freeman, *Everyday Life in Early America,* p. 59; Hawke points out that the mortality for mothers was low in New England compared not only to deaths in the south, but in the rest of the western world.

23. See Larkin, Jack, *The Reshaping of Everyday Life: 1790–1840,* pp. 94–98.

24. See chapters 34–36, Boorstin, Daniel J., *The Americans: The Colonial Experience.*

25. Letter from AA to MC 4/21/1790, *New Letters,* p. 45.

26. In chapter 2 of *The Age of Homespun,* Laurel Thatcher Ulrich beautifully depicts the process of spinning in the seventeenth and eighteenth centuries. On pp. 91–92 she writes, "Some writers refer to spinning as unskilled work. They have obviously never tried it. A good spinning wheel helped, but a spinner's ability to draw evenly, maintain the right tension on the yarn, and control the speed of twisting was what really determined the quality of the finished product."

27. Letter from AA to MC 1/31/1767, AFC vol. 1, pp. 60–62, fn2.

28. Evangelicals were not alone in supporting sewing circles, but George Whitfield's followers were in the vanguard of the movement. See pp. 176–191 in Laurel Thatcher Ulrich's *The Age of Homespun* for an informative discussion of the evangelical impact on colonial politics.

29. Letter from ESP to Isaac Smith 10/9/1768, LOC.

30. Letter from AA to Isaac Smith 4/20/1771, AFC vol. 1, pp. 76–78.

31. *Diary and Autobiography of JA,* vol. 2, entry 11/21/1772, p. 67.

32. Ibid., vol. 1, entry 2/19/1756, p. 8.

33. Letter from AA to MOW 7/24/1775, AFC vol. 1, pp. 254–255.

34. Letter from AA to MOW ante 2/27/1774, AFC vol. 1, pp. 97–99.

35. Letter from AA to Isaac Smith, Jr. 4/20/1771, AFC vol. 1, pp. 76–78.

36. Between 1763 and 1783, Catharine Macaulay wrote an 8-volume history of England. Mary Wollstonecraft called her "the woman of the greatest abilities, undoubtedly, that this country has ever produced." (Wollstonecraft, Mary, *Vindication,* p. 206.)

37. Ibid.

38. Hill, Bridget, *The Republican Virago: The Life and Times of Catherine Macaulay, Historian,* Oxford Clarendon Press, 1992.

39. Fraise, Genevieve, *Reason's Muse: Sexual Difference and the Birth of Democracy,* Chicago and London: University of Chicago Press, 1994; see chapter 1.

40. Juliana Seymour, *On the Management and Education of Children: A Series of Letters Written to a Niece,* London, 1754; this book is sometimes credited to John Hill.

41. Letter from AA to John Thaxter, 2/15/1778, AFC vol. 2, pp. 390–393.

42. On Lord Chesterton's Letters, see JA to AA 4/12/1776, AFC vol. 2, pp. 376–377, and AA to JA 4/21/1776, AFC vol. 2, pp. 389–391. In the last letter, AA tells JA, "I give up my Request for Chesterfields Letters submitting intirely to your judgment, as I have ever found you ready to oblige me in this way whenever you thought it would contribute either to my entertainment or improvement."

43. Abigail speaks of her similarity to John in a 9/12/1763 letter, AFC vol. 1, pp. 8–10, where she writes of their natures: "Whether they have both an eaquil quantity of Steel, I have not yet been able to discover, but do not imagine they are either of them deficient."

44. Letter from AA to JA 9/22/1774, AFC vol. 1, pp. 161–163.

45. Letter from AA to JA 8/19/1774, AFC vol. 1, pp. 142–143.

46. *Diary and Autobiography of JA,* vol. 2, entry 3/5/1773, p. 79.

47. The quotes in this paragraph are from McCullough, David, pp. 67–68. The ideas are mine.

48. *Diary and Autobiography of JA,* vol. 2, entry 3/5/1773, p. 79.
49. AA to JQA 2/1/1813, MHS microfilm.
50. Abigail's first mention of this second daughter comes in a 1788 letter explaining Nabby's frequent silences to her new husband's mother: "The Relationship of sister is a Character [Nabby] has no remembrance of, and must in some measure plead for her Native reserve." Letter from AA to Margaret Smith, 4/22/1788, AFC vol. 8, pp. 246–247.
51. The only duty that remained was a small symbolic tax on tea.
52. *Diary and Autobiography of JA,* vol. 2, entry 5/9/1771, pp. 12–13.
53. Ibid., entry 7/23/1771, p. 47.
54. Letter from JQA to Betsy Cranch, undated AFC postulates 1773 because of handwriting, AFC, vol. 1, p. 91.
55. Letter from JA to AA 7/7/1775, AFC vol. 1, pp. 241–243.
56. Letter from AA to MC 1774?, AFC vol. 1, pp. 176–177.
57. Letter from ESP to MC 2/7/1778, LOC, Shaw Family Papers.
58. Letter from ESP to Nabby 11/19/1785, AFC vol. 6, pp. 459–462.
59. Letter from ESP to Isaac Smith preceding letter of 9/10/1771, LOC.
60. Letter from ESP to Isaac Smith 9/10/1771, LOC.
61. Letter from ESP to JA 10/14/1774, AFC vol. 1, pp. 168–170.
62. Letter from ESP to Isaac Smith 6/10/1768, LOC.
63. Letter from ESP to Nabby, 2/14/1786, AFC vol. 7, pp. 57–59.
64. Letter from ESP to Isaac Smith 8/?/?, preceding letter of 9/10/71, 1771, LOC.
65. Letter from ESP to Isaac Smith 9/10/71, LOC.
66. Letter from ESP to Isaac Smith 12/30/1771, LOC.
67. Bobrick, Benson, *Angel,* pp. 82–83.
68. *Diary and Autobiography of JA,* 11/21/1772, vol. 2, pp. 67–68.
69. For reference to civil war, see letter from AA to Mercy Otis Warren, 12/5/1773, AFC vol. 1, pp. 88–90.
70. Letter from Isaac Smith to MC 10/20/1774, AFC vol. 1, pp. 174–176.
71. Letter from MC to Isaac Smith, AFC vol. 1, pp. 171–172.
72. *Diary and Autobiography of JA,* vol. 2, 12/17/1773, pp. 85–87.
73. Letter from ESP to JA 10/14/1774, AFC vol. 1. pp. 168–170.

CHAPTER III

1. Pages on Bridgewater from Mary O'Connell (librarian), Bridgewater Library.
2. *JQA Diary,* p. 398. JQA reports a conversation where he told his uncle John Shaw that "self was the ultimate motive of all actions, good, bad, or indifferent." Shaw opposed the idea and chastised his nephew for disputing with an elder.
3. Letter from AA to MC, 1774?, AFC, vol. 1, pp. 176–177.
4. Unless noted, the quotes in the above paragraph are from ES to AA 2/8/1774, AFC vol. 1, pp. 94–96 and ES to AA 3/7/1774, AFC vol. 1, pp. 103–106.
5. Ibid.
6. See the reference to hops in letter from MC to EC 3/29/1775, Kathy Chamberlain private collection.
7. Letter from MC to AA 8/20/1774, AFC vol. 1, pp. 143–144.
8. Letter from AA to JA 10/16/1774, AFC vol. 1, pp. 172–174.
9. Kerber, Linda K., *Women of the Republic,* p. 35.

10. Letter from RC to "B-c" 9/4/1772, Albany Institute.
11. Ibid.
12. Letter from MC to AA 8/20/1774, AFC vol. 1, pp. 143–144.
13. Letter from MC to AA 12/23/85, AFC, vol. 6, pp. 499–502.
14. In a letter to Richard on 9/18/1774, AFC vol. 1, pp. 159–160, John urges his brother-in-law to "Break open my Letters to my Wife, and then send them as soon as possible."
15. Letter from JA to AA 9/29/1774, vol. 1, pp. 160–161.
16. *Angel,* p. 93.
17. All his life, John Quincy Adams remained grateful to Dr. Warren for sparing him an amputation.
18. Letter from JA to AA 9/18/1774, AFC vol. 1, pp. 157–158.
19. Letter from JA to AA (delivered by Paul Revere) 10/9/1774, AFC vol. 1, pp. 166–167.
20. Letter from AA to JA 9/14/1774, AFC vol. 1, pp. 151–155.
21. Letter from AA to Mercy Otis Warren 2/1775, AFC vol. 1, pp. 183–186.
22. Letter from MC to Betsy Cranch, 3/29/1775, Kathy Chamberlain private collection.
23. Interview with Michael Ryan.
24. Letter from AA to JA 6/22/1775, AFC vol. 1, pp. 225–226.
25. Apparently, Billy blamed his delay on a stolen horse, but a drinking bout seems the more likely cause.
26. Interview with Michael Ryan.
27. Letter from AA to JA 7/5/1775, AFC vol. 1, pp. 239–241.
28. Letter from RC to JA 7/22/1775, AFC vol. 1, pp. 258–260.
29. Letter from AA to JA 7/12/1775, AFC vol.1, pp. 243–245.
30. A Frenchman, Charles Rollins, wrote popular histories, such as *The Ancient History* and *The Roman History,* both of which John Adams owned.
31. Letter from AA to JA 6/16?/1775, AFC vol. 1, pp. 217–220.
32. Letter from JA to AA 6/11 and 6/17/1775, AFC vol. 1, pp. 215–217.
33. Letter from JA to AA 5/26/1775, AFC vol. 1, pp. 206–207.
34. Letter from AA to JA 5/4/1775, AFC vol. 1, pp. 192–194.
35. Letter from AA to JA 10/9/1795, AFC vol. 1, pp. 296–299.
36. Letter from AA to Mercy Otis Warren 8/27/1775, AFC vol. 1, pp. 275–276.
37. Letter from JA to AA 5/29/1775, AFC vol. 1, pp. 207–208.
38. Letter from JA to AA 6/13/1775, AFC vol. 1, pp. 222–224.
39. Letter from AA to JA 7/9/1774, AFC vol. 1, pp. 134–137.
40. Letter from AA to JA 5/7/1775, AFC vol. 1, pp. 194–195.
41. Letter from AA to JA 5/22/1775, AFC vol. 1, pp. 204–206.
42. Letter from AA to JA 6/25/1775, AFC vol. 1, pp. 230–233.
43. Letter from AA to MC 3/15/1800, MHS microfilm.
44. Letter from JA to AA 7/7/1775, AFC vol. 1, pp. 241–243.
45. Letter from AA to JA 10/15/1774, AFC vol. 1, pp. 172–174.
46. The hill was actually Breec's Hill, which stands beside Bunker.
47. Letter from AA to JA 6/25/1775, AFC vol. 1, pp. 230–233.
48. Letter from AA to JA 6/18/1775, AFC vol. 1, pp. 222–224.
49. Letter from AA to JA 6/25/1775, AFC vol. 1, pp. 230–233.
50. Letter from AA to JA 7/4/1775, AFC vol. 1, pp. 238–241.
51. Interview with Michael Ryan.
52. Letter from JA to AA 7/24/1775, AFC vol. 1 pp. 255–258.
53. Ibid.

54. This is one of two letters the British intercepted and printed in their newspapers. The other, to James Warren, singled John Dickinson out for ridicule and caused many delegates to turn against Adams.

55. Letter from AA to JA 7/16/1775, AFC vol. 1, pp. 245–251.

56. Letter from AA to JA 7/25/1775, AFC vol. 1, pp. 260–264.

57. John wrote in his autobiography that he blamed Dickinson for the burning of Charleston: "I have always imputed the Loss of Charleston, and of the brave Officers and Men who fell there, and the Loss of an Hero of more Worth than all the Town, I mean General Warren, to Mr. Dickinson's petition to the King, and . . . to his subsequent unceasing though finally unavailing Efforts against Independence," which "impeded and parralized" the formation of an Army capable to withstand the British attack (vol. 3, p. 324).

58. Letter from AA to JA 6/25/1775, AFC vol. 1, pp. 230–233.

59. Letter from AA to JA 7/16/1775, AFC vol. 1, pp. 245–251.

60. Letter from JA to AA 7/23/1775, AFC vol. 1, pp. 252–254.

61. Letter from AA to JA 8/10/1775, AFC vol. 1, pp. 272–273.

62. Ibid.

63. Letter from AA to Mercy Otis Warren, 8/27/1775, AFC vol. 1, pp. 275–276.

64. What was not known in the 18th century was that dysentery was spread by flies as well as contact with infected feces.

65. Letter from AA to JA 10/9/1775, AFC vol. 1, pp. 296–299.

66. The quotes in the above two paragraphs come from Letter from AA to JA 9/8/1775, AFC vol. 1, pp. 276–278 and letter from AA to JA 9/16/1775, AFC vol. 1, pp. 278–280.

67. Letter from AA to JA 9/25/1775, AFC vol. 1, pp. 284–285.

68. Ibid.

69. Letter from AA to JA 10/9/1775, AFC vol. 1, pp. 296–299.

70. Letter from AA to JA 10/22/1775, AFC vol. 1, pp. 309–311.

71. This eulogy, printed in the *New England Chronicle* or *Essex Gazette* on 10/19/1775 was probably written by Richard Cranch, who retains a first draft in his files, now at the Albany Institute.

72. Letter from JA to AA 10/13/1775, AFC vol. 1, pp. 300–301.

73. Letter from JA to AA 10/29/1775, AFC vol. 1, pp. 316–317.

CHAPTER IV

1. The bluestocking Mary Wortley Montagu first observed the inoculating process when her husband was British ambassador to Turkey. She introduced smallpox inoculation in London in 1721. Cotton Mather was so inspired by her reports that he brooked powerful opposition to introduce it to the colonies.

2. Letter from JA to AA 10/29/1775, AFC vol. 1, pp. 317–318.

3. Letter from AA to JA 10/21/1775, AFC vol. 1, pp. 305–309.

4. Letter from AA to JA 11/27/1775, AFC vol. 1, pp. 328–331.

5. Letter from AA to JA 11/12/1775, AFC vol. 1, pp. 324–326.

6. Letter from JA to AA 11/27/1775, AFC vol. 1, pp. 328–331.

7. Letter from JA to AA 10/7/1775, AFC vol. 1, pp. 294–296.

8. Letter from JA to AA 10/29/1775, AFC vol. 1, pp. 318–319.

9. Letter from AA to JA 12/10/1775, AFC vol. 1, pp. 335–338.

10. Women in all the colonies made these coats for the soldiers and sewed their names and the towns they came from inside. See Berkin, Carol, *Revolutionary Mothers,* pp. 42–43.

11. With only a few powder mills left over from the French and Indian War, gunpowder was scarce, and women could help out by "boiling together wood ash and earth scraped from beneath the floors of their house, adding charcoal and sulfur to produce the powder." See Berkin, Carol, *Revolutionary Mothers,* p. 43.

12. Letter from AA to JA 3/31/1776, AFC vol. 1, pp. 369–371.

13. Colonel Henry Knox won great respect from Washington by orchestrating this complicated plan.

14. Letter from AA to JA 2/21/1776, AFC vol. 1, pp. 350–352.

15. Paine, Thomas, *Common Sense,* p. 72.

16. See Kramnick, Isaac, Introduction to *Common Sense,* Penguin Classics, 1986, p. 28.

17. According to Paine, *Common Sense* sold 120,000 copies in its first three months in print, ibid., p. 8.

18. Adams, John, *Thoughts on Government,* pp. 11–13.

19. Here JA thoroughly agrees with John Locke and opposes David Hume and the Scottish school of philosophers that so influenced Thomas Jefferson.

20. Adams, John, *Thoughts on Government,* p. 27.

21. Letter from JA to AA 3/19/1776, AFC vol. 1, pp. 362–365.

22. Letter from AA to JA 2/21/1776, AFC vol. 1, pp. 350–352.

23. The troops shot from three spots—Roxbury, Cobble Hill, and Lechmere Point—outside Boston, in order to divert the British attention from their plans to entrench on Dorchester Heights.

24. For an excellent detailed account of these events, see McCullough, David, *1776,* pp. 70–112.

25. Letter from AA to JA 3/16/1776, AFC vol. 1, pp. 357–361.

26. Ibid.

27. McCullough, David, *1776,* p. 99.

28. Letter from AA to JA 3/16/1776, AFC vol. 1, pp. 357–361.

29. Amazingly, all that was stolen from John Hancock's house was a backgammon board.

30. Letter from AA to JA 3/31/1776, AFC vol. 1, pp. 369–371.

31. Interestingly, John here is espousing the evangelical/Scottish Enlightenment view that passion is more powerful than reason.

32. Letter from JA to AA 3/14/1776, AFC vol. 1, pp. 381–383.

33. Letter from JA to AA 4/12/1776, AFC vol.1, pp. 376–377.

34. Letter from JA to AA 4/15/1776, AFC vol. 1, pp. 383–385.

35. Letter from JA to Nabby 4/18/1776, AFC vol. 1, pp. 387–388.

36. Letter from AA to JA 4/21/1776, AFC vol. 1, pp. 389–391.

37. Letter from AA to JA 5/7/1776, AFC vol. 1, pp. 401–403.

38. Letter from AA to MOW 4/27/1776, AFC vol. 1, pp. 396–398.

39. Letter from JA to AA 6/2/1776, AFC vol. 2, pp. 3–4.

40. Letter from JA to Mary Palmer 7/5/1776, AFC vol. 2, pp. 34–35.

41. See Gay, Peter, *The Enlightenment,* on Montesquieu's *De l'esprit des lois,* p. 470.

42. Adams, John, *Thoughts On Government.*

43. Letter from JA to AA 4/15/1776, AFC vol. 2, pp. 383–385.

44. Letter from JA to AA 5/22/1776, AFC vol. 2, pp. 412–413.

45. Letter from JA to AA 4/28/1776, AFC vol. 2, pp. 398–401.

46. *Angel in the Whirlwind,* p. 190.

47. Ibid., p. 100.

48. Letter from JA to AA 4/28/1776, AFC vol. 2, pp. 398–401.

49. Letter from JA to AA 5/27/1776, AFC vol. 2, pp. 419–421.
50. Letter from JA to AA 6/16/1776, AFC vol. 2, pp. 12–13.
51. *Angel,* p. 199.
52. Letters from JA to AA 7/3/1776, AFC vol. 2, pp. 27–33.
53. U.S. National Archives and Records Administration.
54. Letter from RC to JA 7/22/1776, AFC vol. 2, pp. 57–58; and Letter from AA to JA 7/21/1776, AFC vol. 2 pp. 55–57.
55. Letter from AA to JA 8/1/1776, AFC vol. 2, pp. 72–73.
56. Letter from AA to JA 8/14/1776, AFC vol. 2, pp. 93–95.
57. Letter from JA to AA 8/25/1776, AFC vol. 2, pp. 108–110.
58. Letter from AA to JA 8/17/1776, AFC vol. 2, p. 98.
59. Ibid.
60. Letter from MOW to AA 7/4/1776, AFC vol. 2, pp. 118–119.
61. Letter from JA to AA 8/30/1776, AFC vol. 2, pp. 114–115.
62. Letter from MOW to AA 9/4/1776, AFC vol. 2, pp. 118–119.
63. It was believed that sulfur smoke purified germs remaining on the clothes and papers of recovered patients; so anyone coming out of isolation had to be smoked.

CHAPTER V

1. Letter from AA to JA 9/21/1776, vol. 2, pp. 129–130.
2. See Morgan, Edmund S., *Inventing the People,* chapter 7, "The People in Arms."
3. The material on the post office is referenced from *Journal of Hugh-Finlay: Surveyer of Post Roads on the Continent of North America between Falmouth and Casco Bay,* Frank A. Norton, 1867; Ernst, Carl William, *Postal Service in Boston,* The Boston History Company, 1894; Fuller, Wayne E., *The American Mail: Enlarger of Common Life,* University of Chicago Press, 1972; Scheele, Carl H. *A Short History of the Mail Service,* Smithsonian Institute Press, Washington D.C., 1970; Wooley, Mary E., *Early History of the Colonial Post Office,* Papers from the Historical Seminary of Brown University, Edited by Franklin Jameson, Providence, RI, 1894; Letter from JA to AA 2/10/1777, AFC vol. 2, pp. 158–159.
4. *Diary and Autobiography of JA,* vol. 2, pp. 108–110.
5. Letters from JA to AA 2/10/1777, AFC vol. 2, pp. 192–193, and 4/8/1777, AFC vol. 2, pp. 203–204.
6. The only evidence of anyone sharing Abigail's intense dislike for Shaw is in a letter to Abigail from her cousin John Thaxter after the birth of the Shaws' first child, where he writes, "I hope [the baby] is 'bettered by the Mother's side' . . . else I pity it." Letter from John Thaxter to AA 9/11/1778, AFC vol. 3, pp. 88–89.
7. In her letter to JA, 4/17/77, AFC vol. 2, pp. 211–213, AA alludes to this agreement, observing that "certain circumstances," namely her pregnancy, came about "upon [the] condtion" that John be home for the birth.
8. Letter from JA to AA 8/21/1776, AFC vol. 2, pp. 103–105.
9. Letter from JA to AA 6/2/1777, AFC vol. 2, pp. 252–254.
10. Letter from AA to JA 3/26/1777, AFC vol. 2, pp. 186–188.
11. Letter from JA to AA 2/3/1777, AFC vol. 2, pp. 152–153.
12. Letter from JA to AA 3/22/1777, AFC vol. 2, p. 181.
13. Letter from AA to JA 3/8/1777, AFC vol. 2, pp. 171–174.
14. Letter from AA to JA 4/17/1777, AFC vol. 2, pp. 211–213.

15. Letter from JQA to JA 3/3/1777, AFC vol. 2, pp. 167–168, talks of the snow.
16. Letter from AA to JA 4/2/1777, AFC vol. 2, pp. 193–195.
17. Letter from AA to JA 4/17/1777, AFC vol. 2, pp. 211–213.
18. Ibid.
19. Letter from AA to JA 6/1/1777, AFC vol. 2, pp. 250–252.
20. Ibid.
21. Letter from AA to JA 4/17/1777, AFC vol. 2, pp. 211–213.
22. Letter from AA to JA 5/23/1777, AFC vol. 2, pp. 269–270.
23. Letter from JA to AA 2/7/1777, AFC vol. 2, pp. 153–154.
24. See *Angel,* chapters 8 and 9.
25. Letter from AA to JA 3/23/1777, AFC vol. 2, pp. 185–186.
26. Letter from AA to JA 5/6/1777, AFC vol. 2, pp. 231–233.
27. Letter from AA to JA 7/12/1777, AFC vol. 2, pp. 272–274.
28. Letter from AA to JA 6/15/1777, AFC vol. 2, pp. 265–267.
29. Letter from AA to JA 6/23/1777, AFC vol. 2, pp. 269–270.
30. Letter from JA to AA 7/8/1777, AFC vol. 2, pp. 276–277.
31. Letter from JA to AA 6/29/1777, AFC vol. 2, pp. 270–271.
32. Letter from AA to JA 6/23/1777, AFC vol. 2, pp. 269–270.
33. Letter from JA to AA 7/10/1777, AFC vol. 2, p. 278.
34. Letter from AA to JA 7/9/1777, AFC vol. 2, pp. 277–278.
35. Letter from AA to JA 7/10/1777, AFC vol. 2, pp. 278–280.
36. Letter from John Thaxter to JA 7/13/1777, AFC vol. 2, p. 282.
37. Letter from AA to JA 7/16/1777, AFC vol. 2, pp. 282–283.
38. Letter from JA to AA 7/28/1777, AFC vol. 2, p. 292.
39. Letter from AA to JA 8/12/1777, AFC vol. 2, pp. 308–309.
40. Letter from AA to JA 8/5/1777, AFC vol. 2, pp. 300–302.
41. Letter from JA to AA 4/2/1777, AFC vol. 2, pp. 195–196.
42. Schama, Simon, *Citizens,* Random House, pp. 48–49.
43. Letter from JA to AA 8/2/1777, AFC vol. 2, pp. 298–299.
44. Letter from JA to AA 8/5/1777, AFC vol. 2, pp. 300–302.
45. Letter from AA to JA 9/21/1777, AFC vol. 2, pp. 346–349.
46. Ibid.
47. Letter from JA to AA 8/11/1777, AFC vol. 2, pp. 305–306.
48. Letter from JA to AA 7/13/1777, AFC vol. 2, pp. 281–282.
49. Letter from JA to AA 8/24/1777, AFC vol. 2, pp. 327–328.
50. Letter from JA to AA 8/30/1777, AFC vol. 2, pp. 333–334.
51. Since the arrival of the first settlers at Plymouth and Jamestown, Thanksgivings had been celebrated locally usually once or twice a year—to commemorate important days or celebrate happy events like the end of a drought. This was the first Thanksgiving celebrated at the same time throughout the colonies.
52. Letter from AA to JA 10/25/1777, AFC vol. 2, pp. 358–359.
53. Letter from AA to Isaac Smith, Jr. 10/30/1777, vol. 2, pp. 362–365.
54. Letter from JA to AA 11/14/1777, AFC vol. 2, pp. 366–367.
55. In Abigail's letter to John on 10/20/1777, AFC vol. 2, pp. 354–356, she merely notes Betsy's wedding among a list of other recent and upcoming nuptials.
56. Morgan, Edmund S., *The Puritan Family,* pp. 47–48; Morgan writes that love "was a duty imposed by God on all married [Puritan] couples . . . If husband and wife failed to love each other above all the world, they not only wronged each other, they

disobeyed God." And he cites a passage in *Compleat Body of Divinity* where the early minister Samuel Willard states, of the husband's love: "If therefore the *Husband* is bitter against his wife, beating or striking of her (as some vile wretches do) or in any unkind carriage, ill language, hard words, morose, peevish, surly behavior; nay if he is not kind, loving tender in his words and carriage to her; he then shames his profession of Christianity, he breaks the Divine Law, he dishonours God . . . The same is true of the Wife too."

57. Letter from ESP to Nabby, 11/27/1786, LOC, Shaw collection.

58. Letter from ESP to MC 1/10/1778, AFC vol. 2, pp. 380–382.

59. *To Forward Well-Flavored Productions: The Kitchen Garden in Early New England,* by James E. McWilliams, *New England Quarterly,* Brunswick; 3/2004, vol. 77, Iss. 1; pp. 25–51.

60. Ibid.

61. The high roll, modeled on the coiffures of European royalty, was now all the rage in Boston and Philadelphia. Women spent hours in front of the mirror or hired male hairdressers to stretch their tendrils to the limit, often buttressing their own hair with hair from corpses and enhancing the finished product with festoons a la Marie Antoinette.

62. See Kate Haulman's amusing and informative "Object Lessons: A Short History of the High Roll" in *Common-Place,* vol. 2, no.1 10/20001. Elizabeth Shaw's "elaborate and queenly headress" is alluded to in Bartless, Albert LeRoy, *The Story of Haverhill in Massachusetts,* p. 283.

63. Letter from ESP to MC 1/10/1778, AFC vol. 2, pp. 380–382.

64. All the information on Haverhill comes from essays, articles, and books suggested by the enormously knowledgeable librarian of the Haverhill library, Gregory Laing. The writings include "Some Annals of Old Haverhill," by Albert L. Bartlett, *New England Magazine,* July, 1890; "Haverhill, 1840" by John B. D. Cogswell, from *History of Essex County, Mass.,* vol. 2, 1888; "Early Church History in Haverhill" by Vera L. Lindsley; "Sketches of Some Old Houses And Families of Haverhill," by Mrs. Robert M. Carleton, for the "Ladies' Monday Club," May, 1890; Felt, Joseph B., *Memorials of William Smith Shaw,* S. K. Whipple & Co., 1852.

65. JQA Diary, 11/4/85, vol. 2, p. 357.

66. JQA Diary, 12/21/85, vol. 2, p. 374.

67. Letter from ESP to MC 1/10/1778, AFC vol. 2, pp. 380–382.

68. Ibid.

69. *Diary and Autobiography of JA,* vol. 4, pp. 1–3.

70. Letter from AA to James Lovell, ca. 12/15/1777, AFC vol. 2, pp. 370–372.

71. Letter from John Thaxter to AA 1/20/1778, AFC vol. 2, pp. 385.

72. Letter from AA to MC 7/6/1784. AFC vol. 5, p. 358 of sea diary.

73. Letter from AA to ESP 3/1778, AFC vol. 2, pp. 406–408.

74. Letter from AA to John Thaxter, 2/15/1778, AFC vol. 2, pp. 390–393.

75. Ibid.

76. Letter from ESP to AA 4/5/1778, AFC vol. 3, pp. 4–5.

CHAPTER VI

1. Letter from Nabby Adams to Betsy Cranch 2/4/1779, AFC vol. 3, pp. 159–160.

2. Letter from Nabby Adams to Betsy Cranch 2/13/1779, AFC vol. 3, p. 169.

3. Letter from Nabby to Betsy 11/9/1782, AFC vol. 5, pp. 31–33.

4. Letter from Nabby to Betsy 2/13/1779, AFC vol. 3, p. 169.

5. "The Republican Wife: Virtue and Seduction in the Early Republic," by Jan Lewis, *The William and Mary Quarterly,* 3rd series, vol. 44, no. 4, p. 698.

6. Notebook with heading "Eliza Cranch, Haverhill, April 15th 1786" (pp. 3–4); Kathy Chamberlain private collection.

7. See a fascinating discussion of courtship by proxy in the 18th century in "The Cornerstone of a Copious Work: Love and Power in Eighteenth-Century Courtship," Nicole Eustace, *Journal of Social History,* 34.3 (2001), pp. 517–546.

8. Portions of these articles from magazines of the times are quoted in "The Republican Wife: Virtue and Seduction in the Early Republic," Jan Lewis, *The William and Mary Quarterly,* 3rd series, vol. 44, no. 4 (Oct. 1987) pp. 689–721.

9. Letter from Nabby Adams to Betsy Cranch 1/24/1779, AFC vol. 3, 156–157.

10. Letter from Nabby Adams to Betsy Cranch 12/22/1782, AFC vol. 5, pp. 51–52.

11. Journal of Elizabeth Cranch, 10/5/1785, p. 5, Kathy Chamberlain private collection.

12. Ibid. 2/3/1786, p. 30.

13. Letter from JA to AA 12/2/1778, AFC vol. 3, pp. 124–126.

14. Letter from AA to JA 7/17/1782, AFC vol. 4, pp. 343–348.

15. Letter from Nabby Adams to Betsy Cranch, 10/20/1779, AFC vol. 3, pp. 223–224.

16. JQA Diary p. 345.

17. Ibid.

18. Letter from AA to MC 10/12/86, AFC vol. 7, pp. 366–370.

19. Letter from Betsy to Lucy Cranch, 8/1/1783, Wisconsin Historical Society.

20. Letter from Betsy Cranch to Jacob Norton 3/6/1788, Kathy Chamberlain private collection.

21. Journal of Elizabeth Cranch, 1/27/1786, p. 28, ibid.

22. Journal of Elizabeth Cranch, 1/17/1786, p. 26 Kathy Chamberlain private collection.

23. Letter from AA to JA 6/8/1779, AFC vol. 3, pp. 199–202.

24. Letter from JA to RC 8/6/1778, AFC vol. 3, pp. 70–72.

25. Letter from Nabby to Betsy 1/24–26/1779, AFC vol. 3, pp. 156–157.

26. Letter from AA to Mercy Warren 12/10/1778, AFC vol. 3, pp. 132–133.

27. Letter from JQA to Nabby 9/27/1778, AFC vol. 3, pp. 93–94. The reference is to a David Garrick play called *Miss in Her Teens.*

28. Letter from Nabby to Betsy 3/15/1779, AFC vol. 3, pp. 188–189.

29. Letter from Nabby to Betsy 12/22/1783, AFC vol. 5, pp. 51–54.

30. Letter from AA to JA, 12/27/1778, AFC vol. 3, pp. 139–141.

31. Letter from AA to JA ca. 7/15/1778, AFC vol. 3, pp. 59–62.

32. Letter from AA to JA, 11/12–23/1778, AFC vol. 3, pp. 118–120.

33. Letter from AA to JA 10/21/1778, AFC vol. 3, pp. 108–109.

34. In a letter from AA to Lovell 6/18–26/1779, AFC vol. 3, pp. 206–208, Abigail stipulates that the distance between her house and Richard Cranch's is "a dozen mile[s]."

35. Letter from AA to John Thaxter 8/26/1778, AFC vol. 3, pp. 80–81 and JA to AA 8/27/1778, AFC vol. 3, pp. 81–82.

36. In a letter from AA to JA 7/15/1778, AFC vol. 3, pp. 59–62, Abigail tells John she needs him to send her some "saleable items" to put her "more upon an eaquel footing with my Neighbors."

37. Letter from AA to JA 12/13/1778, AFC vol. 3, pp. 137–139.

38. Letter from JA to AA 4/25/1778, AFC vol. 3, p. 17.

39. Letter from AA to JA 6/30/1778, AFC vol. 3, pp. 51–53.

40. Letter from AA to MOW 12/10/1778, AFC vol. 3, pp. 132–133.
41. Letter from AA to JA 12/13/1778, AFC vol. 3, pp. 135–136.
42. Schiff, Stacy, *A Great Improvisation,* p. 193.
43. *Diary and Autobiography of JA,* vol. 2, pp. 182–183.
44. Ibid., vol. 4, pp. 118–119.
45. See Schiff, Stacy, *A Great Improvisation,* pp. 182–184, pp. 216–217, pp. 203–204.
46. *Diary and Autobiography of JA,* vol. 4, pp. 106–108.
47. Jouve, Daniel, *Paris: Birthplace of the U.S.A.,* Grund Press, 1995.
48. *Diary and Autobiography of JA,* 4/10/1778, vol. 2, p. 298.
49. Ibid., 4/11/1778, vol. 2, pp. 298–299.
50. Ibid., 4/27/1778, p. 306.
51. Letter from JA to AA 12/2/1778, AFC vol. 3, pp. 124–126.
52. *Diary and Autobiography of JA,* vol. 1, 4/11/1778, pp. 298–299.
53. Ibid., 5/26/1778, pp. 314–315.
54. Ibid., 4/27/1778, p. 306.
55. Letter from JA to AA 6/3/1778, AFC vol. 3, pp. 31–33.
56. Letter from JA to AA 7/26/1778, AFC vol. 3, pp. 66–67.
57. Letter from JA to AA 12/27/1778, AFC vol. 3, pp. 141–142.
58. Letter from JA to AA 12/18/1778, AFC vol. 3, p. 138.
59. Letter from AA to JL ca. 12/15/1777, AFC vol. 2, pp. 370–372.
60. Letter from JL to AA 2/22/1778, AFC vol. 2, pp. 393–394.
61. Letter from AA to JL 6/24/1778, AFC vol. 3, pp. 48–50.
62. Letter from JL to AA 6/13/1778, AFC vol. 3, pp. 43–44.
63. Letter from AA to JL 6/12/1778, AFC vol. 3, pp. 41–42.
64. Letter from JL to AA 4/1/1778, AFC vol. 3, pp. 1–2.
65. Letter from AA to JL 6/24/1778, AFC vol. 3, pp. 48–50.
66. Letter from AA to JL 8/19/1778, AFC vol. 3, p. 76.
67. Letter from AA to John Thaxter 7/23/1778, AFC vol. 3, pp. 64–66.
68. Letter from JA to AA 2/13/1779, AFC vol. 3, pp. 169–171.
69. Letter from JA to AA 2/20/1779, AFC vol. 3, p. 175.
70. Letter from JA to AA 2/26/1779, AFC vol. 3, pp. 178–180.
71. Letter from JA to AA 2/28/1779, AFC vol. 3, pp. 181–182.
72. Letter from JA to AA 6/14/1779, AFC vol. 3, pp. 205–206.
73. Letter from JL to AA 7/28/1779, AFC vol. 3, pp. 214–215.
74. Letter from ESP to AA 4/5/1778, AFC vol. 3, pp. 4–5.
75. Letter from JA to AA 12/2/1778, AFC vol. 3, pp. 124–126.
76. Constitution of the Commonwealth of Massachusetts, ratified on 6/16/1780, Chapter V, Section II: *"The Encouragement of Literature, etc,"* p. 18.
77. AFC vol. 3, fn 3, pp. 224–233.
78. Letter from AA to JA 11/14/1779, AFC vol. 3, pp. 233–234.
79. Ibid.
80. Letters from JA to AA 11/14/1779 and 11/15/1779, AFC vol. 3, pp. 234–236.
81. Letter from AA to JL 11/18/1779, AFC vol. 3, p. 236.

CHAPTER VII

1. Letter from ESP to MC 4/6/1781, AFC vol. 4, pp. 98–100.
2. JQA Diary, vol. 2, 4/21/1788, p. 394 and 4/21/1786, p. 20.

3. Letter from Nabby to John Thaxter, 5/25/1781, AFC vol. 4, pp. 131–132.

4. Letters from RC to MC 1/21/1782 and 1/30/1782, Richard Cranch Papers 1749–1928, MHS.

5. Part of Sea letter AA to MC 7/30/1784, AFC vol. 5, p. 382.

6. Letter from WC to JCA 12/14/1784, AFC vol. 6, pp. 32–34.

7. Letter from RC to WC 6/19/1783, LOC, Cranch collection.

8. Letter from RC to WC 1/7/1784, LOC, Cranch collection.

9. Letter from AA to JQA 1/9/1780, AFC vol. 4, pp. 268–269.

10. Even when they were paid, the troops' salaries varied widely because they were determined by the individual states, not a central government.

11. Letter from JL to AA 5/29/1781, AFC vol. 4, pp. 145–146.

12. Letter from JL to AA 6/4/1781, AFC vol. 4, p. 208.

13. *Angel,* p. 57.

14. *Boston Evening Post,* 10/25/1781, New York Public Library.

15. *Angel,* p. 56.

16. Letter from RC to JA 10/30/1781, AFC vol. 4, pp. 239–240.

17. Letter from RC to JA 11/3/1781, AFC vol. 4, pp. 240–243.

18. Letter from AA to JA 12/9/1781, AFC vol. 4, pp. 255–261.

19. Letter from JA to AA 12/2/1781, AFC vol. 4, pp. 249–251.

20. This plan involved a truce arbitrated by a third party, either Russia or Austria. In the end England as well as the United States flatly turned it down. *Angel,* p. 439.

21. Letters from JA to AA 2/28/1780, AFC vol. 3, pp. 390–391 and 3/15/1780, AFC vol. 3, p. 302. For a good description of Abigail's entrepreneurial activity, see Gelles, *Portia,* pp. 41–44.

22. Letter from JA to AA 5/12/1780, AFC vol. 3, pp. 441–443.

23. fn to Letter from John Thaxter to JA 8/7/1780, AFC vol. 3, pp. 388–395.

24. Ibid.

25. A letter to an Elizabeth Adams, which was mistakenly delivered to Abigail, spoke of Ben Franklin's "blackening" John's character. Letter from AA to JL 6/30/1781, AFC vol. 4, pp. 164–166.

26. Letter from AA to JA 5/27/1781, AFC vol. 4, pp. 137–138 and letter from AA to JL 7/14/1781, AFC vol. 4, pp. 176–179.

27. I combine two letters. The first is AA to JA 8/1/1781, AFC vol. 4, pp. 190–192. The succeeding sentences are from AA to JA 9/29/1781, AFC vol. 4, pp. 220–222.

28. Letter from AA to JA 7/16/1780, AFC vol. 4, pp. 375–377.

29. Letter from JL to AA 7/14/1780, AFC vol. 3, pp. 373–374.

30. Letter from AA to JL 1/3/1781, AFC vol. 4, pp. 57–58.

31. Letter from AA to JL 9/20(?)/1781, AFC vol. 4, pp. 215–217.

32. Letter from AA to JL 3/17/1781, AFC vol. 4, pp. 91–93.

33. Letter from JL to AA 6/16/1781, AFC vol. 4, pp. 148–152.

34. Letter from AA to JL 7/[14]/1781, AFC vol. 4, pp. 176–179.

35. Letter from AA to JL 9/20(?)/1781, AFC vol. 4, pp. 215–217.

36. Ibid. 12/30/1782, AFC vol. 5, pp. 61–63.

37. Letter from ESP to AA 2/1/1783, LOC, Shaw Collection.

38. Letter from AA to JA 12/23/1782, AFC vol. 5, pp. 54–59.

39. Letter from Nabby to Betsy 6/1782, AFC vol. 4, pp. 335–337.

40. Letter from MC to AA 10/10/1782, AFC vol. 5, pp. 470–471.

41. Letter from Nabby to Betsy, 11/9/1782, AFC vol. 5, pp. 31–33.

42. Letter from JA to AA 8/1782, AFC vol. 4, pp. 364–365.

43. Ibid.

44. Letter from Nabby to Betsy 6/1782, AFC vol. 4, pp. 335–337.

45. Letter from Nabby to Betsy 9/1782, AFC vol. 4, pp. 389–390.

46. Letter from AA to JA 10/8/1782, AFC vol. 5, pp. 4–8.

47. Letter from Nabby to Betsy 11/9/1782, AFC vol. 5, pp. 31–33.

48. Letter from Nabby to Betsy 10/2/1782, AFC vol. 5, p. 2.

49. Letter from ESP to AA 2/1/1783, LOC, Shaw Collection.

50. Letter from AA to JA 10/25/1782, AFC vol. 5, pp. 21–24.

51. Letter from AA to JA 1/10/1783, AFC vol. 5, pp. 66–68.

52. Letter from AA to JA 6/17/1782, AFC vol. 4, pp. 326–329.

53. Letter from AA to JA 12/23/1782, AFC vol. 5, pp. 54–59.

54. Letter from JA to AA 1/22/1782, AFC vol. 5, pp. 74–76.

55. Letter from AA to JA 5/7/1783, AFC vol. 5, pp. 151–155.

56. Letter from ESP to AA 2/1/1783, LOC, Shaw Collection.

57. Letter from Nabby to Betsy, ca. 1/4/1783, AFC vol. 5, pp. 63–64.

58. Letter from ESP to AA 2/1/1783, LOC, Shaw Collection.

59. Letter from JA to AA 11/8/1782, AFC vol. 5, pp. 28–30.

60. McCullough, *John Adams,* p. 278.

61. McCullough, *John Adams,* p. 280.

62. See McCullough's thoughts on this issue, pp. 276–278.

63. Letter from JA to AA 7/1/1782, AFC vol. 5, pp. 337–339.

64. Letter from JA to AA 1/22/1783, AFC vol. 5, pp. 74–76.

65. Letter from JA to AA 1/29/1783, AFC vol. 5, pp. 82–83.

66. Letter from AA to JA 4/7/1783, AFC vol. 5, pp. 116–119.

67. Letter from AA to JA 6/20/1783, AFC vol. 5, pp. 179–184.

68. Letter from AA to JA 11/20/1783, AFC vol. 5, pp. 270–272.

69. Letter from ESP to MC and AA 3/15/1783, AFC vol. 5, pp. 105–107.

70. Letter from AA to JA 6/20/1783, AFC vol. 5, pp. 179–184.

71. Letter from AA to JA 6/30/1783, AFC vol. 5, pp. 188–191.

72. Letters from JA to AA 7/9/1783 and 7/13/1783, AFC vol. 5, pp. 198–200.

73. Letter from ESP to AA 5/20/1787, AFC vol. 8, pp. 49–55.

74. Letter from AA to JA 9/20/1783, AFC vol. 5, pp. 253–255.

75. Letter from ESP to AA 3/4/1784, LOC, Shaw Collection.

76. Letter from AA to JA 10/19/1783, AFC vol. 5, pp. 258–261.

77. Letter from JA to AA 2/14/1763, AFC vol. 1, p. 3.

78. Lovell was assigned to the office of continental Receiver of taxes in Massachusetts, according to AA to JA 4/10/1782, AFC vol. 4, pp. 305–308; also see AA to JL 1/8?/1782, AFC vol. 4, pp. 273–275, fn4.

79. Letter from ESP to MC 6/5/1784, AFC vol. 5, pp. 337–338.

80. Abigail wrote of her departure in a diary she kept during her voyage (see *Diary and Autobiography of JA,* "Abigail Adams' Diary of her Voyage from Boston to Deal," pp. 154–167): "I left my own House the 18 of June. Truly a house of mourning; full of my Neighbours. Not of unmeaning complimenters, but the Honest yeomanary, their wifes and daughters like a funeral procession, all come to wish me well and to pray for a speedy return.—Good Heaven, what were my sensations? Hitherto I had fortified my mind. Knowing I had to act my little part alone, I had possessd myself with calmness, but this was too much for me, so I shook them by the hand mingling my tears with

theirs, and left them. I had after this to bid my neices, adieu. And then another scene still more afflictive, an aged Parent [John's mother] from whom I had kept the day of my departure a secret knowing the agony she would be in. I calld at her door. As soon as the good old Lady beheld me, the tears rolled down her aged cheek, and she cried out O! why did you not tell me you was going so soon? Fatal day! I take my last leave; I shall never see you again . . . I was obliged to leave her in an agony of distress, myself in no less. My good Sister Cranch who accompanied me to Town endeavourd to amuse me and to console me.'

CHAPTER VIII

1. Ibid., p. 151.
2. Letter from AA to ESP 7/11/1784, AFC vol. 5, pp. 393–396.
3. In an article called "Precautions to be Used by those Who are about to undertake a Sea Voyage," (April, 1790) from Colbert, William, *Emigrant's Guide in Ten Letters* (1830), Dr. Franklin writes, "The most disagreeable thing at sea, is the cookery, for there is not, properly speaking, any professed cook on board. The worst sailor is generally chosen for that purpose, who for the most part is equally dirty and unskillful."
4. Shipboard letter from AA to MC, 7/6/1784, AFC vol. 5, pp. 358–385.
5. Ibid. p. 361.
6. Letter from AA to ESP 7/11/1784, AFC vol. 5, pp. 393–396.
7. Letter from Nabby Adams to Betsy Cranch 7/30/1784, AFC vol. 5, pp. 410–412.
8. Buchan, William, *Domestic Medicine,* 1784 edition, Early American Imprints, first series, no.18384, p. 104.
9. Ibid., p. 65.
10. Shipboard letter from AA to MC 7/7/1784, AFC vol. 5, p. 363.
11. Baize is a coarse cotton or wool fabric textured to feel like felt.
12. Shipboard letter from AA to MC 7/6/1784, AFC vol. 5, p. 360.
13. Ibid., 7/16/1784, p. 366.
14. AA's shipboard Diary from *Diary and Autobiography of JA,* vol. 3, p. 166.
15. Ibid.
16. Letter from MC to AA 4/22/1787, AFC vol. 8, pp. 15–23.
17. Letter from RC to JA 1/20/1784, AFC vol. 5, pp. 300–301.
18. Letter from ESP to MC 8/24/1784, AFC vol. 5, pp. 424–425.
19. Letter from MC to AA 8/7/1784, AFC vol. 5, pp. 419–422.
20. MC to AA 11/5/1784, AFC vol. 5, pp. 479–481.
21. Letter from ESP to AA 10/ca. 15/1784, AFC vol. 5, pp. 472–476.
22. Ibid.
23. See Hareven, Tara K., *Family Time & Industrial Time,* pp. 85–119.
24. Letter from ESP to AA 9/7/1785, AFC vol. 6, pp. 347–350. Also see Edith B. Gelles on "Kin keepers," *Portia,* pp. 116–123.
25. See Morgan, Edmund S., *The Puritan Family,* p.77 and Hareven, Tara K., *Family Time & Industrial Time,* pp. 85–119.
26. Letter from Nabby to Betsy 7/1783, AFC vol. 5, pp. 207–209.
27. Letter from ESP to MC 3/28/1780, AFC vol. 3, pp. 318–319.
28. Letter from JA to AA 7/26/1784, AFC vol. 5, pp. 399–400.
29. Shipboard letter from AA to MC., fn 42, vol. 5, p. 385.
30. Letter from AA to ESP 7/28/1784, AFC vol. 5, pp. 402–408.

31. Letter from AA to Betsy Cranch 8/1/1784, AFC vol. 5, pp. 414–415.

32. Letter from AA to ESP 7/28/1784, AFC vol. 5, pp. 402–408.

33. Journal entry 8/27/85, *Journal and Correspondence of Miss Adams,* ed. by Caroline Smith Dewitt, NY and London, Wiley and Putnam, 1841, p. ix.

34. Letter from Nabby to Betsy 7/30/1784, AFC vol. 5, pp. 410–412.

35. *JA Diary & Autobiography,* vol. 3, fn 2, pp. 170–171.

36. Letter from AA to MC 12/9/1784, AFC vol. 6, pp. 14–23.

37. Shipboard letter from AA to MC, AFC vol. 5, p. 383.

38. Letter from JA to JQA 8/1/1784, AFC vol. 5, p. 416.

39. Letter from JA to Nabby 7/17/1784, AFC vol. 5, pp. 400–401.

40. Rousseau, Jean Jacques, *The Basic Political Writings,* Hackett Publishing Company, U.S., 1987.

41. Letter from AA to MOW 9/5/1784, vol. 5, pp. 446–453.

42. Letter from AA to Lucy Cranch, 9/5/1784, AFC vol. 5, pp. 436–439.

43. Letter from AA to MC 9/5/1784, vol. 5, pp. 439–445.

44. Letter from AA to MC 12/9/1784, AFC vol. 6, pp. 14–23.

45. Letter from AA to MC 9/5/1784, AFC vol. 5, pp. 439–446.

46. Letter from AA to ESP 1/11/1785, AFC vol. 6, pp. 55–59.

47. Letter from AA to Betsy Cranch, 12/3–13/1784, AFC vol. 6, pp. 3–10.

48. Letter from Nabby to Betsy 5/6/1784, AFC vol. 6, pp. 123–127.

49. Letter from AA to MC 2/20/1785, AFC vol. 6, pp. 67–71.

50. Letter from AA to John Thaxter 3/20/1785, AFC vol. 6, pp. 78–81.

51. Letter from JA to RC 4/27/1785, AFC vol. 6, pp. 109–111.

52. Letter from AA to John Thaxter, 6/6/1785, AFC vol. 6, pp. 169–173.

53. Letter from AA to MC 9/5/1784, AFC vol. 5, pp. 439–445.

54. Letter from TJ to AA 6/21/1785, *The Adams-Jefferson Letters,* pp. 33–36.

55. Letter from AA to TJ 6/6/1785, *A/J Letters,* pp. 28–30.

56. Letter from AA to MC 5/8/1785, AFC vol. 6, pp. 118–120.

57. Letter from ESP to AA 10/ ca 15/1784, vol. 5, pp. 472–477.

58. Ibid.

59. Letter from AA to ESP 12/14/1784, vol. 6, pp. 28–32.

60. Letter from AA to ESP 1/11/1785, AFC vol. 6, pp. 55–59.

61. Letter from ESP to AA 4/25/1785, AFC vol. 6, pp. 101–103.

62. Letter from AA to Royall Tyler 7/10/1784, AFC vol. 5, pp. 390–393.

63. Letter from AA to MC 12/9/1784, AFC vol. 6, pp. 14–21.

64. Letter from MC to AA 4/25/1785, AFC vol. 6, pp. 92–100.

65. Letter from MC to AA 6/4/1785, AFC vol. 6, pp. 164–165.

66. Letter from ESP to MC 4/30/1785, AFC vol. 6, pp. 116–117.

CHAPTER IX

1. Letter from AA to John Thaxter 3/20/1785, AFC vol. 6, pp. 78–81.

2. Letter from TJ to JA 7/11/1786, *A/J Letters,* pp. 142–144.

3. Letter from AA to John Thaxter 3/20/1785, AFC vol. 6, pp. 78–81.

4. Letter from AA to Cotton Tufts 5/2/1782, AFC vol. 6, pp. 103–109.

5. Letter from AA to MC 4/15/1785, AFC vol. 6, pp. 82–85.

6. Letter from JA to RC 4/27/1785, AFC vol. 6, pp. 109–111.

7. *Journal and Correspondence of Miss Adams,* entry 5/9/1785, p. 74.

8. Letter from AA to Cotton Tufts 5/2/1785, AFC vol. 6, pp. 103–109.

9. Letter from AA to MC 4/15/1785, AFC vol. 6, pp. 82–85.

10. In the same letter Abigail, while asking Mary to draw money for John Quincy's financial needs from their Uncle Tufts, makes a point that "there is to be no extraordinary expences on account of the publick Character which Mr. Adams sustains, because he is not half so able to bear them, as he would have been if he had been only a private citizen. In short I am weary of being obliged to eat and drink up all we have."

11. *Journal and Correspondence of Miss Adams,* 2/14/1785, p. 48.

12. AA to JQA 6/13/1786, AFC vol. 7, pp. 216–217. Here Abigail reminisces about their talks in Auteuil: "You was then frequently witness to a regard and attachment" on Nabby's part, greeted by Tyler with "repeated proofs of neglect."

13. Letter from AA to Cotton Tufts, 5/2/1785, AFC vol. 6, pp. 103–109.

14. Letter from Nabby to Lucy Cranch 6/23/1785, AFC vol. 6, pp. 183–186.

15. Letter from JQA to Nabby 5/17/1785–5/20/1785, AFC vol. 6, pp. 148–151.

16. Letter from AA to TJ 6/6/1785, A/J Letters, pp. 28–30.

17. Letter from AA to Charles Storer 5/18/1785, AFC vol. 6, pp. 151–152.

18. Letter from John Thaxter to AA 6/4/1785, AFC vol. 6, pp. 165–169.

19. John Adams's friend Benjamin Rush.

20. Rush, Benjamin, "Account of the Progress of the Population, Agriculture, Manners, and Government in Pennsylvania, *Columbian Magazine* 1 (Nov. 1786), p. 120. For an insightful view of American perceptions of the West during this period, see Peter S. Onuf's "Liberty, Development, and Union: Visions of the West in the 1770s in *William and Mary Quarterly* serial, 43, 1986.

21. Letter from ESP to MC 3/14/1784, LOC, Shaw Collection.

22. The friend who carried Shaw's first letters was murdered in an Indian massacre.

23. Letter from Betsy Cranch to AA 9/5/1785, AFC vol. 6, pp. 335–340.

24. Letter from Betsy Cranch to AA 4/25/1785, AFC vol. 6, pp. 90–92.

25. Letter from MC to AA 7/19/1785, AFC, vol. 6, pp. 231–240.

26. Letter from MC to AA 10/3/1784, AFC vol. 5, pp. 467–469.

27. Letter from JQA to Nabby 10/1/1785, AFC vol. 6, pp. 398–406.

28. During his brief stay in Braintree, JQA was overwhelmed with emotion at the sight of his childhood farmhouse, impressed by Richard Cranch's conversation, and bored by Parson Wibird's sermons, often on their third or fourth time around.

29. Letter from John Thaxter to AA 6/4/1785, AFC vol. 6, pp. 165–169.

30. Letter from John Thaxter to Nabby 8/28/1781, AFC vol. 4, pp. 131–132.

31. Letter from John Thaxter to AA 6/4/1785, AFC vol. 6, pp. 165–169.

32. Journal of Elizabeth Cranch 10/23/1785, p. 10.

33. Journal of Elizabeth Cranch 11/9/1785, p. 13.

34. Letter from MC to AA 11/29/1785, vol. 6, pp. 475–477.

35. Ibid., p. 16.

36. Ibid., p. 18.

37. Ibid., p. 17.

38. Ibid., p. 19.

39. *JQA Diary* vol. 1 12/21/1785, p. 374.

40. Journal of Elizabeth Cranch, p. 32.

41. entry 3/13/1785, Elizabeth Cranch's unpublished journal, Carleton College Library.

42. Ibid., entry 3/14/1785.

43. Diary of Betsy Cranch, 4/6/1786. Kathy Chamberlain private collection.

44. These passages are from two letters JA wrote TJ, the first from Montreuil sur mer and the second from Calais: Letter from JA to TJ 5/22/1785, *A/J Letters,* pp. 21–22; Letter from JA to TJ 5/23/1785, p. 22.
45. Jefferson, Thomas, *Notes on the State of Virginia,* Electronic Text Center, University of Virginia Library, p. 184.
46. Ibid., pp. 264–265.
47. Letter from JA to TJ 5/22/1785, *A/J Letters,* pp. 21–22.
48. See John Brewer's *The Pleasures of the Imagination,* especially pp. 325–356 on "The Georgian Stage."
49. Letter from JA to TJ 6/7/1785, *A/J Letters,* pp. 31–32.
50. Letter from AA to TJ 6/6/1785, AFC vol. 6, pp. 169–174.
51. In fact, the move to London sealed Abigail's separate friendship with Jefferson, who, replying to her first letter wrote, "I have received duly the honor of your letter, and am now to return you thanks for your condescension in having taken the first step for settling a correspondence which I so much desired; for now I consider it settled and proceed accordingly." Letter from TJ to AA 6/21/1785, *A/J Letters,* pp. 33–36.
52. See Chapter 4 of this book.
53. See Stella Tillyard's brilliant interpretation of this aspect of George III's personality in *A Royal Affair,* Random House, 2006, particularly the Introduction.
54. Letter from JA to John Jay 6/2/1785, *The North American Review,* "Diplomatic Correspondence," pp. 315–318.
55. Letter from AA to MC 6/24/1785, AFC vol. 6, pp. 186–194.
56. The George Washington quote can be found in *Diary and Autobiography of JA,* vol. 3, p. 183.

CHAPTER X

1. Letter from MC to AA 8/14/1785, AFC vol. 6, pp. 268–275.
2. Letter from AA to MC 9/30/1785, AFC vol. 6, pp. 392–395.
3. Letter from MC to AA [ca. 23] 10/1785, vol. 6, pp. 440–441 and MC to AA 7/19/1785, AFC vol. 6, pp. 231–239.
4. Letter from MC to AA 8/14/1785, AFC vol. 6, pp. 268–275.
5. Ibid.
6. Letter from MC to AA 7/19/1785, AFC vol. 6, pp. 231–240.
7. Letter from Cotton Tufts to AA 10/12/1785, AFC vol. 6, p. 424.
8. Letter from Nabby to JQA 7/4/1785, AFC vol. 6, pp. 204–223.
9. Letter from AA to MC 8/15/1785, AFC vol. 6, pp. 276–230.
10. Letter from AA to Betsy Cranch 9/25/1785, AFC vol. 6, pp. 327–330.
11. Letter from AA to MC 4/6/1786, AFC vol. 7, pp. 133–135.
12. Letter from Nabby to JQA 7/4/1785, AFC vol. 6, pp. 204–223.
13. The lyric Abigail discovered was from Two Gentlemen of Verona:
    "I am sorry I must never trust thee more
    But Count the World a stranger for thy sake
    The private wound is deepest; oh time most curst
    Mongst all foes, that a friend should be the worst."
    Letter from AA to MC 7/4/1786, AFC vol. 7, pp. 234–240.
14. Ibid.
15. Letter from AA to Cotton Tufts 8/18/1785, AFC vol. 6, pp. 283–287.

16. The ill-wishers Abigail refers to were mostly American Tories.
17. Jacobs, Diane, *Her Own Woman,* p. 291, chapter 2, fn 3.
18. "Observations on the Importance of the American Revolution," 1785 http://www.constitution.org/price_price_6txt, pp. 24–25.
19. Abigail wrote John Quincy that she would "willingly go much further to hear a Man so liberal so sensible so good as [Dr. Price] is." AA to JQA 6/26/1785, AFC vol. 6, pp. 194–197.
20. Letter from AA to Elizabeth Storer Smith 8/29/1785, AFC vol. 6, pp. 314–316.
21. Letter from AA to Lucy Cranch 8/27/1785, AFC vol. 6, pp. 312–314.
22. George Washington's letter recommending William Smith for a position in the West Indies, 6/1782, quoted by Roof, Katharine Metcalf, *Colonel William Smith and Lady,* pp. 36–37.
23. Ibid., p. 90. Roof quotes from Colonel Smith's letter to Baron Steuben.
24. Letter from AA to JQA 9/6/1785, AFC vol. 6, pp. 342–346.
25. Letter from WS to Baron Steuben, quoted in Roof, Katharine Metcalf, p. 94.
26. This was the first time Abigail had even seen Mrs. Siddons, who starred as Desdemona. She chose a quote from Milton to describe her reaction to the Colonel: "Grace was in all her steps heaven in her Eye/And every Gesture dignity and Love."
27. Letter from AA to WS 6/18/1785, AFC vol. 6, pp. 365–369.
28. Letter from Nabby to JQA, AFC vol. 6, pp. 204–223.
29. Roof writes enigmatically that (pp. 37–38) William fell "violently, if briefly, in love with a certain devastating Miss Read," and implies that she broke his heart.
30. Letter from AA to WS 7/13/1785, AFC vol. 6, pp. 266–267.
31. Ibid.
32. Letter from AA to MC 5/13/1786, AFC vol. 7, pp. 217–220. In this letter to Mary, Abigail gives an intriguing glimpse into the family dynamics: "Upon perusing the Letter mrA. Was much affected I read it—but I knew the Hyena too well, I knew his *cant* and *grimace.* I had been so often the dupe of it myself. I then thought it my duty to lay before mrA Some letters from you, which he had never seen and he returned the Letter of mr T's to your Neice and told her the Man was unworthy of her, and advised her not to write him a line."
33. Letter from WS to John Jay 12/6/1785, Roof, pp. 117–125.
34. Letter from WS to AA 9/5/1785, AFC vol. 6, pp. 340–342.
35. Letter from AA to WS 9/9/1785, AFC vol. 6, pp. 365–369.
36. Letter from TJ to AA 11/20/1785, AFC vol. 6, pp. 462–464.
37. Nabby, choked with emotion, finds it difficult to articulate the end of her love for Tyler and her hopes for a life with William Smith, even in her diary, where, after Smith's return in December, 1785 she writes: "The thread has broken, and I have to begin again; it is in vain trying to join it where I last left it, for I find it impossible. Some events have taken place respecting myself, in which, perhaps, my future happiness may be interested; I have one consolation, the perfect rectitude of my intentions. To that Being, under whose guidance I would fain believe all our actions to be, I must submit, and leave the events; Heaven grant they may prove propitious to my happiness and peace." *Journal And Correspondence of Miss Adams.*
38. Letter from WS to AA 12/29/1785, AFC vol. 6, pp. 508–509.
39. Letter from AA to MC 12/2/1784, AFC vol. 6, pp. 14–23.
40. Letter from AA to MC 1/2/1786, AFC vol. 7, pp. 29–31.
41. Letter from Nabby to Betsy 2/14/1786, AFC vol. 7, pp. 54–56.

42. Ibid.

43. Letter from JQA to Nabby 9/19/1785, AFC vol. 6, pp. 369–377.

44. Letter from AA to JQA 2/16/1786, AFC vol. 7, pp. 62–70.

45. Letter from AA to ESP 3/4/1786, AFC vol. 7, pp. 80–85.

46. Letter from AA to MC 2/26/1786, AFC vol. 7, pp. 77–80.

47. Letter from ESP to AA 6/18/1786, AFC vol. 7, pp. 221–224.

48. On the subject of American debt AA wrote MC (4/29/1786, AFC vol. 7, pp. 147–149) "It is really painful living in this Country at this time, because there is but too much foundation for many of their reproaches against our Country. There does not appear any symptom of a political change in the sentiments of this people, or their Rulers, they say Congress has no power and that the States can not unite. They depend upon our continuing their dupes, and we appear [I] think quite enough disposed to do so."

49. Letter from AA to MC 1/26/1786, AFC vol. 7, pp. 29–31.

50. Letter from AA to JQA 2/16/1786, AFC vol. 7, pp. 62–70.

51. Letter from AA to ESP 3/4/1786, AFC vol.7, pp. 80–85.

52. Letter from Nabby to JQA 2/9/1786, AFC vol. 7, pp. 33–46.

53. Letter from MC to AA 2/9/1786, AFC vol. 7, pp. 46–50.

54. Letter from AA to Charles Storer 3/23/1786, AFC vol. 7, pp. 113–116.

55. Letter from MC to AA 5/22/1786, AFC vol. 7, pp. 190–193.

56. Letter from ESP to Nabby 5/4/1786, vol. 7, pp. 213–216. The closeness of Nabby and Aunt Elizabeth (in contrast to Nabby's strained relationship with her aunt Mary) is touchingly revealed in the latter's complaint: "And now, my dear niece, I will plainly tell you that I feel hurt that so many vessels have arrived without one line to your aunt Shaw who loves you so tenderly, and feels as interested in every thing that befalls, or can happen to my dear friend, as any one in America . . . I cannot believe my niece so wholly devoted to scenes of dissipation as to forget her friend; nor will I believe that her new connection has engrossed all her time and attention. If I thought this to really be the case, I would petition Colonel Smith to permit you to appropriate a certain portion of your time to write and to think of me. I assure you your descriptions, your sentiments, your reflections, constituted a great part of my pleasure and happiness."

57. Letter from AA to MC 6/13/1786, AFC vol. 7, pp. 217–221.

58. Letter from MC to AA 10/8/1786, AFC vol. 7, pp. 354–356.

59. I have modernized the punctuation in this last quote to clarify the meaning.

CHAPTER XI

1. Letter from MC to AA 9/24/1786, AFC vol. 7, pp. 341–344.

2. Ibid.

3. Letter from MC to AA 11/26/1786, AFC vol. 7, pp. 396–401.

4. Letter from AA to JQA 11/28/1786, AFC vol. 7, pp. 405–406.

5. Letter from AA to ESP 3/10/1787, AFC vol. 8, pp. 4–6.

6. Georgia and Pennsylvania were exceptions to this rule.

7. Letter from AA to JQA 3/20/1787, AFC vol. 8, pp. 11–13.

8. Preface to vol. 1, *Defense of the American Constitutions,* Da Capo reprint of first edition, London, 1787–1788.

9. *Thoughts on Government,* p. 3.

10. *A/J Letters,* 12/6/1787, pp. 213–214.

11. Letter from AA to JA 12/30/1786, AFC vol. 7, pp. 413–416.

12. Letter from JQA to AA 12/30/1786, AFC vol. 7, pp. 417–423.

13. Letter from AA to TJ 1/29/1787, *A/J Letters,* pp. 168–169.

14. Kerber, Linda K., *Women of the Republic,* pp. 164–165.

15. Kerber, Linda K., *Women of the Republic,* pp. 211–212. One of the maxims this Academy distributed on the cover of their copy books sounds almost feminist: "That learning belongs not to the female character, and that the female mind is incapable of a degree of improvement equal to that of the other sex, are narrow and unphilosophical prejudice . . . Learning is equally attainable, and I think equally valuable, for the satisfaction arising from it, to a woman as to a man."

16. Kerber, Linda K., *Women of the Republic,* p. 205.

17. Letter from AA to Lucy Cranch 4/26/1787, AFC vol. 8, pp. 24–27.

18. Letter from MC to AA 12/31/1786, AFC vol. 7, pp. 420–423.

19. Letter from ESP to AA 11/1/1786, AFC vol. 7, pp. 384–388.

20. Betsy Cranch's commonplace book, 4/16/1788, Kathy Chamberlain private collection.

21. Letter from MC to AA /10/1787, AFC vol. 7, pp. 430–432.

22. Betsy Cranch's diary, 11/15/1786, MHS.

23. *JQA Diary* vol. 2, 10/29/1786, p. 119.

24. Letter from Betsy Cranch to AA 1/7/1787, AFC vol. 7, pp. 426–428.

25. Betsy Cranch's diary 1/22/1787, MHS.

26. Alamode beef was a braised stew covered with bacon and served with a rich brown gravy. Made from the rump of the beef and much like our current pot roast, it had been a popular dish in Europe for a century and had appeared in cookbooks circulated in America since Eliza Smith wrote about it in *The Compleat Housewife* in 1727. A half century later, Lincoln would serve it at his second inaugural dinner. See *All The Presidents' Tables: A Lincoln Inaugural Beef a la Mode,* posted by C. Berlelsen on Google, 10/27/2008.

27. Letter from ESP to AA 7/22/1787, AFC vol. 8, pp. 134–138.

28. Letter from MC to AA 7/16/1787, AFC vol. 8, pp. 121–123.

29. Betsy Cranch's diary 8/27/1787, Kathy Chamberlain private collection, p. 1.

30. Letter from JA to TJ 3/1/1787, *A/J Letters,* pp. 175–177.

31. Letter from JA to RC 2/21/1787, AFC vol. 7, pp. 466–467.

32. Letter from AA to MC 2/25/1787, AFC vol. 7, pp. 469–474.

33. Letter from MC to AA 7/12/1786, AFC vol. 7, pp. 250–256.

34. Letter from AA to MC 10/12/1786, AFC vol. 7, pp. 366–370.

35. Letter from ESP to AA 7/2/1786, AFC vol. 7, pp. 289–296.

36. Letter from AA to MC 5/25/1786, AFC vol. 7, pp. 202–203.

37. Letter from MC to AA 7/10/1786, AFC vol. 7, pp. 248–250.

38. Letter from MC to AA 7/10/1786, AFC vol. 7, pp. 248–250.

39. Letter from AA to MC 4/28/1787, AFC vol. 8, pp. 28–34.

40. Letter from MC to AA 7/14/1786, AFC vol. 7, pp. 250–256.

41. Letter from AA to MC 10/12/1786, AFC vol. 7, pp. 366–370.

42. Letter from AA to ESP 3/10/1787, AFC vol. 8, pp. 4–6.

43. Letter from Nabby to Betsy Cranch 7/19/1787, AFC vol. 8, pp. 127–129.

44. Letter from Lucy Cranch to AA 8/18/1787, AFC vol. 8, pp. 141–143.

45. Letter from MC to AA 7/21/1787, AFC vol. 8, pp. 132–134.

46. Ibid.

47. Letter from MC to AA 4/22/1787, AFC vol. 8, pp. 15–23.

48. Letter from AA to Lucy Cranch 4/26/1787, AFC vol. 8, pp. 24–27.

49. Letter from AA to ESP 5/12/1787, AFC vol. 8, pp. 37–39.

50. The "throat distemper" was probably strep throat.

51. Letter from ESP to AA 7/22/1787, AFC vol. 8, pp. 134–138 and Letter from AA to ESP 7/19/1787, AFC vol. 8, pp. 126–127.

52. Interview with Michael Ryan, and letter MC to AA 10/21/1787, AFC vol. 8, pp. 196–198, and letter ESP to AA 11/17/1787, AFC vol. 8, pp. 204–206.

53. Letter from AA to MC 2/10/1788, AFC vol. 8, pp. 224–227.

54. Letter from Cotton Tufts to JA 6/13/1787, AFC vol. 8, p. 89.

55. Letter from Cotton Tufts to AA 10/31/1787, vol. 8, pp. 200–201.

56. Letter from JQA to AA 12/23/1787, vol. 8, pp. 213–216.

57. Letter from JA to TJ 11/10/1787, *A/J Letters,* p. 210.

58. Letter from John Adams to Cotton Tufts 1/23/1788, AFC vol. 8, pp. 220–221.

59. Letter from Nabby to JQA 2/10/1788, AFC vol. 8, pp. 227–231.

60. Letter from MC to AA 12/22/1787, AFC vol. 6, pp. 212–213.

61. The authors named themselves Publius in honor of the idealistic Roman republican, Publius Valerius Publicolo.

62. Ellis, Joseph J., p. 156, quoting from a letter to John Taylor.

63. Wills, Gary, *Explaining America,* p. 188.

64. Letter from AA to Margaret Smith 3/22/1788, AFC vol. 8, pp. 246–247.

65. Letter from AA to MC 2/25/1787, AFC vol. 8, pp. 469–474.

66. Letter from AA to Cotton Tufts 1/1/1788, AFC vol. 8, pp. 216–217.

67. Letter from AA to MC 2/10/1788, AFC vol. 8, pp. 224–227.

68. *Diary and Autobiography of JA,* vol. 3, p. 215.

CHAPTER XII

1. Letter from MC to AA 6/29/1787, AFC vol. 8, pp. 94–96.

2. Letter from MC to AA 9/23/1787, AFC vol. 8, pp. 170–173.

3. Tyler's first theatrical comedy, *The Contrast,* had just opened to rave reviews in New York, and he showed no inclination to return to his windmills in Braintree.

4. Letter from MC to AA 9/30/1787, AFC vol. 8, pp. 173–175.

5. Ibid.

6. Letter from Betsy Cranch to AA 9/23/1787, AFC vol. 8, pp. 168–170.

7. Letter from ESP to MC 5/8/1788, AFC vol. 8, pp. 259–261.

8. Journal of Elizabeth Cranch, Kathy Chamberlain private collection, p. 13.

9. Ibid.

10. Letter from ESP to AA, 6/22/1788, AFC vol. 8, pp. 275–276.

11. Betsy Cranch noted John Adams's joy in her diary on 6/28/1788, Kathy Chamberlain private collection, p. 14.

12. Journal of Elizabeth Cranch, May 1788, Kathy Chamberlain private collection, p. 9.

13. Letter from AA to Nabby 8/6/1788, AFC vol. 8, pp. 284–286.

14. Letter from JA to Nabby 7/16/1788, AFC vol. 8, pp. 278–280.

15. Letters from AA to Nabby 7/7/1788, AFC vol. 8, pp. 275–276 and 8/6/1788, pp. 284–286.

16. Letter from Nabby to AA 5/18/1788, AFC vol. 8, pp. 261–266.

17. Letter from Nabby to AA 9/7/1788, AFC vol.8, pp. 293–296.

18. Letter from WS to Nabby, 6/6/1789, AFC vol. 8, pp. 77–78.

19. Chernow, *Hamilton,* p. 268.

20. Letter from Nabby to JQA 9/28/1788, AFC vol. 8, pp. 299–301.

21. Letter from JA to Nabby 7/16/1788, AFC vol. 8, pp. 278–280.

22. Berkin, Carol, *A Brilliant Solution*, p. 188.

23. Chernow, *Hamilton*. See pp. 262–269 for a detailed discussion of the New York Convention.

24. Letter from JA to AA 12/2/1788, AFC vol. 8, pp. 312–313.

25. Letter from TJ to JA 2/26/1788, *A/J Letters*, pp. 227–228.

26. Letter from JA to TJ 12/10/1787, ibid., pp.214–215. Note the early date of this letter. Eighteen months before the start of the French Revolution, Adams had the prescience to imagine its outcome.

27. Letter from Nabby to Betsy, 8/31/1788, Kathy Chamberlain private collection.

28. Letter from Betsy Cranch to Jacob Norton 3/1/1788, Kathy Chamberlain private collection.

29. Letter from Betsy Cranch to Norton 4/5/1788, MHS, Betsy Cranch's diary.

30. Betsy Cranch's diary 3/11/1788, p. 6, Kathy Chamberlain private collection.

31. Letter from MC to Jacob Norton, 2/22/1789. Kathy Chamberlain private collection.

32. Letter from Betsy Cranch to Jacob Norton 3/6/1788, Kathy Chamberlain private collection.

33. Letter from Jacob Norton to Betsy Cranch, 1/5/1789, MHS.

34. The information on the parsonage comes from *The Journal of Margaret Hazlitt: Recollections of England, Ireland, and America,* edited and annotated by Ernest J. Moyne, The University of Kansas Press, Lawrence, Kansas, 1967, pp. 62–72.

35. Betsy Cranch diary February 1788, Kathy Chamberlain private collection,

36. Letter from MC to AA 2/14/1788, AFC vol. 8, pp. 317–318.

37. Dinkin, Robert J., *Campaigning in America: A History of Election Practices,* Greenwood Press, NY, 1789.

38. See JA to AA 12/2/1788 and 12/28/1788, AFC vol. 8, pp. 312–313 and 323–324.

39. Letter from AA to MC 2/15/1788, AFC vol. 8, pp. 320–323.

40. Ibid.

41. Letter from MC to AA 12/14/1788, AFC vol. 8, pp. 317–318

42. Letter from AA to Sarah Livingston Jay, 2/20/1789, AFC vol. 8, pp. 328–329.

43. Why the Shaws were not present is not mentioned in any of the correspondence. Probably the weather or the health of one of them prevented a winter trip.

44. Letter from Betsy to Lucy Cranch, sometime between 1789 and 1790, MHS, Betsy Cranch Norton collection.

45. Letter from ESP to AA 2/14/1789, AFC vol. 8, pp. 327–328.

46. That Abigail has not replied is made clear by Elizabeth's subsequent, May 2, 1789 letter to Abigail, where she continues chastising her sister in the same vein.

47. Letter from AA to JA 4/22/1789, AFC vol. 8, pp. 333–335.

48. Letter from ESP to AA 5/2/1789, AFC vol. 8, pp. 343–344.

49. Letter from MC to AA 11/1/1789, vol. 8, pp. 433–434.

50. Smith, Thomas E.V., *The City of New York in the Year of Washington's Inauguration,* Chatham Press, 1889.

51. *Diary and Autobiography of JA,* 8/23/1774, vol. 2, pp. 108–109.

52. Burrows, Edwin G. and Wallace, Mike, *Gotham,* Oxford University Press, p. 301.

53. McCullough, *John Adams,* p. 402 and Chernow, *Alexander Hamilton,* p. 278, also see *Gotham,* chapter 20.

54. *Memoir of the Life of Eliza S.M. Quincy,* 1861, noted in Stokes, Phelps, vol. 5, p. 1241.

55. The Comte de Moustier, plenipotentiary of France, wrote this on 6/6/1789. He is quoted in Stokes, Phelps, *The Iconography of Manhattan Island,* vol. 5, p. 1244.

56. Smith, *The City of New York in the Year of Washington's Inauguration,* p. 227–232.

57. McCullough, *John Adams,* p. 403.

58. Letter from JA to AA 5/1/1789, AFC vol. 8, pp. 340–341.

59. Letter from AA to JA 5/1/1789, AFC vol. 8, pp. 338–340.

60. Letter from AA to JA 5/31/1789, AFC vol. 8, pp. 364–366.

61. Letter from AA to MC 6/19/1789, AFC vol. 8, pp. 373–375.

62. Letter from RC to MC 4/20/1787, MHS, Cranch Family Papers.

63. Letter from MC to AA 6/21/1789, AFC vol. 8, pp. 375–377.

64. Letter from AA to MC 7/12/1789, AFC vol. 8, pp. 388–391.

CHAPTER XIII

1. Letter from ESP to AA 6/11/1793, AFC vol. 9, pp. 436–438.

2. Letter from ESP to AA 12/31/1792, AFC vol. 9, pp. 362–364.

3. It is clear that at this point John was still unaware of Hamilton's attempt to turn the electoral vote against him and looked upon him as a brilliant young man and friend.

4. Letter from AA to JQA 5/30/1789, AFC vol. 8, pp. 362–363.

5. Letter from AA to MC 8/9/1789, AFC vol. 8, pp. 397–401.

6. Letter from AA to Cotton Tufts 9/1/1789, AFC vol. 8, pp. 405–406.

7. Letter from AA to MC 10/11/1789, vol. 8, pp. 420–422.

8. Letter from AA to MC 1/5/1790, vol. 9, pp. 1–3.

9. Letter from AA to MC 8/9/1787, AFC vol. 8, pp. 397–401.

10. Letter from AA to Lucy Ludwell Paradise 9/6/1790, AFC vol. 9, 101–103.

11. Letter from AA to MC 1/5/1790, AFC vol. 9, pp. 1–3.

12. George Washington's letter recommending Colonel Smith for a position in the West Indies, 6/1782, quoted by Roof, Katherine Metcalf, *Colonel William Smith and Lady,* pp. 36–37.

13. AFC vol. 9, p. xx.

14. The author was in fact Edward Church. Abigail attributed the poem to his grudge against Adams because the latter had not answered his letter requesting a government job.

15. Letter from WC to JQA 10/1/1789, AFC vol. 8, pp. 412–413.

16. See Ellis, Joseph J., *Founding Brothers,* chapter 2, "The Dinner."

17. Letter from AA to MC 4/20/1792, AFC vol. 9, pp. 277–279.

18. Letter from Lucy Cranch to AA 10/23/1789, AFC vol. 8, pp. 428–429.

19. Bartlett, Albert LeRoy, "A Little Town and a Great Event: Haverhill '789," 1932, Haverhill Library.

20. Letter from AA to MC 1/5/1790, AFC vol. 9, pp. 1–3.

21. Letter from AA to JQA 8/20/1790, AFC vol. 9, pp. 92–94.

22. Letter from JQA to WC 6/5/1790, AFC vol. 9, pp. 65–68.

23. Letter from ESP to AA 3/14/1797, AFC vol. 9, pp. 24–25.

24. Letter from AA to MC 4/3/1790, AFC vol. 9, pp. 39–40.

25. Letter from AA to Lucy Ludwell Paradise, AFC vol. 9, pp. 101–103.

26. Letter from JA to TJ 1/2/1789, *A/J Letters,* p. 234.

27. Letter from TJ to JA 7/17/1791, Ibid., pp. 245–247.

28. Letter from JA to TJ 7/29/1791, Ibid., pp. 247–250.

29. Letter from AA to Lucy Ludwell Paradise, 9/6/1790, AFC vol. 9, pp. 101–103.

30. AFC vol. 9, fn 4, p. 103.

31. Enrico Caterino Davila was an Italian historian who wrote a 1630 book on the French civil wars, which Adams uses as springboard for his discussion of the French mentality.

32. Adams, John, *Discourses on Davila: A Series of Papers on Political History By An American Citizen,* The Works of John Adams, vol. 6, The Online Library of Liberty.

33. Letter from MC to AA 5/16/1790, AFC vol. 9, pp. 58–61.

34. Ellis, Joseph J., *His Excellency: George Washington,* p. 190–191.

35. Letter from AA to Cotton Tufts 5/30/1790, AFC vol. 9, pp. 63–65.

36. Letter from AA to MC 5/30/1790, AFC vol. 9, pp. 61–63.

37. Letter from AA to Cotton Tufts 5/30/1790, AFC vol. 9, pp. 63–65.

38. Letter from AA to MC 5/30/1790, AFC vol. 9, pp. 61–63.

39. Ellis, Joseph J., *His Excellency,* p. 191.

40. Letter from AA to Cotton Tufts 5/30/1790, AFC vol. 9, pp. 63–65.

41. Letter from AA to MC 8/8/1790, AFC vol. 9, pp. 84–86.

42. Letter from AA to JQA 8/20/1790, AFC vol. 9, pp. 92–94.

43. Draft of a letter from AA to JQA 7/11/1790, AFC vol. 9, fn 6, p.78.

44. Letter from AA to JQA 8/20/1790, AFC vol. 9, pp. 92–94.

45. The quotes in this and the previous paragraphs are from AA to MC 10/3/1790 and 10/10/1790, AFC vol. 9, pp. 127–128 and 130–131.

46. John Thaxter had married Betsy Duncan, and this was their only child. Thaxter had proved as emotionally vulnerable and physically delicate as Betsy Norton, and Mary—correctly—predicted that he would not long survive his child's death.

47. Letter from ES to AA 9/28/1790, AFC vol. 9, pp. 122–124.

48. Letter from MC to AA 8/9/1790, AFC vol. 9, pp. 86–89.

49. Letter from MC to AA 9/1790, AFC vol. 9, pp. 119–121.

50. Fifty years later, he still remembered the pain of leaving her, writing in his diary (AFC vol. 9 fn 5 pp. 43–44) "Dearly!—how dearly did the sacrifice of her cost me, voluntary as it was—for the separation was occasioned by my declining to contract an unqualified engagement, forbidden by my father, and by the advice of her cousin to her, to insist upon a positive engagement or a separation."

51. AFC vol. 9, fn 5, pp. 43–44.

52. Letter from AA to JQA 7/11/1790, AFC vol. 9, pp. 77–78.

53. Letter from JQA to WC 6/5/1790, AFC vol. 9, pp. 65–68.

54. Letter from WC to JQA 6/10/1790, AFC vol. 9, pp. 69–71.

55. Letter from Nabby Smith to Betsy Norton 2/7/1791, AFC vol. 9, pp. 187–188 and letter from AA to Nabby 1/9/1791, AFC vol. 9, pp. 179–181.

56. Letter from AA to Nabby 1/25/1791, AFC vol. 9, pp. 181–182.

57. Mary Cranch saw Nabby's loneliness quite differently. In a letter to Abigail on 2/20/1791(MHS microfilm), she exclaimed, "[Nabby] does not know it but this feeling of hers is intirely owing to that uncommon reserve which marks her character." We are made for society, Mary insists, "and must forever stand in need of the assistance of each other let our stations be ever so exalted or our circumstances so affluent. There is an affability and desire to make ourselves agreeable to thus around us which is laudable and which will never fail of procuring us agreable companions—you my dear sister know this well to be a truth." Clearly, Mary was still smarting from Nabby's aloofness earlier in life.

58. Letter from AA to Abigail Bromfield Rogers 9/5/1790, AFC vol. 9, pp. 97–99.
59. AA to MC, 10/10/1790 and 10/25/1790, AFC vol. 9, pp. 130–131 and 140–141.
60. Letter from AA to MC 12/12/1790, AFC vol. 9, pp. 155–157.
61. Letter from MC to AA 1/7/1791, AFC vol. 9, pp. 173–174.
62. Letter from AA to Nabby Smith 12/26/1790, AFC vol. 9, pp. 167–168.
63. Letter from AA to Nabby Smith 1/8/1791, AFC vol. 7, pp. 177–179.
64. Letter from AA to Nabby Smith 2/21/1791, AFC vol. 7, pp. 193–194.
65. Smart, James, *Historic Philadelphia: An Illustrated History,* Lammert Publications, Inc., 2001.
66. Letter from AA to ESP 4/16/1800, MHS microfilm.
67. AFC vol. 9, p. 173, fn1.
68. Letter from ESP to AA 2/14/1791, AFC vol. 9, pp. 190–192.
69. Letter from JA to WS 3/14/1791, AFC vol. 9, pp. 202–203.
70. Oberholtzer, Ellis Paxson, *Philadelphia: History of the City and its People,* S.J. Clarke Publishing Company, 2/12/1937.
71. Letter from AA to Cotton Tufts 3/11/1791, AFC vol. 9, pp. 202-203.
72. His salary as supervisor of New York State and New York City has not been reported, but he was also appointed supervisor of revenue for the District of New York at the beginning of 1791, and this job paid a very respectable $800, plus ½ of 1% of the revenues he brought in. AA to Cotton Tufts, 3/11/1791, AFC vol. 9, pp. 196–200, fn #6.
73. Letter from AA to WS 3/16/1791, AFC vol. 9, pp. 203–205.
74. Letter from MC to AA 1/25/1791, AFC vol. 9, pp. 183–184.

CHAPTER XIV

1. Letter from ESP to MC and AA 9/24/1795, MHS microfilm.
2. Pleck, Elizabeth, *Domestic Tyranny: The Making of American Social Policy against Family Violence from Colonial Times to the Present,* pp. 30–31.
3. Ibid., pp. 3–13.
4. Letter from ESP to MC 4/21/1793, AFC vol. 9, pp. 422–424.
5. Letter from JQA to WC 8/17/1791, AFC vol. 9, pp. 222–224.
6. Letter from ESP to AA 9/10/1794, MHS microfilm.
7. The data was provided by Dr. Buchan, whose book Abigail had discovered on her sea journey to England and who was now the most-read medical expert in the English-speaking world.
8. Letter from AA to MC 10/30/1791, AFC vol. 9, pp. 237–238.
9. Letter from MC to AA 6/10/1798, MHS microfilm. In this letter, Mary refers to Elizabeth's response to a later family crisis, but her words are equally applicable to her sister's sorrow over Billy's broken leg.
10. Letter from ESP to AA 8/26/1792, AFC vol. 9, pp. 301–32.
11. Letter from ESP to MC 4/24/1793, AFC vol. 9, pp. 422–424.
12. Jacobs, Diane, *Her Own Woman,* pp. 102–103.
13. Letter from ESP to AA 6/11/1793, AFC vol. 9, pp. 436–438.
14. Letter from JA to AA 2/3/1793, AFC vol. 9, pp. 389–391.
15. Letter from ESP to MC 4/21/1793, AFC vol. 9, pp. 422–424.
16. Ibid. The Shakespearean quote is from King Henry VIII, Act III, scene 2, lines 352–357 and reflects Elizabeth's frame of mind at the time:
    This is the state of Man: to day he puts forth

The tender leaves of Hope: tomorrow blossoms,
And bears his blushing honours thick upon him;
The third day comes a frost, a *killing frost,*
And when he thinks good easy man, full surely
His Greatness aripening, *nips his root.*

17. Letter from ESP to AA 8/26/1792, AFC vol. 9, pp. 301–303.
18. Letter from ESP to William Shaw 9/1/94, LOC, Shaw and Peabody collection.
19. My italics.
20. Letter from ESP to AA 9/10/1794, AFC vol. 10, pp. 228–229.
21. Letter from ESP to MC and AA 9/24/1795, AFC vol. 11, pp. 33–36.
22. Letter from ESP to MC 1/2/1795, LOC, Shaw and Peabody papers.
23. AA quotes Elizabeth in her letter to JA 12/26/1794, AFC vol. 10, pp. 323–325.
24. Letter from JA to JQA 12/2/1794, MHS microfilm.
25. Adams lodged with the Secretary of the Senate Samuel Otis and his wife.
26. Letter from JA to AA 1/24/1793, AFC vol. 9, pp. 380–381.
27. Letter from AA to JA 12/31/1793, AFC vol. 9, pp. 494–496.
28. In 1792 the North Precinct of Braintree, where the Adamses and Cranches resided, was combined with the farms of Squantum into a separate town, named Quincy in honor of the sisters' grandparents.
29. Letter from JA to AA 1/24/1793, AFC vol. 9, pp. 381–382.
30. In 1792, Adams received a serious challenge from New York's anti-Federalist Governor Clinton, but still won by a comfortable 27 votes.
31. To simplify, I will from here on refer to them simply as Republicans.
32. Wood, Gordon S., *Empire of Liberty,* p. 140 fn.1 references Richard Hofstadter, *The Idea of a Party System: The Rise of Legitimate Opposition in the United States, 1780–1840,* Berkeley, 1969.
33. Wood, Gordon S., *Empire of Liberty,* p. 155.
34. Jefferson thought every generation should create government anew. Estimating that a generation lasted nineteen years, he believed all laws and debts, public and private, should then cease to exist. (Considering that Jefferson was living on credit, this plan was not altogether disinterested.) Hamilton, on the other hand, favored a stable legislature and a President seated for life.
35. Lafayette was accused of treason and ultimately jailed in an Austrian prison because he was suspected of assisting the King's doomed Austrian flight.
36. Letter from JA to AA 2/4/1794, AFC vol. 10, pp. 65–68.
37. See chapter 5 of Gordon S. Wood's *Empire of Liberty* for a thoughtful comparison between the American and the French Revolutions.
38. Diary entry *Diary and Autobiography of JA,* volume 2, 1771–1781, p. 354.
39. Letter from JA to AA 12/20/1793, AFC vol. 9, pp. 479–480.
40. Ibid.
41. At this point, the Terror was in motion, and because of his family's former monarchist sympathies, Genet feared for his life if he returned to France. He settled in America where he married Governor Clinton's daughter and became a citizen of the United States.
42. Letter from JA to AA 1/8/1794, AFC vol. 10, pp. 29–31.
43. Letter from JA to CA 1/2/1794, AFC vol. 10, pp. 2–3.
44. Letter from JA to JQA 1/3/1794, AFC vol. 10, pp. 3–4.
45. Letter from AA to JA 1/18/1794, AFC vol. 10, pp. 43–45.

46. Letter from JQA to ESP 7/8/1795, AFC vol. 11, pp. 4–5.
47. Letter from AA to JA 11/23/1794, AFC vol. 10, pp. 270–271.
48. Letter from AA to JA 12/12/1794, AFC vol. 10, pp. 295–298.
49. Local newspaper articles on the history of the town over the following years and decades would confirm Abigail's observation about Haverhill's high regard for Elizabeth. See folders in Haverhill library.
50. Letter from ESP to MC 12/21/1794, LOC, Shaw Collection.
51. Ibid.
52. Ibid.
53. Letter from ESP to AA 1/24/1795, AFC vol. 10, pp. 358–360.
54. Letter from AA to WS 6/28/1798, LOC, Shaw Collection.
55. Letter from ESP to AA 11/24/1795, AFC vol. 10, pp. 358–360.
56. Letter from ESP to AA 6/13/1795, AFC vol. 10, pp. 447–449.
57. Stephen Peabody's diary, 8/20/1770, AFP (Adams Family Papers), MHS.
58. Ibid.
59. The student was Samuel Gilman. The story is recounted in several pamphlets about Atkinson in the Haverhill Library and in the book of Harvard records Sibley's for the class of 1790, pp. 207–217.
60. This is reported in the book of Harvard records Sibley's for the class of 1769, pp. 207–217.
61. Todd, William C., *Biographical and Other Articles,* New Hampshire Historical Society. Lee And Shepard, Boston 2008.
62. ESP to AA 10/31/1795, AFC vol. 11, pp. 50–51. The novelty of the agreement is perceptively discussed in Holton, Woody, *Abigail Adams,* pp. 296–297.
63. Letter from ESP to MC and AA 9/24/1795, AFC vol. 11, pp. 33–36.
64. Ibid.
65. From the late sixteenth century on, "making love" implied romance and courtship. In the eighteenth century it could also mean flirting.

CHAPTER XV

1. Nabby was preoccupied by politics, as her correspondence reveals and as her husband remarks in a letter to JA (10/5/1792, AFC vol. 9, pp. 310–312): "Mrs. Smith has written to Mrs. Adams & I suppose given a greater detail of politicks than I have time to enter into. She loves it; you may guess where she got it from, & her Judgement on those points are astonishingly good."
2. Letter from JA to AA 12/18/1796, AFC vol. 10, pp. 446–448.
3. Letter from AA to JA 12/6/1794, AFC vol. 10, pp. 288–289.
4. Letter from JA to JQA 4/23/1794, AFC vol. 10, pp. 150–153.
5. Letter from JA to AA 3/2/1793, AFC vol. 9, pp. 415–416.
6. Madame Roland ran one of the most influential salons in Paris before she was guillotined for her political views. While Abigail clearly admired Roland, she criticized her for upstaging her husband, writing JQA on 5/20/96, AFC vol. 11, pp. 295–298: "however brilliant a woman tallents may be, she ought never to shine at the expence of her Husband. Government of States and Kingdoms . . . I am willing should be solely administerd by the Lords of Creation . . . I shall only contend for Domestick Government and think that is best administered by the Female."
7. Letter from AA to Nabby, 3/10/1794, AFC vol. 10, pp. 106–108.

8. In a 2/29/1796 letter to JQA (AFC vol. 11, pp. 194-197), AA writes, "Sally is an amiable virtuous Girl, with every disposition to make [Charles] a good Wife and it will be his fault, if he is not in future what he now is."

9. Letter from WC to LC 4/10/1794, Albany Institute.

10. Letter from LC to WC 4/6/1794, Ibid.

11. Letter from WC to MC 4/21/1794, Ibid.

12. Se Wood, Gordon S., *Empire of Liberty,* pp. 201–206.

13. Letter from JA to AA 3/25/1796, AFC vol. 11, pp. 227–228.

14. Letter from JA to AA 3/29/1796, AFC vol. 11, pp. 234–235.

15. In a 1/9/1797 (AFC vol. 11, pp. 486–487) letter to AA, JA wrote: "Hamilton I know to be a proud spirited, conceited mortal always pretending to morality with as debauched morals as old Franklin . . . His intrigues in the election I despise. That he has Talents I admit but I dread none of them . . . I always had and maintain the same conduct toward him I always did, that is keep him at a distance."

16. Letter from AA to JA 11/27/1796, AFC vol. 11, pp. 417–419.

17. Letter from JA to AA 12/7/1796, AFC vol. 11, pp. 438–439.

18. The final vote showed Adams ahead by only three points. He had 71 electoral votes to Jefferson's 68. Pinkney received 59 votes, Burr 30.

19. Letter from JA to AA 12/20/1796, AFC vol. 11, pp. 450–451.

20. Letter from AA to Elbridge Gerry 12/28/1796, AFC vol. 11, pp. 475–476.

21. Letter from AA to JA 1/1/1797, AFC vol. 11, pp. 478–479.

CHAPTER XVI

1. Letter from MC to AA 7/26/1797, MHS microfilm.

2. Letter from AA to MC 5/24/1797, *New Letters,* pp. 91–93.

3. Letter from MC to AA 6/27/1797, MHS, Cranch Family Papers.

4. Letter from AA to MC 3/27/1798, *New Letters,* pp. 147–149.

5. Letter from WC to MC 5/28/1797, MHS, Cranch Family Papers.

6. Letter from AA to MC 5/7/1798, *New Letters,* pp. 168–170.

7. Letter from MC to AA 5/29/1797, MHS microfilm. Here Mary states that Wibird will receive "fifty pounds" of the new minister's salary. The salary offered the candidate was $500. I am conjecturing that Mary meant dollars rather than pounds.

8. Conversation with Reverend Sheldon Bennett of the First Church of Quincy 10/6/2010.

9. Letter from AA to Louisa Adams, 1/3/1818, Levin, Phyllis, p. 474.

10. Peter Whitney's father was a strong supporter of the Revolution.

11. Letter from MC to AA 5/4/1797, MHS microfilm.

12. Peter Whitney's father, an old friend of John Adams, was also a minister. The son may have visited to ask for the elder Whitney's advice.

13. Letter from MC to AA 5/29/1797, MHS microfilm.

14. Letter from AA to MC 6/6/1797, *New Letters,* pp. 96–98.

15. Letter from MC to AA 6/20/1797, MHS microfilm.

16. Letter from ESP to AA 7/10/1797, MHS microfilm.

17. Letter from MC to AA 5/20/1797, MHS microfilm.

18. Letter from ESP to AA 7/9/1797, Ibid.

19. Letter from JA to AA 11/1/1797, AFC vol. 11, pp. 495–496.

20. Letter from JA to AA 2/4/1797, Ibid., p. 538.
21. Letter from JA to AA 3/17/1797, MHS microfilm.
22. Letter from JA to AA 4/1/1797, Ibid.
23. Letter from JA to AA 4/11/1797, Ibid.
24. Letter from JA to AA 4/24/1797, Ibid.
25. Letter from AA to ESP 4/9/1799, LOC, Shaw Family Papers.
26. Letter from AA to ESP 2/10/1797, LOC, Shaw Family Papers.
27. Abigail was so impressed by Elizabeth's prose she sent the letter to John, who called it "lovely."
28. Letter from ESP to AA 1/10/1797, MHS microfilm.
29. Mary Smith was the daughter of the sisters' dead brother William.
30. Letter from AA to JA 4/26/1797, *Letters of Mrs. Adams,* pp. 429–430.
31. Letter from AA to JA, Ibid. and letter from AA to JA 4/26/1797, Ibid.
32. Letter from AA to MC 4/30/1797, Ibid., pp. 86–88.
33. Letter from MC to AA, 6/13/1797, MHS microfilm.
34. Letter from AA to MC, 5/16/1797, *New Letters,* pp. 89–91.
35. Letter from AA to MC 3/15/1800, *New Letters,* pp. 238–242.
36. Letter from AA to MC 5/24/1797, *New Letters,* pp. 91–93.
37. The Boston Chronicle claimed John Quincy was 23 rather than nearly 30 years old and implied he was making a larger salary than any other minister abroad.
38. Letter from AA to MC 6/6/1797, *New Letters,* pp. 96–98.
39. Letter from MC to AA 2/18/1798, MHS microfilm.
40. Letter from AA to MC 7/6/1797, *New Letters,* pp. 100–103.
41. Letter from AA to MC 7/21/1797, *New Letters,* pp. 104–105.
42. Letter from AA to Cotton Tufts, 7/12/1797, MHS microfilm.
43. Letter from AA to MC 7/6/1797, Ibid.
44. Letter from AA to MC 6/6/1797, Ibid.
45. Letter from AA to MC 7/21/1797, Ibid.
46. Letter from MC to AA 10/15/1797, MHS microfilm.
47. Letter from MC to AA 6/27/1797, Ibid.
48. Letter from RC to Jacob Flint 6/26/1797, MHS, Cranch Family Papers.
49. Letter from MC to AA 11/2/1797, MHS microfilm.
50. Letter from AA to MC 12/26/1797, *New Letters,* pp. 119–120.
51. Letter from MC to AA 6/27/1797, MHS microfilm.
52. Letter from MC to AA 11/2/1979, Ibid.
53. In an unquoted section of this sentence, Abigail unflatteringly compares Massachusetts to New Jersey, where in a 1776 constitution women with cash or property were given the right to vote. This right was revoked in 1807.
54. Letter from AA to JA 3/31/1776, AFC vol. 1, pp. 369–371.
55. Letter from AA to MC 11/15/1797, *New Letters,* pp. 110–113.
56. Letter from MC to AA 11/2/1797, MHS microfilm.
57. Letter from AA to MC 12/12/1797, *New Letters,* pp. 115–120.
58. Letter from MC to AA 11/29/1797, MHS microfilm.
59. Letter from AA to MC 12/12/1797, *New Letters,* pp. 115–120.
60. She meant dromedary or camel.
61. Letter from MC to AA 11/2/1797, MHS microfilm.
62. Letter from AA to ESP 6/22/1798, LOC, Shaw Family Papers.
63. Letter from ESP to AA 7/3/1797, MHS microfilm.

64. Gilman, Samuel, *Contributions to Literature,* "Reverend Stephen Peabody and Lady" (first published as an article in 1847), Crosby, Nichols, and Company, 1856.

65. Letter from Nabby to JQA 11/4/1797, MHS microfilm.

66. Letter from AA to MC 11/15/1797, *New Letters* pp. 110–113, Letter from MC to AA 12/17/1797, MHS microfilm.

67. Letter from ESP to AA 12/19/1797, MHS microfilm.

68. Letter from ESP to AA 1/28/1798, Ibid.

69. Letter from AA to ESP 6/22/1798, LOC, Shaw Family Papers.

70. Letter from ESP to AA 5/15/1798, MHS microfilm.

71. Letter from MC to AA 5/18/1798, MHS microfilm.

CHAPTER XVII

1. Letter from AA to MC 12/12/1797, *New Letters,* pp. 115–119.

2. Letter from AA to MC 2/1/1798, Ibid. pp. 126–130.

3. Letter from AA to MC 3/20/1798, Ibid. pp. 146–147.

4. Wood, Gordon S., *Empire of Liberty,* p. 242.

5. Letter from MC to AA 4/15/1798, MHS microfilm.

6. Letter from AA to MC 4/7/1798, *New Letters,* pp. 153–155.

7. Letter from AA to WS 3/24/1798, MHS microfilm.

8. The men's names were Hottinguer, Bellamy, and Hauteval.

9. Wood, Gordon S., *Empire of Liberty,* pp. 241–243. The statement was made by Charles Pinckney.

10. Letter from AA to MC 3/5/1798, *New Letters,* pp. 139–142.

11. Wood, Gordon S., *Empire of Liberty,* p. 263.

12. Letter from AA to MC 4/26/1798, *New Letters,* pp. 164–166.

13. Letter from AA to MC 5/10/1798, Ibid., pp. 170–172.

14. Letter from MC to AA 5/18/1798, MHS microfilm.

15. Letter from MC to AA 6/4/1798, Ibid.

16. Letter from MC to AA 5/18/1798, Ibid., and AA to MC 5/26/1798, *New Letters,* pp. 179–182, also see Holton, Woody pp. 116–117 on significance of John's consulting Abigail before sending this letter.

17. Letter from AA to MC 5/26/1798, *New Letters,* pp. 179–182.

18. An excellent discussion of the Alien and Sedition Acts in the context of their times can be found in Wood, Gordon S., pp. 247–265.

19. Letter from MC to AA 6/1/1798, MHS microfilm.

20. Benjamin Franklin's grandson died in his prison cell of yellow fever that coming September before he was tried.

21. Webster's defines a bobbin as "a narrow cotton cord formerly used by dressmakers for piping."

22. Letter from AA to MC 3/14/1798, *New Letters,* pp. 144–146.

23. It wasn't until the end of the nineteenth century that screened windows and doors came into use.

24. Letter from AA to Catherine Nuth Johnson (Louisa's mother) 6/26/1798, Harvard College.

25. Letters from AA to MC 11/15/1797, *New Letters,* pp. 110–113 and 12/26/1797, Ibid., pp. 119–120.

26. Letter from AA to MC 2/28/1798, *New Letters,* pp. 136–138.

27. Letter from WC to AA 11/21/1797, MHS microfilm.

28. Letter from JA to AA 11/12/1798, MHS microfilm.

29. Abigail told John Quincy that John had observed that the Colonel's frequent absence was her grandsons' salvation. AA to JQA 6/20/1798, MHS microfilm.

30. Letter from AA to JQA 7/20/1798, Ibid.

31. Letter from AA to JQA 11/15/1798, Ibid.

32. Letter from MC to AA 6/29/1798, Ibid.

33. Letter from AA to JQA 6/12/1798, Ibid.

34. Letter from ESP to AA 6/22/1798, LOC, Shaw Family Papers.

35. Letter from Nabby to JQA 9/28/1798, MHS microfilm.

36. Letter from ESP to William Shaw, 9/24/1798, LOC, Shaw/Peabody collection.

37. Letter from Nabby to JQA 9/28/1798, MHS microfilm.

38. Letter from JA to AA 11/12/1798, MHS microfilm.

39. Letter from JA to AA 2/22/1798, Ibid.

40. Letter from AA to JA 11/22/1798, Ibid. Abigail had earlier told John Quincy, "I have hopes that [my sickness] will wear away as the cold weather approaches. AA to JQA 11/13/1798, Ibid.

41. Letter from JA to AA 12/13/1798, MHS microfilm.

42. Letter from AA to JA 11/25/1798, Ibid.

43. Letter from JA to AA 2/22/1799 John expanded on his chagrin about Charles by ruing that he ever had children. Abigail's reaction was, first, to agree she too had "but faint hope" of "reforming" this middle son, adding "It is so painfull and distressing a subject to me, that what I suffer is in silence" (2/14/1799, Ibid.); but then to chastise John for regretting that they'd had children since Charles's siblings had all turned out so well.

44. Letter from JA to AA 12/13/1798 and 12/17/1798, Ibid.

45. Letter from AA to JA 11/29/1798, Ibid. John's response was to worry that she'd expended too much energy making pies and puddings.

46. Letter from ESP to AA 11/26/1798, MHS microfilm.

47. Letter from ESP to William Shaw 3/20/1799, LOC, Shaw/Peabody collection.

48. Ibid.

49. Like Adams, Murray disparaged Montesquieu's theory that virtue was essential to democracy and touted the importance of laws.

50. Bailyn, Bernard, *The Ideological Origins of the American Revolution,* Belknap Press, Cambridge, 1992, pp. 371–372.

51. Letter from AA to ESP 7/19/1799, LOC, Shaw Family Papers.

52. Letter from ESP to WS 11/20/1799, AFC MHS, Ibid.

53. They were among the few to celebrate Thanksgiving in Philadelphia since at this time the holiday was confined to New England states.

54. Letter from AA to MC 12/11/1799, *New Letters,* pp. 219–222.

55. Letter from ESP to AA 1/17/1800, MHS microfilm.

56. Letter from AA to ESP 2/4/1800, LOC, Shaw Collection.

57. John raved against the "dissolution of the family" caused by lack of patriarchal authority in a letter to TA shortly after he left East Chester (JA to TA 10/17/1799, MHS microfilm). He wrote Abigail that he renounced Charles on 10/12/1799, Ibid. He went further in the latter to condemn his middle son as "a mere Rake, Buck Blood and Beast," while acknowledging his feelings of impotence: "I grieved, I mourned but could do no more." He never visited Charles again, but with Abigail exerted himself to help Sally, whom he saw as blameless—like Nabby.

58. Letter from AA to MC 10/31/1799, *New Letters,* pp. 210–212.

59. Letter from AA to MC 12/22/1799, Ibid. pp. 222–223.

60. Letter from MC to AA 1/5/1799, MHS microfilm.

61. Letter from AA to MC 12/30/1799, *New Letters,* pp. 224–226.

62. Letter from MC to AA 1/7/1798, MHS microfilm.

63. The reasons Captain Beal and Captain Baxter gave Mary for their opposition was that "he makes it so difficult to get to heaven" and "Mr. W. is forever bringing up a future day of retribution." Since Mr. Whitney was known to be liberal and soon after became a Unitarian, these Calvinist-like statements were obviously calculated to gain the support of the more orthodox, and Captain Beal and Captain Baxter surely understood the minister's motives. The quotes come from MC to AA 12/15/1799, MHS microfilm.

64. Letter from MC to AA 12/8/1799, MHS microfilm.

65. Letter from AA to MC 12/11/1799, *New Letters,* pp. 219–222.

66. Letter from RC to Peter Whitney, 12/9/1799, Albany Institute of History & Art.

67. Address written by Peter Whitney to the First Church of Quincy and read by his friend Dr. Ware, 1/5/1800, Albany Institute.

68. Letter from MC to AA 2/9/1800, MHS microfilm.

69. Letter from AA to MC 2/27/1800, *New Letters,* pp. 234–236.

70. Letter from AA to MC 5/26/1800, *New Letters,* pp. 252–253.

CHAPTER XVIII

1. What disease Mary suffered from is never specified. Her body was covered with boils, which suggests a persistent fever.

2. Letter from AA to ESP ca. 2/1801, MHS microfilm.

3. Buckland, Gail, *The White House in Miniature,* W.W. Norton & Company, New York, 1994, p. 179.

4. Letter from MC and RC to AA 11/7/1800, MHS microfilm.

5. Letter from AA to MC 11/2/1800, *New Letters,* p. 254.

6. Letter from WC to MC 1/11/1801, MHS, Cranch Family Papers.

7. Letter from MC to AA 12/7/1800, MHS microfilm.

8. Letter from AA to JQA 5/30/1801, Ibid.

9. Letter from AA to MC 11/10/1800, *New Letters,* pp. 254–256.

10. Letter from AA to TA 12/13/1800, MHS microfilm.

11. Charles died on Sunday, November 30.

12. Letter from AA to MC 12/8/1800, New Letters, pp. 261–262.

13. Letter from AA to Sally Smith Adams, 12/8/1800, private owner.

14. Letter from JA to TA 12/17/1800, Ibid.

15. Letter from MC to AA 4/25/1800, MHS microfilm.

16. Letter from AA to MC 5/13/1800, *New Letters,* pp. 249–250.

17. Letter from ESP to AA 12/15/1800, MHS microfilm.

18. Letter from ESP to AA 12/15/1800, Ibid.

19. Letter from ESP to AA 1/17/1800, Ibid.

20. Letter from ESP to WS 2/23/1800, LOC, Shaw Family Papers.

21. A chariot in the 18th c. was a fashionable coach for two.

22. Letter from AA to ESP, 1801, LOC, Shaw Family Papers.

EPILOGUE

1. Ironically, the current head of the Senate was Vice President Thomas Jefferson.
2. Adams had been encouraged to resume communication with Jefferson by their mutual friend, Dr. Benjamin Rush.
3. Letter from JA to TJ 1/1/1812, *A/J Letters,* p. 290.
4. Letter from TJ to JA 1/21/1812, Ibid., pp. 190–192.
5. Letter from RC to WC 3/15/1811, MHS, Cranch Family Papers.
6. Letter from AA to ESP 6/22/1810, LOC, Shaw/Peabody Collection.
7. Ibid.
8. 8/15/1813, item # 162 in Cranch collection, Albany Institute.
9. Letter from ESP to AA 11/1/1786, AFC vol. 7, pp. 384–388.
10. Quaker, New England, and Kersey Genealogy, item 872, listing: Joseph Barlow Felt.
11. Letter from AA to ESP 7/10/1811, LOC, Shaw/Peabody Collection.
12. Letter from RC to RC Norton, 6/10/1811, MHS, Cranch Family Papers.
13. Letter from AA to ESP 7/5/1809, *Letters of Mrs. Adams.*
14. Letter from AA to WC 10/17/1811, *Letters of Mrs. Adams.*
15. Letter from AA to ESP 4/2/1811, LOC, Shaw/Peabody Collection.
16. Letter from AA to ESP, Ibid.
17. Richard Cranch died of a stroke at 81, Mary of consumption at 70.
18. Elizabeth was 65 at her death, her husband was 78 at his.
19. AA to ESP 12/30/1814, *Letters of Mrs. Adams.*
20. Gelles, Edith, *Portia,* p. 168.
21. Holton, Woody, *Abigail Adams,* pp. 403–404.
22. Letter from AA to F.A. Vanderkemp, 2/3/1814, *Letters of Mrs. Adams.*
23. Letter from AA to ESP 6/5/1809, *Letters of Mrs. Adams.*
24. Abigail was 74.

Index

[Page numbers in *italic* refer to captions.]

in Shaw's home, 60–61, 173

smallpox epidemic and, 91, 92, 93

Adams, Charles Frances, 429

Adams, Elihu, 60, 66

Adams, John, 9, 17, 25, 253, 373, 402

accomplishments of, 419

American homecoming of,
282–83, 284, 286

in American mission to France,
115–16, 126, 127–30, 131–32,
134–36, 137–38, 145–49, 159,
160, 161–62, 178–79, 182–88,
197–98, 199

on America's destiny, 26–27

beliefs about democracy and
governance of, 76–77, 82–84,
136–37, 256–59, 274–75, 319,
320–21, 373–74

Boston law practice of, 35, 41

childhood home of, 20, 23

children of, 23–24, 41–42, 99,
102–5. *see also* Adams, Charles;
Adams, John Quincy; Adams,
Nabby; Adams, Thomas

Colonel Smith and, 239, 242, 244

on concept of equality, 346–47

Copley portrait of, 177

courtship of Abigail by, 19–21

Cranch and, 17, 19, 21, 22, 91, 124,
155

in creation of Declaration of
Independence, 86, 87–88

death of, 428

elected and inaugurated vice-
president, 286, 289, 294,
297–302

elections of 1800 and, 410–11, 416,
418–19

Elizabeth Smith and, 43, 62–63,
114–15, 343–44

in England, 163–64, 199, 215, 218,
219–21, 235, 264–65, 348

family background of, 18

in First Continental Congress, 48,
56–57

French Revolution and, 290, 319,
320–21, 340, 360

grandchildren of, 332

Hamilton and, 297

in Holland, 148, 155, 158–59, 175

Jefferson and, 189, 258–59, 319,
347, 349–50, 393, 427–28

Lovell and, 131, 138

marriage of, 3, 22, 35, 39–40,
61–62, 83–84, 93, 156, 344–45

personal qualities of, 17–18, 35–36,
219

in political conflicts during
Washington administration,
345–46

presidency of, 363–66, 372–75, 378,
379–81, 392–93, 395, 396–97,
403, 405–6

Price and, 236, 237

public perception of, in U.S.,
299–300, 313, 322, 379–80, 395

religious and philosophical
convictions of, 18–19, 321, 347,
403–4

on repeal of Stamp Act, 30

Revolutionary War and, 48, 61,
62, 63–64, 65–67, 72–73, 107–8,
109

on status and rights of women, 82,
83, 90–91, 339

Tyler and, 157, 164, 172, 229, 243

About the Author

DIANE JACOBS is the author of *Her Own Woman: the Life of Mary Wollstonecraft, Christmas in July: The Life and Art of Preston Sturges, But We Need the Eggs: The Magic of Woody Allen,* and *Hollywood Renaissance: the New Generation of Filmmakers and Their Works.* She has a BA from the University of Pennsylvania and an MFA from Columbia University. Jacobs has taught at Dartmouth College, the Columbia University School of the Arts, and the NYU School of Continuing and Professional Studies, and has contributed to such publications as *The New York Times* and *The Village Voice.* She lives in New York City.

About the Type

This book was set in Granjon, a modern recutting of a typeface produced under the direction of George W. Jones (1860–1942), who based Granjon's design upon the letterforms of Claude Garamond (1480–1561). The name was given to the typeface as a tribute to the typographic designer Robert Granjon (1513–89).